University Textbook Series

February, 1980

Especially Designed for Collateral Reading

HARRY W. JONES
Directing Editor
Professor of Law, Columbia University

ADMIRALTY, Second Edition (1975)
Grant Gilmore, Professor of Law, Yale University.
Charles L. Black, Jr., Professor of Law, Yale University.

ADMIRALTY AND FEDERALISM (1970)
David W. Robertson, Professor of Law, University of Texas.

AGENCY (1975)
W. Edward Sell, Dean of the School of Law, University of Pittsburgh.

BUSINESS ORGANIZATION AND FINANCE (1980)
William A. Klein, Professor of Law, University of California, Los Angeles.

CIVIL PROCEDURE, BASIC, Second Edition (1979)
Milton D. Green, Professor of Law Emeritus, University of California, Hastings College of the Law.

COMMERCIAL TRANSACTIONS, INTRODUCTION TO (1977)
Hon. Robert Braucher, Associate Justice, Supreme Judicial Court of Massachusetts.
Robert A. Riegert, Professor of Law, Cumberland School of Law.

CONFLICT OF LAWS, COMMENTARY ON THE, Second Edition (1980)
Russell J. Weintraub, Professor of Law, University of Texas.

CONSTITUTIONAL LAW, AMERICAN (A TREATISE ON) (1978) with 1979 Supplement
Laurence H. Tribe, Professor of Law, Harvard University.

CONTRACT LAW, THE CAPABILITY PROBLEM IN (1978)
Richard Danzig.

CORPORATIONS, Second Edition (1971)
Norman D. Lattin, Professor of Law, University of California, Hastings College of the Law.

CORPORATIONS IN PERSPECTIVE (1976)
Alfred F. Conard, Professor of Law, University of Michigan.

CRIMINAL LAW, Second Edition (1969)
Rollin M. Perkins, Professor of Law, University of California, Hastings College of the Law.

ESTATES IN LAND & FUTURE INTERESTS, PREFACE TO (1966)
Thomas F. Bergin, Professor of Law, University of Virginia.
Paul G. Haskell, Professor of Law, Case Western Reserve University.

i

PRINCIPLES

OF THE

LAW OF PROPERTY

By

JOHN E. CRIBBET

Dean and Professor of Law, University of Illinois

SECOND EDITION

Mineola, N. Y.
THE FOUNDATION PRESS, INC.
1975

Cribbet, Prin. Laws of Prop. 2nd Ed. UTB
5th Reprint-1980

"In civilized society men must be able to assume that they may control, for purposes beneficial to themselves, what they have discovered and appropriated to their own use, what they have created by their own labor and what they have acquired under the existing social and economic order. This is a jural postulate of civilized society as we know it. The law of property in the widest sense, including incorporeal property and the growing doctrines as to protection of economically advantageous relations, gives effect to the social want or demand formulated in this postulate."—**Pound, An Introduction to the Philosophy of Law 192 (1922).**

*

PREFACE TO THE SECOND EDITION

The first edition of Principles of the Law of Property was published more than a decade ago in 1962. I still agree with most of what I stated in the preface to that edition, especially about the importance of the "big picture" for the student of land law. There is a plethora of detail available in the multi-volumed treatises, the law review articles, and the reported cases, but the sheer bulk of this material is more likely to confuse than to enlighten the student. If our property law has a rational base, disclosed in the principles enunciated by the courts and legislatures (and I believe it does), then an overview of those principles will be helpful as a partial chart through the maze. This is particularly true in a period of unprecedented change and in the light of a developing fragmentation in the property curricula of the law schools.

Prior to World War II, property law was typically taught in a series of more or less related courses which left the student with a disjointed view of the common thread which united all property law. In the decades since 1945, the casebook editors have consolidated these courses into two principal packages—the "live" area (estates, landlord-tenant, titles, vendor-purchaser, and land use) and the "dead" area (trusts, wills, and future interests) plus related courses, such as land financing, natural resources, etc. By 1970, these packages had begun to unravel under the pressure of social change and a drive for a kind of limited "specialization", even in law school. I view this new fragmentation as unwise and believe that the integrity of the two basic packages should be maintained in the first two years of law school leaving the third year for specialized seminars, problem courses, and the more technical subject matter areas. Every student should be introduced to the basic principles and then encouraged to go further into those areas which appeal to him. This, incidentally, is the approach being followed by the multi-state bar examination and this textbook has the same scope as the outline for the subject of property on that examination, plus a treatment of the land-use area, without which an understanding of the modern law of land is impossible.

Much of the second edition parallels the first. Some principles have altered very little and the historical background, so important in our tradition-centered institution of private property, has been retained. Errors have been corrected, new cases and statutes have been cited, and the book has been updated to 1975.

Large portions of the book are new, however, and it is these portions, reflecting the rapidly changing land law, which required a second edition, lest the student be misled in relying on the first. The landlord-tenant materials have been rewritten in light of the shift toward tenant's (consumer's) rights; similar changes have been made in the sale of land, disclosing the fall of *caveat emptor*; materials on condominium and environmental controls have been added; and the public control of land-use segments have been expanded appreciably to acquaint the student with developments in this most volatile of all property areas.

While it would be presumptuous to call this a book on the jurisprudence of property, I have tried to infiltrate some philosophy into the prosaic fodder and I hope it will be sufficient to help the student form his own judgments as to the relative roles of private volition and public interest. I am convinced that property law is not dull, grubby stuff and I have tried to enliven the text with enough humor to make even the Statute of Uses readable. If attempted levity reduces the level of scholarship, I am apologetic but not contrite.

Finally, I am indebted to the University of Illinois for granting me an administrative leave from my decanal duties so that I could complete this edition in London, while refreshing my knowledge of the English common law which supplied the consistent thread on which the American law of land is based. This edition is dedicated * to my wife, Betty, who encouraged me to persevere despite the siren call of day-to-day administrative and teaching duties.

JOHN E. CRIBBET

Champaign, Illinois
December, 1974

---

* Not to be confused with a common-law or statutory dedication, carrying with it the profits à prendre, if any.

PREFACE TO THE FIRST EDITION

Property, which once dominated the law school curriculum by occupying from one-fourth to one-third of the total class time, is now being reduced to a more modest role in most American colleges of law. The shrink in quantity does not necessarily mean a decline in quality; it does herald a less leisurely approach to this significant segment of the law. The modern first year property course now encompasses no less than six traditional favorites —personal property, estates in land, landlord and tenant, vendor and purchaser, titles (conveyancing), and rights in land (land use). Although property books are legion, ranging from excellent multi-volumed treatises to concise outlines of the subject, none of the textbooks are tailored to the "new look" in the law school curriculum. This volume has been prepared with that gap in mind.

Principles of the Law of Property has two primary objectives: (1) to give the reader the "big picture" of "basic" property law, both in depth (history) and in breadth (scope of the subject); (2) to make the student aware of the changing nature of property law and the need for critical, responsible reform in what is all too often conceived as a static field of jurisprudence.

A true episode will illustrate the first objective. During the closing days of World War II, the author was aide de camp to Lt. General Troy Middleton, senior corps commander in General George Patton's Third United States Army. Patton's headquarters was in Luxembourg City and, following his return from SHAEF in Paris and a conference with General Eisenhower's chief of staff, General Smith, the colorful Patton told his assembled staff of his frustrations. While arguing for a swift, rapier-like thrust into the heart of Germany to end the war, Patton had been rebuffed and General Smith, after explaining that supplies must be diverted to General Montgomery in the north, had patted him patronizingly on the back, saying, "The trouble with you is, Georgie, you just don't understand the big picture!" As Patton told the story, his English bulldog, Willie, lay at his feet. Now Willie, when bored, was apt to yawn and when yawning it looked suspiciously as if he were smiling. He chose this moment to yawn and Patton, launching a kick which nearly carried him off his feet, yelled, "Laugh you little S.O.B., laugh, you don't know the big picture either!" As events have turned out, I doubt if Willie did know the big picture, it seems likely

ix

that General Patton did not, and most days I wonder if anyone did. I am convinced, however, that it is necessary for lawyers to know the "big picture" of property and to discern how its complex principles interact to form a coherent institution.

Obviously, a mass of detail is necessary before the lawyer can handle concrete situations but there are excellent volumes available for that purpose. The real danger is that the student will bog down in the narrow technicalities of property law and fail to *understand* the role of property as an institution and the law as a molder of that institution. Viewing the various strands of property law in a rather brief compass should offset that danger and give new insight into our property system.

As to the second objective, it is ironic that just as curricular time is contracting the law of property is expanding. On top of the always-important traditional areas of property has been piled the exciting new subject of land use with its heady infusions of public policy. The subject has not even been carefully defined as yet but it clearly includes zoning, planning, subdivision controls, water problems, public development of land, etc. While these matters must be left principally to senior seminars or advanced courses of as specialized sort, their impact is felt in the basic course and some coverage is essential so that the student will early be aware of the social, as well as the private, side of property rights. Some elementary understanding of zoning, for example, will do more to show the changing nature of property law than any amount of abstract discussion about how "law must grow or it will die."

Basically, this is a book on the law of land and personal property is treated only incidentally to illuminate certain property principles, such as the nature of gifts and the importance of possession. This approach has been followed for two reasons: (1) the most important aspect of personal property—commercial transfer—is the subject matter of specialized courses in the curriculum (Sales or Commercial Law) and requires textual treatment of its own and (2) Professor Brown's one-volume text on Personal Property is so complete that any extended duplication of that subject matter is unwarranted. At appropriate points in the text citations have been made to the Brown volume and the serious student should incorporate the cited materials by reference in order to complete "the big picture" of the law of property.

Finally, any contemporary writer in so ancient and fundamental a field as that covered by this book owes virtually everything but the organization and the sentence structure (and parts of those too!) to others more able than himself. To single out any specific group for special mention would be unfair and, in any case, appropriate documentation throughout the book discloses this debt to the past.

JOHN E. CRIBBET

Urbana, Illinois
June, 1962

*

SUMMARY OF CONTENTS

*

TABLE OF CONTENTS

TABLE OF CONTENTS

xvii

TABLE OF CONTENTS

†

PRINCIPLES OF THE LAW OF PROPERTY

Part One

INTRODUCTION TO THE CONCEPT OF PROPERTY

Chapter 1

WHO OWNS BLACKACRE?

Blackacre is the most celebrated tract of land in the world of the law—a world which you are now entering. Blackacre is wholly mythical, yet totally real. It is a concept, living in the realm of the mind and doubly valuable since much of the law of property has the same type of reality. The small farm at the edge of town, the big estate in the country, the apartment building, the skyscraper, your father's house, the squalid tenement, the majestic cathedral—they are all Blackacre and the law of property deals with the rights and duties of people in relation to the Blackacres of this planet. (At the present rate of scientific progress in space this statement may need enlarging.) How does one acquire Blackacre? What are his rights and duties while he owns it? What happens to it on his death? How can he give or sell it to others? How many of the decisions about land use are subject solely to private volition? How many of the decisions must be made by society, speaking through various levels of government? In the complex answers to these simple questions lie the law of property.

Who owns Blackacre? Surely the answer is simple enough: Henry Jones does; he inherited it from his father, John. It may be, but consider the following facts about Blackacre. When John Jones died the tract was mortgaged to *A* for half its value and the debt has not been paid. John had contracted in writing to sell the place to *B*, subject to the mortgage, but the sale has not been completed. John made a will in which he left one-half of Blackacre to his wife for her life, then to his son Henry in fee simple absolute. The will left one-quarter to *C* in trust for the benefit of John's alma mater and the remaining one-quarter to his daughters, *D* and *E*, not as tenants in common but as joint tenants with right of survivorship. It is rumored that the wife is dissatisfied with the will and plans to renounce it and seek either dower or her statutory share of the land. *F*, who owns an adjacent farm, has for many years used a road across Jones' tract to reach the highway and claims to have a right to continue doing so in spite of Henry's protest. *F* also claims the right to remove stone from the northern part of Blackacre under an old oral agreement. *G* was in actual possession of the parcel at John's death and has a written five-year lease as a tenant farmer which antedates both the mortgage and the contract. *H*, an oil company, has come forward with a written lease of the mineral rights under the surface of Blackacre. This lease was not recorded in the county recorder's office at the date of John's death and there is some contention that it is invalid. Blackacre is still raw farm land but the county has zoning laws and, in the master plan for the area, the tract is zoned for future residential development only. *B*, the contract purchaser, had planned to use the premises for a chemical plant if he were able to acquire a good title to the land. The state and federal governments are concerned about the environment and any major change in land use may require the filing of an environmental impact statement with the appropriate body. *J* claimed . . . ; but that's enough for purposes of illustration.

Who owns Blackacre? What does it mean to ask such a question in the light of the facts just given? Later, perhaps, you can answer these questions. Now, it is sufficient if you see why they are significant to an understanding of the law of property. The hypothetical case is most appropriate to a tract of land (real property), but you will recognize that many parts of it could also be applied to automobiles, animals, goods of various kinds, stocks and bonds (personal property or chattels). This gives you an insight into one of the basic aspects of property law—you must distinguish between the thing (*res*) and the estates, interests, or claims which people may own in the thing. As a layman you are accustomed to speak of the thing itself as property; as a lawyer you must come to realize that property is a concept, separate and apart from the thing. Property consists, in fact, of the legal relations among people in regard to a thing.[1]

---

1. "The term 'property' is one which is often abused and seldom defined or subjected to a careful analysis. It is generally used to denote a subject matter of a physical nature, such as a house, a car, or a cow. It is also used to denote a complex group of jural relations between the owner of a physical subject and all other individuals." Nelson v. La Tourrette, 178 N.E.2d 67, 68 (Ind.App.1961).

If the concept of property as defined in the previous paragraph is correct, an intriguing question arises as to which individuals have standing to sue to protect their property rights. In Sierra Club v. Morton [2], the United States Supreme Court gave the traditional answer. An environmental group, like the Sierra Club, has standing, i. e., a property right, only if it or its members would be affected in a particular way by a development which would change the natural environment (in this case a Disney Enterprises ski resort in what had been a part of the Sequoia National Forest). Mere special interest in such environmental changes is not enough. Dissenting justices took a less restrictive view and the controversy is far from over but it is clear that individuals or organizations have standing only if they can, at least, show a special reason for suing to protect the *res*. It is true that Mr. Justice Douglas, in dissent, felt that the trees themselves should be able to sue, through a representative, thus giving a new definition to the term property, but that position is unlikely to prevail.[3] For the indefinite future it remains true that property, in a legal sense, consists of the legal relations among people in regard to a thing (*res*).

In a complex society the relations between individuals are certain to be complicated. It follows that property law will be complicated as well since it is the product of society, the rules designed to maintain order in the acquisition, transmission, and use of things. Of course, these things constitute wealth, power, status, security, and many more verbal images which can be conjured up by the simple term, property. In the pages which follow, an attempt has been made to state the basic principles which govern the Anglo-American law of property. Even when reduced to broad principles the *corpus* of the law is complex, but it should be more manageable than when viewed in a multi-volumed treatise or even in a single, large text. These principles should serve as a chart to guide the beginning law student so that he will not lose his way in the maze and as a refresher to the older lawyer to remind him of the rational basis of our property law.

2. 405 U.S. 727, 92 S.Ct. 1361, 31 L.Ed.2d 636 (1972).

3. See Stone, Should Trees Have Standing? Toward Legal Rights for Natural Objects, 45 So.Cal.L. Rev. 450 (1972) and Baude, Sierra Club v. Morton: Standing Trees in a Thicket of Justiciability, 48 Ind.L.J. 197 (1973).

Chapter 2

THE INSTITUTION OF PROPERTY

————

It could be argued, not very plausibly I am afraid, that even animals have an institution of property. My pet beagle, Samantha, certainly treats a choice T-bone, once in her possession, as if it were a species of private property. Other dogs are warned off with appropriate indicia of ownership and even I trespass with respect after the original gift has been made. Why then is the bone not her property? Aside from man's conceit in refusing to extend human institutions to orders lower than himself, Samantha loses out because her rights in the juicy morsel are not protected by law. They are protected solely by brute force and while that may be sufficient for animals it is not enough, or should not be enough, for man. Jeremy Bentham, the great English legal reformer, put it thus: "Property and law are born together, and die together. Before laws were made there was no property; take away laws and property ceases".[1] Note that the thing, land or chattel, would still be there even in a state of anarchy and that man could stand over it, growling like a dog, but we could no longer call it property. The best simple definition of property that I know was given by Professor Cohen: "That is property to which the following label can be attached. To the world: Keep off unless you have my permission, which I may grant or withhold. Signed: Private citizen
       Endorsed: The state." [2]

Thus analyzed, it will be seen that property can exist in relation to an infinite number of things, real and personal, tangible and intangible. It is obvious enough that land, automobiles, and a cask of rare amontillado can be the subject of property. It is just as true, but less obvious, that checks, promissory notes, debts due from one person to another, documents of title such as bills of lading and warehouse receipts, stocks, bonds, shares, patents, trademarks, copyrights, and even good will can be brought within the ken of property. If a thing so intangible as good will can be classified as property, where does the long embrace end? Can an idea, the merest wisp of something that is to be, enter the fold? Perhaps, as the court in Belt v. Hamilton National Bank said: "The law now gives effect to a property right in an idea even

1. Bentham, Theory of Legislation, Principles of the Civil Code, Part I, 112, Dumont, ed., Hildreth Trans. (1864).

2. Cohen, Felix S., Dialogue on Private Property, 9 Rutgers L.Rev. 357 (1954).

though the idea may be neither patentable nor subject to copy-right. Such a concept, however, in order to receive the protection of the law, must be more than a mere abstraction. It must be re-duced to a concrete detailed form. It must, of course, be novel." [3]

Occasionally, in your reading of cases, you will find a court saying, "We cannot grant the relief requested by the plaintiff be-cause no property interest is involved and in this class of cases the court acts only to protect property rights." Is not this rea-soning in reverse? If the court grants the protection, it has cre-ated a species of property, as in the Belt case. If it refuses the remedy then no property can be said to exist because "take away laws and property ceases." No particular harm is done by the legal formula set forth above so long as you realize that property is not a mystical entity established by some fiat outside the framework of the law.

To the Western mind, the term property automatically trans-lates as *private* property. It is the individual's relationship to the *res* that comes to mind, not the state's. We are aware of a large amount of public ownership and of a growing quantity of public interest and control even in private ownership, but the funda-mental concept remains individualized. Not surprisingly, Anglo-American law reflects this view of property to a high degree. But we must not suppose that this craving for *"my* rights in a thing" is solely Western or is confined to the growth of the higher civil-izations. In fact, it seems to be universal, both in time and space. Although at one time it was supposed that primitive man lived in a state of true communism and claimed nothing, save collective-ly with his brethren, the later writers [4] establish that private property of a rudimentary sort did exist even in very early times.

If primitive man had some notion of private property, what happens to the idea that law is the basis of property? Did law, with its courts and enforceable remedies, also exist in these early societies? Obviously not, but there was custom and taboo and a kind of "obedience to the unenforceable" which stood in the stead of the formal law to come. Some writers would call this law of sorts and would not stick to the narrower definition of law which requires an effective sanction before a rule can be classified as law.[5]

3.   108 F.Supp. 689, 691 (D.D.C.1952).

4.   See Lowie, Incorporeal Property in Primitive Society, 37 Yale L.J. 551–554 (1928).

5.   For a lucid presentation of this point of view see Goodhart, English Law and the Moral Law 18–28 (1953). Professor Goodhart states that he borrowed his theory from Sir Frederick Pollock. "After pointing out that history shows that law precedes the organised society which we know as a State and that it can exist without a formal sanc-tion, he concludes that: 'Law is en-forced by the State because it is law: it is not law merely because the State enforces it.'" Goodhart calls this the obligation theory of

No modern society has ever been without some species of private property; it is the extent of private ownership, the quantum of rights that the individual has over the thing, not the fact of private ownership, that has varied. Even the Russian Communists did not abolish *all* private property; it was the means of production that Marx and Engels proposed to put in the hands of the proletariat.[6] In present day Russia, a large quantity of private property remains and the ownership of a house, for example, may not differ materially from that in the West.[7] Of course, a great chasm yawns between the property systems of the communist world and the free world, but common elements remain.

Although the right to private property is one of the pillars of Western faith, its moral justification has always posed a bit of a problem for the philosophers, economists, and all those who must rationalize the existence of institutions. The difficulty has been particularly great in the case of land, since it existed in a state of nature, apparently created by God for the use of all of his creatures. How did it happen that some individuals had rights over so much of it and some none at all? It was easier in the case of man-created things, for then you could say that the individual was entitled to the fruit of his labor. This whole subject is an intriguing one and you may want to explore it further,[8] but for the moment it will be sufficient to state that at least five theories have been propounded as the justification for private property— the occupation theory, the natural rights theory, the labor theory, the legal theory, and the social utility theory. The latter theory furnishes the most satisfying rationalization. "Thus we are finally driven to *the social utility theory*. This is really implied in the preceding theories and supplies the link that binds them all together. In ancient as in modern communities, the individual is helpless as against society, however much under modern democracy society may see fit to extend the bounds of individual freedom. If we allow the individual to seize upon unoccupied wealth, if we recognize the existence of certain rights in what are deemed to be the products of labor, if we throw the mantle of the law around the elements of private property—in every case society is speaking in no uncertain voice and permits these things because it is dimly conscious of the fact that they redound to the social welfare. Private property is an unmistakable index of social progress. It originated because of social reasons; it has grown under continual subjection to the social sanction. It is

law and adds: "I should therefore define law as any rule of human conduct which is recognised as being obligatory."

6. Marx and Engels, The Communist Manifesto.

7. Gunther, Inside Russia Today 374–375 (1958).

8. For a brief discussion see Seligman, Principles of Economics 131–134 (1905).

a natural right only in the broad sense that all social growth is natural." [9]

I would add two comments to the preceding analysis. First, the universality of private property is itself an argument for its continued existence. It appeals to all societies, at all stages of historical development. It is wise to harness that which has so deep an appeal to human nature and to concentrate on devising the best possible system of property which will serve the needs of both the individual and the public. A later portion of the book will deal with that problem in the modern world.[10] Second, the paramount argument for private property is that it best protects the rights of the individual. The old argument about property rights versus individual rights is passé; they are one and the same. Only as the individual has specific, and to a limited extent exclusive, rights over a thing, does he have that liberty of action which is vitally necessary to the preservation of a free society.[11] Absolute dominion by the individual is out of the question; absolute control by the state is unthinkable. The great problem of the law, and of those who develop and administer it, is to find the golden mean between the two extremes. Professor Powell has said it perfectly, "So then, the test of goodness must be some mean between the concept of the complete dominance of the individual and the idea of the all-importance of the state. It is an assumption of any society based on private property that it is good for the individuals to have liberty of a high order in the use of things they own. It is a postulate of any society which hopes to survive that there be limits imposed on the absoluteness of property so as to assure rules which will be accepted as fair for the distribution of scarcities. Whenever a change in the institution of property is being tested for its quality, the change is unadulteratedly bad if it restricts an individual and contributes nothing to the social welfare. If, however, as is usually the case, it restricts the individual but contributes something to the social welfare the disadvantage and the advantage must be weighed against each other and such action taken as the tipping of the scales thus found may dictate. This falls far short of a clear chart to wisdom but it provides an approach which will force persons to face squarely questions of social values, while preserving the benefits of private property." [12]

Now, we must turn our attention from the consideration of property as an institution on a universal basis to the specifics of Anglo-American property law. This is the system which you will be called upon to administer and, I hope, improve. Let us, then, tackle the principles of our property law.

9. Id. at 134.

10. Part Four, Chapter 3, Public Regulation of Land Use, p. 397 infra.

11. Lippman, The Method of Freedom 100–102 (1934).

12. 1 Powell, The Law of Real Property 33, 34 (1949).

*

Part Two

THE SCHEME OF OWNERSHIP IN ANGLO-AMERICAN LAW

Chapter 1

SOME BASIC CONSIDERATIONS

The study of any technical subject is plagued by its terminology and by the wealth of detail that needs explaining before the broad outlines make much sense. Where do you begin? It's no good replying, "at the beginning," because this is an Alice in Wonderland world and the origins are lost behind the mirrors. Professor Llewellyn has suggested the "bramble bush" approach [1] but its appeal lies mainly in retrospect. This chapter is an attempt to solve the dilemma by weeding out a few basic problems before proceeding to the main body of the subject.

SECTION 1. REAL AND PERSONAL PROPERTY

Our first basic consideration is the distinction between real and personal property. Real property relates to land and those things, such as houses, barns, and office buildings, which are more or less permanently attached to it. Personal property describes all other things which are subject to individual rights, whether they are tangible or intangible. This simple definition blurs at

---

1. The nature of this approach is suggested by the verse quoted in the introductory page of The Bramble Bush:

    "There was a man in our town
    And he was wondrous wise.
    He jumped into a bramble-bush
    And scratched out both his eyes—
    And when he found that he was blind,

    With all his might and main
    He jumped into another one—
    And scratched them in again."

    This cold plunge technique has much to commend it but you, as a beginning student, doubtless prefer a more gradual immersion. Nonetheless, you should read all of Professor Llewellyn's classic lectures on law and its study.

the edges and it is not always easy to tell whether a specific item is realty or personalty, e. g., what about growing timber, a pig pen on runners, household appliances that are attached to the plumbing, etc.? A body of decisions has developed to help you predict the correct category when the need arises.

The terminology used here makes no sematic sense because a car is just as "real" as a farm and the family mansion is more "personal" to the owner than shares of stock. The explanation lies, not in the history of property but of procedure. At early common law a real action (so called because it led to the return of the thing itself) was used when land was wrongfully detained by another but a personal action (which gave only a money claim against the wrongdoer) was proper where things other than land were involved. Thus, the *res* took the name of the action and we have, to this day, real property and personal property. The latter is also called a chattel, derived from cattle, the most frequent form of personal wealth in the early days.

This was not just a matter of terminology but a distinction of great importance. The law governing realty was quite different from that relating to personalty and many of these distinctions exist today, although their impact is gradually diminishing. Reference will be made to this bifurcation throughout the book and distinctions will be pointed out. It should not be supposed, however, that the classification is a wholly meaningless accident of history. There is a genuine difference in kind between these two categories of property and all systems of law take some notice of the cleavage. The distinction is really between movables, in the main created by man, and immovables, based on the raw earth which is our common heritage. Artificial distinctions which obfuscate the law and complicate its practice should be abolished but the real difference should never be lost to sight.

SECTION 2. ACQUISITION OF PROPERTY

A second basic consideration relates to the acquisition of property. How does a specific *res* become the subject of individual rights? The most obvious answer is by transfer from a prior owner, either by sale or by gift during the life of the donor or at his death. The rules governing these transfers comprise a large part of the law of property and are discussed in Part Three of this book. But this leaves the basic question unanswered. How was the property right acquired in the first instance? Here the personal versus real property distinction is significant.

Most personalty is created specifically for sale or use by the creator and clearly belongs to its producer. Thus, a new automobile is the property of the manufacturer, a new calf the property of the owner of the mother, and a new story, piece of music or design pattern, the property of the holder of the copyright or patent. There may be complications, of course, and the applicable law of patent or copyright must be carefully followed if ownership is to be fully protected. Moreover, there are special problems arising when the chattel is a wild animal never before subject to human dominion (it usually belongs to the first effective possessor of the animal *ferae naturae*, although this is complicated if the capture is made on the land of another) ; a lost article not reclaimed by the original owner (it typically belongs to the finder as against all but the "true" owner, although again the rights of the owner of the land where found [locus in quo] may give a bit of trouble) ; or a finished product, the result of materials belonging to one individual with labor furnished by another, without agreement between them, so that ownership is difficult to ascertain (the rules governing accession are applicable here). But in most cases, the issue of original ownership of chattels is easy to settle and does *not* become increasingly difficult with the passage of time. The life of most items of personal property is relatively short and they are consumed or pass into the rubbish heap without causing much of a legal tangle.

Land furnishes an interesting contrast to chattels. It is permanent, immovable, and, with minute exceptions, not produced by man. Moreover, it is the source from which most other property must come. He who controls the land does, in fact, control the destiny of man. This monopoly, which we call private property in land, must come by a grant from the sovereign. It would be possible to grant quantities of land to an individual for his life, or for so long as he could profitably use it, and then return it to the state for regrant to another. In practice, we have not followed this pattern and once the land has been granted it belongs to that individual to sell or give to another. The state may take it back for public purposes (eminent domain) or, if a man dies without a will and without heirs, it may revert to the state (escheat), but each of these events is the exception, not the rule. A major question should leap into your mind! How can you ever be sure that you are dealing with the true owner of land when the chain of title must go back many years to a government grant? This puzzler will be discussed in Part Three but you should note now that it is a factor in land law which is largely absent from the law of chattels.

In England, the acquisition of original title goes back for centuries (usually to 1066 and the Norman Conquest) and the pattern of distribution of the land will be treated in some detail in a succeeding chapter. In the United States, the origin of land titles is much more recent but also more diverse since the land came from various sources by conquest, purchase, and cession. However, the fundamental principle remains constant: the ownership of land is initially acquired from the state and passes by an ever-lengthening chain of title to the succeeding generations.

SECTION 3.   POSSESSION, SEISIN, TITLE, AND OWNERSHIP

Our third basic consideration lands us squarely in the middle of a semantic jungle. We must sort out, in a preliminary way, the meanings of several closely related words—possession, seisin, title, and ownership.

"Possession is nine points of the law." This old saw happens to be true and in many a legal controversy involving property rights the principal issue can be phrased, "Who had the prior possession of this thing?" The common-law forms of action which were used to recover a detained *res* or its value (trover, detinue, replevin, ejectment) were usually phrased in terms of possession or of a right to possession and while more complicated questions of title could be raised it was not always necessary to do so. Suppose *A* finds an antique silver plate and then *B* takes it from *A's* house. *A* can recover the plate in an action of replevin, based on his prior possession, even though he cannot be said to be the owner of it. *A* simply has a better right than *B*. Or suppose Blackacre belongs to *O*, who has moved away and apparently forgotten his land, but it is being farmed by *A* who recently moved into the vacant land without permission. If *B* should eject (dispossess) *A* without any authority from *O*, then *A* can recover Blackacre by an action in ejectment. Clearly, *A* does not own the land but he has a protected interest in it. Of course, if *B* sets up the title of *O* and establishes that he is the agent or is acting with authority from *O*, then *A* will lose. *O* was not in possession but he did have the right to possession, based on his ownership. Suppose *B* simply asserts *O's* title but does not tie himself to it, i. e., suppose *B* says, "I do not own Blackacre but neither do you; *O* does?" This is technically known as a plea in *jus tertii* (title in a third person) and there is some authority that it is a good defense to a possessory action.[2] The more recent cases, however, reject such a defense and allow *A* to recover on his prior possession.[3]

Possession, then, is something different from title and ownership but it is an exceedingly valuable property right. Indeed, if continued long enough and adverse to the interests of the owner, it can ripen into absolute ownership by operation of the statutes of limitation or the doctrine of prescription. These matters will be discussed in Part Three of this book.

What is possession? The watch on my wrist and the wallet in my pocket are clearly in my possession. So is the farm which I am cultivating daily or the house in which I am living. These are simple illustrations and mask the difficulty of the question. Actually, possession is one of the most illusive concepts in the law and you will have to wrestle with it for a long time before you see the dimensions of the problem. This is because possession, like many other words, has a lay meaning and a legal meaning and they are not identical. The law may say that a man has possession of a thing when the man in the street would hoot at the notion. Thus, if a master gives a watch to a servant to take to a friend, the watch is never out of the possession (legally) of the master. The servant does not have possession of it, he has only custody and if he converts the watch to his own use he is guilty of larceny, which requires a taking from the possession of the owner.[4] This example is illustrative of a host of similar situations in which the word possession becomes very slippery indeed. As your study progresses you will see why this is so; lawyers and courts are using the term to express certain legal consequences and the word may be expanded or contracted to make it better serve its purpose. This is confusing to the neophyte but essential to the sophisticated practitioner.

The difficulty is further confounded by the practice of speaking of *actual* possession and *constructive* possession.[5] The former tends to correspond to the lay concept of the term while the latter is a fictional use of the word to cover situations where the law requires a certain result but the facts fail to fit actual possession. Thus, two people may have possession of the same *res* at the same time although the individuals are widely separated geographically. The classic example is the gratuitous bailment [6]

2. Doe ex dem. Jefferson v. Howell, 1 Houst. (Del.) 178 (1855).

3. Bradshaw v. Ashley, 180 U.S. 59, 21 S.Ct. 297, 45 L.Ed. 423 (1901).

4. State v. Schingen, 20 Wis. 74 (1865).

5. In one classic case the court was forced to deal with three types of possession—actual, constructive, and constructive actual. New York-Kentucky Oil & Gas v. Miller, 187 Ky. 742, 220 S.W. 535 (1920). This would seem to be carrying a good thing too far.

6. A bailment is a transfer of possession of personal property, without the transfer of ownership, for the

of a chattel. *A* loans his car to *B* to use to go to a party. *A* retains the constructive possession (sometimes defined as the right to immediate possession) of the car; *B* has the actual possession of the vehicle. If it is stolen or damaged, either party can maintain a possessory action against the wrongdoer since each has the requisite possession. Compare this with the master-servant situation where the former has possession, the latter custody, and make some sense out of the distinction, if you can!

Note that if the bailment were for hire, i. e., if *B* paid *A* to let him use the car for one week, a different result would obtain. *B* would then have the actual possession of the automobile but *A* would no longer have constructive possession (no right to immediate possession). *A* would then have a reversionary interest which would entitle him to possession of the vehicle at the end of the bailment, but not before, unless there was a breach of its terms. Similarly, in a lease of land, the lessor would have the reversionary interest and the lessee the possessory interest.

Professor Lawson offers a definition of possession that is worth pondering: "In practice indeed possession is often said to be a social rather than a physical fact, in the sense that a person will be held to possess a thing if he has the sort and extent of control that society, considered as being represented by the ordinary reasonable man, would regard as appropriate to the kind of thing and the circumstances of the case." [7]

Seisin is an even more mystical concept than possession. Although it has been argued that seisin applied to chattels as well as to realty,[8] for most practical purposes we can confine the term to real property. Its importance is largely historical but no understanding of our real property system is possible without some grasp of its meaning. For reasons which will be clarified later, the early English landholder seldom was thought of as owning the land, rather he was seised of it. The protected interest of value to him was his seisin. When he transferred his interest he did so by "livery of seisin", accomplished by going on the land and physically transferring a clod of earth or a twig to the new holder of the land. If an intruder ousted him from the land, he was said to have been disseised and until he re-entered the land, either by self help or by the appropriate legal remedy, he had lost his seisin. This could be disastrous since, if the original holder of the land died without regaining his seisin, the land did not descend to his heirs, while on the death of the disseisor the seisin would go to the latter's heirs by "descent cast."

accomplishment of a particular purpose. Gratuitous means that no consideration was paid and the bailor can reclaim the chattel from the bailee at will.

7. Lawson, Introduction to the Law of Property 33 (1958).

8. Maitland, The Seisin of Chattels, 1 L.Q.Rev. 324 (1885).

In other words, seisin carried with it many aspects of ownership and was a vital part of the early land law. Just how vital
will become more apparent when we discuss the types of common-
law estates. But what was seisin? Many learned articles [9] have
tried to answer this question but we can "get by" if we treat it
as possession plus a mystical something which described a man's
claim to an estate of freehold in land. If this seems a bit sticky,
I apologize and ask your indulgence until we clarify freehold and
non-freehold estates in a subsequent chapter. Non-freehold estates correspond to what the layman thinks of as leasehold interests in land and seisin, for historical reasons, had no application
to them. The tenant had possession of the leased property but he
was not seised. The landlord (owner) did not have possession
but he did have seisin, for his was the freehold estate (a reversionary interest, it is true). The owner of a chattel who had it
under his control was said to be in possession of it but the owner
of Blackacre in a similar situation was said to be seised of the
land.

Title is a term frequently used as synonomous with ownership. While this is not strictly accurate we must recognize that
it is so used or we will be unnecessarily confused. It certainly
means something more than mere possession, although frequently
"proof of title" is made solely by establishing prior possession;
but one can have title to a thing and never have been close to possession of it. I prefer the definition that: "Title is a shorthand
term used to denote the facts which, if proved, will enable a plaintiff to recover possession or a defendant to retain possession of a
thing." [10]

The following illustrations should illuminate the definition.
(1) *A* disseises *B* and holds Blackacre for twenty years (the relevant statute of limitation) adversely to *B's* interests. After
twenty years, *A* has a better title than *B*. (2) *A* finds a ring
which *O* purchased from its manufacturer. *B* takes the ring
from *A*. *A* has a better title to the ring than *B* (based on prior
possession); *O* has a better title to the ring than *A* (based on *O's*
ownership by purchase). (3) *A* lives in a house on Blackacre and
has an abstract of title (history of the various deeds, mortgages,
etc. relating to the land) going back to a patent deed from the
United States. *B* has never been in possession of Blackacre but
has a warranty deed to the land for which he paid a large sum of
money to *C* in good faith, relying on documents which *C* showed
to him. These documents were forged. *A* has a better title to
Blackacre than *B*.

9. For one of the best, see Maitland,   10. Lawson, Introduction to the Law
    The Mystery of Seisin, 2 L.Q.Rev.   of Property 35 (1958).
    481 (1886).

You will note that in each case one person was said to have had a better title than another person. Most titles are relative and all that is necessary in the particular case is to say that *A* has a better title than *B, C,* or *D.* Seldom does the law speak of absolute title in the sense that *A* has title as against the whole world. The layman frequently does so and the lawyer may do so as a matter of convenience, but he recognizes that title is relative even when he speaks as if it were absolute. This is perfectly illustrated in real estate transactions where the vendor of land must have a merchantable title in order to force the purchaser to take it. An absolute or perfect title is not required, just a title which meets the ordinary demands of the market place. It may have slight flaws in it, but so long as a reasonable man would not object to them that is all which the law requires. Absolute title to land has meaning only in the Torrens system of land registration where the title to Blackacre is in fact registered in a public office and guaranteed by the state. Only a small proportion of land titles in the United States are of this sort, although registered titles are common in England and the rest of the common-law world. The registered title to an automobile is an analogous example in the personal property field.

This brings us, finally, to ownership. The interesting fact is that we could talk about the law of property and never mention ownership if it weren't for the significant lay meaning of the term. Early in the introduction we asked, "Who owns Blackacre?" We rather quickly saw that this was a meaningless question except as interpreted to read, "Who owns various estates or interests in Blackacre?" Legally, it would be more correct to say, "Who has title to these various estates, etc.?" Or, "Who has possession or the right to possession of various geographical parts of Blackacre?" Or even, "Who is seised of Blackacre?"

The simple truth is that Anglo-American law has not made much use of the term ownership in a technical sense. The Roman law has, and *dominium* in the civil-law countries means ownership in the absolute sense of that term. In the next chapter we will explore the matter a little further and show why ownership in the sense of *dominium* never became a vital concept in the English, and hence American, law.

This still leaves the basic question unanswered. What is the *usual* meaning of ownership when it appears in our law? Apparently, it is the general concept of absolute title or at least of merchantable title. It is that quantum of rights in a thing that cause most people to assume that the thing "belongs" to the individual. In the case of land it is an estate in fee simple absolute (to be explained in due course) and in the case of chattels it is the same concept *sans* name.

SECTION 4. LAW AND EQUITY

The fourth and final basic consideration deserts property law entirely for a brief excursion into the adjective law and a quick look at those engaging twins—common law and equity. One of the unique features of Anglo-American law is that during its period of gestation the embryo split into two parts and although an attempt was made to weave the two into one the seams still show. The common law developed in the royal courts of King's Bench, Common Pleas, and Exchequer and was administered through the rigid common-law forms of action which prescribed the relief to be given when certain facts were established. The common-law system of estates was worked out within this framework; the rights of property protected by these courts were called legal rights; and the recognized estates and interests were referred to as legal in character.

The rigidity of the common-law remedies, plus certain other factors,[11] led to the denial of justice in many instances and the litigants appealed to the king, the source of all English justice, for additional relief. Instead of referring the parties to the law courts which had already denied relief, the king entrusted these matters to his chancellor, who in those days was usually an ecclesiastic. Slowly, a separate body of law grew up which was supposed to represent the king's conscience and to be more equitable and just than the common law. At first it was erratic and

---

11. The rise of a separate court of equity was due to many factors but Professor Delmar Karlen points out four common-law inadequacies of major importance:

"1. **Remedies.** Substantially all the forms of action yielded only money judgments. The only important exception was the action of ejectment which could be used to recover the possession of real property. There was no practicable remedy for recovery of possession of a chattel, because replevin, as we have noted, was limited to cases of unlawful distress, and detinue allowed the defendant the option of returning the chattel or paying its value.

"The greatest deficiency in common law remedies was the lack of any machinery to prevent wrongs, or to force a defendant to perform a contract or other obligation.

"2. **Harsh Rules.** Some of the rules administered in the common law courts were harsh and contrary to common notions of fairness. There

was a good deal of emphasis upon formalism and ritual, particularly in the field of contract and property law. The tendency was to insist upon a literal interpretation of anything in writing.

"3. **Jury Trials.** While trial by jury was a vastly better method of determining facts than the methods which it supplanted, it had the disadvantage that juries were sometimes incapable of understanding complicated transactions, and in the Middle Ages, frequently subject to corruption or intimidation by powerful men. Thus the character of prospective litigants in some cases determined the feasibility of resort to the common law courts.

"4. **Blind Spots.** Some institutions and areas of conduct were not covered by the common law at all. Conspicuous were trusts and the administration of estates of persons who had died." Karlen, Primer of Procedure 149 (1950).

followed no set precedents, indeed the decrees were said to vary
with "the length of the chancellor's foot." Not surprisingly, the
chancery eventually fell into the hands of lawyers and became
more systematic and "legal" in its approach.

At this point of development it was apparent that there were
two rival systems of "law" in England—one was the common law
and the other was equity, administered by the court of chancery.
An epic struggle ensued [12] and out of the conflict emerged a kind
of truce which allowed the two systems to co-exist in the legal
world. In case of direct clash, equity was supreme but in the
course of time the gears came to mesh well and the two parts became a satisfactory whole which represented English law. In
1873, in the Supreme Court of Judicature Act, England finally
combined the courts themselves into a single High Court of Justice but separate branches remained for law and equity. In general, the American states had followed the English pattern and
either set up separate courts of law and equity or created two
divisions of the same court to handle the subject matter falling
into the two areas. Starting with the Field Code in New York
in 1848, the American legal reformers tried to wipe out the procedural distinctions between law and equity and develop a unified
system. This process of amalgamation of law and equity is still
going on but the split has left deep marks which may never be
fully eradicated.

This is not the forum to explore the various differences between law and equity, the former with its jury trial as a matter
of right and its so-called judgments *in rem*, the latter with its
judge (chancellor) and master in chancery in lieu of a jury and
its decrees *in personam*. What is important, here, is that certain
parts of property law came to be administered in equity rather
than in the common-law courts and another difficulty to ready
understanding of property terminology arose. The rights and
interests recognized by chancery were called equitable and so we
have legal title and equitable title, legal rights and equitable
rights.

Two of the principal heads of equitable jurisdiction will illustrate the point. (1) All trusts are administered on the equity
side of the court (the historical reason for this will be clarified
later) and although the trustee is said to have the legal title to
the property interest, i. e., the title to the land or chattel is transferred to him by a method recognized by the law courts, the equi-

12. This struggle came to a head in
Courtney v. Glanvil, Cro.Jac. 344
(1615), when the Court of King's
Bench released, on a writ of habeas
corpus, an individual who had been
imprisoned for contempt of a decree
of a court of equity. King James,
desiring to assert his supremacy
over all judges, appointed a committee of lawyers to look into the conflict. On the basis of their report,
he decided in favor of chancery.
Cases of outright conflict were few,
however, and, in the main, equity
complemented law rather than
clashing with it.

table title to the *res* is said to be in the beneficiary. This means that equity will protect the interests of the beneficiary and force the trustee to deal fairly with him. (2) If either party to a written contract [13] for the sale of an interest in land fails to carry out his bargain, equity will grant a decree for specific performance, i. e., force the vendor to deed the land to the purchaser and the latter to pay the purchase price. The only remedy at law is money damages for breach of contract and, since that is felt to be inadequate for a *res* so unique as land, equity asserts its extraordinary jurisdiction. The result is that the vendor has legal title until the deed conveying the interest in land is delivered to the purchaser but the purchaser is said to have equitable title just as soon as an enforceable contract for the sale of land is executed. This result arises from a maxim of the court of chancery, "Equity regards as done that which ought to be done." Since the vendor ought to convey the interest in land on performance by the purchaser, equity will treat the matter as if he had done so and give the buyer equitable title to the land. This doctrine had but limited application to personal property since chattels were seldom treated as unique (one plow was just as good as another) and money damages at law were adequate.

Like the distinction between real and personal property, this division into law and equity makes some sense aside from history, because of the inherent difference in the procedural relief involved. But the separate courts of law and equity have, all too frequently, created a chasm where none needed to exist. Even merger of the two courts has not always bridged the chasm.[14] Keeping in mind essential differences, the legal reformer should strive to eliminate all of the non-essentials.

With some of these basic considerations out of the way, we are now ready to turn our attention to the English law's principal contribution to the institution of property—the doctrine of estates.

13. In general, an oral contract for the sale of land is unenforceable because of the Statute of Frauds, the original English version of which reads in part: ". . . no action shall be brought . . . upon any contract or sale of lands, tenements or hereditaments, or any interest in or concerning them . . . unless the agreement upon which such action shall be brought, or some memorandum or note thereof, shall be in writing, and signed by the party to be charged therewith, or some other person thereunto by him lawfully authorized." An Act for Prevention of Frauds and Perjuries, Statute 29 Charles II, Chapter 3 (1677).

Under proper circumstances the doctrine of part performance may allow the equity court to grant specific performance of even an oral contract. See p. 127 infra.

14. "The most important obstacle to complete procedural unification in the United States is the presence in the federal constitution and in most state constitutions of guarantees of trial by jury in civil cases at law. As it has been graphically put, this guarantee of jury trial 'is the sword in the bed that prevents the complete union of law and equity.'" Scott and Simpson, Cases and Other Materials on Civil Procedure 246 (1950).

Chapter 2

THE CONCEPT OF ESTATES IN PROPERTY

The peculiar Anglo-American doctrine of estates can only be appreciated in the light of history. Indeed, Mr. Justice Holmes' famous aphorism, "There are times when a page of history is worth a volume of logic", fits property like a glove. Furthermore, a detailed discussion of each permissible estate is required to give any real substance to this area of the law. Both of these techniques will be applied in succeeding chapters, but we must clarify the concept of an estate before we pick its bones. The doctrine of estates is sometimes treated as if it made no sense except as an accident of history. This can scarcely be true or the doctrine would not have survived through the centuries. The law and lawyers may be a conservative force in society but they are not so hidebound as to retain a thoroughly worthless system of property law out of blind veneration of the past. F. H. Lawson, Professor of Comparative Law in the University of Oxford, successfully disposes of this bugaboo in *The Rational Strength of English Law* and concludes that, following some basic simplification of the law in England in 1925, "it (property law) is not only one of the finest parts of our law, but . . . in its main principles and structure it is superior to all foreign laws dealing with this subject." [1]

Once the student has mastered the full panoply of estates and interests in land (for it is to real property that most of this relates) he is apt to feel that it is the only system of land ownership and to forget that Anglo-American law represents but one way of dealing with the problem. Before this attitude has a chance to develop, let your mind speculate on the wide range of possible ownership schemes. As a starter, consider the following. (1) The state could own all of the land within its borders and (a) lease to its citizens for a set period of time, (b) lease to them for life, or (c) lease to them for so long as they use it wisely and economically. (2) The state could transfer outright the ownership of all of the land to its citizens for a fixed price and then regulate the extent of the interests which the new owner might have in the land, e. g., (a) allow the citizen to use it for life but then require that it go to his eldest son, etc., or (b) allow the citi-

---

1. Lawson, The Rational Strength of English Law 76 (1951). Pages 75–106 of this book deal with property and are eminently worth reading.

zen to own it absolutely, to do with it as he sees fit. (3) The state could grant land to families rather than individuals and give every member of the family a collective share in ownership so long as he remains loyal to the group. (4) The state could adopt the view that the land belongs to the person in possession of it and that all rights depend on possession and use. Abandonment of possession would leave the land open to the first taker by peaceful means.

This should be enough to suggest the wide range of possibilities. Note that all of those listed start with the state doling out certain rights in the land. This is essential at some point of time, although it may be in the forgotten past and may be only a recognition of an existing situation, since our earlier discussion established that property exists only as a creature of law, which presumes an organized state. It is the scheme of ownership which the law allows, after the land is distributed by the state, which is the important point to us.

The two principal legal systems of the West are the common law and the civil law (derived from the Roman law and the basis of most continental European law). The former developed the doctrine of estates as the scheme of land ownership, the latter settled on *dominium,* which denoted a nearly absolute property right. "The owner had an absolute title, he had an absolute right to dispose of the thing he owned, and his right to use it was limited by so few restrictions of a public-law character that it, too, could almost be called absolute. The kinds of incumbrances with which it could be burdened were kept down to the lowest possible number, and where they existed they were carefully distinguished from the *dominium* over the thing, which was regarded as retaining its character of a general undifferentiated right over the thing capable of resuming its original plenitude by the mere disappearance of the incumbrance." [2] This does not mean that the Roman law failed to recognize any interests outside that of *dominium.* It allowed hiring (*locatio conductio*), similar to a lease for a term of years and *usufruct,* not unlike a life estate. But these interests were subservient to the *dominium,* the true ownership of the land. They existed as mere rights issuing out of the land of another and not as separate estates of temporary ownership. Even the *fideicommisa,* which looked like a trust for purposes of a family settlement and required the *heres* (heir) to transfer to a third person designated by will, was bound by the idea of absolute ownership because the *heres* took the entire *dominium.*[3]

2. Lawson, The Law of Property 87 (1958).

3. For a more elaborate discussion of this point see Hargreaves, An Introduction to the Principles of Land Law 44–57 (3d ed. 1952).

If the preceding paragraph sounds a bid muddy, it boils down to the fact that in the civil law a thing has one absolute owner and while other individuals may have claims arising out of the thing they are personal claims (rights *in personam*) and not separate estates with real claims of ownership (rights *in rem*).   The contrast with the common-law system will be apparent in a moment.

The estate concept is the child of feudal notions of tenure. Feudalism is long dead and tenure has modern meaning only in the landlord-tenant relationship, but the child has reached a healthy maturity.   When the English king granted land to a powerful noble in return for military service, and that noble in turn allowed a lesser noble to use it, and so on down the line, it was difficult to speak of any one individual as owning the land. There was a tenurial relationship between the parties but what was the relationship of the parties to the land?   The king could be said to own it ultimately, but what did the first noble, the second noble, etc., down the line, own?   Of course, you could have said that they each had a personal right issuing out of the land, but with the development of forms of action it came about that the land itself could be regained, if there had been improper disseisin, and thus each party seemed to have a real right in the land.   Each person in the tenurial chain owned an estate in the land but not the land itself.   This was the crude beginning for what has become a highly sophisticated concept.

The estate and the land are two separate things.

Blackacre, the land	*Some Possible Estates in Blackacre*
	1. Life estate—owned by *A*
	2. Contingent remainder—owned by *B*
	3. Reversion—owned by *C*

The estate is purely conceptual, yet it is treated by the law as if it were a real thing with an identity of its own.   The land is, of course, a physical thing that is permanent, immovable, and continues to exist regardless of the changing character of the estates that relate to it.   Note that the term estate is *not* being used in the lay sense, "Mr. Henry Blythe White has a beautiful country estate."   The layman equates estate with Blackacre; the lawyer sees it as a separate entity.

A brief look at some of the basic estates will be sufficient to clarify the concept.   Later, after a dip into history, we will spend some time on a detailed analysis of the permissible estates.   By far the most common estate is the fee simple absolute.   This shorthand expression (its origin will be explained later) signifies that the owner of it has the full quantum of rights possible in Black-acre. A familiar illustration is to visualize each right as a stick and say that in the fee simple absolute (usually shortened to fee simple) the owner has the complete bundle of sticks. This estate comes closest to the Roman-law concept of *dominium* and to the lay concept of absolute ownership. Subject to the rights of the state, to zoning laws, and to the rights of adjoining landowners that no nuisance [4] be committed on the premises, it could be said, without too much inaccuracy, that he who owns a fee simple es-tate in Blackacre owns Blackacre. Of course, the fee simple own-er may decide to mortgage his estate or incumber it in various ways and while he would still be said to have a fee simple its util-ity would be greatly reduced.

Assume that *O* has an estate in fee simple in Blackacre. He has a wife, *W*, and one son, *S*. *O* would like to leave the land to the son eventually but *S* is now a young boy and *O* wants to be sure that the mother is provided for during her lifetime. To ac-complish both results,[5] *O* can carve his estate into two new es-tates, either by an *inter vivos* conveyance (a deed delivered dur-ing his lifetime) or by a testamentary disposition (a will which speaks at his death). He can give *W* an estate for her life, fol-lowed by an estate in fee simple to *S*. This latter estate would be called a remainder, i. e., it is what remains after the life es-tate in *W*.

Several important points must be made. The moment *O* dies, if a will has been employed, *O's* fee simple estate becomes two new estates, one in *W* for life, the other by way of remainder in *S*. But the land, Blackacre, is physically unchanged, it has not been carved into two parts nor will it be. Only the estates have changed and they exist apart from the land. Moreover, both es-tates are *presently* in existence even though one of them, the re-mainder, will not become possessory until a future date, the death of *W*. *W's* estate is a present, possessory estate of indeterminate duration. So long as she lives she is entitled to the possession of Blackacre, to its rents and its profits. Subject to the doctrine of waste,[6] she can treat it as her property but, of course, will have some difficulty in selling or mortgaging her estate because of its

4. The law of nuisance is based on an old Latin maxim, *sic utere tuo ut alienum non laedas* (use your own property in such a manner as not to injure that of another). The maxim suggests the scope of the doctrine.

5. *O* could also use a trust and place the legal title in a trustee, directing him to pay the proceeds to *W* for life and then convey the land to *S* on *W's* death.

6. Waste is the legal doctrine which determines the obligations of the life tenant to a remainderman or reversioner. Thus, a life tenant cannot remove the top soil, tear down a building, or cut the growing timber without being called to ac-count for "wasting" the estate.

uncertain duration. Does she own Blackacre? Of course not, but she does own a life estate *in* Blackacre.

S also has a present estate in Blackacre but it is not now possessory. He must wait for his estate to "fall in" on the death of his mother before he can claim a right to rents and profits. *S's* estate is also called a future interest [7] to distinguish it from a possessory interest. Note that *S* did not receive his estate from *W* but from *O*. He will not inherit Blackacre from *W* on her death; it has been his in remainder since the death of his father. Since *S* has a present estate, he can sell it or mortgage it and on his death intestate it will pass to his heirs. Its present value is diminished only by the existence of *W's* life estate. In this case, *S's* remainder is in fee simple because *O* gave him all of the bundle of sticks except the life estate. The remainder could itself be a life estate, however, as when *O* devises to *W* for life, remainder to *S* for life, remainder to another son, *X*, in fee simple.

If *O*, in the illustration above had conveyed the land to *W* for life but made no further provision as to disposition of the land, it is apparent that a large part of the bundle of sticks would have remained in *O*. This transaction could be viewed in several ways. (1) *O*, who had the fee simple before, could be said to have it still, subject to a life estate in *W*. (2) *O* could be said to have converted his present, possessory interest in Blackacre into a future interest. (3) *O* could be said to have changed his fee simple absolute into two estates, a life estate in *W* and a reversion in himself. The estate in reversion which *O* now has will be seen to be quite similar to *S's* remainder in the previous example. If the interest following a particular estate (the life estate in *W*, so called because it is only a fragment—*particula*—of *O's* estate) is transferred to a third person it is called a remainder but if it is retained by *O*, either expressly or by implication (as where nothing is said about what is to happen to his estate after *W's* death) it is called a reversion. Technically, the estate doesn't revert to *O*, he had it all the time, but the right to possession does revert to him and hence the name of the estate. Whenever an owner fails to dispose of all of his estate in the land there will be a reversion in him or in his successor to the title.

While still dealing with the broad concept of estates, we should take a preliminary look at the difference between a vested and a contingent remainder. A remainder is vested when its owner would be entitled to take possession of Blackacre immediately upon termination of the particular estate (usually by the

---

7. This terminology, "future interest", can be quite misleading. Some courts say the remainder is a present estate but a future interest. Actually, it is a present interest as well; only the enjoyment by way of possession is postponed. But, since the usage is so common, you must be prepared to deal with it.

death of the owner of the life estate). The first example above was of a vested remainder because S would take possession just as soon as W died. Both the person to take the estate and the quantum of the estate were known. No condition had to be fulfilled other than the death of the life tenant. In the second example, the reversion too was vested, since the identity of the reversioner was known and O was to take as soon as the particular estate came to an end. Technically, these estates are said to be vested *in interest;* they do not vest *in possession* until the life tenant's death.

Consider the following example. O conveys to W for life, remainder to the first son of O to reach the age of twenty-one. O and W are childless at the time. There is a remainder all right but in whom is it vested? If S, a son of O, aged one year were alive, in whom would it be vested? This is an illustration of a contingent remainder and there are two contingencies to be fulfilled: (1) a son must be born to O (although W would not necessarily need to be the mother) and (2) that son must live to be twenty-one years of age. When both conditions are met the remainder will vest in the son, but not until then. It is not enough for the particular estate to come to an end; the contingencies too must be fulfilled.

What would happen if the contingencies were not met? Then, the estate would revert to O or his successors in title. Thus, whenever you have a contingent remainder you always have a reversion which will be effective if the condition is not satisfied. However, the reversion itself is conditional since it will give the estate back to O only if the contingent remainder fails to vest. Despite this attribute, the interest in O is still called a reversion and *not* a contingent reversion. Note that a contingent remainder is not truly an estate at all, but only the "expectancy" of an estate if the proper events take place. Nonetheless, even this "expectancy" came to be alienable (transferable) if the proper form of deed was used and it is common to speak of the owner of a contingent remainder just as we do of a vested remainder.

In this chapter we have dealt with the estates concept in terms of real property and it is true that its full development took place in relation to land. At the time when estates were evolving most of the wealth was in the soil and there was no need for a complicated system for the few chattels of importance. There is no necessary block which prevents the application of the doctrine of estates to personalty today and to some extent the idea of a split between the *res* and the estate is to be found in the modern law of personalty. This is especially true in shares of stocks and bonds. But the essential distinction between realty and personalty remains and there will never be a need for an extensive system of estates in items so short lived as most chattels. It is, after all, the permanency of land which creates the desire to control its destiny far into the future and this is the *raison d'être* for much of the doctrine of estates.

It has been the purpose of this chapter to introduce you to the idea of estates, to show you how a split between the *res* and the estate in the *res* can lead to flexibility and to a diverse pattern of ownership. Before we turn our microscope on the individual estates, we shall take a broad look at the historical setting which gave rise to our present system.

Chapter 3

THE HISTORICAL BACKGROUND OF ANGLO-AMERICAN PROPERTY LAW

————

Law is a child of its past; property law still suffers from its infantile repressions. Our law of property was born in feudalism and came to maturity as feudalism was dying. It is a tribute to the intellect of the early property lawyers that the system has so long survived the society that gave it birth. Our task is to try to understand the origins of the law so that we may grasp its modern essence. Only then can we be sure of retaining that which is meaningful and rejecting that which has outlived its social usefulness. This is not the place for a detailed or profound historical study,[1] but the sketch which follows should carry us forward in our search for the principles of the law of property.

————

SECTION 1. THE RISE OF FEUDALISM

————

Feudalism grew out of the chaos of the Dark Ages, the period from the fifth to the tenth centuries A.D. It is difficult for us to visualize the total collapse of Western civilization which followed the decline of the Roman Empire. It was not just the fall of a single state but the disintegration of all law and order. Even the habit of or feeling for a stable society gradually disappeared. It became once again, as in the dawn of history, a world of disorganized individuals who looked to their own might for the minimum essentials of life. Unfortunately, we can best visualize the scene by realizing that we live on the brink of a similar precipice. A total nuclear war could reduce modern society to the same horrendous condition that preceded the rise of feudalism.

The need for security and some sense of stability survived the collapse of the Roman peace. Since it could not be found in the state, the individual turned to the strongest of his fellows and put his fate in hands which appeared to be more capable than his own. Thus arose the practice of *commendation* by which a

1. For a more detailed coverage with citations to a number of leading sources see 1 Powell, Real Property 35–66 (1949).

weaker man became the vassal of a stronger man, the lord, through a ceremony of homage which promised mutual duties of support and protection. The vassal needed protection for more than just his family and himself; he needed security for his property which consisted almost solely of land. The land was his means of livelihood and if he lost it to marauders he might as well lose life itself. Feudalism, from the start, was both a system of government and a method of holding property. The lord was, in effect, given the land which he must then protect. The vassal no longer owned what had been his land, he "held" the land "of" the lord as if he were a tenant. This method of land-holding had little in common with the modern law of landlord and tenant, except the name, and should not be confused with it. The land which the vassal now held was called his "fief", "feudum," or "feud" and has become the "fee" of our modern law.

This system of feudal tenure did not end with a simple relationship between one lord and one vassal but became, by the process of "subinfeudation," a lengthening chain between the top feudal lord and the actual possessor of the land. There was no theoretical limit to subinfeudation and as many as five or six mesne lords might be involved, each serving as a link between the lord above and the vassal below. As the central state began to reassert its strength, the king became the lord at the top of the heap and the only one who was always a lord and never a vassal. Even this last statement needs modification, for William the Conqueror was himself a vassal of the King of France. The pattern was much as follows:

King
|
Tenant in chief (*in capite*)
|
Mesne lords (both lord and vassal)
|
Tenant in demesne (the vassal in possession of
the land)

This feudalistic system was general over all of western Europe but it never became the sole method of land ownership on the Continent. There were isolated pockets that held out, where the landowners did not become tenants of some powerful noble. This land was called *allodial* [2] as opposed to tenurial and it was subject to various fates. Some of it developed into petty kingdoms and other tracts were linked to the kings of France or Germany by non-feudal ties. In England, on the other hand, all of the land was subjected to feudalistic tenure by William the Conqueror and

2. Allodial means free, not held of
any lord or superior.

allodial lands were eventually unknown. This point is significant because the universality of feudalism in England led to the consolidation of the law into a systematic whole, while no such result followed on the Continent since the "law of the feuds" could not be applied to the *allodial* land.

English land law begins, for all practical purposes, with 1066 and the Battle of Hastings. The Anglo-Saxon England which existed before the Norman conquest had its own system of law, undoubtedly influenced by the feudalism of the Continent, but within a generation it had been absorbed into the new Norman scheme. How this happened is a fascinating story in its own right, but the key factor is that one powerful noble, William the Bastard, stood at the top of the landholding pyramid and all of the land in England was "held" of him. This complete feudalisation of England is eloquently evidenced by the Domesday Book, a register of landholders compiled by William for tax purposes. The pages of the book reveal the substitution of the formula, "*A* holds of *B; B* holds of the King," for any prior conception of land ownership.

What was this law of the feuds? How was the relationship of tenure controlled between the king, the lords, and the vassals? The first question requires a look at the incidents of feudal tenures; the second a survey of the courts and remedies of twelfth century England. Tenures must, at the outset, be classified as free and unfree. Feudalism was an aristocratic concept and you can be sure that no overlord would be found plowing in the field. He restricted himself to such gentlemanly pursuits as warfare, hawking, hunting, and the ravishing of lovely ladies. The free tenures stopped just short of the actual tillers of the soil, the *villeins* who were bound to the land by an unfree tenure. We will first discuss free tenures and then turn briefly to the unfree type, followed by a quick look at the court structure which enforced them both.

SECTION 2. FREE TENURES

There were four types of free tenure, each of them designed to fulfill a particular need. The principal need was for *security* and the typical tenure therefore was *knight service*.[3] The

---

3. Knight service and serjeantry tenure are sometimes classified together under the broader heading of military tenure.

name fairly well describes the tenure. In return for his feud (fee), the tenant agreed to furnish forty days of armed service to the lord per year. At first this probably was done by the tenant himself but later he hired men to serve in his stead and as the need for a private army diminished, with the growth of the central government, a money payment (scutage) was substituted for the original personal service.

A second need was for *splendor,* for the full panoply of pomp and circumstance which went with a medieval aristocracy. Since there was no money economy, the lord bought these things with land and *serjeantry* tenure was the result. Serjeantry was subdivided into grand and petty; the former being restricted to tenants in chief who performed ceremonial services for the king and the latter covering the less august types of service. Examples of serjeantry tenure included: butlers, cooks, sword bearers, suppliers of military transport and weapons, and such improbable duties as "holding the head of our Lord the King between Dover and Whitsand as often as he should happen to pass over sea between those ports." [4]

A third need was for things of the *spirit.* In those rough times the days on this earth were none too pleasant at best and even a bloodthirsty old lecher had hopes of life eternal. How better make sure of the joy to come than by giving lands for that express purpose? *Frankalmoin* tenure resulted and while it took many forms the tenant was always a priest or a religious body.

The fourth and final need of the times was for *subsistence,* for the crops and products of the soil without which life could not continue. Out of this great need arose *socage* tenure. Actually, it was a kind of residual tenure and Professor Hargreaves [5] suggests that the only accurate way of defining it is to say that it comprised any free tenure which did not fall within the other three types. However, it frequently included labor services on the demesne land of the lord and hence is thought of as the subsistence tenure. It should not, however, be confused with the unfree tenures which will be discussed later and which also related to tilling the soil. Socage tenure was less aristocratic than the other three, in fact it had aspects of the non-feudal, and this had interesting consequences in the development of the law.

In each of the four free tenures certain characteristic services were due from the tenant to the lord, but there were also other rights and obligations involved called the incidents of tenure. These incidents fell into two general classes, first, those which arose during the lifetime of the parties and which involv-

4. Blount, Ancient Tenures 57 (2d ed. 1784).

5. Hargreaves, Introduction to Land Law 29 (3d ed. 1952).

ed the personal relationship of the lord and tenant and, second, those which arose on the death of the tenant and hence might be called feudal problems of inheritance. The first class included homage, fealty, and the aids. The second was composed of escheat, relief, wardship, and marriage.

Homage was the ceremony by which the tenant became the lord's man.[6] Fealty was the oath taken by the tenant in which he promised to be loyal to the lord. The duty of the tenant to supply financial support to the lord on specific occasions was called an aid and eventually there came, in England at least, to be three such aids. They were the ransoming of the lord, the knighting of his eldest son, and the marriage of his eldest daughter.

The second class of incidents requires a bit more discussion. What happened to the feud when the tenant died? If he died without an heir [7] there was no problem. The land was originally the lord's, "held" of him by the tenant. Remove the tenant by death without an heir and the land simply returned to him who "owned" it before. This incident was called escheat and is the name still given to the similar process by which the state succeeds to the property of a man who dies intestate without heirs.[8] In feudal times the land also would revert to the lord if the tenant committed a felony. This *forfeiture* of the feud was said to occur because the felon's blood was attainted or corrupted.[9]

6. Littleton describes homage as follows: "For when the tenant shall make homage to his lord, he shall be ungirt, and his head uncovered, and his lord shall sit, and the tenant shall kneel before him on both his knees, and hold his hands jointly together between the hands of his lord, and shall say thus: 'I become your man from this day forward of life and limb and of earthly worship, and unto you shall be true and faithful, and bear to you faith for the tenements that I claim to hold of you, saving the faith that I owe unto your sovereign lord the king'; and then the lord, so sitting, shall kiss him." Littleton, Tenures, bk. II, c. 1, s. 85.

7. The heir at this date was the eldest son, under the doctrine of primogeniture. England followed this doctrine until 1925 using the Canons of Descent to determine heirship. For a discussion of the Canons see Atkinson, Wills 41–50 (2d ed. 1953).

8. Heirs today are determined by the statute of descent in force in the particular state. The pattern of distribution varies but if there is a surviving spouse and children the former usually takes one-third, the latter two-thirds. If there is no surviving spouse, the children take all. Issue of deceased children take by representation, i. e., they take the share of their deceased parent. The statutes then proceed to spell out a complete scheme of heirship, including collateral as well as lineal heirs and usually ending with a provision for escheat in default of known heirs. See p. 112 infra. For the modern role of escheat see In re O'Connor's Estate, 126 Neb. 182, 252 N.W. 826 (1934).

9. In one situation the feud was forfeited directly to the king and did not escheat to the lord. This was when a tenant committed high treason—usually the outcome of having guessed wrong in the frequent struggles for the crown.

Suppose the tenant had an heir who had attained his majority and was ready and able to succeed to the feud? The tenurial relationship was a highly personal one and just because the lord was willing to be served by the father was no reason that he should have to accept the son. The lord might want the land back so that he could give it to an entirely different person as a tenant. It was finally settled, however, that the land should pass to the heir but that he must pay a sum of money, called a relief,[10] to his lord for this privilege. This may not have been the origin of the modern estate and inheritance taxes but at least it was a feudal incident that had the same effect as our "death duties."

Suppose the tenant died leaving an heir who had not yet attained his (21 years) or her (14 years) majority? This placed a heavy burden on the overlord since the infant could not be of immediate service. To compensate for this difficulty the lord was allowed the profitable right of wardship and marriage. Wardship bore no resemblance to the modern law of guardian and ward, in fact it was the antithesis of it. The lord was allowed full use of the land during the period of minority and was under no obligation to render an account of his stewardship. Even upon attaining majority, the ward had to sue for possession of the land and pay a half year's profits for the privilege of receiving it.

Marriage, the other incident attending minority, was also quite onerous to the infant. Blackstone described it as follows: "While the infant was in ward, the guardian had the power of tendering him or her a suitable match, without disparagement or inequality: which if the infants refused, they forfeited the value of the marriage to their guardian: that is, so much as a jury would assess, or anyone would *bona fide* give to the guardian for such an alliance: and if the infants married themselves without the guardian's consent, they forfeited double the value." [11]

Not all of the incidents, just described, applied to all four types of free tenure. For example, wardship and marriage, which were so prominent in knight service, did not apply to socage. In this latter tenure, the guardian was the nearest relative who was incapable of inheriting the land (a very wise requirement) and the guardian had to account for the profits at the end of his stewardship. Moreover, he could not give or sell the ward in marriage.

In addition to the usual tenures there were certain abnormal patterns which existed in some districts of England, e. g., gavelkind, borough-English, and ancient demesne. Gavelkind was

10. When the relief was due to the king from the tenants *in capite* it was called primer seisin.

11. Blackstone, Vol. ii, p. 70.

the name given to socage tenure in the county of Kent and involved several peculiarities, including the fact that on intestacy the land descended to all the sons equally rather than passing by primogeniture and the land itself was devisable at a period when testamentary distribution was unknown for land generally. Borough-English was the custom, found in some parts of the country, by which the land descended to the youngest son to the exclusion of the rest of the children.[12] Ancient demesne was land held by freehold tenants which had belonged to the Crown in the time of Edward the Confessor and William the Conqueror. The ancient demesne tenants were subject to special restraints but also had special immunities.

SECTION 3.   UNFREE TENURES

In spite of these variations, all of the free tenures had much in common and represented a generally coherent scheme of land distribution—a scheme which served the needs of a feudal society quite as efficiently as the present law serves our twentieth century society. But the feudal pattern did not stop with the free tenures, it included another important type of land holding— copyhold tenure, which grew out of the old custom of villeinage. Copyhold was an unfree tenure and was reserved for those who actually tilled the soil. It can be understood best by a brief glance at the medieval manor.

The manor was the basic unit on which English feudalism was built. The typical manor consisted of: "(a) the land belonging to the lord, which was called his demesne, (b) the land held of the lord by free tenants whether in socage or knight service, (c) the land held of the lord by persons called villein tenants, (d) rights of jurisdiction exercisable by the lord over the free tenants in the Court Baron, and over the villeins in the Court Customary, and (e) waste land on which the tenants were entitled to pasture their cattle."[13] As we have pointed out previously, the free tenures were essentially aristocratic (especially knight service, serjeantry, and frankalmoin) so it was left to the

---

12. If the custom of *prima nox*, allowing the lord the privilege of the first night with the tenant's bride, could be definitely established as having existed in England, as it did on the Continent, then this method of inheritance would make

some sense. The youngest rather than the eldest son would have the better chance of being his father's heir.

13. Cheshire, Modern Real Property 23 (8th ed. 1958).

villeins to do the backbreaking work of medieval farming. They were not free men but serfs who belonged to the manor and thus to the lord. It is true that some socage tenants also farmed the land but they held their feud according to the established incidents and were free men.

The position of the villein was not quite so precarious as it might seem and he was entitled to certain protection in the customary court of the manor. But he did not have any access to the king's court because he was thought of as a creature of the lord over whom the king had no direct control. With the passage of the centuries, the role of the villein changed and he was freed from the soil by processes the discussion of which lie beyond the scope of this book.[14] Suffice it to say that the individual became a free man but that the tenure itself continued to be classified as unfree and the nomenclature changed from villeinage to copyhold tenure. The term copyhold arose as follows: "The copyhold tenant, like his predecessor the villein, held at the will of the lord, but yet at the same time he held on the conditions which had become fixed by the customs of his particular manor. The lord's will could not be exercised capriciously, but only in conformity with custom. He still held a court, and that court kept records of all transactions affecting the lands. These records were called the rolls of the court. When, for instance, a tenant sold his interest to a third party, the circumstances of the sale would be recorded, and the buyer would receive a copy of the court rolls in so far as they affected his holding. Inasmuch as he held his estate by copy of court roll, he came to be called a copyholder." [15]

SECTION 4. COURTS, LEGISLATION, AND THE DECLINE OF FEUDALISM

This, then, was the law of the feuds. Of course, it was not written down in the form of legislation and much of it was more accurately custom [16] than law. It was enforced, when need be,

14. Many factors contributed to the villeins' new status, including the shortage of labor caused by the Black Death which made the individual's services more valuable.

15. Cheshire, op. cit. supra note 13, at 25.

16. Some of the customs were not only strange but downright hilarious. Consider for example: "The manors of East and West Enborne, in the county of Berks, have this custom, that if a copyhold tenant die, the widow shall have her free-bench in all his copyhold lands whilst she continues sole and chaste (dum sola et casta fuerit); but if she commits incontinency, she forfeits her widow's estate; yet, after

by the courts of the period and they worked out the details of the feudal structure. Originally, the local courts of the lord handled most of the problems of the manor and there was no law common to all of England. But the king too had a court and from the early days of the Conquest the tenants-in-chief had access to the jurisdiction of the Crown when their land was in dispute. The developing writ system [17] gave them a *praecipe in capite*, a species of the Writs of Right for the recovery of land. Since the writ was so ancient it was dilatory, cumbersome, and subject to the defect of trial by battle.[18] The evolution by which this archaic remedy was ultimately replaced by writs of entry and, finally, by the action of ejectment makes a complicated story. The history of these early forms of action is really the history of the law of land, for within the mystic language of the writs was worked out the full significance of possession, seisin, and the relativity of title.[19] Beginning in 1154, with the accession of the great lawgiver Henry II, the royal courts gradually took over most of the controversies involving the land held by free tenure and eventually even the copyhold tenant found justice in the king's court.

By the early years of the thirteenth century the feudalistic system of tenures was firmly rooted in England. The later history of tenures is a tale of steady disintegration under the inexorable pressures of a changing society. The first departure of major significance came in 1290 with the statute of *Quia Emptores,* one of the most important pieces of legislation in the history of land law. *Quia Emptores* is still on the statute books in England and is considered to be a part of the law of most American states.[20] Simply put, it abolished subinfeudation and pro-

---

this, if she comes into the next court held for the manor, riding backward upon a black ram, with his tail in her hand, and says the words following, the steward is bound by the custom to readmit her to her free-bench:

'Here I am,
Riding upon a black ram,
Like a whore, as I am;
And for my crincum crancum,
Have lost my bincum bancum;
And for my tail's game,
Am brought to this wordly shame:
Therefore, good Mr. Steward, let me have my lands again.' "

Hazlitt, Tenures of Land and Customs of Manors (Blount) 109 (4th ed. 1874).

17. For a brief summary of the development of the forms of action

(writs) see Shipman, Common-Law Pleading 54–65 (3d ed. 1923).

18. This method of trial was brought from Normandy by William and allowed the accuser to fight the accused, in the belief that heaven would give victory to the one in the right. The modern jury is a distinct advance over this more primitive type of warfare!

19. Since judgment would be awarded to the one who had a better or prior right to possession, it was not necessary to decide who was the "owner" of the land, only whether *P's* title was relatively better than *D's.*

20. In most states *Quia Emptores* is considered a common-law statute and is treated as a part of the law brought by the colonists to this

vided that all future alienations of land must be by substitution. For various reasons [21] it was to the interest of the great lords to prevent a further lengthening of the feudal chain and this could be done only by ending subinfeudation. As a result, when a mesne lord conveyed his feud to a stranger the latter stepped into the conveyor's shoes (was substituted for him) instead of becoming a tenant of the conveyor. Since 1290, it has been legally impossible to alienate a fee simple absolute [22] so that there shall be tenure between grantor and grantee; the grantee holds the land as tenant of the grantor's lord. It should be noted that *Quia Emptores* also provided that no more tenures in frankalmoin could be created.

It was impossible to devise land until 1540, with the passage of the Statute of Wills. This meant that prior to that time the land frequently escheated to the overlord for want of an heir. Treason was a common offense, since the landholder was likely to choose the wrong side in the continuous struggle with the king.[23] This meant forfeiture of the land because of the tainted blood. Both escheat and forfeiture gradually reduced the length of the feudal chain and, since *Quia Emptores* had put an end to further subinfeudation, more and more land came to be held directly of the king.

Other forces were also at work, reducing the significance of the various obligations of tenure. Even in the twelfth century the money payment of scutage had taken the place of military service and by the sixteenth century most of the services due in socage tenure had been commuted to a fixed money rent. With the inflation resulting from the discovery of the wealth of the New World these fixed rents ceased to be valuable and indeed were hardly worth the trouble of collecting.[24] Wardship and marriage continued to be important since they gave actual control of the land but they never applied to socage tenure and eventually came to be of value only to the king in knight service. In the seventeenth century even they were abolished and the king

country and incorporated into the common law of the state.

21. The principal reason was that each addition to the chain carried the overlord further from control, by wardship, of the land itself.

22. It must be noted that this applied only to a fee simple absolute. It was still possible to carve out estates less than a fee simple absolute, as we shall see in the next chapter.

23. Witness the effect of the War of the Roses on the land titles of England.

24. An occasional trace survives, even in the atomic age, as see *Time*, Sept. 15, 1947, p. 27: "The owner of the Red Rose Inn in West Grove, Pa., solemnly went through the yearly ceremony stipulated by a 216-year old deed, handed over one red rose to the heir of William Penn." This species of subinfeudation was possible even after *Quia Emptores* because the statute was held not to apply to the king or his immediate tenants, of which William Penn was one.

received an hereditary excise on beer, cider, and spirits in their stead. In 1660, the Statute of Tenures marked the end of the strictly feudal period of English land law. It turned knight service and serjeantry into socage tenure, destroying all incidents of value except escheat. The honorary services of grand serjeantry were retained but this had no real significance to land law. The aids were abolished and this ended the last burdensome incident of socage tenure. Frankalmoin was not affected by the Act of 1660 and, in theory, it may still exist if created prior to *Quia Emptores* (1290), but the tenure has no practical modern significance.

The Statute of Tenures applied only to freeholds; copyhold tenure continued in England until the twentieth century. However, the special incidents of copyhold, which included the rights of the lord to the mines and timber of the tenant, could be sold to the copyholder and the great proportion of copyhold land had become freehold by the end of the nineteenth century. The last vestiges of the old distinctions were finally swept away in England on January 1, 1926, when a series of acts, known collectively as "The Property Legislation of 1925," came into effect. All copyholds were automatically converted into socage tenure. Escheat was abolished, even for those cases where an intervening lord could be discovered, and when a tenant dies intestate without any heirs his estate now goes directly to the Crown as *bona vacantia* (property without an owner).

Professor Hargreaves sums up the present law of England: "It follows that for practical purposes all land is now held directly of the King by socage tenure, though the services and incidents have now disappeared, and that consequently the existence of tenure no longer has any direct effects. Its indirect effects, however, still remain, for they are the basis of the modern doctrine of estates. . . ."[25]

SECTION 5.   TENURE IN THE UNITED STATES

This chapter has been devoted entirely to English history, for obvious reasons. Feudalism never existed in the United States and, but for its vital role in shaping modern land law, could be omitted from our study. Except for Louisiana, the com-

25.   Hargreaves, op. cit. supra note 5, at 36.

mon law of England is the basis for our legal institutions. "When the American colonies were first settled by our ancestors, it was held as well by the settlers, as by the judges and lawyers of England, that they brought hither as a birthright and inheritance, so much of the common law as was applicable to their local situation and change of circumstances." [26] This reception of the English common law into the American stream is a complicated matter and it varies from state to state,[27] but it is clear enough that the broad framework of property law is English, with all of its strengths and weaknesses.

The American colonies recognized, to some extent, the law of tenure and some of the charters provided that the land was to be held in free and common socage. In several colonies attempts were made to set up a "quit rent" system—the reservation of an annual rent on the grant of a tract of land. Some manors were even established, following the English manorial system but apparently no form of military tenure was ever recognized. The American Revolution destroyed any tenurial relationship between American landowners and the English king but left open the question of whether the state succeeded to the position of the king as an overlord. In theory, this did happen in some states and a tenurial relation continued; in other states, there was an indication that the land was to be considered as allodial and that tenure had ceased to exist, even in theory, after the Revolution. It is interesting to speculate on this distinction between theories of land holding and whether it makes any practical difference which view a particular state adopts, but for our purposes it seems best to conclude, with Chancellor Kent, that in the United States "every real vestige of tenure is annihilated." [28]

This discussion of the historical background of Anglo-American property law has omitted any mention of the Statute of Uses and its widespread influence on property concepts. This statute and the role of the chancery court in the development of the law will be the subject of a later chapter. First, we must make a more detailed analysis of the permissible common-law estates.

26.   State v. Campbell, T.U.P.Charlton 166, 167 (Ga.1808).

27.   See for example Ill.Rev.Stat. ch. 28 (1973). Illinois became a state in 1818 and its law included the enactments of the Northwest Territory which embraced an act of 1795 receiving the English common law and statutes as of the fourth year of James I. The fourth year of James I covers the period beginning March 24, 1606, and ending March 23, 1607.

28.   4 Kent Comm. *24. For an excellent short discussion of tenure in United States with references to the leading articles and books, see 1 American Law of Property 57–60 (Casner ed. 1952).

Chapter 4

PERMISSIBLE ESTATES AT COMMON LAW

Now that we know something about the concept of estates and the feudal society out of which that concept grew, we must turn our attention to the estates themselves. Here, we shall be concerned with the estates not only as they were but as they now are, and an attempt will be made to indicate the contemporary law in each instance. The term estate apparently referred originally to status, i. e., it described the position of the landholder in feudal society. Later the word lost its significance as to status but the terminology remained. Thus, our first major classification is between freehold estates and non-freehold estates. The first category includes the various types of fees simple, the fee simple conditional, the fee tail, and the life estate. The second grouping encompasses the estate for years, the estate from period to period, the estate at will, and the estate at sufferance. These were the only estates that were recognized by the courts of common law and hence they are referred to as legal estates. Eventually, the rise of a separate court of equity enlarged the scheme of permissible estates and we will discuss the enlarged pattern in due course. The common-law courts were quite rigid in their handling of estates and unless the grantor of land followed the prescribed formula the conveyance was likely to be void or to reach an unexpected result. The owner of land was not free to create new types of estates just because they happened to strike his fancy.

The non-freehold estates should not be confused with the unfree tenure of copyhold. The latter was a part of the feudal scheme and a tenant could have a freehold estate (a fee simple, for example) in an unfree tenure. The non-freehold estates, on the other hand, were outside the feudal pattern and historically were not considered to be real property at all. The tenant who leased land for a term of years could not recover his leasehold by a real action but had to resort to a personal action for money damages. Thus, the leasehold was treated as personal property and called by the ambiguous name of chattel real. This term, and some of the legal consequences, have stuck to the non-freehold estates to this day.

SECTION 1. THE FREEHOLD ESTATES

A. THE FEES SIMPLE

When we say fee simple, or even fee, we normally mean the fee simple absolute, the largest quantum of interest that a landowner can have in Anglo-American law. However, there are two other kinds of fees simple which are of some importance: the fee simple determinable and the fee simple subject to a condition subsequent. These latter two estates are covered by the generic term defeasible fees or determinable fees and are also frequently called base or qualified fees. We are now in an area where exact terminology is called for so you must be careful not to confuse terms which, on the surface, seem very close to each other.

---

(1) THE FEE SIMPLE ABSOLUTE

This estate has several attributes which distinguish it from all other estates in land. It is the most common of all the estates and corresponds most closely to what the layman means by ownership. It is freely alienable, i. e., the owner of a fee simple absolute has all of the "bundle of sticks" and can transfer them to anyone whom he may choose, either for value or gratuitously. It is freely devisable, i. e., the owner of this estate can leave it, by will, to any person of his own choosing since the estate is not subject to control by the owner's heirs. (Both of these last statements are modified by the marital rights of a spouse, a matter for subsequent discussion.) If the owner dies intestate, the fee simple will be inherited by his collateral heirs if there are no lineal heirs and no spouse, i. e., the estate can pass, not only to descendants of the owner, but also to uncles, aunts, nephews, nieces and cousins, depending on the statute of descent in the particular jurisdiction. Finally, the owner is entitled to the full protection of the law in safeguarding his estate. He does not have absolute and sole dominion over the land, but so long as he complies with the public law and does not commit a nuisance on the land he can expect the full help of the state in preserving his bundle of rights in Blackacre.

The sum of these attributes means that the fee simple absolute, as an estate, has a potentially infinite duration. The original owner may sell it, give it away, devise it, or die intestate, but the estate itself continues merrily on its way. It can end· only if the owner dies intestate without heirs, in which case it escheats to the state. Of course, the state can also acquire all or a part of it by eminent domain but this is true of any estate or interest in land.

At common law, there was only one way to convey [1] a fee simple absolute. It had to be done by a conveyance "to A and his heirs." Language which varied from this formula would not suffice; thus a grant "to A", "to A forever," or even "to A in fee simple absolute" would result in a life estate in A rather than a fee simple absolute. This bit of mysticism seems odd to us now and, indeed, the need for the phrase "and his heirs" has been rather universally abolished.[2] A grantor, who has a fee, can now convey it by any language which indicates an intention to transfer an absolute estate. It is significant that the key phrase never was necessary to *devise* a fee simple absolute. But then this latter method of land transfer was not possible until relatively late in legal development—1540, with the passage of the Statute of Wills.

In legal analysis, "and his heirs" were said to be words of limitation rather than words of purchase. "To A", on the other hand, were words of purchase. This cryptic language meant that A took an estate by the terms of the conveyance itself. Purchase was not used to imply that A paid for or purchased the estate—it might in fact be a gift—but only that he took the land by conveyance or devise. *A's* heirs, however, took nothing by the terms of the grant (if they ever received the estate it would have to be by descent) so the phrase "and his heirs" described or limited the estate held by A, i. e., a fee simple absolute. Note that when we speak of words of limitation we are using limitation in the old sense of bounding or describing, rather than in the sense of cutting down or holding back. The grant, "to A and his heirs", describes the fact that A takes a fee simple absolute rather than creating a joint estate in A and *A's* heirs. Even today, a conveyance "to A and his heirs" creates a fee simple absolute

1. Convey is a word of art which means to transfer an estate in land *inter vivos.* When an estate in land is transferred by will it is said to be devised.

2. The Illinois statute is typical. "Every estate in lands which shall be granted, conveyed or devised, although other words heretofore necessary to transfer an estate of inheritance be not added, shall be deemed a fee simple estate of inheritance, if a less estate be not limited by express words, or do not appear to have been granted, conveyed or devised by construction or operation of law." Ill.Rev.Stat. ch. 30, § 12 (1973).

in *A* although, as previously pointed out, the cumbersome formula is no longer necessary.

"And his heirs" were also said to be words of inheritance since they indicated an inheritable estate, as opposed to a life estate which died with the life tenant. Moreover, they were words of general inheritance in contrast to "and the heirs of his body" which created a fee tail and were words of special inheritance, limiting the estate to descendants of *A*. No one is quite sure of the origin of this famous phrase, "and his heirs",[3] but you should note that it accurately described the estate in the very early days. At a time when *A* could neither alienate or devise land, it had either to revert to the overlord (if a life estate) or pass to the heir (primogeniture was in effect) if one existed. So, the words described an estate which would pass on death to *A*'s heir, thence to *A*'s heir's heir, etc. The change in the nature of a fee in the direction of free alienability and devisability made the words meaningless in the original sense but their vitality carried on until recent times.[4]

---

(2) The Defeasible or Determinable Fees

Assume *O* has an estate of fee simple absolute in Blackacre. *O* is a crusading teetotaler and, while he wants to sell Blackacre to *A*, he abhors the thought of a tavern on the old home place. *A* is dry as a bone and could be counted on to keep out the demon rum, but *A* will not live forever and moreover he might sell at any time. Rather than sell *A* the full "bundle of sticks", *O's* lawyer advises him to convey a defeasible fee. The conveyance reads: "To *A* and his heirs *so long as* the premises are not used for the sale of spirituous beverages." *A* now has a fee simple determinable or a fee on common-law limitation.[5] It has all of the characteristics of a fee simple absolute, except one—it is not of infinite duration because it will terminate if the premises are used for the sale of liquor. The grant says nothing about what will happen if the forbidden act occurs, but the law will supply this omission. The estate will go back to *O* (or his heirs), who will then own it in fee simple absolute again. Perhaps liq-

---

3. For a good account of the historical background of this phrase see Bigelow, Introduction to the Law of Real Property 21–23 (3d ed. 1945).

4. The words "and his heirs" may still be necessary in some states. See Cole v. Steinlauf, 144 Conn.

629, 136 A.2d 744 (1957). See also, Dennen v. Searle, 149 Conn. 126, 176 A.2d 561 (1961) and Grainger v. Hamilton, 228 S.C. 318, 90 S.E. 2d 209 (1955).

5. First Universalist Society of North Adams v. Boland, 155 Mass. **171**, 29 N.E. 524 (1892).

uor will never be sold on the land, so *O* is not at all sure that he, or his heirs, will ever possess Blackacre again; thus it is not possible to call *O's* retained interest a reversion (as would be the case if *A* had been given a life estate). *O* has a possibility of reverter, the technical name for the future interest which follows a fee simple determinable.

O could have accomplished the same result by a slightly different technique. He could have conveyed Blackacre "to *A* and his heirs *on the condition that* the land is never used for the sale of liquor and if it is then *O* and his heirs may *re-enter* and repossess the land." This would create a fee simple subject to a condition subsequent. This estate is also called a fee on condition subsequent. *O* would then be left with a future interest, called a right of entry for condition broken or a power of termination. Both of these terms are used but the latter seems to be the more modern terminology. The fee simple determinable and the fee simple subject to a condition subsequent are obviously twins [6] with a great deal in common, but there are times when it is necessary to make a sharp distinction between the two.[7] The former estate terminates automatically on the happening of the named event, whereas the latter requires the affirmative act of re-entry by *O* or his heirs before the estate can be said to be back in the grantor.

It is not always easy to distinguish between the two types of defeasible fees, and poor draftsmanship often confuses the issue even further. As a general guide, however, the words "so long as", "until", etc., denote a fee simple determinable in *A;* the words "on the condition that", "on condition", or words setting up an affirmative right of re-entry in any fashion indicate a fee simple subject to a condition subsequent. Professor Gray [8] thought that the fee simple determinable should have been impossible after the statute of *Quia Emptores* because the estate involved a continuing relation of tenure between the grantor and the grantee, whereas the statute allowed only a conveyance by substitution. Whatever may be said for Gray's position,[9] it was not adopted by the courts and both of the estates are very much alive today.

6. See Dunham, Possibility of Reverter and Powers of Termination —Fraternal or Identical Twins?, 20 U.Chi.L.Rev. 215 (1953).

7. Oldfield v. Stoeco Homes, Inc., 26 N.J. 246, 139 A.2d 291 (1958). For a more extended discussion see Williams, Restrictions on the Use of Land: Conditions Subsequent and Determinable Fees, 27 Texas L.Rev. 158 (1948).

8. Gray, The Rule Against Perpetuities §§ 31–32 (4th ed. 1942).

9. The adoption of Gray's position would have simplified the law of estates and prevented the clouding of many real estate titles. On the other hand, the estate must have some social utility since it has been so widely used in practice.

The future interests which follow these estates, the possibility of reverter and the power of termination, have caused a great deal of difficulty in the law. The courts have held that they are not subject to the Rule Against Perpetuities [10] and hence they can continue to exist for an indefinite period of time. The problem is further confounded by the fact that in many states these particular future interests are held to be neither alienable nor devisable.[11] They can descend to the heirs at law according to the local statute of descent or be released to the holder of the defeasible fee, thus giving him a fee simple absolute by way of merger of the present and future estates. The title situation becomes clear when we refer to the previous illustrations. In either case, O could release his interest to A and settle the matter, but he is not likely to do so since it was he who established the defeasible fee in the first instance. Years pass, the sentiment against liquor drinking fades, and X wants to buy the land from A's heirs to use for a hotel which will include a bar. From whom must X get conveyances? Obviously, he wants a deed from the present holders of the defeasible fee but he must also extinguish the future interest or run into difficulty later. O is long since dead and so are his immediate heirs, but the lawyer must trace the pattern of descent to discover the present owners of the possibility of reverter or power of termination and then buy their interests in the land.

In order to eliminate some of these title problems, the various states have passed statutes of limitation which bar the future interest after a period of time. Some of these statutes [12] put a time limit on the enforcement of a claim after the specific event has occurred, e. g., O or his heirs must re-enter the land or bring suit for possession within seven years after Blackacre is used for the sale of liquor. Other statutes [13] provide that the possibility of reverter or power of termination will cease to be effective after a gross period (say, forty years) from the date of creation of the estate. Note that these latter statutes have the effect of turning defeasible fees into fees simple absolute

10. Leach, Perpetuities in Perspective: Ending the Rule's Reign of Terror, 65 Harv.L.Rev. 721, 739–740 (1952).

11. See Ill.Rev.Stat. ch. 30, § 37b (1973): "No possibility of reverter or right of re-entry for breach of a condition subsequent is alienable or devisable . . ." In other states the problem can be even more complex since a distinction is drawn between these two future interests and a power of termination is destroyed by an attempt to alienate (assign) it while a possibility of reverter is not so destroyed. Rice v. Boston and Worcester R. R. Corp., 12 Allen 141 (Mass.1866); Halpin v. Rural Agricultural School District No. 9, 224 Mich. 308, 194 N.W. 1005 (1923); contra, Jones v. Oklahoma City, 193 Okl. 637, 145 P.2d 971 (1943).

12. Ill.Rev.Stat. ch. 83, §§ 1a, 1b (1973).

13. Id., ch. 30, § 37e.

after the passage of a sufficient length of time. They do not abolish defeasible fees but they lessen their impact considerably.

Two additional points should be mentioned before passing to the next estate. First, defeasible estates are not confined to the fee simple category. You can have a determinable life estate, i. e., an estate for the life of *A* or so long as he uses the premises for school purposes. Similarly, you can have an estate for years subject to a power of termination in the lessor, e. g., "to *A* for ten years on condition that he pay the rent the first of every month and keep the premises in repair, if he does not the lessor to have the power to terminate the estate." In these latter two situations, the possibility of reverter and the power of termination are incident to a reversion in the grantor and will pass to anyone who acquires the reversion. Thus, if the lessor sells his reversion to another person, the purchaser will have the power to terminate *A's* estate for years for non-payment of rent. This should be contrasted with the future interests following defeasible fees, which are not incident to any reversion and, in many states, can only descend to the heirs of the creator of the interests.

Second, there is a third type of defeasible fee which we have not discussed at this point—the fee simple subject to an executory limitation. This estate was not permissible at common law and came into existence only after the Statute of Uses (1535). It will be explained in a later chapter but one or two comments should be made here. At common law, the only estates that were permissible after a fee simple were the possibility of reverter and the power of termination. Neither of them could be created in a third party, i. e., they could exist only in the grantor. If *O* tried to convey "to *A* and his heirs for so long as the land is used for school purposes, then to *B* and his heirs", the latter part of the conveyance was void. This was an attempt to create a shifting interest, shifting the fee from *A* to *B* on the happening of a certain event. After the Statute of Uses this became a permissible estate and today *A* would have a fee simple subject to an executory limitation and *B* would have an executory interest in the land, similar to a possibility of reverter.

B.   THE FEE SIMPLE CONDITIONAL AND THE FEE TAIL

The temptation is great to spend a long time on the fascinating estate of fee tail but the impulse must be resisted because the estate does not have much significance for the twentieth-century lawyer. It cannot be safely ignored, however, because the grant "to *A* and the heirs of his body" or "to *A* and his issue" may still be encountered in title search and we must have a clear idea of what it means.

The entailed estate represents one stage in the long struggle to tie up the family land in such a way that it would never cease to be family land. Coupled with the rule of primogeniture and, at a later date, the strict settlement,[14] it led to the perpetuation of a landed aristocracy in England which never had a real counterpart in this country. The idea was basically simple. Since a grant "to *A* and his heirs" gave *A* the full estate in fee simple absolute with free alienabiliy and devisability, *A* could easily run through the estate and leave nothing for the next generation. A formula was needed which, in effect, gave *A* a life estate, followed by a life estate in his eldest son, followed by a similar estate in his eldest son, and so on down through the generations. Then *A* could never sell, devise, or incumber more than the estate for his own life, his son would be similarly bound, etc. The attempted solution was for *O* to grant the land "to *A* and the heirs of his body", "to *A* and his bodily heirs", or "to *A* and his issue."

In the very early days of the common law (prior to 1285), this device was not wholly successful, for the courts held that this created a fee simple conditional, which had the following consequences: (1) if *A* had no issue (heirs of body) he could make no conveyance during his lifetime and *O*, who had a reversionary interest would take the property on *A's* death; (2) if issue were born alive to *A*, then he could convey a fee simple to a third party, thus cutting off the inheritance by his issue and also *O's* reversion; (3) if, after the birth of issue alive, *A* did not convey the estate it passed to the issue in fee simple conditional and the same consequences followed in the hands of the new holder. This meant that the original purpose of the conveyance could be defeated and there was no assurance that the property would stay in the family line. To remedy this situation the Statute *De Donis Conditionalibus* was passed in 1285, resulting in the fee tail estate. Since *De Donis* is a part of the received law of most American states, the fee simple conditional never existed in most of the United States. However, in a few states the statute *De Donis Conditionalibus* was never adopted and the old fee simple

14. The strict settlement was an English device by which land was limited to a parent for life, then to his first and other sons or children in tail, with trustees interposed to protect contingent remainders. For a good, short discussion see Casner and Leach, Cases and Text on Property 382–384 (1951).

conditional is still a possible estate.[15] You should be careful not to confuse this anachronistic estate with the fee simple determinable and the fee simple subject to a condition subsequent, both of which sound similar to it but are quite different creatures.

The name fee tail comes from the French *tailler* (to carve) and probably meant that the grantor was able to carve a fee to his exact prescription. This carving could be carried to great lengths and the land could be limited to male descendants generally—fee tail male general; to female issue—fee tail female; or to issue of a specific wife—fee tail special. In the latter case, if the specified wife died, the holder of the estate was said to have a fee tail with possibility of issue extinct—a type of life estate. Note, however, that the limiting language must mean successive generations of bodily heirs, not just the bodily heir or heirs determined at the death of the first taker. Thus, a grant "to A and his children"[16] did not create a fee tail at all since this was a particular group of bodily heirs rather than an indefinite line of succession.

Assume a grant by *O* "to *A* and the heirs of his body." *A* dies survived by three sons, the eldest of whom is *X*. Under primogeniture, *X* would inherit the fee tail estate, but what if he died later without issue? The estate would then pass to *O* or *O's* heirs, if he were dead. Every estate tail was followed by a reversion since it was always possible that a given holder of the estate tail would die without bodily heirs. However, the grantor could create a remainder after a fee tail instead of keeping the reversion himself. This was done by the following language: "To *A* and the heirs of his body, but if *A* dies without issue then to *B* and his heirs." Remember, however, that no remainders could be created following any fees simple.

For about two hundred years after the Statute *De Donis Conditionalibus* the fee tail was in its hey-day. Then the lawyers, with the cooperation of the courts, developed techniques for defeating the purpose of the grantor by allowing the tenant in tail to convey a fee simple absolute to a stranger. The stranger could then reconvey the fee simple to the former tenant in tail who would now own the land free of the entail. These disentail-

---

15. South Carolina is the most conspicuous example of this group. See Blume v. Pearcy, 204 S.C. 409, 29 S.E.2d 673 (1944) and 2 Powell, Real Property 67–70 (1950).

16. This language called for the application of the Rule in Wild's Case (Wild's Case, 6 Co.Rep. 16b [1599]). If *A* had children at the time of the conveyance or devise, *A* and the children shared equal concurrent estates. If *A* had no children, the original Rule called *A's* estate a fee tail if created by a devise, but gave *A* a life estate with a remainder to the children of *A*, if any were born, if created by deed. The modern tendency is to apply the latter rule to both devises and deeds. At least one court has given *A* a fee simple in the latter situation. See Herrick v. Lain, 375 Ill. 569, 32 N.E.2d 154 (1941).

ing devices were called the fine and the common recovery [17] and they represent the rankest fictions in the history of the common law. Nonetheless, they undoubtedly served a purpose in the period when the fee tail was outgrowing its usefulness and can be cited as another example of the common law's capacity for growth without the intervention of legislation. Although the fine and the common recovery crippled the effectiveness of the fee tail they did not make it the same estate as a fee simple. If the tenant in tail failed to make a disentailing conveyance the land could not pass under his will and it would descend only to his lineal, not his general, heirs or if there was a failure of issue it would pass to the reversioner or remainderman. Moreover, the disentailment could be made only by a tenant in possession and out of this requirement grew the English system of strict settlement which from about 1650 to 1925 was used to keep English land in the family line.

The American colonies did not take kindly to entailed estates or to primogeniture. These twin attributes of a landed aristocracy did not mesh with democratic ideals and the state constitutions and statutes were used to prohibit this part of the English common law. Thomas Jefferson led the way with his draft of the Virginia constitution.[18] Despite the ban on the fee tail estate, the language "to A and the heirs of his body" continued to creep into the deeds and wills in this country and even today the lawyer may be faced with this ghost from the remote past. When he encounters this apparition there is no excuse for palpitation of the heart, since he can consult the statute books and cases in his particular jurisdiction and usually find an answer to the legal effect of "to A and his issue."

Although there are many variations among the states, the present treatment of the fee tail can be generally classified under four heads. (1) Some states still retain the fee simple conditional.[19] (2) Some states (New York falls in this category) treat the language as creating a fee simple absolute.[20] This is

17. See Williams, Cases and Materials on the Law of Property 163–166 (1954) for a short account of how these fictional law suits operated.

18. 1 Schachner, Thomas Jefferson 146 (1951): "On the day after he brought in his court bill, Jefferson launched the first of his major assaults on the ancient regime—a request for leave to bring in a bill 'to enable tenants in taille to convey their lands in fee simple.' And, as if this revolutionary attack on the fundamental base for an aristocracy were not sufficient for a day, he

followed it immediately with a demand for complete and drastic revision of the laws of Virginia." Incidentally, Schachner uses an interesting description of the fee tail estate when he writes, "The real title was in the biological family and not in the temporary individual."

19. Iowa, Oregon, and South Carolina are usually listed in this category although the estate seems to be important only in the latter jurisdiction.

20. More than twenty states have a statute of this type. Even with

probably the least complicated expedient. (3) Some states (e. g., Delaware) retain the fee tail but allow the tenant in tail to execute a simple disentailing conveyance. This is a streamlined version of the fine and common recovery.[21] (4) Still other states (the Illinois statute is of this type) attempt to give some meaning to the language by giving *A*, the first taker, a life estate followed by a remainder in fee simple in *A's* issue.

Once you depart from the common-law pattern it is easy to make property law hard. This aphorism is neatly illustrated by the judicial gloss put on the Illinois disentailment statute. The Act reads: "In cases where, by the common law, any person or persons might hereafter become seized, without applying the rule of property known as the rule in Shelley's Case, in fee tail, of any lands, tenements, or hereditaments, by virtue of any devise, gift, grant or other conveyance, hereafter to be made, or by any other means whatsoever, such person or persons, instead of being or becoming seized thereof in fee tail, shall be deemed and adjudged to be, and become seized thereof, for his or her natural life only, and the remainder shall pass in fee simple absolute, to the person or persons to whom the estate tail would, on the death of the first grantee, devisee or donee in tail first pass, according to the course of the common law, by virtue of such devise, gift, grant or conveyance." [22] The Illinois Supreme Court [23] has interpreted this to mean that, in a grant "to *A* and his bodily heirs," *A* will take a life estate and so long as *A* has no issue the grantor, *O*, will have the reversion. As soon as the first child is born to *A* the remainder vests in him subject to partial divestiture to let in after-born children. *O's* reversion is, of course, cut off by the birth of this first child. As successive children are born to *A* they each take their aliquot share of the remainder, thus cutting down on the share of the first child. Moreover, since the remainder vests in each child, as born, there is no requirement that he survive *A* in order to take his share. Death in the lifetime of *A* will cause the child's portion to pass to his heirs or devisees. This interpretation flies in the teeth of the general rule that a living person has no heirs and hence a child, not being a bodily

such an act all is not beer and skittles, however. The New York statute reads: "Estates tail have been abolished; and every estate which would be adjudged a fee tail . . . shall be deemed a fee simple; and if no valid remainder be limited thereon, a fee simple absolute. Where a remainder in fee shall be limited on an estate which would be a fee tail . . . such remainder shall be valid, as a contingent limitation on a fee, and shall vest in possession on the death of the first taker, without issue living at the time of such death." New York Consolidated Laws ch. 50, § 32. Try your hand at the interpretation of this statute.

21. See Caccamo v. Banning, 6 Terry (Del.) 394, 75 A.2d 222 (1950).

22. Ill.Rev.Stat. ch. 30, § 5 (1973).

23. Danberg v. Langman, 318 Ill. 266, 149 N.E. 245 (1925); Stearns v. Curry, 306 Ill. 94, 137 N.E. 471 (1922).

heir until *A's* death, should have to survive *A* in order to take. Arkansas,[24] which has a statute similar to that in Illinois, has adopted the latter interpretation and holds that *A* takes a life estate, followed by contingent (conditioned on outliving *A* and hence being his heir of body) remainders in *A's* issue. In a given case, widely divergent results could be reached under statutes which read almost the same. This should warn you that the fee tail can still be a tricky business and should be treated with proper respect.

C. THE LIFE ESTATE

Apart from the fee simple absolute, the life estate is the most common and the most important of the freehold estates. Although its origin was commercial—it was granted in return for rent in the period when a term of years was not entitled to "real" protection from the law—at the present time it is used primarily as a part of a family settlement, either inter vivos or testamentary. In some areas of the United States it is still common for the husband to leave Blackacre to his wife for life, remainder to his children. It is a growing practice, however, to establish a trust in these circumstances and leave Blackacre to *X*, a trustee with power of sale, to hold for the benefit of the wife for life and then to distribute the land or the proceeds of a sale to the children. This gives the wife an equitable life estate rather than a legal one.

Life estates are divided broadly into two classes, legal and conventional. The former are those estates created by operation of law rather than by act of the parties. Under this heading come curtesy, dower, and some of the other marital interests in land.[25] Logically, these legal life estates should be discussed at this point but functionally they represent an attempt by society to provide security for a spouse by giving him or her an interest in the real property of the other. Hence, all such interests will be treated later under an appropriate heading.[26]

24. Ark.Stat.Ann. § 50–405 (1947).

25. At common law, during the joint lives of husband and wife, the husband was seised of his wife's freeholds *jure uxoris*. The fee tail after possibility of issue extinct was also a legal life estate. It arose in the case of a fee tail special (where the estate was limited to the bodily heirs of a named spouse). After the named spouse died, her husband had a fee tail with possibility of issue extinct. Do you see why this was a life estate?

26. See Chapter 6, Section 1, Marital Interests, p. 85, infra.

Conventional life estates are themselves subdivided into two classes, ordinary life estates and estates *pur autre vie* (for the life of another). The former are by far the most frequent and, if the creating language is ambiguous, the presumption always favors the use of the grantee's life as the measuring stick. Typically, the estate is created by *O* granting or devising "to *A* for life," although it should be remembered that a grant "to *A*", without the addition of the mystic words "and his heirs", created a life estate in *A* at common law. If no further limitation by way of remainder appears there is, of course, a reversion in *O*. The ordinary life estate is obviously not an estate of inheritance and must end with the death of the life tenant. It can end earlier by merger with the reversion or the remainder and, at common law, it could also be terminated by forfeiture. This point will be mentioned again when we discuss the destructibility of contingent remainders. During the lifetime of *A*, both the seisin and the right to possession are in *A*. This means that the life tenant has the right to receive the rents and profits and is treated for most purposes as the "owner" of Blackacre, subject to the law of waste. It is always possible to run into difficult problems of construction of a testator's language,[27] but in the main the ordinary life estate is a rather simple creature.

The estate *pur autre vie* can be created in two ways. *O* can convey Blackacre "to *A* for the life of *B*." *B*, whose life is thus used as a measuring stick, is called the *cestui que vie* and he takes nothing by the grant. Sometimes, several people's lives may be used as the measuring device and the courts usually interpret this to mean that the estate of *A* continues until the death of the last *cestui que vie*.[28] The estate can also come into existence when an ordinary life tenant conveys his interest to a third party. The life tenant clearly has an alienable interest but just as clearly he can grant no more than he possesses. Thus when *A*, a life tenant, grants to *B*, the latter has a life estate measured by the life of *A*.

The common law was much disturbed by the death of the holder of an estate *pur' autre vie* during the life of the *cestui que*

27. What estate does the following language create? "The remainder of my property to go to my wife Virginia Simpson as long as she remains my widow. In the event of her marrying then said remainder of my property is to be equally divided between my sons . . ." See Dickson v. Alexandria Hospital, Inc., 177 F.2d 876 (4th Cir. 1949) holding that this language created a defeasible fee simple in Virginia Simpson, which became a fee simple absolute when she died without having remarried. There are cases holding that similar language creates a defeasible life estate.

See also, Lewis v. Searles, 452 S.W. 2d 153 (Mo.1970); Kautz v. Kautz, 365 Pa. 450, 76 A.2d 398 (1950); and Chesnut v. Chesnut, 300 Pa. 146, 151 A. 339 (1930).

28. 2 Powell, Real Property 90 (1950).

vie. Because it was a life estate it was not inheritable by the heirs of the tenant, the *cestui que vie* had no interest, and the estate of the reversioner or remainderman could not vest in possession because the measuring life had not ended. The dilemma was solved by treating the land as being without a tenant and allowing the first person to occupy it after the death of the tenant to claim the seisin as a "general occupant." This claimant was entitled to hold the estate until the death of the *cestui que vie*. If, however, the original grant was "to A *and his heirs* for the life of B", the heir of A was allowed to occupy the land, not because he had inherited it, but as a "special occupant." Thus, it came about that the words "and his heirs" had some significance even in a life estate. This mumbo jumbo of special and general occupancy has now been altered by statute so that the unexpired estate descends like other estates in land.[29]

SECTION 2. THE NON-FREEHOLD ESTATES

The law of the non-freehold estates is the law of landlord and tenant. A more extended discussion of leaseholds will follow later in the book,[30] but at this point we must see the relevance of the estates for years, from period to period, at will, and at sufferance to the "big picture" of the legal estates. Never a part of the feudal pattern, the estate for years, for example, grew out of an attempt to evade the usury laws. *O* would grant his land to *A* for a term of years in exchange for a sum of money, badly needed by *O*. The term would be sufficiently long so that the rents would repay not only the principal sum but a goodly profit as well. Because of its lowly origin, the estate was not well thought of by the courts and many of the consequences persist even in the twentieth century. The earlier real actions would not protect the leasehold tenant and the law treated him as having only possession of the premises while the seisin remained in the lessor. Moreover, the non-freehold estates were called by the ambiguous name chattels real and were treated as personal property for various purposes. Thus, on the death of the lessee the estate would pass to the executor or administrator as personal property rather than to the heir as real property. This latter characteristic still persists except that most statutes of descent now treat both classes of property in the same way.

---

29. Restatement, Property, § 151 (1936).

30. See Part Three, Chapter 4, Voluntary Transfer by Lease, p. 189, infra.

A. THE ESTATE FOR YEARS

The estate for years is also referred to as a tenancy for a term and a tenancy for a period. Its principal characteristic is that it must have a fixed beginning and ending. While this is normally stated in express terms, e. g., "To A for five years" or "To A from January 1, 1955 to December 31, 1960", it is sufficient if a gross period can be determined by implication from the language used. So long as a gross period is stated it remains an estate for years even though subject to earlier termination. Thus, you may have a determinable estate for years or an estate for years subject to a condition subsequent. The latter is particularly common, since the lessor may wish to keep a power of termination for failure of the lessee to pay rent or to perform certain other covenants in the lease. This may even take such an extreme form as allowing the lessor to terminate the estate at any time upon an event within his own control.[31] This does not convert the tenancy into one at will, if a gross period is set out in the lease.

Any lease for a fixed period is called an estate for years, regardless of the length of the period. "To A for one day", "To A for six months," and "To A for nine hundred ninety nine years" [32] are all examples of estates for years. The estate will expire automatically upon the termination of the stated period, and, in the absence of a provision in the lease, no notice of any kind need be given by either the landlord or the tenant.

The estate for years involves a continuing relationship between the parties and thus differs materially from the conveyance of a fee simple which normally severs all contacts between the vendor and purchaser after the deed is delivered. Because of the Statute of Frauds,[33] leases for a term in excess of a certain period, usually one year, must be in writing in order to be enforceable. Quite apart from the statute, it is apparent that all but the most simple leases should be reduced to writing in order to hold disputes between the parties to a minimum. The average lease bristles with covenants, dealing with all manner of things that may or may not be done for the duration of the estate for

31. Cleveland Wrecking Co. v. Aetna Oil Co., 287 Ky. 542, 154 S.W.2d 31, 137 A.L.R. 352 (1941).

32. Restatement, Property, § 19 (1936).

33. The English Statute of Frauds, 29 Car.II, c. 3 (1677) required that any lease for more than three years had to be in writing or it would create an estate at will. Present statutes vary but a majority of the states have reduced the period to one year.

years. The lease thus falls into two major areas of the substantive law—property and contract. It is a conveyance of Blackacre for a fixed period of time and it is also a contract between the lessor and lessee regulating their respective rights for that same period. Much of the ambivalence of landlord and tenant law is explained by this simple fact.[34]

B. THE ESTATE FROM PERIOD TO PERIOD

Also referred to as a periodic tenancy, the estate from period to period is characterized chiefly by the element of continuity. Whereas the estate for years will terminate automatically, the periodic tenancy, once created, will continue on its way until proper steps are taken to put it to death. The notice which either party must give in order to terminate the estate is rather technical and the statutes of the particular jurisdiction must be carefully checked in each situation.[35] As a general guide, at common law a tenancy from year to year required six months' notice and a tenancy for a lesser period required a notice equal to the length of the period, e. g., a month-to-month tenancy required a month's notice, etc. Moreover, the notice had to be given so as to terminate the estate at the end of a period and not in the middle of it. Thus, in a month-to-month tenancy which began on January 1, 1959, the notice to terminate on May 1, 1959, would have to be given on April 1. A notice on April 15 to terminate on May 15 would have no effect.[36]

An estate from period to period can be created expressly, as "To *A* from month to month, beginning on January 1, 1960", but, in fact, many such tenancies arise by implication. This can come about in several different ways. We have already mentioned that some leases must be in writing in order to be enforceable. Sup-

---

34. There are many examples of this property-contract dichotomy, one of the best being the mitigation of damages problem. In contract law the non-breaching party must make a reasonable effort to reduce damages or he cannot recover his full loss. The majority of landlord-tenant cases, however, require no such mitigation by the lessor and he can let the premises lie idle following an unjustified vacation by the lessee. Lawson v. Callaway, 131 Kan. 789, 293 P. 503 (1930). This mitigation doctrine is subject to reexamination in the various states and will be modified in the proper case, as see Wohl v. Yelen, 22 Ill. App.2d 455, 161 N.E.2d 339 (1959). See also p. 190, infra.

35. For a collection of these statutes see Lesar, Landlord and Tenant, § 3.90 (1957).

36. May v. Rice, 108 Mass. 150 (1871).

pose that *O* leases to *A* for eighteen months in a jurisdiction which has a Statute of Frauds requiring all leases in excess of one year to be in writing. If *A* enters the land under this voidable lease, he will not be a trespasser and so long as he pays no rent he will probably be treated as a tenant at will. If he tenders the first month's rent, however, and *O* accepts it this will *probably* convert the tenancy into one from month to month and *A* can continue until either party elects to terminate by proper notice.[37] Similarly, if *O* should lease to *A*, without any statement of the term of the lease, and then *A* should pay rent on a monthly basis, a tenancy from month to month would result.[38] Or suppose *O* leases to *A* for one year and *A* holds over at the expiration of the year. Then, if *O* accepts the monthly rental from *A*, the holdover tenant, it is probable that a tenancy from year to year has been created.[39]

C. THE ESTATE AT WILL

As in the case of the periodic tenancy, the estate at will can be created by the express agreement of the parties. So long as no gross period is stated,[40] any lease "To *A* at the will of *O*" creates an estate at will. An estate at the will of *O*, the lessor, is automatically an estate at the will of *A*, the lessee. The converse of this statement is not universally true because some jurisdictions treat an estate at the will of the lessee as if it were a life estate rather than an estate at will.[41] This means that *A* can ter-

37. Note the use of the word *probably*. In Maine and Massachusetts the Statute of Frauds provides that any oral lease creates only a tenancy at will and in other states, while a periodic tenancy of some sort results, it may be month to month or year to year depending on whether the unenforceable lease for a term reserved an annual rent or a monthly one. See Lesar, Landlord and Tenant, § 3.27 (1957).

38. Williams v. Apothecaries Hall Co., 80 Conn. 503, 69 A. 12 (1908). Here again, the way the rent is paid or reserved determines the period. Indeed, in some cases the reservation of the rent without actual pay-

ment has been held sufficient and some statutes so provide. Ala.Code, tit. 31, § 4 (1940); Kan.Gen.Stat. § 67–503 (1935).

39. The tenancy usually is from year to year if the original lease was for a year or more; if for less than a year, the period is based on the way the rent was reserved. See Note, 108 A.L.R. 1464 (1937).

40. If a gross period is stated then a determinable term of years is created. See p. 53, supra.

41. Gunnison v. Evans, 136 Kan. 791, 18 P.2d 191 (1933). For a contrary view see Foley v. Gamester, 271 Mass. 55, 170 N.E. 799 (1930).

minate the estate if he so desires but that *O* has no power to do so except for breach of some of the covenants of the lease.

Usually, however, the estate at will is created by implication and arises whenever *A* takes possession of *O's* land with the latter's implied consent. Thus, an unenforceable contract for the sale of land may result in a purchaser in possession being treated as a tenant at will. We have already mentioned how the Statute of Frauds may give rise to an estate at will, at least until such time as some of the rent is tendered and accepted.

It was a common-law characteristic of this estate that it could be terminated by either party without any notice whatever. The harshness of this rule has been mitigated in some states by statutes which require a notice equal to the rent-paying period.[42] The effect of such statutes is to turn the estate at will into something very like the estate from period to period. In addition to termination by either party, the estate will come to an end automatically if either party dies or attempts to convey his interest. It is apparent that the tenancy at will is a very frail interest, but nonetheless it falls under the majestic cloak of an estate in land.

D. THE ESTATE AT SUFFERANCE

The tenant at sufferance does not have any estate in land, but because some writers have listed an estate at sufferance as one of the non-freeholds we should mention it here to complete the pattern. This wispy interest arises only in the case of a holdover tenant. If *O* leases to *A* for five years, *A* is supposed to vacate the premises at the termination of the period. If he does not do so, he would seem to be a mere trespasser and entitled to no more consideration than any other wrongdoer. However, this could, in some cases, work against the interests of *O*. The statute of limitations would begin to run immediately and if *A* stayed on the land a sufficient length of time he might get title by adverse possession. To prevent this unfortunate result, the courts have sometimes referred to *A* as a tenant at sufferance, not holding adversely to *O*. It is clear that *O* in these cases has an election and can either evict *A* by the proper proceedings, probably a suit in forcible entry and detainer, or treat him as a holdover tenant and bind him to an estate from period to period.[43]

42. Mass.Gen.Laws Ann. c. 186, § 12.

43. The problems of the holdover tenant are discussed further at p. 200, infra.

SECTION 3. THE SURVIVAL OF SOME
ANACHRONISTIC RULES

———

One of Mr. Justice Holmes' wisest utterances ran: "It is revolting to have no better reason for a rule of law than that so it was laid down in the time of Henry IV. It is still more revolting if the grounds upon which it was laid down have vanished long since, and the rule simply persists from blind imitation of the past." [44] Since law, by its very nature, is precedent bound, many rules do survive whose principal claim to fame lies in services that they have long ceased to render. The law of property is particularly susceptible since it must be fairly stable if it is to be useful. Men cannot order their affairs if the law changes every time some inventive judge has a bright idea. On the other hand, occasional revision is essential lest the whole system bog down under the accumulated weight of centuries. Much of the supertechnical aspect of property law has been abandoned or remodeled and we have tried to deal here only with those antiquities which have modern relevance. Only in a full scale history of the law of land could all of those intricate snarls be unravelled. However, some of the anachronisms we have with us still, or, if buried, they have sufficient vitality to be felt beyond the grave. The three most important of these survivals from a darker age are, the Rule in Shelley's Case, the Doctrine of Worthier Title, and the destructibility of contingent remainders.

———

A. THE RULE IN SHELLEY'S CASE

———

You will recall that in a grant "to *A* and his heirs" the last three words were treated as words of limitation rather than of purchase, thus giving *A* a fee simple absolute. What would be the result, at common law, of a conveyance "to *A* for life, remainder to his heirs"? Logically, it would seem to create a life estate in *A*, a contingent remainder in the heirs of *A* (contingent because a living person has no heirs), with a reversion in *O*, the grantor. This would also seem to square with the intent of the grantor (or the testator) since by varying the formula, "to *A*

———

44. Holmes, The Path of the Law, in
Collected Legal Papers 187 (1921).

and his heirs" he must have had a different result in mind. Moreover, the very words "remainder to his heirs" or "remainder to the heirs of *A*" would seem to indicate that the heirs were to take by "purchase." Similarly, a grant or devise "to *A* for life, remainder to the heirs of his body" seems to call for a life estate in *A*, contingent remainder in the bodily heirs of *A*, and a reversion in *O*. But, by the rule laid down in the famous (notorious might be a better word) Shelley's Case [45] the first grant would result in a fee simple absolute in *A*, the second in a fee tail in *A*.

Property experts differ as to the exact reason for this peculiar rule,[46] but since Shelley's Case dates from 1581 it has long been accepted as a part of the common law and applied without much analysis of the forces that called it into being. It applied to both deeds and wills and acquired such a sacrosanct character that it overrode even a clear indication of contrary intent,[47] i. e., it was treated as a rule of law and not merely as a rule of construction. Although some fantastic results have flowed from tortured application of this ancient rule, it has had at least one beneficent influence. Its application has led to freer alienability by giving a fee simple to *A* instead of creating a life estate followed by contingent remainders; but this has been an incidental effect and scarcely explains the hardy survival of the Rule.

Stripped of its legal jargon,[48] the Rule provides that where in the same instrument a freehold estate is limited to *A* with a purported remainder to the heirs of *A* (or the heirs of his body) and the estates are of the same quality (both legal or both equitable) then the purported remainder becomes a fee simple (or fee tail) in *A*. It is important to note that the Rule spends its force by changing the remainder in the heirs to a remainder in *A*, thus giving *A* a life estate followed by a remainder in fee simple (or fee tail) in *A*. This results in a fee simple in *A* be-

45. 1 Co.Rep. 93b (1581). Actually, the rule goes back to Abel's Case, Y.B. 18 Edw.II, 577 (1324).

46. Perhaps the most likely explanation is that it prevented landowners from avoiding their feudal obligations since the estate had to pass to the heirs by inheritance rather than being given to them by the terms of the original grant.

47. Perrin v. Blake, 1 W.L. 672 (1769); Havely v. Comerford, 343 Ill. 90, 174 N.E. 830 (1931).

48. A classic statement of the rule appears in Hancock v. Butler, 21 Tex. 804, 808 (1858): " '. . . when a person takes an estate of freehold, legally, or equitably, under a deed, will, or other writing, and in the same instrument, there is a limitation, by way of remainder, either with or without the interposition of another estate, of an interest of the same legal or equitable quality, to his heirs or heirs of his body, as a class of persons, to take in succession, from generation to generation, the limitation to the heirs entitles the ancestor to the whole estate.' 4 Kent 215. This result would follow, although the deed might express that the first taker should have a life estate only. It is founded on the use of the technical words, 'heirs' or 'heirs of his body,' in the deed or the will."

cause, by the doctrine of merger, the life estate and the remainder, being lodged in the same person, unite (or merge) to form the greater estate in fee. This may strike you as a minor analytical point but observe its consequences in the following devise. O devises to A for life, to B for life, remainder to the heirs of A. What result? Does A have a fee simple and, if so, what happens to *B's* life estate? A will have a life estate, followed by a life estate in B, followed by a remainder in fee simple in A. But so long as B lives, A will not have a present fee simple because *B's* life estate separates *A's* two estates and prevents merger. Of course, if B dies in the lifetime of A then merger can occur. You should analyze the various possibilities inherent in this situation and see why a precise understanding of the Rule is essential.

Broken into its component parts the elements of the Rule are:

(1) The estates must be created by one and the same instrument, i. e., by the same deed or the same will.

(2) The instrument must give A a freehold estate; a term of years in A will not invoke the Rule. "To A for five years, remainder to his heirs", means just what it says. Usually, the estate in A will be a life estate but it could be a fee tail.

(3) The estate in the heirs must be a remainder. At early common law the only future interest possible in a stranger was a remainder but, as you will see later, the Statute of Uses (1536) permitted certain other future interests (springing and shifting uses). However, the Rule never had any application to these "new" interests.

(4) The Rule applies only when the remainder is limited to *A's* heirs or the heirs of *A's* body. A grant "to A for life, remainder to *A's* children" does not give A a fee simple. It might well be that *A's* children will in fact turn out to be his heirs but that makes no difference. The word heirs has to be used in its technical sense. But what is the technical sense of "heirs"? This question was one of the greatest litigation producers in the application of the Rule. The refinements are too involved for an elementary text, but the puzzle can be illustrated by the following grant, "to A for life, remainder to those persons who, according to the statutes of Illinois, would take *A's* real estate if he should die intestate." [49] Does the Rule apply, thus giving to A a fee simple absolute? It does, if those persons who will take *A's* real estate when he dies intestate are the same as "heirs," used in a technical sense. It does not, if the word "heirs" must mean "heirs taking in succession in infinite generations" as opposed to heirs taking at the death of A. This "how-many-angels-can-

---

49.   People v. Emery, 314 Ill. 220, 145 N.E. 349 (1924).

dance-on-the-head-of-a-pin" argument must have delighted the property expert of another generation and the English courts followed the latter view thus refusing to apply the Rule. The American courts, however, tended to ignore this esoteric distinction and applied the Rule as if "heirs" meant those individuals who would take *A's* real estate immediately on his death.

(5) The Rule applies even though the freehold estate in *A* is separated from the remainder in the heirs by an intervening estate. This was illustrated earlier by the devise "to *A* for life, to *B* for life, remainder to the heirs of *A*."

(6) The Rule applies to future interests as well as to present possessory estates. Thus, in a grant "to *A* for life, to *B* for life, remainder to the heirs of *B*," *A* will take a life estate followed by a remainder in fee simple in *B*.

(7) The Rule applies only when the freehold estate and the remainder are both of the same quality, i. e., are both legal or both equitable. Assume a grant "To *A* for the life of *B*, in trust to collect the rents and profits and pay them to *B*, remainder to the heirs of *B*." The Rule does not apply to give *B* a fee simple. *B's* life estate is equitable since *A* holds the land in trust for him to pay out the proceeds, but the remainder in the heirs of *B* is legal since they will take the estate in fee simple on *B's* death. Had the grant provided that *A*, as trustee, was to hold the remainder in trust for *B's* heirs also, then the Rule would have governed because both estates would have been equitable.

This brief analysis does not exhaust the infinite possibilities of the Rule, but it should suffice to put you on notice and enable you to spot the situations in which the Rule may be involved. Indeed, for many students the Rule in Shelley's Case is not unlike a communist and is often seen hiding under every bed. At the present time the Rule has been abolished in most American jurisdictions [50] but it still has full force in a few. Even when abolished it may continue to be important in title examination since the statutes are not retroactive and in many instances have been passed quite recently. Abolition of the Rule was designed to allow the courts to follow the intent of the grantor or testator so that a conveyance, "To *A* for life, remainder to his heirs," will now result in the logical estates mentioned at the outset of this section. It should be mentioned in closing that the Rule in Shelley's Case does not generally apply to personal property since its whole excuse for being grew out of feudal land concepts.[51]

50. 2 Powell, Real Property 24 (1950). For an interesting case applying the Rule see Sybert v. Sybert, 152 Tex. 106, 254 S.W.2d 999 (1953). Later Texas abolished the Rule see Tex.Civ.Stat.Ann., Art. 1291a (1964). As in most cases, the abolition was not retroactive.

51. 1 Simes and Smith, The Law of Future Interests § 367 (2d ed. 1956).

B. THE DOCTRINE OF WORTHIER TITLE

Somewhat akin to (and frequently confused with) the Rule in Shelley's Case is the Doctrine of Worthier Title. Actually, it is a completely separate rule and should be treated as such. Its name comes from the maxim that a title by descent is worthier than one by grant or devise. This is errant nonsense except to the lord in a feudalistic society. He might think it worthier because if the title to land passed by descent to the heirs the lord would be entitled to a relief and, if the heirs were infants, to wardship and marriage. If the title passed to the heirs by devise the lord would get none of these feudal incidents. This fact probably explains the origin of the Doctrine; nothing adequately accounts for its hardy survival.

The Doctrine consists of two separate rules, the first of which has little modern significance. It runs: If a will purports to give a freehold estate to an individual and that estate is of the same quality and quantity which he would have received by the statutes of descent if the testator had died intestate, then the estate passes by descent rather than by devise. Thus, if *O* devises Blackacre "to *A* in fee simple absolute" and *A* turns out to be *O's* only son and heir then *A* will take Blackacre by descent rather than by the terms of the will. In modern times this will make no difference to *A*—he gets Blackacre in fee simple in either event—and this part of the Doctrine has been largely forgotten.[52]

The second rule still has teeth in it. If a fee simple owner of Blackacre purports to grant a life estate or an estate tail to *A*, with a remainder to the grantor's heirs, the latter take nothing by the grant but must take, if at all, by descent from the grantor, i. e., the remainder is void and the grantor is left with a reversion.[53] Note that this is like the Rule in Shelley's Case in that it turns an express grant to the heirs of an individual into an estate in the individual himself. An illustration is required to make much sense out of this Doctrine.

O grants "to *A* for life, remainder to *my* heirs." This would seem to give *A* a life estate, with contingent remainder in the

For a case to the contrary see Fowler v. Lanpher, 193 Wash. 308, 75 P.2d 132 (1938) commented on in 15 Wash.L.Rev. 99 (1940).

52. Unfortunately, it has occasionally been resurrected and given unwarranted effect. See Leach,

Cases on Future Interests 13–19 (2d ed. 1940).

53. For a detailed discussion in a modern case, see Braswell v. Braswell, 195 Va. 971, 81 S.E.2d 560 (1954).

heirs of *O*. But the Doctrine says, in effect, it is worthier for
O's heirs to take the estate by descent from *O* when he dies intestate than to take it by grant in this present conveyance, therefore *O's* heirs get nothing and *O* still has the reversion. But, of
course, if *O* still has the reversion his heirs may never get anything at all. Why? Because *O* now has a future interest, a
reversion in fee simple following the life estate in *A*, and he may
sell it during his lifetime, creditors may levy on it in satisfaction
of *O's* debts, or *O* may devise it to someone other than his heirs
when it comes time for him to die. Only if *O*, in fact, dies intestate, still owning Blackacre, will it pass to his heirs. Note
that this aspect of the rule applies only to a grant (an inter
vivos transfer) by *O* and not to a devise by him. If he devises
"to *A* for life, remainder to *my* heirs," it will make no difference
since the heirs will take in either case.

The Doctrine has been abolished in a few states but it remains in full effect in many others.[54] It has even been unnecessarily extended to personal property by treating it as a principle
of construction rather than as a technical rule of law.[55] In states
where the Doctrine has been abolished, a grant by *O* "to *A* for
life, remainder to *my* heirs" has the following result. *A* takes a
life estate, followed by a contingent remainder in the heirs of *O*.
If *O* dies in the lifetime of *A*, the remainder immediately vests
in the heirs of *O*. If *O* is still alive when *A* dies, the estate reverts to *O* but is subject to an executory limitation in the heirs of
O, i. e., as soon as *O* does die the estate will shift to the heirs in
fee simple absolute. This latter type of estate is one made possible by the Statute of Uses and will be discussed in more detail
in the next chapter.

C. THE DESTRUCTIBILITY OF CONTINGENT REMAINDERS

The third anachronism was the rule that under certain circumstances a contingent remainder could be destroyed so that
the holder of the expectant estate would never come into enjoyment. Bluntly stated, a contingent remainder is destroyed unless

---

54. It was abolished in England in
1833. Stats. 3 and 4 Wm.IV, c. 106,
§ 3 (1833). Illinois followed this
trail-blazing lead in 1955! Ill.Rev.
Stat. ch. 30, §§ 188, 189 (1973). The
only modern justification for the

rule is that normally a person making an inter vivos transfer does
not intend to create irrevocable interests in his eventual heirs.

55. Doctor v. Hughes, 225 N.Y. 305,
122 N.E. 221 (1919).

it vests at or before the termination of the preceding freehold estate. *O* grants Blackacre "to *A* for life, remainder to the first child of *A* who attains the age of twenty-one." If *S*, a son of *A*, attains his majority during *A's* lifetime the remainder vests in *S* and all is well. Even if *S* dies the day after his twenty-first birthday, it does not affect the estate. *S* died owning a vested remainder and it will descend as such, if *S* died intestate, or pass by his will. If, however, *A* dies while *S* is only twenty years old, the contingent remainder is destroyed and Blackacre reverts to *O*. Even if *S* now lives to be twenty-one it makes no difference, the contingent remainder has been destroyed and cannot be revived.

This doctrine originated in the feudal rule that there could be no abeyance of seisin and, since the contingency had not occurred at the end of the particular estate, *S* could not be seised of the land. Blackacre could have reverted to *O*, however, thus giving him the seisin until *S* satisfied the condition by reaching twenty-one and then the land could have been automatically transferred to *S* who would then have had the seisin. This would have solved the abeyance problem but it ran smack into another difficulty—the common-law rule against springing and shifting interests. This rule held (1) that a freehold could not be created to commence in the future and (2) that a condition could not be reserved in a stranger. Stripped of a lot of verbiage, this meant that once a freehold estate had been created in one person it could not be cut short by the happening of a condition and shifted over to someone else. Applied to the present situation, it meant that once the estate reverted to *O* he had it in fee simple absolute and it could not spring [56] out of him to *S* when the latter reached the age of twenty-one. Oddly enough, even when the Statute of Uses allowed the creation of springing and shifting interests this had no effect on the doctrine of destructibility and *S's* estate would still be lost for failure to vest in the lifetime of *A*.

The situation was even more complicated than this initial analysis would indicate because a life estate could end in other ways than by the death of the life tenant. It could cease by forfeiture or by merger and frequently these methods were used to destroy the contingent remainder and bring the reversion into immediate enjoyment. Forfeiture (usually by renunciation of fealty or by a tortious conveyance, purporting to convey a fee when only a life estate was owned) has little modern significance,

56. Technically, this would be called a springing interest because it would have to "spring out" of the estate of *O*, the original grantor; a shifting interest was one which would cut short an estate in a prior grantee and shift it over to a new one.

but merger is quite another matter. We have already noted that if both the life estate and the remainder came into the ownership of the same individual the two estates would merge to form a fee simple absolute. It is this principle which clever lawyers used to destroy the contingent remainder.

Assume that *O* grants "to *A* for life, remainder to the first child of *A* who attains the age of twenty-one." If *A* wants to destroy the contingent remainder, and if *O* is willing, *A* can buy the reversion from *O* and the life estate will merge into the reversion, thus ending the contingent remainder. The life estate has ceased to exist and since no child of *A* is yet twenty-one the contingent remainder is lost. The same result would be reached if *O* had purchased the life estate from *A*. You can see that there are numerous possibilities if careful use is made of the doctrine of merger.[57]

There is one situation, however, in which the doctrine of merger does not automatically apply. If the life estate and the next vested estate (usually it will be a reversion) are created in the same person simultaneously, they will not merge to destroy the contingent remainder. Assume that *O* devises Blackacre "to *A* for life, remainder to *A's* first child in fee." *A*, in fact, has no child at the time of *O's* death so the remainder is contingent. *A* turns out to be *O's* sole heir and therefore he takes the reversion by the statute of descent. Despite the fact that *A* now owns both the life estate and the reversion there will be no merger; the two estates were created in the same person simultaneously. (Of course, if *A* now has a child the estate will vest in him, cutting off *A's* reversion.) But even in the simultaneous creation situation, *A* can easily destroy the contingent remainder if he so desires. This is true, because if the two estates unite in a third party merger will take place. Thus, if *A* conveys his life estate and his reversion to *X*, the latter will have the fee simple and the contingent remainder will vanish. Since *X* can be a straw party who will reconvey Blackacre to *A*, purged of the contingent remainder, you can see how easy it is for *A* to accomplish his purpose.

Like the Rule in Shelley's Case, this anachronistic doctrine has at least one merit, it promotes a freer alienability of land by allowing a fee simple to be conveyed without waiting for all of the possible contingencies to occur. On the other hand, it thwarts the apparent desires of the grantor or testator and deprives the parties who "own" the contingent remainder of their

57. See, for example, Stoller v. Doyle, 257 Ill. 369, 100 N.E. 959 (1913).

natural expectancy. Because this has not seemed fair to the modern mind, many states have abolished the doctrine entirely and the judicial decisions have whittled away at its common-law rigidity in those states where it has not been totally rescinded.[58] But, like its fellow survivors from the past, it can still be a vicious trap for the unwary.

Since the vested remainder could not be destroyed it was often necessary to distinguish between types of remainders. There were other reasons for making the distinction as well, e. g., vested remainders could be freely alienated whereas contingent remainders were subject to more restrictive rules and in case of involuntary transfers (attachment by creditors, bankruptcy, etc.) might be totally inalienable.[59] Today, most courts allow both types of remainders to be transferred by deed or by will and to be subject to claims of creditors so the reasons for making this distinction are fading. Nonetheless, you must be aware of the classification since it may be important in the state where you practice and it is frequently involved in the Rule against Perpetuities,[60] a common-law development designed to prevent remoteness of vesting and thus the tying up of property over too long a period of time.

It may be helpful to point out a more complete classification of remainders to illustrate how complicated the distinctions could be. Thus, a remainder could be (1) indefeasibly vested (to *A* for life, remainder to *B* and his heirs); (2) vested subject to open, also called vested subject to partial divestiture (to *A* for life, remainder to the children of *B* and their heirs—*B*, having at the time of transfer one or more children with the possibility of further issue); (3) vested subject to total divestiture, also called vested subject to a condition subsequent (to *A* for life, then to *B* and his heirs, but if *B* fails to survive *A*, then to *C* and his heirs)—*C* has a shifting or executory interest, not possible until after the Statute of Uses; or (4) contingent, also called subject to a condition precedent (to *A* for life, then to *B* and his heirs if *B* survives *A*, but if *B* does not do so, then to *C* and his heirs)—*B* and *C* have alternative contingent remainders, sometimes called contingent remainders with a double aspect. It is apparent that there is little difference between (3) and (4) above, but so long as legal consequences flow from the vested-contingent classification, property rights may depend on just such semantic fine points.

58. Restatement, Property, § 240 (1936).

59. Kost v. Foster, 406 Ill. 565, 94 N.E.2d 302 (1950). See also 1 Amer-

ican Law of Property, §§ 4.65, 4.66 (Casner ed. 1952).

60. See pp. 79 to 82, infra.

Chapter 5

THE ROLE OF EQUITY

Writing about the Anglo-American law of property subjects one to a peculiar handicap, not unlike boxing with one arm in a sling. The writer, as he slugs it out with the common-law estates, must constantly be alert for the equitable estates but he cannot pause to take them on at the same time. Hence, he makes veiled references to chancery and statements that such and such is true except in equity. It is almost with a sigh of relief that he finally turns to the role of equity in shaping the modern law of property. It is chronologically proper to take up equity at this point since the chancery court did not appear on the scene until the basic common-law doctrine of estates was well established.

The law of the feuds was ideally adapted to serve the society that produced it, but by the time that law had matured feudalism was already dying as a *political* system. The strong central government, under the king, was now able to maintain the peace and the various feudal incidents lived on as burdens to the landowner without much benefit in return. Unable to destroy the burdens directly by legislation, since the rudimentary parliament was under the domination of the king who was the principal recipient of the incidents, the landowners turned to legal subterfuge. They adapted to their needs an ancient device, the conveyance to uses.

SECTION 1. THE RISE OF THE USE

The use was essentially a simple tool and not even a new one. For various purposes, the fee simple owner of land might convey it to another person to hold for certain specified uses. For example, the Franciscans, having taken a vow of poverty, could not own land, so religious followers would convey the necessary dwelling to some trusted individual to hold "for the use of" the friars. A similar transaction might be utilized to set up an estate for minor children while the father was on a crusade. The feudal lawyers were apparently as alert as contemporary ones and they hit upon the scheme of transferring Blackacre to two or more joint tenants to hold "for the use of" the grantor or such persons as he might specify. The transferee was called the "feoffee to uses" and the person for whose benefit he was to hold was called the *cestui que use*. Note that the feoffee to uses had the legal title, i. e., he was seised of the fee simple estate recognized by the courts while the *cestui que use* had only a beneficial interest, in reality a claim that the feoffee hold the proceeds of the estate for him.

Now comes the beauty of the scheme. The feudal incidents attached only to the legal estate, not to the beneficial interest which the law did not even recognize. Thus, if the *cestui que use* died no incidents were due and the feoffee to uses simply held Blackacre for the person or persons designated by the original grantor. Since wills were not permitted at this time,[1] probably because the king wanted all land to descend to the heir so he could have the feudal dues, the feoffment to uses also served as a method for passing the land at death to someone other than the heir at law. But suppose the feoffee to uses died, wouldn't he have to ante up the incidents since he had the legal title? He clearly would have had to do so but since two or more persons were used as joint tenants the land was held by the survivor and the feudal dues were defeated. Moreover, as soon as one joint tenant died a new one was introduced into the picture so that seldom would any obligations be incurred.

This conveyance to uses had one weak spot. If the feoffee to uses were dishonest or unfaithful to his "trust" the *cestui que use* was left without a remedy. The courts recognized that the feoffee was seised of Blackacre since a fee simple estate had been transferred to him and so they would not interfere to make him perform his promise. When the device was infrequently used this caused but little difficulty, but with its rapid growth in the fourteenth century the frauds began to multiply. A solution had to be found or the use abandoned.

In this dilemma the *cestui que uses* turned to the king who was the source of all justice in the realm. Most justice was dispensed by the common-law courts but the king retained a residue of power which he exercised through the chancellor and which could be utilized in extraordinary cases where there was no relief at the common law. Why the king should have intervened to help landowners who were engaged in depriving him of the cherished feudal incidents is not clear, but at any rate the chancellor did order the feoffee to uses to carry out the "trust" or be held in contempt of the royal prerogative. This is not the place to trace the rise of the court of chancery as a rival to the com-

---

1. It was not until 1540 that the Statute of Wills, 32 Hen. 8, c. 1, made land generally devisable in England.

mon-law courts [2] but a few comments must be made to clarify the operation of the feoffment to uses.

At first, the chancellor acted solely at his discretion and was not bound by any rules of precedent but eventually the chancery accumulated its own principles and equity became a separate system of "law" administered by an independent tribunal.[3] However, the chancery did not come into direct conflict with the common-law courts and did not attempt to interfere with the common-law estates. In fact, it adopted the same scheme of ownership so that you could have an equitable fee simple, fee tail, or life estate with the same consequences that we have already discussed. Equity went even further in permitting the creation of new interests in land and, since chancery was not bound by some of the more technical rules of the common law, it was possible to have springing and shifting uses as well as the more usual estates. Equity acted solely *in personam* by ordering the feoffee to uses to do certain things and then fining or imprisoning him for failure to do so. Thus, if *O* granted "to *A* and his heirs, to hold for the use of *B* for life, remainder for the use of *C* and his heirs", *A* had a legal fee simple while *B* had an equitable life estate followed by an equitable vested remainder in *C*. Equity recognized *A's* fee simple but if *A* refused to give the rents and profits to *B* during his lifetime or tried to sell Blackacre as his own, the chancellor, on request by *B*, would step in and see that the use was properly carried out. This power of the equity court extended to successors in interest of *A* and therefore an heir or devisee of *A* would take Blackacre subject to the use as would any purchaser from *A* who had notice (i. e., knew or should have known) of the use. The only person who could take free of the use would be a bona fide purchaser for value without notice (b.f.p.). Even in this last case, the *cestui que use* would have an action against the feoffee to uses for breach of confidence.

By the sixteenth century the use was a highly-developed device and vast quantities of English land were held to uses. Equitable titles were almost as common as legal ones and, since in each case the king was being deprived of his feudal incidents, it is not surprising to find an attempt being made to end the whole system.

2. For a brief account of the role of equity in Anglo-American law see de Funiak, Handbook of Modern Equity 1–26 (2d ed. 1956). See also p. 17, supra.

3. Equity has been defined as "that portion of remedial justice which is exclusively administered by courts of equity, as distinguished from courts of common law." Malone v. Meres, 91 Fla. 709, 109 So. 677 (1926).

SECTION 2. THE STATUTE OF USES

It was that multi-wived monarch, Henry VIII, who finally forced the issue. He seems to have been perpetually pressed for funds and a survey of the assets of the kingdom disclosed how the feudal incidents were slipping through the royal fingers. In 1535, he forced the Statute of Uses upon a reluctant parliament. It is a peculiar statute since it attacked the use only indirectly; it did not abolish the device or prohibit conveyances to uses but, rather, *executed* the use. It accomplished this by providing that the seisin, and therefore the legal estate, should be vested in the *cestui que use*, passing right on through the feoffee to uses. Thus, the feudal incidents would become due to the lord of the fee as soon as the *cestui que use* died. The statute reads: "Where any person or persons stand or be seised . . . to the use, confidence or trust of any other person or persons or to any body politic . . . that in every such case all and every such person or persons and bodies politic that have . . . any such use in fee simple, fee tail, for term of life or for years . . . or in remainder or reverter shall stand and be seised . . . in lawful seisin estate and possession of the same . . . lands . . . to all intents of and in such like estates as they had or shall have in the use." [4]

The theory of the Statute was simple. Suppose O granted Blackacre "to A and his heirs for the use of B and his heirs." The statute executed the use and B received a *legal* estate in fee simple absolute. A did not receive anything but merely served as a conduit through which the legal title flowed from O to B. Moreover, the *cestui que use* received a legal estate of exactly the same type as the equitable one which he would have had before the passage of the Statute. Thus, if O grants "to A and his heirs to hold for the use of B for life, remainder for the use of C and his heirs", A takes nothing, B receives a legal life estate in possession and C a vested remainder in fee simple absolute (legal).

The immediate result of the Statute of Uses was to restore the feudal incidents to the overlord and nullify the point of a feoffment to uses. It had a side effect—destruction of the use as a method of devising property on death, the pre-1535 equivalent of a will. The latter effect seems to have caused the most immediate reaction because the habit of devising land to individuals other than, or in addition to, the heir was widespread.

---

4. 27 Hen. 8, c. 10 (1535).

Henry VIII was forced to compromise on this issue and five years after the Statute of Uses, in 1540, the Statute of Wills was passed. It did not allow complete testation but it was adequate for the purpose and met the demands of the landowners. The Statute of Wills did not require the intervention of the use but allowed the testator to execute a document, under proper safeguards, which passed the legal title directly to the named devisees.

SECTION 3. THE MODERN SIGNIFICANCE OF THE STATUTE OF USES

The Statute of Uses has been called the most important single piece of legislation in the Anglo-American law of property. It is still on the statute books of many American states and is considered as a part of the adopted common law of England [5] in many more. Why should an essentially revenue-raising act of Henry VIII have had so profound an influence on property law? Paradoxically, it is because (1) the Statute was not successful in its primary aim and (2) the Statute had some totally unforeseen consequences. It is a perfect example of the unplanned growth of English law. The Statute's lack of success gave rise to the modern law of trusts, and the unforeseen consequences led to new methods of conveying real property and to the possibility of new estates in land. Let us look at each of these points in turn.

A. THE MODERN TRUST

It must have occurred to you that the ancient use bore many similarities to what we now call a trust. The feoffee to

---

5. The Statute of Uses was repealed in England as a part of the property reform legislation of 1925. Speaking of the abolition of the Statute, the Lord Chancellor said: "I am told that there is one most respected practitioner, grown grey in the practice of the Chancery Law, sixty years of whose successful and brilliant life has been spent in the exposition, not unremunerative exposition, of the Statute of Uses, who, when he heard, not from my lips but from lips perhaps less sympathetic, that at last the Statute of Uses was abolished, definitely and irrevocably announced his intention not to survive it, and that he resigned his practice at once."

uses was the trustee, the *cestui que use* was the beneficiary, and the grantor of Blackacre was the settlor or trustor. In the modern trust, the trustee takes the legal title but must hold it for the benefit (use) of the beneficiary who thus has equitable title. In our modern courts, with their merger of law and equity, the trust is still the creature of equity and is handled on the chancery side of the court.[6] It is obvious that none of this could have come about if the Statute of Uses had been successful, for its avowed purpose was to destroy the split between legal and equitable ownership and return to the earlier concept of legal estates only. In fact, the Statute probably had this effect for nearly a century, but eventually loopholes were discovered in the legislation and through them crawled the equitable jurisdiction of chancery to fashion the modern trust. These loopholes were three in number: (1) the Statute did not apply to a use on a use; (2) it did not apply to personal property; and (3) it did not apply to active, as distinguished from passive, uses.

(1) USE ON A USE

Suppose *O* granted Blackacre "to *A* and his heirs for the use of *B* and his heirs for the use of *C* and his heirs." Prior to the Statute of Uses, *A* would take the legal title and *B* would have the equitable one. *C* would take nothing, since *O* had exhausted his estate in the grant to *B* and the further limitation to *C* would be repugnant to it. After the Statute, you would normally assume that the legal title would pass to *C* since Blackacre was to be held to his ultimate use. The Statute should execute the two uses and *A* and *B* should both become mere conduits for the legal title. However, the chancellors finally decided that the Statute would operate only once and then, with its force spent, would retire from the scene. The state of the title would then be as follows: the Statute would execute the first use, so *A* would take nothing and *B* would have the legal fee, but the Statute would not execute the second use, so *B* would hold Blackacre in trust for *C*, who now had the beneficial interest. By this bit of hocus pocus, equity was able to reassert its jurisdiction and in 1738 Lord Chancellor Hardwicke could claim that the Statute "has had no other effect than to add at most three words to a conveyance." If all of this seems, as the English say, "a bit much", you should remember that in 1660 the Statute of Tenures had finally ended the feudal incidents and the crown no longer cared

6. See Karlen, Primer of Procedure 165–172 (1950) for a brief discussion of the fusion of law and equity in the modern judicial system.

whether the Statute of Uses was thwarted. Of course, the Statute could have been repealed, but why bother when the desirable results of a trust could be attained by the simple device of a use on a use?

The use *on* a use should be distinguished from the use *after* a use, for in the latter case the Statute was fully operational. Suppose *O* grants Blackacre "to *A* and his heirs for the use of *B* for life, remainder to the use of *C* and his heirs." This is a use *after* a use, first a use to *B* for life, followed by a use to *C* in remainder. As we have already pointed out, the Statute will operate to give *B* the legal life estate and *C* the legal vested remainder. Contrast this with the result in the previous paragraph where a use *on* a use was involved.

----

(2) Uses of Personal Property

The Statute of Uses was not concerned with personalty for no feudal incidents were involved. The Statute applied only where one person was *seised* to the use of another and seisin had no application outside of the freehold estates. If *O* gave a herd of cattle to *A* to hold for the use of *B*, you had a split between the legal and the equitable ownership and chancery would enforce the "trust" in favor of *B*, after, as well as before, the Statute. Suppose *O* granted Blackacre "to *A* for ninety-nine years, to hold for the use of *B* and his heirs." Would the Statute apply? It would not, because *A* was not *seised* to the use of *B*. *A* had only a non-freehold estate and, as we have already discussed, that was a species of personal property, a chattel real. Thus, *A* would be the trustee and *B* would have an equitable interest for the ninety-nine years, at the end of which time the land would revert to *O* or his heirs. Here, again, equity could retain its jurisdiction and while personal property did not bulk large in the seventeenth-century scheme of things, it makes up a large proportion of modern trust property. The most common ingredient of the contemporary trust *res* is likely to be stocks and bonds.

----

(3) Active Uses

Prior to the Statute of Uses, the feoffee to uses seldom had any duties to perform. After all, the use was only a scheme to evade the feudal incidents and perhaps to have the benefits of a will. The feoffee was in reality a straw man, holding a naked legal title for the true owner. Because of this fact, the common-law courts came to the conclusion that the Statute did not apply if, in fact, the feoffee was given some active duties to perform. It was reasoned that in such a case he was more than a straw man and must have the legal title if he were to successfully perform those duties. Moreover, the duties did not have to be very extensive before the court would say that the Statute had no application. Thus, if *O* granted Blackacre "to *A* and his heirs upon trust to collect the rents and profits and pay them to *B*", the legal title remained in *A*, for how else could he justify his collection of the rents? Similarly, a trust for sale of the land by *A* was beyond the reach of the Statute, since *A* would have to hold the legal title in order to sell the estate. It was still possible to have a dry or passive trust where no duties were involved, but this became progressively less likely to happen. The typical, modern trust literally bristles with all sorts of duties for the trustee.

It should be clear that in these three areas where the Statute of Uses did not operate, there was sufficient room for the gigantic edifice which is the modern trust. Although the law of trusts is obviously a part of the law of property in the broad sense, it has become so specialized a subject that we will not spend further time on it in a book on the basic principles of property law. We will now turn our attention to two areas in which the Statute of Uses did operate, but with unforeseen consequences.

B. NEW METHODS OF CONVEYANCING

There were a number of methods of conveyancing at common law [7] but all of them were cumbersome and subject to various disadvantages. The most frequently used, the feoffment, involved the formal ceremony of livery of seisin and required the parties to be physically present on the land so that the clod of dirt or twig could be handed over to symbolize the transfer of seisin. Although a charter of feoffment was later given to memorialize the conveyance, the livery of seisin was the operative part of the feoffment. This bit of pageantry was undoubtedly

7. Among those in normal use were the feoffment, the fine and common recovery, the lease, the grant, the lease and release, and the surren-der. For a good, short discussion see Tiffany, Real Property 654–666 (New Abridged Edition, 1940).

appealing to the medieval mind but it was hardly the method on which to build the commercial use of land. Eventually, some simpler scheme for conveying real property was bound to be developed and the Statute of Uses happened to be the catalyst which called forth the modern deed. Like most brief descriptions of legal phenomena, this is an over-simplification of what actually happened but it should clarify the importance of the Statute in the field of conveyancing. The two new methods of transferring title were the bargain and sale and the covenant to stand seised.

Before the passage of the Statute, the feoffment to uses had become so common that a presumption existed that any conveyance was for the use of the grantor unless there was evidence to the contrary. Thus, if *O* enfeoffed *A*, nothing more appearing, *A* received the legal title but he held it for the use of *O*. This was called a resulting use, since the use came back or resulted to *O*. It was a justifiable conclusion, since *O* was probably trying to put the legal title in *A* to avoid the feudal incidents. Of course, this presumption could be rebutted by showing that *A* paid value (consideration) to *O* or that there was an express declaration of use, such as "to *A* and his heirs for the use of *A* and his heirs" or "to *A* and his heirs for the use of *B* and his heirs." There was a corollary to this presumption in the case of the feoffment. Suppose *O* "bargained and sold Blackacre to *A* and his heirs", i. e., suppose *A* paid value to *O* for the land but did not take a common-law conveyance. This bargain and sale might be oral or it might be evidenced by a written contract, but in any case no formal conveyance was made and so the legal title to the land remained in *O*. Since value had been paid, however, it was presumed that the parties had intended *A* to become the beneficial owner and equity would treat *O* as holding to the use of *A*. What was the result after the passage of the Statute of Uses? The Statute executed the use, since *O* was seised to the use of *A*, and the legal as well as the beneficial interest passed to *A*.

The way had now been cleared for a simple, efficient method of land transfer. After the Statute, the parties could gather in the lawyer's office, he could draft a "deed" of bargain and sale, the purchaser could pay the money to the vendor, the Statute would automatically execute the use, and the purchaser could walk out of the office as the new owner of Blackacre. The bargain-and-sale form of deed is still much used in the United States and while many states have a simplified form of statutory conveyance [8] others still rely on the Statute of Uses to give vitality to their land transfers.

8.   3 American Law of Property 221–224 (Casner ed. 1952).

The effectiveness of the bargain and sale depended upon the payment of consideration to raise the presumption of use in the payor. A parallel development gave rise to the covenant to stand seised where no "valuable" consideration (money or money's worth) was involved but where "good" consideration (a legal relationship based on blood or marriage) was found to exist. If *O* covenanted to stand seised—promised under seal to hold Blackacre—to the use of *A*, and *A* was a stranger, the covenant had no legal consequence. There had been no legal conveyance to *A* and since value had not been paid there was no basis for a presumption of a use in *A*. But suppose *A* was the wife or son of *O*? Equity would now presume that, because of the close ties between *O* and *A*,[9] the equitable title was in *A* while *O* continued to hold the legal title for the former's use. After the Statute, the use would, of course, be executed and the full legal title would be in *A* although no common-law conveyance of the land had been made.

Henry VIII and his advisors had never intended to affect the common-law conveyancing structure of England; the Statute was designed to be a reactionary, not a liberal reform, measure. But, due to the accidents of history and the adaptability of the common-law lawyers, a modern system of land transfer was born.

C. THE CREATION OF NEW ESTATES IN LAND

In Chapter 4,[10] we discussed the permissible estates at common law and found them to be divided into two categories—freehold and non-freehold. The latter group was unaffected by the Statute of Uses but the freehold estates were expanded by the admission of certain types of future interests which had been impossible at common law. You will recall that the fees simple, the fee tail, and the life estate were the permissible freehold estates and the chancery court recognized equitable equivalents of each of them. The freehold estates could be further divided into present (possessory) estates and future interests. The future interests were also present estates but their owners were not en-

---

9. Just how close these ties must be is an open question. See Dawley v. Dawley's Estate, 60 Colo. 73, 152 P. 1171 (1915), where the court decided an agreement to hold property to the use of an *adopted* son was a good covenant to stand seised.

10. P. 39, supra.

titled to possession until the preceding estate had ended, i. e., they were vested in interest but not in possession.   These common-law future interests were the reversion, the vested remainder, the possibility of reverter, the right of entry for condition broken (power of termination), and the contingent remainder.   Our prior discussion of these future interests pointed out that the first two were true estates in land, i. e., they represented interests that were certain to accrue to the holder or his heirs once the preceding possessory estate ended.[11]   The latter three, however, were subject to further conditions and might, in fact, never become true estates.   More accurately, they should be called expectancies but long usage has led to their classification generally as species of future interests.

In recognizing these future interests the common law was typically rigid and required a strict following of the rules.   In Section 3 of Chapter 4 [12] some of these anachronistic rules—the Rule in Shelley's Case, the Doctrine of Worthier Title, and the destructibility of contingent remainders—were explored and it was pointed out that they have survived into modern times.   The Statute of Uses should have affected some of these rules [13] but it did not do so and they were adopted by the chancery, apparently as a part of the maxim that equity follows the law.   But there were some further technical rules of the common-law courts that were not blindly followed in equity.   These rules had to do mainly with seisin and the common-law insistence that seisin always be lodged in a specific person to whom the overlord could look for the feudal incidents.   These rules were: (1) no freehold could be limited to begin *in futuro*; (2) no remainder could be limited after the grant of a fee simple; (3) no remainder could be limited so as to vest in possession prior to the normal ending of the preceding estate; and (4) no power of appointment could be used to vest in a third party an interest greater than that owned by the donee of the power.[14]   It is necessary to look at each of these, in turn, and see the change wrought by the Statute of Uses.

(1) No freehold could be limited to begin *in futuro*.   *O*, on January 1, grants "to *A* and his heirs from September 1."   There might be many reasons why *O* would desire to do this, e. g., September 1 might be the marriage date of *A*, and *O*, going on a long journey, might want to make a present gift of Blackacre.   At common law such a grant would be void because it must be made

---

11. This is not strictly accurate since a reversion could be subject to a condition precedent, e. g., any reversion following a life estate and a contingent remainder.   However, most reversions are of the vested type, i. e., following a life estate or an estate for years.

12. P. 57, supra.

13. It clearly should have ended the destructibility of contingent remainders doctrine.   Do you see why?

14. Hargreaves, Introduction to Land Law 105–106 (3d ed. 1952).

by a livery of seisin and once that was done A would be the owner. There could be no abeyance of seisin. (Of course, you realize that O could grant to X for eight months, then to A, but that was interpreted as a present grant to A, subject to an estate for years in X). This problem was easily solved by a use. O granted "to X and his heirs for the use of A and his heirs from September 1." The seisin passed to X immediately, thus no abeyance, and equity would enforce A's rights after September 1. Prior to that time, there would be a resulting use in O since X had given nothing of value and the language of grant was silent as to the intervening months. With the passage of the Statute of Uses, these equitable interests became legal ones and, in effect, O kept the legal estate until September 1 when the legal estate passed automatically to A. Thus, it was possible, after the Statute, to limit a freehold to begin *in futuro*. A new type of future interest had been added to the closed categories of the common law.

(2) No remainder could be limited after the grant of a fee simple. O could create a fee simple determinable or a fee simple subject to a condition subsequent and, if he did so, he would retain, respectively, a possibility of reverter or a power of termination. No other future interest was possible following a fee simple. Assume O granted "to A and his heirs, but if A shall marry a tradesman's daughter, then to B and his heirs." At common law, the limitation to B was void since it would result in shifting the seisin from A to B and would offend the rule under discussion. However, O could grant "to X and his heirs for the use of A and his heirs, but if A shall marry a tradesman's daughter, then to B and his heirs." Prior to the Statute, X would hold first for A, then if the condition occurred, he would hold for B. After the Statute, the use would be executed and both interests would be legal, the shift occurring automatically upon the happening of the contingency. Note, however, that B would not have a contingent remainder but a shifting use or interest, called an executory devise if it appeared in a will. A's estate would be a defeasible fee, technically referred to as a fee simple subject to an executory limitation.[15]

15. If you have been following this discussion closely, you will now see why the Statute of Uses should have ended the destructibility doctrine. Suppose, after 1536, O bargains and sells "to A for life, remainder to A's first son who shall reach twenty-one." A dies, survived by a minor son. The court should say that the land reverts to O in fee simple subject to an executory limitation and the minor son will take the land by a springing use when he reaches twenty- one. Such interests are now possible because of the Statute of Uses. Instead, in Purefoy v. Rogers, 2 Wms.Saund. 380 (1670) the court announced the rule: "No limitation capable of taking effect as a contingent remainder shall, if created inter vivos, be held to be a springing use under the Statute of Uses, or, if created by will, be held to be an executory devise under the Statute of Wills." The quote is from White v. Summers, L. R. [1908] 2 Ch. 256 but it is known

To be accurate, it should be explained that the term executory interest (or executory limitation) is generic and includes the shifting use (interest) and the springing use (interest). The former has just been illustrated and arises whenever the happening of the condition destroys a legal estate vested in a grantee and shifts that estate over to another party. The latter term refers to an estate which springs out of the original grantor, i. e., where the happening of the condition destroys the original estate of the grantor. Thus, the estate in the immediately preceding subsection (1) is a springing use since it will spring into existence on September 1 and destroy the estate of *O*, the grantor. Similarly, *O* might grant "to *X* and his heirs for the use of *A* and his heirs when *A* shall attain the age of twenty-one." After the Statute, such a grant would leave *O* with a fee simple subject to an executory limitation and would give *A* a springing use.

(3) No remainder could be limited so as to vest in possession prior to the normal ending of the preceding estate. This rule is similar to the preceding one and, indeed, is another way of explaining why there could be no springing or shifting interests at common law. It is included here because it is a broader statement of the proposition and illustrates that any interest following a common-law estate had to wait for the natural end of its predecessor—"after you, my dear Alphonso!." Thus, if *O* granted "to *A* for life, but if he marries a tradesman's daughter, then to *B* for life", the grant to *B* was void since it might destroy *A's* estate prior to its normal termination on *A's* death. Again, it is apparent that this result could have been reached by a use and would now be possible because of the Statute of Uses.

(4) No power of appointment could be used to vest in a third party an interest greater than that owned by the donee of the power. Among the most flexible of the modern methods for the disposition of property is the power of appointment. By this device, a power can be given to a trusted friend or a bank to designate a person or persons who will ultimately take the property, without the donee of the power having any interest in the property himself. This could not be done at common law. A grant "to *A* for life, remainder to such children of *A* as *X* shall appoint" would give *A* a life estate but the power would be void

as the Rule of Purefoy v. Rogers. As you know from the previous discussion, the doctrine of destructibility has now been changed by statute in most states. For a case where the distinction between contingent remainders and executory interests determined the outcome see Stoller v. Doyle, 257 Ill. 369, 100 N.E. 959 (1913).

Since executory interests were nondestructible it became possible, after the Statute of Uses, to tie up property for an indefinite period and dead-hand control became a distinct reality. This gave rise to the Rule against Perpetuities as a common-law policy opposed to remoteness of vesting.

and *O* would have a reversion. But *O* could grant "to *X* and his heirs for the use of *A* for life then for the use of such children of *A* as *X* (or someone else) shall appoint." Equity would enforce such a use and after the Statute the interests were held to be legal, thus allowing the powers of appointment to be added to the arsenal of the property lawyer. These powers may be either general or special. The former allows the appointment to be exercised in favor of any one, including the donee of the power, while the latter restricts the exercise to members of a specified class.[16]

At the present time, all of these "new" estates in land are so well recognized that it is not necessary to follow the old formula, "to *X* and his heirs for the use of, etc.", in order to take advantage of the greater flexibility of equity. It is fair to say that the four rules just discussed no longer exist and that, in addition to the permissible common-law estates, executory interests and powers of appointment must be included in the list of estates in land.[17]

SECTION 4. THE RULE AGAINST PERPETUITIES AND RESTRAINTS ON ALIENATION

As the preceding section demonstrates, the Statute of Uses led to the creation of new estates in land. The distinction between contingent remainders and executory interests was a narrow one, based on the logic of history, but it had some significant consequences. Contingent remainders could be destroyed at common law but executory interests could not and hence they might vest at some indefinite (and remote) period in the future, thus tying up property interests in perpetuity. Since much of English law had been concerned with the free alienability of land, the courts viewed this prospect with alarm and set about (with all deliberate speed) the task of restraining too much "dead hand" control. The result was the Rule against Perpetuities—a deceptively stated Rule that has led to fantastic amounts of litigation and volumes of learned exegesis, expounding (and complicating) the application of the Rule. A little

16. A full discussion of powers of appointment is beyond the scope of this text. For a brief discussion see Powell on Real Property 479–525. (Abridged Ed. Powell and Rohan (1968).

17. While executory interests, both springing and shifting, have full legal recognition today, they cannot be used to reach a result that is contrary to public policy. Thus, in Capitol Federal Savings & Loan Ass'n v. Smith, 136 Colo. 265, 316 P.2d 252 (1957) the court refused to enforce a shifting interest which would have prevented the sale of land to black persons.

learning is a dangerous thing and no attempt will be made here to explain the full ramifications of the Rule, although you should be aware of its existence and should study it in detail in the advanced course in Future Interests. If you wish a short explanation at this time, you should read the justly popular article, "Perpetuities in a Nutshell" by the late Professor Leach of Harvard.[18] It will show something of the complex character of the Rule.

Professor Gray's classic statement of the Rule was as follows: "No interest is good unless it must vest, if at all, not later than twenty-one years after some life in being at the creation of the interest." It was a rule against remoteness of vesting and so long as the estate was vested in interest, even though not in possession, the Rule was not violated. After all, a fee simple absolute had a potentially infinite duration and that was no obstacle if someone had the power to alienate the land. The vice lay in tying up the land with non-destructible contingent interests in perpetuity. The Rule was designed to allow suspension of vesting for the lifetime or lifetimes of individuals living at the effective date of the deed, will, or trust plus the minority (hence twenty-one years) of someone not yet in being. (Later the twenty-one years was extended to include a period of gestation, twenty-one years plus nine months.) If the estate *might* vest in interest at a period more remote than that it was void for remoteness, being viewed as a perpetuity. The rest of the grant or devise was valid but the "gift over" failed and the intent of the grantor or testator was thwarted. Obviously, a devise to a living person for life, followed by a contingent interest in his issue (vesting on the death of the life tenant or within twenty-one years plus a period of gestation thereafter) was all right but attempts to keep the interest contingent through succeeding generations of the family would raise the spectre of the Rule.

One illustration, with which you are already acquainted, will demonstrate the complexities of the Rule. O devises Blackacre "to A and his heirs for so long as no liquor is sold on the premises." A has a fee simple determinable and O has a possibility of reverter. The Rule does not apply because a possibility of reverter, in common-law theory, is vested in interest (being a reversionary interest) and if liquor is ever sold on the premises (regardless of how long in the future, absent some spe-

---

18. Leach, Perpetuities in a Nutshell, 51 Harv.L.Rev. 638 (1938). Note Professor Leach's own *caveat*. "If this paper fails of its purpose it has, at least, eminent company. Lord Thurlow undertook to put the Rule in Shelley's case in a nutshell. 'But,' said Lord Macnaghten, 'it is one thing to put a case like Shelley's in a nutshell and another to keep it there.' Van Grutten v. Foxwell, [1897] A.C. 658, 671."

cial statute on the matter [19]) O or his heirs will get the land, which will then vest in possession. If, however, O devises Blackacre "to A and his heirs for so long as no liquor is sold on the premises but if liquor shall ever be sold on the premises then to B and his heirs", the interest given to B is void as violating the Rule Against Perpetuities. A had a fee simple subject to an executory limitation and B had an executory interest of the shifting type, which does *not* vest in interest until liquor is, in fact, sold on the premises. Since this *might* be at a time more remote than lives in being plus twenty-one years it is void *ab initio*. A would still have his defeasible fee which he could lose if liquor is ever sold on the premises, but the future interest would be in O or his heirs not in B.[20] Of course, O could have saved the "gift over" to B by stipulating that if liquor is sold during the lifetime of A or twenty-one years thereafter then the land is to pass to B and his heirs.

Similarly, if O devised Blackacre "to A and his heirs at such time as liquor shall be sold on the premises", the interest in A would be void for violating the Rule. A would have had an executory interest of the springing type (springing out of O's heirs if liquor is ever sold on the premises) but, since the interest cannot vest until liquor is in fact sold, that *might* occur at a time more remote than allowed by the Rule and it must fail. O's heirs (or devisees) would take Blackacre freed of the executory interest in A.

This brief look at an intricate Rule should be sufficient to demonstrate why lawyers engaged in the property practice, especially in the drafting of wills and trusts, should have a thorough understanding of the subject. There is no reason why the client's interest cannot be adequately protected at the drafting stage (preventive law) but once the Rule has been violated it may require expensive litigation to settle the rights of the parties.

Somewhat related to the problems covered by Rule Against Perpetuities are the numerous attempts to place restraints on the alienation of land. True, the Rule is concerned solely with the remoteness of vesting but its objective is to allow freer alienability and prevent the accumulation of large interests which no one can transfer. Having been astute to frustrate the landowner's desire to tie up his property in perpetuity by creating non-destructible future interests, the courts could scarcely be expected to allow more direct restraints on aliena-

---

19. See p. 44, supra.

20. First Universalist Society of North Adams v. Boland, 155 Mass. 171, 29 N.E. 524 (1892).

tion which would have the same effect. Thus, a conveyance "to A and his heirs, provided he never sells, mortgages, or otherwise transfers the land" is a direct restraint on alienation and hence void. The basic principle is clear enough but its application can be difficult. If the restraint is a reasonable one, e. g., prohibiting transfer to a small group or for a limited purpose, but leaving a wide range of volition in the grantee, it will be enforceable. The key issue is: what is reasonable? Like the Rule, the range of problems caused by attempted restraints is beyond the scope of this text and must be left to the student's initiative by a perusal of the excellent material on the subject [21] or to later courses in the property field.

SECTION 5 OTHER ASPECTS OF EQUITY

Equity's principal impact on the law of property came through the ancient use, modified into the modern trust. It must not be supposed, however, that this was equity's sole contribution to property law. Chancery's jurisdiction depended, in the main, on the inadequacy of the remedy at law. Thus, you could expect that the chancellor would range across the whole field of the common law and that eventually equity would come to permeate most areas of contract, tort, and property. So extensive was this infiltration that today, following the merger of law and equity, it is often difficult to tell whether a particular rule was legal or equitable in origin. If it really makes a difference which it is, as in cases where the right to a jury trial is in dispute, the lawyer may have to undertake a sizable piece of historical research.

Aside from trusts, the principal areas of equitable concern in property matters are: (1) the specific performance of real estate contracts; (2) the cancellation and rescission of contracts and deeds for fraud, mistake, duress, undue influence, and lack of capacity to contract (insanity, infancy, etc.) ; (3) the enforcement of covenants relating to land under the doctrine of equitable servitudes; and (4) the equity of redemption and certain other features of the law of mortgages. Some of these points are beyond the scope of this book and so will not be mentioned again; others such as the equitable servitude will receive further treatment in connection with later portions of our discussion.

---

21. See, for example, Schnebly, Restraints upon the Alienation of Legal Interests, 44 Yale L.J. 961, 1186, 1380 (1935).

Chapter 6

MULTIPLE OWNERSHIP

The study of law, and indeed the practice of it, involves a process of continual classification. We must call our concepts by name in order to talk about them, to deal with them, and to find out what others have said or done about them. Is a certain interest real or personal, present or future, vested or contingent? Once the classification has been made the problem is *not* solved; it has only been given a handle so we can start solving it. Moreover, the classifications are often vague and overlapping and not infrequently cause as much harm to our thinking as they do good. Consider for a moment the matter of multiple interests in the same *res*.

If the law recognized only one estate, the fee simple absolute, and if Blackacre could be owned by only one man at a time who could do nothing with it but possess and farm it, the law of property would be simple, but the social utility of Blackacre would be quite limited. Instead, the law, in order to increase the social utility, is complex and recognizes many interests in the same *res*. We cannot catalogue them all but it will be useful to direct our thinking to a number of the principal categories.

First, in the field of personal property, we encounter:

(a) *The finder and the "true" owner.* The former has possession and, in general, a claim that is good against the whole world except the "true" owner. The latter, unless he abandons the property, has ownership plus the right to possession if he can locate the finder.

(b) *The bailor and the bailee.* There are many forms of bailment—constructive, involuntary, gratuitous, for hire, etc.— but all of them involve multiple interests in the same piece of personal property. The basic idea is the transfer of the possession of personal property, without the transfer of ownership, for the accomplishment of a particular purpose. Thus, the bailor remains the owner of a pair of trousers left with a cleaner; the bailee has the right to their possession until they have been properly cleaned and pressed.

(c) *The pledgor and the pledgee.* The pledge is really a specialized form of bailment in which a chattel is bailed to a creditor as security for a debt. When the debt is paid the goods are to be returned but, in the meantime, the ownership remains in the pledgor and the pledgee has the right to retain possession only.   Today, most pledges involve stocks and bonds and the pledgee is usually a bank.

(d) *The lienor and the lienee.*   The lien is similar to the pledge since the lienor has the right to possession of the chattel but no ownership of it.   However, the right to the lien arises out of improvements made on the chattel by a repairman or some artisan and the property is simply being retained until the bill is paid.   The common law was very strict in its regulation of the rights of the lienor and if he surrendered possession of the chattel he surrendered his lien as well.   There have, of course, been many statutory changes.

(e) *The chattel mortgagor and the mortgagee.*   The owner of an automobile wishes to borrow $750, using his car as collateral.   He signs a personal note for the $750 plus interest and gives a chattel mortgage on his car to secure the payment.   The mortgagor still "owns" the car but the lending bank has a security interest in the same vehicle and can foreclose the mortgage if the debt is not paid.

(f) *The conditional seller and the buyer.*   Using the previous illustration, if the seller of the car wished to employ the conditional sale device he would keep the "title" to the automobile himself but transfer the possession to the buyer.   The latter would not own the car until he completed all of the payments plus the finance charges.   If he did not meet the payments, the seller would "repossess" the vehicle.

In all of the above situations at least two people have a legal interest in the same *res*.   As you would expect, many areas for dispute exist and the law has developed a series of rules and principles to adjust these difficulties.   The common law covered most of the problems but it was too inflexible and the demands of a commercial society have required many statutory changes.   Moreover, many of the relationships are regulated by special contracts and by the customs of the groups involved in commercial credit.[1]

Second, in the field of real property, we find all sorts of multiple interests in the same piece of land, e. g., the present interest and the future interest (life estate plus remainder), the landlord and the tenant, the vendor and the purchaser, the mortgagor and the mortgagee, the holder of the fee simple absolute and the owner of the non-possessory interest in that same land (easement, profit, restrictive covenant), and the trustee and the beneficiary (the trust device applies to personal property as well).   Most of these interests in land are within the scope of this book; some

1. For a full treatment of these areas see Brown, The Law of Personal Property (2d ed. 1955) and the course in Sales or Commercial Law.

of them, e. g., trusts and mortgages, are too specialized to be covered extensively here.

Third, there are still other types of multiple interests in the same property and they form the principal subject matter of this chapter. These are marital interests and concurrent estates. While these interests are most important in the law of real property some of them have application to personal property as well. The concurrent estates are particularly intriguing since they involve present interests of the same quality in a single *res*. Moreover, these interests may exist in a whole series of individuals.

SECTION 1. MARITAL INTERESTS

In a traditional classification of property interests the materials of this section, except for community property which is *sui generis*, are usually found under the heading "legal life estates", because in the main they tend to be estates for life and because they are created by operation of law rather than by act of the parties through a deed or will. However, with but few exceptions,[2] these legal life estates were created for the protection and use of either the husband or the wife and it is more realistic to look at them in this light. These marital interests were a kind of social security and they gave some assurance that the spouse of a man (or woman) of property would not be left entirely destitute. The interests created have many other effects, however, such as interfering with the rights of creditors, causing added difficulties in the sale of land, etc. Since the interests themselves grew out of the social conditions of the past you should ask the always pertinent legal question, "Have these particular property interests outlived their social usefulness?"

In this section we shall discuss the estate of *jure uxoris*, curtesy, dower, homestead rights, and the doctrine of community property. Since the first three have roots deep in the soil of the common law we shall try to get the feel of these interests by a brief excursion into the past. You should know, in advance, that the estate of *jure uxoris* has little modern significance, that

2. Tenancy in special tail with possibility of issue extinct was a legal life estate created incidentally to a specific type of estate in land; in some states (see Ark.Stat. § 61– 110, 1947) a life estate may be given to a parent by operation of the statutes of descent; and homestead may protect the children as well as the surviving spouse.

curtesy is now merged with dower in many states and that either spouse is then entitled to dower, and that dower itself has been changed by statute in all states so that you are never safe without consulting the latest pronouncement of the legislature.

A. JURE UXORIS, CURTESY, AND DOWER

The common law regarded the husband and wife as one and the husband as the one. The married woman's lack of status was reflected in the law of property. When *H* married *W*, who was seised of an estate of freehold, *H* was entitled to the use, occupancy and profits of the land for the duration of the marriage. The English law, until comparatively recently, did not recognize absolute divorce without a special act of Parliament, so the estate of *jure uxoris* (by right of the wife) in effect gave *H* a right to the land for the joint lives of the spouses. He could sell or mortgage his interest to a third party and the estate was liable for his debts.[3] He could also sue for any injury to his interest. Nonetheless, his estate was only for life and on the death of either spouse, or upon absolute divorce, *H's* interest terminated, and *W*, if *H* died, or *W's* heirs, if she died, became entitled to the land, unaffected by a prior conveyance or incumbrance by *H*. If issue were born of the marriage, the estate *jure uxoris* merged into *H's* estate by curtesy. At an early date, equity interfered to protect the wife's interest in some situations and this reduced the harshness of the common-law rules. Land could be conveyed or devised to trustees for the benefit of a married woman and thus freed of the control of the husband. Eventually, it became possible to convey directly to *W*, "for her sole and separate use," and equity would still protect this "equitable separate estate." Today, the estate *jure uxoris* has been abolished by statutes, either directly or indirectly, and the married woman has full control over her own property, subject to a possible curtesy or dower interest in some states.[4]

3. Mattocks v. Stearns, 9 Vt. 326 (1837).

4. See, for example, G.L.Ann. (Mass.) ch. 209, § 1. "The real and personal property of a woman shall upon her marriage remain her separate property, and a married woman may receive, receipt for, hold, manage and dispose of property, real and personal, in the same manner as if she were sole. But no conveyance by a married woman of real estate shall, except as otherwise provided in this chapter, extinguish or impair her husband's tenancy by the curtesy by statute . . . unless he joins in the conveyance or otherwise releases the same."

"Tenant by the curtesy of England, is where a man marries a woman seised of an estate of inheritance, that is, of lands and tenements in fee simple or fee tail; and has by her issue, born alive, which was capable of inheriting her estate. In this case he shall, on the death of his wife, hold the lands for his life, as tenant by the curtesy of England." [5] Immediately on birth of issue the estate *jure uxoris* was changed to curtesy initiate which in turn became curtesy consummate upon the death of the wife. This distinction between *jure uxoris* and curtesy explains the eagerness with which the first heir was awaited, even by men with few of the normal fatherly characteristics. Blackstone demonstrates the learning on the subject. "The issue must be born alive. Some have had a notion that it must be heard to cry; but that is a mistake. Crying indeed is the strongest evidence of its being born alive; but it is not the only evidence. The issue also must be born during the life of the mother: for if the mother dies in labour, and the Caesarean operation is performed, the husband in this case shall not be tenant by the curtesy; because at the instant of the mother's death he was not clearly entitled, as having had no issue born, but the land descended to the child while he was yet in his mother's womb; and the estate being once vested shall not afterwards be taken from him." [6] Curtesy initiate has been generally abolished by statute so that the husband would have to survive the wife to receive an actual estate in the land. Curtesy consummate has likewise been generally abolished or modified by statute and you should consult the law of the jurisdiction in question. [7]

"Tenant in dower is where the husband of a woman is seised of an estate of inheritance, and dies; in this case, the wife shall have the third part of all the lands and tenements whereof he was seised at any time during the coverture, to hold to herself for the term of her natural life". [8] Note that dower for the wife bore some similarity to curtesy for the husband, but the former did not depend on birth of issue and was a life estate in only one-third of the husband's estate whereas curtesy extended to all of the wife's estate. Moreover, there was no dower initiate, i. e., the wife had no estate in the husband's land until his death. During his lifetime her interest was inchoate and amounted to no more than an expectancy based on her survival. [9]

5. 2 Blackstone Com. 126 et seq.

6. Id.

7. See, for example, Ill.Rev.Stat. ch. 3, § 18 (1961) "A surviving spouse, whether husband or wife, may become endowed of a third part of all real estate of which the decedent was seized of an estate of inheritance at any time during the marriage by electing to take dower. . . . There is no estate of curtesy." In 1972, Illinois also abolished dower. Ill.Rev.Stat. ch. 3, s. 18 (1973).

8. 2 Blackstone Com. 126 et seq.

9. Flynn v. Flynn, 171 Mass. 312, 50 N.E. 650 (1898). The wife claimed

Even inchoate dower has some substance, however, because it attaches to all freehold estates of inheritance owned by the husband during marriage and once attached it can be barred only by the death of the wife in the lifetime of the husband, by release by the wife, or by divorce for the fault of the wife.[10] The usual way to release inchoate dower is for the wife to join in a deed or mortgage of the land but if she fails to do so her interest is unaffected and on the death of the husband she can elect to take dower even though Blackacre is now owned by a third party. By refusing to join her husband in a conveyance of land, a stubborn wife can exert a powerful "blackmail" influence and if the parties inadvertently fail to secure her signature on a deed or mortgage serious problems can arise affecting the merchantability of title.

The husband cannot use fraudulent devices to defeat the wife's dower and where H abstained from paying a mortgage in which W had joined, in order to force a foreclosure, and the property was purchased at the foreclosure sale with money advanced by H, W's dower interest was not destroyed.[11] This case is typical of many in which the courts have given substantial protection to inchoate dower. Moreover, the right of dower will be sustained against the claims of creditors of the deceased husband, if the claims originated after marriage.[12]

After the death of the husband, inchoate dower becomes consummate and an assignment of the dower property must be made if the widow so elects. In the early days, many large English estates had a Dower House on the premises and this was set aside for the widow when the son and heir moved on up to the manor house. The widow would then be entitled to one-third of the rents and profits of the estate for her own life. Today, the Dower House has disappeared and the interest itself survives as a kind of relic of a social security system of the past.[13] Modern legislation typically gives two rights to the widow (and in many cases to the husband as well) which did not exist at common law: (1)

a part of a condemnation award for her inchoate dower but was refused because she did not own any estate or interest in land. Of course, dower consummate is protected fully in eminent domain proceedings. Borough of York v. Welsh, 117 Pa. 174, 11 A. 390 (1887). For a good discussion of the nature of inchoate dower see Opinion of the Justices, 337 Mass. 786, 151 N.E.2d 475 (1958), which upheld the constitutionality of a statute abolishing inchoate dower, and hence all dower in Massachusetts, except where it was already a vested estate (consummate).

10. Divorce for the husband's fault leaves dower intact unless it is disposed of by the divorce decree or by a voluntary divorce settlement. At common law, absolute divorce would prevent the assignment of dower regardless of fault but statutes have rather generally reached the result just stated. 2 Tiffany, Real Property, § 531 (3d ed. 1939).

11. Stokes v. Stokes, 119 Misc. 168, 196 N.Y.S. 184 (1922).

12. 2 Tiffany, Real Property, § 487 (3d ed. 1939).

13. Comment, Does Dower Pay Its Way in Illinois?, 1956 U.Ill.L.F. 487.

if H dies intestate, W is an heir and is usually given one-half of the estate if there is no issue, one-third if there is issue; (2) if H dies testate, W may renounce the will (whether or not she is named in it) and take a statutory share of $H's$ estate (this share will usually be the same as her intestate share). Such legislation makes dower of much less importance than it was at common law when the widow could not claim any of the real property as an heir and had no power to renounce the will of her husband. Some statutes expressly provide that the statutory share of a surviving spouse is in lieu of dower.[14] It should be noted, however, that the statutory share is a more tenuous interest than dower because it attaches only to the property which the husband owns at the time of his death. Thus, he can defeat the claim of the wife by an inter vivos conveyance of the property without her consent.[15]

Dower has survived the passage of time better than curtesy, but even so it has been abolished in more than half the states and has been materially altered in most of the others.[16]

B. HOMESTEAD [17]

The homestead exemption did not grow out of the common law and hence it lacks the thread of consistency that binds *jure uxoris,* curtesy, and dower into some sort of package, untidy though it may be. Texas passed the first homestead statute in 1839 [18] and many states, by constitutional or legislative provision, have followed suit. Homestead represents a policy decision designed to give protection to the family unit by granting a certain exemption to the head of a family against the claims of creditors.[19] The basic idea is simple enough. Many a householder, through circumstances beyond his control, falls on evil days and creditors, seeking to collect their due, strip him to the bone, taking the very roof from over the heads of his family. To prevent a disruption of the home, society grants him an exemption defined in money value, area, or both, and creditors can then reach only the value or area which is in excess of the exemption.[20] As

14. McKinney's N.Y.Consol.Laws, ch. 13, Decedent Estate Law, § 82.

15. Redman v. Churchill, 230 Mass. 415, 119 N.E. 953 (1918).

16. 2 Powell, Real Property, § 217 (1950).

17. Do not confuse the state homestead exemption with federal homestead legislation designed to allow an occupying claimant to acquire title to unappropriated public land. "Homesteading" the West is popular on the television screens but has nothing to do with our present subject.

18. Marshall, Homestead Exemption —Oregon Law, 20 Ore.L.Rev. 328 (1941).

19. Waples, Homestead and Exemption, § 3 (1893).

20. Burby, Real Property 365 (2d ed. 1954).

with many another good idea, the execution has fallen short of the conception. Originally, the exemption was probably large enough to preserve the home intact, but much of the legislation has not kept pace with changing economic conditions and today the dollar amount is often too small to protect the home although large enough to cause title problems when land is conveyed without the proper release of the exemption. In Illinois, the amount was $1,000 until 1957 when it was increased to $2,500.[21] At today's prices this might save a garage roof, but little else.

"Few statutory enactments have met with such a variety of interpretations as has been accorded to the homestead exemption laws. Statutes containing identical language have led the courts to entirely different conclusions in their application, and even the courts of the same jurisdiction have felt free to deviate from and ignore former opinions without much concern about stare decisis. 'Fireside equity' has found a fertile field among the Homestead Acts, and this, coupled with frequent amendments, repeals, and re-enactments has thrown the law of homestead into a state of conflict and confusion." [22] A few general principles can be discerned, however, and a brief statement will help clarify the modern role of homestead.

Strictly speaking, homestead is broader than a marital interest since it is available to the head of a family whether or not he is married. Thus, any person who has a legal or moral duty to support dependent persons living with him may be considered the head of a family.[23] In Minnesota, any resident of the state, whether or not he is head of a family, may claim the exemption.[24] Some states allow the acquisition of homestead by the mere occupancy of real property as a home; others require a declaration filed of record in order to make the claim;[25] and at least one state (Texas) provides the exemption for land occupied for business purposes.[26] In spite of these variations, the usual situation involves a husband or wife who claims the privilege as protection for the family unit.

What exactly is homestead? Most writers contend that it is no more than an exemption from debts and does not rise to the dignity of an estate. Tiffany, for example, says that it is difficult to see how the right of an owner to hold land exempt from liability for debts can be an estate and that even where a statute expressly declares it to be an estate, a new meaning must be given

21. Ill.Rev.Stat. ch. 52, § 1 (1961). By 1972, Illinois had increased the exemption to $10,000, thus saving the roof and the foundations.

22. Note, The Illinois Homestead Exemption, 1950 U.Ill.L.F. 99.

23. Webster v. McGauvran, 8 N.D. 274, 78 N.W. 80 (1899).

24. Note, Homesteads—Application of Minnesota Statutes, 25 Minn.L. Rev. 66 (1940).

25. 2 Thompson, Real Property, § 987 (1939).

26. Tex.Const. art. XVI, § 51.

to that term.[27] But there is no reason why a legislature may not create a new estate unknown at common law, and the fact that a rise or decline in value of land set off as homestead does not change its boundaries shows that we may be dealing with an interest that is more than an exemption and may, indeed, be called an estate. The Illinois act speaks of an estate of homestead and the Illinois courts have reluctantly called it that.[28] In fact, in Illinois, "if a conveyance of real estate is made without waiving homestead, then at the death of the homesteader, the title to the homestead estate descends to his heirs at law or passes to the devisees under his will as in the case of other real estate. Thus, where the householder conveys homestead property worth in excess of [$2,500] and fails to waive homestead, he retains the title to [$2,500] worth of the property. Upon his death this [$2,500] worth of the homestead property, if not conveyed by the householder before his death, passes to his heirs or devisees." [29]

Regardless of the jurisdiction, it is apparent that purchasers or mortgagees must be careful to see that homestead is waived at the time of the sale or mortgage so that they will not be plagued by the interest at a future date. The statutes prescribe how this must be done and, as a general rule, they require certain formalities, such as an acknowledgment by the grantors and the signatures of both spouses on the deed or mortgage.[30] Since dower also requires joinder in the conveyance by the wife (or husband in some states) both of these marital interests may be extinguished by the same act.[31]

C. COMMUNITY PROPERTY

Homestead makes a statutory break with the common-law tradition of marital interests; community property springs from a completely separate tradition and is borrowed from the civil law of Spain and France. The eight jurisdictions [32] where the

---

27. 5 Tiffany, Real Property, § 1332 (3d ed. 1939).

28. Browning v. Harris, 99 Ill. 456 (1881).

29. Fitch, Real Estate Titles in Illinois 380 (1948).

30. 2 Thompson, Real Property, § 1005 (1939).

31. Acknowledgment, i. e., attestation before the proper official, usually a notary public, is typically required to release homestead but not dower.

32. Arizona, California, Idaho, Louisiana, Nevada, New Mexico, Texas, and Washington. Note that the Spanish background of Louisiana

doctrine of community property now exists do not have curtesy or dower although they do have the homestead exemption. Except in Louisiana, the basic principles of the common law, including the concept of estates and interests in land, have full play in these states but the special rules of community property must also be considered in giving sound legal advice. Since the system is a creature of statute there are wide variations among the states and no attempt will be made to do more than sketch the general outline of the doctrine.[33]

It is the theory of community property that the husband and wife should share *equally* that property acquired by their joint efforts during marriage. The marriage itself is a "community" to which both partners contribute and it makes no difference whether the husband or the wife is the actual breadwinner. This one-half-to-the-husband, one-half-to-the-wife approach seems to be the ultimate in marital interests. It makes a startling contrast with the old common-law estate *jure uxoris*!

Where the doctrine prevails, the first big problem is to distinguish between community property and separate property because not everything a spouse owns falls under the community veil. Property acquired by the earnings of either husband or wife during marriage, income from community property, and property acquired by the sale of community property, must be shared equally. On the other hand, property owned by either spouse before marriage, acquired by gift, inheritance, or devise after marriage, and income from such property is considered to be separate and subject to control by the spouse concerned. Thus, a husband (or wife) has the power to transfer inter vivos any separate property he may own and can devise it freely, subject only to the possible right of the other spouse to renounce the will and take a statutory forced share. It is true that community-property jurisdictions typically give a surviving spouse a larger share on intestacy than is normal in the other states. It should be noted that a presumption exists that all property of a married couple is community property and so careful records as to source of acquisition should be kept in order to rebut the presumption.

The earlier community-property doctrine paralleled the common law and gave the husband full control but this has now been changed by statute and transfers of such property do not affect the wife's interest, unless she joins in the deed or mortgage. At death, either party can devise one-half of the community property but, of course, the other half remains vested in the surviving

and Mexico accounts for five of these states having adopted community property. Idaho, Nevada, and Washington were converted in the early stages of their settlement.

33. For a complete treatment see McKay, Community Property (2d ed. 1925) or de Funiak, Principles of Community Property (1943).

spouse. If the death is intestate, the statutes vary considerably but in some instances they give all to the survivor. If the marriage tie is severed by divorce, the community property is divided equally but the court has the power to reach the separate property of the husband, or even his one-half of the community property, if the circumstances require it.

Does the community-property doctrine have sufficient social value to commend it to the forty-two states that have remained loyal to the common law? Professor Powell does not think so. "When adopted at the beginning of a society's existence, community property may be as good as its proponents claim. Any attempt to shift from the customs, practices and rules of a state having the common law traditions to the community property system involves changes in so many aspects of society that it is a shift not lightly to be undertaken. There is at present no apparent likelihood that the system will spread in continental United States to more than the eight states which have grown up in its practices." [34]

Prior to 1948, there was a swing toward community property because of the great tax advantage arising from the fact that one-half of the husband's earnings was his income and one-half was his wife's income. Michigan, Nebraska, Oklahoma, Oregon, Pennsylvania, and Hawaii passed community-property legislation, designed to secure for their citizens the tax reduction enjoyed by the "old" community-property states.[35] The Revenue Act of 1948 eliminated this inequity by extending to all married couples the opportunity to split income, thus reaching about the same result as that prevailing in community-property states. Interest in community-property doctrine receded apace and five of the jurisdictions repealed their acts. The sixth, Pennsylvania, solved the problem more neatly when the Supreme Court of Pennsylvania held its statute unconstitutional.[36] In the five states where the legislatures repealed the acts, there will be haunting problems for years to come since the doctrine was in force from the date of passage to the date of repeal and could affect titles during that period. In Pennsylvania, the court's action means that the statute was void *ab initio* and property rights are unaffected by this venture into "alien principles."

34. 4 Powell, Real Property 675, 676 (1954).

35. de Funiak, The Community Property Trend, 23 Notre Dame Law. 293 (1948).

36. Willcox v. Penn Mutual Life Ins. Co., 357 Pa. 581, 55 A.2d 21 (1947).

SECTION 2. CONCURRENT ESTATES

———

Most of the multiple interests in the same *res* are successive in character, e. g., a life estate followed by a remainder, or are different in quality, e. g., a mortgage (security interest) on a fee simple estate.   In this section, we develop the concept of concurrent ownership where the parties, at one and the same time, have the same quality of rights in one and the same *res*.   These co-owners have simultaneous interests in every portion of the thing, but no separate interest in any particular portion of it.   They have a claim, determined by the extent of their share, to every part of the whole.   Thus, if *O* dies intestate, survived only by three sons, they will take his property as tenants in common, owning no specific part in severalty but each having an undivided one-third of the whole.   The relevant estates developed early in English history, during the fifteenth century, and have survived, with varying degrees of modification, to the present day.   These concurrent estates are: coparcenary, tenancy by the entirety, joint tenancy, and tenancy in common.   Although the interests originated as estates in land, they find modern application to personalty as well, in such interests as joint bank accounts, jointly payable government savings bonds, etc.   Moreover, there are certain modern developments, such as partnership property and cooperative apartments, which are properly classified under the broad umbrella of concurrent estates.

———

A.   COPARCENARY

———

This form of co-ownership is virtually extinct in United States and deserves space primarily to show the historical development of the law.   It arose as a corollary to primogeniture and applied when there were no sons so that the daughters had to share equally as heir.   (It applied by special custom in some English localities, where the land descended to two or more males.)   The coparceners [37] took but a single estate and were viewed col-

---

37. "The name parcener is derived from the fact that, apart from statute, such a tenant had the right to compel partition at a time when joint tenants and tenants in common had no such right." Moynihan, Preliminary Survey of the Law of Real Property 135 (1940).

lectively as a single heir. Note that this idea was consistent with the feudal policy against dividing the ownership of the land among numerous heirs. Nevertheless, the estate in coparcenary was like the tenancy in common, in that no right of survivorship prevailed among the parceners and the share of each would go to that parcener's heir who would then hold in coparcenary with the survivors. Only if there was a partition would the land again be held in severalty. The term is still used occasionally, but to-day the individuals who share an inheritance are usually called tenants in common.

B. TENANCY BY THE ENTIRETY

Reference has been made previously to the common law's view of the husband and wife as one, giving rise to the husband's estate of *jure uxoris* in the wife's land. That estate has passed into limbo but the idea behind it survives, in many jurisdictions, in the tenancy by the entirety. That estate came into being when property was transferred to husband and wife; since they were one they received but a single estate, an entirety. So strong was this presumption that, if land was conveyed to a man and his wife and a third person, the spouses took a one-half interest by the entirety and the third person took a one-half interest which he held as a joint tenant or tenant in common (depending on the presumption) with the spouses. It follows that the estate could be created only where the legal unity of husband and wife existed, and a conveyance to two unmarried persons "as tenants by the entirety" resulted in a tenancy in common.[38] If the marriage bond were severed by an absolute divorce it severed the estate as well, since the unity was gone and a tenancy in common would result.[39]

The tenancy by the entirety's nearest relative was the joint tenancy since both carried the important right of survivorship which did not attach to the tenancy in common or to coparcenary. Indeed, the estate by the entirety so resembles a joint tenancy that it has been called a joint tenancy "modified by the common law doctrine that husband and wife are one person."[40] Despite the similarities, however, the two estates are different both con-

38. Perrin v. Harrington, 146 App. Div. 292, 130 N.Y.S. 944 (1911).

39. Andrews v. Andrews, 155 Fla. 654, 21 So.2d 205 (1945).

40. Pray v. Stebbins, 141 Mass. 219, 221, 4 N.E. 824, 825 (1886).

ceptually and practically. To lapse into the mystical Latin of the property lawyer, tenants by the entirety were seised *per tout et non per my*, joint tenants were seised *per my et per tout*. This is shorthand for saying that the former own the whole interest collectively but not any individual share whereas the latter own both the whole interest and a share. This mysticism is clarified by the practical consequences: the estate by the entireties could not be partitioned except by the voluntary act of *both* parties or by divorce, nor could the estate be defeated by an act on the part of a single spouse, i. e., by voluntary conveyance of his interest or by a sale on execution to reach his assets; the joint tenancy could be partitioned and was, in fact, severed by a voluntary or involuntary conveyance by a single party.

The modern role of the tenancy by the entirety varies widely from state to state. In Massachusetts, it retains most of its common-law glory and seems unaffected by the emancipation of women.[41] In more than half of the states, however, the tenancy has no modern significance and a conveyance to husband and wife will give rise to a joint tenancy or a tenancy in common, depending on the language used. This result has been reached for a variety of reasons, the most common being the Married Women's Property Acts which were held to destroy the spousal unity. Some states have simply rejected this type of property ownership as "repugnant to our institutions and to the American sense of justice to the heirs and therefore not the common law." [42] Between the extremes, other states have retained the common-law concept while modifying its practical consequences, usually by giving the parties equal rights in the control and enjoyment of the land rather than vesting these rights in the husband alone. Aside from the divorce problem, there has been little litigation between the spouses themselves and most of the cases arise when a creditor seeks to reach the interest of one of the parties.

A Massachusetts creditor would find that he could not do with the interest of a tenant by the entirety that which the tenant could not do. Thus, since the wife could not sell the land alone, her creditor could not sell it by resort to attachment and levy on an execution in an action at law.[43] All the wife has, in effect, is a right of survivorship and this apparently is not assignable either voluntarily or involuntarily.[44] It follows that the hus-

41. Licker v. Gluskin, 265 Mass. 403, 164 N.E. 613 (1929) ; Hoag v. Hoag, 213 Mass. 50, 99 N.E. 521 (1912).

42. For a complete discussion of ownership by the entireties with reference to specific states see 4 Powell, Real Property 653–671 (1954).

43. Note 41 supra.

44. This latter point seems inconsistent with the Massachusetts rule that "a contingent interest is assignable if the chance of the contingency happening is not so uncertain as to make it a mere speculative possibility." Newhall, Future

band's interest can be reached for his life at least, but will be defeated if the wife survives. In the jurisdictions where the tenancy is extinct, the creditor has the right to reach the respective shares of either spouse and this same result is reached in those states which retain the tenancy but allow the spouses to share the beneficial ownership equally. A third position is taken by a number of states which hold that the creditors of neither spouse can reach the land, since to allow such involuntary transfer would be too great an interference with the other spouse's use and enjoyment.[45] This last position is particularly undesirable since it allows a married couple to render a large portion of their estate inaccessible to creditors and this can be especially inequitable in a jurisdiction which allows the tenancy to exist in personal property as well. In 1944, a committee of the American Bar Association recommended that the tenancy by the entirety be abolished in all states and it seems high time for this vestige of an older day to join *jure uxoris* and coparcenary in the real property museum.

Until such time as tenancy by the entirety is abolished in all states it will continue to cause some interesting litigation. Suppose, for example, a house held by the entireties is destroyed by fire. Will the insurance proceeds be impressed with the tenancy or should they be paid equally to H and W? In Hawthorne v. Hawthorne,[46] the Court of Appeals of New York held that W was entitled to one-half of the insurance proceeds. "Since personalty cannot be held by the entirety this ends the question as far as a legal estate or title is concerned unless equity demands exact equivalence in both quantity and quality of ownership in all cases resembling 'involuntary conversion'." In a case involving a condemnation award, the New York court had held that the survivorship right continued into the substituted *res* but that was a true case of "involuntary conversion" and, moreover, the issue of severability was not raised, only the right to the proceeds as survivor. Since there was no question of survivorship in the insurance case, both H and W were alive, the insurance proceeds (being personal property) were severable and the wife was entitled to her share. This seems to be the correct result if tenancy by the entirety is restricted to land, as in New York, but the problem would be different in states allowing such tenancies in personalty.

Interests in Massachusetts, § 13 (1938).

45. Fairclaw v. Forrest, 130 F.2d 829 (D.C.Cir. 1942); Ward Terry and Co. v. Hensen, 75 Wyo. 444, 297

P.2d 213 (1956) (this case contains an excellent analysis of the various American views).

46. 13 N.Y.2d 82, 242 N.Y.S.2d 50, 192 N.E.2d 20 (1963).

An even more intriguing problem was presented in Benson v. United States.[47] H and W had owned land as tenants by the entirety but were later divorced. In all jurisdictions except the District of Columbia the divorce would have ended the entireties and H and W would have become tenants in common. A special statute in the District allowed the tenancy by the entireties to continue even after divorce, if there was a valid antenuptial or postnuptial agreement in relation to its continuance. Since the entireties still continued in this case, the property was not subject to a federal tax lien against the husband alone. The tax lien could not attach until H survived W; if W survived H it would not attach at all. Of course, if the tax lien had been against both H and W it would have attached to the property.

While the two previous examples are, admittedly, unusual cases they do illustrate the complex problems caused by the continued existence of an outmoded concurrent estate. Incidentally, it should be pointed out that, while a tenancy by the entireties was non-severable by the unilateral act of either H or W, both could join in a conveyance of the full fee in severalty (or otherwise) to a third party. Similarly, either spouse could convey his interest to the other. Indeed, in Union Planters National Bank v. United States [48] H conveyed his interest in a tenancy by the entireties to W as a completed gift, without reserving any legal title, right, or interest therein to himself, and even though he continued to live with his wife in the home until his death, the value of the residence was not included in his taxable estate for federal estate tax purposes. The court did point out that, "in some situations this may prove to be an unfortunate test of one's partner's judgment of the security of the marriage."

C. JOINT TENANCY

The outstanding feature of the joint tenancy is the right of survivorship which is inherent in it. When one joint tenant dies the other is the sole owner; if there are several joint tenants, the deceased's share is owned by the survivors jointly. The deceased's share does not "pass to" the survivor, as in a testate or

47. 143 U.S.App.D.C. 197, 442 F.2d   48. 361 F.2d 662 (C.A.Tenn.1966).
     1221 (1971).

intestate succession, since each joint tenant is conceived as owning the whole, subject to the equal rights of the other or others. Thus, when one dies the estate of the survivor is simply freed from the former's rights in the property. This can have some interesting consequences, as when one joint tenant murders another [49] or when joint tenants die simultaneously.[50]

The common-law presumption favored the creation of a joint tenancy over a tenancy in common when the exact nature of the concurrent estate was not specified. This was consistent with the doctrines of primogeniture and coparcenary since it carried out the feudal desire to keep the land in a single ownership, if possible. There is no modern justification for the survivorship principle, unless the parties expressly wish this feature to apply, and it can be dangerous since the surviving tenant will exclude the heirs and devisees of the decedent, frequently contrary to the intent of the parties. Consequently, the common-law presumption has been universally reversed and many states have statutes which provide that there shall be no joint tenancy unless the right of survivorship is expressly provided for in the creating instrument.[51] A few states do not permit joint tenancies in land at all. Usually, an exception is made for fiduciaries (trustees, executors, etc.) since the survivorship principle aids them in the performance of their duties. The exact language necessary to rebut the presumption of a tenancy in common is far from clear. Since it depends on the intent of the parties, as shown by the creating instrument, you may be sure that the cases are not consistent. If the grantor desires to create a joint tenancy, he should make this wish crystal clear by some such language as, "to *A* and *B*, not in tenancy in common, but in joint tenancy, with right of survivorship." [52] The worst possible language is, "to *A* and *B* jointly", since this conjures up images

49. In Welsh v. James, 408 Ill. 18, 95 N.E.2d 872 (1951), Comment, 1951 U.Ill.L.F. 172, the right of survivorship was held to take its customary course, but this case was overruled in Bradley v. Fox, 7 Ill.2d 106, 129 N.E.2d 699 (1955).

50. The Uniform Simultaneous Death Act, § 3 provides: "Where there is no sufficient evidence that two joint tenants or tenants by the entirety have died otherwise than simultaneously the property so held shall be distributed one half as if one had survived and one half as if the other had survived. If there are more than two joint tenants and all of them have so died the property then distributed shall be in the proportion that one bears to the whole number of joint tenants." This statute, which has the effect of treating the parties as having died as tenants in common, has been adopted in some forty states.

51. The New York Real Property Law, § 66 is typical. "Every estate granted or devised to two or more persons in their own right shall be a tenancy in common, unless expressly declared to be in joint tenancy; but every estate, vested in executors or trustees as such, shall be held by them in joint tenancy."

52. See Ill.Rev.Stat. ch. 76, § 1 (1973).

of both types of estates and is thoroughly ambiguous. It would seem that the courts should treat this language as not sufficiently rebutting the presumption and thus creating a tenancy in common.[53]

There is no way to prevent people from using language outside the legal norm and when this occurs litigation may be the only recourse for clearing the title. In these cases, the court's role will be to ascertain the intent of the parties as disclosed by the deed or will. Sometimes, the parties are attempting to create a non-severable estate with a right of survivorship and this can be done if the correct language is used. A grant to "A and B for their joint lives with the remainder vesting in the survivor of them" would seem to do the job. This does not create a joint tenancy, although it is similar to such an estate in many ways. While both A and B are alive they have life estates measured by their joint lives with a contingent remainder in the survivor, vesting in one on the death of the other. There would be no way to sever this estate other than by the joint action of A and B.

Similarly, a grant to "A and B and their heirs, and to the survivor of them" could be construed as conveying to B a life estate as a tenant in common, plus a remainder in fee (or executory interest) if he survives A or it could be held that the deed creates a tenancy in common in fee plus a somewhat anomalous "right of survivorship".[54] Either construction would seem to create a non-destructible right of survivorship.

If the language is ambiguous, the court will have to choose between a construction which creates a somewhat anomalous estate in the land and a more conventional joint tenancy with its inherent right of severance. For two interesting cases where the court wrestled with this problem. See Bernhard v. Bernhard [55] and Palmer v. Flint.[56] In the former, the Alabama Court seems to have been led astray by the statute abolishing joint tenancies as they existed at common law; in the latter the trial court was led astray but the Supreme Court of Maine returned to basic principles and decided the parties had intended to create a joint tenancy, despite the ambiguous language.

According to common-law dogma, a joint tenancy could be created only where the four unities of time, title, interest, and

53. Taylor v. Taylor, 310 Mich. 541, 17 N.W.2d 745, 157 A.L.R. 559 (1945).

54. Runions v. Runions, 186 Tenn. 25, 207 S.W.2d 1016, 1 A.L.R.2d 242 (1948) and Anson v. Murphy, 149 Neb. 716, 32 N.W.2d 271 (1948).

55. 278 Ala. 240, 177 So.2d 565 (1965), overruled in Nunn v. Keith, 289 Ala. 518, 268 So.2d 792 (1972).

56. 156 Me. 103, 161 A.2d 837 (1960).

possession were present. It followed that any severance of these four unities would also end the joint tenancy. A brief analysis of each of these unities is called for: *time* meant that the interests of the joint tenants must vest at the same time; *title* meant that the parties must take their interests by the same instrument —deed, will, etc.; *interest* meant that they must have estates of the same type and duration; and *possession* meant that the joint tenants must have undivided interests in the whole, not divided interests in the several parts. This legal formula was fully expounded by Blackstone [57] and found its way into American law where it has shown surprising vitality. As a general proposition it is harmless enough and, indeed, can be viewed as little more than descriptive of the nature of the estate, but it, like many a common-law rule, has caused a few real hangovers. Suppose *A* owns Blackacre in fee simple absolute and decides he would like to convey it to himself and his new bride, *B*, as joint tenants, so she will have a right of survivorship and thus avoid the necessity of making a will. If he makes a deed directly to "*A* and *B*, as joint tenants" he will fail in his purpose and will create only a tenancy in common because two of the four unities— time and title—are missing. At common law a party could not convey to himself, that would be a nullity, so the wife received her interest at a different time and by a different instrument than the husband. The intent to create a joint tenancy was clear but, because of this "pitfall for the unwary," *A* failed to accomplish his purpose. To avoid this result the device of a straw man was used; *A* conveyed to *X*, who in turn reconveyed to "*A* and *B* as joint tenants." Now the four unities were present and, *voila*, a joint tenancy resulted. For an interesting Maine case involving this bit of legal sleight of hand see Strout v. Burgess.[58] To avoid this weird result and do away with the necessity for a straw party, several states have passed legislation which allows the creation of a joint tenancy by direct conveyance.[59] The spirit behind these statutes was urged on the court in the Maine case but the judge wrote, as is so frequent in the property field, "If the law with relation to the creation of joint tenancies or with relation to survivorship between co-owners is to be further modified it should be accomplished by the Legislature and not by the Court."

Once a joint tenancy has been created it is easy to destroy it —a simple conveyance by one of the joint tenants will do the job. If *A* and *B* hold as joint tenants and *B*, with or without the permission of *A*, conveys to *C* the severance is complete since the unities are no more. The result is that *A* and *C* now hold as

57. 2 Blackstone Com. 180 et seq.

58. 144 Me. 263, 68 A.2d 241 (1949).

59. See, for example, Ill.Rev.Stat. ch. 76, s. 2.1 (1973).

tenants in common. Of course, *B* could not convey more than he owned and in the hypothetical case that was an undivided one-half interest. If *A, B,* and *C* are joint tenants and *C* conveys to *D,* then *A* and *B* continue as joint tenants in an undivided two-thirds of the estate and *D* has an undivided one-third as a tenant in common with *A* and *B*.[60] While it is clear that a conveyance of the fee by one joint tenant will work a severance, there is some dispute as to the effect of a mortgage, a lease, a contract of sale, etc. Since these transfers, although of limited interests, can be said to destroy the essential unities the tendency is to hold that they, too, cause a severance.[61] It follows that a sale of a joint tenant's interest under execution severs a joint tenancy just as a voluntary conveyance does.[62]

Unlike the tenancy by the entirety, the joint tenancy has considerable social utility so long as it is clear that this is the estate which was intended to be created. Since the estate is severable, it does not serve as a bastion from which to repel the attacks of creditors and the survivorship feature allows it to serve as a "poor man's probate." According to *property* theory, the survivor's share would not be subject to death taxes since the deceased's estate did not pass to the survivor at death but was his from the inception. You may be sure, however, that *tax* theory (whatever that may be) plugged this loophole at an early date and the hopes for tax savings proved to be illusory. The same result was reached as to the tenancy by the entirety.[63] It is fair to say that the problems of joint ownership can be considerable, both taxwise and otherwise, and that the lawyer should tread this area of property law with great care.[64]

60. For an interesting example of this point see Jackson v. O'Connell, 23 Ill.2d 52, 177 N.E.2d 194 (1961).

61. For a more extended discussion see 2 American Law of Property, § 6.2 (Casner ed. 1952).

The issue of severance in these cases will depend on the legal effect of the mortgage, or other legal instrument in the particular jurisdiction. Thus, in People v. Nogarr, 164 Cal. App.2d 591, 330 P.2d 858, 67 A.L.R. 2d 992 (1958) a mortgage by H alone did not sever a joint tenancy and the surviving W took the property free of H's mortgage. This was because California followed a lien theory of mortgages; if they had followed a title theory the court admitted a severance would have occurred.

62. Albright v. Creel, 236 Ala. 286, 182 So. 10 (1938); Young v. Hessler, 72 Cal.App.2d 67, 164 P.2d 65 (1945).

63. U. S. v. Jacobs, 306 U.S. 363, 59 S.Ct. 551, 83 L.Ed. 763 (1939) rejected any differences between the two estates as "shadowy and intricate distinctions of common law property concepts and ancient fictions."

64. To get a further idea of the complexities of these rather simple-appearing estates, see a symposium of five articles on the Problems of Joint Ownership, 1959 U.Ill.L.F. 883–1040.

D.   TENANCY IN COMMON [65]

By this time, the tenancy in common has been identified by a process of elimination. It is that concurrent estate which results if none of the estates in Sections A, B, and C are created. Today, it is the most common of all concurrent estates and is favored by a statutory presumption which must be rebutted by the expressed intent of the parties. The unity of possession is the only essential unity involved in a tenancy in common and Blackstone wrote, "For indeed tenancies in common differ in nothing from sole estates but merely in the blending and unity of possession." [66] There is no right of survivorship between tenants in common and it is accurate to say that the share of each tenant is several and distinct from that of his cotenant, except that it is an undivided interest so that he cannot lay claim to any specific portion of the whole until there is a partition in kind. Tenants in common may receive their respective interests by different instruments of conveyance, at different times, and their interests need not be equal either in size of share or in quantum of estate. Thus *O*, owning Blackacre in fee simple absolute, may convey a one-quarter interest to his wife, *W*, by warranty deed and then die testate, devising an interest in one-eighth of the land to two of his children and a one-half interest to a third child. A tenancy in common would ultimately result, with *W* owning an undivided one-quarter, two children an undivided one-eighth each, and one child an undivided one-half. It follows that each tenant can transfer his own interest as he sees fit (further subdividing the tenancy perhaps) and that his creditors can reach the estate just as if he owned it in severalty.

The basic distinction between a joint tenancy and a tenancy in common is illustrated by the marital rights of a spouse in each case. Assume *A* and *B* are brothers, owning Blackacre as joint tenants, and both are married. The wife of neither can be said to have an inchoate dower in Blackacre because neither is seised of an estate of inheritance. If *A* dies first, *B* has the whole estate and *A's* wife has no claim, although at this point *B's* wife acquires an inchoate dower. On the other hand, if *A* and *B* own as tenants in common, the wife of each has an inchoate dower in the undivided share of her husband since he has an estate of inheritance. Of course, if dower has been abolished in the par-

---

65. Note the tenant in common was seized *per my et non per tout i. e.* by the share or moiety but not by the whole.

66. 2 Blackstone Com. 180.

ticular jurisdiction, this illustration would have no application but the same principle would apply to statutory rights of descent. On the death of a joint tenant or a tenant by the entirety, the surviving tenant owns the property whereas the interest of a tenant in common descends to his heirs or passes under his will.

There are some problems that are inherent in concurrent estates and which arise regardless of the specific tenancy involved. These difficulties cluster around the concept of unity of possession and the legal relationship among co-owners of the same *res*. By definition, each tenant is entitled to possession of the entire parcel of land yet he cannot exercise that possession without coming into conflict with the reciprocal right of his cotenant. So long as one tenant occupies the whole without objection from his fellows no particular problem ensues since the law treats the possession of one cotenant as the possession of all, but disputes can easily arise and joint possession can be difficult.[67] As one court colorfully remarked, "Two men cannot plow the same furrow." [68] If one tenant excludes his cotenants from the whole or any part of the land, he is guilty of an ouster and ejectment will lie at the option of the dispossessed tenant. One tenant can get title to the whole estate by adverse possession if he ousts his cotenant and then occupies himself for the requisite statutory period. In these cases, however, the ouster must be clear-cut and the claimant must "hoist his flag high and keep it flying." Some states even hold "that in order to start the running of the Statute of Limitations against a cotenant, it must be shown that the tenant in possession gave *actual* notice to the tenant out of possession that he was claiming adversely, or that the tenant out of possession had received notice of such claim of the tenant in possession by some act which would amount to an ouster or disseizin." [69] This is clearly a higher standard than required for adverse possession generally; and it should be, because of the close legal relationship between the parties.[70]

The nature of this legal relationship between cotenants cannot be defined but it can be partially described. In Andrews v.

---

67. Note this is true even of joint occupants, like two lessees of an apartment, who do not have a technical concurrent estate in the sense used in this Section. See Tompkins v. Superior Court of San Francisco, 59 Cal.2d 65, 27 Cal.Rptr. 889, 378 P.2d 113 (1963).

68. Mastbaum v. Mastbaum, 126 N.J. Eq. 366, 372, 9 A.2d 51, 55 (1939).

69. Mercer v. Wayman, 9 Ill.2d 441, 445, 137 N.E.2d 815, 818 (1956).

70. Goergen v. Maar, 2 A.D.2d 276, 153 N.Y.S.2d 826 (1956) called it "a quasi trust relationship" and held that in an accounting for profits the statute of limitations on the accounting does not ordinarily begin to run until the termination of the relationship of the cotenants, by a sale of the property.

Andrews,[71] the Florida Supreme Court pointed out that each tenant by the entirety owes the other the highest degree of confidence and trust and proceeded to hold that one tenant could not eliminate the interest of the other by purchasing at a tax sale in his own name, after a default in payment of taxes. If one tenant purchases the joint property at a tax sale, his act benefits all the cotenants and discharges the lien. Of course, the confidential relationship is higher in the entireties' situation because of the marriage but the same principle applies to other cotenancies and to mortgage redemptions as well as tax sales.[72] The cotenant who made the expenditure is entitled to contribution from his fellows and although he may have difficulty in a direct suit for reimbursement he can adjust his rights in a suit for partition.[73] Similarly, adjustments can usually be made for improvements, repairs, insurance, etc., which have been paid for by one cotenant in excess of his aliquot portion of the estate. The principal difficulty will be one of finding the proper remedy, since many states will not allow a direct suit for these items alone.

A particularly troublesome problem can arise as to the duty of one cotenant to account to his fellows for rents and profits derived from the common land. At common law, there was such a duty if one tenant agreed to act as bailiff or manager, if the land was rented to a third party who paid all or a disproportionate share to one tenant, or if one tenant excluded his fellows from possession. But if a cotenant entered the land, not excluding or interfering with his cotenants, he was not liable for the profits of his occupancy.[74] This view still prevails in some states but others have repudiated it. "No practical or reasonable argument can be advanced for allowing one in possession to reap a financial benefit by occupying property owned in common without paying for his personal use of that part of the property owned by his cotenants. The fairest method in cases in which the cotenant occupies and uses common property, instead of renting it out, is to charge him with its reasonable rental value." [75]

The ultimate destiny of many a concurrent estate is the chancery side of a court of general jurisdiction and a suit in partition. Here the chancellor will endeavor to do what the cotenants presumably have failed to do—reach an equitable severance

71. 155 Fla. 654, 21 So.2d 205 (1945).

72. Knesek v. Muzny, 191 Okl. 332, 129 P.2d 853 (1942).

73. Kirsch v. Scandia American Bank, 160 Minn. 269, 199 N.W. 881 (1924).

74. Pico v. Columbet, 12 Cal. 414 (1859).

For a detailed analysis of this point see Baird v. Moore, 50 N.J.Super. 156, 141 A.2d 324 (1958).

75. McKnight v. Basilides, 19 Wash. 2d 391, 407, 143 P.2d 307, 315 (1943).

of the interests and make the parties owners in severalty at last. Today, this usually means a sale with an apportionment of the proceeds rather than partition in kind.[76] The proceeding will probably be regulated by statute and discussion of it is beyond the scope of this book but a good review of its history and theory can be found in the Michigan case of Henkel v. Henkel.[77] It should be noted that while partition is normally an absolute right of any cotenant (other than a tenant by the entireties) the courts will enforce an explicit agreement between the parties not to partition, at least so long as the agreement does not bind the parties for an unreasonable time and run afoul of the Rule Against Perpetuities or become an unreasonable restraint on alienation.[78]

E. CONCURRENT ESTATES IN PERSONALTY

The concurrent estates discussed in the preceding sections can exist in personal property as well as in land, except that a tenancy by the entirety may be restricted to real property in many states. Indeed, in modern society, the joint bank account (checking or savings), the jointly owned government bonds, the joint ownership of the family automobile, etc., may be the most striking manifestations of these property concepts. It is the survivorship feature that has the most appeal and the popularity of the joint bank account is due, in part at least, to the fact that a testamentary disposition can be made without the expense of drafting a will or the delay of probate proceedings. Despite the deceptive simplicity of these joints interests, they can be real sources of trouble, as attested by the volume of litigation involving ownership of joint bank accounts.[79]

The basic difficulty is that the courts have not agreed on the theory to be used to sustain such joint interests. At least four theories, with varying results, have been utilized: the gift the-

76. For two interesting cases involving the issue of partition in kind versus partition by sale see Johnson v. Hendrickson, 71 S.D. 392, 24 N.W.2d 914 (1946) and White v. Smyth, 147 Tex. 272, 214 S.W.2d 967, 5 A.L.R.2d 1348 (1948).

77. 282 Mich. 473, 276 N.W. 522 (1937).

78. Michalski v. Michalski, 50 N.J. Super. 454, 142 A.2d 645 (1958).

79. For a brief discussion of the point see Comment, The Joint and Survivorship Bank Account, 1957 U.Ill.L.F. 655.

ory,[80] the trust theory,[81] the contract theory [82] and the joint tenancy theory.[83] Oddly enough, none of the theories fit exactly, e. g., the joint bank account cannot be a true joint tenancy because the four common-law unities—time, title, interest and possession—are lacking and the trust theory is so "far-fetched" that only Maryland follows it today. Oregon has faced the issue squarely saying, "It is not important that the interest created has no well-settled legal name. . . . It is enough that it was intended to be created, and that it violates no rule of statute or common law. . . . Out of the practice, now extensively engaged in, of keeping money in joint bank accounts, there has grown up a considerable body of law, reflecting the view held by a majority of courts that such arrangements, when entered into in good faith, are not opposed to any policy of the state, and that the purposes which are sought to be accomplished by them should not be set at naught by employing in too narrow and technical a spirit the legal principles which are found to be involved." [84]

The joint account is typically created by a deposit agreement, signed by both parties and reading: "As joint tenants, with right of survivorship and not as tenants in common." The bank is usually protected by statute and can pay either of the parties without fear of a later claim by the other.[85] Because the creating instrument gives either party the power to withdraw all the funds during his lifetime, the issue of ownership generally does not arise until after the death of one of the depositors (typically the husband) and the contending parties are then the estate of the deceased and the surviving "joint tenant." The following hypothetical problem illustrates the point.

H, a businessman, has his wife, *W*, working as his secretary and for convenience in his operations he deposits all funds in a joint checking account with his wife, using the form quoted in the previous paragraph. *H* and *W* have three grown children and, becoming estranged from his wife maritally although continuing to find her an excellent secretary, *H* leaves the bulk of his estate to the children by will. *H* dies, a major asset of his estate is the business cash, and *W* claims it all as surviving joint tenant while the executor claims it for the children. If the jurisdiction follows a strict contract theory, the wife takes it all under the

80. Estate of Schneider, 6 Ill.2d 180, 127 N.E.2d 445 (1955).

81. Kornmann v. Safe Deposit Co., 180 Md. 270, 23 A.2d 692 (1942).

82. Castle v. Wightman, 303 Mass. 74, 20 N.E.2d 436 (1939).

83. Tacoma Sav. and Loan Ass'n v. Nahm, 14 Wash.2d 576, 128 P.2d 982 (1942).

84. Beach v. Holland, 172 Or. 396, 417, 418, 142 P.2d 990, 998, 149 A.L.R. 866 (1943).
For a good, recent analysis of the entire problem see Miller v. Riegler, 243 Ark. 251, 419 S.W.2d 599 (1967).

85. Ill.Rev.Stat. ch. 76, § 2(a) (1973); Mass.Gen.Laws Ann., c. 334, § 1 (1953); Tenn.Code Ann. § 45–412.

terms of the agreement.   Similarly, she is the winner if a joint tenancy was created.[86]   But, if the basis of the joint account is the gift theory, then the wife can succeed only if there was donative intent on the part of *H*.   Since such intent can be rebutted by the facts of the case (business convenience, not the desire to make a gift to the wife, was the reason for the joint account) the children have an excellent chance of reaching the joint funds.[87] As so frequently happens in the law, two basic policies conflict here—certainty and fairness.   To refuse to go behind the joint-account mask frequently may be unfair to the parties; to do so introduces a flexibility in the concurrent estate concept which may destroy much of its utility.   At the present time, these varying policies have not been wholly reconciled, so even the innocent-appearing joint bank account may have booby-trap tendencies.

Brief mention should be made of the Totten trust, christened for the case which popularized the device—Matter of Totten,[88] because it is closely related to the joint bank account, although sustained on another theory.   "Typically, it involves a deposit of his own money by *A* to the account of '*A*, in trust for *B*.' After careful consideration, the New York court concluded that such a deposit should be deemed the declaration of a 'tentative trust'—one which the donor-depositor may revoke by withdrawing the fund or by changing the form of the account.   The transfer of ownership becomes complete only upon the depositor's death; thereafter the donee may effectively claim any amount credited to the account, but he has no enforceable claim during the depositor's lifetime, nor may he recover any sum which the depositor has withdrawn from the account.   Occasionally a court is candid enough to recognize such a device as the Totten trust or the joint bank account with right of survivorship as 'the poor man's will.' " [89]

86.   It is, perhaps, misleading to say W wins.   She takes the legal title as the survivor under the contract and joint tenancy theories but that does not end the matter.   Equity may impress the proceeds with a constructive trust and order the survivor to hold them as a part of the deceased's estate, if it can be clearly and satisfactorily proved that the joint account was for convenience only.   There is, in effect, a rebuttable presumption that the donor depositor intended a right of survivorship in the cotenant.   In re Estate of Michaels, 26 Wis.2d 382, 132 N.W.2d 557 (1965).   Note this same device, the constructive trust, has been used to reach a just result in a case where one co-owner of a joint bank account has allegedly murdered the other.   See Vesey v. Vesey, 237 Minn. 295, 54 N.W.2d 385, 32 A.L.R.2d 1090 (1952).

87.   Imirie v. Imirie, 246 F.2d 652 (D.C.Cir.1957);   Estate of Schneider, 6 Ill.2d 180, 127 N.E.2d 445 (1955).

As the discussion in the previous footnote points out, the final result *may* be the same under any of the theories but the process of legal reasoning is different and indicates the continuing confusion of legal thought about joint accounts.

88.   179 N.Y. 112, 71 N.E. 748 (1904).

89.   Cribbet, Fritz and Johnson, Cases and Materials on Property 237 (3d ed. 1972).

Part Three

TRANSFER OF OWNERSHIP

In Part One, we discussed property as an institution and sought some insight as to the role of private property in modern society. In Part Two, we explored the scheme of ownership as developed in Anglo-American law with slight references to other systems of jurisprudence. Now, assuming you understand such esoteric matters as freehold versus non-freehold estates, seisin versus possession, etc., we turn our attention to the transfer of ownership from one party to another. There are various ways to categorize these transfers but the broad division is between voluntary and involuntary. The former are more important for our present purpose since they include the major commercial aspects of property law—sale, mortgage, and lease—but the latter will be discussed first in order to provide perspective. None of these transfers are of maximum utility unless the title itself is merchantable, i. e., capable of being transferred profitably to others, so this part of the book will close with a look at the modern methods of title assurance.

Chapter 1

INVOLUNTARY TRANSFER

Although we tend to think first of a sale, a gift, or perhaps a lease, when we visualize transfers of ownership from one party to another, many changes in title take place against the express desires of the owner. Judgments may be obtained which will be liens against the property, resulting in levy of execution and sale;[1] involuntary bankruptcy proceedings may force the debtor to strip himself of his limited assets;[2] adverse possession by a rival claimant may ripen into a new title under the Statute of Limitations;[3] title to personal property may be changed due to doctrines of accession and confusion;[4] the boundary-changing

1. See Brown, The Law of Personal Property 40–50 (2d ed. 1955).

2. See generally MacLachlan, Handbook of the Law of Bankruptcy (1956).

3. Discussed herein as a method of title assurance at p. 300 infra.

4. Brown op. cit. supra at 51–82.

propensities of rivers may take land from one riparian owner
and give it to another; [5] etc.   While all of these title changes
may involve serious legal problems, they cannot be discussed in
a short, elementary book.   One type of involuntary transfer,
however, does call for our attention—transfer at death.

Testate and intestate succession, i. e., transfer through a
will or by operation of a statute of descent in absence of a will,
are frequently classified as gratuitous transfers, operating as a
type of gift.   This is a useful concept since it separates these
transfers from commercial transactions and highlights the donee
aspect of the recipient.   It may seem odd to call a testamentary
disposition an involuntary transfer since the making of the will
is clearly voluntary and may have been accompanied by estate
planning of a high order.   Still, it is doubtful if many testators
voluntarily slip over the great divide so that the objects of their
bounty may enjoy the material possessions left behind.   If there
were pockets in shrouds, no doubt the man of property would depart this life heavily laden.   Hence, the title of this chapter
seems appropriate.

SECTION 1.   INTESTATE SUCCESSION

It is difficult to separate intestate and testate succession for
discussion, but it may clarify our thinking to see the distinct
categories represented by the two methods of transfer.   The former was the more ancient method and, so far as land was concerned, it was the middle of the sixteenth century in England [6]
before fee simple estates were freely devisable.   Here, again,
the split between realty and personalty played a key role in the
development of the law since personal property could be disposed of by will from very ancient times.   It was, at one time,
thought to be a religious duty to bequeath all of one's chattels and
the church, through the ecclesiastical courts, exerted a powerful
influence to see that no person of wealth died intestate.   You
may be sure that this religious interest was not wholly altruistic
and the worldly position of the church was enhanced by the
wealth acquired through carefully planned wills.   One English
historian writes that "this abandonment of jurisdiction [over
personal property] to the ecclesiastical courts has tended, more

5.   3 American Law of Property, §   6.   The Statute of Wills was passed
   12.113 (Casner ed. 1952).   in 1540.

than any other single cause, to accentuate the difference between real and personal property; for even when the ecclesiastical courts had ceased to exercise some parts of this jurisdiction, the law which they had created was exercised by their successors." [7]

Even if we grant the power to the individual to dispose of his property at death more or less as he sees fit, we are a long way from settling the issue. While it might seem that no aspect of private property is more basic than the power to choose the objects of one's bounty, many individuals will die without exercising this power even where it is available to them. The law must then decide how the deceased's estate shall be distributed. Of course, it could be argued that, due to the former owner's lack of personal concern, all of the property should pass to the state to be used for the general welfare, but this extreme position has not in fact been taken, except in the rare cases where there are no heirs at law or next of kin and the property escheats to the state. More than three hundred years ago Grotius said that the purpose of the intestate succession law was to provide that the property of a dead man would descend "to the person to whom it is especially probable that the dead man had wished that it should belong." Writers and courts have generally taken this position since that time so that we seem to have a mandate to make our law conform to the probable wishes of the community. [8]

Any detailed historical analysis of intestate succession [9] is out of place in a book of basic principles but it would show the constant striving, inept at times and full of digressions, of the parliament in England and the state legislatures in this country to make the law conform to the social needs and the probable wishes of the community at any given time. Thus, in the modern law, primogeniture and the canons of descent have been confined to the ash heap and vigorous efforts have been made to remove the differences between real and personal property. This latter reform is not yet complete in all states but the distinctions are fast disappearing. The present law of intestate succession is wholly controlled by local statutes and the details vary from state to state, yet, not too surprisingly, the general "running gears" are pretty much the same throughout the United States and an understanding of one such statute makes it easy to work with others. The pattern of distribution is about the same with the "one-third to the spouse, two-thirds to the children" apparently representing the wishes of the community. A typical stat-

7. 1 Holdsworth, History of English Law 625 (7th ed. 1956).

8. For an excellent discussion of this point, including how we are supposed to discover the wishes of the community see Dunham, Social Science Research for Legislative Reform, 46 A.B.A.J. 1020 (1960).

9. See Atkinson, Wills 1–158 (2d ed. 1953).

ute follows, together with comments, so that you may put some flesh on the skeleton just outlined.

Illinois Law of Descent [10]

"§ 11. *Rules of Descent and Distribution.)* The intestate real and personal estate of a resident decedent and the intestate real estate in this state of a non-resident decedent after all just claims against his estate are fully paid, descends and shall be distributed as follows:

"(1) If there is a surviving spouse and also a descendant of the decedent: one-third of the entire estate to the surviving spouse and two-thirds to the decedent's descendants per stirpes.

"(2) If there is no surviving spouse but a descendant of the decedent: the entire estate to the decedent's descendants per stirpes.

"(3) If there is a surviving spouse but no descendant of the decedent: the entire estate to the surviving spouse.

"(4) If there is no surviving spouse or descendant but a parent, brother, sister, or descendant of a brother or sister of the decedent: the entire estate to the parents, brothers and sisters of the decedent in equal parts, allowing to the surviving parent, if one is dead, a double portion and to the descendants of a deceased brother or sister per stirpes the portion which the deceased brother or sister would have taken if living.

"(5) If there is no surviving spouse, descendant, parent, brother, sister, or descendant of a brother or sister of the decedent, but a grandparent or descendant of a grandparent of the decedent: (a) one-half of the entire estate to the decedent's maternal grandparents in equal parts or to the survivor of them, or if there is none surviving, to their descendants per stirpes, and (b) one-half of the entire estate to the decedent's paternal grandparents in equal parts or to the survivor of them, or if there is none surviving, to their descendants per stirpes. If there is no surviving paternal grandparent or descendant of a paternal grandparent, but a maternal grandparent or descendant of a maternal grandparent of the decedent: the entire estate to the decedent's maternal grandparents in equal parts or to the survivor of them, or if there is none surviving, to their descendants per stirpes. If there is no surviving maternal grandparent

10.   Ill.Rev.Stat. ch. 3, § 11 (1973).

or descendant of a maternal grandparent, but a paternal grandparent or descendant of a paternal grandparent of the decedent: the entire estate to the decedent's paternal grandparents in equal parts or to the survivor of them, or if there is none surviving, to their descendants per stirpes.

"(6) If there is no surviving spouse, descendant, parent, brother, sister, descendant of a brother or sister or grandparent or descendant of a grandparent of the decedent: (a) one-half of the entire estate to the decedent's maternal great-grandparents in equal parts or to the survivor of them, or if there is none surviving, to their descendants per stirpes, and (b) one-half of the entire estate to the decedent's paternal great-grandparents in equal parts or to the survivor of them, or if there is none surviving, to their descendants per stirpes. If there is no surviving paternal great-grandparent or descendant of a paternal great-grandparent, but a maternal great-grandparent or descendant of a maternal great-grandparent of the decedent: the entire estate to the decedent's maternal great-grandparents in equal parts or to the survivor of them, or if there is none surviving, to their descendants per stirpes. If there is no surviving maternal great-grandparent or descendant of a maternal great-grandparent, but a paternal great-grandparent or descendant of a paternal great-grandparent of the decedent: the entire estate to the decedent's paternal great-grandparents in equal parts or to the survivor of them, or if there is none surviving, to their descendants per stirpes.

"(7) If there is no surviving spouse, descendant, parent, brother, sister, descendant of a brother or sister, grandparent, descendant of a grandparent, great-grandparent, or descendant of a great-grandparent of the decedent: the entire estate in equal parts to the nearest kindred of the decedent in equal degree (computing by the rules of the civil law) and without representation.

"(8) If there is no surviving spouse and no known kindred of the decedent: the real estate escheats to the county in which it is located; the personal estate physically located within this state and the personal estate physically located or held outside this state which is the subject of ancillary administration of an estate being administered within this state escheats to the county of which the decedent was a resident or, if the decedent was not a resident of this state, to the county in which it is located; all other personal property of the decedent of every class and character, wherever situate, or the proceeds thereof, shall escheat to this state and be delivered to the Director of Financial

Institutions of the State of Illinois pursuant to the provisions of the 'Uniform Disposition of Unclaimed Property Act'.

"In no case is there any distinction between the kindred of the whole and the half blood."

The opening paragraph of the statute betrays the history of the subject. Reference is made to both real and personal estate —not just to property or to the estate—and it descends and shall be distributed. Real property was said to descend to the heirs at law on the instant of death (note this typically meant pass by descent to the eldest son—primogeniture) while personal property was collected by the administrator, the debts were paid, and then it was distributed to the next of kin, who might be different parties than the heirs. Note that this modern statute has abolished all distinctions between real and personal property so far as descent is concerned. This simplifies the problems and eliminates one area of potential litigation. Dower, which applied only to real property, was abolished in Illinois in 1972.[11]

The statute uses the quaint language, *per stirpes*, to describe how the property shall pass to descendants. The Model Probate Code prepared by the American Bar Association substitutes the more meaningful phrase, "by representation", but they both come out at the same place. *Per stirpes*, Latin for by roots or stocks, is a term taken from the civil law and describes the method for dividing an intestate estate so that a group of distributees take the share that their deceased ancestor (root?) would have been entitled to take, i. e., they inherit by virtue of representing such ancestor rather than as so many individuals, *per capita*. Thus, in the first paragraph, if a father is survived by his wife, a son and two grandchildren, descendants of a deceased daughter, the wife will take one-third, the son one-third, and the two grandchildren will share the deceased daughter's one-third. If the son were deceased, leaving four children, they would take only his one-third, so that the deceased daughter's children would take twice as much as the deceased son's children because of the *per stirpes* doctrine. Contrast this with a *per capita* gift by will to all of the grandchildren. It follows that no descendant can take *per stirpes* while his root or stock is still alive, i. e., the grandchildren take nothing if the parent survives the intestate.

The statute is progressive in the sense that in applying it you move from paragraph to paragraph to determine the pattern of distribution. Paragraph seven, for example, has no application until you exhaust all of the preceding six paragraphs and find no relatives that fit the described categories. At that point you

11. Ill.Rev.Stat. ch. 3, § 18 (1973).

move to the rules of the civil law and determine the nearest collateral heirs according to the following formula.

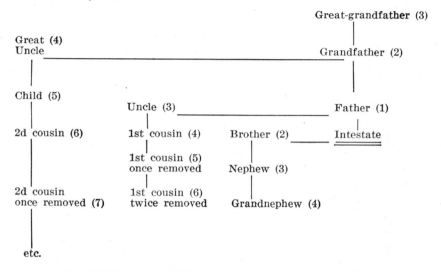

etc.

Ascertain the closest common ancestor of intestate and claimant. Count the steps from intestate to common ancestor and from common ancestor to claimant. The sum of the two figures represents the degree of relationship between claimant and intestate. The claimant who stands in smallest numerical degree of relationship to the intestate takes the property.

In addition to the civil-law rule for determining inheritance by collaterals there was a canon or common-law rule but it need not be considered as a part of the basic principles of intestate succession. There are serious policy questions as to whether distant collateral relatives should be allowed to participate in any case. Typically, these individuals are far removed from the deceased and do not have any real concern for him other than the windfall which has come their way, hence the highly appropriate term, "laughing heirs." [12] This point can be illustrated best by the famous *Wendel* case. "Ella V. von E. Wendel died on March 13, 1931, leaving an estate of about $40,000,000, including 143 parcels of real estate in New York County, bank deposits of $1,-900,000 in New York, and securities of the value of $2,900,000. Her estate was long in the courts, and a total of 2303 claimants appeared to file claims. The court in 146 Misc. 260, 262 N.Y.S. 41 (1933) accepted the claims of 9 claimants of the fifth degree. It denied the claim of another that he was related to the deceased in the fourth degree and referred the matter to the District Attor-

12. Cavers, Change in the American
Family and the "Laughing Heirs",
20 Iowa L.Rev. 203 (1935).

ney for prosecution. [He was sentenced to a three year term on
conviction of conspiracy. Some of the fraud and conspiracy attempted in the litigation is summarized in Matter of Wendel, 159
Misc. 443, 287 N.Y.S. 893 (1936), wherein the Surrogate felt called upon to call to the attention of attorneys canons 30 and 31 of
the American Bar Association.]" [13]

If all of the paragraphs (or rules) fail to produce a winner
the eighth paragraph governs and the property escheats. It has
been argued that this listing of the state (or its designate, the
county, state university, etc.) in the statute of descent makes it
an heir, in effect, and thus subject to an inheritance tax. In Re
O'Connor's Estate [14] rejects this argument and holds that escheat
is an incident of state sovereignty and the state's rights set forth
in the last paragraph of the statute do not make it a beneficiary
of the deceased.

The last sentence of the statute erases any distinction between kindred of the whole and half blood and subsequent sections go on to cover all possible problems, such as posthumous
children (they can inherit as if born in the father's lifetime),
adopted children (in general, they can inherit as if they were natural children), heir murdering an ancestor (he is cut out to prevent profit from a Kind-Hearts-and-Coronets situation), and illegitimate children. At common law, the lot of a bastard was a
hard one and he could not succeed to the property of his ancestors or collateral relatives, nor could the latter take from him on
intestacy. His property went to the crown if he died without a
wife or descendants. Today, the law is much kinder [15] and the
illegitimate child can inherit through his mother, although most
statutes still exclude him from the father's estate unless the parents later marry and acknowledge the child. Arizona goes all the
way and provides: "Every child is the legitimate child of its
natural parents. . . . Every child shall inherit from its natural parents and from their kindred heir, lineal and collateral,
in the same manner as children born in lawful wedlock. . ." [16]

At this point, it would be wise for you to conjure up several
fact situations of your own and try your hand at solving them
so that you will be sure to understand the operation of a statute

13. Williams, Cases and Materials
on the Law of Property 108 (1954).

14. 126 Neb. 182, 252 N.W. 826 (1934).

15. This is due not only to a more
civilized society but to the recognition that bastards have contributed
much to their fellows. Bennett
Cerf in his Trade Winds Column in
The Saturday Review told of the

professor who wanted to offer a
course in the lives and talents of
authors of illegitimate birth. He
labelled the course, "Some Miscon-
ceptions in English Literature."

16. Ariz.Rev.Stat. § 14–206. For a
full treatment of illegitimacy problems see Krause, Illegitimacy:
Law and Social Policy (1971).

of descent.   A little speculation will reveal survival patterns which would distribute the estate in ways not likely to be foreseen by the deceased and clarify the reason for a will, even in small estates.

SECTION 2.   TESTATE SUCCESSION

Should a testator be permitted to dispose of his property by will according to his own unrestricted fancy and caprice, without regard to wife, children, kin or charities?   Is the assertion so frequently made, that there is complete freedom of testation in England and America, justified by the facts?   These are fascinating questions and the temptation to rest awhile and talk of jurisprudential matters is hard to resist.   However, Professor Simes has already pre-empted the subject and I remand you to his Cooley Lectures.[17]   Suffice it to say that most societies have put restraints on testation but that the testamentary power has been freer in Anglo-American law than elsewhere.   Thus, France restricts freedom of testation in favor of both descendants and ascendants and Germany protects descendants, parents, and surviving spouses.   Even in England and United States, there are some curbs and while the testator can disinherit his children (even without the device of giving them one dollar and a pat on the head) he typically finds his spouse a protected party.   Modern statutes tend to allow the surviving spouse (widow or widower) to renounce the will and take a stated statutory share of the estate.[18]   The fee tail estate, with its line of descent restricted to lineal heirs, was, at one time, a limiting factor but with modern disentailing statutes [19] this restriction disappears.   Dower, homestead, and community property, in the states utilizing these features of property law, all serve as fetters on testation.   Tax policy, exerted through federal estate taxes and state inheritance taxes, also has an effect on free choice and some estate planning looks as if it were designed more to save taxes than to transfer property to the natural objects of one's bounty.   One wag tells

---

17. Simes, Public Policy and the Dead Hand 3, 7 (The Thomas M. Cooley Lectures, University of Michigan Law School, 1955).

18. See e. g., Ill.Rev.Stat. ch. 3, §§ 16, 16a, and 17 (1973), which gives the surviving spouse who re-nounces: "one-third of the entire estate if the testator leaves a descendant, or one-half of the entire estate if the testator leaves no descendant."

19. P. 48, supra.

the story of the wealthy client who said, "I don't care who gets it so long as the government doesn't."

In the main, however, there is relative freedom of testation in the Anglo-American countries and a decedent can cut off his children while leaving his property to a blonde mistress or a cat and dog hospital. The will may be contested for fraud, duress, or undue influence or its admission to probate may be attacked for improper execution or forgery but that is another matter entirely.

Since the Statute of Wills in 1540, it has been possible for the decedent to transfer his property, both real and personal, to those persons whom he has properly designated. Some degree of formality was demanded even by the Statute of Wills—it required a written instrument but did not specify that the testator must himself write or sign the document—but reliable proof was first required by the Statute of Frauds in 1676. It directed that the will be signed by the testator or, at his direction, by a person in his presence, and that it be attested and subscribed, in his presence, by three or four credible witnesses. The modern requirements are based on these two old statutes but the details vary from state to state and the local law must always be consulted. There are also such things as nuncupative wills and holographic wills. The former is an oral will declared or dictated by the testator in his last illness, before witnesses, and afterwards reduced to writing; the latter is a will entirely written, dated, and signed by the hand of the testator himself. Frequently, these latter types are not allowed by the language of the statute even though they clearly reveal the intent of the deceased. Of course, if the will fails, for any reason, the decedent dies intestate and the property is distributed according to the relevant statute of descent.

The great merit of a will over other types of testamentary disposition, some of which will be discussed in the next chapter, lies in its clarity and in its ambulatory character. Ambulatory (literally walking) means the instrument is revocable and lets the testator change his will whenever he feels the need, providing he uses the proper formalities. Since the will does not speak until the date of death this allows alterations to meet changing conditions and represents the reverse of the deed which becomes effective as soon as delivered. The fact that the will must be in writing, plus the simple formalities, usually means that the pattern of distribution is well thought out, rather than being a sudden whim of the testator.

Chapter 2

VOLUNTARY TRANSFER BY GIFT

There are many forms of voluntary transfer of property but we shall restrict our discussion to gift, sale, and lease. This does not mean that other transfers are unimportant but only that they tend to be more specialized and hence beyond the purview of a book on basic principles. The transfer of property for security purposes, as in a mortgage, raises a host of legal problems and the creation of a trust,[1] involving a transfer of the legal title to a trustee to hold and utilize for the benefit of the original owner or a third party, obviously calls for a complex body of law. Fortunately, these more specialized forms of transfer are built on the basic property foundation and if you understand the principles of gift, sale, and lease you should be able to find your way around in the other types of transfer.

It would seem, at first blush, that an owner ought to be able to give his property away without any legal entanglements other than those arising from the ever-present tax collector. In one sense he can—so long as both parties, donor and donee, agree that a gift has in fact been made, there is no difficulty. This proves nothing, however, since it is rather like saying there are no legal problems unless a dispute arises and that is a difficult proposition to debate. The law of gifts develops principally around the issue of whether the owner ever intended to become a donor. The dispute can arise while the alleged donor is still alive, but more often it develops after his death when the heirs contend no gift was ever made and that the property passed to them either by testate or intestate succession. Thus, it will be seen that the voluntary transfer by gift bears a close relationship to the involuntary transfer by death.

SECTION 1. GIFTS OF PERSONALTY

Gifts of personal property have been analyzed so well by Professor Brown that no extended discussion is required here

---

1. For basic treatment of mortgages and trusts see Walsh, Mortgages (1934) and Bogert, Trusts (3d ed. 1952).

and the student is requested to incorporate by reference the Brown materials.[2] Traditionally, the gift of a chattel required intent, delivery, and acceptance; this was a sacred trinity, like offer, acceptance, and consideration for a contract. Intent could be proved by the facts as later disclosed by admissible evidence, delivery was conceived to be a manual tradition (handing over) of the object of gift, and acceptance could normally be presumed if the gift was a beneficial one. So long as the law was in a period of extreme formalism each element of a gift had to be carefully established and delivery became the touchstone. The *res* had to change possession and pass from the donor to the donee or the gift failed,[3] even though the intent to make a gift was clear. While it is still good doctrine that no parol gift of a chattel capable of manual tradition is valid without the requisite delivery, there are so many exceptions to the basic rule that it is impossible to make dogmatic statements on the subject.

The nature of the problem can be quickly illustrated by a partial catalogue of difficulties. How do you deliver one-fourth of a horse, if you wish to make a gift of this fractional interest in the animal?[4] Can you deliver the property to a third person to hold for the donee? Can you have a symbolic or constructive delivery, as of a key to a safety deposit box, when it is impossible or impractical to transfer possession of the thing itself? How can you make delivery of a chattel already in possession of the donee or in the common possession of the donor and the donee? The list could be extended indefinitely but since, in the proper case, the gift has been sustained in each of the above situations, it is apparent that delivery no longer means manual tradition from the donor to the donee but has become a fiction that is roughly equivalent to intent and may be viewed as one way of proving that the donor wanted to transfer ownership of his property. This is not to say that delivery, in its traditional sense, has no modern importance. It is clearly easier to sustain the gift if it is present, but the gift does not necessarily fail without it. Professor Mechem argued persuasively that the requirement should be retained by the courts because it (1) makes vivid and concrete to the donor the significance of his act, (2) the manual tradition is unequivocal to witnesses to the transaction, and (3) the delivery gives the donee *prima facie* evidence in favor of the gift.[5] On the other hand, the retention of so formal a requisite may cause many gifts to fail in cases where there is little doubt that the donor intended his property to pass to the donee. In

2. Brown, Personal Property 83–225 (2d ed. 1955).

3. Irons v. Smallpiece, 3 B. and Ald. 551 (1819).

4. Cochrane v. Moore, L.R. 25 Q.B.D. 57 (1890).

5. Mechem, The Requirement of Delivery in Gifts of Chattels, 21 Ill. L.Rev. 341, 342–352 (1926).

Foster v. Reiss [6] the conflicting theories of gift collided in a spectacular fashion and a careful analysis of the majority and minority opinions in that case will add immeasurably to your understanding of the problem.

Since the policy of the law is crystal clear in this area—the protection of the owner from ill-founded and fraudulent claims of gift which rest only on oral statements, concerning which the evidence may be doubtful and open to controversy—it might seem reasonable to require that all gifts of chattels be accompanied by a written document, stating the reason for the gift and manifesting the donor's intent. A statute could even require that the document be witnessed after the manner of wills so that proof would be always forthcoming. In fact, a deed of gift (i. e., a sealed document) or other written instrument, in those states where the private seal has lost its significance, is a recognized method of making an effective gift. Probably the instrument would need to be delivered to the donee, or a third party in his behalf, but there would be no need for delivery of the chattel itself.[7] However, this has never been recognized as the exclusive method for making a gift for the very good reason that it is the custom of people generally to give away their property in a much more informal fashion and the law, to some extent at least, must deal with people as it finds them. It seems fair to conclude that most modern courts will sustain a gift of chattels on some theory,[8] so long as they are convinced that the parties intended that result and gave some objective manifestation of that intent.[9]

The motivation for a gift is not normally of any concern to the law. It may spring from the purest of sentiments, such as filial devotion, or it may arise from a less noble source, to wit the gratification of the whim of a mistress. A man's property is his own and the right to dispose of it as he sees fit should be protected. However, there is a situation in which motivation becomes crucial, i. e., the gift *causa mortis*, which is made in apprehension of imminent death. Most gifts are classified as *inter vivos*, i. e., transfers made between living persons where the donor has no particular expectation of approaching death.[10] The cases abound with statements that gifts *inter vivos* must be absolute, uncondi-

---

6. 18 N.J. 41, 112 A.2d 553, 48 A.L.R. 2d 1391 (1955).

7. Note 2 supra at p. 118.

8. The theory may be that of an oral trust which dispenses with delivery entirely since the donor can declare himself a trustee of the *res* for the benefit of the donee. See Smith's Estate, 144 Pa. 428, 22 A. 916 (1891).

9. In re Cohn, 187 App.Div. 392, 176 N.Y.S. 225 (1919); Beach v. Holland, 172 Or. 396, 142 P.2d 990, 149 A.L.R. 866 (1943).

10. Presumably all individuals with the mental capacity to make a gift realize they will die eventually and it could be argued that they are now disposing of their estate due to that mournful fact.

tional, and irrevocable if they are to be valid.[11]   This general
view requires a surrender of dominion and control over the chattel so that a present gift can be sustained.   Like most general
statements, this ban on conditional *inter vivos* gifts is subject to
many exceptions and the courts frequently sustain donations
which are, in fact, revocable.   This is usually done on the theory
that there has been the present transfer of a future interest [12]
or that some present interest, such as a share of a joint bank account, has been transferred even though it may be revoked later
by a withdrawal of the funds.[13]   The fact remains that most *inter vivos* gifts are unconditional and that, if the condition is
precedent to the vesting of present rights, the attempted transfer
is one *in futuro* and hence void.   By way of contrast, the gift
causa mortis is, by its very nature, conditional and will not fail
for that reason.

The conditional aspect of the gift in apprehension of death
is well stated in Allen v. Hendrick [14]:   "A gift *causa mortis* is
made subject to three conditions implied by law, the occurrence
of any one of which will defeat the gift: (1) the recovery of the
donor from the sickness or his delivery from the peril;   (2) revocation by the donor before his death;   (3) death of the donee before the death of the donor."   Aside from the conditional character of such gifts, the essential elements are the same as in *inter
vivos* transfers, i. e., intention, delivery, and acceptance.   However, the courts will scrutinize these gifts with even more care because of the greater opportunity for fraud inherent in a claim
made against the estate of a now deceased person.   Moreover, it
is clear that such gifts are really testamentary in character, par-
taking of the nature of a nuncupative will.   If the law will not
allow a testator to dispose of his property other than by jealously
guarded formalities, why should it sustain a clearly oral and frequently ambiguous donation?

This last question continues to plague the courts and accounts for many of the irreconcilable decisions.   Manual tradition becomes even more important here since it furnishes stronger proof of the purported gift.   A major theoretical hurdle for
the courts is erected out of the conditional aspect of the gift.   If
the condition is precedent, i. e., if the gift becomes absolute only
when the donor dies of the apprehended peril then it is clearly
testamentary, title passing at the instant of death.   If the condition is subsequent, i. e., if the donee's title vests immediately on

11. Grignon v. Shape, 100 Or. 611,
    197 P. 317 (1921).

12. Conlon v. Turley, 56 App.D.C.
    95, 10 F.2d 890 (1926); Innes v.
    Potter, 130 Minn. 320, 153 N.W. 604,
    3 A.L.R. 896 (1915).

13. Malone v. Walsh, 315 Mass. 484,
    53 N.E.2d 126 (1944).

14. 104 Or. 202, 219, 206 P. 733, 738
    (1922).

delivery, subject to revocation if the donor fails to die, then the gift is not testamentary and can be sustained. You can be sure that the majority of cases have accepted the condition subsequent theory in order to sustain such gifts.[15]

SECTION 2. GIFTS OF REALTY

A watch may be physically handed to the donee but Black-acre resists such casual treatment and this makes the gift of realty a more formal affair. It is true that, in earlier times, the symbolic delivery of a clod or twig in the ceremony of livery of seisin came close to manual tradition, but since the passage of the Statute of Frauds a writing has been required for the conveyance of land and this applies to gratuitous transfers as well as to those for value. Occasionally, an oral gift of land will be sustained where the equities are exceptionally strong in favor of the donee, as where the possession has been transferred, valuable improvements have been made on the premises, and it would work substantial injustice or fraud to hold the gift void under the statute.[16] These situations are so rare, however, that we can assume the necessity for a deed in nearly all cases, thus approaching a greater degree of certainty than is possible in the gift of chattels. Assuming the deed is properly executed, along the lines discussed later,[17] the only serious problems are likely to arise in connection with delivery of the document and the always troublesome issue of a conveyance which is meant to be effective only at the donor's death. There is some dispute over the necessity for consideration in order to have a valid deed, but this is easily solved by the recital of "one dollar and other good and valuable consideration" even though no money is, in fact, paid. This minor quibble arises out of the theory under which modern deeds operate. If they are still bargain and sale deeds, functioning by virtue of the Statute of Uses, then consideration is essential. Even if they are covenants to stand seised under the Statute of Uses, they require a consideration of blood or marriage and this might be absent in some gifts. But if they operate under modern conveyancing acts, no consideration is required and the gift is complete on delivery of the deed. Since there is still doubt in some states as to the ex-

15. Note 2 supra, at p. 152.   17. See p. 162, infra.

16. Hayes v. Hayes, 126 Minn. 389,
    148 N.W. 125 (1914).

act nature of a conveyance, it may be well for the careful drafts-man to recite a consideration even in a deed of gift.[18]

The question of delivery of a deed to realty is essentially the same as that discussed in the previous section. It has never been stated better than in Kyle v. Kyle.[19] "That delivery is essential to the effectiveness of a deed to real estate is elementary, but just what amounts to a delivery is sometimes a question of doubt. Ordinarily it is the simple transfer of possession of the written instrument from the grantor to the grantee with intent on part of the grantor to convey and on part of the grantee to acquire title to the property described therein. But an actual manual transfer of the paper is not necessary. A delivery may be effected by acts without words, or by words without acts, or by both words and acts. Assuming the instrument to have been properly executed ready for delivery, acts and words evincing intent to part with it and relinquish the grantor's right over it is a sufficient delivery. . . . It may be made direct to the grantee or to a third person in his behalf. . . . In final analysis it may be said that delivery is a matter of intent, or any distinct act or word by the grantor with intent to pass the title to the grantee by transferring the deed to him or to another for his benefit is a delivery."

The terms *inter vivos* and *causa mortis* are not much used in relation to gifts of realty but the same kind of problem does exist. A gift of land must be unconditional and the donor's attempt to retain dominion and control over Blackacre will normally cause the gift to fail, but if the facts disclose that the donor kept only a life estate and that the remainder passed immediately to the donee then the gift can be sustained.[20] If the deed is delivered directly to the donee but with oral conditions that must be met before the conveyance is to be effective, the majority of cases treat the conveyance as presently valid and ignore the conditions precedent.[21] These statements of general doctrine set the stage for a type of testamentary disposition that does not comply with the Statute of Wills. The donor delivers a deed to a third person with directions to deliver it to the donee on the donor's death. When does the title pass to the donee? If it passes at death, the agency of the third party is revoked by death and the gift fails for lack of delivery in the lifetime of the donor. If, however, the deed is placed beyond the grantor's control, i. e., if he has reserved no right to get it back from the third party, then it is relatively easy

18. Hill v. Bowen, 8 Ill.2d 527, 134 N.E.2d 769 (1956). For a comment on the case see 1956 U.Ill.L.F. 513.

19. 175 Iowa 734, 737, 157 N.W. 248, 249 (1916).

20. Ferrell v. Stinson, 233 Iowa 1331, 11 N.W.2d 701 (1953).

21. Ivancovich v. Sullivan, 149 Cal. App.2d 160, 307 P.2d 989 (1957). But see Chillemi v. Chillemi, 197 Md. 257, 78 A.2d 750 (1951) where the equities in favor of the donor were too strong and the deed was set aside.

to conclude that the donor has retained an estate for his own life and that a future interest by way of remainder passed to the donee with the delivery to the third party.[22] This arrangement is similar to escrow [23] since it involves delivery to a third person with further delivery to the donee on the happening of a condition. However, in this case the condition, death, is certain to occur sometime and in this sense the delivery to the third party is not conditional at all. At any rate, this method of making a gift has been sustained by the courts on so many occasions that it, like joint tenancy, can be said to operate as a will substitute, a poor man's probate.

22. Milligan v. Milligan, 161 Neb. 499, 74 N.W.2d 74 (1955); Mann, Escrows—Their Use and Value, 1949 U.Ill.L.F. 398, 418.

23. Discussed at p. 172, infra.

Chapter 3

VOLUNTARY TRANSFER BY SALE

The commercial transfer of a property interest from one owner to another, while simple in theory, can be complex in actual operation. The law which has developed to protect the parties to a sale is a curious blend of common law, custom, and statute. As usual, the laws of personalty and realty have followed divergent paths, due both to historical accident and to inherent differences between movables and immovables. Much of the schism springs from questions of title to the *res*. In personalty, only a few complicated questions of ownership arise and the sale is readily consummated without a long delay while the title is being searched. Possession usually means ownership and, if the jeweler sells a watch he does not own, the remedy lies in a suit against him for the sale price. Realty is far more complex and, in chapter 5, a discussion of the methods of title assurance will show the need for a gap between the signing of the contract and the delivery of the deed. Of course, many of the principles are the same regardless of the *res* being sold and the lawyer should be thoroughly familiar with both the similarities and the differences.

No attempt will be made here to cover the sale of goods. These transfers are governed largely by statute,[1] plus the inevitable judicial gloss, and appear in law school curricula as a part of the commercial law subjects under the usual title of Sales or Commercial Transactions. A good brief discussion of the elementary aspects of the sale of goods appears in Brown on Personal Property [2] and a perusal of that material will be most helpful before proceeding with the sale of realty.

The sale of land centers around two separate legal documents —the contract to sell and the deed which actually conveys the title. In addition, many commercial transfers involve the use of an escrow agreement and its role must be understood in order to visualize the operation of a sale. Therefore, this chapter will be developed under three headings—contract, deed, and escrow. A fourth document, the mortgage, is a vital partner in most transactions but it will be discussed only incidentally since its complexities call for extended coverage in their own right.[3]

---

1. The Uniform Sales Act and the Uniform Commercial Code.

2. Pages 226–251 (2d ed. 1955).

3. The best brief treatment is found in Casner and Leach, Cases and Text on Property 673–688 (First Standard Ed. 1950).

SECTION 1. THE CONTRACT

It would be possible to sell real estate without the use of a contract. A purchaser, walking down the street, could pick out a house he liked, as he would a melon in the supermarket, exclaim, "I'll take it," and accept a deed forthwith from a willing vendor. In practice, this will seldom happen, not only because of the title search, but also due to the financing details and the multifarious items that must be adjusted before a transfer. All of the law of contracts is applicable at this juncture and the well-drafted instrument covers a host of detail that has only inferential relationship to the law of property. Since the contract is the blueprint of the transaction it is the most important document in the sale and must be carefully handled. However, this is not a book on drafting [4] and we will concentrate here on some of the typical problems involved in all real estate contracts.

A. THE STATUTE OF FRAUDS

Our seventeenth-century friend, the Statute of Frauds, still applies to real estate contracts, even in England.[5] The entire, detailed agreement need not be reduced to writing since the Statute itself provides for a memorandum, but this is designed for the aberrational case and a lawyer would obviously cover the full terms in writing. The sufficiency of the memorandum has been challenged in countless cases, and from them it appears that an adequate memo must identify the parties to the contract, give a sufficient description of the property so that it can be identified, state the terms and conditions of the agreement, and be signed by the party to be charged.[6]

---

4. There are many excellent articles on drafting a real estate contract. For a succinct treatment of the essential points see Friedman, Buying a Home: Representing the Purchaser, 47 A.B.A.J. 596 (1961) and Drafting of Real Estate Contracts, 35 Chi.Bar Record (1954). For an excellent practice book see Friedman, Contracts and Conveyances of Real Property (2d ed. 1963).

5. England has now repealed most of the Statute but the sections on land and suretyship remain. Act 1954, 2 and 3 Eliz. 2, c. 34.

6. Kohlbrecher v. Guettermann, 329 Ill. 246, 160 N.E. 142 (1928). See also Ward v. Mattuschek, 134 Mont. 307, 330 P.2d 971 (1958).

These general principles are so flexible that the courts can decide many cases either way without doing violence to the stated law. What is a sufficient identification of the parties? They need not be mentioned by name and labelled as vendor and purchaser, providing their identity can be ascertained by words contained in the writing, which writing may include hasty notes, memoranda in books, papers, letters, or telegrams.[7] However, the failure to disclose in any way the vendor or the purchaser is fatal as a mere "offer lanced into the void."[8]

What is an adequate description of the property? It need not be a fully accurate legal description in metes and bounds or by governmental survey, but it must point out a specific piece of real property with such particularity that only one tract is identified. A building described by street number is sufficient if the city, county, and state are mentioned. Less than this may cause real difficulty.[9] Property referred to as "my house or building" (meaning the vendor's) is satisfactory if the seller owns only one such piece, but is ambiguous and fatal if he owns more than one tract fitting the description.[10] If the language is restricted to "a frame residence" rather than "my", it may be fatal even if the vendor owns only one such house since it could refer to property he does not yet own but plans to buy.[11]

When are the terms and conditions sufficient? Clearly, they need not be set out with the specificity of a mature contract, but the "key" points must be included if they have been agreed upon. Thus, if special financing has been set up, failure to include it in the memo may wreck the transaction, whereas if no such agreement has been reached the law can imply that the sale is for cash.[12] Even failure to include the price of the land may be over-

---

7. In A. B. C. Auto Parts, Inc. v. Edward Moran, 268 N.E.2d 844 (Mass.1971) a check with a somewhat detailed endorsement was held to be sufficient.

8. This is Mr. Justice Cardozo's language in Irvmor Corporation v. Rodewald, 253 N.Y. 472, 171 N.E. 747, 70 A.L.R. 192 (1930).

9. Some courts are very strict about the description. Martin v. Seigel, 35 Wash.2d 223, 212 P.2d 107 (1949) required the lot number, block, addition, city, county, and state. See 27 Wash.L.Rev. 166 (1952) for a comment on the case. Similarly, Wilson v. Wilson, 134 Ind.App. 655, 190 N.E.2d 667 (1963) invalidated a description which would have been sufficient in many states. Said the court: "Though the re-

cent trend is for American courts to liberally interpret the Statute of Frauds, we believe that a decision to the contrary would completely abrogate a statute of our legislative branch . . . ."

10. Corrado v. Montuori, 49 R.I. 78, 139 A. 791 (1928).

11. Draper v. Hoops, 135 Ill.App. 389 (1907).

12. Much of the difficulty concerning terms relates to financing provisions. Some courts are quite strict while others are very liberal in their requirements. Contrast Montanaro v. Pandolfini, 148 Conn. 153, 168 A.2d 550 (1961) (contract unenforceable for failure to specify when the monthly payments are to commence or the amount of each

looked if no agreement was reached, since the court can insert a reasonable price. This doctrine can have interesting consequences, such as allowing a vendor to prove that, in fact, the parties agreed on a specific price per acre, but failed to put it in the memo and hence made the contract unenforceable because of the Statute of Frauds.[13]

Who must sign the memorandum in order for it to be enforceable? The English statute, and most of the American ones which used it for a model, required only that the memo be signed by the party to be charged. This translates, "by the party being sued." Thus, if the vendor signs he can be sued by the purchaser but he cannot sue in return unless the purchaser signed. The reverse is obviously true. This leads to the anomaly that frequently one party has a remedy, the other none, and seems to fly in the teeth of the so-called mutuality of remedy rule. Nonetheless, it is the law, except in those states that have made some modification of the old rule.

Occasionally, the memo will contain the necessary elements but some of them will be in error. If this is due to a mutual mistake of fact on the part of the vendor and the purchaser, i. e., if they both meant Blackacre but the typist inserted Whiteacre and they signed without realizing it, then a court of equity can reform the memo to correct the error. Reformation is not available, however, to fill in missing elements since this would allow the complainant to hoist himself by his own bootstraps and reform nothing into something.

Most of the memo problems arise when the parties seek no outside advice but rely on their native skill and put something into writing because they vaguely recall that oral land contracts are ineffective. However, the real estate broker [14] causes his share of the difficulties when he uses an informal memo as a receipt or binder on the assumption that a formal contract will be drafted and signed later. Too often the binder stands in lieu of

payment in a purchase money mortgage) with Monaco v. Levy, 12 A. D.2d 790, 209 N.Y.S.2d 555 (1961) (contract on its face satisfied the Statute of Frauds, despite its silence as to the mortgage maturity date and the mortgage interest rate).

13. Hanlon v. Hayes, 404 Ill. 362, 89 N.E.2d 51 (1949). Comment, 1950 U.Ill.L.F. 309.

14. In most states the Statute of Frauds applies to real estate brokerage contracts and many of the same problems covered in this section on the real estate contract arise in the broker's agreement. For example, the adequacy of the description or designation of the property is often in issue. See Owen v. Hendricks, 433 S.W.2d 164, 30 A.L.R.3d 929 (Tex.1968). In some states, the Statute does not apply to real estate brokerage contracts and the broker's agreement may be oral although the contract between the vendor and purchaser remains subject to the provisions of the Statute.

the contract and the parties never get professional legal advice at all.[15]

Even if the contract is entirely oral, all is not necessarily lost. The law courts tend to follow the exact language of the statute and, while not treating the contract as void, refuse to enforce the parol agreement. If the contract is wholly executory there is probably no hope, but if sufficient acts of part performance have taken place, equity may grant specific performance in order to prevent the Statute from working a fraud.[16] The exact reason behind the doctrine of part performance is not too clear but it usually operates on one of two theories—unequivocal referability or equitable fraud. The former phrase was coined by Mr. Justice Cardozo in Burns v. McCormick [17] and means that the acts done must unequivocally refer to the existence of a contract before that contract can be enforced. "The theory of part performance rests on the fact that one sees from the acts of a man that he has title to or some interest in the property or he would not be doing those things." [18] Thus, the purchaser would not have paid money down, gone into possession, and made improvements on the land unless he had a contract to purchase. This view of the doctrine is based on adequacy of proof and the court of equity is allowing the contract to be proved by parol, if the acts of part performance point sufficiently to a contract. The equitable fraud theory holds that, "The foundation of the doctrine is fraud; not necessarily an antecedent fraud, consciously intended by the party making the contract, but a fraud inhering in the consequence of thus setting up the statute." [19] This view is sometimes referred to as estoppel, the court saying the offending party is estopped to deny the existence of a contract because of the acts of the other party. It does not depend so much on proof as it does on the hardship [20] which would result if the defendant were allowed to plead successfully the Statute of Frauds.

15. For the problems that can arise when the informal memo meets the required minimum but contains the phrase, "Formal contract to be signed on or before September 1, 19—", see Levine v. Lafayette Building Corp., 103 N.J.Eq. 121, 142 A. 441 (1928) reversed by the Court of Errors and Appeals 105 N.J.L. 532, 148 A. 772 (1929).

16. Shaughnessy v. Eidsmo, 222 Minn. 141, 23 N.W.2d 362 (1946).

17. 233 N.Y. 230, 135 N.E. 273 (1922).

18. Neverman v. Neverman, 254 N.Y. 496, 501, 173 N.E. 838, 839 (1930).

19. Pomeroy, Specific Performance, § 104 (3d ed. 1926).

20. "Hardship alone, according to the Supreme Court of California, may remove an oral contract from the Statute of Frauds by estoppel. . . . California courts have been clearly progressing toward abrogation of the Statute of Frauds." Note, 3 Stan.L.Rev. 281 (1951).

The two theories are not mutually exclusive, even though they proceed on different premises, and both depend on the same legally significant acts—payment, change of possession, and improvements. There may be other acts of part performance as well but most cases follow the stated pattern. There seem to be at least five different views in this country as to what acts are necessary and each view has substantial adherents. (1) Possession alone is sufficient. (2) Possession accompanied by payment is sufficient. (3) Possession accompanied by the making of valuable and lasting improvements is sufficient. (4) There must be both possession and such a change of position by the purchaser that irreparable injury will result unless the oral contract is enforced. (5) No acts of part performance will be recognized to take an oral real estate contract out of the Statute of Frauds.[21] In none of the states is payment alone sufficient because the purchaser can always maintain an action at law for the return of his money, plus interest. This makes the remedy at law adequate and does not call for the intervention of chancery. In most states, if all three acts appear, in combination, the chance of enforcement is very good. It should be noted that it makes no difference what has been done in part performance of an alleged contract to sell land unless it can be clearly shown that such a contract exists, i. e., the agreement must be proved by oral testimony like any other parol contract, in addition to showing the acts of part performance.[22] These acts, while they may themselves go to the question of proof, are principally significant because they provide a peg on which the chancellor can hang his jurisdictional hat.

If the acts of part performance are done by the purchaser, can the vendor use them to enforce the contract for his own benefit? At first glance, the answer would appear to be no since the vendor has done nothing to entitle himself to specific performance if the purchaser wants out of the contract. This result follows under the equitable fraud theory since it is no fraud on the purchaser if he wants out of the contract.[23] However, under the unequivocal referability theory the acts of the purchaser tend to prove the existence of a contract regardless of which party relies on them and the contract should be enforced even at the suit of the vendor.[24]

Although a lawyer drafts a beautiful contract, the client may scuttle it with an attempted oral modification. The weight of American authority holds that a total rescission of a written contract for the sale of land is permissible on the theory that the Statute applies only to enforcement of the contract, not to re-

21. Chafee, Simpson, Maloney, Cases on Equity 657 (3d ed. 1951).

22. Wright v. Raftree, 181 Ill. 464, 54 N.E. 998 (1899).

23. Palumbo v. James, 266 Mass. 1, 164 N.E. 466 (1929).

24. Pearson v. Gardner, 202 Mich. 360, 168 N.W. 485 (1918).

lease of the rights under it by the parties.[25] On the other hand, a parol modification of some of its terms would be ineffective because you cannot enforce a land contract which is partly written and partly parol.[26] The original contract stands, as written, and the changes fail unless it is possible to enforce them on a theory of estoppel. This latter situation can arise when the vendor agrees to a change in the manner of performance and then on the day for the final payment and delivery of the deed, after the purchaser has relied on the oral change, tries to go back to the written agreement. He may be estopped to deny the change or at least required to give the buyer additional time in which to comply with the written contract.[27]

So much litigation has arisen because of the Statute of Frauds and so many exceptions have been engrafted upon the original, simple prohibition against the enforcement of any oral contract for the sale of land that it may be that the Statute itself should be repealed so far as it relates to contracts and retained only for deeds. At any rate, the moral for the lawyer is clear: put your land contracts in writing when you are involved at the drafting stage and search hard for a precedent allowing specific performance in equity if you come in at the litigation phase of an oral contract.

B.   TIME STIPULATIONS

A real estate contract typically remains in the executory stage for three to five weeks and, in installment land contracts, may continue to incubate for years. The day set for final performance, when the remainder of the purchase money is to be paid and the deed delivered, is called law day. Suppose law day is set for June 1, 19—, but one party cannot perform exactly on that date. What is the result of this failure to meet the contract date? The law courts took the position that time was of the essence in all contracts for the sale of land, unless the document provided otherwise by express or implied agreement.[28] This meant the non-breaching party was excused from performance, provided he was ready, willing, and able to perform and made a proper tender. Law thus treated performance by a day certain as a condition precedent to further rights under the contract.

---

25. Niernberg v. Feld, 131 Colo. 508, 283 P.2d 640 (1955). See Comment, 28 Rocky Mt.L.Rev. 268 (1956).

26. Malken v. Hemming Bros., 82 Conn. 293, 73 A. 752 (1909).

27. Imperator Realty Co., Inc. v. Tull, 228 N.Y. 447, 127 N.E. 263 (1920).

28. Sugden, Law of Vendors and Purchasers 352 (5th ed. 1818).

Of course, it followed that the non-breacher also had a cause of action for damages against the party unable to perform on the set day.

This rigid position led to many hardships, particularly when coupled with a forfeiture clause which might cause the purchaser to lose substantial payments which he had already made. Moreover, the breach was frequently nominal and the party who failed on law day would have had the money in hand, or the title defects cured, a few days later. Accordingly, equity took a more flexible view of the time for performance and treated the time stipulation as a promise rather than as a condition.[29] This allowed the non-breaching party nominal damages (or more if real injury resulted) but did not excuse performance. The contract remained enforceable so long as it could be carried out within a reasonable period. This tended to square with the probable intention of the parties who usually would not attach importance to a specific day. However, time can be made of the essence even in equity due to the nature of the property, surrounding circumstances, or the express stipulation of the parties.[30]

If both vendor and purchaser know that a professor wants a home to live in at the opening of school, September 15, and the contract sets that date as law day, this circumstance may be sufficient to cause time to be of the essence, even in equity. Similarly, if the real property interest being sold is a relatively short term lease that will soon expire or if it is a sale on speculation in times of rapidly fluctuating prices, this may cause chancery to follow the rule at law. The most common situation, however, is where the contract expressly states, "time is of the essence of this agreement." When so specifically drafted that the court feels the meaning is clear to both parties the delay of even half an hour in producing the purchase money has been held to excuse performance by the vendor.[31] Although time is not made of the essence when the contract is first drafted, it can be made so by notice of either party, provided it is given a reasonable length of time before law day.[32] This sounds suspiciously like a unilateral change in the terms of a contract and the view has been criticized by legal writers.[33]

29. King v. Connors, 222 Mass. 261, 110 N.E. 289 (1915); Kasten Construction Co. v. Maple Ridge Construction Co., 245 Md. 373, 226 A.2d 341 (1967).

30. Edgerton v. Peckham, 11 Paige (N.Y.) 352 (1844).

31. Doctorman v. Schroeder, 92 N.J. Eq. 676, 114 A. 810 (1921).

32. Schmidt v. Reed, 132 N.Y. 108, 30 N.E. 373 (1892).

33. Walsh, Equity 361–377 (1930).

Despite Professor Walsh's attack on "unilateral modification" many cases seem to allow it. See Shullo Construction Co. v. Miller, 2 Ohio App.2d 177, 207 N.E.2d 393 (1965).

Because time of the essence clauses are frequently inserted (or left in a standard, printed form) without any real appreciation of their effect, courts naturally struggle to relieve a defaulting, but good faith, vendor or purchaser. The most common relief mechanism is waiver. Thus, repeated acceptance of late payments by a vendor, followed by a sudden decision to cut off the purchaser's rights for one specific delinquency, can lead to a successful plea of waiver by the purchaser. Even here, however, the vendor can rely on the legal effectiveness of the clause by giving proper notice. "The vendor who has, by a practice of accepting later payment, permitted the purchaser to rely on this course of conduct, need only give reasonable notice that thereafter he will insist on strict performance of the contract. Further defaults would entitle him to his foreclosure remedy." [34]

C. FINANCING ARRANGEMENTS—MORTGAGES AND INSTALLMENT LAND CONTRACTS

Real estate financing involves a host of practical and legal problems and only the general "running gears" can be discussed in a basic text.[35] Since few people pay cash for real property, the financing arrangements tend to be the heart of the matter. Frequently, the purchaser signs a contract without being certain as to how he will pay for the property. In order to protect himself, he typically wishes to insert a clause making the contract contingent on his obtaining the proper financing. Unless this clause is carefully drafted, the result may be an ambiguous agreement which will cause litigation. In Gerruth Realty Co. v. Pire [36] the real estate broker inserted the following clause in the offer: "This offer to purchase is further contingent upon the purchaser obtaining the proper amount of financing." The purchaser was in such financial condition that he could not get a conventional mortgage in the amount needed and he sought to escape from the contract and to cancel a $5000 promissory note he had given as a down payment. The Wisconsin Supreme Court felt the ambiguous clause came dangerously close to making the agreement an illusory or aleatory contract. While this difficulty might be cured by reading in a require-

34. Stinemeyer v. Wesco Farms, Inc., 487 P.2d 65 (Or.1971).

35. All law schools offer separate courses in Mortgages or Real Estate Financing which analyze these problems in depth.

36. 17 Wis.2d 89, 115 N.W.2d 557 (1962).

ment that the purchaser make reasonable efforts to secure proper financing, the court felt the contract should fail for indefiniteness. The court apparently believed the real estate agent was more eager to earn a commission than to properly serve his client. "The real estate broker, presumably familiar with the difficulties, details and terms of financing, might have asked the defendant for more details, but was apparently content with putting something in writing and having it signed by the purchasers."

In Anaheim Co. v. Holcombe,[37] the parties were somewhat more specific: "This offer is contingent on obtaining a loan of $25,000." The Oregon Supreme Court held that there was an implied condition that the purchaser use reasonable diligence in procuring a loan. The question of reasonable diligence was for the trial court to decide and the purchaser failed to sustain the burden and could not recover his $5,000 earnest money payment.

These two cases illustrate the perils involved for both vendor and purchaser, but the necessity for some such clause remains since the purchaser may locate the property he wishes to buy before he can fully investigate available financing. In these situations, the clause should specify the exact amount of money needed, the kind of financing sought, including the acceptable term for repayment, interest rates, etc.[38]

Some of the worst financing problems stem from the use of forfeiture clauses, usually coupled with a time of the essence stipulation. Here, we must digress briefly to clarify the elementary aspects of real estate financing. Seldom does the buyer find himself in that happy state of liquidity which would allow him to pay cash for the property, so he will finance through a purchase money mortgage, a mortgage (or trust deed) to a third party (bank, insurance company, or savings and loan association), or an installment land contract. Using the first method, he pays the vendor what he can afford, receives a deed to the land, and gives a mortgage (in lieu of the rest of the purchase money) back to the seller. By the second method, he pays the vendor what he can afford, takes a deed to the land, mortgages the property to a third party and pays the proceeds of the mortgage loan to the seller who bows out of the transaction. In the third method, he pays the vendor what he can afford, the vendor keeps title to the land, the purchaser goes into possession and pays installments to the vendor over so long a period as

37. 246 Or. 541, 426 P.2d 743 (1967).

38. For a discussion of the various issues see Raushenbush, Problems and Practices with Financing Conditions in Real Estate Purchase Contracts, 1963 Wis.L.Rev. 566.

necessary to complete the purchase price. When the purchaser makes the last payment he receives a deed. In all three situations, the buyer is, in effect, borrowing money and must repay it in installments plus interest, but in the first two methods he receives legal title to the land subject to a mortgage, in the latter he does not receive legal title until all payments are made.

The fundamental difference occurs on default. If the buyer fails to pay in the first two cases the mortgage must be foreclosed, accompanied by all of the safeguards that the legislatures and courts have established to protect the mortgagor. Usually, this means judicial foreclosure with an equity of redemption in the buyer-mortgagor. In theory, although sometimes not in practice, it means the property will be sold to the highest bidder, the mortgage loan plus interest, costs, etc., paid to the mortgagee, and the surplus returned to the mortgagor. By contrast, the contract-buyer may find that he forfeits all of his payments to date, if he fails to perform, and is left without his money, land, or even an equity of redemption.[39]

Since the purchaser has less legal protection in an installment land contract, why would he choose this method of financing? He does not choose it, exactly; he is forced into it by lack of capital.[40] When we indicated that the buyer paid down what he could afford and gave a mortgage for the rest, the oversimplification should have been apparent. If he can afford too little— the amount varies but typically one-third to one-fourth of the purchase price is required—mortgage money is not available and his only recourse is to buy "on contract." Naturally, the vendor wants maximum protection for his investment in the property since the buyer has put up very little; the forfeiture on default results. This device is not always as harsh as it sounds since the purchaser has possession, the payments may

39. Pease v. Baxter, 12 Wash. 567, 41 P. 899 (1895).

For a good, brief discussion of the difference between mortgages, with their equity of redemption, and installment land contracts see Osborne, Secured Transactions 217–224 (1967).

40. Not surprisingly, the burden falls more heavily on minority groups and others in the lower income brackets than on the public generally. This was recognized in Rosewood Corp. v. Fisher, 46 Ill.2d 249, 263 N.E.2d 833 (1970) where the contract buyers league (a group of Chicago blacks) sought relief from the harsh terms of installment land contracts. The Illinois Supreme Court allowed the purchasers to raise equitable defenses to a vendor's suit in Forcible Entry and Detainer (summary action for possession for non-payment of installments due), a defense not previously available in Illinois. This case shows a judicial recognition of the problem and allows an approach similar to that being used in landlord-tenant cases. See pp. 235 to 238, infra. For the intriguing story of the contract buyers league see McPherson, "In My Father's House There Are Many Mansions—And I'm Going to Get Me Some of Them Too," 229 Atlantic Monthly 51–82 (April, 1972).

be roughly the equivalent of rent, and the amount forfeited may therefore square rather well with the actual damages on breach.[41]   On the other hand, the contrast with mortgage financing is striking and on occasion the inequity can be substantial.   In these hardship cases, courts of equity, which "abhor a forfeiture", struggle to find some way to allow the defaulting vendee to continue the contract.   Dean Pound has suggested that, "Strict doctrines as to forfeiture inevitably produce loose doctrines as to waiver", and the cases bear out the truth of the aphorism.   The vendor may lose his right to rely on forfeiture by prior acceptance of late payments or other acts and one court has gone so far as to distinguish between notice of intent to declare a forfeiture and *declaration* of a forfeiture.   Since the contract called for the former and the vendor relied on the latter, the purchaser had not lost his rights.[42]

Modern courts have freely stated their "abhorrence of odious forfeitures" and have given relief to defaulting purchasers under a wide variety of circumstances.   Thus, in State v. Superior Court for King County,[43] a purchaser who had been in default for a year was allowed to complete the contract, which contained both time of the essence and forfeiture clauses, upon payment of the full balance plus interest and all expenses incurred by the vendor.   In Land Development, Inc. v. Padgett,[44] the court allowed similar relief by ordering forfeiture only if the purchasers failed to pay the accrued interest within one week and the principal balance within three months.   This last approach is very much like strict foreclosure of a mortgage and, indeed, that technique now seems fairly common.   See Nelson v. Robinson,[45] where the court treated a $48,000 contract, based on a crop payment plan, as an equitable mortgage, setting a six to eighteen month redemption period and Henry Uihlein Realty Co. v. Downtown Develop. Corp.,[46] where strict foreclosure was ordered but the purchaser's demand for restitution to prevent unjust enrichment was denied.   This last point remains a tough problem.   Assuming the purchaser can pay at a later date the courts can act to prevent unfairness but if he is hopelessly insolvent does he have to lose all his payments and improvements or can he seek salvation through further recourse to mortgage doctrine?   It should be clear, in any case, that the courts will not always allow redemption and will usually enforce the con-

41. Bishop v. Beecher, 67 N.M. 339, 355 P.2d 277 (1960).

42. Zeta Bldg. Corporation v. Garst, 408 Ill. 519, 97 N.E.2d 331 (1951).

43. 57 Wash.2d 571, 358 P.2d 550 (1961).

44. 360 P.2d 888 (Alaska 1962).

45. 184 Kan. 340, 336 P.2d 415 (1959).

46. 9 Wis.2d 620, 101 N.W.2d 775 (1960).

tract as written if it involves no real hardship for the purchaser.[47]

The purchaser who relies on the conscience of a court of equity puts his faith in a variable standard, however, and in many situations the buyer cannot continue the contract, even if allowed to do so, because he is insolvent. In these cases he wants restitution for the money he has paid in excess of actual damage, i. e., he would like the favored position of a mortgagor on default. His chances of such treatment are slight unless there has been some statutory change which entitles him to equitable relief.[48] It should be noted that the vendor has problems too. If the installment land contract is recorded, this puts a cloud on the merchantability of title and even when the buyer defaults it may be difficult to clear that title. It is always possible that equity may aid the purchaser and subsequent buyers, having notice of the prior contract, may be unwilling to take that chance.

Forfeiture problems also arise in the standard contract which calls for full settlement on law day. Normally, earnest money is paid at the signing of the contract and the agreement calls for its forfeiture if the purchaser defaults. This down payment or earnest money is usually a small percentage amount (five to ten per cent of the total price) but the general principles just discussed apply to it.

D. MERCHANTABLE TITLE

What does a purchaser expect to get for his money when he signs a contract of sale? Obviously, he wants physical possession of Blackacre, but this will do him little good if the vendor's inter-

---

47. Dorman v. Fisher, 52 N.J.Super. 70, 144 A.2d 805 (1958).

48. Union Bond and Trust Co. v. Blue Creek Redwood Co., 128 F. Supp. 709 (D.C.Cal.1955) illustrates how the California statute rescues the buyer.

An interesting Florida statute, which provides in effect that a contract may be deemed a mortgage where the purpose or intent is to secure the payment of money, was involved in Mid-State Investment Corp. v. O'Steen, 133 So.2d 455, 457 (Fla. 1961). Said the court: "In our opinion the contract before us was clearly intended to secure the payment of money and must be deemed and held to be mortgage, subject to the same rules of foreclosure and to the same regulations, restraints and forms as are prescribed in relation to mortgages, to use the words of the statute."

The general problem is thoroughly discussed in Corbin, Right of a Defaulting Vendee to the Restitution of Installments Paid, 40 Yale L.J. 1013 (1931) and some of the legislation is analyzed in a Note, 52 Harv.L.Rev. 129 (1938).

See also Kratovil, Forfeiture of Installment Contracts in Illinois, 53 Ill.Bar J. 188 (1964).

est turns out to be a life estate or a fee simple determinable. At a minimum, a non-defeasible fee simple is required. Even this may not be enough, since the fee could be subject to various liens, charges, covenants running with the land, etc. The courts have developed the concept of a merchantable title to cover the situation. The words roll off the tongue but their meaning is hazy. The judicial definitions add little. "A merchantable title is a title not subject to such reasonable doubt as would create a just apprehension of its validity in the mind of a reasonable, prudent and intelligent person; one that persons of reasonable prudence and intelligence, guided by competent legal advice, would be willing to take and pay the fair value of the land for." [49] In the last analysis, a merchantable title is one that a court of equity will force an unwilling purchaser to accept in a suit for specific performance. This still begs the question but it makes it perfectly clear that the standard is laid down by the chancellor. Any number of defects, e. g., a break in a chain of record title, an outstanding mortgage, dower, taxes, special assessment, etc., may destroy merchantability and it is clear that equity will not force a man to buy a lawsuit. The full impact of merchantability will be clarified in chapter 5 when we discuss the recording system and the various methods of title assurance.

The contracting parties can handle the title question in any way they see fit. They may contract for something less than a merchantable title, e. g., a defensible title (one that could be defended against a suit in ejectment) or such interest as the vendor may have; or they may require something more, such as title satisfactory to a third party or even to the purchaser himself; or they may demand something that is simply different, to wit, an insurable title. Suppose the contract is silent on the point and calls only for a conveyance of the premises or of the property? Then the courts will imply that a merchantable title is called for: "Although the writing does not say so, the law says so, and the law is part of the writing."[50] This implication will be made even though the contract calls for conveyance by a quitclaim rather than a warranty deed.[51]

Merchantability does not require a perfect title, indeed it is doubtful if many perfect titles exist, but it is not necessary to prove that a title is wholly "bad" in order to destroy its merchantability. It is sufficient if there is enough doubt or uncertainty to form a reasonable basis for litigation.[52] The purchaser cannot wait until law day and then suddenly reject the title as unmer-

49. Eggers v. Busch, 154 Ill. 604, 607, 39 N.E. 619, 620 (1895).

50. Wallach v. Riverside Bank, 206 N.Y. 434, 437, 100 N.E. 50, 51 (1912).

51. Id.

52. Bartos v. Czerwinski, 323 Mich. 87, 34 N.W.2d 566 (1948).

chantable and slip out of the bargain. He must examine the title
and notify the vendor of the defects within a reasonable time so
that they can be removed by the time set for performance. Failure to do this will simply extend the law day, even when time is
of the essence, so that the defects can be cured, unless, of course,
such defects are irreparable.[53]

In the typical real estate contract the parties expect the title
to be merchantable by law day. How does this principle apply
to installment land contracts? Here too, in the absence of a
special provision, the vendor satisfies his part of the bargain if
the title is merchantable on the date set for delivery of the deed.
This means that the purchaser may have to make payments
over many years with no real assurance that he will eventually
get a merchantable title to the land.[54] If it appears that the
vendor is insolvent, so that he could not respond in money damages if the title fails, or if the title is subject to an incurable
defect, equity may grant relief to the purchaser by allowing him
to rescind before law day or by requiring the vendor to clear
his title at an earlier date.[55] The purchaser should not rely on
this "chancy" proposition, however, but should insert a provision
in installment land contracts that the vendor must produce a
merchantable title by a set date in the reasonably near future
or the purchaser is entitled to his money back and is excused
from further performance.

Traditionally, titles based on the annual tax sale deed, where
the original owner was in default for non-payment of taxes, have
not been viewed as merchantable by the courts. This was because the tax deeds were usually issued by administrative officials, such as a county clerk, and any defects in the proceedings
were viewed as jurisdictional, thus opening the title to collateral
attack at any time by the original owner. In recent years, many
states have made the issuance of tax deeds a judicial matter with
the result that they are usually subject only to direct attack
and, after the time for appeal has gone by, such deeds may be the
basis of a merchantable title.[56]

A merchantable title must be a paper title, i. e., one that is
disclosed from the records based on the connected chain of deeds,
mortgages, probate proceedings, etc. While a title based on the

53. Easton v. Montgomery, 90 Cal. 307, 27 P. 280 (1891).

54. Luette v. Bank of Italy Nat. Trust & Savings Ass'n, 42 F.2d 9 (1930).

55. Marlowe Investment Corp. v. Radmall, 26 Utah 2d 124, 485 P.2d 1402 (Utah, 1971); Leavitt v. Blohm, 11 Utah 2d 220, 357 P.2d 190 (1960).

56. Cherin v. R. & C. Co., 11 Ill.2d 447, 143 N.E.2d 235 (1957). See also Young, The Tax Deed—Modern Movement Towards Respectability, 34 Rocky Mt.L.Rev. 181 (1962).

statute of limitations may be good in fact, it is too uncertain to be called merchantable.[57]   The only way to make a title gained by adverse possession merchantable is by a suit in equity to quiet title.   This is also the way to cure other serious defects in title, if in fact they can be proved to be invalid clouds on the owner's claim to the land.[58]

E.   TENDER

Tender calls for brief mention because of its relationship to time stipulations and merchantability of title.   Even if time is made of the essence, performance may be extended beyond law day simply because neither party puts the other in default by tendering his own performance.   For the purchaser, this means proving that he is ready, willing, and able to perform by offering to pay the rest of the purchase money or to deliver a properly executed purchase money mortgage; for the vendor, it means offering to deliver a properly executed deed, sufficient to convey a merchantable title.   The tender need not be absolute since the other party could then accept it with a brief, "thanks", but still remain in default.   Conditional tender—offer to perform if the other party will do so—is sufficient since the principal purpose of this requirement is to fulfill the condition precedent to the right to sue for breach.

Under proper circumstances, tender may be excused if it is clear that the other party would not perform in any case.   The law does not require a person to do a useless act and if the purchaser has already repudiated the contract (anticipatory breach) the vendor need not tender, or vice versa.[59]

While it is clear that tender is a prerequisite to suit on the contract, i. e., a suit for specific performance in equity or for money damages at law, less clarity surrounds a suit for rescission of the contract and a return of the purchase money plus interest. If tender is required before there is a breach, then it is necessary in both cases but if it is only a condition precedent to suit for the benefits under the contract then it is superfluous in rescission. In Christopher v. West,[60] an Illinois appellate court took the for-

57.   Escher v. Bender, 338 Mich. 1, 61 N.W.2d 143 (1953).

58.   Note, Enhancing the Marketability of Land: The Suit to Quiet Title, 68 Yale L.J. 1245 (1959).

59.   Cohen v. Kranz, 12 N.Y.2d 242, 238 N.Y.S.2d 928, 189 N.E.2d 473 (1963).

60.   340 Ill.App. 225, 91 N.E.2d 613 (1950).

mer position but it was reversed on appeal, the Supreme Court saying, "The only question for us here to decide is whether the law imposed upon Christopher, as a necessary condition precedent to the maintenance of this suit to recover back the earnest money paid, the duty of tendering performance to West in order to acquire the right of restitution.   The party who insists upon performance by the other party must show performance on his part, while he who desires to rescind the contract need only show non-performance or inability to perform by the other.   Inability to perform is sufficient excuse on the part of the purchaser for not tendering performance, for, in this event, a tender would be devoid of meaning.   .   .   .   If any claimed defect was such as to affect the merchantability of the title and one which was not cured or curable within a reasonable time as provided in the contract, no tender of the full purchase price was necessary." [61]

At the moment of breach, the future plaintiff does not know what remedy he will ultimately seek and the voice of caution should counsel him to make his tender whether it is strictly necessary or not.   The place of tender can also be confusing since some cases put it at the vendor's place of business, others at the purchaser's.   This matter should be covered in the contract by stating precisely where the settlement is to occur.

F.   ASSIGNMENT

The mystic rites of assignment are better left to texts on contract law, but some reference is required here to complete the picture of the real estate sale.   Many contracts for the sale of land end with this boilerplate: "It is mutually agreed by and between the parties hereunto, that the covenants and agreements herein contained shall extend to and be obligatory upon the heirs, executors, administrators, and assigns of the respective parties." This language adds little to the contract since it simply makes explicit what is implicit anyway.   It may focus the attention of the parties on the free assignability of the contract and, in effect, warn them to place some prohibition on assignment if they desire to deal only with the original parties.

The vendor can assign his contract rights by selling the fee, subject to the contract, and the purchaser can transfer his interest by the usual assignment process.   Of course, neither one can rid himself of obligations incurred in the contract, unless released

61.   Christopher v. West, 409 Ill. 131,
136, 98 N.E.2d 722, 725 (1951).

by the other party, and the assignor will remain secondarily liable, as in contracts generally. A prohibition on assignment may not be very effective, even if coupled with a forfeiture, since equity still abhors a forfeiture and may find that no harm has occurred to the vendor when all that remains to be done is to pay the purchase money and receive the deed.[62] The law has traditionally favored the free alienability of land and since the purchaser has equitable title after signing the contract, as we shall see in the next section, the courts dislike clauses which hamper his power to transfer that title, unless there is some clear-cut reason for it.

G.   REMEDIES

If a lawyer handles the real estate transaction there is less likelihood of litigation than in the do-it-yourself approach, since the attorney will foresee the danger spots and cover them in the contract.[63] However, even the most carefully drafted document cannot avoid occasional controversy and the client's remedy may have to be a judicial one. The property lawyer has a choice from a varied arsenal of weapons when he finds it necessary to engage in combat by trial. His basic choice will lie between an equity action for specific performance or a suit at law for money damages but other options may be possible, depending on the nature of the dispute.

If the purchaser refuses to perform because the title is unmerchantable due to minor but colorable defects, the vendor may be forced to bring a suit to remove cloud on title so that he can make a proper tender to the buyer.[64] If the purchaser is in breach but refuses to vacate the land, actions for the recovery of possession, either ejectment or forcible entry and detainer, may

---

62. Handzel v. Bassi, 343 Ill.App. 281, 99 N.E.2d 23 (1951).

The judicial attitude toward prohibition on assignment of a real estate contract should be contrasted with the approach to identical clauses in landlord-tenant law. See pp. 219 to 223, infra. The difference lies in the continuing relationship between the parties in the lease situation and the early termination of such relationship in the sale.

Some courts do enforce non-assignment clauses in contracts as rigidly as they enforce such clauses in leases. See Rother-Gallagher v. Montana Power Co., 522 P.2d 1226 (Mont.1974).

63. For a detailed illustration of the lawyer's role in draftsmanship note the next section and the relationship of insurance to risk of loss.

64. Holland v. Challen, 110 U.S. 15, 3 S.Ct. 495, 28 L.Ed. 52 (1884).

be in order. At times, the best remedy is to seek rescission of the contract and a restoration of the status quo. In this latter situation, the enforcement of a vendor's or a vendee's lien may be required in order to give priority over assignees with notice of the contract.[65]

Land has long been considered unique, "for the peculiar locality, soil, vicinage, advantage of markets and the like conveniences of an estate contracted for, cannot be replaced by other land of equal value." [66] It follows that the remedy at law is inadequate since it can give only money damages at best and the purchaser is entitled to specific performance in equity in nearly all cases. He need not prove the uniqueness of the *res* in each case, as he would have to do with personal property, but need only establish a valid contract that is certain enough to support the decree. Since the purchaser is entitled to equitable relief, the vendor has the same right in order to give mutuality of remedy and also because "he may not wish the lands, even with the damages, but may prefer to have them off his hands, and he has a right to require that the vendee shall take them and pay the stipulated price." [67]

The draftsman must be careful not to barter away this most valuable of remedies by too much zeal for liquidated damages. For example, in Davis v. Isenstein [68] the contract read, in part: "The willful neglect or failure by either of the parties hereto to perform his or their respective parts of the undertakings hereunder is to subject such party to the payment of the sum of $1500 fixed and liquidated damages to the party injured, and upon such payment thereof this contract is to become null and void." The court held that this created an option to perform or pay the stipulated damages. Since the buyer was prepared to do the latter, the suit was dismissed for want of equity.[69] There is serious doubt about the correctness of this view since the primary objective of contracts is performance rather than non-performance, and the liquidated damages provision should be interpreted as cumulative, or as added security, rather than as creating an option.[70] However, this is clearly a pitfall to be avoided by the alert lawyer.

65. For a collection of cases on the remedies involved in vendor and purchaser, see Handler, Cases and Materials on Vendor and Purchaser 401–491 (1933).

66. Losee v. Morey and Cramer, 57 Barb. (N.Y.) 561, 565 (1865).

67. Id. at 566.

68. 257 Ill. 260, 261, 100 N.E. 940, 941 (1913).

69. See also Duckwall v. Rees, 119 Ind.App. 474, 86 N.E.2d 460 (1949).

70. Nolan v. Kirchner, 98 N.J.Eq. 452, 131 A. 104 (1925).

Sometimes, the vendor is in a position where he can perform in major part but not fully. He may be quite willing to convey the land but an outstanding dower interest, an easement across one corner, a deficiency in quantity, etc., may place him in breach. In these situations the purchaser, still desiring the property but not wanting to pay the full price, may seek specific performance with compensation for the deficiency.[71] This can create very difficult questions of fact in trying to arrive at the amount of compensation, and in some cases the remedy is denied for that very reason.[72] The situation differs considerably if the vendor seeks specific performance with compensation against the purchaser and the courts will rarely grant such relief since to do so would force the purchaser to accept something he did not bargain for on the theory that it is just as good as what he expected to receive.[73]

Specific performance is not always available, as where the vendor has sold the land to a bona fide purchaser for value without notice, and sometimes the parties prefer money damages to equitable relief. In these cases, the usual action at law for breach of contract will be chosen. The principal difficulty here relates to the amount of damages. The rule in personal property cases is straightforward and easy to state. It is aimed at giving the non-breaching party the benefit of his bargain. This is determined by the difference between the contract price of the property and the market price at the time and place when the contract should have been performed. Thus, if the contract price was $10,000 and the market rises to $12,000, the buyer has suffered a $2,000 loss if the seller refuses to perform. If the market falls, the buyer suffers only nominal damages. Conversely, if the market falls to $8,000 and the purchaser refuses to buy, the seller has suffered a $2,000 loss. About half of the American states use this same rule for real property.[74]

As early as 1776, the English courts, in Flureau v. Thornhill,[75] recognized that the personal property cases were not necessarily analogous to the real property ones. Once again, title was the crux. A chattel owner nearly always knows the state of his title and, if he is unable to perform, the breach is usually wilful. The real property owner may have only the vaguest idea of whether his title is merchantable and his failure to convey a

71. For a brief treatment see de Funiak, Handbook of Modern Equity 195–198 (2d ed. 1956).

72. Horack, Specific Performance and Dower Rights, 11 Iowa L.Rev. 97 (1926).

73. Van Blarcom v. Hopkins, 63 N.J. Eq. 466, 52 A. 147 (1902).

74. Doherty v. Dolan, 65 Me. 87, 20 Am.Rep. 677 (1876). See also McCormick, Damages 680–700 (1935).

75. 2 W.Bl. 1078, 96 Eng.Rep. 635 (1776).

satisfactory title may spring from no real fault of his own. To tax him with huge damages for a non-wilful default may be unfair. This is particularly true in times of widely oscillating land values or where the discovery of minerals, unknown at the time of the contract, may cause the damages to skyrocket. The "English" rule, therefore, limited the purchaser, except where the vendor had acted in bad faith, to the money paid down by the purchaser, plus interest and expenses connected with examination of the title.[76] You will note that this is the amount generally recoverable on rescission of the contract. The "English" rule made good sense to many American courts and it has been adopted in about half the states.[77] The biggest difficulty with the "English" rule is the determination of bad faith on the part of the vendor. The English cases have expanded the original idea by holding that if the seller fails to "do his best" to remove a title defect he becomes liable for the value of the bargain. This is fair enough, but it introduces an additional uncertainty. What is meant by "do his best"? This is another example of the age-old conflict between certainty and flexibility in the law.

SECTION 2.   THE CONTRACT AND EQUITABLE CONVERSION [78]

Nowhere does the peculiar nature of the real estate contract appear in such bold relief as in the doctrine of equitable conversion.[79] In one sense, the relationship between vendor and purchaser is wholly *personal*, with the right of either to sue the

76. Bain v. Fothergill, L.R. 7 H.L. (E. and I.App.) 158 (1874).

77. For a good statement of the reasons behind the "English" rule see Crenshaw v. Williams, 191 Ky. 559, 567, 231 S.W. 45, 49, 48 A.L.R. 5 (1921). See also, Kramer v. Mobley, 309 Ky. 143, 216 S.W.2d 930 (1949).

78. The insurance discussion in this section is based on a speech by the author to the Real Property, Probate and Trust Law Section of the American Bar Association, delivered at an annual meeting of the American Bar Association. The full text of the speech appears in Proceedings, Real Property Probate and Trust Law Section, A.B.A. 3–

12 (1961). The material has been updated and numerous non-insurance aspects of equitable conversion have been added.

79. Even when the doctrine is not applied it has a pervasive effect. See Clay v. Landreth, 187 Va. 169, 45 S.E.2d 875, 175 A.L.R. 1047 (1948), where there were zoning changes after the contract was signed so that the purchaser could not use the land for the purpose for which both parties knew he was buying it. The vendor claimed the risk was on the purchaser under the doctrine but the court refused to apply an equitable doctrine inequitably and excused the purchaser from performance.

other in event of breach. In another sense, the contract creates a status of vendor-purchaser and the latter acquires *real* rights in the property due to the possibility of specific performance. Equity, by treating as done those things which should be done, looks upon the purchaser as having equitable title to the land even though the legal title remains in the vendor. If this way of looking at the contract relationship were a matter of academic theory only, we could dismiss it with an explanatory wave of the pen, but it has had a profound influence on the development of the law in at least three areas—creditors' rights,[80] the devolution of property interests on the death of either the vendor or the purchaser while the contract is still executory, and the risk of loss.

In an elementary book of principles, the author usually is forced to sketch in broad outlines, but occasionally a protrait in some detail is called for to illustrate the nature of the problem. Rather than a few general statements about each of the three areas, I will give a greater discussion to the risk of loss problem and tie in creditors' rights and devolution on death at the appropriate points. More extended knowledge of these latter two areas can be obtained by perusal of the appropriate footnote references. This will also make possible a treatment of the relationship of insurance to the real estate contract, without which an understanding of risk of loss is impossible. Furthermore, since this is a book on principles, this will furnish an excellent vehicle to point out a principle gone wrong—a segment of the law which is caught in the toils of its own fictional logic and which needs to re-examine its major premise.

The accurately descriptive, but dull-sounding, title of this section conceals a fascinating controversy which has been raging in Anglo-American law since 1801.[81] While it will never compete in the public press with school integration or space law, particularly in this age when our earthly antics become more and more lunar, it does have its appeal for those who like to inspect a microcosm of the law and draw conclusions about the macrocosm from it. Moreover, judging from the large quantity of appellate litigation in the last few years, there is a practical flavor

80. The doctrine is often invoked where creditors are trying to reach the assets of either the vendor or the purchaser. While the doctrine makes considerable difference in legal theory, in practice the creditor usually reaches the available assets of either, provided he uses the correct remedy for the particular jurisdiction. See First Security Bank of Idaho, National Ass'n v. Rogers, 91 Idaho 654, 429 P.2d 386 (1967).

81. In that year Paine v. Meller, 6 Ves.Jr. 349, 31 Eng.Reprint 1088 (1801), decided that the risk of loss in an executory contract for the sale of real property was on the purchaser.

to the problem which should interest our always pragmatic profession.

Before proceeding to an analysis of the law on this subject, let the late Judge Goodrich of the United States Court of Appeals for the Third Circuit, set the stage for a little playlet, Vogel v. Northern Assurance Co.[82] The judge, a former law teacher and dean, briefs his own case so well that I shall quote rather than paraphrase. "The undisputed facts present a question with all of the tantalizing niceties of the type which examiners pose to law students. Indeed, the problem of the case can be posed in the form of a hypothetical examination question. Here it is:

"*S*, a seller of real property (in the actual case a man named Shank) agrees to sell the land to *V*, the vendee, for $15,000. (The vendee's real name in this case is Vogel, so the initials fit happily.) *S* then takes out fire insurance on the property in the amount of $6,000; *V* does likewise but in the amount of $9,000. Before *S* conveys the property to *V*, a fire occurs, damaging the house on the land to the extent of $12,000. *V* goes ahead and completes his part of the purchase agreement and receives a deed from *S*. Following this, *S* assigns to *V* all of his rights against the insurance company under the policy. *V* then sues both *S's* insurer (Northern Assurance Company, Ltd.) and his own insurer (Mount Joy Mutual Insurance Company). Was the district court correct in giving judgment against each company even though the total recovery exceeds the stipulated loss by $3,000?"

I pause, to see how many students can pass the test. The final paragraph of the opinion gives the answer.

"This brings us out to an affirmance of a judgment for $15,-000, $3,000 more than the loss. This, it is true, seems incongruous in view of the often stated generalization that fire insurance is indemnity insurance. Vance on Insurance, § 14 (3d ed. 1951); 1 Richards on Insurance 3. The incongruity, if there is one, reaches clear back to 1853 in the settled rule in Pennsylvania that the seller can recover fully against the insurance company for a loss occurring between the time of the agreement and final settlement even though the buyer has taken title according to the terms of the contract. We have no doubt that the ingenuity of insurance counsel will draft a provision whereby total recovery can be limited to actual loss if that is an object to be desired. And if this Court has failed in its examination of Pennsylvania law on the subject, it will be compelled to take the course over."

82. 219 F.2d 409 (1955). The case was decided according to Pennsylvania law.

For the reasoning between the two quoted paragraphs I remand you to Judge Goodrich's opinion, with the sole comment that it has something to do with the fact that both the vendor and the purchaser have an insurable interest in the property. It would be unfair to claim that the judge flunked his examination on *existing* Pennsylvania law, but it should be pointed out that the following year the Supreme Court of Pennsylvania, while citing the *Vogel* case with apparent approval, seemed to reverse its field on the issue of indemnity, stating, " . . . the liability of the two insurance companies will properly be limited to the amount of the damage occasioned by the fire, . . . and they will prorate their respective liabilities therefor in accordance with the terms of the policies." [83] The recovery in excess of loss represented by the *Vogel* case is thoroughly explored by Professor William F. Young, Jr., in an article, "Some 'Windfall Coverages' in Property and Liability Insurance",[84] in the *Columbia Law Review*; suffice it for the moment to agree with Mr. Justice Schaefer of the Illinois Supreme Court. "When insured property is in a single ownership, it is not hard to hold to the orthodox concept of an insurance contract as a personal contract of indemnity. But there are inherent difficulties when there are multiple interests in the property. Those inherent difficulties are augmented because the effect given to an executory contract to sell realty, and to the doctrine of equitable conversion, differs significantly from one jurisdiction to another. The result is that neither courts nor commentators are agreed upon proper solutions for the many variations on the vendor-vendee-insurer theme." [85]

Now that the stage has been set, let us proceed to the critic's role in the developing drama.

A. WHO HAS THE RISK OF LOSS?

The executory contract for the sale of real estate is a peculiar beast. It is a creature of equity, enforceable in proper circumstances by a decree of specific performance, and hence caught up in the odd Anglo-American bifurcation of law and equity. In an

83. Insurance Company of North America v. Alberstadt, 383 Pa. 556, 119 A.2d 83 (1956).

84. 60 Col.L.Rev. 1063, 1066–1072 (1960).

85. First National Bank v. Boston Insurance Company, 17 Ill.2d 147, 150, 160 N.E.2d 802, 804 (1959).

action at law the risk was traditionally stated to be on the vendor,[86] whereas in a suit in equity the majority of courts would place it on the purchaser.[87] This ancient distinction has nothing but the logic of historical accident to commend it and is of less importance today because of the continuing merger of law and equity. Even if the action begins at law, an equitable counterclaim will doubtless take precedence and the rule in chancery will prevail. Do not cheer too soon, however, for all is not beer and skittles on the equity side and even the chancellor suffers from the infantile repressions of an undersized boot,[88] the particular boot being the fiction of equitable conversion.

This hoary chestnut has undoubted utility due to the gap between the signing of the contract and the delivery of the deed. During this interval, while the title is being checked [89] and other incidental messes are being tidied, many interesting events can occur. One or both parties may die, become insane, descend into hopeless bankruptcy, be rigorously attacked by determined creditors, or the property itself may be damaged due to fire, flood, earthquake, or governmental action through eminent domain. Who owns what during the gap? The chancellors answered this simple query with a maxim, "Equity regards as done that which ought to be done." This stated a conclusion rather than giving a reason, but after sufficient repetition it acquired the ring of truth. Since the parties obviously intended that the contract should be performed, the equitable title was said to pass to the purchaser as soon as a valid, enforceable contract for the sale of realty was signed. "The vendee is looked upon and treated as *the owner of the land;* an equitable estate has vested in him com-

86. "If a contract be made for the purchase and sale of land which has buildings on it, and, after the making of the contract, but before the conveyance of the land, the buildings be casually destroyed by fire, upon whom will the loss fall? At law it will clearly fall upon the vendor in all cases." Langdell, A Brief Survey of Equity Jurisdiction 58 (2d ed. 1908). Not surprisingly, the decisions on the point are considerably less clear than the Langdell statement would indicate. See, e. g., Handler, Cases and Materials on Vendor and Purchaser, ftn. 27, p. 369 (1933).

87. Cases on the risk of loss are collected in Annot., 27 A.L.R.2d 44 (1953).

See Bleckley v. Langston, 112 Ga.App. 63, 143 S.E.2d 671 (1965), where the court placed the risk of loss on the purchaser after an ice storm had damaged all of the pecan trees on the real property contracted to be sold. Since the purchaser bears the burdens he also gets the benefits, e. g., he is entitled to the award when the property is taken by eminent domain. See Arko Enterprises, Inc. v. Wood, 185 So.2d 734 (Fla.App.1966). In the last case, there was a vigorous dissent on the grounds that the contract was not capable of specific performance at the time the land was condemned.

88. You may recall that discretion in equity was said to be measured by the length of the Chancellor's foot.

89. For a discussion of the mystic rites of modern conveyancing see p. 306, infra.

mensurate with that provided for by the contract, whether in fee, for life, or for years; although the vendor remains owner of the legal estate he holds it as a trustee for the vendee, to whom all the beneficial interest has passed, having a lien on the land, even if in possession of the vendee, as security for an unpaid portion of the purchase-money." [90]

Equitable conversion thus treats the parties as having changed positions, the original estate of each having been converted—that of the purchaser from personal into real property, and that of the vendor from real into personal property. Various legal consequences flow from the application of this fiction, including a change in the devolution of property on death. If the vendor dies, the "personalty" (in the form of the money still due under the contract) descends to the takers of the personal property (although the naked legal title to the land will descend to the takers of the realty, who hold it in trust as the vendor did) whereas, if the purchaser dies, the "realty" will descend to the takers of his real property even though the remaining purchase money must come from the share going to the takers of the personalty.[91] This aspect of equitable conversion has little present-day effect in an intestate succession since the statutes of descent typically treat real and personal property alike, but it may have some unforeseen consequences where either party dies testate.[92] The death cases will not be discussed in detail here, but they do show the pervasiveness of the doctrine and point out that basically

---

90. 2 Pomeroy, Equity Jurisprudence 21 (5th ed. 1941).

91. For interesting cases involving devolution on death see Eddington v. Turner, 27 Del.Ch. 411, 38 A.2d 738, 155 A.L.R. 562 (1944) and Clapp v. Tower, 11 N.D. 556, 93 N.W. 862 (1903).

The former case involved an option to purchase where the vendor died before the option was exercised. While the purchaser could still exercise the option after the vendor's death, the court refused to apply the doctrine of relation back (as some English cases had done) and so invoke equitable conversion. Thus, the vendor died owning realty, not personalty, and the proceeds of the sale were treated as realty in his estate and passed to the takers of the real property. In the latter case, the doctrine was applied even though the contract was forfeited by the personal representa-

tive of the vendor after his death, thus the land was treated as personalty, not realty. The cases are consistent since in each situation it was a question of whether there was a valid, subsisting contract, capable of being enforced in equity, at the instant of the vendor's death. In the former there was not—only an option which might or might not ripen into a contract; in the latter there was even though it was subsequently forfeited.

92. Of course, if realty and personalty descend differently in a particular jurisdiction then the doctrine could have legal significance. Shay v. Penrose, 25 Ill.2d 447, 185 N.E. 2d 218 (1962). The doctrine may also affect survivorship rights in concurrent estates although it is doubtful if it should do so. Panushka v. Panushka, 221 Or. 145, 349 P.2d 450 (1960) and Watson v. Watson, 5 Ill.2d 526, 126 N.E.2d 220 (1955).

it is designed to carry out the supposed intent of the parties. Thus, the making of a contract to sell land previously devised has the same effect in equity as the conveyance of such land would have at law. On the other hand, if the devise is subsequent to the contract and is specific it has been regarded as being, in effect, a bequest of the purchase money due on the contract.[93] In brief, equitable conversion, like all legal theories, should be applied to reach a just result, consistent with the probable intent of the parties. It should *not* be lifted mechanically from its embalmment in black letter text and vigorously applied in all land contract cases.

Viewed in this perspective, it is clear that the risk of loss should not pass automatically to the purchaser the instant he signs an enforceable contract.[94] In the typical situation the vendor remains in possession; he already has his interest insured; and it would never occur to either party that the purchaser assumes the risk prior to the transfer of legal title or possession. Without belaboring the point, it should be noted that the case on which the doctrine is based, Paine v. Meller,[95] did not require such a result and most legal commentators have criticized the unwarranted expansion of *dicta* in the case into different fact situations. The maxim, "equity regards as done that which should have been done," stems from cases in which the vendor and purchaser were ready to perform the necessary acts and the time had arrived for them to do so, but because of mistake, delay, accident, concession to convenience, or some wrongful neglect on the part of the one against whom the maxim was invoked, actual performance had not occurred. Law could not aid the parties, so equity treated the situation as if the transaction had been executed. The maxim simply has no place in cases of loss by casualty before the time for performance has arrived and before the conditions precedent to the conveyance have been fulfilled.

It is precisely because the present majority rule runs counter to the normal intent of the parties and to the logic of the maxim itself, that so many variations on the theme have developed. No less than five different theories have been advanced: (1) the risk of loss should be on the vendor until legal title is conveyed; (2)

---

93. For a good, brief discussion of this whole matter see Chafee, Simpson, Maloney, Cases on Equity 516–522 (1951).

See also Father Flanagan's Boys' Home v. Graybill, 178 Neb. 79, 132 N.W.2d 304 (1964).

94. Note the constant emphasis on *enforceable* contract. If neither party has signed a memorandum sufficient to satisfy the Statute of Frauds or if the title is clearly unmerchantable, equitable conversion does not take place and the risk remains on the vendor. Sanford v. Breidenbach, 111 Ohio App. 474, 173 N.E.2d 702 (1960); Amundson v. Severson, 41 S.D. 377, 170 N. W. 633 (1919).

95. Note 81 supra.

the risk should be on the vendor until the time agreed upon for the conveyance of the legal title, and thereafter on the purchaser, unless the vendor is then in such default as to be unable specifically to enforce the contract; (3) the risk should be on the party in possession, whether vendor or purchaser; (4) the risk should be on the vendor unless there is something in the contract or the relations of the parties from which the court can infer a different intention; and (5) the risk should be on the purchaser from the time the vendor-purchaser relation arises.[96]

Several states have settled the issue by legislation, adopting the Uniform Vendor and Purchaser Risk Act which leaves the casualty risk on the vendor, as long as the contract is executory and the purchaser has not gone into possession. In the other forty-two states the courts still decide the matter, with results ranging from the majority view, following the *dicta* of Paine v. Meller, to the minority view of Massachusetts in Libman v. Levenson [97] where the court said: "It is now settled . . . that the contract is to be construed as subject to the implied condition that it no longer shall be binding if, before the time for the conveyance to be made, the buildings are destroyed by fire. The loss by the fire falls upon the vendor, the owner; and if he has not protected himself by insurance, he can have no reimbursement of this loss; but the contract is no longer binding upon either party. If the purchaser has advanced any part of the price, he can recover it back."

Other states take positions somewhere between the two extremes and hold that the purchaser is the equitable owner only in cases in which he has fulfilled all conditions and become absolutely entitled to a conveyance. In what was long the leading Illinois case, Budelman v. American Insurance Company,[98] the Court put it succinctly: "The law is well settled in this State that an executory contract of sale does not convey title to the vendee. The vendor retains the legal title and the vendee does not even take an equitable title. . . . When the vendee performs all acts necessary to entitle him to a deed, then, and not until then, he has an equitable title and may compel a conveyance." [99]

96. Note 93 at 556–557.

97. 236 Mass. 221, 224, 128 N.E. 13, 14 (1920). See also Anderson. v. Yaworski, 120 Conn. 390, 181 A. 205, 101 A.L.R. 1232 (1935) for a good statement of this view.

98. 297 Ill. 222, 225, 130 N.E. 513, 514 (1921). See also Newman v. Mountain Park Land Co., 85 Ark. 208, 107 S.W. 391 (1908) and Good v. Jarrard, 93 S.C. 229, 76 S.E. 698 (1912).

99. Interestingly enough, the Illinois law is not well settled that an executory contract conveys no equitable title to the purchaser. Indeed, in Shay v. Penrose, 25 Ill.2d 447, 185 N.E.2d 218 (1962), the Illinois Supreme Court specifically applied the doctrine, even in an installment land contract, and, in effect, repudiated the basis of the *Budelman* case. For a good discussion of the Illinois law of equitable conversion see Note, The Doctrine of Equita-

The moral is clear, there is no one hiding place for the button. The real estate lawyer must discover as best he can where the risk of loss lurks in his own state and draft his contract or build his law suit on the basis of that discovery. But even in the jurisdictions which purport to place the risk on the purchaser with the signing of the contract, it may be possible to get the court to revert to first principles and overrule (or distinguish) cases which mechanically apply the doctrine of equitable conversion. For what it is worth, I believe that the Uniform Vendor and Purchaser Risk Act represents the best solution to this phase of the problem. This view is shared by many of the writers who have searched for the *proper* hiding place of the button.[1]

B. FIXING THE RISK BY CONTRACT

In any jurisdiction, it is unwise to leave the risk of loss issue to the operation of law. The contract is the blueprint of the transaction and it should cover all of those contingencies which might arise but which we hope will not. A poorly drafted contract, or even none at all, will serve quite well so long as everything goes smoothly. The test of any legal document is how it stands up in a crisis.

The parties clearly have the right to handle the risk of loss in any way they see fit.[2] Just as clearly, there is no set formula which will fit all situations. A common clause provides: "The risk of loss or damage to said premises by fire is assumed by the vendor until the delivery of the deed." At first blush this appears clear enough, but doubts soon creep in. Loss may occur from windstorm, vandalism, boiler destruction, hurricane, erosion, subsidence and collapse of a retaining wall, etc., and this clause covers only loss by fire. It is obviously too narrow. Moreover, how is the risk of loss to be handled, granting it falls on the vendor? Does this clause merely entitle the purchaser to rescind the contract and receive his down payment or does it allow him to seek specific performance of the contract with substantial abatement from the purchase price? There is authority for both

---

ble Conversion in Illinois, 1955 U. Ill.L.F. 743.

1. But see Pound, The Progress of the Law, Equity, 33 Harv.L.Rev. 813, 826 (1920). Dean Pound disagreed with Professor Williston's argument for possession at the time

of the loss as the proper criterion. Williston's view was adopted by the Uniform Act.

2. Coolidge and Sickler, Inc. v. Regn, 7 N.J. 93, 80 A.2d 554, 27 A.L.R.2d 437 (1951).

positions.[3] Finally, this clause is silent as to possession and would not be helpful in installment land contracts or other situations calling for a transfer of possession prior to delivery of the deed. Brevity has its own virtue but it can be a false god. More detail and more precision is needed here.

Mr. Milton R. Friedman of the New York Bar, in an article on real estate contracts in the *American Bar Association Journal*,[4] lists résumés of three possible clauses :

"A. In case of injury, seller has the option to restore. If seller fails to restore purchaser may : (1) terminate the contract; or (2) accept a deed, without abatement, but with seller's rights to insurance.

"B. (1) If the injury is less than 10 per cent of the purchase price purchaser shall complete the contract; and (2) if the injury is greater than 10 per cent purchaser has the option of completing or terminating the contract. If in either case the contract is completed purchaser is entitled to an abatement commensurate with the damage.

"C. (1) If the injury does not exceed a stated amount purchaser shall accept the premises as damaged, with seller's right to insurance; and (2) if the injury exceeds the sum mentioned purchaser has the option of either completing the contract, and receiving seller's right to insurance, or terminating the contract."

All of these stipulations provide that if the contract is terminated because of the injury the vendor will repay any advance on the purchase price. Each of these clauses has merit, but a little reflection will reveal aspects that will not be entirely satisfactory to both parties. They are sufficient, however, to suggest solutions to the drafting problems and each contract must be approached in light of the peculiar fact situation involved.[5]

Without attempting to reconcile the conflicting theories as to risk of loss, and even without settling the issue by contract, the parties can substantially avoid loss through insurance. There is agreement that both the vendor and purchaser have insurable interests; hence both can be properly insured. A "contract of sale" endorsement can be added to the existing insurance policy,

3. See Lampesis v. The Travelers Insurance Company, 101 N.H. 323, 143 A.2d 104 (1958). In this case the risk of loss being on the vendor apparently gives him the option of repairing the property and enforcing the contract or treating the contract as at an end.

4. Friedman, Buying a Home: Representing the Purchaser, 47 A.B.A.J. 596, 602 (1961).

5. For a discussion of the fire clause with a detailed analysis of the problems which can arise even with well-drafted contracts see Drafting of Real Estate Sales Contracts, 35 Chicago Bar Record 247, 260 (1954). This article was prepared by the Committee on Real Property Law of the Chicago Bar Association.

after first ascertaining that there is sufficient coverage to take care of any loss. This last point is essential since in these days of unending inflation many properties are woefully under-insured at the time the contract is signed. The "contract of sale" clause recites that a contract has been executed between the insured and the named purchaser, and that any loss shall be adjusted with the insured and paid to him and the purchaser as their respective interests may appear. An alternative is to cause the policy to be amended, constituting the purchaser an additional insured, or the latter may secure a separate policy. As an insured he would have the right to participate in the settlement of any controversy as to the amount of the claim, whereas under the "contract of sale" endorsement his only right is to share in the proceeds when paid.[6]

C. WHO RECEIVES THE INSURANCE PROCEEDS?

If the transaction is handled by a lawyer who is familiar with the preceding material (or at least the last few paragraphs of it) all but the most stubborn problems will disappear. Not all vendors and purchasers of real estate are so circumspect as to seek legal assistance, however, and even in this enlightened age some complicated messes can result. It is interesting to note that as long ago as Paine v. Meller the insurance issue reared its head. The vendor had allowed the insurance on the premises to lapse shortly before the fire and the purchaser claimed this was a significant factor in determining the risk of loss. Said Lord Eldon: ". . . For I do not see how I can allow it, unless I say, this Court warrants to every buyer of a house, that the house is insured, and not only insured, but to the full extent of the value. The house is bought, not the benefit of any existing policy. However general the practice of insuring from fire, it is not universal; and it is yet less general that houses are insured to their full value, or near it. The question, whether insured or not, is with the vendor solely, not with the vendee; unless he proposes something upon that; and makes it matter of contract with the vendor, that the vendee shall buy according to that fact, that the house is insured." [7]

6. Although see Dubin Paper Co. v. Insurance Co. of North America, 361 Pa. 68, 63 A.2d 85 (1949) which apparently would allow the purchaser to sue on the vendor's policy.

7. Note 81 supra.

This remains good law and the vendor's failure to insure adequately, or indeed at all, puts no added burden upon him unless he had contracted to so protect the premises. Suppose, however, the vendor has insurance, the purchaser has none, the contract is silent, and the jurisdiction puts the risk of loss on the purchaser—what then? The inexorable logic of the law grinds out the following answer. Both parties have an insurable interest; the vendor protected his interest; the purchaser, like the foolish virgins, did not; insurance is a personal contract, payable only to the insured; the purchaser "has had it." [8] But surely such logic would result in a major windfall to the vendor, since he would have the insurance proceeds to cover his loss plus the right to sue the purchaser for specific performance and receive the full purchase price of the land? The English court had the courage of its misplaced convictions, holding that the vendor, having collected both the insurance and the purchase money, held the latter in trust for the insurer on the principle that the latter was entitled to subrogation against the purchaser.[9] This judicial logic was too much for Parliament and the English rule was changed by statute to provide that the purchaser might claim the insurance money received by the vendor, subject, however, to any stipulation to the contrary.[10]

No such statutory changes have been made in this country and a minority of American jurisdictions still echo the old English view which denies the purchaser any access to the insurance proceeds.[11] These cases follow the *dictum* of Judge Pound in Brownell v. Board of Education: [12] "These reasons [for holding for the purchaser] may savor of layman's ideas of equity, but they are not law. . . .   Insurance is a mere personal contract to pay a sum of money by way of indemnity to protect the interest of the insured. . . .   In common parlance the buildings are insured but every one who stops to consider the nature of the insurance contract understands that they are not. Both in the forum and the market place it is known that the insurance runs to the individual insured and not with the land. The vendor has a beneficial interest to protect, i. e., his own. The vendee has an insurable interest and may protect himself. The trustee as such has no insurable interest and can only act for the *cestui que trust*. Plaintiff may not have the insurance money collected by

8. Rayner v. Preston, 18 Ch.Div. 1 (1881); Brownell v. Board of Education, 239 N.Y. 369, 146 N.E. 630, 37 A.L.R. 1319 (1925).

9. Castellain v. Preston, 11 Q.B.D. 380 (1883).

10. 15 Geo.V, c. 20, § 47 (1925).

11. Cases on the rights of vendor and purchaser, as between themselves, in insurance proceeds are collected in Annot., 64 A.L.R.2d 1397 (1959).

12. 239 N.Y. 369, 374, 146 N.E. 630, 632 (1925).

defendant. It is not a part of the *res* bargained for and no trust relation exists in regard to it."

The amazing vitality of the old Brownell case was demonstrated in Raplee v. Piper.[13] The contract of sale required the purchaser to keep the property insured against fire in the name of the vendor. A loss occurred while the purchaser was in possession and the company paid the vendor $4,650. The purchaser insisted that, while the risk of loss was his under the Uniform Act, the money should be credited on the balance of the purchase price. The vendor refused on the theory that the insurance was his even though the purchaser paid the premiums. The Court of Appeals of New York held for the purchaser, distinguishing the Brownell case, although stating it was still the law of New York, because there the vendor had obtained the insurance at his own cost, for his own protection, and not because of any agreement.

Surely this corollary to the Brownell doctrine is reasonable but there was a vigorous dissent by three judges who felt that even here the purchaser was entitled to no part of the insurance proceeds because of the settled law of New York. Said Judge Burke: "In light of these circumstances we think that this court should adhere to the rule established by the Brownell case. Such adherence, it seems to us, is imperative, not only because this is a well-recognized rule which the legislature has not undertaken to change, but also because many businessmen and their lawyers may have entered into contracts in reliance upon it." [14] It is far from clear, however, that the purchaser, businessman or no, intended to pay the vendor's premiums and receive nothing in return but the opportunity to pay the full purchase price for a damaged building. Fortunately, the majority of the court reached a just result but the litigation itself could have been avoided by a properly drafted contract or even by a more sensible rule of law than that represented by the Brownell case.

13. 3 N.Y.2d 179, 143 N.E.2d 919, 64 A.L.R.2d 1397 (1957).

14. Id. at 184 and 922. Since the law of the Brownell case was judge-made (or was it only judge-discovered?) it would seem that it could be judge-altered if shown to be erroneous. For a fascinating analysis of the modern English attitude toward the judge's role see Davis, The Future of Judge-Made Public Law in England: A Problem of Practical Jurisprudence, 61 Col.L.Rev. 201, 210 (1961). "What is now the orthodox English attitude was stated several centuries ago by Francis Bacon: 'Judges ought to remember that their office is . . . to interpret law, and not to make law, or give law.' My assertion is largely the opposite: Judges ought to remember that the easier part of their office is to discover and to apply previously-existing law to the problems that come before them, but the most important and most difficult task they perform is the molding of a body of case law that will satisfactorily serve the needs of society."

The "inexorable logic of the law," which led to the older English rule and the Brownell case, proved too much for most American courts. Said the court in a leading New Jersey case: "As purchaser under a valid contract of purchase vendee became the equitable owner of the property; in equity the property is regarded as belonging to him, the vendor retaining the legal title simply as trustee and as security for the unpaid purchase money. By reason of this equitable relation of the parties to a contract of sale of land, it has been determined by the great weight of American authority that money accruing on a policy of insurance, where the loss has occurred subsequent to the execution of the contract, will in equity inure to the benefit of the vendee; the vendor still retaining his character as trustee, and the insurance money in his hands representing the property that has been destroyed." [15] The court was correct in calling this view the great weight of American authority, as decisions in at least fifteen states attest.[16] The ever-useful remedy of constructive trust has proved flexible enough to reach a just result and what once savored of a "layman's ideas of equity" has now become the law in most states. Professor Vance suggested, long ago, that in the business world the insurance runs with the land and that the courts should give effect to that understanding.[17] That view should soon prevail generally in this country. One recent state adopting this position was Alabama,[18] in 1958, and the court proceeded to do complete equity by decreeing that the purchaser should reimburse the vendor for the amount of the premiums paid by him.

Even this enlightened view will not solve all problems since the vendor may not be willing to sue the insurance company to collect on the policy and the purchaser, not being a party to it, may be hard up for a remedy. The Dubin case [19] in Pennsylvania comes closest to suggesting an answer here. The fire occurred before the date of settlement under the contract, the purchaser performed his part, and the vendor received checks from his insurance companies to cover the loss but returned them to the companies. (Now why would a vendor behave in that fashion?) The purchaser sued in equity to compel the companies to pay the proceeds to the vendor and asked the court to declare that the vendor held the proceeds as trustee for the plaintiff. The court

15. Millville Aerie v. Weatherby, 82 N.J.Eq. 455, 457, 88 A. 847, 848 (1913).

16. Note 11 supra.

17. Vance, Vendee's Claim to Insurance Money Received by Vendor, 34 Yale L.J. 87 (1924).

18. Alabama Farm Bureau Mutual Insurance Service, Inc. v. Nixon, 268 Ala. 271, 105 So.2d 643 (1958).

19. Note 6 supra.

concluded that the action was well brought and the purchaser was entitled to relief. This, too, may savor of "barnyard equity" but it makes good sense.

Although there is dispute as to the purchaser's rights to the insurance proceeds in the situations discussed in the preceding paragraphs, it seems clear that where the vendor agrees to keep the premises insured for the benefit of the purchaser, or when the vendor assigns his rights under the policy to the purchaser, either before or after the loss, the insurance proceeds belong to the purchaser.[20]

Since the constructive trust theory has been applied to allow the purchaser to reach the insurance proceeds in the hands of the vendor it might seem to follow, in the interest of symmetry if nothing else, that the purchaser too could be held as a constructive trustee for the benefit of the vendor. The equities are not really parallel, however, since the vendor, having been owner all along and being the apparent bearer of the risk of loss, might be expected to carry insurance for the benefit of all interested parties. The purchaser, on the other hand, is a "Johnny-come-lately" to the property and if he insures at all will probably do so solely to protect his own interests. This analysis seems to be reflected in the judicial attitude and, in the absence of a provision in the contract requiring the purchaser to insure for the benefit of the vendor or the presence of some special equities, the purchaser will not be compelled to account for any part of the proceeds paid on a policy taken out to protect his own interests.[21]

Obviously, the words "special equities" in the previous sentence can cover a lot of ground and you can visualize situations in which the vendor might have a claim to the purchaser's insurance. For example, in Cetkowski v. Knutson [22] the vendor had the right to rescind a contract of sale because he was induced to enter it by the purchaser's fraud. The court made the purchaser a trustee of the insurance proceeds for the benefit of the vendor, even though the policy was maintained in the purchaser's name and for his benefit.

---

20. Vierneisel v. Rhode Island Ins. Co., 77 Cal.App.2d 229, 175 P.2d 63 (1946); Allyn v. Allyn, 154 Mass. 570, 28 N.E. 779 (1891).

21. Deming Investment Co. v. Dickerman, 63 Kan. 728, 66 P. 1029 (1901).

22. 163 Minn. 492, 204 N.W. 528, 40 A.L.R. 599 (1925).

D.   A TYPICAL PROBLEM

I began this discussion with a quiz based on a recent Pennsylvania case, and I daresay some of you flunked it. We conclude this section with a question from an Illinois decision [23] to see whether you have shown sufficient improvement to remain in class.   The vendor, holding title as trustee under a land trust, insured a building with four companies, aggregating $46,750. Each of the policies indemnified the insured "to the extent of the actual cash value of the property at the time of loss, but not exceeding the amount which it would cost to repair or replace the property with material of like kind and quality within a reasonable time after such loss .   .   .   nor in any event for more than the interest of the insured, against all direct loss by fire." The vendor then entered into a contract to sell the property to the purchaser for $19,000 of which $3,000 was paid down.   The form contract provided that premiums were to be prorated as of the date of the delivery of the deed and the policies would then be assigned to the buyers.   It also provided, "If, prior to delivery of deed hereunder, the improvements on said premises shall be destroyed or materially damaged by fire or other casualty, this contract shall, at the option of the buyer, become null and void."

The building was totally destroyed by fire before law day and appraisals secured by the insurance adjusters showed reproduction costs in excess of $230,000.   The companies conceded that the building's value was in excess of the $46,750 coverage but refused to pay more than $16,000 to the insured vendor.   Why? Said the companies, the "interest of the insured" under the doctrine of equitable conversion is $16,000, the amount unpaid on the purchase price.   How would you decide this case?

Mr. Justice Schaefer, admitting that the problem presented by the case was not an easy one, held against the companies, pointing out that equitable conversion had evolved as a fiction to carry out the intent of the parties to the contract and should have no effect upon the rights of others.   Had the fire occurred prior to the signing of the contract or had the contract been performed before the fire took place and the policies been assigned to the purchaser, there would have been a recovery for the face amount of the policies.   Legal realism required brushing aside the fiction of equitable conversion and allowing full recovery. The case represents the "old school try" by insurance counsel in a lost cause.   Incidentally, during oral argument and in response

---

23.   Note 85 supra.

to questions from the bench, counsel for the insured vendor stated that the insured was obligated to account to the purchasers for the proceeds.   This caused a flurry of excitement and led to the filing of supplemental briefs since the companies' counsel complained this fact had not been previously revealed.   However, the court held this was immaterial, pointing out that the purchasers had the option to cancel the contract in event of fire and could have left the property entirely in the ownership of the vendor.   Concluded the court: "That contingency [the fire] occurred, and we do not see how the way in which the contracting parties have dealt with the resulting situation can be a matter of concern to the insurers."   This point scarcely puts Illinois in the company of those who make the vendor a trustee of the insurance for the purchaser but it does indicate which way the winds of doctrine are blowing.

We can agree with Professor Young, who stated in the *Columbia Law Review* article [24] cited earlier: "Enough has been said to suggest that the state of the law in a particular jurisdiction depends largely on the order in which the issues arise for appellate consideration.   .   .   .   The doubt and disagreement existing about these relationships cannot be overlooked.   This should not be charged naively to judicial ineptitude.   Rather, it may be supposed that 'proper solutions' cannot be found easily for the issues involved, which are so diverse yet so interrelated, in the fashion of courts, case by case."   Once again the common law needs the helping hand of beneficent legislation.

SECTION 3.   THE DEED

Compared to the contract or the lease, the deed is a simple document.   The first two instruments must govern the relationship of the parties over a long period of time; the deed, in a sense, ends the relationship since its very purpose is to transfer legal title from the grantor to the grantee.   So strong is this terminal character of a deed that, under the doctrine of merger, many of the contract rights of a purchaser are extinguished when he accepts a deed.   Thus, a purchaser who was entitled to a warranty deed conveying merchantable title but who accepted a quitclaim deed found himself without recourse when the premises turned out to be subject to a mortgage.[25]   In the main, this

24. Note 84 supra at 1070.   25. Whittemore v. Farrington, 76 N.
                                              Y. 452 (1879).

doctrine of merger of the contract into the deed applies only to questions of title and does not affect collateral covenants to build or make repairs.[26]   Certainly the restrictive covenants, binding the grantee to specific uses of the land, survive the delivery of the deed, but these matters will be discussed later.[27]

The essential simplicity of the deed is illustrated by the statutory short form warranty deed in use in Illinois.[28]

WARRANTY DEED   DOCUMENT NO. _____

THE GRANTOR__, _____	For Recorder's Certificate Only
of the _____, in the County of _____, and State of _____ for and in consideration of _____ DOLLARS in hand paid, CONVEY__ and WARRANT__ to	
of the _____, County of _____, and State of _____, the following described Real Estate:	

situated in the County of Champaign, in the State of Illinois, hereby releasing and waiving all rights under and by virtue of the Homestead Exemption Laws of the State of Illinois.

_____

_____

Dated this _____ day of _____, A. D. 19__.

_____[Seal]

_____[Seal]

_____[Seal]

_____[Seal]

26. Re v. Magness Construction Co., 49 Del. 377, 117 A.2d 78 (1955).
Even in title situations there is some chipping away at the merger doctrine.   In Mayer v. Summergrade, 111 Ohio App. 237, 167 N.E.2d 516 (1960), the court allowed a purchaser to sue on a covenant against special tax assessments in the contract after delivery of the deed.   There was a vigorous dissent, however, and the case represents a minority position on the title issue.

27. P. 347, infra.

28. Ill.Rev.Stat., ch. 30, §§ 8 and 9 (1973).

STATE OF ILLINOIS, ⎫ ss
Champaign County,   ⎭

               I, the undersigned, a Notary Public
in and for said County and State afore-
said, DO HEREBY CERTIFY, that

[Seal]

_____

_____

personally known to me to be the same
person__ whose name__ _____ subscribed to the foregoing instrument appeared before me this day in person and
acknowledged that __he__ signed, sealed and delivered the said instrument as
_____ free and voluntary act, for the
uses and purposes therein set forth, including the release and waiver of the
right of homestead.

               Given under my hand and Notarial
Seal, this _____ day of _____, A. D.
19__.

My Commission expires _____, A. D. 19__.

_____
                          Notary Public

    The simplicity of the deed should not lead you to underrate its
importance, however. Since it is the operative instrument of conveyance, questions of title turn on its validity and adequacy. The
conveyance of land has had a fascinating history, starting as a
physical act dramatized by the livery of seisin, accompanied by
the words "I give" (Latin, "do") "to him and his heirs" or "to
him and the heirs of his body." [29] The Statute of Frauds required
a writing and the private seal added the touch that made the modern deed. The role of the Statute of Uses, with its new methods
of conveyancing—the bargain and sale and the covenant to stand
seised to uses—has already been explained.[30] Modern conveyancing acts tend to operate independently of the Statute of Uses
and the statute of the particular jurisdiction should be carefully
followed. However, the earlier methods often survive and, while
not regularly used today, they may be invoked to save a conveyance that would otherwise fail.[31]

29. 1 Patton, Titles 3–8 (2d ed. 1957).   **31.** French v. French, 3 N.H. 234
                                                        (1825).

30. P. 73, supra.

A. TYPES AND ELEMENTS OF THE MODERN DEED

While no one form of deed is in universal use, the modern deed does follow a general pattern. There are two basic types— warranty and quitclaim. Either type is sufficient to transfer such interest as a grantor *presently* [32] has, but the former includes personal covenants by the grantor that his title is good. If the deed contains all of the usual covenants, it is classified as a general warranty deed; if it contains only a few or creates some new promises, it is called a special warranty deed. Since these covenants are a type of title assurance they will be discussed in Chapter 5. The warranty deed is typically used where the grantor purports to convey an indefeasible fee simple, while the quitclaim (sometimes called a release deed) is used to surrender such interest as the grantor may happen to have. Thus, if title examination discloses that there is an outstanding dower interest in some prior owner's widow that claim would probably be released by a quitclaim deed from her. Of course, there are various types of deeds which are used for a special purpose, such as mortgage deeds, trust deeds, deeds in trust, etc. These may be either warranty or quitclaim in form. Another classification you may encounter is the indenture versus the deed poll. The former is executed by all parties to it (usually the grantor and the grantee); the latter is executed by the grantor only.[33] Today, virtually all deeds to real property are deeds poll, being signed only by the grantor and his wife or the proper corporate officials. The grantee need not sign since by his acceptance of the deed he becomes bound by its terms.

Traditionally, the deed was divided into four parts—the premises, the habendum, the execution clause, and the acknowledgment. The premises consisted of the names of the grantor and grantee, any recitals of fact explanatory of the transaction, the operative words of conveyance, the consideration, and the legal description of the land. The habendum,[34] sometimes called

---

32. The warranty deed will also pass after-acquired title, whereas the quitclaim will not do so unless there are added representations as to the grantor's title. See p. 278, infra.

33. These odd names derive from the fact that originally the deed poll was on paper that was *polled* or cut in a straight line, whereas the indenture was indented or cut in a wavy line across the top. The indenting practice originated from cutting the deed through the middle of a word and giving each party part of the document.

34. If there was a conflict between the granting clause and the habendum clause, thus creating an ambiguity in the deed, the traditional

the "to have and to hold" clause because it was introduced by those words, described the estate to be taken by the grantee (fee simple, life estate, etc.), contained the declaration of trust, if any, set forth any conditions or powers affecting the grant, and included the covenants of title when it was necessary to state them *in haec verba.*[35]   The execution clause contained the date, the signatures of the grantor and his wife, the seal (if still required) and, in some states, the signatures of witnesses.   The acknowledgment—attestation by a public officer—completed the instrument.   The acknowledgment might not be necessary to the passage of title, but it was frequently a prerequisite to recording and was required as a condition to the admission of the deed into evidence without further proof of execution.   Its role was to add to the authenticity of the document and cut down on the likelihood of fraud or forgery.   The modern deed usually contains these traditional parts, but a conveyance may be sustained even though it consists only of the names of the parties, the consideration, the words of conveyance, and the description of the land.[36]

As always in the law, there is considerable gulf between what competent draftsmanship requires and what a court may be induced to sustain under proper circumstances.[37]   For example, the general rule of law is that a deed is a nullity until the name of the grantee is lawfully inserted therein.[38]   Yet in Womack v. Stegner,[39] a Texas court stated: "It appears to be well settled in Texas that when a deed with the name of the grantee in blank is delivered by the grantor with the intention that the title shall rest in the person to whom the deed is delivered, and that person is expressly authorized at the time of delivery to insert his own or any other name as grantee, title passes with the delivery."   In that case, the court used the concept of equitable title, which passed at the time of the delivery, and even the subsequent death of the grantor, before the authority was exercised and the blank filled, was immaterial.   Similarly, the law clearly requires operative words of conveyance, i. e., words like convey, grant,

view was that the granting clause prevailed.   This view was rejected in Grayson v. Holloway, 203 Tenn. 464, 313 S.W.2d 555 (1958).   "The technical rules of the common law as to the division of deeds into formal parts have long since been disregarded in this state, and the rule now is that all parts shall be examined to ascertain the intention."

35.   Modern statutes allow the use of a single word, such as *warrant*, to stand for the usual covenants.   See p. 268, infra.

36.   For a more detailed analysis, see Tiffany, Real Property 670–681 (New Abridged Edition, 1940).

37.   See, for example, the discussion in Hinchliffe v. Fischer, 198 Kan. 365, 424 P.2d 581 (1967) and Cribbet, Fritz and Johnson, Cases and Materials on Property 616 (3d ed. 1972), where a valid deed in the form of a poem is reproduced.

38.   Hedding v. Schauble, 146 Minn. 95, 177 N.W. 1019 (1920).

39.   293 S.W.2d 124 (1956).   See Comment, 35 Tex.L.Rev. 435 (1957).

bargain and sell, which show the grantor's intent to transfer an interest to the grantee. So strong is this requirement that words of reservation or exception in a deed normally are insufficient to create a new interest; they can only retain something out of an estate conveyed.[40] But in a South Carolina case, the court held that a husband could "reserve" a life estate to his wife, even though she had no previous interest in the premises, other than inchoate dower.[41] While this might not be strictly logical, "pure logic for its own sake, should not be allowed to frustrate the clearly ascertained intention of a grantor which does not violate an established rule of construction or law."

B. EXECUTION OF THE DEED

Aside from the type of deed used and the elements it must contain, there are certain acts which must be done before the document becomes anything more than a piece of paper. This execution of the deed is summed up in the old saw, "signed, sealed, and delivered." As we have already seen it may have to be attested and acknowledged as well. Some states require the affixing of documentary tax stamps but fortunately the conveyance is valid even though the stamps are omitted. All of these matters of execution are mechanical and require little discussion except for the subject of delivery. Delivery is the final operative act and without it the whole transaction fails. We have already discussed this requirement under gifts and since the same principles control in commercial transfers we will not repeat that material.[42] The most important additional aspect of delivery arises from the use of the escrow agreement and that will be covered in some detail in the next section.

Acceptance should also be considered as a part of execution. Seldom does it raise any real difficulties, since if the conveyance is beneficial it will be presumed and if, in fact, acceptance does not occur until much later because the grantee did not know of the conveyance, then it will be held to relate back to the delivery of the deed. Occasionally, intricate problems can arise and it has been determined that the fiction of relation back will not be used to cut off the intervening rights of a third party, usually a bona fide purchaser for value without notice.[43]

40. Leidig v. Hoopes, 288 P.2d 402 (Okl.1955).

41. Glasgow v. Glasgow, 221 S.C. 322, 70 S.E.2d 432 (1952).

See also Willard v. First Church of Christ Scientist, 7 Cal.3d 473, 102 Cal.Rptr. 739, 498 P.2d 987 (1972)

and Johnson v. Republic Steel Corp., 262 F.2d 108 (6th Cir. 1958).

42. P. 123, supra.

43. Although in Green v. Skinner, 185 Cal. 435, 197 P. 60 (1921) the court refused to relate the acceptance back to cut off the interest of a surviving joint tenant.

C. DESCRIPTION OF THE LAND

It is hard to overestimate the importance of an accurate legal description of the land conveyed. Unless the land can be accurately located, the deed is void and a sloppy description may make the title unmerchantable, even though it can ultimately be sustained in court. The improvements on the land need not be identified since they are included in the legal description of the real estate. Conveyancing customs vary in different sections of the country and no attempt will be made to give a technical account of this phase of the law. All descriptions are based on a survey of the land and, in the final analysis, a new survey may be called for to determine the exact boundaries of a plat of land. The governmental or rectangular survey system controls in vast areas of the nation and the familiar "Southeast one quarter of the southwest one quarter of Section 6 in Township 4 North, Range 4 East of the Third Principal Meridian in _____ County, State of _____" will be the formula for much agricultural acreage.[44] In the East, the metes and bounds description is much more common and this requires a careful drafting of the calls and distances, related to the established monuments which furnish the points of departure. Urban descriptions will usually be based on a subdivision plat which has been recorded and which leads to: "Lot 1 in Block 10 of the McAdams Addition to the City of Pleasantville in the State of Ohio."

The legal standard involved in descriptions is simple—so describe the land that only one possible tract can be identified by the language used. But suppose this simple standard is not met, does the deed fail? Since courts exist to settle disputes, you may be sure that some of these problems will land in the judge's lap. The court has one basic principle to guide it—the intent of the parties, as gathered from the four corners of the deed. All so-called rules of construction are simply guides for ascertaining the intent. There is a strong tendency for the courts to sustain the deed if at all possible, since it is apparent that the parties intended for something to be conveyed or they would never have been involved in the transaction. It is this underlying assumption which accounts for some of the weird descriptions which are upheld.

44. See Maley and Thuma, Legal Descriptions of Land (Pamphlet published by Chicago Title and Trust Co., 1955); Ward, Illinois Law of Title Examination 69–74 (2d ed. 1952).

The cases on legal description are legion but a "feel" for the judicial construction problem may be obtained by a look at ten canons of construction. They are as follows.

1.   The construction prevails which is most favorable to the grantee, i. e., the language of the deed is construed against the grantor.   If the deed contains two descriptions, the grantee can select that which is most favorable to him.   This canon is based on the presumption that the grantor drafted the deed and, if an ambiguity has resulted, he has only himself to blame.   As in insurance law, where the policy is typically construed against the insurer, this canon is frequently the unstated premise in a case otherwise inexplicable.[45]

2.   If the deed contains two descriptions, one ambiguous and the other unambiguous, the latter prevails in order to sustain the deed.   This is not so likely to happen with modern, short form deeds but with the old, prolix instruments it was not uncommon.

3.   Extrinsic evidence will be allowed to explain a latent ambiguity but a patent ambiguity must be resolved within the four corners of the deed.[46]   This old chestnut has lost much of its validity but it still must be reckoned with.   It was based on the idea that if the defect was latent (not apparent to the parties when the deed was drafted) evidence of surrounding circumstances should be admitted to clarify intent, but if it was patent (apparent on the face of the document) the parties must have been aware of it when the deed was executed and no extrinsic evidence is necessary.   It has long been clear that this canon is easily controlled by the determination of what is latent or patent and many writers have called for abolition of the distinction.[47]

4.   Monuments control distances and courses;   courses control distances;   and quantity is the least reliable guide of all.[48]   In a metes and bounds description, it is relatively easy to start with a known monument (the side of a road, a stream, a rock, etc.), move in a stated direction or course for a set distance, and end up with an impossible description because one of these elements is in error.   This canon tries to set up a priority of reliability, based on presumed intent of the parties.   Most monuments would be difficult to mistake so they are probably identified correctly.   A course, "northerly at a 90° angle", is more certain than a distance, "thence eighty feet," since most people cannot measure dis-

45.   See Hall v. Eaton, 139 Mass. 217, 29 N.E. 660 (1885) which makes little sense on any other basis.

46.   Walters v. Tucker, 281 S.W.2d 843 (Mo.1955).

47.   McBaine, The Rule Against Disturbing Plain Meaning of Writings, 31 Cal.L.Rev. 145 (1943). In a footnote it is pointed out that the distinction "is gradually disappearing" and the hope is expressed that the time will soon come "when it will be of interest only to students engaged in tracing the history of law through periods of formalism to a period of realism."

48.   Pritchard v. Rebori, 135 Tenn. 328, 186 S.W. 121 (1916).

tances with any degree of accuracy with the naked eye. Quantity, which is always hard to estimate, logically brings up the end of the list.

5.   Useless or contradictory words may be disregarded as mere surplusage. The difficulty with this canon is patent. Which are the useless or contradictory words? Nonetheless, it states a useful truth since many prolix, confusing descriptions can be pared down to meaningful size to sustain a deed.

6.   Particular descriptions control over general descriptions, although a false particular may be disregarded to give effect to a true general description. Any more questions?

7.   A description, insufficient in itself, may be made certain through incorporation by reference. This is a particularly useful canon since it enables shorthand reference to be made to involved descriptions in other documents. It can create major merchantability problems, however, if the instrument referred to is not recorded and hence not available for title search.

8.   If an exception in a deed is erroneously described, the conveyance is good for the whole tract and title to all of the land passes. Frequently, the grantor will convey Blackacre "except for" a described area. If the description of the exception is faulty, it could be argued that the entire deed should fail but this canon would sustain the larger grant at the expense of the grantor who made the error.

9.   When a tract of land is bound by a monument which has width, such as a highway or a stream, the boundary line extends to the center, provided the grantor owns that far, unless the deed manifests an intention to the contrary.[49] The converse of this canon would lead to undesirable policy results. Suppose *A*, who owns to the center of a highway, conveys to *B*, but the description uses the edge of the road as one boundary. Years pass and the highway is vacated so that the easement of public use is removed. At this point, the narrow strip of land becomes valuable due to the discovery of oil or a change in the direction of urban growth. Who owns the strip? If the parties thought of it at all, they probably intended to transfer whatever land the grantor owned since the retention of a strip under an existing highway would be unreasonable. To prevent endless litigation over narrow strips and gores of land, the courts, in general, have followed the rule stated above.

10.   A description in a deed includes the appurtenances to the tract even though they are not specifically mentioned in the deed.[50] Normally, only that portion of the land passes to the

49.   Bowers v. Atchison, T. and S. F. Ry. Co., 119 Kan. 202, 237 P. 913, 42 A.L.R. 228 (1925).

For an excellent recent discussion of this canon and the exceptions to it

see City of Albany v. State of New York, 28 N.Y.2d 352, 321 N.Y.S.2d 877, 270 N.E.2d 705 (1971).

50.   Stockdale v. Yerden, 220 Mich. 444, 190 N.W. 225 (1922).

grantee which is specifically described in the deed.   However, there are interests in the land which are appurtenant to the described tract in such a way that they have no existence apart from their parasitical attachment to the host premises.   Thus, if *A* owns Blackacre and has an access road across Whiteacre to the highway, a conveyance of Blackacre to *B* will include the appurtenant easement even though not described in the conveyance.[51]

A study of the canons will reveal that they overlap in their statements of law and that some of them are contradictory. Moreover, it should be clear that any one of them will yield to a clear manifestation of intent, which is always the courts' major guideline.   Even so, they serve a useful purpose, if only as a point of departure, and do give some degree of predictability in an uncertain area of the law.

Two additional points should be brought to your attention. Even though the description in the deed is unambiguous it may no longer state the true boundaries of the land.   The parties may have orally agreed to a new fence line, built the fence, and treated it as the boundary for a long period of time.   Thus, the doctrine of acquiescence may have settled a boundary that is, in fact, different from that shown by the records.[52]   Only a physical inspection of the premises and, perhaps, a survey can clarify this situation.   The Statute of Limitations may affect the case also since title to land not described in the deed may have been acquired by adverse possession.[53]

Occasionally, the description is so general that a look at the deed tells you little, yet the intent of the parties is clear.   Thus, a conveyance of "all lands and real estate belonging to the said party of the first part, wherever the same may be situated," has been sustained.[54]   A more difficult problem is the conveyance of a stated number of acres out of a much larger tract, without indicating where the land is located in the larger area.   This little gem has received a variety of judicial reactions, ranging from a determination that the conveyance was void because too indefinite and uncertain.[55] to a finding that an undivided interest in the whole was transferred, making the grantor and the grantee tenants in common of the land.[56]   An interesting mid-point was reached where the description called for "one acre and a half in the northwest *corner* of section five."   This was held to mean a

51. For further treatment of easements see p. 335, infra.

52. Provonsha v. Pitman, 6 Utah 2d 26, 305 P.2d 486 (1957).

53. Gregory v. Thorrez, 227 Mich. 197, 269 N.W. 142 (1936).

54. Pettigrew v. Dobbelaar, 63 Cal. 396 (1883).

55. Harris v. Woodard, 130 N.C. 580, 41 S.E. 790 (1902).

56. Morehead v. Hall, 126 N.C. 213, 35 S.E. 428 (1900).

square of that quantity in the corner since the governmental survey laid out the state in rectangular forms.[57]

Even this brief discussion should be sufficient to establish the truth of the earlier statement that the courts struggle to uphold the validity of a deed where at all possible. The lawyer, as draftsman and property planner, should strive for accuracy and certainty, but the lawyer as litigator must realize that he can build a successful case on precious little, if the intent can be established.

SECTION 4. THE ESCROW AGREEMENT

The sale of real property can be conducted without the use of an escrow agreement. In rural areas and in smaller communities it is not usually involved because the parties know and trust each other and the title questions tend to be less complex. In big metropolitan centers it is much more likely to be a part of the transaction and frequently is as common as the contract and the deed. Also, an understanding of escrow will throw considerable light on the always troublesome issue of delivery. For these reasons, plus the fact that escrow usually receives scant treatment in basic property texts, an extended discussion is included here.[58]

For at least five centuries, the escrow has served as a convenient mechanism for closing real estate transactions.[59] The use of this familiar device involves the deposit of a deed or other document with a third party to be held by the latter pending performance of certain conditions. When those conditions have been

57. Bybee v. Hageman, 66 Ill. 519 (1873).

58. The rest of the material on escrow is taken, in edited form, from an article, "Escrows—Their Use and Value," by John Mann, formerly associate general counsel of the Chicago Title and Trust Company. This article was first published in 1949 University of Illinois Law Forum 398 as a part of a symposium on real estate transactions. At that time the author of this text was faculty editor of the Law Forum. The article states so clearly the principles called for at this point that it seemed wiser to use it, with the author's permission, than to draft a new statement. Certain changes have been made in the text and many of the copious footnotes have been omitted.

59. The practice of depositing deeds as escrows was recognized by the English common law courts at least as early as the first half of the fifteenth century. 4 Tiffany, The Law of Real Property, § 1052 (3rd ed. 1939). The general subject of escrows is dealt with by early law commentators. Coke, Commentary Upon Littleton 36a (1628); Sheppard's Touchstone *58–59 (7th ed. by Hilliard 1820).

performed, the third party is authorized to deliver the deed or other document to the person then entitled thereto.

Perhaps the simplest illustration of such an escrow transaction is the deposit by the vendor of his deed with a third party to be delivered over to the purchaser upon payment of the purchase price. Thus a nonresident vendor of an Illinois farm may forward his deed to an Illinois bank or trust company in the city where the purchaser resides with instructions to deliver the deed to the purchaser if and when the purchase money has been duly deposited for the vendor's account. In this way the vendor can guard against delivery of the deed without concurrent receipt of the purchase price. Or a vendee who has entered into a contract for the purchase of a home where the purchase price is to be paid in monthly installments over a period of years may insist that the vendor deposit his deed with a bank or trust company to be delivered if and when the purchase price has eventually been paid in full. The deed will thus be available for delivery when the last installment is paid some years later, even though the vendor may have died in the interim.

Generally this basic type of escrow transaction between vendor and purchaser, sometimes referred to as a "Deed and Money Escrow," involves conditions relating to title. Thus it may be provided that the third party is to deliver the deed to the purchaser and turn over the purchase money to the vendor only if and when the abstract of title has been examined and approved by the purchaser's attorney. In Cook County, where the great volume of instruments continuously passing through the recorder's office makes it impossible to check the status of a title as of any current date, the third party is frequently authorized to record the vendor's deed as soon as the purchase money has been deposited by the purchaser and before any investigation has been made with respect to title. In addition to the purchase money, the purchaser also deposits with the third party a quitclaim deed back to the vendor. After the vendor's deed has been recorded, a title examination is made up to and including the recording of that deed, and if the title is ready to be guaranteed in the purchaser or is otherwise approved, the third party disburses the purchase money to the vendor and returns the quitclaim deed to the purchaser. If the title cannot be guaranteed or is not found good in the purchaser, the third party records the latter's quitclaim deed in order to put the vendor back in status quo and returns the purchase money to the purchaser.

There may, of course, be many variations in the form of a "Deed and Money Escrow," depending upon the facts of the particular case. For example, the third party is frequently authorized to use a part of the purchase money in discharging liens and encumbrances on the property so that the purchaser will receive an unencumbered title, as agreed.

Another common type of escrow transaction is that known as a "Money Lender's Escrow." In general this involves deposit of the proceeds of a mortgage loan with a third party to be disbursed as directed when satisfactory evidence has been furnished showing the mortgage to be a valid first lien. This type of escrow transaction not only provides the mortgagee with a convenient method of protecting its interests, but it may also be used to advantage by an owner who has made a mortgage loan for the purpose of refunding an existing mortgage or of paying accumulated taxes and special assessments, judgments, mechanic's liens, or other encumbrances on the property. . . . [60]

The foregoing illustrate only a few of the varied forms which escrow transactions may assume.[61] In essence, however, they involve as their basic framework the deposit of deeds and other documents with a third party to be delivered upon the performance of specified conditions.

It is well settled, of course, that the use of escrows is not restricted to real estate transactions. Instruments other than deeds for the conveyance of real estate may legally be deposited as escrows.[62] Indeed, the Illinois Supreme Court has said that "the term 'escrow,' though usually applied to deeds, is equally applicable to all written instruments." [63] This section, however, is limited to a discussion of "escrows" in relation to real estate transactions. It deals entirely with the escrow as a device for the closing of sales of real estate and the transfer of title between vendors and purchasers.

60. An extended discussion of a "Deed and Money, Proceeds-of-Loan Escrow" is omitted.

61. A very common type of transaction used in Cook County in closing sales of real estate is that known as the "Joint Order Escrow." Here the contract for the sale of real estate and the earnest money are deposited with a bank or trust company, subject to the joint direction of the parties in interest. The vendor is thus assured that in event the transaction fails, the contract will not be recorded, clouding his title, and the purchaser is assured that in event the deal fails, the earnest money will be available for repayment to him.

62. The term has been applied, although technically somewhat inaptly, it is said, to money deposited to be held until the performance of a condition. Nash v. Normandy State Bank, 201 S.W.2d 299 (Mo. Sup.Ct.1947). Compare American Service Co. v. Henderson, 120 F.2d 525 (4th Cir. 1941).

63. Main v. Pratt, 276 Ill. 218, 224, 114 N.E. 576, 578 (1916).

A. TERMINOLOGY

An "escrow" has been defined to be "any written instrument which by its terms imposes a legal obligation, and which is deposited by the grantor, promisor or obligor, or his agent, with a stranger or third party, to be kept by the depositary until the performance of a condition or the happening of a certain event and then to be delivered over to the grantee, promisee or obligee." [64] It thus appears that the term "escrow" in its strict technical sense characterizes the instrument while it is being held by the third party awaiting performance of the condition upon which it is to be delivered. An instrument for the conveyance of real estate while so held on deposit is not accurately speaking a deed because it has not been completely delivered. It is, on the contrary, an "escrow." Thus it has been said that an escrow differs from a deed only in respect to its delivery.[65]

Present-day usage, however, would seem to justify some enlargement of this technically correct terminology. Both judges and lawyers alike so commonly refer to "deeds" being deposited as escrows that this convenient form of expression would now seem to have the sanction of common usage. Furthermore, the term "escrow" is often used in a broad sense to describe the general arrangement under which an instrument is deposited with a third person to be delivered upon the performance of a condition. Thus instead of speaking of an instrument being deposited "as an escrow," it is often said today that it is deposited "in escrow." It has likewise become common usage to refer to the parties as "creating an escrow" for the purpose of closing a real estate transaction. There would appear to be no reason why this modern and enlarged use of the term "escrow" should lead to any confusion or misunderstanding.

64. Johnson v. Wallden, 342 Ill. 201, 206, 173 N.E. 790, 792 (1930).

65. Fitch v. Bunch, 30 Cal. 208, 212 (1866). In his Commentaries, Blackstone said: "A delivery may be either absolute, that is, to the party or grantee himself; or to a third person, to hold till some conditions be performed on the part of the grantee; in which last case it is not delivered as a *deed*, but as an *escrow*; that is, as a scroll or writing, which is not to take effect as a deed till the conditions be performed; and then it is a deed to all intents and purposes." 2 Bl. Comm. 307 (1765).

The third-party depositary is sometimes called the "escrow agent" or "escrowee." [66] The directions to the depositary are frequently characterized as the "escrow agreement." [67]

B. WHY ESCROWS ARE USED

Inasmuch as the escrow has been so long used as a convenient device for closing sales of real estate between vendors and purchasers, it is obvious that it possesses certain practical advantages. Some of these may be enumerated as follows:

1. The use of an escrow renders the transaction less likely to "fall through." The sale in its material aspects is very largely executed by one or both of the parties at the time the contract is signed or shortly afterwards. Only mechanical details are left to be carried out through the instrumentality of the third-party escrowee.

2. Where an escrow is not employed, death of the vendor after the contract of sale has been executed but before the transaction has been finally closed often raises complications with respect to the subsequent execution of a proper deed. A judicial proceeding may even be necessary in such a case.[68] However, where the vendor has executed a deed and deposited it as an escrow during his lifetime, the escrowee may, notwithstanding the grantor's death, properly deliver the deed upon performance of the conditions, and a deed so delivered will operate as a valid conveyance to the purchaser.[69]

---

66. The term "escrowee" is probably to be preferred over "escrow agent" inasmuch as there seems to be a growing tendency to regard the third-party depositary as being in effect a trustee. Dodson v. National Title Ins. Co., 159 Fla. 371, 31 So.2d 402 (1947); Tomasello, Jr., Rec'r, v. Murphy, 100 Fla. 132, 129 So. 328 (1930); Stark v. Chicago Title and Trust Co., 316 Ill.App. 353, 45 N.E. 2d 81 (1st Dist. 1942); Moslander v. Beldon, 88 Ind.App. 411, 164 N.E. 277 (1928); Nash v. Normandy State Bank, 201 S.W.2d 299 (Mo.Sup.Ct. 1947); Levin v. Nedelman, 141 N.J. Eq. 23, 55 A.2d 826 (1947); Farago v. Burke, 262 N.Y. 229, 186 N.E. 683 (1933); 19 Am.Jur., Escrow, § 13 (1939). And see Squire v. Branciforti, 131 Ohio St. 344, 2 N.E.2d 878 (1936).

67. This terminology is used in Clodfelter v. Van Fossan, 394 Ill. 29, 37, 67 N.E.2d 182, 183 (1946). And see Home Insurance Co. v. Wilson, 210 Ky. 237, 241, 275 S.W. 691, 692 (1925).

68. Ill.Rev.Stat. ch. 29, §§ 2–8 (1973).

69. The conveyance will in such a case be sustained as against a claim that the grantor's death terminated the escrowee's authority to make a valid delivery, on the theory that the deed relates back to and takes effect as of the time of its original deposit with the escrowee. The deed would also be sustained on like

3. If an escrow is used, the concurrent acts involved in a sale of real estate can ordinarily be performed in such a manner as to protect more adequately the interests of both vendor and purchaser. Thus where a sale is closed without an escrow and the vendor delivers a deed to the purchaser and receives the latter's check (frequently large) in return, there is sometimes a lurking fear in the mind of the vendor, which he may hesitate to express, that the check may not clear. It is a simple matter, however, to provide at the outset in an escrow agreement that the purchaser's check be cashed by the escrowee and the deed delivered only when the check has cleared. The utility of the escrow where problems of concurrent performance are involved can also be illustrated by the situation which arises where current property taxes are to be prorated between the parties but the amount of the tax bill has not been ascertained at the time the sale is closed. If a final adjustment is made on the basis of the known taxes for the preceding year, one party will actually lose if the current tax bill when later rendered should differ from that of the preceding year. There generally is a variance, and where a large transaction is involved, the loss could be substantial. The parties may be required, however, under the terms of an escrow agreement to leave a sufficient amount on deposit with the escrowee to cover the current tax bill when it comes out. The bill can then be paid by the escrowee, and the excess remaining in its hands can be so distributed as to adjust the rights of the parties exactly.

4. Particularly is the escrow convenient in closing complex real estate transactions involving the interests of a number of different parties. For example, an escrow may be used by a purchaser as a convenient means of borrowing money on the security of property he is about to acquire and of using the proceeds of the loan as a part of the purchase price.[70] It may, as already indicated, be used to consummate a four-party transaction whereby an existing mortgage is replaced by a new mortgage concurrently with the completion of the sale between vendor and purchaser. It may be used to advantage in closing a transaction looking to the consolidation of numerous titles into one ownership. In general the escrow is a particularly convenient closing device in that type of case where a clearing house is needed for involved real estate transactions.[71]

reasoning in event of the grantor's subsequent incompetency.

70. In such a situation the seller is willing to convey, provided he receives the purchase money. The mortgage lender, who is supplying a substantial part of the purchase money, is willing to pay out the proceeds of the loan, provided he receives a valid title. Use of the escrow assures each party he will receive that which his particular interest in the transaction requires.

71. In fact it would seem that the lawyer might well give consideration to the use of an escrow when planning the mechanical procedure for closing any complicated trans-

5. The use of the escrow often proves of advantage to the real estate broker by relieving him of mechanical details, which he might otherwise be expected to perform. Where an escrow is used, the earnest money, which would ordinarily be held by the broker, can be deposited with the escrowee; and at the same time, provision can be made in the escrow agreement under which the broker will still be authorized in effect to look to the earnest money for the payment of his commission. The broker is thus relieved of the responsibility and clerical detail of maintaining the earnest money as a separate trust account.

6. In a large county such as Cook, where the volume of daily transactions in the recorder's office is so great that it is physically impossible to ascertain the actual state of a title at any precise current moment, the use of an escrow may be required in order to make certain that the purchaser's interests are protected. In a smaller county it is often possible for the parties to meet at the courthouse, check the records in the recorder's office and in the offices of the clerks of the circuit and county courts from the date of the last abstract continuation down to the current moment so as to make certain that nothing recent has occurred to affect the vendor's title, and thereupon close the transaction forthwith and record the deed to the purchaser. Under such circumstances the purchaser can be reasonably sure, in most instances, that his interests have been protected against any last minute changes in title. In Cook County, however, the volume of daily business at the county courthouse is so great that it is impossible to ascertain from the records the status of a title as of any current point of time. There, as previously indicated, this situation is frequently met by use of the escrow, the escrowee being authorized to record the deed to the purchaser as soon as the purchase money is in its hands but before it is disbursed to the grantor. The title can then be later checked to include the actual recording of the deed, and when title is ready to be guaranteed in the purchaser or is otherwise approved, the escrowee is authorized to disburse the purchase money to the vendor. A quitclaim deed from the purchaser back to the vendor is customarily deposited with the escrowee to be recorded in event the title should not be found good in the purchaser. In the absence of such an arrangement, a purchaser who pays the purchase money to the vendor and receives the vendor's deed in concurrent transactions must necessarily be without positive knowledge at the

action, whether one involving real estate or not, particularly where a number of interests are involved. Thus the escrow has often been used to advantage in working out complex compromises of pending litigation where the concurrent adjustment of various adverse interests is required.

time of such payment as to the condition of the record title during the highly important interval of time immediately preceding the completion of the sale.

C. SELECTION OF THE DEPOSITARY

One of the first questions presented to a vendor and a purchaser who desire to close the sale by means of an escrow is the selection of an escrowee. In general it would seem clear that the escrowee selected should be a third party who is a stranger to the transaction.

The Illinois Supreme Court has said that the "rule is established in this State that a deed cannot be delivered to the grantee as an escrow, to take effect upon a condition not appearing upon the face of the deed, but such deed becomes absolute at law unless delivery is made to a stranger." [72]   In the early case of Price v. Pittsburg, Ft. Wayne and Chicago R. R. Co.,[73] it was contended that deeds to a railroad company had been deposited as escrows with an attorney for the company to be delivered only upon the performance of certain conditions. The Illinois Court held, however, that since the deposit had not been made with a stranger but with the grantee's attorney, the deeds took effect immediately. This holding does not appear to have been overruled or modified by subsequent decisions.[74]

It is true that the modern tendency seems to be to relax in some measure the rigidity of the "third-party stranger" rule,[75] and delivery of a deed as an escrow to the attorney who advised the grantor and drew the deed for him has in some cases been sustained.[76] In order to eliminate any possible question, however, it would appear to be the prudent course for the parties to select a disinterested third party as escrowee who is neither the agent nor attorney for either vendor or purchaser.

72. Szymczak v. Szymczak, 306 Ill. 541, 546, 138 N.E. 218, 220 (1923).

73. 34 Ill. 13 (1864).

74. See Clark v. Harper, 215 Ill. 24, 74 N.E. 61 (1905).

75. Gronewold v. Gronewold, 304 Ill. 11, 136 N.E. 489 (1922). And see Levin v. Nedelman, 141 N.J.Eq. 23, 55 A.2d 826 (1947); 19 Am.Jur., Escrow, § 15 (1939); Note, 11 A.L. R. 1174 (1921).

76. Van Epps v. Arbuckle, 332 Ill. 551, 164 N.E. 1 (1928).

D. REQUIREMENTS AS TO WRITINGS

Another important preliminary problem which may arise where a sale of real estate is to be closed by means of an escrow relates to the nature and extent of the writings or memoranda necessary in order to meet the requirements of the Statute of Frauds.

The Illinois rule is that a binding and irrevocable escrow between a vendor and purchaser must be based on a contract of sale between those parties which is enforceable under the Statute of Frauds. The Illinois Supreme Court has held that in the absence of such a contract, a deposit by the vendor with a third party of a deed in ordinary form for the conveyance of the real estate to be delivered to the purchaser upon payment of the purchase price constitutes a mere revocable transaction only, and the vendor may, under such circumstances, cancel the instructions to the third party and recall the undelivered deed at any time before there has been a performance by the vendee sufficient to take the case out of the Statute.[77] Some commentators have criticized this view on principle,[78] but it, nevertheless, appears to be in accord with the weight of authority from other jurisdictions.[79]

77. Johnson v. Wallden, 342 Ill. 201, 173 N.E. 790 (1930); Main v. Pratt, 276 Ill. 218, 114 N.E. 576 (1916); Kopp v. Reiter, 146 Ill. 437, 34 N.E. 942 (1893). See also Mode v. Whitely, 30 F.Supp. 129 (D.C.Ill.1939). It is indicated by the language in Main v. Pratt, supra, and Johnson v. Wallden, supra, that this principle would not apply to the situation where a deed is delivered to a third person with instructions to deliver it to the grantee therein named upon the happening of an event certain to occur, such as the death of the grantor. In the latter type of case, the decisive issue of whether the grantor did or did not intend to reserve control over the deed at the time it was delivered to the third person may be shown by what the grantor said and did at the time. McReynolds v. Miller, 372 Ill. 151, 22 N.E.2d 951 (1939); Johnson v. Fleming, 301 Ill. 139, 133 N.E. 667 (1922).

78. Aigler, Is a Contract Necessary to Create an Effective Escrow?, 16 Mich.L.Rev. 569 (1918); Comment, Aigler, Necessity of Valid Contract to Support Escrow, 15 Mich.L.Rev. 579 (1917). Compare, however, Bigelow, Conditional Deliveries of Deeds of Land, 26 Harv.L.Rev. 565, 567–75, 578 (1913). See, in general, Ballantine, Nature of Escrows and Conditional Delivery, 3 Ill.L.Bull. 3, 14–18 (1920); Ballantine, Delivery in Escrow and the Parol Evidence Rule, 29 Yale L.J. 826, 830–32 (1920); Note, 17 Minn.L.Rev. 817 (1933).

79. Ballantine, Nature of Escrows and Conditional Delivery, 3 Ill.L. Bull. 3, 14–18 (1920). In this article (pp. 15, 16), Dean Ballantine observed: "Tiffany says that the view that a contract is necessary to a conditional delivery 'has no considerations of policy or convenience in its favor. No doubt the courts have been influenced in their present tendency to require a contract to uphold escrows by an instinctive hostility to this method of evading the statute of frauds and the parol evidence rule. There is a strong policy against having contracts and conveyances of land rest any more than is necessary in

It has also been held that a deed in ordinary form does not in and of itself supply the necessary written memorandum.[80]

A further question, however, still remains. Is it essential in such a case that the instructions to the third-party escrowee also be reduced to writing and signed by the latter?

While this question does not appear to have been fully discussed in the Illinois decisions, yet in Osby v. Reynolds [81] the Illinois Supreme Court pointed out that it was "well settled that the conditions upon which a deed is delivered in escrow may be proved by parol evidence." That statement is not, it would seem, inconsistent with the Illinois holdings previously mentioned [82] to the effect that an enforceable escrow for the closing of a sale of real estate must rest on a contract between the vendor and purchaser enforceable under the Statute of Frauds.[83] The agreement between the vendor and purchaser which fixes the basic rights of those contracting parties may be distinguished, it seems, from the escrow arrangement which merely provides the mechanics by which those basic rights are to be carried out.

This distinction was long ago pointed out by Mr. Chief Justice Ryan of the Wisconsin Supreme Court in the following apt language:

"I have no doubt that an *escrow* may be proved by parol. The difficulty here is not in the proof of the alleged *escrow*, but in the proof of the contract of sale and purchase itself. When there is a valid contract under the statute, the papers constituting it, or executed in compliance with it, may be delivered in *escrow*, and the *escrow* may be proved by parol. But the validity of the *escrow* rests on the validity of the contract; and the validity of the contract rests on the statute." [84]

It would seem, therefore, that in view of the above-mentioned principle a vendor and a purchaser should be able to create by parol a valid and binding escrow agreement with a third-party escrowee, under which a deed deposited by the vendor as an escrow is to be delivered to the purchaser upon the performance of certain conditions—provided, of course, that the rights of the vendor and purchaser have been definitely fixed by a written

parol, or having title depend upon the performance of unwritten conditions.' "

80. Cases cited under note 77 supra.

81. 260 Ill. 576, 583, 103 N.E. 556, 559 (1913) citing 1 Devlin, The Law of Real Property and Deeds, § 312a (3d ed. 1911).

82. Note 77 supra.

83. Stanton v. Miller, 58 N.Y. 192 (1874); Akers v. Brooks, 103 Okl.

98, 229 P. 544 (1924); McLain v. Healy, 98 Wash. 489, 168 P. 1 (1917); Nichols v. Oppermann, 6 Wash. 618, 34 P. 162 (1893); Jozefowicz v. Leickem, 174 Wis. 475, 182 N.W. 729 (1921); Campbell v. Thomas, 42 Wis. 437, 24 Am.Rep. 427 (1877).

84. Campbell v. Thomas, supra note 83.

agreement between themselves sufficient to meet the requirements of the Statute of Frauds.

There appear to be strong practical considerations, however,
why the directions to the escrowee should be reduced to writing.

In the first place, it is doubtful whether a responsible escrowee would consent to act unless its duties were clearly and
specifically defined by written instructions. The sound view undoubtedly is that aside from the proposition that an enforceable
escrow agreement may rest in parol, nevertheless, where such
an agreement has been reduced to writing and is neither ambiguous nor uncertain, parol evidence is inadmissible to modify or
vary its terms.[85] Hence where the instructions to the escrowee
have been reduced to writing, the latter is in a position to rely on
such written instructions as specifically defining and limiting its
duties and responsibilities. Without instructions in writing,
misunderstanding and uncertainty with respect to the escrowee's
duties might well result, and a responsible escrowee would doubtless insist upon obviating such possible difficulties.

In the second place, this effect of written directions to obvi-
ate possible misunderstanding and uncertainty with respect to
the escrowee's duties likewise operates to the benefit of the vendor and the purchaser. An escrowee, in reasonable doubt as to
the proper performance of its duties, is not required to decide close
questions at its own risk.[86] It is accordingly to the interests of
both vendor and purchaser to have the duties of the escrowee
clearly and certainly defined in writing since that will tend to
eliminate the possibility of delay and expense which would likely
ensue if a controversy over the exact terms of the directions to
the escrowee should make it necessary for the latter to resort to
a judicial proceeding for a determination of its rights and duties.

Finally, written instructions to the escrowee tend to mini-
mize any risk that the vendor and the purchaser may inadvertently run afoul of the Statute of Frauds. It is easy enough in
theory to differentiate between the contract of sale, which must
be evidenced by writing to satisfy the Statute, and the incidental
instructions to the escrowee, which may rest in parol. In actual
practice, however, there is always the lurking danger that the

85. Clodfelter v. Van Fossan, 394
Ill. 29, 67 N.E.2d 182 (1946); Note,
49 A.L.R. 1529 (1927). In Colorado
Title & Trust Co. v. Roberts, 80
Colo. 258, 259, 250 P. 641 (1926),
the court said: "Defendant claims
that the rule against the variation
of written contracts by parol does
not apply to escrow instructions. It
would seem that in reason the rule
ought to be especially beneficial

there. How can a bank holding
perhaps scores of escrows be expected to remember oral instructions given in connection with written ones? We are not willing to
assent to the claim of the defendant
in error."

86. Stark v. Chicago Title and Trust
Co., 316 Ill.App. 353, 45 N.E.2d 81
(1st Dist. 1942). And see Note, 60
A.L.R. 638 (1929).

two may through inadvertence not be kept separate and distinct. A note of warning is sounded in Jozefowicz v. Leickem,[87] wherein the Supreme Court of Wisconsin says:

"To constitute a true escrow the contract of sale must be fully executed and nothing left but the transfer of title when the terms of the escrow are complied with. Those terms, however, cannot embody a substantive part of the contract of sale, resting in parol, though the fact of escrow may be shown by parol."

E. SPECIFIC DIRECTIONS TO ESCROWEE

Regardless of whether the directions to the escrowee are made a part of the contract of sale between the vendor and vendee or whether they are set forth in a separate escrow agreement, it is important that the draftsman should see to it that they are complete, detailed, and specific.

The need for particularity is well illustrated by Ortman v. Kane.[88] The directions to the escrowee were, in that case, incorporated in the basic contract between the vendor and purchaser. This contract, after setting forth the terms and provisions of sale between the vendor and purchaser, recited that a deed had been executed by the vendor and delivered to the third-party escrowee (naming him) together with a copy of the contract. It was provided that the deed should be held by the escrowee in escrow and delivered to the purchaser upon his full compliance with the provisions of this contract. Except for a stipulation that upon default of the purchaser the escrowee was to surrender all papers, including the deed, to the vendor, nothing further was said with respect to any steps to be taken by the escrowee.

The Court pointed out that under these facts, the escrowee was not authorized "to accept the balance of the purchase money or to do anything else in connection with the transaction except deliver the deed after the contract had been complied with" by the purchaser. "The depositary of an escrow," said the Court, "is a special and not a general agent. His powers are limited to the conditions of the deposit."

Ordinarily an important object of an escrow transaction is to authorize the depositary to receive the balance of the purchase money in order that the vendor may be sure that the purchase

---

87. 174 Wis. 475, 478–79, 182 N.W. 729, 730 (1921).

88. 389 Ill. 613, 621, 60 N.E.2d 93, 97 (1945).

money has actually come into its hands for his account before the deed is delivered over to the purchaser. The Ortman case makes it clear, however, that in order to effectuate that purpose, express authority must be conferred upon the escrowee to receive such payment. The same principle would apply, it seems, to other steps to be taken by the escrowee, such as proration of taxes and similar items, return of the deed and other papers to the vendor in certain eventualities, and even the affixing of proper revenue stamps to the deed before it is finally delivered to the purchaser. Each step to be taken by the escrowee should be covered with certainty and particularity.

F. WHEN DEED TAKES EFFECT

Where a sale of real estate between vendor and purchaser is to be closed by means of an escrow, with final delivery of the deed by the escrowee dependent upon the performance of some uncertain future condition, the general rule is that the escrow will have no effect as a conveyance, and no estate will pass until the event has happened and the second delivery has been made, or at least until the grantee has become absolutely entitled to such a delivery.[89]

This general rule is, however, subject to the important qualification that where the condition has been fully performed, and the deed delivered by the escrowee, it will under certain circumstances be treated as relating back to and taking effect at the time of its original deposit as an escrow.[90] Thus the Illinois Su-

---

89. Fitch v. Miller, 200 Ill. 170, 65 N.E. 650 (1902); Skinner v. Baker, 79 Ill. 496 (1875). The sound view appears to be that upon full performance of the condition, title will be regarded as having vested in the grantee notwithstanding a want of formal delivery of the deed by the escrowee. Park Avenue Church v. Park Avenue Colored Church, 244 Ill.App. 148 (1st Dist. 1927); 19 Am.Jur., Escrow, § 25 (1939).

90. In general the doctrine of "relation back" does not come into play unless the condition upon which the instrument was deposited as an escrow has been fully performed. County of Calhoun v. American Emigrant Company, 93 U.S. 124 (1876). Thus where both parties abandon the escrow agreement, a subsequent delivery of the deed will not relate back. Whitney v. Sherman, 178 Cal. 435, 173 P. 931 (1918). And where the grantee wrongfully obtains possession of the instrument held as an escrow, the doctrine of "relation back" will not be applied even though the grantor afterward ratifies the delivery. Mosley v. Magnolia Petroleum Co., 45 N.M. 230, 114 P.2d 740 (1941); Carlisle v. National Oil & Development Co., 108 Okl. 18, 234 P. 629 (1924). And see Illinois Central R. R. Co. v. McCullough, 59 Ill. 166 (1871). However, in Meyers v. Manufac-

preme Court has said that "the instrument will be treated as relating back to and taking effect at the time of its original deposit in escrow, where a resort to this fiction is necessary to give
the deed effect to prevent injustice, or to effectuate the intention
of the parties." [91]

G. INSTANCES OF "RELATION BACK"

The operation of this doctrine of "relation back" can be best
illustrated by reference to certain concrete situations.

Death of grantor. Where the grantor dies before the condition is performed, his death would, if the doctrine of "relation
back" were not employed, operate as a revocation of the escrowee's authority to make a valid delivery to the grantee upon
subsequent performance. Accordingly in such a case, the rule
is universal that the transaction will be effectuated by holding
the conveyance operative as of the time when the deed was originally deposited as an escrow, and the grantee's title will for such
purpose relate back to that date.[92]

Dower of grantor's widow. Likewise, where the grantor dies
before the condition is performed, the doctrine of "relation back"
has been applied to protect the grantee against a claim of dower
by the grantor's widow where such a claim could not have been
properly asserted had the grantor's deed been unconditionally delivered at the time it was deposited as an escrow.[93]

Incompetency of grantor. The doctrine of "relation back" is
also applied to effectuate the escrow transaction where the gran-

turers & Traders Nat. Bank, 335
Pa. 180, 2 A.2d 768 (1938), where
a deed to the purchaser at a tax
sale was deposited by county commissioners as an escrow, to be delivered to the purchaser (who had
also deposited the purchase money)
when title had been adjudged good,
it was held the grantee could, in
view of the doctrine of "relation
back," maintain a suit to confirm
title before final delivery of the
deed.

91. Clodfelter **v.** Van Fossan, 394
Ill. 29, 37, 67 N.E.2d 182, 186 (1946).

92. The authorities generally are collected in a Note, 117 A.L.R. 69, 74–

78 (1938). Some later cases are
Ryckman v. Cooper, 291 Mich. 556,
289 N.W. 252 (1939); Anselman v.
Oklahoma City University, 197 Okl.
529, 172 P.2d 782 (1946); Morris v.
Clark, 100 Utah 252, 112 P.2d 153
(1941), cert. denied 314 U.S. 584, 62
S.Ct. 357 (1941).

93. Bucher v. Young, 94 Ind.App.
586, 158 N.E. 581 (1927); First Nat.
Bank & Trust Co. v. Scott, 109
N.J.Eq. 244, 156 A. 836 (1931);
Vorheis v. Kitch, 8 Phila. 554 (Pa.
1871). Compare Tyler v. Tyler, 50
Mont. 65, 144 P. 1090 (1914), where
the escrow agreement was in the
form of an option to purchase real
estate.

tor becomes incompetent before the condition has been perform-ed.[94]

Death of grantee. Where the grantee dies after the deed has been deposited as an escrow but before the condition has been performed, the doctrine of "relation back" will be applied to sustain the transaction, and the deed may, after the condition has been performed, be delivered by the escrowee to the grantee's heirs.[95]

Conveyance by grantor to a third party. Where the grantor has deposited his deed as an escrow but thereafter, pending performance of the condition, he conveys to a third-party purchaser with notice, it has been held that the doctrine of "relation back" will be applied to protect the title of the grantee under the deed previously deposited as an escrow.[96] However, it appears that the doctrine will not be so applied where the third party to whom the grantor conveys is a bona fide purchaser for value without notice of the escrow.[97]

. . . [98]

"Relation back" for one purpose and not others. The fact that the doctrine of "relation back" is applied for one purpose does not necessarily mean that it must be applied for all other purposes in the same transaction.[99]

The fiction of "relation back" would seem to afford an apt illustration of the flexibility of the common law in adapting itself to practical situations. The escrow has long been a convenient mechanism which serves a useful and practical end.[1] The doctrine of "relation back" is the method by which the common law has exempted that particular transaction from certain general rules governing delivery of instruments so that parties may avail themselves of the escrow as a useful, workable device.

94. This is recognized in Price v. Pittsburg, Ft. Wayne and Chicago R. R. Co., 34 Ill. 13, 34 (1864). Authorities generally are collected in the Note, 117 A.L.R. 69, 80 (1938).

95. Authorities generally will be found in the Note, 117 A.L.R. 69, 79 (1938).

96. Leiter v. Pike, 127 Ill. 287, 20 N.E. 23 (1889); Emmons v. Harding, 162 Ind. 154, 70 N.E. 142 (1904).

97. Heffron v. Flanigan, 37 Mich. 274 (1877); Waldock v. Frisco Lum-ber Co., 71 Okl. 200, 176 P. 218 (1918).

98. The discussion of ten other instances of relation back is omitted since they are simply further illustrations of the basic principle.

99. Stone v. Duvall, 77 Ill. 475, 480–81 (1875).

1. "An escrow fills a definite niche in the body of the law." Squire v. Branciforti, 131 Ohio St. 344, 353, 2 N.E.2d 878, 882 (1936).

H. UNAUTHORIZED DELIVERY AND BONA FIDE PURCHASERS

Where a deed has been deposited as an escrow, the general rule is that unauthorized delivery by the escrowee before the conditions have been complied with conveys no title.[2]

Suppose, however, that the grantee in such a case records the deed, and thereafter the property passes into the hands of an innocent third party who purchases in good faith and for value in reliance on the public records. Is the latter protected notwithstanding the unauthorized delivery? This question is one upon which there is much conflict of authority.[3] There are strong considerations, it would seem, to support the view that the bona fide purchaser should be protected. One well-known commentator, after stating that this is the better view upon principle and the one supported by the weight of authority, advances the following persuasive reasons why the bona fide purchaser should be accorded protection.[4] The first is based on the familiar doctrine that when a loss has occurred which must fall on one of two innocent persons, it should be borne by him who is the occasion of the loss. A deed deposited as an escrow is ordinarily regular on its face and is capable of clothing the grantee with apparent title. Consequently when the maker of such an instrument has voluntarily parted with the possession of it and delivered it into the care and keeping of a person of his own selection, he should be responsible for the use that may in fact be made of it in a controversy subsequently arising between himself and a bona fide purchaser. Second, a contrary view would tend to render titles insecure. Many real estate transactions are today closed by means of escrows with nothing of record to indicate that fact. If a purchaser could acquire such a title only at his peril, the merchantability of real estate generally as an article of daily commerce would be impaired. These considerations should, it is believed, carry weight with the courts.[5]

Aside from the principle just considered, it is to be noted that a grantor may ratify an unauthorized delivery by the es-

2. Tucker v. Kanatzar, 373 Ill. 162, 166, 25 N.E.2d 823, 825 (1940).

See also Blakeney v. Home Owners' Loan Corp., 192 Okl. 158, 135 P.2d 339 (1943) and Clevenger v. Moore, 126 Okl. 246, 259 P. 219, 54 A.L.R. 1237 (1927).

3. 4 Thompson, Commentaries on the Modern Law of Real Property, §§ 3953–3955 (1924).

4. Id. §§ 3954–55.

5. See Tutt v. Smith, 201 Iowa 107, 204 N.W. 294 (1925); Schurtz v. Colvin, 55 Ohio St. 274, 45 N.E. 527 (1896); Note, 16 Calif.L.Rev. 141–46 (1928).

crowee or estop himself by his conduct from questioning such delivery.[6]

6. 4 Thompson, op. cit. supra note 88, § 3959. And see Harris v. Geneva Mill Co., 209 Ala. 538, 96 So. 622 (1923); Home Owners' Loan Corp. v. Ashford, 198 Okl. 481, 179 P.2d 905 (1946); Beck v. Harvey, 196 Okl. 270, 164 P.2d 399 (1944); Hansen v. Bellman, 161 Or. 373, 88 P.2d 295 (1939); Smith v. Goodrich, 167 Ill. 46, 47 N.E. 316 (1897); Illinois Central R. R. Co. v. McCullough, 59 Ill. 166 (1871); Eichlor v. Holroyd, 15 Ill.App. 657 (2d Dist. 1885); Note, 48 A.L.R. 405, 424 (1927). Compare Chicago & Great Western Railroad Land Co. v. Peck, 112 Ill. 408, 443–44 (1885).

Chapter 4

VOLUNTARY TRANSFER BY LEASE

The gift and the sale, providing they are of the full interest in the property, sever the donor-donee and the vendor-purchaser relationship. A new ownership is created as the old one is terminated. The lease stands on a different footing. The lessor merely carves a new estate out of his total interest, creating a non-freehold estate and retaining the reversion. The types of non-freehold estates and their general nature were discussed earlier in order to make the permissible interests in land more meaningful.[1] You should now re-read that portion of the book in order to refresh your memory before proceeding to a more detailed explanation of the modern lease.

Today, leasehold interests are almost as important as fee simple ownership in the property structure of the nation. Not only do millions of people live in rented property, countless farmers operate on leased land, and many small businesses carry on in short-term leaseholds, but some of the largest corporations utilize long-term leasing almost exclusively and many of the nation's largest buildings are constructed on non-freehold estates. The legal principles which govern these wide variety of interests are much the same regardless of the purpose for which the leased land is used. Thus, there is more similarity between the mimeographed nine-month lease which you signed for a student room or apartment and the printed multi-paged lease for a major shopping center than you would normally suppose. Since the lease is both a conveyance of land and a contract it is apparent that the parties can alter the basic principles by provisions in the lease so long as they are not illegal and do not contravene public policy. However, this is a question of draftsmanship and beyond the scope of this book.[2] We are concerned here with the basic principles of real estate leases which apply in those cases where no specific lease provisions are included or with the normal judicial construction of some of the more common clauses.

1. P. 52, supra.
2. There are many excellent materials on the drafting of leases. One short pamphlet which you may want to consult is Friedman, Preparation of Leases (Practising Law Institute, 1955).

SECTION 1. THE SURVIVAL OF THREE PECULIAR DOCTRINES

Before we turn to an analysis of these principles, it should be made clear that landlord-tenant law suffers severely from senility. As Mr. Justice Holmes remarked, "The law as to leases is not a matter of logic in vacuo; it is a matter of history that has not forgotten Lord Coke." [3] As you now know, this is true of most property law but the non-freehold estate appears to have even harder arteries than some of its brethren. This point is illustrated by the survival of three peculiar doctrines—the mitigation of damages rule, the Rule in Spencer's Case, and the Rule in Dumpor's Case. None of the three has its common-law vigor, it is true, but they still manage to get around.

A. MITIGATION OF DAMAGES

It is a basic principle of contract law that damages are compensatory, not punitive. Therefore, the non-breaching party cannot recover damages which he could have averted by reasonable activity on his own part, i. e., he must mitigate or lessen damages. You would assume then, if a tenant were forced to vacate the premises, for whatever purpose, that the lessor would be expected to try to re-rent the property and thus cut down on the rent due from the first tenant. But the lease was also a conveyance of real property and, since the tenant owned a non-freehold estate, it was no concern of the lessor if he chose not to occupy it, i. e., the landlord did not need to mitigate damages but could fold his hands and hold the tenant for rent for the full term. If the lease contained a prohibition on assignment or sub-leasing without the consent of the lessor, the landlord could refuse to accept a new, and apparently satisfactory, lessee even though the original tenant procured him for the lessor. This rule was applied in 1956 in a Minnesota case [4] where the new and reputable tenant was the United States Post Office. The court discussed the rule at some length, admitted that there was contrary authority, and that leading writers had attacked the doctrine, but concluded that it would follow the "majority" rule. [5]

3. Gardiner v. Wm. S. Butler and Co., 245 U.S. 603, 38 S.Ct. 214 (1918).

4. Gruman v. Investors Diversified Services, 247 Minn. 502, 78 N.W.2d 377 (1956).

5. There are persuasive cases to the contrary. See, for example, Wohl v. Yelen, 22 Ill.App.2d 455, 161 N.E. 2d 339 (1959) and Comment, 1960 U. Ill.L.F. 332.

Although the Minnesota case states what is still the prevailing view, the trend is toward the adoption of a mitigation requirement as the effect of contract doctrine because more influential in the leasehold area. Thus, in Wright v. Baumann,[6] the Oregon Supreme Court used strong language favoring the mitigation rule. "Writing in 1925, McCormick predicted that eventually 'the logic, inescapable according to the standards of a jurisprudence of conceptions which permits the landlord to stand idly by the vacant, abandoned premises and treat them as the property of the tenant and recover full rent, will yield to more realistic notions of social advantage which in other fields of the law have forbidden a recovery for damages which the plaintiff by reasonable efforts could have avoided.' We believe that it is time for McCormick's prediction to become a reality." It is true that in Wright v. Baumann the court was dealing with a contract to make a lease, rather than a lease itself, so that the narrow holding could be distinguished, but the dicta is a clear indication of a changing judicial attitude. Similar straws in the wind can be discerned in a wide range of cases going back over a number of years. For example, in Novak v. Fontaine Furniture Co.,[7] the Supreme Court of New Hampshire stated that, "in any case involving a breach of contract the plaintiff must make reasonable efforts to curtail his loss." It then proceeded to decide a surrender case as if the mitigation doctrine applied to leases as well as to contracts generally.

Naturally, there are some good arguments for the peculiar landlord-tenant rule or it would not have survived so long, but the point is that, as a general doctrine, it is archaic. The principal virtue of the rule arises from the fact that a re-entry by the landlord may result in a court later calling this act an acceptance of the tenant's surrender of the premises thus destroying the latter's liability without giving the lessor assurance of a new lessee.[8] So that he will not be caught on the horns of such a dilemma, it is argued that the lessor should be allowed to sit tight and hold the lessee for the full rent. It would seem that a more just solution would be to treat the leasehold as surrendered only where the landlord *clearly* agreed to such a release and require mitigation of damages with a retained action against the lessee for the actual damage suffered.[9]

6. 239 Or. 410, 398 P.2d 119 (1965).

7. 84 N.H. 93, 146 A. 525 (1929).

8. See Kanter v. Safran, 68 So.2d 553 (Fla.1953).

9. For a discussion of the surrender problem see Schnebly, Operative Facts in Surrenders, 22 Ill.L.Rev. 117, 130 (1927).

B.   SPENCER'S CASE

"According to the two propositions declared in Spencer's Case, an assignee of either the reversion or the leasehold estate cannot be held liable for breach of covenant, (1) if the covenant pertained to a thing not *in esse* (in being or existence), unless the covenant was in terms made binding upon assignees, or (2) if the covenant does not touch and concern the land." [10]   This rule involves the running of covenants with the land and attempts to state a test for deciding when successors in interest to the leasehold will be liable for promises made in the original lease.   This "running of the covenants" has caused difficulty throughout the law of property because it binds a party to a promise he never specifically made just because he now owns the property interest in question.   Lacking privity of contract (unless there was an assumption of the promises in the lease), the courts hung the liability on privity of estate.   It was not hard to find the latter in landlord-tenant cases because of the tenure relationship between the parties, and their assignees clearly succeeded to this same tenure. The problem was much greater in conveyances of the fee where covenants for title and restrictive use covenants were involved, but that point will be discussed later.[11]

Spencer's first proposition would bind an assignee to a promise pertaining to a thing not in being only if the lease expressly bound assigns.   Thus, if the lease called for the tenant to build on the land and then repair and maintain the structure, that promise could not be enforced against a successor tenant unless the lease stated it was to be binding on assigns.   To turn the result on a technical use of language seems unduly formalistic to the modern mind and courts now are willing to determine intention from surrounding circumstances and the general "tone" of the lease.[12]   Nonetheless, the old doctrine has some life and it is best to make the intent of the parties clear when drafting the lease.

Spencer's second proposition is very much alive because it still makes good sense.   Regardless of the parties' intentions, the covenants will not run with the land unless they "touch and concern" the land.   What does "touch and concern" mean?   Aye, there's the rub.   Dean Bigelow has been said to have presented a workable test: "If the covenant tends to increase or diminish the rights, privileges, or powers of the tenant in connection with

10.   Burby, Real Property 196 (2d ed. 1954).   Spencer's Case, 5 Co.Rep. 16A, 77 Eng.Rep. 72, was decided in 1583.

11.   Pp. 268 and 347, infra.

12.   Purvis v. Shuman, 273 Ill. 286, 112 N.E. 679 (1916).

the enjoyment of the leased land, then the covenant is one that touches and concerns the leasehold estate, and may be enforced by and against any subsequent assignee of the estate." [13] Opposed to the covenant which meets this test is the collateral or personal promise which does not run with the land. The broad idea is clear enough, even though application to specific cases gets a bit sticky. If the promises are those you would normally expect to find in a lease and if they relate to the subject matter of the lease —a covenant to build on the land, to repair, to pay rent, to renew or extend, etc.—they undoubtedly "touch and concern" the land. If they are abnormal and seem to relate to the personal relationship of the parties rather than the lease relationship—a promise to marry the lessor's daughter or buy ale at his pub—they are collateral. Thus, a covenant by the tenant to pay taxes on the leased property "touches and concerns" the land, while a covenant to pay taxes on other than leased land does not "touch and concern" the estate and cannot be enforced by or against remote parties.[14] However, since rent always runs with the land it is easy enough to provide that the payment of taxes on the unleased land of the lessor is a part of the rent and then it will run. It should be apparent that the great bulk of the promises in leases will run with the land and in the material which follows the "runnability" will be assumed unless there is a statement to the contrary.

C. DUMPOR'S CASE

The Rule in Dumpor's Case [15] has even less to commend it than the other two rules. In that case, the lease contained a condition against assigning without the consent of the lessor. One consent was granted and the lease assigned. The assignee then assigned without consent and the landlord tried to declare a forfeiture of the lease. Probably because the court abhorred a forfeiture, it was held that the condition was entire and that the consent to one assignment ended the condition and made the lease freely assignable. It is true that the policy of the law favors free alienability of interests in land, but there is no reason to apply this policy in the face of the clear intent of the parties. Moreover, the Rule is ridiculously easy to circumvent by giving only a qualified consent, i. e., conditioned on no further assignments,

13. Note 10 supra at 197. Bigelow, The Content of Covenants in Leases, 12 Mich.L.Rev. 639 (1914).

14. Gower v. Postmaster-General, 57 L.T.Rep., N.S. 527 (Ch.Div.1887).

15. 4 Coke 119b, 76 Eng.Rep. 1110 (1603).

so that it is only a trap for the uninitiated. Some courts have held it applies only to *conditions* and not to *covenants* against assignment,[16] since the latter are divisible, but this only further complicates the law by drawing another distinction between conditions and covenants, a matter discussed further on in this section. The Rule was abolished long ago in England [17] but, despite decisions to the contrary,[18] it still has followers in this country.[19]

A good discussion of the typical American reaction is found in Childs v. Warner Bros. Southern Theatres, Inc.,[20] where the court put the Rule in historical perspective. "The Dumpor Case was followed in England and perhaps crossed the Atlantic in the Mayflower and took root in America, because many of the earlier cases in the American Courts followed the reasoning and applied the doctrine announced by the English courts". The court then drew a distinction between single and multiple covenants in a lease, the covenants being multiple if they extended to heirs and assigns. Since in *Childs* the lease did bind heirs and assigns the Rule did not apply and one assignment with consent did not make the lease freely assignable thereafter. Such a technical distinction, turning on the use of the mystical language "heirs and assigns" illustrates the bankruptcy of the Rule. Rather than confuse the issue with distinctions between covenants and conditions, single and multiple covenants, etc., it would seem preferable to simply declare the Rule in Dumpor's case inoperative.

Other examples of outmoded doctrine will be noted in the material which follows, but these three rules are so extreme that they seemed to call for preferential treatment. We now proceed to an analysis of the major principles of the landlord-tenant relationship.[21]

16. Williams v. Dakin, 22 Wend. (N. Y.) 201 (1839); contra: Reid v. Wiessner Brewing Co., 88 Md. 234, 40 A. 877 (1898).

17. 22 and 23 Vict., ch. 35 (1859).

18. Kendis v. Cohn, 90 Cal.App. 41, 265 P. 844 (1928); Investors' Guaranty Corp. v. Thomson, 31 Wyo. 264, 225 P. 590, 32 A.L.R. 1071 (1924).

19. Aste v. Putnam's Hotel Co., 247 Mass. 147, 141 N.E. 666, 31 A.L.R. 149 (1923).

20. 200 N.C. 333, 156 S.E. 923 (1931).

21. Some portion of the material which follows in this section was taken, in edited form, from an article, "Basic Principles of Real Estate Leases," by David Levinson of the Chicago Bar. This article was first published in 1952 University of Illinois Law Forum 321 as a part of a symposium on contemporary real estate leases. At that time, the author of this text was faculty editor of the Law Forum. Major changes have been made in the text to reflect developments over the past two decades, new material has been added, and the footnotes have been materially altered.

SECTION 2. ORIGIN OF THE LANDLORD AND
TENANT RELATIONSHIP

The origin of the law of landlord and tenant, in common with most other property law, was in the feudal system. It arose as a related system to the doctrine of tenure. Under that doctrine, all land was originally derived by a grant from the crown. The word "tenure" defines the relationship created. Before the statute of *Quia Emptores*,[22] each grantee of land in turn might grant his land to others, creating a sub-tenure between himself and his grantee who in turn was required to perform the duties and services to his lord. The statute of Quia Emptores prevented such sub-infeudation and thereafter the grantee of land was to hold of the same person of whom the grantor had held. The statute did not apply when the grantor retained a reversion in the property, i. e., conveyed less than his entire estate. Under these circumstances the relationship created was designated imperfect tenure.[23]

Because the land owners realized that they could exploit their large land holdings best by leasing them to tenant farmers, this practice soon became common and much of the land in England was cultivated by those not owning the land.[24] As is well known, traces of the feudal system still exist and much of its technical language is retained, as well as many of its rules, both arbitrary and otherwise.

Estates for years were not recognized as estates or interests in land by the early feudal law. The lessee had no interest which the law would protect against third persons, nor against even the lessor unless the interest rested in a covenant by deed, in which case if the lessor wrongfully ejected the lessee, the sole remedy of the lessee was by action on the covenant as in the case of any other covenant under seal.

A new writ *(quare ejecit infra terminum)* was introduced about the middle of the thirteenth century, giving the lessee a right to recover possession of the land when wrongfully ejected and not merely damages for breach of covenant. In later years new writs were established giving the tenant additional rights in the land.[25] The modern tenant of a leasehold for a term of years, although not a freehold, now has an interest in the land it-

---

22. 18 Edw. 1, c. 1 (1290).

23. 1 Tiffany, Landlord and Tenant, § 1 (1910).

24. 7 Holdsworth, History of English Law, § 7 (1926).

25. Digby, History of the Law of Real Property 176 et seq. (5th ed. 1897) ; 2 Pollock and Maitland, History of English Law, c. 4, § 4 (2d ed. 1903).

self,[26] and not merely a right by way of contract. However, leasehold estates were and still are considered inferior to estates of freehold. Thus, a life estate, being a freehold, is a larger estate than a term of years, however long.

SECTION 3. CREATION OF THE MODERN LANDLORD AND TENANT RELATIONSHIP

Leasehold estates have been termed "chattels real," classified as personal property, and governed in part by the rules of law pertaining to personal property. Thus, upon the death of a tenant for years the property will pass to his personal representative, who may sell it without an order of court, as is required in cases of freehold estates.[27] Moreover, there is no dower in leasehold estates.[28] The relationship, however, now does have many aspects of real property in that it is an interest in the land itself.[29]

A. CONTRACTUAL BASIS OF THE LEASE

Generally, the landlord and tenant relationship arises from an express contract between the parties, usually called a lease. It does not matter what the instrument is called; if the intent

26. People ex rel. Healy v. Shedd, 241 Ill. 155, 89 N.E. 332 (1909), aff'd Shedd v. People of the State of Illinois ex rel. Healy, 217 U.S. 597, 54 L.Ed. 896, 30 S.Ct. 696 (1909); Leonard v. Autocar Sales and Service Co., 325 Ill.App. 375, 60 N.E.2d 457 (1st Dist. 1945), aff'd 392 Ill. 182, 64 N.E.2d 477 (1946).

27. Jacquat v. Bachman, 26 Ill.App. 169 (2d Dist. 1888).

28. Hayes v. Hayes, 259 Ill.App. 600 (1st Dist. 1931), holding that the inchoate right of dower attaches

to the freehold estate and only to that estate.

29. Much of the "chattel real" concept has been relegated to the legal museum. Statutory changes, not directly related to leaseholds, have reduced the concept to distinctions without meaningful differences. The widespread abolition of dower see, e. g., Ill.Rev.Stat. ch. 3, s. 18 (1973), the changes in statutes governing the administration of estates, etc. have all contributed, willy nilly, to the simplification of the law of land generally.

to create a tenancy was present, a tenancy will have been created. Thus the instrument can be designated a contract, and it might even be agreed in the contract to execute a formal lease thereafter, yet if all the essential terms are present, the instrument will operate to create an interest in the land. The case of Illinois Life Insurance Co. v. Beifeld [30] illustrates this proposition in a rather dramatic fashion. In that case the memorandum showed upon its face that a formal contract of leasing was to be subsequently prepared, and few of the usual covenants and conditions were mentioned as having been agreed upon in the memorandum; nevertheless it was held that since the essential provisions were present, the mere fact that a formal instrument was to be subsequently prepared did not change the result. The court said that if it affirmatively appeared from the language of the memorandum that all terms were not agreed upon, then the instrument could not convey any rights in the land since in such case no agreement in fact would have been reached. In drafting such memoranda it is well therefore to state specifically that no lease is intended until the formal instrument has been executed.

Nor are formal words of hiring or leasing necessary. Whatever is sufficient to show that the owner intends to divest himself of possession and that the proposed tenant intends to come into possession for a definite time and for a fixed rental, amounts to a valid lease. Of course, to these requirements must be added the necessity for a definite agreement as to the extent and bounds of the property leased.[31]

Many terms and conditions other than the essential terms may be incorporated in a lease, dealing with such usual subjects as restrictions on use of the premises, repairs, insurance, taxes, liability of the parties, rights of inspection, holding over, assignment, subleasing, default remedies, and numerous other subjects mentioned later in this chapter, but they are not essential (although, as is well known, highly desirable) since the law of landlord and tenant will supply for the parties the rights and obligations not expressly dealt with by them. Because these rules of law may produce different results than the lessor, lessee, or both may have intended, it is best to execute a formal lease providing for all contingencies then foreseeable. For this reason written leases, even for a small apartment, have become rather formidable documents and the oft-repeated assertion that the contingency not considered is the one that inevitably occurs has been a challenge to those who have drafted written leases, rather than a deterrent to the exercise of legal imagination.

30.   184 Ill.App. 582 (1st Dist. 1914).   31.   Tips v. United States, 70 F.2d 525 (5th Cir. 1934).

Throughout the material which follows the contractual basis of the lease will be stressed.   There has been an almost revolutionary change in American leasehold doctrine over the past decade—a change from stress on property concepts to emphasis on the contractual nature of a lease, at least in residential leases. Although this change might appear to have been legally neutral, it has in fact reversed the time-honored maximum protection for the landlord and brought the tenant into his own.   I used to tell my students that the law of non-freehold estates was essentially the law of the landlord, derived from English common-law judges who were themselves members of the land owning class. This is no longer true and the landlords, like the New York Yankees, have fallen from grace.   When in doubt as to the result, guess that the court will try to sustain the tenant's claim. *O tempore!   O mores!*

This general point is well illustrated by a recent law review article [32] the introductory portion of which reads.

"The concept of a real property lease has been undergoing change throughout the life of Anglo-American jurisprudence; however, this change has often been so slow as to give the appearance of dormancy.   Until recent years real property leases have been encrusted with property law characteristics to such an extent that other characteristics which they may possess have been largely hidden from view.   Yet, there is an aspect of such leases that has been inherent in them for many years and is now beginning to break through to the surface and be recognized and used.   This aspect—the contractual nature of real property leases—forms the subject matter of this article.

"There are two interrelated factors that have affected the concept of a leasehold interest in real property as it exists today. First, the historical setting of a lease has changed from that of rural England, where raw land, devoid of any but the most simple improvements, was leased for agricultural purposes to that of urban America, where space provided by valuable and extensive improvements on the land serves both residential and commercial needs in our society.   The leased farm and pasturage of our English and American ancestors has largely given way to the multistoried apartment complex or office building or industrial plant of late-twentieth century America.

"Second, the property characteristic of a lease of real estate was the one which best served the needs of our recent ancestors when they were concerned with the leasing of unimproved land

32. Hicks, The Contractual Nature of Real Property Leases, 24 Baylor L.Rev. 443 (1972). This article is based on an LL.M. thesis which

Associate Professor Hicks wrote under my supervision at the University of Illinois College of Law.

for agricultural purposes or for pasturage. Although this characteristic of a lease was not the first it possessed, having gone through earlier evolutionary stages, it is the characteristic which has been carried into the twentieth century and with which our present society must cope. Although our society has changed dramatically from that known by our recent ancestors, the leasehold in real property, as a functional tool, has not kept pace. More and more the judicial, educational and professional segments of the legal profession are calling for a redefinition of a real property lease to include a contractual aspect in order that this legal tool may better serve our present needs.

"There have been three sources injecting contract principles into real property leases. The first source has been public policy, used by the judiciary to mold common law leasehold principles to fit modern day needs. The second source has been federal and state statutes. Some statutes have been directly aimed at real property leases; others, in particular, the Uniform Commercial Code, which is enjoying wide adoption across the United States, have been indirectly affecting attitudes toward leases. The third source has been local ordinances, such as housing codes, that have placed the rights and responsibilities of lessors and lessees in a new light. Each of these sources has been more useful than the others in dealing with certain aspects of leases; yet, all three have been needed for a full development of the contractual nature of real property leases."

B.   IMPLIED LEASES

An express contract is not essential. As in the case of other implied contracts, leases are said to be implied when their terms have not been stated in words. The distinction is not one of legal effect, but of the way in which mutual assent is manifested.[33] Thus the so-called contract implied in fact is a real contract in which the parties manifest assent by acts rather than words. In no case, however, does the law "imply" a tenancy when none in fact exists, that is, where the landlord or tenant or both did not in words or by conduct agree to the occupation of the land. One who enters another's land without his permission is a trespasser, not a tenant, and the court will not imply otherwise. Obviously

---

33.   1 Williston, Contracts, § 3 (Williston and Thompson, revised ed. 1936).

no value is accorded here to those cases where the courts have incorrectly appraised the evidence adduced in the cases. The courts will "imply" a tenancy only where from the evidentiary facts an agreement therefor may be inferred. No attempt will be made to cite opinions dealing with such factual situations since of course each case presents an example only of the variables possible. The rule is illustrated, however, by the case involving the possession under a contract to purchase, where after breach of contract it was held that no tenancy by implication was created.[34]

Perhaps the most common situation in which the relation arises by conduct of the parties (without express agreement) is where the tenant remains on the premises after the termination of a valid lease, usually described by the words "hold-over." Under these circumstances the courts will imply a renewal of the tenancy relationship, provided that there is no showing of a contrary intention on the part of the landlord who has the election of treating the occupant holding over as either a trespasser or a tenant. By the acceptance of rent after the termination of the lease the landlord has been held to have elected to treat the occupant as a tenant. The intent of the former tenant in holding over is not material. Even though he did not intend to renew, he may still be treated as a tenant if the landlord so elects.[35]

The tenancy created by a hold-over will effect a renewal of the lease upon the same terms as the expired lease, so far as they are applicable, and the duration of the term will be for a year and thereafter from year to year,[36] except where the expired lease is for less than a year, in which case the term of the new tenancy will be the same as the previous term. Thus, where the original tenancy was for a period of eleven months, the new tenancy was held to be on an eleven months basis rather than a month-to-month or year-to-year basis.[37] If the landlord notifies his tenant, before the expiration of the lease, that if he continues to occupy the premises he must do so on a different basis, and the tenant holds over, the terms of the hold-over will be those of the original lease as modified by the landlord. The reason for the rule is that the expired lease is only evidence of the agreement between the parties, rather than the contract itself. Such agree-

34. McNair v. Schwartz, 16 Ill. 24 (1854).

35. The landlord cannot be unconscionable in his election, however, and where a tenant made every effort to vacate an apartment but slept there one additional night no new tenancy resulted. Commonwealth Building Corporation v. Hirschfield, 307 Ill.App. 533, 30 N.E. 2d 790 (1940).

36. Goldsborough v. Gable, 140 Ill. 269, 29 N.E. 722 (1892).

37. Heun v. Hanson, 331 Ill.App. 82, 72 N.E.2d 703 (1st Dist. 1947); see also Sinclair Refining Co. v. Shakespeare, 115 Colo. 520, 175 P.2d 389, 171 A.L.R. 1058 (1946).

ment therefore can be changed by a subsequent agreement.[38]
The landlord, because of his rights in the property, can state the
terms of a lease, and to permit the tenant to change the terms,
by merely remaining in possession, would deprive the landlord
of control of his property.[39]

SECTION 4.   STATUTE OF FRAUDS

At common law a lease was valid without a writing.   Section 1 of the Statute of Frauds,[40] first adopted in England, provided in part that all leases for longer than three years not in
writing should have the effect of leases at will only.   Most modern statutes of frauds are essentially the same.   However, under
most statutes, oral leases for a term of one year or less are now
valid.   Thus the Illinois statute provides: "No action shall be
brought to charge any person upon any contract for the sale of
lands, tenements or hereditaments or any interest in or concerning them, for a longer term than one year, unless such contract or
some memorandum or note thereof shall be in writing, and signed
by the party to be charged therewith. . . . "[41]   The courts
hold that a leasehold is an interest in land within the meaning
of this section and thus is within the scope of its terms.[42]
Section 1 of the Illinois statute[43] provides that no action
shall be brought to charge any person upon any agreement not
to be performed within one year.   Because of this section a
verbal lease to begin *in futuro* for a greater period than one year
including the time before the commencement of the term is unenforceable.[44]

The problem last mentioned is not free from difficulty.
While Illinois and many other jurisdictions[45] hold that both the

38.   Sherriff v. Kromer, 232 Ill.App.
589 (1st Dist. 1924).

39.   See, however, Welk v. Bidwell,
136 Conn. 603, 73 A.2d 295 (1950),
where in a periodic tenancy the
court felt the landlord's attempt to
change the terms resulted in a tenancy at sufferance.

40.   An Act for Prevention of Fraud
and Perjury, 29 Car. 2, c. 3, § 1
(1677).

41.   Ill.Rev.Stat. ch. 59, § 2 (1973).

42.   Chicago Attachment Co. v. Davis
S. M. Co., 142 Ill. 171, 31 N.E. 438
(1892).

43.   Ill.Rev.Stat. ch. 59, § 1 (1973).

44.   Leindecker v. Schaeffer, 194 Ill.
App. 508 (1st Dist. 1915).   This appears to be the weight of authority
but there are cases to the contrary.
Williams, Cases and Materials on
the Law of Property 225 (1954).

45.   See, for example, Luster v. Estate of Cohon, 11 Ill.App.3d 608,
297 N.E.2d 335 (1973) and Shaughnessy v. Eidsmo, 222 Minn. 141, 23
N.W.2d 362 (1946).

contract section, requiring all contracts not to be performed within one year to be in writing, and the leasehold section must be met, other well-reasoned decisions take a contrary position. Thus, in Bell v. Vaughn [46] the Arizona Supreme Court held that an oral lease for one year or less was valid even if it began in futuro. With impeccable logic, the Court wrote: "Most leases, and indeed, we may say all, with here and there an exception, take effect in futuro. Farm leases, for instance, are made, as a rule, one, two or three months before commencement of the term. Many of these are for one year, commencing not in praesenti, but on a subsequent day. And in view of the general custom . . . if construed as appellant claims would have but little practical force or value. Verbal leases are made, and the statute contemplates their validity under certain circumstances. And to hold that the year commences to run from the date of the contract, would almost necessarily render invalid all those where the term is for the full year."

Many of the cases turn on statutory construction of the language of the Statute of Frauds, but this can be an arid intellectual exercise and the pragmatic approach of the Arizona Court is probably fairer to both parties. Of course, the result may turn on judicial attitudes toward the Statute of Frauds and strict constructionists, who favor forcing the maximum number of contracts into the written mold, will probably prefer the Illinois view.

SECTION 5. COVENANT FOR QUIET ENJOYMENT

It had been recognized at an early date that the relationship of landlord and tenant gave rise to certain implied covenants on the part of the lessor. These covenants are independent of the contract, and ordinarily include acts by the lessor, those claiming under him, and those claiming under title paramount.[47] Acts of a wrongdoer are not impliedly covenanted against. The reason

---

46. 46 Ariz. 515, 53 P.2d 61, 111 A.L.R. 460 (1935).

47. Title paramount may not be entirely self explanatory. If the landlord has only a life estate, even though he thinks he has a fee simple absolute, his interest, and the tenant's lease, will end with his death. The reversioner or remainderman would have title paramount and could oust the tenant unless the former had signed the lease. Any time the landlord's title fails and one with a superior claim intervenes the tenant has recourse to the covenant for quiet enjoyment because of the theory of title paramount.

for the rule is that if a wrongdoer disturbs the lessee's possession, the latter has his remedies at law against the wrongdoer.   However, if the acts are done by the landlord, those claiming under him, or those claiming under title paramount, the tenant can only redress his wrongs by an action against the landlord.   These principles were stated in the Year Books of Henry VI's reign and have been adhered to ever since.[48]   The covenant for quiet enjoyment is among those implied.

A few jurisdictions will imply a covenant for quiet enjoyment only if the words "demise," "let," or "lease" are used.   According to the weight of authority, however, the covenant arises by operation of law independently of the presence of any particular words in the lease, and therefore it exists even if the contract is not in writing.[49]   This covenant, in common with other implied covenants, is not breached through acts of a stranger, nor is it breached through acts of the sovereign.

The covenant for quiet enjoyment is breached by an eviction. Evictions are divided into two classes: actual eviction and constructive eviction.   In an actual eviction, the tenant must be physically removed from all or a part of the premises.   In an actual eviction of a part of the premises, the tenant may remain in possession of the remaining part but is not required to pay any rent because of the wrongful acts of the lessor.[50]   A constructive eviction is established when it is shown that the landlord in some way has prevented the tenant's enjoyment of his interest in the property.   Generally, the acts must have been of such grave and permanent character as to deny the tenant the enjoyment of his possessory rights.   It is not complete until the tenant, dissatisfied with the condition of the premises, vacates, within a reasonable time, after which his liability for rent ceases, and he also has a cause of action against the landlord for breach of covenant.[51]

48.   7 Holdsworth, History of English Law 251 et seq. (1926).

49.   Cohen v. Hayden, 180 Iowa 232, 163 N.W. 238 (1917).

In at lease one state, New Jersey, there is no implied covenant of quiet enjoyment in any lease, oral or written.   Adrian v. Rabinowitz, 116 N.J.L. 586, 186 A. 29 (1936). Of course, the parties may include an express covenant of quiet enjoyment and would normally do so.

50.   See Fifth Avenue Building Co. v. Kernochan, 221 N.Y. 370, 117 N.E. 579 (1917) for an expanded treatment of this point.

See also Mr. Justice Holmes' explanation of the reason for this rule in Smith v. McEnany, 170 Mass. 26, 48 N.E. 781 (1897).   Note this does not mean that the tenant could occupy a portion of the premises without obligation.   While not liable for rent under the lease because of the landlord's partial eviction, he would be answerable in quasi-contract for any benefit conferred.   In fact, this might not be too dissimilar from an apportionment of the rent, provided the rent was roughly the same as the fair market value for a comparable non-freehold estate.

51.   Jackson v. Paterno, 58 Misc. 201, 108 N.Y.S. 1073 (1908).

SECTION 6. COVENANT TO DELIVER POSSESSION

Another implied covenant on the part of the lessor is with respect to delivery of possession of the premises at the beginning of the term. In a majority of jurisdictions this covenant is very limited, the extent of it being to confer upon the lessee the right to possession. The lessor covenants that neither he, nor one holding title paramount will withhold possession from his lessee. The covenant does not extend to a wrongdoer including a former tenant who is wrongfully holding over, since the lessor gives to his lessee a complete and perfect right of possession to the demised premises and thus has done all that he is required to do by the terms of the lease, absent an express covenant enlarging the landlord's obligation. The tenant assumes the burden of enforcing the right of possession as against wrongful possessors.[52] A few jurisdictions hold, contra to this rule, that it is the landlord's duty to put the tenant in possession. They reason that the implied covenant includes the undertaking that premises shall be open to the tenant's entry.[53]

A lease gives the lessee the right of possession as against the whole world, including the landlord. Any acts of the landlord which tend to violate the exclusive possession of the tenant are wrongful and the latter may recover in an appropriate action against the landlord. If the landlord leases to one and then wrongfully leases the same premises for the same time to another, the second tenant may sue the landlord for breach of covenant of possession, but of course cannot acquire possession unless he is a b.f.p.

52. Hannan v. Dusch, 154 Va. 356, 153 S.E. 824, 70 A.L.R. 141 (1930).

This is the so-called "American" rule and while strictly logical from traditional landlord-tenant principles, it has been much criticized. Certainly, a tenant would expect to get actual possession, not the mere right to legal possession. No tenant would wish to buy a law suit and, of course, he could prevent this result by inserting an express covenant requiring that the landlord put him in actual possession.

53. Adrian v. Rabinowitz, 116 N.J.L. 586, 186 A. 29 (1936), explains the so-called "English" rule. Said the court: "The English rule, so-called, is on principle much the better one. It has the virtue, ordinarily, of effectuating the common intention of the parties—to give actual and exclusive possession of the premises to the lessee on the day fixed for commencement of the term."

SECTION 7. FITNESS OF THE PREMISES

The first edition of this book (1962) contained the follow-ing two paragraphs. They are reprinted here because they correctly state traditional doctrine and still represent the state of the law in many jurisdictions. Everywhere, however, this area of landlord-tenant law is in a state of flux, under the im-pact of recent court decisions and statutory changes. New principles, based on contractual concepts, are letting a breath of fresh air into the stale atmosphere of leasehold law. The remainder of this section will deal with the new principles.

There is no implied covenant on the part of the landlord that the premises at the time of the letting are in tenantable condition, nor that the physical condition of the premises shall remain un-changed during the term.[54] This is especially true where the ten-ant inspects the premises before executing the lease. An excep-tion to this rule occurs in the case of latent defects in which case the landlord is liable if he has knowledge of such defects. Courts hold that a tenant has a right of action against the landlord for injuries resulting from a latent defect only where the tenant can show the following essential elements: (1) that the landlord had actual knowledge of such defect; (2) that the defect was one which the tenant could not be expected to discover upon reason-able inspection, and (3) the landlord failed to disclose his knowl-edge of this defect. The stated theory upon which recovery is based is sometimes that of fraud.[55]

The lessor is not bound to repair the premises unless he has expressly agreed to do so in the lease. The reason for the rule that the landlord is not required to repair the premises, absent a covenant so to do, is that exclusive possession is given to the tenant and that possession excludes the right of the landlord to enter the premises to ascertain and make the necessary repairs. Most printed forms require the tenant to make the necessary re-pairs and give the landlord the right to enter in order to inspect the property, and make the repairs himself in case the tenant does not.

The traditional doctrine, just stated, caused grave problems for the tenant. Since there was no implied covenant of fitness (habitability), the tenant had the "gracious protection" of *caveat emptor* and his eyes were his bargain—not a bad concept

54. Hughes v. Westchester Develop-ment Corporation, 77 F.2d 550 (D.C. Cir.1935).

55. Borggard v. Gale, 205 Ill. 511, 68 N.E. 1063 (1903).

if the parties dealt at arms length and the premises were unimproved agricultural land. Obviously, this gave the landlord a powerful position in large, urban, residential complexes where the lease was essentially a contract of adhesion. The tenant took the landlord's lease, as offered, and had little legal opportunity to complain when the apartment turned out to be egregiously uninhabitable. In theory, he could insist on the protection of express covenants but his economic and social position precluded him from doing so in practice.

The problem was accentuated by the theory of independent covenants. Under contract law, substantial covenants were held to be dependent and, under the doctrine of constructive conditions, performance by one party was held to be a condition precedent to recovery against the other party.[56] Not so in landlord-tenant law. Even if the landlord expressly promised to paint, repair, etc., that was an independent covenant and he could collect the rent while failing to keep his part of the bargain. Of course, the tenant could sue the landlord for breach of the independent covenant but that proved to be a frail reed for most economically pressed tenants. The covenants could be made expressly dependent, i. e., the landlord's promise could be made a condition precedent to the tenants duty to pay rent but this was seldom done since the landlord prepared the lease. Coupled with the lack of any implied covenant of habitability, the tenant was in a precarious position. This deficiency in the law had long been recognized but legal inertia, a devotion to historical doctrine, and sympathy for the landlord's rights blocked any material reform of the law.

There was one traditional escape route for the tenant in particularly harsh situations—the doctrine of constructive eviction. This doctrine allowed the courts to remain consistent with existing theory but still prevent some obvious injustices. Suppose, for example, the landlord expressly promise to provide heat in a multi-story building where only he had access to the furnace. This was an independent promise, for breach of which he could be sued, but the rent was still due. However, if, after protest by the tenant, the leased premises remained too cold for occupancy, the tenant could claim he had been constructively evicted, move out, and contend that no rent was owing because of his constructive eviction.[57] This salved the conscience of the legal purist but was scant solace to the tenant. If he did not move out promptly, he was held to have waived the breach; if

56. See Corbin, Contracts 620–642 (One volume ed., 1952) or Williston, Contracts 695–727 (Students ed., 1938).

57. For a good discussion of constructive eviction see Reste Realty Corp. v. Cooper, 53 N.J. 444, 251 A.2d 268, 33 A.L.R.3d 1341 (1968).

he did move out he acted at his peril since a court might later hold that the landlord's acts, or failure to act, was not so substantial as to amount to constructive eviction, in which case the tenant remained liable for the rent.   The tenant might seek a declaratory judgment before vacating to avoid a portion of the peril, but this was time-consuming and expensive.   Moreover, if this was the tenant's sole recourse there was a tendency to treat every slight dereliction by the landlord as constructive eviction and an excuse for "breaking the lease."   This tendency worked to the disadvantage of landlords as well as tenants and constructive eviction came to be one of the "hoary chestnuts" of the law.

There was an obvious way out of the dilemma, which after all was court created and could be judicially cured.   The courts could treat the lease like all other contracts, except that a nonfreehold estate had been conveyed, and make the covenants dependent and subject to the doctrine of constructive conditions.   Furthermore, the courts could imply covenants of habitability, just as they had long done by implying covenants of fitness for a particular purpose in the sale of goods.   This required overruling old cases and modernizing the law of landlord and tenant.   By the late 1960's and early 1970's, social conditions were ripe for this "bold venture" and a long series of recent cases have been moving in that direction.   The process is still underway but the trend of the developing law is now clear.   Indeed, Professor Roberts refers to it as one aspect of the vanishing law of property[58] and would treat landlord-tenant law today as part of the law of contracts.   Nonsense!   It is still a part of the law of land, hauled kicking and screaming into the twentieth century.

Initial breaches in the dike occurred in the early 1960's as a series of state courts recognized the inadequacies of constructive eviction and allowed a trickle of contract principle to soften the hard clay of property law.[59]   But the dike finally burst under the pressure of a series of cases from the District of Columbia starting in 1968.   In Brown v. Southall Realty Co.[60] the District of Columbia Court of Appeals held a lease to be an illegal contract when certain housing code violations existed at the time the lease was made.   Even though the code violations could have been the subject of separate law suits by the enforcement authorities, as a matter of public policy they made the habitation unsafe and unsanitary so that the tenant, herself, could raise the issue.   If

58. See Roberts, The Demise of Property Law, 57 Cornell L.Rev. 1 (1971).

59. See, for example, Pines v. Perssian, 14 Wis.2d 590, 111 N.W.

2d 409 (1961) through Reste Realty Corp. v. Cooper, 53 N.J. 444, 251 A.2d 268, 33 A.L.R.3d 1341 (1968).

60. 237 A.2d 834 (D.C.App.1968).

the lease was illegal no rent could be collected, independent covenants or no. Wrote Judge Quinn: "Neither does there exist any reason to treat a lease agreement differently from any other contract in this regard."

Brown v. Southall left many questions unanswered, however. Suppose the code violations had occurred after the tenant moved in? Suppose the tenant remained in possession in spite of the violations, would any rent be due? (In *Brown* the tenant had vacated the premises after discovering the violations.) How far would the courts go in implying covenants of habitability?

Many of the questions were answered by Judge J. Skelly Wright in a masterful opinion which is now the leading case on the subject.[61] Code violations occurring subsequent to possession under the lease are sufficient to breach the lease. Part of the tenant's rental obligation had been suspended because of the violations but part of the unpaid rent was indeed owed, as determined by a jury. The landlord is not entitled to a judgment for possession if the tenant pays the partial rent but if he refuses to pay the portion due a judgment for possession will be entered. Finally, wrote Judge Wright: "We now reverse and hold that a warranty of habitability, measured by the standards set out in the Housing Regulations for the District of Columbia, is implied by operation of law into leases of urban dwelling units covered by those Regulations and that breach of this warranty gives rise to the usual remedy for breach of contract."

Judge Wright discussed the history of landlord tenant-law, the changing social climate, and the need for reform to bring the tenants' rights into line with those of the consumers' of personal property. Every student should read the opinion in order to catch the full flavor of modern landlord-tenant law, at least in the field of housing. It remains an open question as to how far these new principles will be incorporated into landlord tenant-law generally, e. g., commercial and business leases, farm leases, etc. Certainly, the rationale is not the same in these latter areas since it is clear that the housing codes have provided the peg on which to hang the hat of implied covenants. Distinctions remain to be drawn but much of the law has been clarified.

The principles enunciated in *Javins* had an immediate impact across the nation. Illinois, which had long followed the traditional view, quickly granted the tenants new rights, based on an implied covenant of habitability arising from the Chicago

61. Javins v. First National Realty Corp., 138 U.S.App.D.C. 369, 428 F.2d 1071, cert. denied 400 U.S. 925, 91 S.Ct. 186, 27 L.Ed.2d 185 (1970).

Building Code. In Jack Spring, Inc. v. Little, et al,[62] the Illinois Supreme Court allowed violation of the implied covenant to be raised as an affirmative defense in a summary dispossession action (forcible entry and detainer) for failure to pay rent. Since, prior to *Jack Spring*, the only relevant issue would have been payment or non-payment of the rent, the decision seems to bring landlord-tenant law into harmony with the new consumerism and provides a formidable weapon for tenant unions and community action groups.

The Illinois Court raised the issue of whether the parties to the lease could waive the protection of an implied covenant of habitability and indicated that they could. This position is directly contrary to dicta in *Javins*, where Judge Wright said: "The duties imposed by the Housing Regulations may not be waived or shifted by agreement if the Regulations specifically place the duty upon the lessor." Unless the courts insist that private agreements to shift the duties are illegal and unenforceable, much of the impact of *Javins* and its progeny will go down the drain since waiver of the implied covenant will rapidly become a stock clause in every landlord's lease.

SECTION 8. WASTE

In the absence of an express agreement, the law imposes on the lessee an obligation to treat the premises in such a way that no injury shall be done to the property during the continuance of the lease. The tenant is thus liable for his negligence in his use of the property. This rule does not require the lessee to make substantial or lasting repairs, but only such repairs as are necessary to prevent waste or decay of the premises.

There are two general types of waste. Voluntary waste consists in the commission of some affirmative act causing injury to the premises, such as wrecking a building, or changing the character of the reversion, this latter under certain circumstances being referred to as meliorating waste. Permissive waste consists in the mere neglect or omission to do that which will prevent injury from decay for want of repairs. Meliorating waste is nevertheless waste although the value of the premises

62. 50 Ill.2d 351, 280 N.E.2d 208 (1972).

is increased, for example, if the tenant removes a small building from the property and replaces it with a large modern building.[63]

The tenant is liable for all acts constituting waste. He is liable also if a stranger commits acts which would have been classed as waste if committed by the tenant.[64] The tenant will be left to his remedy against the stranger in this situation. If the tenant has an option to purchase the property, however, his liability for the waste will be suspended until it is known whether or not he will exercise the option.[65]

The waste doctrine appears in many guises and can be flexibly used to achieve what a given court views as a just result. Thus, in Crewe Corporation v. Feiler [66] a lessor had covenanted to pay all taxes on the leased premises. The lessee, who had an option to purchase the property, then made major improvements on the land with the knowledge of the lessor but without his express consent. The improvements more than doubled the tax bill and reduced the lessor's yearly rental yield by 36%. Following an excellent discussion of the doctrine of waste, the majority of the court concluded that the lessor could have stopped the improvements on the premises but, having allowed the lessee to proceed for his own advantage (lessee would undoubtedly exercise his option to purchase), the lessor should be able to collect the increased taxes from the lessee. A dissenting judge vigorously disagreed, noting that "hard cases make bad law" and complaining that the majority had rewritten the lease for the benefit of the lessor.

Whatever the merits of the controversy in *Crewe*, it shows the continued vitality of the waste doctrine even in a period when the principal emphasis seems to be on a kind of "waste" by the landlord, i. e., his failure to repair and maintain multi-family housing in defiance of the municipal codes. Of course, this latter situation is not called waste (how can a landlord waste his own land?) but isn't the principle somewhat the same? A landlord can expect his tenant to maintain the leased premises and sue in waste if he doesn't; the tenant can expect his landlord to, at least, comply with housing codes and sue for breach of an implied covenant of habitability (or defend a suit for rent) if he

63. Willing v. Chicago Auditorium Ass'n, 20 F.2d 837 (7th Cir. 1927), rev'd 277 U.S. 274, 48 S.Ct. 507, 72 L.Ed. 880 (1927). It does not always follow that the tenant must respond in damages for meliorating waste. See, for example, Melms v. Pabst Brewing Co., 104 Wis. 7, 79 N.W. 738 (1899) for a good discussion of the point in a case involving a life tenant.

64. Consolidated Coal Co. v. Savitz, 57 Ill.App. 659 (4th Dist. 1894).

65. Keogh v. Peck, 316 Ill. 318, 147 N.E. 266 (1925).

66. 28 N.J. 316, 146 A.2d 458 (1958).

doesn't. It would seem that landlord-tenant law is now approaching mutuality of remedy in this area.

SECTION 9. COVENANT LIMITING USE OF PREMISES

In the absence of any provision to the contrary, a lessee has the right to possess and enjoy the property and to put it to such use as he pleases. A few jurisdictions have held that the use to which he puts it must be a reasonable one under the circumstances, depending upon the purpose for which the building was built and the use for which that type of building is usually employed.[67] These limitations do not appear in other cases.

However, the lessor may restrict the use of the premises as he sees fit as an incident to his right to control his property and the tenant may not avoid the effect of the expressed restriction on the ground that it is unreasonable. The law does not favor restrictions upon use of land and thus any such clause will be construed most strongly against the lessor.[68] However, equity will enforce a clear restriction on the use of the property if the clause is unambiguous, and will enforce these covenants even though the lessor does not suffer any damages.[69]

The mere statement in the lease that the premises may be used for a purpose mentioned does not prohibit the use for any other purpose. It has been held that such a clause is permissive and descriptive only; but where the statement is made in the lease that the premises may be used for given purposes only and for no other purposes, equity will enforce the agreement according to the generally accepted meaning of the words.[70] Any express covenant limiting the use of the premises runs with the land and thus will apply with equal force to subtenants or assignees of the lease.

Closely related to the lessee's freedom to use his non-freehold estate as he sees fit is the question of his duty to continue to operate a business on the premises, rather than let the property lie idle while he pays the rent. This issue is likely to arise only in a percentage lease since in a flat rental lease the lessor

67. Bovin v. Galitzka, 250 N.Y. 228, 165 N.E. 273 (1929).

68. Dickey v. Philadelphia Minit-Man Corp., 377 Pa. 549, 105 A.2d 580 (1954).

69. Thibodeaux v. Uptown Motors Corp., 270 Ill.App. 191 (1st Dist. 1933).

70. Lyon v. Bethlehem Eng. Corp., 253 N.Y. 111, 170 N.E. 512 (1930).

has no direct stake in the lessee's financial success. As a general rule, a statement of the purpose for which premises are leased does not imply a covenant by the lessee that he will continue to engage in that use. Some courts have implied such a covenant in percentage leases on the theory that a lessee would reasonably have intended to continue the business in good faith as a part of his rental arrangement.[71] Obviously, however, the lessor should make this an express covenant rather than leave the matter for litigation. If the lease contains a provision for minimum rent in addition to the percentage clause, most courts would be unwilling to imply any covenant of continued use. In Lippman v. Sears Roebuck and Co.,[72] the California Supreme Court did imply such a covenant even though a minimum monthly rental was included. However, *Lippman* was based on its peculiar facts, including prior negotiations which proved that the minimum was really a nominal payment and bore no relationship to the expected return for the lessor and a special clause that provided for the percentage rent of the previous year to be used as the base rent in the event of assignment. This result required the admission of extrinsic evidence (not always permissible) and does not represent a true conflict with the usual rule.

SECTION 10. ILLEGALITY

The law is well settled that there is an implied obligation in every lease that the lessee will use the property for lawful purposes only.[73] If the premises are leased to be used for an unlawful purpose, the lease is void and there can be no recovery upon it. A problem often arises as to the effect of a lease for lawful purposes, which subsequently become illegal. Where subsequent legislation is enacted prohibiting a certain business and a lease limits the use of the premises to that business, the tenant will be relieved from further liability to pay rent on the ground that performance has become impossible due to this legislation.[74] However, where a lease provides that the tenant might pursue multiple purposes in his use of the premises and only some of these purposes subsequently become unlawful, the tenant is not ex-

------

71. See 170 A.L.R. 1113, 1117–1121.

72. 44 Cal.2d 136, 280 P.2d 775 (1955).

73. Bogden v. Lasswell, 331 Ill.App. 395, 73 N.E.2d 441 (3d Dist. 1947).

74. Levy v. Johnston and Hunt, 224 Ill.App. 300 (1st Dist. 1922).

cused from liability for the rent. As long as the tenant is authorized to perform any lawful acts under the lease, despite the fact that the value of the remaining lawful purposes is substantially diminished, the tenant is still required to pay the rent.

A related group of cases deals with the rights of the parties when the use of the premises is not made unlawful, but the business which the lessee is to transact is materially restricted. Under the general rule, if there is a total frustration in the purposes for which the use of the premises was originally contemplated, the lessee will be excused. In the case of Deibler v. Bernard Bros., Inc.,[75] an appellate court construed a lease as providing that the premises could be used as an automobile showroom and for no other purpose. Subsequent government restrictions made the sale of new automobiles difficult, if not impossible. It was held that the sale of automobiles was not prohibited, only restricted; therefore, the lessee was not relieved from his obligations under the lease. The fact that business was not as good as usual would not alter the decision. This opinion would seem to commit the court to a very strict interpretation of the general rule. However, on appeal to the Supreme Court the case was affirmed on the ground, seemingly sound, that the lease contained no use restriction.[76]

As discussed previously,[77] the court in Brown v. Southall Realty Company [78] used the illegality principle to nullify a lease which was not in compliance with the D. C. Housing Code at the time of leasing. This marks a material extension of the illegality doctrine and opens a new field of potential litigation, particularly in the area of multiple family dwellings.

SECTION 11. ESTOPPEL TO DENY LANDLORD'S TITLE

While not an implied covenant, the rule that the tenant in possession of the premises is estopped to deny his landlord's title as of the time of the demise should be mentioned here. It has been stated that the tenant in possession under one title can make no valid attornment to one not in privity with that title.[79] An-

---

75. 319 Ill.App. 504, 48 N.E.2d 422 (1st Dist. 1943).

76. Deibler v. Bernard Bros., Inc., 385 Ill. 610, 53 N.E.2d 450 (1944).

77. Pp. 207–208 supra.

78. 237 A.2d 834 (D.C.App.1968).

79. Kepley v. Scully, 185 Ill. 52, 57 N.E. 187 (1900).

other statement of the rule is that where a party is in possession of premises under a lease he is estopped to deny his landlord's title.[80] The basis of the estoppel doctrine is the possession of the tenant. The tenant can assert an adverse title only after he has vacated the premises.

Some examples of the application of the rule follow: If the lessee takes a second lease from a third person, that lease is void and cannot constitute adverse possession as against the original lessor.[81] The tenant is estopped to assert that the lessor had no title in defending an action on the lease for rent.[82] The lessee may, where there are conflicting titles, take a lease from each of the claimants; if he is not deceived by their assertions, he will be required to pay both since he cannot deny the title of either or the right of either to lease to him.[83] If the tenant claims through a better title than his landlord, he must give up possession before asserting his claim to the better title.

There are certain exceptions to this rule. If the tenant is induced by fraud concerning the title to accept a lease, he is permitted to avoid it by proof of such facts as would warrant relief in equity from any other obligation created by deed.[84] Although the tenant cannot deny his lessor's title as it existed at the beginning of the tenancy, he can show that the lessor had a limited estate which has since terminated through its limitation or has been divested by operation of law. The tenant can also show that he or some third person acquired title from the lessor. In such case the tenant does not acquire title adversely and is permitted to show the true title. Thus, in the case of Spafford v. Hedges,[85] the lessor had title to certain property subject to mortgage. The lessee acquired title from the purchaser at the foreclosure sale. It was held that because the tenant did not acquire an adverse title but rather acquired title through the landlord, he could show such title in an action for rent. This same rule applies also to the purchase of property by the lessee at a tax sale.

80. Orthwein v. Davis, 140 Ill.App. 107 (4th Dist. 1908).

81. Supra note 79.

82. Pearce v. Pearce, 83 Ill.App. 77 (3d Dist. 1898). This view may be subject to change in light of the relaxed attitude toward defenses against summary actions for possession. If a tenant can show the breach of an implied covenant of habitability in such an action, why could he not show that his lessor was in total breach because he had no title to the land?

83. Koelmel v. Kaelin, 374 Ill. 204, 29 N.E.2d 106 (1940).

84. Carter v. Marshall, 72 Ill. 609 (1874).

85. 231 Ill. 140, 83 N.E. 129 (1907).

SECTION 12. COVENANTS AND CONDITIONS

There is a difference in legal effect between a covenant and a condition. Ordinarily a breach of covenant will subject the promisor to a suit for damages. It will not work a forfeiture of the tenant's interest or terminate the relationship of landlord and tenant. On the other hand, a breach of condition ordinarily will terminate the relationship. Whether a given provision should operate as a condition or covenant or both is held to be a matter of the intention of the parties. It is often difficult, however, to decide whether a promise (covenant) or a condition is intended. Because courts do not favor forfeitures an effort is made to construe provisions as covenants rather than as conditions. This results in confusion in some of the cases where if the exact language used in the provisions were followed none would exist. Thus the fact that the words "on condition" are used is not decisive [86] when to give these words their natural meaning might lead to the disfavored forfeiture. In the case of Kew v. Trainor,[87] it was held that although courts incline to interpret language as a covenant rather than a condition, the intention of the parties, when clearly ascertained by the instrument, must control. In this case an agreement not to assign, together with an express provision for re-entry on default, was held to be a condition upon which the term depended.

Distinction must be made between covenants which are dependent and those which are independent. With respect to dependent covenants, the performance by each party of his covenant is a condition precedent to his right to recover for the breach of the covenant of the other. If the covenants are independent, it is no excuse for the non-performance by one party that the other has not performed. Most covenants in a lease are held by the courts to be independent covenants—and thus the general rule is that the covenant of the landlord to repair or make improvements and the covenant of the lessee to pay rent are independent. However, under the rule concerning constructive evictions, if the repairs to be made are of such a character that failure to make them would be equivalent to an eviction, the failure justifies a termination of the term at the election of the lessee.

The previous paragraph correctly states the traditional rule, still prevailing in many states. However, as previously discussed, the courts are now importing contract principles into

---

86. Nowak v. Dombrowski, 267 Ill. 103, 107 N.E. 807 (1915).   87. 150 Ill. 150, 37 N.E. 223 (1894).

the law of landlord tenant and many covenants, particularly implied covenants of habitability and a duty to repair, are being treated as dependent. Where this is done, covenants will be treated as constructive conditions, regardless of the language used, and no recourse to the principle of constructive eviction will be required.

SECTION 13.   TORT LIABILITY IN LANDLORD– TENANT LAW

As a general proposition, a landlord is not liable for the torts of his tenant. While a lease is a contract, it is also a conveyance of a non-freehold estate in land and, after the conveyance, the tenant is normally responsible for his own acts on the premises. A lease is not a partnership. However, some percentage leases skirt very close to the line since, in effect, there is a sharing of profits and a rigidly defined scheme of operation in which the lessor may have a major voice. Losses are not shared, however, except in an indirect sense, and so long as the percentage paid is carefully defined as rent the lessor is not a partner.[88] Neither is there an agency relationship although, again, some ambiguous agreements may run the risk of being so interpreted by the courts.

As with all general rules, there are certain exceptions. In Green v. Asher Coal Mining Company [89], the Court of Appeals of Kentucky held an owner of land leased for strip mining purposes liable to a lower riparian owner who was damaged by debris produced in a strip mining operation. The court listed several examples where a lessor would remain liable following the lease. These included the "sidewalk" cases, the nuisance cases, and the blasting cases. Said the court: "The authorities heretofore discussed recognize that the owner of land may be held liable for acts of his lessee under the following conditions: the particular use or exploitation of land must be such that harm to others is likely to ensue unless precautions are taken; the owner must consent to, authorize or be cognizant of this use; and the injury must be such as can reasonably be anticipated from such use."

Although the lessor is liable in tort to third parties only in exceptional circumstances, he may be liable to his own lessee

88. See Lesar, Landlord and Tenant § 3.66 (1957).

89. 377 S.W.2d 68 (Ky.App.1964).

in a wide variety of situations. Traditionally, this liability too was quite restricted. Thus, the lessor remained liable both to third parties and to his lessee for negligence in maintaining common areas, such as stairways, elevators, and entrance halls, not included in the lease. He was responsible for latent defects, known to him but not disclosed to the lessee, for assuming the responsibility to make repairs whether or not he was required to do so and then performing in a negligent fashion, and for defects in furnished residences where the lessee had no opportunity to inspect before taking possession.[90] In short, *caveat emptor* was the prevailing rule and the lessor was typically liable only where there was no reasonable opportunity to inspect or discover the defect or where the lessor had retained dominion and control of a portion of the property and hence was liable for his own torts.

The most difficult issue has been the legal effect of a promise by the lessor to repair the demised property or to keep it in "good order and repair." In Faber v. Creswick[91] a tenant's wife was injured when she fell through a plaster board floor of an attic. While the court might have decided the case on the latent defect principle, the landlord had promised to "have the house thoroughly clean and in good order and repair at the beginning of this lease", and the court seized the opportunity to clarify the law of New Jersey in such cases. Pointing out that the wife was not in privity with the landlord, since she had not signed the lease, the court overruled a prior case requiring privity and held that the landlord was liable to the wife for her injury. Said the court: "Under modern social conditions, the precept of privity is sterile and no longer serves the interests of justice. And this apart from other influences, for the obvious reason that it is utterly unrealistic to say that when the head of a family leases premises and bargains for an agreement on the part of the lessor to maintain them in good repair, the parties do not recognize that the pact is in the interest and for the protection of members of his household and others who enter thereon in his right. It is likewise inconsistent with reality to suggest that the parties do not accept their mutual engagements with a full awareness that if the necessary repairs are not made, the safety of such persons will be endangered."

The court then dealt with the even more difficult issue of the correct measure of damages in such a case. Historically, the measure of damages was *ex contractu* and the recovery was confined to the cost of making the particular repair, a rather

---

90. See Prosser, Law of Torts 399–412 (4th ed. 1971) for a detailed discussion of tort liability in landlord-tenant law.

91. 31 N.J. 234, 156 A.2d 252 (1959).

hollow victory for the injured party. While some jurisdictions still follow this narrow view, the court felt a majority had shifted to recovery *ex delictu* and would use a tort measure of damages so that the plaintiff could recover for the personal injuries. While this view may have some theoretical inconsistencies,[92] it does move in the direction of greater protection for the tenant and is an additional prod to force the landlord to keep the premises in repair.

The full significance of Faber v. Creswick can be appreciated when its teachings are combined with *Javins*.[93] In *Faber* there was an express covenant to repair, but if implied covenants of habitality (hence to repair) are to be read into residential leases through the impact of state legislation and municipal building codes then the landlord will be liable in tort to the tenant and others upon the land with his consent. This represents a major extension of the traditional tort liability of the landlord.

All of this advance in tenant's rights will come to naught if the landlord can insist on an exculpatory clause which will free him from his own negligence. The concept of freedom of contract would argue that such clauses are valid but this conflicts with the emerging social policy enunciated in *Javins*. In McCutcheon v. United Homes Corporation [94] the Supreme Court of Washington faced this issue squarely in a case involving an injury to a tenant in a common area. Said the Court: "The question is one of first impression. The issue is whether the lessor of a residential unit within a multi-family dwelling complex may exculpate itself from liability for personal injuries sustained by a tenant, which injuries result from the lessor's own negligence in maintenance of the approaches, common passage ways, stairways and other areas under the lessor's dominion and control but available for the tenant's use."

The court carefully explored the issues involved and nullified the effect of such an exculpatory clause, at least in multi-family residential leases. "Under these circumstances it cannot be said that such exculpatory clauses are 'purely a private affair' or that they are 'not a matter of public interest'." The court did enter a caveat as to whether a landlord and tenant could specifically enter into a bargain for an exculpatory clause in a residential lease on the basis of a reduced rental payment. However, that issue was not before the court. *McCutcheon* also left open the use of exculpatory clauses in leases other than

92. See Cribbet, Fritz and Johnson, Cases and Materials on Property (3d ed. 1972) at pp. 329–332 for a detailed discussion of this point.

93. See p. 208, supra.

94. 79 Wash.2d 443, 486 P.2d 1093 (1971).

multiple family residential. The Illinois experience is instructive on this point. In O'Callaghan v. Waller and Beckwith Realty Co.[95] the Illinois Supreme Court upheld exculpatory clauses in leases on the basis of freedom of contract. A few months later, the legislature adopted a statute, based on a New York Model, which nullified such clauses but made an exception for business leases in which governmental units or agencies were involved.[96] The Supreme Court then declared this statute unconstitutional because of the unreasonable classification.[97] The legislature promptly repassed the statute without exceptions.[98] There would appear to be no basis for holding this latest statute unconstitutional and the death knell appears to have been sounded for exculpatory clauses in Illinois. Whether most jurisdictions will follow the Illinois lead is open to conjecture.

SECTION 14. ASSIGNMENT AND SUBLETTING BY LESSEE

All leases, except leases at will, may be assigned provided there is no restriction in the lease itself. A leasehold interest in real estate is personal property and is transferable as such. Although a leasehold is personal property (a chattel real) it is also an interest in land and transfers must comply with the Statute of Frauds. Thus, if the assigned lease has more than one year to run, the transfer must be in writing in order to be enforceable.[99] By an assignment, the tenant conveys all of his interest in the property to a third person for the entire term, whereas in a sublease the tenant conveys all or part of his interest in the property for a period less than the entire term. In Jaber v. Miller,[1] the Supreme Court of Arkansas cast doubt on the historic test, just stated, and said that the issue of assignment versus sublease should be decided on the basis of intent of the parties rather than the feudal concept of retention of a reversion by the landlord. Under this view, the fact that the parties called the transfer on assignment would be material, as would a layman's understanding of what he thought he was doing.

95. 15 Ill.2d 436, 155 N.E.2d 545 (1959).

96. Ill.Rev.Stat., Ch. 80, § 15a (1969).

97. Sweney Gas & Oil Co. v. Toledo, 42 Ill.2d 265, 247 N.E.2d 603 (1969). See Note, 64 N.W.L.Rev. 851 (1970).

98. Ill.Rev.Stat. ch. 80, § 91 (1973).

99. Chicago Attachment Co. v. Davis Sewing Machine Co., 142 Ill. 171, 31 N.E. 438, 15 L.R.A. 754 (1892).

1. 219 Ark. 59, 239 S.W.2d 760 (1951).

However, *Jaber* was based on a peculiar set of circumstances and most courts have continued to follow the traditional rule which, in the typical case, probably does conform to the intent of the parties. In *Jaber* the only "reversion" was the power of the lessor to terminate the transfer if the transferee failed to pay the rent. While some jurisdictions would call this power of termination a reversionary interest [2] others would not.[3] Indeed, the former view has been criticized on the ground that a common-law power of termination (right of re-entry) was a mere chose in action and not a reversionary estate.[4] Hence the traditional view of a sublease, where a set period—even one day —is kept by the landlord, could be consistently retained while ignoring the effect of a power of termination and using intent as the test in those cases. There is a division in the cases as to whether a conveyance of part of the property for the entire term is a sublease or an assignment. Perhaps this is a situation in which the *Jaber* test of intent of the parties could profitably be employed.

Obviously, there will be some situations in which it will be difficult to determine whether an assignment has been made. In Amco Trust, Inc. v. Naylor [5] the lessee mortgaged his leasehold interest and the lessor attempted to treat this as an assignment, holding the mortgagee for the rent. Although the lessee had retained a power of termination, which under Texas law [6] made the transfer a sublease rather than an assignment, the court decided the case more broadly and held that a mortgage was not an assignment until foreclosure by the mortgagee with a subsequent purchase at the foreclosure sale. It pointed out the disparity of views, ranging from treating the mortgage as an assignment immediately (under the title theory of mortgages) through calling it an assignment only if the mortgagee went into possession to requiring foreclosure (under the lien theory) before it could be said to be an assignment. Here, again, the intent of the parties might be a useful test since few mortgagees would think of themselves as assignees, with accompanying liability for rent, simply because they took a security interest in a leasehold.

In general, where the lessee assigns his entire estate without reserving to himself a reversion, a privity of estate is at once

---

2. Dunlap v. Bullard, 131 Mass. 161 (1881).

3. Davis v. Vidal, 105 Tex. 444, 151 S.W. 290 (1912).

4. Tiffany, Landlord and Tenant, § 151 (1910).

5. 159 Tex. 146, 317 S.W.2d 47 (1958).

6. Davis v. Vidal, 105 Tex. 444, 151 S.W. 290 (1912).

created between his assignee and the original lessor, and the lessor then has a right of action directly against the assignee on the covenants running with the land.   But if the lessee sublets the premises, reserving or retaining any reversion, however small, privity of estate between the sublessee and the original landlord is not established and the landlord then has no right of action against the sublessee on covenants contained in the top lease, since there is neither privity of estate nor of contract; however, the landlord may evict the subtenant, if he violates any of these covenants.   The possession of the subtenant is that of the tenant and the termination of the original tenant's lease works a termination of the sublease.   Where all of the lessee's estate is transferred, the instrument will operate as an assignment notwithstanding that words of demise instead of assignment are used. Even if the instrument is called a sublease, it will be an assignment if that is the effect of the language used.   An excellent summary of the pertinent rules of assignment is found in Kewanee Boiler Corp. v. American Laundry Machinery Co.[7]

An assignee of the lessee's interest under a lease who does not assume the obligations of the lease during the balance of the term, may be held liable for performance only during the period of his occupancy.[8]

An assignee in a "losing" lease may wish to be rid of the burden of the lease and, if he did not assume, he will be eager to end his privity of estate with the lessor.   This is fairly easy to do, since, absent a fraudulent or colorable assignment, he can "dump" the lease on a new assignee.   As stated in A. D. Juilliard and Co. v. American Woolen Co.[9]   "If such assignee, by a new assignment, fairly relinquishes not only possession of the leased premises but also all benefits therefrom, it is immaterial that the new assignee may be financially irresponsible, or that he gave no consideration, or even that he received a bonus as an inducement to accept the assignment of the lease."

At first blush, this may sound unfair to the landlord, but note that he retains the liability of the original tenant (unless released by a novation), could have required the assignee to assume if there was a prohibition on assignment without the lessor's consent, and still has the ownership of the land which he can return to his own possession if the rent is not paid.

When the assignee goes into possession of the leased premises and assumes the obligations under the lease, both privity of

7.   289 Ill.App. 482, 7 N.E.2d 461 (1st Dist.1937).

8.   69 R.I. 215, 32 A.2d 800, 148 A.L.R. 187 (1943).

9.   Id.

contract and of estate are established between the assignee and the lessor. The privity of estate is terminated when he surrenders possession. However, the privity of contract remains, therefore he may be held liable by the lessor for performance while he is in possession of the premises and after re-assignment. He is liable also to the original lessee, and any intermediate assignee who, being liable to do so, has performed the lease. Where the original lessee makes good the assignee's default, he may recover from the assignee, even though the default occurred after the assignee vacated the premises because privity of contract continues. When a novation occurs, however, the lessee is thereby released.[10]

Throughout this section the terms assignment, assumption, sublease, release, and novation have been freely used. While the law dictionaries define the terms, perhaps a word of explanation will be useful. The typical assignment is written on the lease itself: "I hereby assign all my right, title, and interest in this lease". It can be oral if the Statute of Frauds does not come into play. The assignee makes no express promise to pay the rent or be bound by the terms of the lease but becomes liable, so long as he does not reassign, because of privity of estate, i. e. he has the same estate the lessor granted to the lessee. If he adds: "I assume the obligations of this lease and promise to pay the lessor (or lessee) the rent", then he is brought into privity of contract with the lessor and remains liable until released.

Even if he promises to pay the lessee he is bound to the lessor on principles of third party beneficiary contracts. Of course, if the transfer is for less than the full remaining period of the lease, it is a sublease under principles previously discussed. In no case is the original lessee freed of his liability unless expressly released by the lessor, in which case there is a novation and the assignee steps completely into the assignor's shoes. Occasionally, an argument is made for an implied assumption or release but usually this fails.[11] Once an assignment has been made the assignee becomes primarily liable on the lease and the assignor is secondarily liable, i. e., suretyship principles apply, with the assignor being a surety for the assignee. Of course, the lessor can sue either party (or both) but is entitled to only one satisfaction. The factual situations vary widely but most cases will fall within the outlined principles. The problems involved in covenants against transfer are complicated by the Rule in *Dumpor's* Case and by the doctrine of miti-

---

10. Of course, the original lessee remains liable to the landlord whether there is assignment, subletting, or assumption. Only release by the landlord ends his lia-bility. Cauble v. Hanson, 249 S.W. 175 (Tex.1923).

11. Cauble v. Hanson, 249 S.W. 175 (Com.App.1923).

gation of damages.[12]   If landlord-tenant law eventually adopts fully the contracts principle as to mitigation of damages, the landlord may have less freedom to reject a satisfactory, solvent assignee even if the lease does require his consent prior to transfer.

SECTION 15.   COVENANTS AGAINST TRANSFER

A covenant in a lease against assignment or subletting, although not favored by the law, will be enforced, but will not be extended beyond express stipulation.   Thus, the courts have held that where the tenant under a restrictive clause takes another into copartnership with him and lets him into joint possession of the premises, it is not a breach of this covenant.   Also, subletting the premises will not violate a covenant against assignment and vice versa.[13]   Many leases contain covenants that no assignment will be permitted unless the landlord expressly assents thereto. A landlord can be arbitrary in refusing to give such assent; however, if the lease provides further that his consent shall not be unreasonably withheld, the court's judgment is substituted for that of the landlord.   Thus, the landlord in Edelman v. F. W. Woolworth Co.[14] was not permitted to refuse to consent to the assignment to a business competitor, merely because he was a competitor, when in all other respects he was a suitable tenant. The court held that if the lessor had desired to prevent the assignment of the premises to a business competitor, or to some other objectionable person, he should have expressly so stated. A provision restraining the assignment of a lease includes only voluntary assignments and is not operative against an assignment effected by law or through an order of the court,[15] unless it appears that the proceedings were voluntary and collusive on the part of the tenant in order to defraud the landlord of his rights.

The landlord may waive the effect of a covenant against assignment expressly or by conduct.   Thus, where he accepts rent from an assignee with knowledge of the facts, this may constitute a waiver.

12.   See p. 190, supra for a discussion of these issues.

13.   Union Trust Co. v. First Trust and Savings Bank, 252 Ill.App. 337 (1st Dist. 1929).

14.   252 Ill.App. 142 (1st Dist. 1929).

15.   Sinclair v. Sinclair, 224 Ill.App. 130 (2d Dist. 1922).

SECTION 16.   ASSIGNMENT BY LESSOR

The lessor's interest during a tenancy is a reversion, and carries with it the right to transfer the reversion. A transfer of a reversion is unlike an assignment of a chose in action, since in order to perfect an assignment of a chose notice must be given to the debtor. However, where a reversionary interest in land is transferred, constructive notice is given to all the world, including the lessee, by recording the deed. Actual notice, therefore, is not necessary.

After the lessor has transferred his reversion, the tenant's rights and liabilities remain the same. The grantee of the reversion is given by statute in many states the same remedies for the recovery of rent or the enforcement of the other covenants of the lease as the lessor might have had.[16] The early cases, before the passage of these statutes, held that an attornment would be necessary in order to create privity of contract between the tenant and the grantee so as to enable the grantee to recover rent. The statutes have changed this requirement and an attornment is no longer necessary.[17]

A conveyance by the landlord of the premises is naturally subject to the rights of tenants under prior valid leases. The grantee of the lessor has constructive notice of the lessee's rights under the lease, by virtue of the lessee's possession of the premises.[18] The lessee's possession of the premises gives to the grantee not only constructive notice of all rights which he may have had under the original lease but it also gives him constructive notice of any rights to options for extensions or agreements between the landlord and the tenant, such as a contract or an option to purchase the land. However the tenant's possession does not give notice of the rights of the landlord's grantee. To give notice of these rights, the assignment must be recorded.[19]

After the lessor transfers the reversion, he no longer has any rights with regard to the property and he has been relieved of some of his liabilities by virtue of the fact that he is no longer in privity of estate with the lessee. He is still liable on certain

16. Ill.Rev.Stat. ch. 80, § 14 (1973) (based on the statute of 32 Hen. 8, c. 34, § 1 [1540]).

17. Compare Fisher v. Deering, 60 Ill. 114 (1871), with Barnes v. Northern Trust Co., 169 Ill. 112, 48 N.E. 31 (1897).

18. Nelson v. Joshel, 305 Ill. 420, 137 N.E. 389 (1922).

19. Bullard v. Turner, 357 Ill. 279, 192 N.E. 223 (1934).

promises which he made in the contract, however, since a party cannot by his own act relieve himself of a contractual liability without the consent of the other party, and although he is no longer in privity of estate with the lessee, the privity of contract remains. The benefits of the contract go to the grantee, including rent which accrues after the transfer, and the original landlord can no longer sue on a breach of the contract occurring after the transfer. The grantee becomes liable for all obligations to the tenant arising after the transfer. However, he is not liable for obligations which have arisen pursuant to the lease before the transfer unless he expressly assumes them.

If the lessor conveys property, reserving nothing to himself, the effect will be to convey the lessor's interest in the lease on the property and the right to receive all unaccrued rentals, since unaccrued rentals are not personal property but incorporeal hereditaments. They are an incident to the reversion and follow the land. They pass with the conveyance or devise of the land and although separable from the reversion, they are, until such separation, a part of the land. However, rent may be excepted in a grant of a reversion, since rent is not an inseparable incident of the reversion. A transfer of the rent alone does not transfer an estate or interest in the land but operates to transfer a mere chose in action. It need not be in any particular form and it is not necessary that it be recorded.

A lessor may mortgage property which is occupied by his tenant. Where the lease is made subsequent to the mortgage, the mortgagee can extinguish the right of the tenant by foreclosing the mortgage. However, when the mortgage is subsequent to the lease, the mortgagee must respect the rights of the tenant, and, regardless of foreclosure, the tenant cannot be evicted prior to the expiration of the lease, unless he joined in the mortgage. The mortgagee has the same constructive notice of the lessee's rights by virtue of his possession as has a grantee of the lessor. The mortgagee is not bound by any advance rent payment made by the tenant to the mortgagor, and on appointment of a receiver, or on the mortgagee's taking possession of the land, the tenant with actual or constructive notice of the mortgage will nevertheless have to pay rent thereafter to the receiver or mortgagee, even though he has already paid his rent in advance to the mortgagor.[20]

---

20. Rohrer v. Deatherage, 336 Ill. 450, 168 N.E. 266 (1929). See also, First Nat. Bank of Chicago v. Gordon, 287 Ill.App. 83, 4 N.E.2d 504 (1st Dist. 1936), in which the court did not allow rent reduction given by the mortgagor to the tenant shortly before foreclosure.

Cribbet, Prin.Laws of Prop. 2nd Ed. UTB—15

SECTION 17. TERMINATION OF THE NON–
FREEHOLD ESTATE

Unlike the fees simple, with their potentially infinite duration, and the life estate or the fee tail with their indefinite duration, most non-freehold estates have a set time for termination.
True, the estate from period to period will continue until proper
notice is given by one party or the other and an estate at will
may last for an unstated period, but the most prevalent form,
an estate for years, has a definite terminal point. Of course,
even the latter may end earlier due to breach by the landlord or
the tenant but that is a premature death caused by failure to
live up to the bargain. Some premature terminations cause difficult legal problems, e. g., surrender and destruction of the estate due to eminent domain or disasters caused by fire or acts
of nature.

Surrender is a word of art describing a transfer of the reversion to the tenant or of the non-freehold estate to the landlord. Surrenders are either express or implied. The former
causes few problems since it is a simple conveyance of the estate
of one party to the other. If the period involved is for more
than one year, it must be in writing to comply with the Statute
of Frauds.

Implied surrender is a more difficult concept.[21] Whenever
the tenant abandons possession to the landlord and the latter
accepts dominion and control of the estate, the former is apt
to claim there has been a surrender by operation of law since
the landlord's acts are inconsistent with a continuation of the
non-freehold estate. This is particularly true if the landlord
relets to another, thereby creating the logical dilemma of two-
non-freehold estates in the same land at the same time. The
problem is exacerbated by the peculiar doctrine of no mitigation of damages so that the landlord would have been justified
in doing nothing and holding the tenant for rent, a solution
which may work to the disadvantage of both parties.

While there is no easy solution to the problem of implied
surrenders, Novak v. Fontaine Furniture Co.[22] offers the best
analysis. "The question whether, upon the tenant's abandonment of the premises, the landlord may lease them to another
without thereby causing a surrender of the lease, and conse-
quent termination of the tenant's liability for rent, is one of
great practical interest, upon which the authorities are not in

---

21. See Schnebly, Operative Facts in   **22.** 84 N.H. 93, 146 A. 525 (1929).
Surrenders, 22 Ill.L.Rev. 117 (1927).

accord. There are a number of decisions to the effect that the landlord may so 'relet' to another and still hold the former tenant. By others it is regarded as necessary, in order that such reletting shall not effect a surrender, that the landlord, before making the new lease, inform the tenant that he is about to do so on the latter's account, that is, that the purpose is to reduce, but not necessarily to extinguish, the latter's liability for rent. By still another line of decisions it is adjudged that the reletting will terminate the liabilities under the previous lease, without any suggestion being made that a notice to the previous tenant would prevent this result." The court then proceeded to state its own test. " 'The real question in such cases is what is the intent of the landlord in taking possession.' . . . Notice of proposed reletting is merely evidence on that issue." This seems a sensible solution of the problem, since most landlords would not intend to accept a surrender by attempting to mitigate damages (whether required by law to do so or not) and few tenants would have that result in mind at the time they abandoned the premises—that thought occurs later when they are looking for a defense to an action for rent. Of course, the landlord would be well advised to give the tenant full notice of his actions since that would help clarify the issue of intent.

Destruction of the premises by fire or other cause, without the fault of either party, might be thought to terminate the non-freehold estate but this is not normally the case. Once the lease is signed the tenant assumes the risk of loss on his estate and must still pay rent even though the improvements are damaged or destroyed, unless the lease provides otherwise. He can use the land for some other purpose and should have insured against his loss. Both parties have an insurable interest since each has an estate which may be damaged. This can give rise to complicated insurance problems which are beyond the scope of this basic text, but it should be pointed out that where the lessor carries the insurance, by agreement of the parties, and the lease provides for return of the premises in good condition "loss by fire, casualty, providence and deterioration excepted", the tenant will be protected even though the loss was due to his own negligence.[23] This is true because most insurance policies are intended to protect against losses caused by the insured's own negligence and the tenant would naturally expect this result when he left the insurance coverage to the lessor by agreement.

The risk of loss doctrine was based on a lease of land plus improvements and would not apply where the lease was of an

23. Rock Springs Realty Inc. v. Waid, 392 S.W.2d 270, 15 A.L.R.3d 774 (Mo.1965).

apartment in a building or where the fire, etc. destroyed the subject matter of the lease itself. Where the estate from which the rent issues ceases to exist the landlord is not entitled to recover rent for the remainder of the term, i. e., the lease is terminated.[24]

Closely related to destruction by fire or other catastrophes, is the taking of the estate by eminent domain proceedings. Here too, the tenant bears the risk of loss to his non-freehold estate. The rent is not even abated *pro tanto*, if a portion of the non-freehold estate is taken but that which is left is "susceptible of occupation." The tenant must pay the full rent for the remainder of the period but is entitled to a proportionate share of the condemnation award. While there is some dissent from this position it seems to represent the weight of authority. Only if the entire non-freehold estate is taken by the condemning authority is the lease terminated, on the theory that no rent can then issue from a non-existent estate.[25] As in the case of destruction by fire, this entire matter can be regulated by the terms of the lease.[26]

SECTION 18. DAMAGES IN EVENT OF BREACH

Damage issues can arise in a number of ways during the lifetime of a lease and some of these issues have been discussed in the interstices of the preceding material. If the landlord breaches the lease and fails to give the tenant possession initially, or ousts him later, the measure of damages, in the absence of special circumstances attending the making of the lease and communicated to the landlord, is the difference between the actual rental value and the rent reserved for the period the tenant is out of possession.[27] Thus, if the tenant had promised to pay $1,000 a month rent but premises of equivalent market value were renting for $1,200, the tenant could recover $200 a month on breach by the landlord. This measure of damages is designed to give the tenant the benefit of his bargain so far as the leasehold *qua* leasehold is concerned, but it may leave the tenant far from whole, due to lost profits, inconvenience in mov-

24. Norman v. Stark Grain and Elevator Co., 237 S.W. 963 (Tex.Civ. App.1922).

25. For a detailed discussion, see Elliott v. Joseph, 163 Tex. 71, 351 S.W. 2d 879 (1961).

26. Garrett, Lease Provisions Against Special Contingencies, [1952] U. of I. Law Forum 395.

27. Adrian v. Rabinowitz, 116 N.J.L. 586, 186 A. 29 (1936).

ing to another location, loss of good will, etc. These items may be difficult to include as damages because of their speculative nature and the use of the foreseeability test which applies to leases as well as to contracts generally.

If the tenant breaches, by refusing to pay rent, he can normally be ousted [28] but he can also be sued for the rent due and there may be no duty on the landlord to mitigate damages by seeking a new tenant.[29] A troublesome problem arises as to whether the landlord can sue for future rent or must wait and seek recovery as the rent accrues. Here, again, the traditional view, based on independent covenants, was that there could be no anticipatory breach of a lease despite the development of such a doctrine in contract law generally. Although there is still a split of authority in this country, there is growing recognition that anticipatory breach doctrines do apply to leases and, in line with the general shift to contract principles that trend can be expected to continue.[30] Of course, there must be a repudiation of the lease by the tenant, not just the failure to pay a rent installment, and some cases require that there be an actual breach along with the repudiation in order to invoke the doctrine.

This issue is most likely to arise in long term bases where the tenant goes bankrupt or for some other reason desires to repudiate the lease. Typically, this will occur in a falling market so that the rental value of the land is less than the tenant agreed to pay. The damage test there is the difference between the agreed rent and the actual rental value, over a period of years, discounted to its present value. This is highly speculative since the market oscillates over time and is probably one reason why many states stick to the older rule. The same result can be reached even in those jurisdictions, however, by the use of an acceleration clause in the lease so the problem is not necessarily avoided. As a result of the high degree of speculation involved, courts are likely to limit the number of years of recovery in long term leases, rather than try to determine damages over the entire period. For example, in Hawkinson v. Johnston [31] the recovery was limited to a ten year period.

Another example of the intricate damage problems that can arise is found in the eminent domain cases discussed above.[32] If the entire non-freehold estate is taken the rent is abated and the lease terminated but how much of the award (damages) does the lessee get? If the rental value of the premises and the

28. See, however, implied covenant of habitability cases, p. 208, supra.

29. See discussion p. 190, supra.

30. 122 F.2d 724 (1941).

31. Id.

32. P. 228, supra.

rent reserved are identical (or if the latter is more) he probably will get nothing since he is freed from any further obligation to pay rent. If, however, the rental value is in excess of the rent reserved, likely to be true in an inflationary economy, then the tenant has been deprived of a valuable estate and is entitled to a portion of the award.

SECTION 19.   TYPICAL PROVISIONS OF A LEASE

Subject to the previous discussion, the ordinary rules of construction of contracts apply in construing a lease. Ordinarily a lease is construed in favor of the tenant, since it is presumed that the landlord drew the lease and that he, therefore, could have inserted any provisions desired. Any ambiguity of language, therefore, or absence of provisions, will be construed against the lessor.

A.   ESSENTIAL TERMS

The usual, often termed essential, parts of the lease are (1) the names of the parties, (2) the extent and boundaries of the properties let, (3) the term of the lease, (4) the amount of rent, (5) the time of payment, and (6) the execution by the parties.

It is common practice to require rent to be paid in advance monthly or quarterly. Unless the time of payment is fixed, rent will not be due until the expiration of the period or term.[33]

The description of the premises must be certain, but the defect is cured if the lessee enters into possession.[34] Special care should be used in the complete description of the premises, in order that the lease will not be void for uncertainty and so that improvements will not be included or excluded against the intent of the parties.

The time when the lease is to begin must be stated and also the duration of the lease. Where no time or duration is stated,

---

33. McFarlane v. Williams, 107 Ill. 33 (1883).

34. Bulkley v. Devine, 127 Ill. 406, 20 N.E. 16 (1889).

the lease is merely a tenancy at will and confers few, if any, rights to the parties under it.[35]

The amount of rental should be fixed with definiteness. However, seemingly in opposition to this rule, it has been held that where the amount of rent is omitted, the law will supply the omission and assume that the parties intended to pay the reasonable value of the premises.[36] The signature of the lessor is necessary to give effect to a lease, but it is not essential (although in practice it is done) to obtain the lessee's signature, if he accepts and acts upon the lease.[37] Formalities of execution as set out in the applicable statute must also be complied with strictly.

B. ADDITIONAL TERMS

In addition to the essential terms, the parties may insert any other lawful terms in the lease. Common terms and conditions as stated in a check list for long term leases include the following subjects: names of lessor and lessee; description of premises, including buildings; statement concerning title and acceptance by lessee thereof; and if landlord's interest is mortgaged, consent of mortgagor, if procurable; term; rental, how payable, place of payment; taxes and assessments, with special provision for inheritance, transfer and income taxes, and right of lessee to contest taxes, if required to pay them; maintenance and care of buildings; indemnification to lessor against loss or damage; compliance with statutes, ordinances, and restrictions on use, if any; insurance, covenants against liens; covenants against waste; advances by lessor upon lessee's default; wrecking of old buildings and construction of new buildings; security for rent, and application of security; rebuilding in case of injury or destruction; alterations; improvements; notice of ejectment proceedings and other suits; buildings to be part of realty, to vest in lessor at end of term; defaults and remedies; lien of rent; receipt of rent after notice and after re-entry; notice with respect to default; mortgage by lessor of reversion; interest on defaulted payments; indemnity to lessor, including payment of attorney's fees; provision for receiver in case of default; reme-

---

35. Foley v. Gamester, 271 Mass. 55, 170 N.E. 799 (1930). There the lease read, "for as many years as desired by the party of the second part (the tenant)." There is some authority that this gives the tenant a life estate, as see the cited case.

36. 1 American Law of Property, § 3.64 (Casner ed. 1952).

37. Henderson v. Virden Coal Co., 78 Ill.App. 437 (3d Dist. 1897).

dies cumulative; frontage consents; assignment of lease; mortgage of leasehold estate; sub-leases; party wall agreements and sub-sidewalk space and rights in adjacent streets and alleys; covenant for quiet enjoyment; adjustment of rights of lessee and lessor in event of condemnation; covenants to run with the land; no waiver of breach to constitute waiver of succeeding breaches; notices, how given.

C. REPAIRS

In the absence of a covenant to repair, the lessor, traditionally, was under no obligation to repair premises in the control of the lessee. The extent to which this view is changing has been previously discussed.[38]

The lessor was, and is, however, obligated to use reasonable care to keep in safe condition premises over which he retains control. Thus where the landlord leases separate portions of a building to different tenants, and reserves control of parts of the building used in common by all of the tenants, he is bound to use reasonable care to keep those parts in safe condition.[39]

Because of the traditional view of repairs and the continued ambiguity of the developing position, it is quite common to spell out the duty to repair in some detail. Subject to the fact that the lessor may not be able to shift the burden to the lessee in multi-family residential leases protected by housing codes,[40] the courts will usually enforce the covenant to repair as written. In many instances, the tenant is allowed to make the repairs himself and then deduct the reasonable cost from the rent due, if the burden was placed on the landlord by express provision or by implied covenant. Where the repairs are not made and the tenant or others rightfully on the premises with his permission are injured recovery may be had under principles previously discussed.[41]

38. See p. 205, supra.

39. For the tort liability of the parties generally see Harris v. Lewistown Trust Co., 326 Pa. 145, 191 A. 34, 110 A.L.R. 749 (1937).

40. See p. 209, supra.

41. See p. 216, supra.

D. TAXES

In the absence of express provisions, the lessor must pay the taxes on the premises since he is the fee simple owner of the land.[42] In any case, the tax bill will be sent to him and failure to pay can result in the land being sold at the annual tax sales. Frequently, this burden is shifted to the lessee by covenants in the lease, in which case the rent should be adjusted accordingly. The lessee should pay the additional taxes due because of improvements which he erects on the premises. In the absence of express provision to this effect, the courts will probably imply such a promise on the lessee's part if the tenant is to have the benefit of the enhanced assessed valuation.[43]

E. INSURANCE

Neither the landlord nor the tenant is under any obligation to insure the property. If there is no insurance, the tenant runs the risk of being obligated to continue paying rent even though a portion of the demised premises is damaged, and, of course, the landlord risks bearing the loss on the destruction of his property. In the absence of express provision to the contrary, if a lease includes both land and improvements, the tenant is not relieved from the payment of rent in case of damage or even total destruction by fire or other casualty. On the other hand, if the leased premises consist only of the improvements, the tenant may be relieved from the payment of rent if the improvements are so damaged or destroyed that nothing remains to which the lease may attach. However, if the premises are partially destroyed the tenant remains liable on his covenant to pay rent. The tenant is released from this covenant only where the subject matter of the contract is extinguished.[44]

Both the landlord and the tenant have an insurable interest in the property, and both may insure to the extent of their interest. If the lessee, under no obligation, insures his interest in the

42. Bournique v. Williams, 225 Ill. App. 12 (1st Dist. 1922).

43. See p. 210, supra for a discussion of this point.

44. Humiston, Keeling & Co. v. Wheeler, 175 Ill. 514, 51 N.E. 893 (1898); Smith v. McLean, 123 Ill. 210, 14 N.E. 50 (1887).

See also discussion p. 228, supra.

property and collects the proceeds from the insurance company, the landlord can recover no part of this, even if the lessee, though not entitled to do so, receives a greater amount than the value of his interest in the property.[45]

F. FIXTURES

The lease should always contain provisions for the handling of fixtures, if the tenant contemplates making improvements on the premises which fall in this category. The common law solved this problem in a simple fashion. Absent provisions to the contrary, anything added permanently to the freehold became a part of the real property and belonged to the landlord on the termination of the lease. This is still generally true so far as buildings and permanent improvements or alterations of existing structures is concerned. If the tenant wishes to protect his interest in these improvements, he must include an option to purchase the premises, an agreement that the landlord will pay a set price for the improvements, or an agreement that the improvements can be removed in some fashion.

The rigidity and unfairness of the common-law rule has now been modified by the doctrine of trade fixtures, however, and even if the lease is silent, the tenant may remove certain personal property which he has affixed to the premises in order to carry out his commercial venture. This doctrine is based both on the presumed intent of the parties and a public policy designed to allow the tenant the greatest latitude in the removal of such trade fixtures to encourage trade and industry. "So today it is the general rule, in the absence of agreement to the contrary, that a tenant may remove whatever he has erected or installed for the purpose of carrying on trade, usually referred to as trade fixtures, provided they can be severed from the freehold without material injury thereto and that such removal is affected before he yields possession of the premises." [46]

Obviously, however, it is better, even in the case of trade fixtures, to cover this matter specifically in the lease.

45. Griffin v. Pfeffer Lumber Co., 285 Ill. 19, 120 N.E. 583 (1918).

46. Handler v. Horns, 2 N.J. 18, 65 A.2d 523 (1949).

SECTION 20. CONTINUING DEVELOPMENTS IN LANDLORD–TENANT LAW

It is difficult to write a text on *Principles of the Law of Property* in an era when the principles are changing rapidly. In 1962, when the first edition of this book was prepared, there were some signs of a peaceful revolution in landlord-tenant law but traditional doctrine was essentially intact. It still is in many jurisdictions and that fact must be borne in mind when applying these new principles to the law of a particular state, but the direction in which the winds of doctrine are blowing is clear. We now have separate doctrines for commercial leases and for residential leases. The former adhere to traditional property concepts; the latter are heavily infiltrated with contract concepts. The result may be that the same language in two similar leases, dealing with space in the same building but containing different use clauses, will result in diverse consequences. This may well be justified as courts and legislatures seek to treat residential tenants as consumers of an important product— housing—but it does not make for a tidy set of legal principles. Moreover, the state of the law, even in residential leases, is difficult to predict.

It is safe to assume that the trend toward greater protection of the residential tenant will continue. Thus, in Berzito v. Gambino,[47] the New Jersey Supreme Court granted tenants the right to affirmatively sue their landlords for breach of the implied warranty of habitability and held that damages could be awarded retroactively to the inception of the lease or to the date of breach, even though the rent had in fact been tendered and accepted. This was another major step forward for the tenant since previously in New Jersey, as elsewhere, he had been limited to a choice between making the repairs himself and deducting the cost from the rent or relying on constructive eviction.[48] Now he can rely almost completely on contract principles and recover for failure to get the benefit of his bargain.

As a result of *Berzito*, the principles in New Jersey can now be summarized:

"(1) the residential tenant and landlord relationship is governed by laws of contract rather than property;

"(2) the tenant's covenant to pay rent and the landlord's covenant to deliver and maintain the premises in habitable condition are mutually dependent upon each other;

---

47. 63 N.J. 460, 308 A.2d 17 (1972).   48. Marini v. Ireland, 56 N.J. 130, 265 A.2d 526 (1970).

"(3) the legal doctrine of caveat emptor is no longer applicable to residential rentals;

"(4) tenants cannot waive the warranty of habitability or their newly vested right to sue upon a breach thereof; and most importantly,

"(5) tenants may institute affirmative retroactive damage actions against their landlords for breach of the warranty of habitability." [49] How long will be it be before a majority of other states follow this lead? [50]

Despite the sweeping developments in the case law, the major changes may well come through legislation. Historically, landlord-tenant statutes have tended to be sketchy acts, not true codes, and largely confirmatory of the common law.[51] Today, the statutes are wide-ranging, although almost all of them are designed to redress the balance in favor of the tenant. For example, there are now acts which require the landlord to make a security deposit with a governmental agency to assure that he will comply with housing codes, a unique twist on the landlord's habit of requiring a security deposit from the tenant against the latter's defaults.[52] Other acts regulate strictly the landlord's use of the tenant's security deposit, a device long thought sacrosanct in the arsenal of landlord's remedies.[53] The impetus for the new wave of legislation has come from many groups but certainly the legal service agencies have played a major role in both judicial and legislation change.[54]

The most ambitious, and potentially the most influential, of the legislative developments is the proposed Uniform Residential Landlord and Tenant Act prepared by the Commissioners on Uniform State Laws. Although not yet submitted in final form, following criticisms from various interest groups the proposed Act will recommend major alterations in the existing law. "In drafting this proposed law, the Commissioners adopt the view that residential lease provisions should be interpreted according to contract law principles and not according to the principles of real property law. Thus, they have abandoned the 'rent for possession' theory in favor of the view that the residential

---

49. Blumberg and Robbins, Retroactive Rent Abatement: A Landmark Tenant Remedy, 7 Clearinghouse Review 323 at 326 (1973).

50. See Developments in Contemporary Landlord-Tenant Law: An Annotated Bibliography, 26 Vanderbilt L.Rev. 689 (1973).

51. See, for example, Ill.Rev.Stat. ch. 80 (1973).

52. See Blumberg and Robbins, The Landlord Security Deposit Act, 7 Clearing House Review 411 (1973).

53. Furner, From the Legislatures: Uniform Residential Landlord-Tenant Act, 2 Real Estate Law Journal 481 (1973).

54. Note, Legal Services and Landlord-Tenant Litigation: A Critical Analysis, 82 Yale L.J. 1495 (1973).

tenant not only bargains for quiet possession but also for services and a definite quality of housing .   . . . The Commissioners seem to have departed to the greatest extent from real property principles and even, in some cases, from previously enacted statutory guidelines in their treatment of security deposits, in their efforts to ensure habitability of the dwelling units and in their attempt to restrict the action of landlords in terminating leases." [55]

The American Law Institute is also at work, under the direction of Professor Casner of Harvard, on a new Restatement of the Law of Landlord and Tenant. Once completed, this Restatement will undoubtedly have a profound effect on the judicial doctrine in this vital area of the law.

Many critics, while applauding the new trend towards tenant's rights—rent abatement, rent escrow, receivership, tenants right to repair and deduct, tenant unions, and protection against landlord retaliation, see this as a mere palliative which does not reach the heart of a difficult social problem.[56] They believe the underlying cause of housing deterioration arises out of malfunctions in the economic, rather than the legal system.

"The legal relationship between landlords and tenants is an outmoded, unworkable, and mischievous anachronism that is dangerously maladjusted to the needs of an urban democracy. It is a relationship that was created to meet the needs of an agrarian and feudal society. The relationship survives today, albeit precariously, in a state of rapid deterioration. Symptoms apparent to everyone are blatant tenant hostility toward landlords; widespread neglect and wholesale abandonment of properties by landlords; increasing reluctance of investors and lenders to become enmeshed in the maze; and a critical shortage of housing accommodations for low- and moderate-income tenants.

"Most statutory proposals for landlord-tenant reform are mere palliatives that will only postpone the ultimate end of the landlord-tenant relationship. This is not to demean proposals for interim improvement, but only to point up the short-range impact of the remedies thus far proposed. Long-range reform requires fundamental changes in the underlying economic, social, and political causes of maladjustment." [57]

55. Strum, Proposed Uniform Residential Landlord and Tenant Act: A Departure from Traditional Concepts, 8 Real Property, Probate and Trust Journal 495 (1973). Mr. Strum approves of the purpose of the Act but is critical of many of its technical provisions. He believes both property and contract principles should be used, depending on which will result in "equitable treatment of both landlord and tenant."

56. See, e. g., Rose, Landlords and Tenants: Do They Have A Future? 3 Real Estate Review 92 (1973).

57. Id. at 92.

The diagnosis is easier than the cure. The housing crisis, worldwide, will not be solved by changes in law alone. Professor Rose writes: "Our evaluation of the present landlord-tenant relationship shows the need for a complete transformation from private and public landlords to mutual ownership. Mutual ownership (in the form of a cooperative, condominium, or home association) offers tenants the security of residential permanence, the pride of home ownership, the tax and economic benefits of real estate investment, and an opportunity to participate in the management of the residential community. This fundamental change in the landlord-tenant relationship may be the primary basis of successful housing reform." [58]

Just how this fundamental change is to be brought about is far from clear but it is apparent that the static days of landlord-tenant law have passed. Further changes in economic, social, and legal structures appear to be inevitable.

---

58. Id. at 96. Mr. Rose is Professor of Urban Planning at Livingston College, Rutgers University and Editor of the *Real Estate Law Journal*. He is author of a new book, *Landlords and Tenants, a Complete Guide to the Residential Rental Relationship*.

Chapter 5

VOLUNTARY TRANSFER—CONDOMINIUM

The preceding chapter on leases ended with Professor Rose's suggestion that landlord-tenant relationships should eventually be replaced by some form of mutual ownership (cooperatives, condominium or home associations).[1] The demise of traditional leasing arrangements for housing is far in the future, if, indeed, it ever occurs, but Professor Rose is right in suggesting that new legal structures offer distinct advantages to the tenant and, hence, to society as a whole. The spectacular rise of the condominium demonstrates the partial correctness of his analysis. Even a text on basic principles would be incomplete today without some discussion of this old-new concept which combines elements of both sales and lease. There is a rich lode of legal material on condominia[2] and the student of the subject can delve as deeply into the literature as he desires, but some elementary treatment is called for to complete the "big picture" of the modern law of property. The present chapter is designed to explain the importance of condominia as a tool for dealing with housing (and to some extent, commercial) problems. It uses a comparative, historical approach, discusses the basic principles involved and ends with an analysis of the advantages and disadvantages of condominium as a method of land ownership.[3]

The past decade has witnessed no real let up in the intense competition between East and West, despite the current efforts for detente. In the race for the conquest of space, in the battle

1. P. 238, supra.

2. See for example, Rohan and Reskin, Condominium Law and Practice (1973).

3. The material in this chapter is based on an article by the author in the Michigan Law Review. See Cribbet, Condominium—Home Ownership for Megalopolis? 61 Mich.L. Rev. 1207 (1963).

"Some two thousand years before the first European settlers landed on the shores of the James River, Massachusetts Bay, and Manhattan Island, a group of ancient people, planning a new city-state in the Peloponnesus in Greece, called it *Megalopolis*, for they dreamed of a great future for it and hoped it would become the largest of the Greek cities. Their hopes did not materialize. Megalopolis still appears on modern maps of the Peloponnesus but it is just a small town nestling in a small river basin. Through the centuries the word *Megalopolis* has been used in many senses by various people, and it has even found its way into Webster's dictionary, which defines it as 'a very large city.' Its use, however, has not become so common that it could not be applied in a new sense, as a geographical place name for the unique cluster of metropolitan areas of the Northeastern seaboard of the United States. There, if anywhere in our times, the dream of those ancient Greeks has come true." Gottmann, Megalopolis 4 (1961).

of national rates of economic growth, in the propaganda struggle to fix the responsibility for nuclear testing, in the earlier trial of strength over Cuba, in the more recent confrontation in the Middle East, and in countless other areas, each bloc leader continued to measure achievement against the rival's successes or defeats. The cold war is a deadly business and produces little to warm the cockles of a man's heart, but, if only the threat of nuclear destruction *could* be averted, there is something of fascination and, indeed, high-spirited adventure in this clash between powerful societies founded on different economic, political, social, and religious theories. To the lawyer (or layman for that matter) interested in the institution of property, the struggle for superiority has an added fillip—the opportunity to see basic principle tested in times of great stress and change. The worldwide population explosion, the mass migration to urban and suburban areas, and the accelerating rate of technical advance call for a legal response to the needs of the new society without abandoning the heritage of the past. This broad generality becomes concrete when we look at the specific problem of home ownership in the United States of America and in the Union of the Soviet Socialist Republics. Here is a facet of the domestic economy that touches the quick of every individual. A society [4] which fails to provide satisfactory housing for its citizens has stubbed its toe at the threshold of the good life.

Until August 1962, the prime example of private property in Russia was the individual home. It resisted collectivization and flourished, even under Stalin, primarily because of the acute housing shortage. By 1960, thirty-one percent of all living space in Soviet cities was privately owned, although built on land rented from the state.[5] Many of these homes were built by factory managers and government officials with construction loans obtained from the state bank. Due to shortage of building materials, to embezzling public servants who invested hoarded rubles in private houses, and to Chairman Khrushchev's propaganda that the imminent shift from socialism to communism would make privately-owned houses unnecessary, the August decree [6] banned all future private construction while allowing

4. I am not using "society" as synonymous with "government," although the latter must play a role if the normal functions of the economic system leave large numbers of people beyond the pale of decent housing.

5. Time, Aug. 17, 1962, p. 21, col. 3. For an interesting statement of how the Soviet Government views its own housing position vis-à-vis the West, see Sosnovy, Book Review, 22 Slavic Review 169 (1963).

6. State and Law, Current Digest of the Soviet Press No. 41, Nov. 7, 1962, p. 23. Actually, the words "August decree" are misleading. Rather, a series of decrees passed in several of the republics culminated in the stated ban on private construction.

the existing private houses to continue as before.   The new thrust was to be toward cooperatives, similar to the big apartment houses that already dot the Moscow landscape.   Whether Khrushchev's decree runs so counter to basic human drives for "my own home" that it will founder in the relatively more relaxed atmosphere of present-day Russia remains to be seen.

It is clear, however, that the Western yearning to have an individual castle for everyman's home is running into a barrier that is just as real, though stemming from a different source. American presidents have issued no decree against private home building, but choice construction sites have all but disappeared in megalopolis, and suburban sprawl has added to the cost and inconvenience of the traditional house and lot.   Unless there is a major reversal in present trends, people are likely to be "forced" back into the central city or into the close-lying peripheral areas, at an accelerating rate, in order to avoid prohibitive commuting distances and to reduce the cost of dwelling units.[7] This inevitably means apartment living of some sort, which has traditionally required the head of the family to be a tenant rather than a homeowner.   Even in a cooperative apartment he is not technically the owner, although he has many of the indicia of ownership.   This tenant half of the landlord-tenant relationship, whatever its considerable advantages, runs counter to a deep strain in the American psyche.   Long ago, Mr. Justice Story commented on this trait as it related to agricultural life in America: "One of the most remarkable circumstances in our colonial history is the almost total absence of leasehold estates.   .   .   .   The philosophical mind can scarcely fail to trace the intimate connexion which naturally subsists between the general equality of the apportionment of property among the mass of a nation, and the popular form of its government." [8] Admittedly, this drive for individual ownership is less in the city

---

7.   The alternative is increased decentralization of the city so that the job moves to the man and so that manageable-sized dwelling areas can grow up around the smaller core. I do not propose to debate the desirability or inevitability of these alternatives, since both of them will probably occur at the same time. The current trend toward apartment dwelling is quite apparent, however.   "More and more American families are moving into apartment houses, and the dramatic shift in their mode of living is having a profound effect in construction and real estate.   .   .   .   Realty men attending the annual convention of the National Association of Real Estate Boards discussed today the growing public preference for apartment living.   .   .   .   The foremost reason for the increase in apartment living, the realty men agreed, was the high cost of land in and around the nation's large cities.   This has made the cost of buying land and creating single-family homes prohibitive to builders in many areas."   N.Y. Times, Nov. 14, 1962, p. 63, col. 5.

8.   1 Story, Commentaries on the Constitution of the United States 159, 166 (1833).

than in the rural areas, and less in the atomic age than in the colonial era, but millions of American renters still regard their fate as a temporary one and long for the full benefits of ownership *cum* mortgage.

If the preceding analysis is correct, it would seem that the law should provide some format that would allow private ownership of the individual unit involved in communal living. In fact, this format is now available under the esoteric heading of condominium, *i. e.,* "individual ownership in fee simple of a one-family unit in a multifamily structure coupled with ownership of an undivided interest in the land and in all other parts of the structure held in common with all of the other owners of one-family units."[9] It is the purpose of this chapter to explore this old-new concept and evaluate its utility for modern society.

SECTION 1. THE HISTORY OF CONDOMINIUM

It is tempting to remark that while the Russians have moved away from what little private property their system provides, the Americans have developed a legal technique which allows private ownership in the midst of mass living, and then add, "It could only happen in America."[10] That it could happen anywhere, however, is evidenced by the fact that condominium had its genesis in Europe during the Middle Ages, has had a marked renaissance there since World War II, has flourished in Puerto Rico in recent years, and has belatedly burst upon the scene in the United States, following the Housing Act of 1961 which extended FHA mortgage insurance to condominium projects.[11] Some writers seem to think that the concept found its origin in ancient Rome,[12] but this seems doubtful since classical Roman

---

9. Ramsey, Condominium: The New Look in Co-ops 3 (pamphlet published by Chicago Title & Trust Co., 1961). For a more scholarly definition which should be sufficient to confuse the engineers, see Black, Law Dictionary 391 (3d ed. 1933): "In the civil law. Co-ownerships or limited ownerships, such as *emphyteusis, superficies, pignus, hypotheca, ususfructus, usus,* and *habitatio.* These were more than mere *jura in re alienâ,* being portion of the *dominium* itself, although they are commonly distinguished from the *dominium* strictly so called."

10. This recalls the two women in New York City who watched the parade for Lord Mayor Robert Briscoe, the Jewish mayor of Dublin, and then commented, "It could only happen in America."

11. Housing Act of 1961, 75 Stat. 160, 12 U.S.C.A. § 1715y (Supp. III, 1961).

12. "[T]he concept of property ownership to which it pertains is literally as old as the hills—the hills of ancient Rome where it is said to have had its beginning." Ramsey, op. cit. supra note 9, at 3.

law followed the principle *superficies solo cedit*—whatever is attached to the land forms part of it—and did not visualize separate ownership of floors in a dwelling. During the Middle Ages, however, the ownership of floors of houses, and even separate rooms, appears to have been common in various parts of Europe. There is recorded history of such ownership (*Geschosseigentum* or *Stockwerkseigentum*) back to the twelfth century in German cities, and similar evidence exists as to the late Middle Ages in France and Switzerland.[13]

Apparently, the splitting up of ownership of housing units became excessive, and, since there were no clear rules as to repair and maintenance of the structure, disputes became common. These difficulties, plus the reception of Roman law principles, so jeopardized the whole concept that some of the codifications by German states either failed to recognize this form of ownership or even prohibited outright the ownership of parts of buildings. The Code Napoleon, however, recognized the separate ownership of floors of a building, in line with established customary law, as a special type of co-ownership of an immovable. Through the years it became common to define the rights of the various floor or flat owners by special agreement, the *réglement de copropriété*, which prevented some of the earlier disputes. However, doubtful points remained, including the fact that the special agreement did not bind successors in title. Legislation in 1938, amended in 1939 and 1943, cured most of the defects.[14] The purpose of the legislation, as described by a French property lawyer, was three-fold:

> "First, it was to clarify the rights and obligations of the owners of flats with regard to the common parts of the buildings.

> "Second, it was to create an organization of the various flat owners in a building by (a) giving binding force to the *réglements de copropriété*, and (b) giving a majority of flat owners the right to make decisions binding on all.

> "Third, it was to provide for the appointment of a person (the syndic) authorized to represent the flat owners and to contract on their behalf." [15]

13. For a detailed treatment of the historical background, see Leyser, The Ownership of Flats—A Comparative Study, 7 Int'l & Comp.L.Q. 31, 33–37 (1958). For a presentation of the French law on fee ownership of apartments and an explanation of why this is blocked in Lousiana, see Comment, Individual Ownership of Apartments in Lousiana, 19 La.L. Rev. 668 (1959).

14. Law of June 28, 1938, [1938] Collection des Lois 654, as amended by order (Décret Loi) of Nov. 29, 1939, [1939] Collection des Lois 1408, and Law of Feb. 4, 1943, [1943] Collection des Lois 70 (Fr.).

15. Planiol & Ripert, 3 Traité Pratique de Droit Civil Français 314 (Picard 2d ed. 1952).

West Germany now allows ownership of individual flats in a building, as do most other European countries. Switzerland is one of the few continental states which has no legislation enabling an individual to own a flat, and changes in the law are contemplated even there.

> "Although the creation of ownership rights in individual flats has thus now been made possible in most Continental countries, the legislation is by no means uniform. Not only are there differences in the concept of the right itself, but there are interesting variations in other aspects, such as the organisation and representation of the community of flat owners in a building, the binding force of statutory provisions, and the role of the courts in the administration of flat ownership schemes." [16]

In contrast to the Roman law, the common law developed no aversion to separate floor or room ownership, and hence no special legislation is required to allow the creation of condominia in countries whose legal system is based on English law. At first blush this seems odd, since the concept comes from the continent of Europe, but it is another example of the flexibility and capacity for growth inherent in the common law. Ownership rights in a portion of a building are mentioned in *Coke on Littleton,* and such "superimposed freeholds" have existed in England for a long period of time.[17] Many of the American states have long recognized the legality of conveying a freehold estate in a portion of a building.[18] The difficulty is that the interest created in the grantee may be a defeasible fee simple which will determine with the destruction of the building, the title reverting to the owner of the soil.[19] This falls short of the requirements desired by the purchaser of a home. Although the common law is broad enough to allow separate ownership of individual units in a building, it is only recently that much interest has developed in the condominium concept as a large-scale solution to housing shortages. The immediate impetus in this country has come, not from Europe, but from Puerto Rico,

---

16. Leyser, supra note 13, at 37.

17. Buckland & McNair, Roman Law and Common Law 78 (1936). The authors mention specifically New Square, Lincoln's Inn, where the houses consist of layers of freehold sold as such centuries ago.

18. Thompson v. McKay, 41 Cal. 221 (1871); McConnel v. Kibbe, 43 Ill. 12 (1867); Townes v. Cox, 162 Tenn. 624, 39 S.W.2d 749 (1931). See also Ball, Division into Horizontal Strata of the Landscape Above the Surface, 39 Yale L.J. 616 (1930).

19. Weaver v. Osborne, 154 Iowa 10, 134 N.W. 103 (1912); Hahn v. Baker Lodge, No. 47, 21 Or. 30, 27 P. 166 (1891); Bell, Air Rights, 23 Ill. L.Rev. 251, 257 (1928). For a contrary English view, see George, The Sale of Flats 29 (2d ed. 1959); Watts, The Conveyance of a Flat— The Question of Defeasibility, 1 Austl.L.J. 363 (1928).

where *condominios,* as the buildings themselves are called, enjoy a wide popularity.

Three factors are apparent in the Puerto Rican picture.
First, the island is faced with a major housing shortage that
appears in a particularly acute form because of the expanding
population and the lack of good building sites. Second, the average Puerto Rican has a great desire for home ownership which
is certain to be thwarted if he has to wait for an individual house
and lot. Third, the cost of construction and the monthly payments on a mortgage have proved to be less in a cooperative venture of the condominium type than in any other form of comparable housing. The legality of this plan of ownership was
first established in 1951,[20] and the present "Horizontal Property
Act" was approved June 25, 1958.[21] The latter act includes virtually all of the provisions of the former, but it goes into much
greater detail and has become the model for much of the current legislation being enacted in the various states. Several
aspects of the act will be discussed later in connection with proposed legislation, but it should be mentioned here that its provisions apply only to those buildings where the parties expressly
declare by a public deed, recorded in the Registry of Property,
that they intend to submit the structure to the "Horizontal
Property Regime." [22] Thus, while it may be possible to have
split-unit ownership outside the act, a deliberate decision is required in order to receive the advantages provided by legislation. This is significant because, in discussion of the relative
advantages of condominium and cooperative apartments, or other legal devices, it will be demonstrated that the former has
problems all of its own. Even though this new tool is not a panacea, there seems to be no reason not to make the benefits available by statute for those who elect to follow it.

This brief historical sketch brings us to the present and the
sudden surge of American interest in condominium. The same
factors that account for its Puerto Rican popularity are undoubtedly at work in the states. Modern megalopolis has caused a
land shortage formerly found only in small countries, and California, Florida, Illinois, Michigan, and New York, no less than
Puerto Rico, may need new legal devices to satisfy old human
needs. The current interest has been sparked, however, by the
Housing Act of 1961, which promised to provide the necessary
financing, and by the willingness of title companies to insure the

20. P.R.Laws Ann. tit. 31, §§ 1275–
     93k (1955 & Supp. 1962).

21. P.R.Laws Ann. tit. 31, § 1291
     (Supp.1962).

22. For a detailed analysis of the
     Puerto Rican Act, see Ramsey, op.
     cit. supra note 9, at 8–13.

title, so long as correct procedures are followed in setting up the condominium. The role of the title insurance companies has been particularly interesting since they have been devoting considerable space in their house organs to the new device, and the members of their legal staffs have been writing articles and making speeches on the subject. For example, an issue of Lawyers Title News has a handsome picture of the leaning tower of Pisa on the cover with the following marginal comment:

> "A Way-Out Example—If the leaning tower of Pisa in Italy bordering the Gulf of Genoa had been built as a condominium, its famed 'leaning' would now be the world's most extreme example of encroachment on adjoining air rights. All buildings settle and constantly shift; yet, the space lot conveyed to condominium purchasers theoretically never changes. To cure the problem of possible encroachments and to preserve marketability of title . . . [the] author . . . suggests that the deeds contain reciprocal easements to exist as long as the building stands." [23]

This brief statement not only illustrates a typical problem in condominium, and a possible solution, but it shows the growing role of title insurance companies in shaping the American law of property.[24]

Before proceeding to an analysis of the practical advantages and disadvantages of condominium, cooperative apartments, etc., it may be well to take a further look at the classical property concepts involved in this type of ownership.

23. Lawyers Title News, Sept. 1962. See also the August 1961 issue of the same publication, which is referred to as the "Condominium Issue." Reference has already been made in note 9 supra to the pamphlet by Mr. Ramsey, a title officer for the Chicago Title and Trust Company.

24. Some commentators feel that the role of title insurance is already too great and is crowding the lawyer out of his traditional position in the real estate practice. See Payne, In Search of Title (pts. 1–2), 14 Ala.L. Rev. 11, 278 (1962). "The basic issue before conveyancers today is whether title insurance will spread and become the dominant form of conveyancing or whether the system of direct records examination can be restored. . . . The economic stakes involved are enormous, and the professional interests of the bar deeply involved. In this struggle the title insurance companies have the marked advantage, in that if they can simply block any action, the movement toward title insurance will undoubtedly continue. The bar, on the other hand, must take decisive action if the present trend is to be reversed. Whether the bar is capable of mobilizing its forces so as to achieve such a result will determine the course of future events."

SECTION 2.   THE CONCEPT OF CONDOMINIUM

The common law has long recognized multiple interests in a single *res*. Indeed, much of the law of property deals with the complex rules and principles developed to regulate the relationships among the owners of these multifarious interests. Ranging from the relatively simple problems of bailment in personal property to the intricate snarls of the Rule Against Perpetuities in future interests, the law has struggled, more or less successfully, with the concept of a *single* thing subject to *multiple* rights. The nearest approach to condominium, aside from the sub-surface, surface, and air rights cases, has been in one form or another of cotenancy. But whether coparcenary, tenancy by the entirety, joint tenancy, or tenancy in common, the legal concept has always called for unity of possession. The shares of each owner need not be equal, e. g., tenancy in common, but the possession of one is the possession of all, and, in legal theory if not in fact, each owner has a claim to every square inch of Blackacre subject only to correlative claims by the other cotenants. Only on partition, whether by voluntary action or suit in equity, does the individual owner have a claim to his specific share of the res. At that point the ownership ceases to be joint and becomes several. A concept of ownership which is joint, i. e., in common, as to part of the res, but several as to another part, goes beyond the ordinary theory of cotenancy. It means, in effect, that the owner of one unit in the structure has a fee simple absolute as to that unit, accompanied by the broad right to exclude others, which is of the essence of a fee, plus a tenancy in common with others as to the land and certain common elements of the building.

Although, as suggested in the previous section, the common law recognized the rights of ownership in separate floors, rooms, etc., it did not, prior to the development of condominium, work out a theory of several plus joint rights which could be fixed in space and would survive even the destruction of a building. Nothing in the common law would prevent this from being done by special agreement among the parties,[25] but it scarcely stands alone as a separate type of property ownership like joint tenancy or tenancy in common. This may be significant in deciding

---

25. It has been pointed out that, in England, vesting of the common parts of the premises in the ownership of freehold titles to flats as tenants in common is impossible due to the Law of Property Act of 1925 [15 & 16 Geo. 5, c. 20, §§ 1(6), 34(2)]. See Leyser, supra note 13, at 51. However, this is due solely to legislation which itself modified the common law, and no such barrier exists in this country.

whether a statute is needed in a particular jurisdiction to serve as a kind of enabling act for this form of multiple ownership. If the concept were well recognized in the legal system, it might be best to let it develop without legislative interference, but, where the concept itself is new, a more specific charter seems required.

One illustration should be sufficient to illuminate the conceptual difficulty. The typical cotenancies carry with them the right to partition, and lawyers are accustomed to thinking of this right as one of the "sticks in the bundle." This right, transferred to condominium, could wreck a project since the land plus certain common elements must remain unsevered, although attached to the ownership of the individual air space represented by an apartment, office, or store. These common elements must pass, like easements appurtenant, to the successive owners of the individual unit. Interestingly enough, the right to partition has not always been an incident of co-ownership and, in the early common law, the joint tenancy had to remain joint in order to maintain the socially desirable unity of title. Indeed, coparcenary's very name was derived from the fact that, without benefit of a statute, the parceners could compel partition at a time when joint tenants and tenants in common enjoyed no such right.[26] In many states, the tenancy by the entirety is still non-severable, except on divorce, just as it was at early common law.[27] Thus, although the common law is flexible enough to deny partition of the common elements, the issue may be confused since condominium does not yet have sufficient status to stand alone as a type of new estate in the law. The concept will have to be delineated in a case-by-case approach, after the method of the common law, or clarified by specific statutory authority.

SECTION 3.   THE COMMON–LAW APPROACH TO CONDOMINIUM

Apart from the specific concept of condominium, cooperative ownership of apartments is old hat in this country.[28] The

26. Moynihan, Preliminary Survey of the Law of Real Property 135 (1940).

27. Licker v. Gluskin, 265 Mass. 403, 164 N.E. 613 (1929); Hoag v. Hoag, 213 Mass. 50, 99 N.E. 521 (1912).

28. The earliest reported case in this country involving a cooperative apartment is Barrington Apartment Ass'n v. Watson, 38 Hun 545 (N.Y. Sup.Ct.1886). Among the many excellent discussions of cooperative ownership, see Hennessey, Co-opera-

familiar pattern is to vest the title to both building and land in a corporation or trust. The tenant-owner holds stock in the corporation or a certificate of beneficial interest in the trust plus a proprietary lease of a particular apartment in the building. The rights and duties of the tenant-owners are covered in great detail in the lease, charter, bylaws, or trust agreement. This type of cooperative ownership is easily accomplished without the necessity for statutory authorization. The relative advantages and disadvantages of this legal device vis-à-vis condominium will be discussed later, though a detailed analysis is beyond the scope of this text.

As suggested earlier, the common law recognized the separate ownership of rooms or floors in a building, and, since air rights could be conveyed apart from the fee in the land,[29] it has long been possible to have condominium-type developments *sans* the esoteric name. Indeed, a 1947 example in New York City is discussed in some detail by Mr. Ramsey in his pamphlet, Condominium: The New Look in Co-ops.[30] This project involved a six-story building, containing twelve apartments, and conveyances of each unit were made separately by the legal description of a cube of space.

Similarly, the California "Own Your Own Apartment" plan functions without a statute on condominium and seems to have been attractive to both purchasers and lenders in that boom state.

"Under this method a purchaser receives a deed which conveys an undivided fractional interest in the land and building, subject, however, to the reservation by a grantor of the exclusive use and right to occupy all the apartments in the building as shown on a plat attached to and made a part of the deed, excepting from such reservation such rights of occupancy and use as are thereinafter granted to the grantee. A subsequent clause then grants to the grantee the exclusive right to occupy a particular apartment identified by number on the above mentioned plat." [31]

The California experience, plus an analysis of the problems that may arise in any jurisdiction, is thoroughly discussed in an ex-

tive Apartments and Town Houses, 1956 U.Ill.L.F. 22; Yourman, Some Legal Aspects of Cooperative Housing, 12 Law & Contemp. Prob. 126 (1947); Note, 61 Harv.L.Rev. 1407 (1948). For a discussion of the tax problems, see Jacobson, Tax Problems of Sponsor and Tenant-Stockholder of Co-operative Housing Corporation, 13 J. Taxation 28 (1960).

29. See Note, 1960 U.Ill.L.F. 303. For a major, recent example, note the forty-one story Prudential Building in Chicago, erected in air lots over the Illinois Central Railroad tracks.

30. Ramsey, op. cit. supra note 9, at 6–7.

31. Id. at 7.

cellent note in the California Law Review.[32] Most of the common-law precedents are mentioned, and the authors make it apparent that condominium can function effectively without the
interposition of a legislative enabling act.   Nonetheless, there
are strong reasons for preferring the legislative approach, and
some writers feel that legislation is a virtual necessity.   Thus,
Mr. J. Leonard Smith, Jr., a member of the Legislative Committee of the Real Property, Probate and Trust Law Section of
the Pennsylvania Bar Association, urged immediate adoption
of a condominium act in Pennsylvania. He stated:

> "The same problems have arisen in California where
> several condominium type projects have been built with-
> out the benefit of specific condominium legislation.   One
> California developer stated flatly that although he was
> more than pleased with his condominium project and the ac-
> ceptance of it, he would not be inclined to do another one
> until something was done to remove some of the legal and
> practical roadblocks." [33]

Whatever the common-law possibilities of condominium,
the real future for projects of this sort appears to lie with a
sound enabling act, and attention is now turned to that phase
of the problem.

SECTION 4.   THE LEGISLATIVE APPROACH TO CONDOMINIUM

There are two principal reasons for preferring the legislative approach to condominium: (1) a carefully drafted statute
can clarify many of the uncertainties which would otherwise
have to wait for the answers to be produced by judicial decision,
and (2) such an act will provide uniformity in the creation of
projects and thus ease title and financing difficulties.   Since
the statutes are permissive, and therefore govern the condominium only if the owner or owners elect to follow the legislative plan, there seem to be no real arguments against the passage of enabling legislation.   It is possible, however, that statutes will tend to freeze projects into a common mold and thus reduce valuable experimentation, but this seems a slight risk in
view of the desirable features of a statute.

32. See Note, Community Apart-
     ments: Condominium or Stock Co-
     operative?,   50   Calif.L.Rev.   299
     (1962).

33. J. L. Smith, The Case for a Con-
     dominium Law in Pennsylvania, 33
     Pa.B.A.Q. 513, 516 (1962).

Puerto Rico led the way with its 1951 act, followed in 1958 by the "Horizontal Property Act," a somewhat confusing name for a well thought out statute. Arkansas [34] and Hawaii [35] were the first states to take up the Puerto Rican challenge, and Arizona, Kentucky, South Carolina, and Virginia [36] quickly joined the parade. Over the last decade the interest has been increasing at a rapid rate, and, by 1974, a large number of states had passed such legislation. The best way to illustrate the role of legislation would be to set forth an actual act and comment on its provisions. However, that approach is too detailed for a basic text and the interested student is referred to special works dealing solely with the subject of condominium.[37]

One provision of the Puerto Rican act, should be mentioned —the right of first refusal. This provision gives to the unit owners the first right to purchase any unit when it is offered for sale. If they fail to purchase within a reasonable time,[38] the vendor can then accept the outside offer on the terms originally proposed. If the unit owner sells without giving the co-owners the option to buy, they have the right to redeem from the sale. This right of first refusal is thought to be necessary in a cooperative enterprise so that the unit owners will have a voice in the selection of their neighbors. Does it violate the doctrine of restraints on alienation of fee interests? Mr. Ramsey thinks that it does not, because "the purpose of such a provision is not to restrain an owner from selling, but rather to enable a particular person to buy." [39] However, the provision was purposely omitted from the Hawaiian act and does not appear in some of the other acts. It should be noted that the provision does not afford complete protection in all cases since it deals only with voluntary sale and does not cover transfer by gift, judicial sale, or devolution on death.

The omission of this provision from the particular legislation does not prevent the inclusion of a similar clause in the by-laws if the owners so desire. While the right of first refusal may be valid if attacked solely as an unreasonable restraint on

---

34. Ark. Acts 1961, No. 60, § 2(a).

35. Hawaii Rev.Laws § 170A (Supp. 1961).

36. See 60 Mich.L.Rev. 527 (1962).

37. For comments on the Illinois Act see ftn. 3 supra at 1219–1234. For a discussion of American statutes generally see Rohan and Reskin, Condominium Law and Practice (1973).

38. The Puerto Rican act sets the period at ten days, but this seems an unreasonably short time within which to expect the other unit owners to respond.

39. Ramsey, op. cit. supra note 9, at 21. See also Gale v. York Center Community Co-op., Inc., 21 Ill.2d 86, 171 N.E.2d 30 (1961) (upholding a comparable restraint).

alienation,[40] it could raise questions under the doctrine of Shelley v. Kraemer [41] if it becomes apparent that the provision is but a mask to conceal restrictions on racial or religious grounds.

SECTION 5. ADVANTAGES OF CONDOMINIUM

The advantages of all things are relative.[42] The advantages of condominium must be stated in relationship to ordinary apartment dwelling, to ordinary home ownership, and to other types of cooperative apartments. Moreover, as the advantages to the purchaser will be different from the advantages to developers, lenders, and brokers, they must be stated separately for each group. Finally, since some of the advantages will turn out to be illusory, and because certain disadvantages exist which will offset some of the rosy claims made for condominium, a group-by-group analysis of advantages must be followed by a realistic look at the other side of the coin.

A. ADVANTAGES TO THE PURCHASER

---

1. *Compared to Ordinary Apartment Dwelling.* The advantages of condominium as compared to ordinary apartment dwelling are roughly those claimed for any form of cooperative ownership. It is possible to compile a list of fifteen to twenty specific advantages, depending on the zeal with which the advocate of cooperative dwelling approaches his task.[43] Basically, however, these advantages fall into two large categories: first, the improved financial situation of the owner vis-à-vis the tenant, and second, the added security and sense of status that accompanies ownership of a dwelling unit.

There is no denying that substantial savings can be realized in a well-run cooperative. The landlord's profit is eliminated,

---

40. It could also run afoul of the Rule against Perpetuities as an unlimited option to purchase, but for § 20 of the act. See Eastman Marble Co. v. Vermont Marble Co., 236 Mass. 138, 128 N.E. 177 (1920); Starcher Bros. v. Duty, 61 W.Va. 373, 56 S.E. 527 (1907).

41. 334 U.S. 1 (1948).

42. This is best illustrated by an old canard. A man greeted his friend with, "Life is odd isn't it?" Came the reply, "Compared to what?"

43. For illustrations, see Teitelbaum, Representing the Purchaser of a Cooperative Apartment, 45 Ill.B.J. 420 (1957); Wall St.J., March 8, 1962, p. 1, col. 1.

and all of the economies produced by mass purchase of supplies, fuel, public utilities, etc., can be passed on to the unit owners. Tax deductions for interest on the mortgage payments and real estate taxes should be most attractive to prospective purchasers. Moreover, under the proper circumstances, a purchaser may receive deferred capital gains treatment as a seller of a home who reinvests in a new residence under section 1034 of the Internal Revenue Code.[44] Since the owner is building an equity in his unit, which can later be sold, he is adding to the total of his estate rather than paying out rent which disappears with each passing day. It has even been noted that the homestead exemption laws would apply to the unit so that something might be salvaged if the owner fell on evil days. However, since lenders will invariably require a waiver of the homestead right, this is likely to be one of the illusory advantages.

The sense of ownership that goes with cooperatives in all forms, and which is strongest in condominium, may well be the principal advantage over a normal tenancy. The owner can sink his roots into his apartment with an assurance of tenure that would be lacking if he could be evicted by a landlord at the termination of any given period of the lease. He can make alterations, decorate his own unit to his individual taste, and have a voice in managing the entire structure in a way not possible except through cooperative ownership. It is true that he must share the management with others, but even this has its advantages since he may find a sense of purpose and fellowship in the united effort for maintenance and improvement of the building and grounds. The exclusiveness of this type of ownership is usually listed as an advantage—the ability to choose one's neighbors, in a way denied to the tenant, being heavily stressed. It is easy to overplay this point, however, since the initial subscribers may have no right to pass on other initial subscribers and the developer may dispose of the remaining units, in a slow-moving cooperative, without much thought of exclusivity. Later sales may also fall short of the ideal if the project runs into financial difficulties, and a situation may develop in which any solvent buyer begins to look better than the burden of extra assessments.[45] Nonetheless, the cooperative in any form is likely to be more exclusive than ordinary apartment living, and the right of first refusal in the condominium has a distinct appeal to many purchasers.[46]

---

44. For a treatment of this and other tax problems, see Anderson, Cooperative Apartments in Florida: A Legal Analysis, 12 U.Miami L.Rev. 13, 29 (1957).

45. Id. at 15.

46. See text supra at 251–252 for a discussion of this point.

2. *Compared to Ordinary Home Ownership.* Many of the advantages just discussed are inherent in ordinary home ownership. The merit of the cooperative device is that it makes these advantages available in urban areas where land scarcity and high cost cause individual home ownership to be next to impossible. Cooperative units of all types tend to combine the values of separate home ownership with the economy and stability of a large-scale enterprise. It becomes possible to have landscaping, garden areas, swimming pools, and other luxuries infrequently found in the "cheesebox on a raft" type of large-scale, individual unit subdivisions. These can be financed at a lower cost per unit because of the "one basement, one roof, high rise" approach to urban dwelling. In short, the advantages of apartment living with the freedom from worry over the petty details of day-to-day maintenance and operation can be combined with the pride of ownership that strikes a common chord for most Americans. These apartment-type advantages are likely to be particularly appealing to the older generation whose children are grown and away from home. Since the life expectancy tables disclose increasing prospects of longevity for the average American, this advantage of condominium may be of prime importance.

3. *Compared to Other Types of Cooperative Apartments.* An extensive brief could be prepared for condominium as opposed to other types of cooperative apartments currently in operation. However, most of the arguments can be reduced to a single claim, i. e., condominium combines the advantages of cooperative dwelling and separate home ownership. Thus, the unit owner's tenure is more akin to a fee simple title than would be the case under a proprietary lease with stock in a cooperative corporation. Granting that he is bound by the cooperative aspects of the declaration and bylaws, he comes as close as it is possible to get to "true ownership" of his apartment. This is important, not only psychologically, but in many, more tangible ways. The history of cooperative apartments, especially during recessions, has been an unfortunate one,[47] and the liability under a blanket mortgage is enough to scare away many interested purchasers. The unit owner is not quite so financially dependent upon the activities of his fellows. He negotiates his own mortgage and can make accelerated payments much as he could on a separate home. He pays his own taxes, and thus can avoid forfeiture and the ignominy of a tax sale. Although the condominium purchaser is not entirely free from the defaults of others (as will be seen in the later dis-

<hr>

47. Postwar Co-ops, Architectural
Forum, June 1948, p. 93.

cussion of disadvantages), he probably avoids the worst hazards of the other types of cooperatives.[48]

The unit owner's greater degree of financial independence is illustrated in another way. He may sell his unit at market price and thus reap a capital gain, instead of being required to sell his shares to the corporation for the amount originally paid in, as is frequently the case in the ordinary cooperative. Even if the other owners have a right of first refusal, they must exercise it at the market level. This can be of major importance in an era of steadily rising real estate values. Moreover, the owner has assurance that his family will have a place to live on his death without undergoing scrutiny from other members of the cooperative as to popularity and financial resources. In other forms of cooperatives, leases frequently terminate on death, with a right of the family to remain for a limited period only.[49]

It is well known that owning a home offers several significant income tax advantages over renting. These same benefits should be available to a unit owner in a condominium, although they may not accrue to the participant in a typical cooperative. Thus, the unit owner should be entitled to casualty loss deductions, to interest and property tax deductions, to deferred recognition of gains on sale of an old residence and to a depreciation allowance if he rents the unit to another.[50]

B.   ADVANTAGES TO THE DEVELOPERS, LENDERS AND BROKERS

In essence, the advantages to the developers, lenders, and brokers arise from the advantages to the purchaser. If the consumer finds condominium to be an attractive investment, then the suppliers of housing are certain to fulfill the demand. The present impetus toward condominium is furnished principally by the 1961 amendments to the federal housing laws, which recognized this concept of real property ownership and authorized the FHA to insure a first mortgage given to secure the unpaid purchase price on individual units.[51] As late as 1958, commentators noted that mortgage loans for ordinary coopera-

---

48. For a good analysis of these hazards, see Note, 68 Yale L.J. 542 (1958).

49. Note 61 Harv.L.Rev. 1407, 1419 (1948).

50. Note, supra note 32, at 332.

51. Housing Act of 1961, 7 Stat. 160, 12 U.S.C.A. § 1715y (Supp. III, 1961).

tives were "practically unobtainable," even with federal insurance, because the terms were too long and the maximum interest rate too low.[52] Condominium should alleviate this problem with its smaller individual mortgages, rather than a single blanket one, and with negotiated down payments that may well run higher than that possible for the entire structure. As with any cooperative, the builder or promoter can find equity capital from the potential purchasers, rather than being forced to provide his own. Moreover, smaller lending institutions may be able to participate in financing the individual units in situations where they could not have financed the entire project.

There may be less "red tape" in the sale of condominium units than in the handling of a stock cooperative. The latter must meet the requirements of the appropriate state blue sky laws, whereas condominium, since involving the sale of real property, should be regulated by the real estate laws of the several states.[53] However, since real property interests have on occasion been held to be securities, the developer will want to check carefully the law of his own jurisdiction.[54]

The advantages to the real estate broker are easy to visualize since each unit becomes a potential listing. One enthusiastic writer outlines five distinct advantages to the realtor and sums it up this way.

"The condominium subdivision is an answer to the land scarcity problem. The two-dimensional subdivision that passage of time and increase of land values has rendered obsolescent and uneconomic, is transformed by the condominium into a three-dimensional subdivision, section stacked vertically upon section. It restores the realtor's base of individually owned, single family units destroyed in land clearing operations, but in a new and different form." [55]

SECTION 6. DISADVANTAGES OF CONDOMINIUM

Ironically, the advantages of condominium carry the seeds of disadvantage. The more you strengthen individual unit ownership the more you weaken cooperative control by the group. It may be true "that condominium is simply another form of

52. See Note, supra note 48, at 569.

53. See Brothers v. McMahon, 351 Ill.App. 321, 115 N.E.2d 116 (1953).

54. Note, supra note 32, at 338.

55. Maki, Condominiums: New Prospects for Realtors, Lawyers Title News, Nov. 1962, p. 5.

cooperative ownership of real property," [56] but the very security of the fee simple title runs counter to the traditional view of a cooperative. This is but a legal affirmation of the truth in the saw, "you can't have your cake and eat it too." It is not an argument against condominium, as such, since all legal devices have weaknesses as well as strengths, but it does suggest caution in dealing with overly optimistic claims about the merits of this kind of project.

A.   DISADVANTAGES TO THE PURCHASER

As in the case of advantages, a long list of claimed disadvantages of condominium to the purchaser could be compiled. The problem areas can be isolated under three heads, however: first, the cumbersomeness of this legal device, especially if unaccompanied by statutory authorization; second, the lack of control by the co-owners of the activity of a recalcitrant owner; and third, the legal problems peculiar to any new technique that has not been fully developed by the case law.[57]

The first point has been well stated by Professor Powell, writing before the current impetus for condominium and not mentioning the concept by name.

> "The legal patterns employed in creating cooperative apartments fall into four categories, of which two are extremely rare. . . . Under the second of the rare patterns, each tenant acquires the legal ownership of the cubic footage constituting his apartment but a joint tenancy or tenancy in common is established as to the areas used in common, such as halls, stairways and grounds.[58] Few persons have resorted to these cumbersome and unsuitable patterns for the creation of a cooperative apartment relation." [59]

---

56. Ramsey, Condominium, The New Look in Cooperative Building, in Proceedings of the American Bar Ass'n Section of Real Property, Probate and Trust Law, Part II, Real Property Law Division 4–5 (1962).

57. The point can be illustrated by the true story of a lawyer who visited Minneapolis for the first time. On his way in from the airport, he spotted a mammoth building complex and asked the taxi driver, "What is that big building?" "Oh", said the cabby, "that's one of them new pandemoniums!"

58. See, e. g., Woods v. Petchell, 175 F.2d 202 (8th Cir. 1949), where the result was found to be a cooperative apartment. [Footnote by Professor Powell.]

59. 4 Powell, Real Property 709–10 (1954).

In a footnote, Professor Powell adds:

> "The inconvenience of requiring the joinder of many persons in deeds, leases or mortgages, the complete absence of a simple method of forcing the individual participant to perform his financial obligations, and the risk of heavy individual personal liability, combine to prevent both of these devices from ever having popularity."

The previous discussion in this chapter indicates that some of these objections have been met by the Puerto Rican experience and by carefully drafted statutes and bylaws, but others remain, and the whole idea will undoubtedly strike many purchasers as too complicated for their tastes. Just as the sale of realty can never be made as simple as the transfer of personalty, neither can the sale of a condominium unit be reduced to the simplicity of the deed, mortgage, and closing statement to which individual home owners are accustomed. Moreover, the expense may be increased because of the separate fees and separate mortgages. The latter will require more servicing and may carry a one-half percent higher interest rate than a blanket mortgage on the same project.[60]

The appeal of individual ownership may also be lessened when the purchaser realizes the necessity for a long-term mortgage on which he will remain personally liable even after he leaves the project. In ordinary cooperatives the agreement usually has an "escape clause" which allows a member to get out after the payment of a fixed sum. Although the separate mortgage makes the owner more financially independent of his fellows, it also means that he cannot take advantage of any reserves which might be built up and which could be available to carry him through a temporary default.

The second disadvantage comes down to this—it may be difficult to get rid of a "bad egg" if one owns a fee. The lessee can be evicted by summary proceedings, but the owner has a security of tenure which protects the undesirable participant as well as the desirable one. Remedies do exist, but lien foreclosures and breach of covenant suits can be costly and protracted if the built-in social pressures fail to resolve a dispute. Moreover, it may be difficult to insure, even through restrictive covenants in the deed and the binding force of the statute and bylaws, that future purchasers will be desirable and financially

---

60. See Note, supra note 48, at 603.

Perhaps the financing problems of condominia are no more complex than those of other large projects but they can be staggering. For example, a businessman went to Florida to look over a huge hotel that was for sale. He called his partner, "I've got some good news and some bad news. The good news first. They only want $10,000,000 for a building worth $15,000,000. The bad news? Oh, they want a $1,000 down!"

responsible.[61] The principal difficulty, however, lies with the owner who becomes *in*voluntarily undesirable, i. e., one who, for reasons beyond his control, cannot pay his share of the common expenses and taxes. These defaults are anticipated in the various statutes, and remedies are provided. They should work well when the defaults are few and the bulk of the owners are solvent, but what will happen in times of recession or of major depression? It was the latter which broke the back of the old-style stock cooperative, and no one knows how condominium would fare in such troubled times. The mortgages are several but the common expenses are joint.

The third area of disadvantage is the most difficult to handle. Condominium has a long history, but it is only now being tried in the crucible of twentieth-century America. An inventive mind can visualize numerous problems for which the solutions are not at hand. The more cautious investor may wish to let others provide the answers before casting his own lot with condominium. Central to this problem is the exact nature of the management association and its relationship to the unit owners. It has been suggested that the board of managers might be considered an "association" and taxable as a corporation.[62] This seems doubtful since there is no intent to carry on a business for joint profit;[63] but it would be possible to show a profit in a given year, and one is never too sure about tax matters. On the other hand, the management group is not incorporated and hence there is no limited liability either in contract or tort. This may not cause difficulty since the role of the board is carefully circumscribed; it deals principally with the common elements, and proper insurance coverage is mandatory. Nonetheless, one can foresee situations where the coverage would be inadequate, and the unit owner might find himself liable for a sizable judgment with no protecting corporate screen.[64] Similarly, on the insurance point, would a breach of warranty by one co-owner (say, in a fire insurance policy) void the policy for all? Can the management association sue a unit owner, or a third party, without joining all other owners? What

61. See Comment, 13 Hastings L.J. 357 (1962).

62. See Int.Rev.Code of 1954, § 7701 (a)(3). For a detailed discussion of the point, see Note, supra note 32, at 334.

63. Treas.Reg. § 301.7701–2(a)(2) (1960) states that "the absence of [either associates or an objective to carry on business for joint profit] will cause an arrangement among co-owners of property for the development of such property for the separate profit of each [or for no profit] not to be classified as an association."

64. Note, supra note 32, at 312. The board of managers could be set up as a not-for-profit corporation to avoid some of these problems. This is being done in some condominia.

if some refuse to join? What can be done to facilitate class actions by the association?

Other questions come readily to mind. In an eminent domain proceeding, is each unit owner entitled to a separate hearing on his fee or can the condemning authority proceed against the entire building? Many statutes of limitations read, "No person shall commence an action for the recovery of lands . . . unless within twenty years," etc.[65] Is a unit land, and, if not will the contract statute apply? There is no point in continuing this list since the moral should now be clear. None of these objections are, in any sense, fatal, but collectively they must be treated as some of the disadvantages of a new legal tool like condominium.

B. DISADVANTAGES TO THE DEVELOPERS, LENDERS, AND BROKERS

The disadvantages to the developers, lenders, and brokers follow the same pattern as those to the purchaser. The principal objection is administrative complexity. At the outset, the developer must make two applications for FHA insurance, one for a blanket mortgage for the project, the other for individual mortgages for the unit owners. Each must comply with the FHA regulations and the developer may run into delay while individuals arrange for FHA approval. If the developer is unable to sell all the units, he may have difficulty in discharging the original project mortgage, with the result that the entire venture could bog down.[66] Moreover, the lender may be restive under a security which is subject to rules and assessments imposed by a management group over which he has little or no control. This is particularly true if incompetent amateurs are in the position of running the show.

Prior discussion has indicated other administrative problems. In the absence of statute, the building may be taxed as a whole, and even with statutory authorization some assessors may be less than cooperative in carrying out their duties.[67] The developers may have to comply with subdivision regulations which would not be involved in ordinary apartment houses.[68] In short, the suppliers of condominia will find that all is not beer and skittles, and that they, too, must deal with the cumbersomeness inherent in this type of multiple unit housing and with some of the uncertainties involved in the new and the different.

65. Ill.Rev.Stat. ch. 83, § 1 (1973).

66. See Note, supra note 32, at 330.

67. See Annot., 80 A.L.R. 867 (1932).

68. See Note, Community Apartments: Condominium or Stock Cooperative? 50 Calif.L.Rev. 299, 336 (1962).

SECTION 7.   THE FUTURE OF CONDOMINIUM

Will condominium help provide home ownership for megalopolis? The advantages and disadvantages to the purchaser, the developer, the lender, and the broker are relevant in answering that question, but the issue for society as a whole is how to provide more and better housing for a rapidly expanding urban population. On balance, condominium should be a useful legal tool because it appeals to the basic American urge for private ownership and provides a greater degree of independence from one's fellows than is normally available in the landlord-tenant relationship or in the traditional cooperative. While it is far from perfect and while some of its advocates seem to be overly optimistic in its praise,[69] condominium is more than an attractive gimmick designed to lure reluctant capital into the housing market. It has more to commend it than the availability of FHA insurance, and, if approached with the usual legal skepticism and caution, it should join its older cousins as a respectable member of the property family. Although not strictly required, condominium should be undergirded by a well-drafted statute, and the bar should watch its growth closely so that needed changes can be made as experience discloses the weak spots in the pioneer projects.

Finally, it should be noted that condominium is, in a sense, a new type of subdivision—vertical rather than horizontal—and it has much of the same potential for development that we have seen in subdivision growth generally since the end of World

---

69. "Think of a condominium as a high-rise apartment building, a garden-type housing development of detached and semi-detached units each consisting of one or more stories, a row of attractive town houses, an office building in which each occupier owns his own office space, a shopping center where each shopkeeper owns his own storeroom, an industrial complex where each industry owns its own plant or facilities, a warehouse or terminal with ownership of areas divided among the occupiers—think of a condominium as any conceivable type of project where it is desirable for the various occupiers to own their respective areas and to have joint control of common areas or facilities. The possibilities are unlimited. Think, also, of the unlimited possibilities for land development and redevelopment and the possibilities for more and better housing, as well as urban renewal and rejuvenation. Do not overlook the possibilities for commercial and industrial expansion and all of the economic advantages that can accrue to our Commonwealth and its residents, *if* we are farsighted enough to provide the legislation and legal working tools so that condominium projects will be feasible in Pennsylvania." Smith, supra note 33, at 514. As Mr. Smith correctly points out, condominium is useful for many projects other than housing and, if it operates sucessfully in the apartment field, it will undoubtedly be used in a variety of commercial ventures.

War II. It has the same vulnerability to exploitation that un-
regulated growth of traditional subdivisions has already disclosed but also the identical opportuniy for decent housing if
properly planned and controlled.[70]   The discussion in this chapter should be compared with the later material on land use generally.[71]

70. See Krasnowiecki, Townhouse
Condominiums Compared to Con-
ventional Subdivisions With Homes
Association, 1 Real Estate Law
Journal 323 (1973).

71. Pp. 397 to 472 infra.

Chapter 6

METHODS OF TITLE ASSURANCE

Much of the Anglo-American law of land is explicable only in the light of man's search for title security. No great problem with chattels, since possession normally indicates ownership and the buyer can sue the seller if title proves defective, assured ownership of the vendor still plagues the real property lawyer. In this chapter, we shall discuss the legal principles involved in the various methods of title assurance and then conclude with a critique of the present systems, plus some suggestions for conveyancing reform. This approach will involve sections on covenants for title, the recording system and the methods based on it —examination from the records (or an abstract) and title insurance, title registration (Torrens system), and Statutes of Limitation. Bear in mind that all which has gone before in this text is of no avail if the purchaser, lessee, or mortgagee cannot be assured of receiving a merchantable title.

SECTION 1. IMPLIED COVENANTS OF HABITABILITY

Before proceeding to a discussion of the methods of title assurance, however, it is necessary to take a look at the dwindling role of *caveat emptor* in areas other than title to land. Of course, implied covenants of habitability have nothing to do with title to the land; one can have merchantable title to an uninhabitable dwelling. But, since there were no implied covenants of title, traditionally there were no implied covenants of *any* kind in a deed. Therefore, it is logical to explore the rise of the implied covenant of habitability before analyzing the title issues.

We have previously discussed the role of implied covenants of habitability in landlord-tenant law and have noted the dramatic change in the past few years.[1] A similar development has occurred in the freehold estates and for essentially the same reasons. As recently as 1961 an American court could say: "The great weight of authority does not support implied warranties in real estate transactions but requires any purported

1. Pp. 235 to 238 supra.

warranties to be in written contractual form. . . . No decision has come to our attention which permitted recovery by the vendee of a house upon the theory of implied warranty.[2] The Alabama decision was typical of the prevailing judicial attitude which put the full burden on the purchaser to inspect and discover defects before he accepted the deed. After delivery of the deed, it was too late to complain unless he had had the unusual foresight to include an express covenant or unless there was actual fraud on the part of the vendor. In the Alabama case the plumbing was not even connected to the sewer system and the waste was discharged under the house but, no matter, *caveat emptor* applied. There was an express covenant involved but it was for a limited period only and had expired.

It requires no extended discussion to see the full implications of such a rule in an era of tract housing, frequently shoddy workmanship, and an increasingly mobile population. Some cases and many legal commentators began to attack the inequity of this legal doctrine and by the late 'sixties *caveat emptor* was everywhere in full retreat. In Humber v. Morton[3], the Texas Supreme Court carefully analyzed the entire problem and correctly stated the modern rule that covenants of habitability can be implied. Said the court:

"If at one time in Texas the rule of caveat emptor had application to the sale of a new house by a vendor-builder, that time is now past. The decisions and legal writings herein referred to afford numerous examples and situations illustrating the harshness and injustice of the rule when applied to the sale of new houses by a builder-vendor,[4] and we need not repeat them here. Obviously, the ordinary purchaser is not in a position to

---

2. Druid Homes, Inc. v. Cooper, 272 Ala. 415, 131 So.2d 884 (1961). By 1971, Alabama had reversed its position. See Cochran v. Keeton, 287 Ala. 439, 252 So.2d 313 (1971).

3. 426 S.W.2d 554, 25 A.L.R.3d 372 (Tex.1968).

4. In the vendor-builder situation, Professor Roberts seems inclined to agree with Mr. Bumble's estimate of the law and points out that when caveat emptor is retained with regard to the sale of new houses, the law seemingly concerns itself little with a transaction which may and often does involve a purchaser's life savings, yet may afford relief by raising an implied warranty of fitness when one is swindled in the purchase of a two dollar fountain pen. 52 Cornell L.Rev. 835. Similarly, in 111 Solicitors' Journal 22, 1. c. 25 (London), it is pointed out that, "the purchaser buying a new house with legal assistance is often less well protected legally than the purchaser buying a chattel without legal assistance." It is further urged that, "The legal profession should have made it their business to insure proper protection for the purchaser without waiting for building societies to take the initiative" for their own protection since most builders "try to do a good job (but) the reputation of all may be injuriously affected by the low standards of a few."

ascertain when there is a defect in a chimney flue, or vent of a heating apparatus, or whether the plumbing work covered by a concrete slab foundation is faulty. It is also highly irrational to make a distinction between the liability of a vendor-builder who employs servants and one who uses independent contractors. Compare, Connor v. Conejo Valley Development Co., 61 Cal.Rptr. 333 (App.1967). The common law is not afflicted with the rigidity of the law of the Medes and the Persians 'which altereth not,' and as stated in Cardozo in 'The Nature of the Judicial Process,' pp. 150–151 (quoted in 415 P.2d 698):

> 'That court best serves the law which recognizes that the rules of law which grew up in a remote generation may, in the fullness of experience, be found to serve another generation badly, and which discards the old rule when it finds that another rule of law represents what should be according to the established and settled judgment of society, and no considerable property rights have become vested in reliance upon the old rule. . . .'

"The caveat emptor rule as applied to new houses is an anachronism patently out of harmony with modern home buying practices. It does a disservice not only to the ordinary prudent purchaser but to the industry itself by lending encouragement to the unscrupulous, fly-by-night operator and purveyor of shoddy work."

The shift is not yet complete in all jurisdictions and difficult problems of proof remain, but the purchaser, like the lessee, now has legal protection almost totally lacking a decade ago. The implied covenant doctrine is typically restricted to unfinished buildings and new structures. For obvious reasons, it has little application to older buildings and there the purchaser's eyes remain his bargain, unless he can convince the vendor to include an express warranty. There are situations, however, in which even the purchaser of an old building may have some legal recourse. In Maser v. Lind [5] the purchaser sued the vendor due to termite infestation and recovered on the basis of a representation that the buildings were "in good sound condition", although there was no express warranty against termites. In an A.L.R. comment on the case, it was noted: "In a few recent decisions, however, the courts have held that termite infestation can obviously become a serious and dangerous condition and, if known to the vendor, must in good faith be disclosed to the purchaser, since caveat emptor is no longer rigidly applied to the complete exclusion of any moral and legal obliga-

---

5.   181 Neb. 365, 148 N.W.2d 831, 22 A.L.R.3d 965 (1967).

tion to disclosed material facts not readily observable upon reasonable inspection by the purchaser, and that the object of the law is to impose on parties to the transaction a duty to speak whenever justice, equity, and fair dealing demand it." [6]

The growing protection for the purchaser was carried even further in Halpert v. Rosenthal [7] where the buyer was permitted to rescind for an innocent misrepresentation by the seller regarding termites. Even the fact that the agreement contained a merger clause providing that the agreement was subject to no understandings, conditions, or representations did not require the purchaser to prove fraudulent misrepresentation.

Obviously, the law is in a state of transition as consumer rights come to the fore in real property as well as in personal property. It is impossible to predict how far the law will move in its reversed direction but there are many straws in the wind. For example, in a precedent-shattering California case, Connor v. Great Western Savings and Loan Association [8], the court allowed purchasers of tract housing to sue a savings and loan association which had financed the project and was heavily involved in various stages of the development. The purchasers' homes had suffered serious damage from cracking caused by poorly-designed foundations that could not withstand the expansion and contraction of the adobe soil. The case depended on its peculiar facts. "In undertaking these relationships, Great Western became much more than a lender content to lend money at interest on security of real property. It became an active participant in a home construction enterprise." There were vigorous dissents, even given the special facts, and the court realized that the implications of its decision would end the traditional isolation of the financing institution from any liability for injury to the ultimate consumer. This is a major step since frequently the vendor-developer is insolvent and a suit against him for breach of an implied covenant of habitability is a hollow victory. Carried to its logical conclusion this decision would place a responsibility on the lending institution which is now largely absent. [9]

6. 22 A.L.R.3d 965, 975 (1967).

7. 267 A.2d 730 (R.I.1970).

8. 69 Cal.2d 850, 73 Cal.Rptr. 369, 447 F.2d 609 (1968).

9. See also Bradler v. Craig, 274 Cal.App.2d 466, 79 Cal.Rptr. 401, (1969) where the purchasers sued the general contractor and the construction and purchase money lender to recover damages for alleged negligent construction of a house. The court cited the principal case with apparent approval but held that any legal duty to protect the purchasers had expired by lapse of time. The plaintiffs had purchased the house eighteen years after its construction.

The *Connor* case became one of the most widely noted and debated California civil cases of the '60's.[10]

In 1969, the California legislature passed the following statute: "Liability of lender financing design, manufacture, construction, repair, modification or improvement of real or personal property.

"A lender who makes a loan of money, the proceeds of which are used or may be used by the borrower to finance the design, manufacture, construction, repair, modification or improvement of real or personal property for sale or lease to others, shall not be held liable to third persons for any loss or damage occasioned by any defect in the real or personal property so designed, manufactured, constructed, repaired, modified or improved or for any loss or damage resulting from the failure of the borrower to use due care in the design, manufacture, construction, repair, modification or improvement of such real or personal property, unless such loss or damage is a result of an act of the lender outside the scope of the activities of a lender of money or unless the lender has been a party to misrepresentations with respect to such real or personal property. (Added by Stats.1969, c. 1584, p. 3222 § 1.)" [11]

The statute was obviously designed to reverse the result of the *Connor* decision,[12] but the door has now been opened and the issue is unlikely to go away as the pressure for consumer protection continues to rise. While a full discussion of the fascinating problems involved in the merchandising of housing developments is beyond the scope of this text, each student should be aware of the implications of such statutory devices as the Interstate Land Sales Full Disclosure Act [13] and related state legislation.

10. See for example, Comment, "New Liability in Construction Lending: Implications of Connor v. Great Western Savings and Loan," 42 S.Calif.L.Rev. 353 (1969) and Comment, "Liability of Institutional Lender for Structural Defects in New Housing," 35 U. of Chi.L.Rev. 739 (1968). The latter comment was prepared while the case was at the intermediate appellate level.

11. West's Ann.Cal.Civ.Code, § 3434.

12. See Lascher, Lending–Institution Liability for Defective Home Construction, 45 State Bar of Calif. J. 338 (1970).

13. See, e. g., a letter from the Department of Housing and Urban Development, published in 19 Real Property Newsletter (I.S.B.A.) (1973).

"The purpose of this letter is to alert you to consequences which may ensue from your failure to understand fully the Interstate Land Sales Full Disclosure Act and its implementing regulations.

"The 1968 Interstate Land Sales Full Disclosure Act became effective April 28, 1969, and has now been operative for nearly four years. Although the Office of Interstate Land Sales Registration (OILSR) has processed thousands of registrations on both domestic and foreign subdivisions, it is nevertheless likely that an even larger number

SECTION 2. COVENANTS FOR TITLE

The doctrine of *caveat emptor* finds its natural home in the law of titles. In the absence of express covenants for title the full risk of title failure falls on the purchaser. The common law did not allow covenants to be implied and so strong is that doctrine that even the promises made in the contract are merged or extinguished when the deed is accepted.[14] This means that any right to sue the grantor, for title failure, in absence of fraud, mistake, duress, etc., must be based on covenants for title in the deed. If these covenants are included they give the purchaser of land some of the same protection which the buyer of personal property would have but they do not establish that the vendor definitely owned the interest he purported to convey.

In feudal times the grantor of a fee was typically a lord with large estates at his disposal.[15] He owed protection to the

of subdivisions covered by this Act are still unregistered.

"Unless exempt, any developer having 50 or more lots or parcels of subdivided land who sells these lots by using the U. S. mails or any other instruments of interstate commerce, without first registering with OILSR and providing the purchaser in advance of sale with an approved property report, is in violation of the law and may be sentenced to a jail term of 5 years or a $5,000 fine, or both.

"In addition, all such contracts are voidable at the absolute and unconditional election of the purchaser. Besides refunding the purchase price of the lot, the developer may be required to pay the reasonable costs of all improvements on the lot or lots. Once an unregistered developer is faced with the wholesale repurchasing of properties previously sold, many of which have already been improved, his bankruptcy is more than a remote possibility. All developers should be forewarned to reassess their positions on the need for registration before it is too late.

"Attorneys who have developers as clients have a professional responsi-

bility to familiarize themselves with the provisions of the Interstate Land Sales Full Disclosure Act and its implementing regulations, and to advise their clients accordingly.

"In addition to the direct penalties that the developer may face, there may be serious derivative consequences for the accountants, bankers and title companies, and even the real estate brokers of unregistered developers under certain circumstances.

"We urge you to read and study the Interstate Land Sales Full Disclosure Act and the OILSR Regulations. We are ready at all times to answer any questions from concerned parties."

Sincerely,
George K. Berstein
Interstate Land Sales
Administrator
Department of Housing
and Urban Development
Washington, D. C. 20410

14. P. 163 supra.

15. The following twelve paragraphs are reprinted from Cribbet, Fritz, Johnson, Cases and Materials on Property 776–779 (3d ed. 1972).

grantee, his vassal, in return for homage and other feudal services. If the vassal happened to be ousted from possession the
lord simply furnished another fief of equal value. This feudal
warranty operated rather like specific performance of a contract
in equity, but it was not based on contract at all; it arose out of
the tenurial relationship between the lord and his vassal. The
warranty could be enforced either by a real action against the
disseisor, where the warrantor was impleaded and forced to defend the title, or by a writ of *warrantia chartae* brought by the
grantee directly against the grantor. If the warrantor lost he
was forced to give up land of equal value (the value of the original land at the time of the grant) or, if he did not possess sufficient land for this purpose, he was assessed damages to make up
the difference. This feudal warranty had a complicated history
and was subjected to many statutory modifications. It gradually became too cumbersome for modern times, fell into disuse, and
finally was abolished in 1834.

Modern covenants find their genesis in the feudal warranty,
but they are quite different in scope and operation. The basic
difference is that today's covenants are contractual in nature;
hence they can be molded to fit the needs of the particular case.
While this section will deal only with the traditional or so-called
usual covenants, you should remember that the lawyer can draft
any covenant which suits his purpose so long as it does not run
counter to public policy. Legislation has played a major role in
this area so that you must always check the statutes before attempting to draft a deed in an unfamiliar jurisdiction. Typically, the statutes provide for a short-form warranty deed, the
usual covenants, or some of them, being implied from the use
of such key words as "grant," "bargain and sell," or "warrant."
This means that in present-day practice you may never run into
the exact language of a covenant set forth in the deed itself.

In the present section we are concerned with the operation
of these covenants and with the answers to several crucial questions. Why should there be more than one covenant? What is
the meaning of each covenant? Do the covenants in fact overlap? Can the same act breach more than one covenant? Do they
run with the land; i. e., do they protect successors in interest or
only the original warrantee? How much protection do they actually give to a purchaser?

But first it is important that we try to define and classify the
six usual covenants. They are as follows: (1) the covenant of
seisin; (2) the covenant of right to convey; (3) the covenant
against incumbrances; (4) the covenant for further assurance;
(5) the covenant of quiet enjoyment; and (6) the covenant of
warranty. Collectively they are called covenants for title to

distinguish them from restrictive covenants of the type discussed in Part Four of this book. The first three are called present
covenants because they are breached, if ever, as soon as the deed
is delivered. The last three are referred to as future covenants
because they may be breached at some future date when actual
injury accrues to the warrantee. A word about each of them
will be helpful before we proceed with our discussion.

Of Seisin. This covenant is so entwined with the mysteries
of seisin that its usefulness tends to be reduced. Maupin, a leading writer on marketable titles, states: "A covenant for seisin is
usually expressed by the formula 'that he, the said (vendor), is
lawfully seised of the said premises,' but as a matter of prudence
in some of the states, and of necessity in others, it is customary
for the grantee to require a covenant that the grantor 'is seised
of an absolute, perfect and indefeasible estate in fee simple.'
This is to avoid the rule established by those cases which hold
that a covenant that the grantor is 'lawfully seised' is satisfied
by a mere seisin in fact, whether with or without right. . . .
It is a rule of property in several of the states that a covenant
that the grantor is 'lawfully seised' does not require that the
grantor should have an indefeasible estate, and is satisfied by an
actual though tortious seisin, provided it be under claim of title.
The rule thus announced applies in but few of the states and has
been distinctly repudiated in others." [16]

The covenant is broken by any lessening of the corpus or
physical extent of the granted property, or by any diminution of
the quantity of the estate; e. g., the conveyance of a life estate
rather than a fee simple. On the other hand a mere incumbrance,
such as an outstanding judgment, mortgage, lease, easement,
dower, etc., does not amount to breach of the covenant, since none
of these operates as a divestiture of the warrantor's technical
seisin. The seisin passes to the warrantee but subject to the incumbrance.

An eviction is not necessary, as the mere existence of an
outstanding paramount title is a breach of the covenant if it is
properly worded. This raises some interesting questions regarding the statute of limitations and the amount of damages,
but we shall discuss these points later.

Right to convey. This covenant usually is included with
the covenant of seisin and is considered coextensive with it.
Oddly enough this identity holds true even in those states where
the covenant of seisin is satisfied by delivery of seisin in fact.
Like its twin, the covenant operates *in praesenti,* and an out-

16. Maupin, Marketable Title to   Covenant of Seisin in an Ohio Deed,
     Real Property 270, 272 (3d ed. 1921).   21 U.Cinc.L.Rev. 293 (1952).
     See Note, Scope and Effect of a

standing paramount title at the time the deed is delivered amounts to breach. No eviction is essential.

Against incumbrances. To quote Maupin again: "The precise legal definition of the term *incumbrance* is a matter of some nicety. In a popular sense, it means a clog, load, hindrance, impediment, weight. Perhaps the best judicial definition of the term is that of Chief Justice Parson: 'Every right to or interest in the land granted, to the diminution of the value of the land, but consistent with the passing of the fee.' Hereunder all incumbrances may be classed as: (1) Pecuniary charges on the granted premises; (2) Estates or interests less than a fee in the premises; and (3) Easements or servitudes to which the premises are subject."[17]

Examples of the first class are mortgages, judgment liens, taxes, special assessments, and mechanics' liens; of the second, leaseholds, life estates, or dower rights; and of the third, restrictive covenants, affirmative obligations burdening the property, rights of way, and easements generally. This covenant, like the first two, operates *in praesenti* and is breached by existence of an incumbrance at the time of the conveyance. Again, eviction is not necessary.

Further assurance. This covenant is the least important of the six and is not much used in the United States, although it has more vitality in England. In essence it is a promise by the grantor that he will, in the future, make any conveyance necessary to vest in the grantee the title intended to be conveyed. The covenant may be specifically enforced in equity and bears some similarity to the old feudal warranty. Although there has not been much litigation over its effect, there is no apparent reason why a draftsman could not use it to good purpose.

Quiet enjoyment and warranty.[18] These two covenants are virtually the same and should be considered together. The covenant of warranty should not be confused with its feudal ancestor, since it does not require the warrantor to provide lands of equal value. The warrantor can, however, be held liable for damages resulting from eviction. The covenants may be either general, protecting the grantee against the claims of all persons; or they may be special, protecting him only against persons claiming through or under the covenantor.

The covenants are prospective, operating *in futuro,* and breach does not occur until eviction. They do not promise that the title is indefeasible—that is the role of the first two covenants—they do promise that the grantee will not be evicted by

17. Id. at 310.

18. For a detailed analysis of the broadest and most effective of the

usual covenants for title see Comment, The Covenant of Warranty, 14 Baylor L.Rev. 77 (1962).

the holder of a paramount title. Note that while these covenants do not include the covenants of seisin and against incumbrances, a violation of these latter covenants, followed by an eviction, will result in a breach of quiet enjoyment and of warranty.

A. RUNNING OF COVENANTS WITH THE LAND

You will recall our earlier discussion of this problem in connection with leases.[19] There the principal difficulty was "touch and concern", a matter of no great moment here since a promise relating to title clearly "touches and concerns" the land. But the basic question remains, how can a subsequent purchaser of the land sue on a promise never made to him? So far as the three present covenants were concerned the answer of the common law was clear—he could not! These covenants, being breached as soon as made—i. e., when the deed was delivered the grantor either was or wasn't seised, either did or didn't have a right to convey, and the land was either incumbered or it wasn't—became choses in action and hence unassignable at common law.[20] The original grantee could sue for breach but when he sold the land his grantee's sole cause of action was against him, not the remote grantor. The non-assignability of choses in action has largely disappeared into the limbo it so richly deserves, but the bulk of American courts still follow the common-law doctrine. England and some American states, both by decision and by statute, have abandoned this "technical scruple" and allowed even the present covenants to run with the land.[21]

19. P. 192 supra.

20. Mitchell v. Warner, 5 Conn. 498 (1825).

For a good analysis of California law, which is fairly typical, see Comment, Covenants of Title Running with the Land in California, 49 Calif.L.Rev. 931, 945 (1961). The writer concludes: "Present covenants cannot run with the land however, for the whole concept of present and future covenants precludes this. Nevertheless, there is no reason why virtually the same result could not be accomplished by holding that covenants of title are assigned by operation of deed. If this were done the only reason for distinguishing between present and future covenants would be to determine when the statute of limitations begins to run." See also Comment, Covenants for Title— Protection Afforded Buyer of Realty in Florida, 7 U.Miami L.Rev. 378 (1953).

21. Schofield v. The Iowa Homestead Co., 32 Iowa 317, 7 Am.Rep. 197 (1871); Colo.Rev.Stat. ch. 118, art. 1–21 (1953).

Some states have solved the runability problem by a simple stat-

The future covenants do not raise this problem since they are not breached until an eviction occurs, which may be years and many grantees in the future. Granting, however, that the particular covenant runs with the land there must be privity of estate, i. e., the remote grantee must prove that he now owns the estate once conveyed from the remote grantor to the first grantee. If he fails to so prove or must rely on the Statute of Limitations to take the place of a missing link in his title chain, he cannot sue.[22] A more serious problem arises when there is a total failure of title from the start. If the grantor never owned an estate to convey to the grantee, how can the covenants attach to nothing and run with a non-existent estate? This may sound like another quibble, but it appealed to courts, not too happy with the "runnability" of covenants anyway, and many of them held that this barred a suit by a remote grantee. If possession passed, although no title, the covenants could latch onto the possession, but if neither title nor possession was transferred the paradox was complete. Nevertheless, some courts were friendly to suits by the remote grantee even in these cases.[23] One court stated it this way: "We should be inclined rather to say, that although the covenant of warranty is attached to the land, and for that reason is said in the books, to pass to the assignee, yet this certainly does not mean that it is attached to the paramount title, nor does it mean that it is attached to an imperfect title, or to possession, and only passes with that, but it means simply, that it passes by virtue of the privity of estate, created by the successive deeds, each grantor being estopped by his own deed from denying that he has conveyed an estate to which the covenant would attach." [24]

ute. See, for example, Colorado Revised Statutes, c. 118, art. 1–21 (1953): "Covenants of seisin, peaceable possession, freedom from incumbrances, and of warranty, contained in any conveyance of real estate, or of any interest therein, shall be held to run with the premises, and to inure to the benefit of all subsequent purchasers and incumbrancers."

Such a statute does not solve the problem of the time of breach and the resulting difficulty as to when the statute of limitations will bar a suit by the covenantee. See Bernklau v. Stevens, 150 Colo. 187, 189, 371 P.2d 765, 768, 95 A.L.R.2d 905 (1962). "The purpose of C.R.S. '53, 118–1–21, as to such covenants, is not to change the time of the accrual of the cause of action, but

rather to extend the benefit of such covenants to subsequent purchasers and incumbrancers. Wheeler v. Roley, 105 Colo. 116, 118, 95 P.2d 2 (1939). Thus the accrual of a cause of action still depends upon the time of breach; and the time of breach varies with the particular covenant. Consequently whether defendants' counterclaim is barred by the statute of limitations depends upon the particular covenants alleged to have been breached."

22. Deason v. Findley, 145 Ala. 407, 40 So. 220 (1906).

23. Solberg v. Robinson, 34 S.D. 55, 147 N.W. 87 (1914).

24. Wead v. Larkin, 54 Ill. 489, 499 (1870).

Assuming that the particular covenant will run with the land, it is not essential that all of the deeds in the chain be warranty deeds. Thus, if *A* delivers a warranty deed to *B*; *B*, a quitclaim deed to *C*; *C*, a warranty deed to *D*; and the title is now in *E* by virtue of a sheriff's deed coming through a mortgage foreclosure against *D*; *E* may have the following choices, in event of a title failure which antedates *A's* conveyance. He may sue *C* or *A* on the covenants running with the land, but he cannot sue *B* or *D* who gave no covenants for title.

B.　BREACH OF COVENANT

Apart from the right of a remote grantee to sue when a covenant is breached, difficult questions arise as to the breach itself. There is general agreement that the present covenants are breached as soon as made, if ever, but this scarcely solves the matter. Although there is a technical breach of the covenant of seisin, for example, the grantee may be undisturbed in possession so that no actual damage accrues. The third party who, in fact, owns all or a portion of the estate may be unaware of it and may slumber on his rights until the grantee's title is perfected by adverse possession. To allow the grantee damages prior to ouster, or threat thereof, may thus be unfair. On the other hand, if the grantee is forced to wait, the relevant statute of limitations (typically five to ten years on a written contract) may run so that the grantee will lose his cause of action against the grantor. If he sues presently and recovers only nominal damages, he runs the risk of a successful plea of *res judicata* when actual damage occurs because of ouster. This dilemma was faced squarely in the leading case of Bolinger v. Brake [25] and full damages were allowed to the grantee when he proved title failure, even though his possession was undisturbed. Other cases have ignored the dilemma and restricted the grantee to nominal damages until an eviction occurs.[26] This problem is non-existent with future covenants since they are not breached prior to eviction.

Future covenants, then, require eviction; present covenants, except for the one against incumbrances, may demand the same test. But what is eviction? Certainly, it must be by a person claiming under title paramount, for the covenants never promise

------

25. 57 Kan. 663, 47 P. 537 (1897).

26. For a collection of cases see Burby on Real Property 479, ftn. 35 (2d ed. 1954).

freedom from interference by a stranger to the title. Actual ouster by self help, ejectment, etc., clearly qualifies as a breach of covenant. Constructive eviction, that ever-helpful legal fiction, may also qualify. Thus, if the grantee is faced with ouster under a decree in partition, foreclosure, etc., he need not wait until the sheriff places him in the street, but may pay the sum due to the paramount title holder to prevent such drastic results. If he relies on constructive eviction, however, he should notify his warrantor (grantor) of the pending suit and, preferably, request him to appear and defend.[27] Failure to do this will not be fatal to his cause, but in a second suit by the grantee against the grantor on the covenant he will have to prove that the payment was justified, whereas had the grantor been notified and requested to defend that issue would have been *res judicata*. It follows that any time the grantee pays a third party claimant without suit he does so at his peril since the warrantor may later deny the validity of the claim.

The covenant against incumbrances does not necessarily require eviction in order to prove breach. An outstanding easement or restrictive covenant may interfere with the grantee's possessory rights but still leave him in control of most of the premises. In these situations, all the warrantee has to prove is the existence of the outstanding incumbrance. One troublesome question arises when the grantee knows of the existence of an easement but accepts a covenant against it. May he later sue for breach if the easement is not extinguished? The classic answer is yes, since knowledge of the outstanding incumbrance may be the very reason for insisting on a covenant against it.[28] This yes must be qualified and tempered with reason, however, for sometimes it is clear that the parties did not intend to remove the incumbrance. "Some of the cases are decided upon the theory that, whenever the actual physical conditions of the property are apparent, and are in their nature permanent, and irremediable, such conditions are within the contemplation of the parties when contracting, and are therefore not included in a general covenant against encumbrances. These principles have led to a conflict among the authorities, especially in the cases where a public highway or railroad right of way existed upon the land conveyed." [29]

27. Morgan v. Haley, 107 Va. 331, 58 S.E. 564 (1907).

28. Jones v. Grow Investment and Mortgage Co., 11 Utah 2d 326, 358 P.2d 909 (1961); Lavey v. Graessle, 245 Mich. 681, 224 N.W. 436, 64 A. L.R. 1477 (1929).

29. 64 A.L.R. 1479, 1480 (1929). See also Merchandising Corp. v. Marine Nat. Exchange Bank, 12 Wis.2d 79, 106 N.W.2d 317 (1960).

Although an easement is clearly an encumbrance, it is not always easy to determine whether a particular interference with a purchaser's rights amounts to breach of the covenant against encumbrances. The mere existence of use restrictions by way of zoning or building codes does not constitute an encumbrance but violation of these restrictions prior to sale may be sufficient to cause a breach of the covenant in the warranty deed. Thus in Lohmeyer v. Bower,[30] the court decided that the location of a structure in violation of a zoning ordinance specifying a minimum distance from the rear lot line exposed the owner to the hazard of litigation and made the title doubtful and unmarketable. Similarly, in Brunke v. Pharo,[31] the court held that violation of a building code, prescribing standards of safety to be met by apartment buildings, constituted an encumbrance violative of the grantor's covenant, where the agency charged with enforcement of the code had begun official action before conveyance and such action was thus imminent when the deed was delivered.

C. DAMAGES

We are immediately confronted by another dilemma. If the title proves defective it may not be discovered for many years and, by this time, the land may have increased greatly in value and major improvements may have been added to the premises. Is the damage to be determined by the actual loss suffered at the future eviction or will it be restricted to the purchase money paid to the warrantor? A small minority of states (all in New England) have followed the former rule and thus given the warrantee the maximum protection under the future covenants.[32] The overwhelming majority of the states have felt this placed too great a burden on the warrantor, especially in a society where the trend of land values appears to be always upward, and have restricted recovery to the purchase price, or a proportionate share thereof for partial breach, plus interest.[33] Interest is usually allowed, however, only in the cases where the grantee has not had the benefit of the rents and profits from the land or has had to sur-

---

30. 170 Kan. 442, 227 P.2d 102 (1951).

31. 3 Wis.2d 628, 89 N.W.2d 221 (1958).

32. For a collection of cases and a more detailed discussion of the damage question see McCormick on Damages 700–709 (1935).

33. Id. For a good discussion of the reasons behind the majority rule see Davis v. Smith, 5 Ga. 274, 48 Am.Dec. 279 (1848).

render them to the paramount title holder. As an additional sop, the grantee can usually recover the costs, including attorney's fees, for an unsuccessful defense of his title against a paramount owner. In the case of an incumbrance, the warrantee can recover the reasonable cost of removal, not to exceed the purchase price paid to the warrantor, or if the claim cannot be extinguished, as in the case of an easement where the holder refuses to release it, the diminution in value of the estate due to the incumbrance.[34]

When the covenants run with the land all sorts of puzzles are possible. Try this one for size. *A* delivers a warranty deed to *B* for $10,000. *B* delivers a warranty deed to *C* for $8,000. *X*, a paramount title holder, ousts *C*. *C* can recover $8,000 from *B*, but since the covenants of warranty and quiet enjoyment run with the land he can also sue *A*. He is restricted, of course, to one satisfaction. How much can *C* recover from *A*? Brooks v. Black,[35] in a well-reasoned opinion, allowed *C* to recover $10,000, i. e., the court held the original warrantor liable for the full price received by him, even though the remote grantee paid less to his own grantor. Other courts have limited recovery to the amount paid by the plaintiff to his own grantor.[36]

The purchaser of land who makes improvements in good faith, relying on his supposed ownership, may nonetheless be ousted later by a stranger who in fact owns the property. If a warranty deed was used the grantee may be able to recover a portion of his loss, but it will probably fall short of his real damages. Can he recoup any portion of this loss from the stranger-owner? At common law, the innocent improver was considered to be an interloper without legal remedy and since the buildings were annexed to the soil they became the property of the true owner. To modify this rigid rule, occupying claimants acts have been passed which, on a theory of unjust enrichment, allow substantial relief to the innocent grantee. Madrid v. Spears,[37] analyzes these statutes and demonstrates how they fit into the total damage picture.

34. Note 28, supra.

35. 68 Miss. 161, 8 So. 332, 24 Am. St.Rep. 259 (1890).

36. Taylor v. Wallace, 20 Colo. 211, 37 P. 963 (1894); Taylor v. Allen, 131 Ga. 416, 62 S.E. 291 (1908).

37. 250 F.2d 51 (10th Cir. 1957). See also City of Poplar Bluff v. Knox, 410 S.W.2d 100 (Mo.App.1966).

D. ESTOPPEL BY DEED (AFTER-ACQUIRED TITLE)

A conveys land he does not own to *B* by warranty deed. Later *A* acquires the title from *C*. Who now owns the land? Since *A* owned nothing at the time of the conveyance, nothing passed to *B* and *A* would appear to own Blackacre. If so, *B* can sue *A* on the covenants in the deed and recover the purchase price. To avoid this "circuity of action" the courts have long held that the title passed to *B*, thus giving him what he should have had all along and ending any suit on the covenants.[38] Suppose the deed to *B* had been quitclaim in form? If the avoidance of circuity of action is the sole basis for the doctrine of after-acquired title then *A* is the owner still, because *B* could not sue *A* on a quitclaim deed. However, the better view bases the doctrine on estoppel, i. e., *A* is estopped to deny that the title passed to *B* since he represented, at the time of the original deed, that he owned Blackacre.[39] This estoppel would nearly always work when a warranty deed was involved, hence we discuss it under covenants for title because it does give the grantee some further title assurance. It *might* also work with a quitclaim deed, however, providing the intent of the grantor, gathered from the deed, was to convey the full interest and not just release any possible claim he might have. Thus, the usual quitclaim deed would not carry after-acquired title but if there were recitals, such as "*A*, being seised of a fee simple absolute, conveys and quitclaims to *B*", this could form the basis of an estoppel by representation. A number of the states have clarified the doctrine by statute.[40]

Although the point is in conflict, the better view is that the doctrine operates to "feed the estoppel", i. e., it transfers the title automatically to *B*, rather than furnishing him with an equitable defense if sued by *A* or his privies.[41] This is the better view because it allows the title examiner to rely on this after-acquired title as a link in the chain of title. It can cause complications, however, if the grantee, *B*, does not want to accept this after-acquired title but prefers to sue on the covenants instead. Although the doctrine normally works *eo instante*, it would seem that in this last situation the grantee should have his option to accept the title or sue.[42]

38. Robben v. Obering, 279 F.2d 381 (1960). This case gives a good, general discussion of the doctrine and holds it applies to leases as well as to deeds.

39. Hagensick v. Castor, 53 Neb. 495, 73 N.W. 932 (1898).

40. See, for example, Ill.Rev.Stat. ch. 30, § 6 (1973).

41. Perkins v. Coleman, 90 Ky. 611, 14 S.W. 640 (1890).

42. Resser v. Carney, 52 Minn. 397, 54 N.W. 89 (1893).

SECTION 3. THE RECORDING SYSTEM (HEREIN OF TITLE EXAMINATION AND TITLE INSURANCE)

The previous section demonstrates that covenants for title leave much to be desired as a method of title assurance. Aside from their technical defects they require a lawsuit, unless the warrantor pays willingly, and if he is insolvent they are worthless. Moreover, even at best, they will not enable the purchaser to keep his land and he will have to settle for money damages. The buyer of land wants assurance that the vendor has a merchantable title which he can transfer to him. The recording system helps give him that assurance.

"Apart from the recording acts priority between deeds, mortgages, judgments and other liens or titles, is determined by the order in point of time in which they become effective. Where *A* conveys land by a valid deed to *B*, and conveys or mortgages the same land to *C*, nothing passes to *C* since *A* had nothing to convey to him, having already conveyed the same property to *B*. So, if *A* mortgages the land to *B* and later conveys or mortgages it to *C*, the right secured by *C* is subject to *B's* mortgage. This is true though *C* be a purchaser for value without notice of *B's* deed or mortgage. The doctrine that a purchaser for value without notice will be protected against prior claims applies only to cases where the legal title has passed to such purchaser and the prior claims are equitable and not legal rights. This doctrine is purely equitable, equity refusing to disturb the legal title by enforcing a prior equity where such title is held by a purchaser for value without notice. Apart from the statutes, therefore, a valid title or lien existing and enforceable at law is never cut off or affected by a subsequent deed or mortgage executed by the same vendor or owner to another person, whether a purchaser for value or not." [43]

There is logic in the "first in time, first in right" scheme of priority, but it is the logic of theory, not of practice. In a complex society purchasers have no way of checking on the status of title unless they can rely on some official record which shows all of the transactions in regard to the land in question. In the United States [44] the recording system has furnished the solution

43. 2 Walsh, Commentaries on the Law of Real Property 487, 488 (1947).

44. "Except as registration of title under a Torrens law obtains in the city and county of London, and except lands affected by the registry acts for the counties of Middlesex and York, proof of title in England is to this day by possession of the property and by exhibition of the original title deeds. . . . But, with the exception first noted, there has never been any provision in England by which proof of title may be made from public and semi-public records alone, as is now so universally the case in this country." 1 Patton, Titles 8 (1957).

to the purchaser's dilemma by creating a permanent record which can be examined by anyone wishing to buy land or lend money on it as a security interest. The net effect of the system is to introduce by statute the equitable concept of bona fide purchaser for value without notice so that the b.f.p. takes free of prior deeds, mortgages, leases, etc., if they are not recorded as required by the particular act.

The acts set forth the instruments which are authorized to be recorded, and while there is considerable variation they generally include deeds, mortgages, assignments of mortgages, leases, and executory contracts. Some acts are broad enough to include virtually any document: "Deeds, mortgages, powers of attorney, and other instruments relating to or affecting the title to real estate." [45] These instruments are copied (originally in a flowing script unknown today and now by photostatic means) into books kept in a public office in the local unit of government (usually a county) where the land is located. Typically the instruments go into the record as tendered, without regard to the names of the parties or the location of the tracts being conveyed. (Indeed in some areas little attention is paid to the instruments themselves and one wag tells of the county clerk who would put a menu on record if a fee were tendered.) Since in many counties there will be hundreds of books and thousands of instruments, it is apparent that careful indexing is required if the recording system is to make any sense whatever.

There are two basic systems of indexing—the grantor-grantee system and the tract system. The present trend is to reduce the number of indexes and use only one grantor-grantee index, but many states have a separate index for each type of instrument (mortgagor-mortgagee, mechanic's lien, index to miscellaneous documents, etc.). For example, Idaho has twenty-four different indexes.[46] Note how these indexes work in practice.

"A title searcher tracing title by means of the public records employs an official index of names, called the Grantor-Grantee Index.[47] Suppose, for example, that the United States Govern-

---

45. Ill.Rev.Stat. ch. 30, § 27 (1973).

46. Idaho Code, § 31-2404 (1948) provides for the following indexes: Grantors, grantees, mortgagors of real property, mortgagors of personal property, mortgagees of real and personal property, releases of real property mortgages in the name of the mortgagor, releases of personal property mortgages in the name of the mortgagor, two similar indexes for releases in the name of the mortgagee, powers of attorney, lessors, lessees, marriage certificates in the name of the husband, same in the name of the wife, assignors (of mortgages and leases), assignees (of mortgages and leases), wills, official bonds, mechanics' liens, judgments, attachments, notices of actions (lis pendens), separate property of married women, possessory claims, homesteads, real property agreements, mining claims, water rights, and federal tax liens.

47. The following five paragraphs are quoted from Kratovil, Real Estate Law 94–95 (3d ed. 1958).

ment records show that the United States sold a particular tract of land to John Jones on March 15, 1840. The title searcher will turn to the Grantor Index, which is arranged alphabetically, and, beginning with the date March 15, 1840, he will look under the letter 'J' for any deeds or mortgages made since March 15, 1840, by John Jones. Naturally he would not expect to find any deeds or mortgages of that land made by Jones prior to March 15, 1840, because Jones did not acquire title until that date. Therefore, except in a few states, the law does not require him to look for any such deeds or mortgages prior to that date. Suppose he finds that John Jones conveyed the land to Joseph Smith by deed dated September 10, 1860, and recorded November 1, 1860. He will now look under the letter 'S' for any deeds or mortgages made by Smith on or after September 10, 1860, the date when Smith acquired title. This process is repeated until he has brought the title down to date. This process is called running the chain of title.

"Suppose, however, that Joseph Smith had made a mortgage on the land in question, dated September 5, 1860, and recorded September 6, 1860. Observe that both of these dates are prior to the date of the deed by which Smith acquired title, namely, September 10, 1860. A title searcher would not find this mortgage, since he would not look under the name 'Smith' for any deed or mortgage prior to September 10, 1860. Such a mortgage is not in the line of title. It is also said that the mortgage is not in the *chain of title*. The legal result is the same as though the mortgage had not been recorded at all. A person buying the land not knowing of the existence of this mortgage would get good title free and clear of the mortgage.

"In other words, the records show the ownership of land passing from one person to another, and the name of each successive owner must be searched during the period of his ownership to see what recorded deeds and mortgages he has signed. The person searching the name indexes must always have some point of time to mark the beginning of his search of a name that appears on the records, and as a rule, where the records show that Smith became the owner of the land, the searcher need not look for documents that may have been executed by Smith prior to the date on which the records show Smith became the owner of the property. [However, in a few states, a warranty deed or mortgage executed and recorded by Smith, who does not *then* own the land, is, nevertheless, binding on all persons dealing with the land after the deed *to* Smith is recorded. Ayer v. Philadelphia Brick Co., 159 Mass. 84, 34 N.E. 177. This is a poor rule, for it requires searchers of the records to check a name for an indefinite time *prior* to the time such party acquired ownership of the land, merely to guard against the possibility of such 'wild' deeds and mortgages executed by him prior to his acquisition of ownership of the land. 2d ed. 1952.]

"In a few states, the name index (grantor-grantee index) has been superseded by a *tract index*. This index allocates a separate page in the index to each piece of property in the county, and if you are interested in a particular piece of property, you simply locate the proper page in the index, and there you will find listed all recorded deeds and other documents relating to this piece of property.

"In virtually all states, including those in which the only official index is the grantor-grantee index, abstract and title companies maintain their own private tract indexes."

A. GENERAL OPERATION OF THE SYSTEM

With minor exceptions, recording adds nothing to the validity of a legal document except as that document affects the rights of a b.f.p.[48] Title will pass from the grantor to the grantee as soon as the deed is delivered. Recording the deed simply assures the grantee that the world has constructive notice of the conveyance thus cutting off the grantor's power to defeat the former's interest by a new conveyance to a b.f.p. In the early days of the recording acts, the courts were somewhat bothered by the legal theory of the acts. If *A* conveyed the legal title to *B*, what did *A* have left to transfer to *C*, even if the latter was a b.f.p.?[49] The best answer seems to be that *A* has the apparent title, as disclosed by the records, even though *B* has the actual title. This apparent title does not give *A* a *right* to convey the land again but it does leave him with a *power* to do so until *B* records his deed.

Nor can recording give validity to a void deed or mortgage.[50] Recording places on file, in a public place, the written evidence

48. In Mountain States Telephone and Telegraph Co. v. Kelton, 79 Ariz. 126, 285 P.2d 168 (1955) the court held a contractor, owning no interest in the land, did not have a duty to search for recorded underground telephone line easements and thus was not negligent in damaging the lines, since he was unaware of their presence. "It is sometimes said that the record of a deed is constructive notice to all the world. That, it is evident, is too broad and unqualified an enunciation of the doctrine. *It is constructive notice only to those who are bound to search for it.*"

49. Earle v. Fiske, 103 Mass. 491 (1870) illustrates the remnants of this theoretical difficulty although the court decided correctly for the b.f.p.

50. Stone v. French, 37 Kan. 145, 14 P. 530, 1 Am.St.Rep. 237 (1887).

of a conveyance; if that conveyance was void for want of delivery, forgery, lack of capacity in the grantor due to infancy or insanity, etc., it is void still. Some statutes do make recording conclusive evidence of delivery in favor of a b.f.p.,[51] but beyond that concession the title examiner takes the record as he finds it, subject to numerous possible defects that are not disclosed on its face.

The recording acts were drafted to apply to written or paper titles that depend for their proof on a connected chain of deeds, contracts, mortgages, leases, etc. This will cover the bulk of the ownership problems but, even today, there are good titles which do not depend on a written document. Adverse possession of land for the requisite statutory period (typically twenty years) will give a good title to the adverse possessor but its proof will depend entirely on physical acts, not written words. This sets the stage for conflict. *A* has record title; *B* has possessed adversely for twenty years, but has temporarily left the land so his current possession gives no constructive notice of his claim; *C*, a b.f.p., buys from *A* on the strength of the record. Who owns the land? Mugaas v. Smith [52] gave judgment for *B*, the adverse possessor, since the recording acts do not apply to this type of title and once *B* has perfected his ownership he need not keep his "flag flying forever" on the land in order to be protected. This clearly cuts into the effectiveness of the acts, but they could be amended to require the adverse possessor to, at least, file for record an affidavit of his claim in order to protect innocent parties. It is true, of course, that he could not record his title, since he has nothing in writing, unless he brings a quiet title suit to confirm his claim by a decree in equity.

Mistakes will inevitably occur in the administration of a recording system. In the early days, when the documents were copied by hand, it was easy to misdescribe the land and, while photostating largely eliminates that error, it is still possible to index a document improperly. An instrument mistakenly indexed or not indexed at all is worthless to the title searcher, but who must bear the loss? The recording party has done all required of him, he can scarcely be expected to supervise the work of the recorder's office; the b.f.p. has relied on the records as they appear to him and has no possible way of discovering the error. The cases split on this tough issue and tend to turn on whether the particular act makes indexing an essential part of recording or whether it treats recording as complete in itself and covers indexing separately.[53] Mortensen v. Lingo,[54] a relatively

51. Mass.Gen.Laws Ann. ch. 183, § 5.

52. 33 Wash.2d 429, 206 P.2d 332, 9 A.L.R.2d 846 (1949).

53. 4 American Law of Property, § 17.25 (Casner ed. 1952).

54. 99 F.Supp. 585 (1951).

recent and well-reasoned case, promoted the integrity of the recording system by holding for the b.f.p. This case may represent the trend of modern authority. In any case, the injured party should have an action against the recorder on his bond.

A nagging problem under the recording acts concerns the effect of a defective, but not void, instrument which fails to comply with certain statutory requirements. The most common defect is a faulty acknowledgment but others may be involved. If the statute requires acknowledgment or attestation and the deed is recorded without it, does the instrument give constructive notice of a conveyance? The general rule seems to be that it does not, since there has been a failure to follow the statute.[55] While this may be a good way to put teeth into the statute and force proper acknowledgment, etc., it seems unfair to allow a subsequent purchaser to ignore a recorded document just because of a technical error. He can scarcely claim that he had no constructive notice of the grantor's effort to make a valid conveyance. This view has led to some statutory changes which declare that the document in question shall be notice to subsequent purchasers and creditors even though not acknowledged.[56]

Up to this point the discussion has proceeded as if the recording acts were all of one piece. It is true that they all seek the same general end, but there are substantial differences in detail. Moreover, you have probably noticed that the acts are strictly construed and, at times, seem hypertechnical. This is because they are deemed to be in opposition to the common law, which followed the "first-in-time, first-in-right" system of priorities, and hence fall under the old canon of statutory interpretation that statutes in derogation of the common law must be strictly construed. This means that no case under the recording acts should be considered without first analyzing the statute in the particular jurisdiction, plus its judicial interpretation.

It would be pleasant if the recording acts were all based on a uniform statute and the problems could be mastered by an analysis of the basic pattern. But statutes never seem to be passed to give pleasure to students, and the acts are far from uniform. Fortunately, however, there are not fifty separate

55. Nordman v. Rau, 86 Kan. 19, 119 P. 351 (1911); Messersmith v. Smith, 60 N.W.2d 276 (N.D.1953).

56. Ill.Rev.Stat. ch. 30, § 30 (1973). The extreme importance of specific statutes is illustrated by Flexter v. Woomer, 46 Ill.App.2d 456, 197 N.E. 2d 161 (1964). Despite Illinois' liberal position in regard to acknowledgments, the court held that a recorded mortgage was not constructive notice to a subsequent b.f.p. when it did not state the maturity date or the amount of the note. The statute required the mortgage to recite the nature and amount of the indebtedness. Should not the defectively recorded mortgage at least put the purchaser on notice of a prior lien and force him to make inquiry as to the date and amount?

types.　Most writers have classified the acts into four categories.

(1) *Pure race.* Under an act of this type the grantee who first places his deed on the proper records prevails over other conveyances from the common source of title. The first party to record is protected even though he took with notice of a prior unrecorded conveyance.[57] Some states use this pure race concept only for certain types of conveyances; e. g., mortgages or oil and gas leases; others apply it across the board.

(2) *Period of grace.* This type of act is designed to protect the first conveyee for a set period of time whether or not he records. If he still has not recorded at the end of the period he loses the special protection. This type was quite common at an earlier day when it took some time to travel to the county seat and when such trips might be infrequent for the landowner. Few states still have this feature, and those which do tend to reduce the period of grace from the earlier pattern of ninety days to, say, fifteen days. The provision for a period of grace is found in combination with one of the other types of recording act; i. e., race-notice or notice.[58]

(3) *Race-notice.* Acts of this type require that the subsequent purchaser be without notice at the time the conveyance is made and the consideration paid. In addition, the subsequent buyer without notice must record first.[59]

(4) *Notice.* Acts following this pattern protect the junior conveyee against a prior unrecorded conveyance if he has paid value and is without notice. They differ from race-notice acts, since the junior conveyee is protected even though the senior conveyee records after the grant to the junior and before the junior records, or even if the junior does not record at all.[60] In some states with acts which appear to be of the notice type, the race-notice principle prevails because of judicial interpretation.[61] Although notice acts originally were prevalent, at the present time notice and race-notice statutes appear to be about evenly divided. Acts of one type or the other are in force in most states.[62]

57. Dulin v. Williams, 239 N.C. 33, 79 S.E.2d 213 (1953).

58. 21 P.S. § 444 (Penn.1955). Pennsylvania has now repealed their period of grace statute. See 21 P.S. §§ 329, 330.

59. Mich.Comp.Laws Ann. § 565.29 (1953).

60. Mass.Gen.Laws Ann. c. 183, § 4 (1955).

61. Simmons v. Stum, 101 Ill. 454 (1882).

62. For a detailed history and analysis of the recording acts see 4 American Law of Property, §§ 17.4–17.36 (Casner ed. 1952).

B. PERSONS PROTECTED BY THE SYSTEM

The recording acts do not announce to the world, "*X* owns Blackacre"; they simply furnish a source of information on which the individual dealing with the land can, more or less, rely. The key to discovering who is protected by the acts lies in the word "rely." A donee, having parted with nothing of value, cannot be said to have relied on the system.[63] A purchaser, who knows the truth about prior but unrecorded transactions, has not relied on the acts. However, the buyer need not actually have searched the records in order to be protected and he takes free of unrecorded claims even though he negligently failed to look for them. While this appears, initially, to negative reliance it is actually a compromise with practicality, making the test objective rather than subjective. If the individual fits into the protected class he gets the full benefit of the system. The basic test remains: is he a bona fide purchaser for value without notice? In the pure race jurisdictions a purchaser with notice who records first is protected too, but this is important in only a few states.

The meaning of "for value" is the first hurdle. A valuable consideration is money or something that is worth money as opposed to a good consideration which refers to a relationship of blood or marriage. It is not necessary that the consideration be adequate and even though small or nominal it will suffice, in the absence of fraud.[64] Again, this view seems designed to make the system workable since an inquiry into the adequacy of consideration for each transfer would be intolerable. This is particularly true for past transactions in the chain which may well recite "for one dollar and other good and valuable consideration" even though a large sum was, in fact, paid. If the value paid was merely colorable or fraud was involved that is another matter. The authorities are split as to whether a grantee under a quitclaim deed is a protected party.[65] Good arguments can be made for either position since a quitclaim deed could be said to give notice on its face that the title may be defective and yet full value might well have been paid for the conveyance. Certainly, the position that "a purchaser for value by quitclaim deed is as much within the

---

63. Colorado is the only state to reach a contrary position. Due to the peculiar wording of the Colorado statute, even a donee is protected in that jurisdiction. Eastwood v. Shedd, 166 Colo. 136, 442 P.2d 423 (1968).

64. Strong v. Whybark, 204 Mo. 341, 102 S.W. 968 (1907).

65. Morris v. Wicks, 81 Kan. 790, 106 P. 1048 (1910).

protection of the registry act as one who becomes a purchaser by a warranty deed",[66] is more in line with the spirit of the acts and is a major help to the examining attorney.

If a buyer has paid only a portion of the purchase price when he discovers a prior conveyance, mortgage, or valid lien, he makes further payments at his peril since he is entitled to protection only to the extent that he has been "hurt." This is called protection *pro tanto* and the rule is applied in various ways depending on the equities of the parties and the facts surrounding the transaction. "Some of the courts adopt that rule that allows the innocent purchaser to retain of the land purchased the proportion paid for. Some admit a lien in favor of the innocent purchaser upon the land for the amount of the purchase money paid. Other courts give to the innocent purchaser all the land, with a right in the real owner to recover from him the purchase money unpaid at the time of notice." [67]

Is a lessee a purchaser under the recording system? The answer is yes, according to Egbert v. Duck.[68] "Although a lessee is considered a purchaser, as a practical matter this means very little to the lessee, since he is protected only to the extent of rent paid prior to notice and must vacate the premises at the end of the period for which such rent was paid. This may result in a great hardship when the lessee has made expensive improvements or has otherwise substantially changed his position, as a lessee for a long term may well have done." [69]

Once the land comes into the hands of a b.f.p. it is, in effect, cleansed of its outstanding, but unrecorded, equities and even if it comes thereafter into the ownership of a purchaser with notice or a donee the title remains clear. This rule is essential to a proper functioning of the system since otherwise a b.f.p. would have less than full ownership of the land. If, however, the title comes back to one who was party to a fraudulent transfer or to a former owner who held subject to outstanding equities the defects revive and attach to the land in his hands. This prevents a holder of the title from using the b.f.p. as a "filter" to cleanse his de-

---

66. Note 64, supra at 347 and 969.

67. Durst v. Daugherty, 81 Tex. 650, 654, 17 S.W. 388, 389 (1891).

In Alexander v. Andrews, 135 W.Va. 403, 64 S.E.2d 487 (1951) the court held that a purchaser who was paying the price in installments received notice of a prior unrecorded deed as soon as it was recorded. This places an intolerable burden on the buyer since he would have to examine the records immediate-ly before paying each installment. It would seem preferable to require actual notice to the b. f. p. similar to that required of a subsequent judgment creditor. See First Security Bank of Idaho v. Rogers, 91 Idaho 654, 429 P.2d 386 (1967).

68. 239 Iowa 646, 32 N.W.2d 404 (1948).

69. Johnson, Purpose and Scope of Recording Statutes, 47 Iowa L.Rev. 231, 235 (1962).

fective ownership.　He would scarcely be in good faith under these circumstances.[70]

The pre-existing debt, which is discharged as consideration for a conveyance of land, qualifies the grantee as a b.f.p. in some states but not in others.　The crux of the matter lies in a change of position in reliance upon the acts.　In Gabel v. Drewrys Limited, U.S.A., Inc.,[71] a mortgagee carefully searched the records, found the land free of prior liens, and then accepted the mortgagor's notes and mortgage.　In fact, there was a prior mortgage, unrecorded, which was placed of record later.　The mortgagee first mentioned had clearly relied upon the record but since no new consideration had passed to him—he simply took the mortgage to secure debts already due him—he was not entitled to priority and ended up with a second mortgage on the land.　The court felt there had been no change in position and hence he was not entitled to protection.　However, they said: "A definite extension of time for the payment of an existing debt, by a valid agreement, for any period however short, though it be for a day only, is a valuable consideration, and is sufficient to support a mortgage, or a conveyance, as a purchase for a valuable consideration."　Since it is easy enough to draft an instrument which will meet this requirement, it makes the result turn on a very small point indeed.　In the personal property field the matter has been resolved by legislation [72] and the pre-existing debt is sufficient to constitute value.　Consistency and practicality call for the same result in real property.

A related question arises as to the role of the judgment creditor.　*A* owns land that so far as the records disclose is free of all incumbrances.　In fact, *B* has a valid mortgage on the land but has failed to record it.　*C* obtains a judgment against *A* arising from some cause of action—the source is immaterial.　The judgment normally becomes a lien against the land as soon as docketed.　Who has priority?　Once again, the cases are split with the results turning largely on the language of the particular statute.[73]　The answer depends on whether the lien of the judgment extends to the actual title of the debtor or whether it reaches the apparent title as well.　If it is the former, *A* has only a title subject to a mortgage; if it is the latter, he apparently owns it in fee simple absolute, free of all liens.[74]　Note that, as in

---

70. 3 Pomeroy, Equity Jurisprudence 55–57 (5th ed. 1941).

71. 68 So.2d 372, 39 A.L.R.2d 1083 (Fla.1953).

72. Uniform Sales Act, § 76(1); Uniform Negotiable Instruments Act, § 25.

73. Holden v. Garrett, 23 Kan. 66 (1879).

74. Kartchner v. State Tax Commission, 4 Utah 2d 382, 294 P.2d 790 (1956).

the case of the pre-existing debt, you can argue that the judgment creditor is not a b.f.p. because he has not parted with something new in reliance on the debtor's ownership of land. Conversely, you could claim that he would not have bothered to sue and reduce his claim to judgment but for the fact that he expected to have a first lien. While the weight of authority probably favors the view that the judgment creditor is not a protected party, there is substantial authority and much logic to the contrary.

The protected party must not only have paid value in reliance on the record but he must be *bona fide,* and without notice.[75] (This last phrase may be redundant since if he had notice of a prior claim he could not be *bona fide* in his actions.) It is clear that actual notice of a prior conveyance will disqualify the subsequent purchaser, but what about constructive notice? Recording itself is constructive notice and binds a party whether he looks at the record or not. Possession of the land by an apparent stranger to the title has the same effect in most jurisdictions, many of them going so far as to say "he must make inquiry as to the rights or title of the possessor, for possession is equivalent to registration [recording], in that it gives constructive notice of the possessor's rights." [76] This inquiry notice is normally held to bind the purchaser to anything which an investigation of the possessor's claim would have disclosed.[77] In some jurisdictions the purchaser seems to be bound only if he knew of the possession,[78] but even in those states a careful buyer would inspect the premises thoroughly before closing the transaction. Fortunately, a party is not bound by mere rumor as to claims against the land or by the general knowledge of people in the locality that someone has an unrecorded interest.[79] Nevertheless, even in this latter case, the facts may be sufficient to cast doubt on the *bona fides* of the buyer.

75. A troublesome question arises as to the burden of proof when an issue of the purchaser's *bona fides* is involved. In Kindred v. Crosby, 251 Iowa 198, 100 N.W.2d 20 (1959), the court placed the burden on the alleged "purchaser" in a case where she looked suspiciously like a donee. Since she failed to prove her *bona fides,* she lost the case. Clearly, the burden of proof may decide many cases since, all too often, the evidence tends to be ambiguous and conflicting. The cases themselves are in conflict and reflect the diversity of opinion on the operation of the recording system. For a careful analysis of the problem see Johnson, Purpose and Scope of Recording Statutes. 47 Iowa L.Rev. 237–238 (1962).

76. Strong v. Strong, 128 Tex. 470, 474, 98 S.W.2d 346, 348, 109 A.L.R. 739 (1936). See also Wineberg v. Moore, 194 F.Supp. 12 (D.C.Cal. 1961) for a discussion of what constitutes possession and its effect on the recording system.

77. Galley v. Ward, 60 N.H. 331 (1880).

78. Toupin v. Peabody, 162 Mass. 473, 39 N.E. 280 (1895).

79. Note 76, supra.

C. THE CHAIN OF TITLE [80]

Documents affecting title may be recorded and still fail to bind a subsequent b.f.p. if they fall outside the chain of title. This paradox results from the use of a grantor-grantee system of indexing which can mean that a recorded instrument is, for all practical purposes, lost in the vastness of the recorder's office.[81] If a tract system of indexing is used this problem evaporates.

80. For a detailed analysis of the chain of title concept and some suggestions for reform see Cross, The Record "Chain of Title" Hypocrisy, 57 Col.L.Rev. 787 (1957).

For the most extensive chain of title I have been able to discover, note the following story from a column in the Washington Post.

"This is a story about a lawyer—a New Orleans lawyer—who called at the Reconstruction Finance Corporation here to arrange a loan for his client. He was told the loan would be okayed if title to the property was good and sufficient so the lawyer returned home and sent a rather voluminous and accurate abstract of title by mail to the RFC office here. Soon afterward he received this letter: 'We received today your letter enclosing application for loan for your client, supported by abstract of title. Let us compliment you on the able manner in which you have prepared and presented the application. Your abstract clearly demonstrates that you are not without ample experience in this line of your profession. We have observed, however, that you have not chained the titles back of the year 1803 and, before final approval can be accorded the application, it will be necessary that title be chained back of that year.'

"The attorney read the letter and his blood pressure shot up. He called his secretary and dictated this letter:

'Gentlemen: Your letter regarding titles in Case No. 198156 received. I note you wish titles to extend further than I have presented them. I was unaware that any educated man in the world failed to know that Louisiana was purchased by the United States from France in 1803.

'The title to the land was acquired by France by right of conquest from Spain. The land came into the possession of Spain by right of a discovery made in 1492 by a Spanish-Portugese sailor named Christopher Columbus, who had been granted the privilege of seeking a new route to India by the then reigning monarch, Queen Isabella.

'The Good Queen, being a pious woman and careful about titles (almost as careful, I might say, as the RFC) took the precaution of securing the blessings of the Pope of Rome upon the voyage before she sold her jewels to help Columbus. Now, the Pope, as you know, is the emissary of Jesus Christ, who is the Son of God, and God, it is commonly accepted, made the world. Therefore, I believe it is safe to presume that he also made that part of the United States called Louisiana—and I hope to HELL you're satisfied.' "

81. The chain of title concept may also protect title insurance companies where the defect falls outside the chain. See Ryczkowski v. Chelsea Title and Guaranty Co., 85 Nev. 37, 449 P.2d 261 (1969). The issue is less likely to arise there, however, since most title insurance companies maintain their own system of tract indexes and would usually find the claim, if recorded.

The chain of title concept is illustrated by the following case. *A* leases to *B*, who neither records nor takes possession. *B* assigns the lease to *C* who records the assignment but does not enter into possession. *A* then gives a warranty deed to *D*, a b.f.p., who records. *D* will take free of the lease, even though its assignment was recorded, because it is outside the chain of title. In using the grantor-grantee index, *D* would find no prior conveyance indexed under the name of *A* as grantor. How could he ever discover the assignment since it would be indexed under names that are strangers to his chain of title? A contrary holding would make the system unworkable since no one could search every document in the recording office. Note that if a tract system were in use all instruments relating to that particular piece of property would be indexed in the same place and the assignment would then be discovered, giving notice of the prior unrecorded lease. If, under the above facts, *A*, prior to the warranty deed to *D*, had given an option to purchase (recorded) to *E* and that option had recited that it was subject to a prior lease to *B* that would have been sufficient to bind *D*. This is so, because the option is in the chain of title and the subsequent purchaser takes subject to all facts disclosed by the terms of the option, i. e., he is put on inquiry notice by the recital.[82]

There are many variations of the basic situation just discussed but it is safe to conclude that any time a document affecting title is left unrecorded, subsequent transactions based on that document will be out of the chain of title and hence will not give constructive notice to a subsequent b.f.p. from the original owner.[83] Of course, if the claimants under the unrecorded instrument enter into possession that will be constructive notice in itself.

Must a purchaser search the records for a conveyance recorded *after* a prior grantor in the chain parted with title? *A* conveys to *B* but the latter does not record. *A* then conveys to *C* who promptly records but is not a protected party because he knew of the prior deed to *B*. *B* then records, but some time after the recorded conveyance to *C*. *C* then conveys to *D*, a b.f.p., who records. Who has priority? The better view would prefer *D*,

82. Guerin v. Sunburst Oil and Gas Co., 68 Mont. 365, 218 P. 949 (1923). The reference to claims outside the chain, in recitals in documents inside the chain, has clouded many titles. This is particularly troublesome if the reference is vague and gives no real clue as to the nature of the claim or the identity of the claimant. This problem has been dealt with by statutes in some states and the acts tend to protect the b. f. p. and promote merchantability of titles. See L. C. Stroh and Sons, Inc. v. Batavia Homes and Develop. Corp., 17 A. D.2d 385, 234 N.Y.S.2d 401 (1962).

83. Capper v. Poulsen, 321 Ill. 480, 152 N.E. 587 (1926), is another variation on the theme in which a recorded affidavit, which would have put the subsequent purchaser on notice, failed to have that effect because it was out of the chain of title.

since he is a b.f.p. and the deed to *B* is now out of the chain of title.[84] A contrary position, based on the fact that *B's* deed was recorded before the conveyance to *D*, has been adopted in some states.[85] The importance of the problem lies in the light it throws on the chain of title concept. It is impractical for a purchaser to search the grantor index for a period after the title has been conveyed because there would literally be no place to stop, short of the day when the purchaser's deed is recorded, and this would have to be done for every title holder in the chain, back to the patent deed from the government.

The converse of the situation discussed in the preceding paragraph is also interesting. Must a purchaser search the records for a conveyance recorded *before* a prior grantor in the chain acquired title? *A* conveys by warranty deed to *B*, who promptly records. Unfortunately, *A* has no title at the time since the land is really owned by *X*. Subsequently, *A* acquires *X's* interest and the deed is recorded. *A* then conveys to *C*, a b.f.p., who records. Who has priority? Again, the better view prefers *C* since he is a b.f.p. and the deed to *B* is out of the chain of title.[86] However, since this situation involves the doctrine of estoppel by deed it is possible to argue that the title acquired by *A* from *X* passed immediately to *B* under the warranties in the deed and hence left nothing for *C*. Several cases have so held [87] but this position has been vigorously attacked by Professor Walsh. "This obsolete doctrine of estoppel by deed has been applied . . . in obvious disregard of the recording acts and the necessary rule incident to their application that the recorded instrument must be in the chain of title. They have held that estoppel by deed binds all subsequent purchasers, though for value and without notice, and therefore the recording acts do not protect them—a shocking exhibition of technicality and ignorance of legal history. . . . Though the principle of legal estoppel is recognized, its application in these cases to defeat the recording acts by the fiction of relation is without any reasonable basis." [88] This latter view, which prefers *B*, would require the purchaser to search the grantor index for conveyances by the grantor clear back to the beginning—again, a hopeless task since it would have to be done for every grantor in the chain. Of course, a tract index would solve both of these knotty problems.

84. Morse v. Curtis, 140 Mass. 112, 2 N.E. 929 (1885).

85. Woods v. Garnett, 72 Miss. 78, 16 So. 390 (1894).

86. Richardson v. Atlantic Coast Lumber Corporation, 93 S.C. 254, 75 S.E. 371 (1912).

87. Ayer v. Philadelphia and Boston Face Brick Co., 159 Mass. 84, 34 N.E. 177 (1893); Tefft v. Munson, 57 N.Y. 97 (1875).

88. 2 Walsh, Commentaries on the Law of Real Property 511 (1947).

One final illustration should be sufficient to clarify the chain of title problem. *A* subdivides a tract of land into numerous lots, putting restrictive covenants (set back lines, limitations to residential use, etc.) in most of the deeds to his grantees. He fails to put any such covenants in a deed to *B*, a b.f.p., who is unaware of the restricted nature of the area. All of the prior deeds are recorded so that if they give constructive notice *B* is bound by the restrictions.[89] Once more the cases split, with some courts taking the position that the prior deeds are out of the chain of title since "subsequent purchaser" in the recording acts means purchaser of the same tract of land, *not* purchaser from the same grantor.[90] Other courts, claiming to represent the weight of authority, say that the "grantee is chargeable with notice of everything affecting his title which could be discovered by an examination of the records of the deeds or other muniments of title of his grantor." [91] Strict chain of title logic favors the former position, but the latter may be more practical since usually the restricted nature of the subdivision is apparent to the purchaser so that he may be put on inquiry notice as to the covenants.[92]

D. EXAMINATION OF THE RECORDS OR OF AN ABSTRACT OF TITLE

The recording system was designed to protect a purchaser or a mortgagee of an interest in land.[93] That individual has constructive notice of all that appears in the records, and he would be most foolish to invest his money without a careful check at the appropriate offices in the county courthouse. He has constructive notice of matters other than those in the recorder's office; he must check the court records for judgments that may

89. See p. 347, infra, for a discussion of restrictive covenants and the theory by which *B* is bound if he has notice, actual or constructive.

90. Glorieux v. Lighthipe, 88 N.J.L. 199, 96 A. 94 (1915).

91. Finley v. Glenn, 303 Pa. 131, 136, 154 A. 299, 301 (1931).

92. For a more detailed analysis of this point see 4 Am.L.Prop. § 17.24, p. 602 (Casner ed. 1952).

Conveyances of subdivided land can cause other chain of title problems. For example, deeds using metes and bounds descriptions, after the land has been subdivided into numbered lots, may be outside the chain. See Baker v. Koch, 114 Ohio App. 519, 183 N.E.2d 434 (1960).

93. The following five paragraphs are reprinted from Cribbet, Fritz, Johnson, Cases and Materials on Property 822–823 (3d ed. 1972).

be liens against the land, the probate records for proceedings in an intestate or a testate succession, the tax and special assessments records, etc. All of these have indexes, and since they are public records the purchaser himself could make the examination. Obviously this would be a waste of his time since, even if he found the relevant documents, he would have some difficulty in interpreting them. Therefore, the lawyer performs this service and renders his opinion as to the state of the title.

In some areas of the country the lawyer still makes the search, prepares his chain of title, and then gives his opinion. This is slow, detailed work, virtually impossible in large population centers because of the sheer bulk of the records. Private abstract companies have been developed to ease the lawyer's load (and make a good profit). These companies typically keep a duplicate set of records based on the tract index principle. They then prepare an abstract of the record for each piece of property, as the need develops, and the lawyer can examine this abstract in the privacy of his own office, then give his opinion of the title. The abstract company keeps its records up to date by a daily transfer from the various public records to the private set kept by the company. This is usually done by a "take-off man" who operates between the courthouse and the company office.

Once the initial abstract has been prepared, usually starting with the patent deed from the United States or the state, it is relatively easy to keep it up to date by a continuation each time the land is transferred. The abstracter need cover only the period from the last continuation down to date and add this to the constantly increasing bulk of the abstract. Needless to say, the abstract will become a valuable piece of personal property in its own right, frequently being worth several hundred dollars.

The examining attorney does not assume any responsibility for the correctness of the abstract but limits his opinion [94] to the

94. The opinion of title is usually a carefully worded legal document which strictly limits the area of the lawyer's responsibility and concludes that 0 is seized of a merchantable title in fee simple absolute (if this is the case) subject to stated encumbrances, liens, etc. The following opinion of a Texas lawyer is scarcely typical but it may lighten a somewhat dreary discussion.

> *A Slightly Imperfect Title*
> 1214 Marcus Bldg.
> Prewitt, Texas
> January 4, 1928

Mr. Alex Deanton
Prewitt, Texas

Dear Sir:
In accordance with your order, I have examined abstract of title in seven parts covering the South 236½ acres out of the Edmundson Survey in ———— County, Texas, which you are preparing to buy and herewith render my opinion.

Don't buy the G———— d———— land. It has been my sorrow and burden to look over several horrible examples of a title examiner's nightmare, but this alleged title takes the cut-glass flyswatter. It is my private belief that you couldn't cure the defects if you sued everybody from the Spanish Government (who started this mess) on down to the pres-

title disclosed by the abstracted records. Any error in the abstract itself, such as the miscopying of a deed or the omission of a

ent possessor of the land, who is in there by virtue of a peculiar instrument optimistically designated by the abstractor as a "General Warranty Deed."

In the first place, the field notes of the Spanish Grant do not close. I don't think it is possible to obtain a confirmation grant since the late unpleasantness in 1898. In the second place, there were nineteen heirs of the original grantee, and only three of them joined in the execution of the conveyance unto the next party in this very rusty chain of title, which is a major defect in the first place. We might rely on limitation here, except that I am reliably informed that nobody has succeeded in living on this land for a longer period than two years, before dying of malnutrition. Laches might help out, but anybody who undertakes to buy land under a title acquired by laches is (to paraphrase Mark Twain) setting out like the man who set out to carry the cat home by the tail—he is going to acquire experience that will be of great value to him and never grow dim or doubtful.

This land has been sold for taxes eight times in the last forty years. Nobody has ever redeemed one of these tax sales—glad to be rid of it, no doubt. The last purchaser sued the tax collector a month after he bought for cancellation of the sale for fraud and misrepresentation. He doubtless had grounds, but this incident will give you a rough idea of what kind of muzzle-loading smooth-bores have been fritzing this title.

On January 1, 1908, a gentleman who appears suddenly out of nowhere by the name of Ellis Gretzberg executes a quit-claim deed containing a general warranty of title to one Peter Perkinston. Perkinston, the prolific old billygoat, died, leaving two wives and seventeen children, the legitimacy of two of them being severely contested. I am not being funnier than the circumstances indicate; he actually left two wives, and it seems never to have been legally adjudicated who he done wrong by. Each one of these ladies passed away in the fear of

God and the hope of a glorious resurrection and left a will devising this land to their respective brats. A shooting match between the two sets of claimants seems to have assisted the title slightly by reducing the original number to six and substituting eleven sets of descendants. One of the most prevalent causes of defects in this title seems to be the amorous proclivities and utter disregard for consequences prevailing in this neighborhood.

Your prospective vendor derives title by virtue of an instrument concerning which I have previously remarked. It is executed by a fair majority of one set of the offspring of Peter ("Prolific") Perkinston, and is acknowledged in a manner sufficient to pass a County Clerk with his fee prepaid. Outside of the fact that it doesn't exactly describe the property under search, the habendum clause is to the grantors, the covenant of general warranty doesn't warrant a thing and it is acknowledged before it is dated, I suppose it is all right.

I might mention that this land was the subject of a trespass to try title suit between two parties who appear in the abstracts for the first time when the suit was filed, and one of them recovered judgment awarding title and possession. We may waive this as a minor defect, comparatively speaking.

I would advise you to keep the abstracts, if you can. They are a speaking testimonial to the result of notaries public drawing instruments, county clerks who would put a menu on record if a fee was tendered, and jacklegged jugheads posing as lawyers.

You can buy the land if you so desire. There are five hundred and seventy-three people who can give you as good a title as your prospective vendor has, not counting the heirs of the illegitimate son of Prather Linkon who died in the penitentiary in 1889 while serving a term for sodomy.

Yours very truly,
Kress L. Campel

P.S. You owe me two dollars more for headache powders I used.

mortgage, is the fault of the company. Both the lawyer and the abstracter may be liable to the client for any negligence in the areas of their respective responsibilities.[95]

As the term indicates, the abstract is not a reproduction of the original documents but consists of a condensed statement of the key facts in each transfer.[96] Normally the abstracter expresses no opinion as to the legal significance of the instruments but simply sets them forth for the lawyer's judgment.

The only way to clarify this method of title assurance is for you to look at some actual abstracts and try your hand at examining one of them. It would be worthwhile for you, at this point, to look at Mr. Flick's book on Abstract and Title Practice and study the short, but actual, abstract which he reprints there.[97]

It should be noted that while the title insurance company is normally liable only as an insurer and has no duty to search (it could write pure casualty insurance without any search of the records), it may be held to have such a duty and hence be liable for negligence in doing so.[98] This could mean liability in excess of the stated limits of the policy, if the company has overlooked a title defect causing the purchaser to suffer a loss.

95. The abstract company may also be liable to third parties, who have relied on the accuracy of the abstract, on the principle of third party beneficiary contracts. Slate v. Boone County Abstract Co., 432 S.W.2d 305 (Mo.1968). In Chun v. Park, 51 Hawaii 501, 462 P.2d 905 (1969), the court held a title company liable to the buyers and a lending institution where the seller had ordered the title search. The title company was said to owe a duty to those parties, whose identity was known, to use reasonable care in making the search and preparing the certificate of title. The company, however, was liable only for those damages for which its negligence was the proximate cause of the loss. Loss of anticipated profits from resale of the premises and sums expended for plans and specifications for a new building on the land were thus held not to be recoverable. See also Williams v. Polgar, 391 Mich. 6, 215 N.W.2d 149 (1973).

96. If the contract is silent as to who must furnish the abstract (normally the contract provides that the vendor must do so), who must bear the burden of preparing such a document? See Department of Public Works and Buildings v. Halls, 35 Ill.2d 283, 220 N.E.2d 167 (1966). "The option here was to buy certain property for $25,000. There was no reference therein to an abstract of title or a warranty deed, and it is clear that a seller is under no obligation to furnish an abstract (Turn Verein Eiche v. Kionka, 255 Ill. 392, 99 N.E. 684, 43 L.R.A., N.S. 44), or a warranty deed (Morris v. Goldthorp, 390 Ill. 186, 60 N.E.2d 857) in the absence of a specific agreement to do so."

97. 1 Flick, Abstract and Title Practice 22–40 (2d ed. 1958).

98. J. H. Trisdale, Inc. v. Shasta County Title Co., 146 Cal.App.2d 831, 304 P.2d 832 (1956). See also Note, Title Insurance: The Duty to Search, 71 Yale L.J. 1161 (1962).

E.   TITLE INSURANCE

Title insurance introduces no new principle into the law of property. It is based squarely on the recording system and involves a search of the records in the manner which we have just discussed. Its principal advantage lies in title investigation by a group of specialists whose work is then insured by a financially stable institution. More will be said on this point in the critique of modern conveyancing, which follows our present exploration of methods.

Title insurance usually covers defects in the title of record, hidden defects not disclosed by the record, and the costs of defending the title against attack. You will recall some of the hidden defects which no title examiner could discover from his search of the records: disability of a grantor in the chain of title; forgery of an instrument in the chain; fraudulent representation of marital status by a grantor; mistaken identity of a record titleholder and a grantor due to similar or identical names; errors in the record; errors in examination of the record; undisclosed heirs; exercise of a power of attorney after death of the creator of the power; and defects in conveyances in the chain due to lack of delivery.[99] There are also the difficulties in construction of a will, trust, etc., where capable attorneys will differ as to the correct result. Title insurance will, in effect, guarantee the interpretation decided upon by the insurance company. So, too, unjustifiable attacks may be made on the title which the owner can eventually defeat, but only after the expense and difficulty of a lawsuit. Title insurance companies will defend the title, as guaranteed, and thus bear this burden for the purchaser.

On the other hand, title insurance is no panacea and it has the inherent problems of all insurance, including the key one of coverage. The policy must be read carefully since the exceptions can be so broad that they destroy the protection. The companies are not above relying on technicalities to defeat liability,[1] and unless the purchaser has independent legal counsel to interpret the policy and point out areas of potential danger he may end up with something less than he bargained for.[2]

---

99. 2 Fitch, Abstracts and Titles to Real Property 445–446 (1954).

1. Beaullieu v. Atlantic Title and Trust Co., 60 Ga.App. 400, 4 S.E.2d 78 (1939); Mayers v. Van Schaick, 268 N.Y. 320, 197 N.E. 296 (1935).

2. Hocking v. Title Insurance and Trust Co., 37 Cal.2d 644, 234 P.2d 625 (1951).

SECTION 4. TITLE REGISTRATION—THE
TORRENS SYSTEM

It is easy to confuse recording and registration because some of the terms are used interchangeably. However, they are entirely separate systems of title assurance, based on different theories and operating in distinct fashions. "The basic principle of this system is the registration of the *title* of land, instead of registering [recording], as the old system requires, the *evidence* of title. In the one case only the ultimate fact or conclusion that a certain named party has title to a particular tract of land is registered, and a certificate thereof is delivered to him. In the other the entire evidence, from which proposed purchasers must, at their peril, draw the conclusion, is registered [recorded]. Necessarily the initial registration of the title—that is, the conclusive establishment of a starting point binding upon all the world—must rest on judicial proceedings." [3]

The certificate of title to an automobile is the closest personal property analogy to title registration. It purports to show absolute ownership of the car and any liens against the title must appear on the face of the certificate in order to be binding on a b.f.p. Indeed, the concept of title registration was borrowed from personal property by an Australian, Sir Robert Torrens, whose name the system now bears. He had been associated with the shipping industry and saw how simply the title to huge vessels was transferred in contrast to the complexity of real property. He was appointed Registrar General of the Province of South Australia and demonstrated that the certificate system could work satisfactorily for land as well. He drafted the first law for title registration of land and from Australia the system has spread to many parts of the globe. It is not, however, widely used in United States and for that reason the discussion here will be quite limited.

Title is first registered, providing the necessary statutory authority for Torrens exists, by a judicial proceeding similar to a suit to quiet title. An abstract of the records to date is the basis of the registration and all possible claimants are made parties to the proceeding. Service by publication is provided for since this is an *in rem* action. The resulting decree gives the owner a certificate showing the extent of his title and setting forth any exceptions to it. In the absence of fraud, mistake, or lack of jurisdiction, this certificate is conclusive as to title in the holder and

3.   State v. Westfall, 85 Minn. 437,
438, 89 N.W. 175 (1902).

any injured parties must look to an assurance fund, established from charges for registration, for reimbursement.

Transfers of title subsequent to the initial registration follow the same pattern of contract, escrow agreement, and deed already discussed, except that the final act is the cancellation of the vendor's title certificate, and the issuance of a new one to the purchaser. Until that has been done no title passes and the deed itself transfers only equitable title as between the parties until the registration is complete. Of course, the title search by the purchaser is quite simple since he need look only at the certificate; the memorial section will list incumbrances, liens, and similar interests in the land. The particular Torrens Act may make certain items (such as local tax liens) binding on the title even if not filed in the registrar's office, but these are held to a minimum. Even the federal government may be bound by the system and failure to memorialize a notice of a federal tax lien on a certificate of title allows a b. f. p. to take free of the lien.[4] Incidentally, this can be a cause of confusion to the claimant against a land owner in areas where both Torrens and recording are used. A mortgage filed in the recorder's office gives constructive notice to subsequent purchasers of land under the recording system but would have no effect as to Torrens land until filed with the registrar and placed on the memorial. The attorney must always be careful to discover which system applies to the land in question.

No system is foolproof and nice questions of title arise under Torrens too. *A* entrusts his duplicate certificate of title (the original is kept in the registrar's office) to *B* during negotiations for sale. *B* forges a deed to himself and presents it to the registrar who issues a new certificate to *B*. *B* then transfers the title to *C*, a b. f. p. Who owns the land? Mr. Justice Holmes decided for *C*, in affirming a decision of the Illinois Supreme Court under the Illinois Torrens Act.[5] Since a forged deed could not convey good title under the recording acts, even if filed for record, the potency of the certificate of title becomes all the more apparent. If the forged deed had been presented to the registrar without the duplicate certificate, the result might well have been different[6] since Mr. Justice Holmes seemed to put the case on the basic principle, "As between two innocent persons one of whom must suffer the consequences of a breach of trust the one who made it possible by his act of confidence must bear the loss."

4. United States v. Ryan, 124 F. Supp. 1 (D.C.Minn.1954).

5. Eliason v. Wilborn, 281 U.S. 457, 50 S.Ct. 382, 74 L.Ed. 962 (1929).

6. In fact, a later Illinois case held it would be different in a case where the original holder of a Torrens certificate had never parted with it and the whole series of transfers was a fraud on her. Hoffman v. Schroeder, 38 Ill.App.2d 20, 186 N. E.2d 381 (1962).

The relationship of "possession as notice" to title registration is a bit puzzling. Title cannot be obtained by adverse possession to Torrens land since the statutes of limitations do not run against such lands, but that does not solve the notice question. If a claimant is in possession prior to the initial registration and is not made a party to that proceeding his claim survives the suit. The court lacks jurisdiction over his person and failure to follow the statutory provisions would protect him.[7] Possession acquired subsequent to registration, even though based on a valid but unregistered claim, does not give *constructive* notice of the interest and the b. f. p. of the certificate is fully protected.[8] It has been held, however, that *actual* notice of an interest, such as a lease, even though not registered will bind the subsequent purchaser.[9] This leads to the conclusion that, even under Torrens, possession by an apparent stranger to the title may be material and is ignored at the purchaser's peril.

SECTION 5. STATUTES OF LIMITATION

At various points in the book we have referred to title by adverse possession, to prescriptive rights, and to the role of statutes of limitation.[10] However, we have not taken a detailed look at the operation of the statutes, and it is appropriate that we do so in this chapter, since the *principal* role of such legislation is to strengthen the title of the possessor of land. The interest obtained by the adverse possessor is frequently referred to as an original title—i. e., a new title obtained in opposition to the former record owner—as distinct from a derivative title, which is obtained by descent, devise, or purchase. It is possible to obtain an original title in this way, but it would be a rare case in which an individual would set out deliberately to acquire title by adverse possession. He may quite frequently, however, purchase what he thinks is a valid paper title only to find a major flaw in

---

7. Follette v. Pacific Light and Power Corporation, 189 Cal. 193, 208 P. 295 (1922). In that case it was a public utility corporation which had a recorded easement and was using the right of way.

8. Abrahamson v. Sundman, 174 Minn. 22, 218 N.W. 246 (1928).

9. Killam v. March, 316 Mass. 646, 55 N.E.2d 945 (1944).

10. The following three paragraphs are reprinted from Cribbet, Fritz, Johnson, Cases and Materials on Property 869–871 (3d ed. 1972).

the chain. In this situation each year of possession adds to his claim and may thus be said to give him added title assurance. Mr. Justice Holmes, in a letter to William James, stated the "reason behind the rule" with his usual succinctness: "The true explanation of title by prescription seems to me to be that man, like a tree in a cleft of a rock, gradually shapes his roots to his surroundings, and when the roots have grown to a certain size, cannot be displaced without cutting at his life. The law used to look with disfavor on the Statute of Limitations, but I have been in the habit of saying it is one of the most sacred and indubitable principles that we have, which used to lead my predecessor Field to say that Holmes didn't value any title that was not based on fraud or force." [11]

The statutes are of many types and naturally vary from state to state. It is the purpose of this section to explore the principal varieties and to explain their operation. As usual, the roots must be traced to the English common law. From an early date numerous English statutes limited the time within which an action could be brought for a disseisin, but instead of stating a gross period they named a specific year beyond which the pleader could not go. For example, a statute enacted in 1275 barred the remedy by writ of right where the pleader relied upon the seisin of an ancestor before the first year of the reign of Richard I (1189). The modern method of measuring limitation was adopted in 1540, and in 1623 it was provided that no person should thereafter make any entry into any lands, tenements, or hereditaments but within twenty years next after his or their right or title accrued. While this act is the model for most of the statutes in the United States, it has been replaced in England by acts which bar any action to recover land after the statutory period has elapsed, without reference to the character of the defendant's possession. Many difficult questions plague the real estate lawyer in this country as he attempts to discern the character of the possession which the claimant must have for the statutory period in order to bar the rights of the original owner. It is clear that it must be adverse, but what does the term adverse mean?

The Statute of James adopted a gross period of twenty years after the cause of action accrued, and most states have used the same measuring stick, although a few require a greater or a lesser period. Many states have "short limitations" acts where the claimant is in possession under "color of title"; e. g., a judicial decree falsely purporting to vest title in him. Usually these acts require not only "color of title" but also payment of taxes for each year of possession.

11. Lerner, The Mind and Faith of Justice Holmes 417 (1953).

Since adverse possession for the statutory period ripens into title because all other claimants to the land are deprived of a remedy, it would seem that the passage of time would make all titles merchantable. There are at least three reasons why this is not so. First, it is not enough that the possession last for the requisite period; it must also be open, notorious, adverse, continuous, exclusive, and with a claim of right.[12] All of these elements must be established by the adverse possessor, who normally has the burden of proof, and while the title may be defensible so that he could defeat all suits in ejectment it is difficult to negative all possible claims when the parties are not before the court. Second, most statutes do not run against non-possessory interests. Therefore, *A* might occupy for twenty years adversely to *B* but if the latter had only a life estate the statute would not have run at all against *C,* the remainderman, and *A* would have only an estate *pur autre vie.* Third, most statutes have disability provisions so that the interests of minors, insane persons, etc., may survive well beyond the basic period.[13] Since it is difficult, if not impossible, to obtain the necessary information from the record, the purchaser's attorney must assume the worst and he puts little reliance in the statutory period for merchantability purposes.[14] If the time elapsed is so great as to negative all but the barest speculation as to possible claimants, then the court may rely on the statute of limitations and find the title merchantable.[15]

Fortunately, it is not necessary for the same individual to occupy the land throughout the statutory period. The law allows the tacking of successive possessors to make up the full period so long as there is privity of estate between the claimants. If the disseisins are unconnected, e. g., if *A* possesses for less than the

12. See Marengo Cave Co. v. Ross, 212 Ind. 624, 10 N.E.2d 917 (1937) for a good discussion of several of these elements.

13. "Some statutes provide that the duration of disability is not computed as a part of the statutory period. Other statutes provide for a designated time after the disability has been removed within which proceedings may be brought. Mindful of the fact that an exemption provision affects the marketability of land, courts have construed the exemption clause as applicable only to disabilities existing at the inception of adverse possession. In other words, only the disability, or disabilities, existing when the cause of action accrued will postpone the operative effect of the statute of limitations. Further, if land was held adversely when the owner died, a disability of the one succeeding to that interest will not interrupt the running of the statute. This is true even though the owner was under a disability at the time of his death. There is no tacking of disabilities, either with respect to disabilities in the same owner, or with respect to disabilities in successive owners. If an owner was under two or more disabilities when the cause of action accrued, the disability of longest duration will control." Burby, Real Property 396–398 (2d ed. 1954).

14. Simis v. McElroy, 160 N.Y. 156, 54 N.E. 674 (1899).

15. Rehoboth Heights Development Co. v. Marshall, 15 Del.Ch. 314, 137 A. 83 (1927).

period and then abandons and *B* comes in for the remainder, the seisin of the "true" owner revives in the interval and his rights are not barred. "To create such privity, there must have existed as between the different disseisors, in regard to the estate of which a title by disseisin is claimed, some such relation as that of ancestor and heir, grantor and grantee, or devisor and devisee. In such cases, the title acquired by disseisin passes by descent, deed, or devise." [16] The requirement of privity causes difficulty in boundary line disputes when tacking is necessary to make up the statutory period. This is because the deed usually describes only the basic tract and does not include the disputed area that is, in fact, being occupied. Although the cases are in conflict, the better view allows tacking under these circumstances on the theory that it is not the deed which creates the privity but the parol transfer of possession which accompanies the delivery of the deed.[17]

Tacking is clearly allowed on the disseisee side. *A* ousts *B* and, during the statutory period, *B* sells his interest to *C*, who dies leaving the land to his son *D*. At the end of the period, *A* owns the land even though he has occupied for less than the period as against any one of the "true" owners. To put it another way, transfer of the "true" owner's interest does not interrupt the running of the statute, unless there is a termination of the disseisor's adverse possession.

As previously explained, the mere passage of time will not make all titles merchantable even though the claimant has been in possession for the statutory period. This is particularly true where there has been a severance in ownership between the surface and the subsurface. In Failoni v. Chicago and Northwestern Railway Co.,[18] the claimant had been in possession of the surface for more than forty years but earlier the mineral rights had been conveyed to another. While the claimant had title to the surface by adverse possession, she had no title to the subsurface. "To possess the mineral estate, one must undertake the actual removal thereof from the ground or do such other act as will apprise the community that such interest is in the exclusive use and enjoyment of the claiming party." Of course if there has been no severance, the possession of the surface will carry with it the possession of the entire land and adverse possession may ripen into title to the whole.

16. Sawyer v. Kendall, 10 Cush. (Mass.) 241, 244 (1852).

17. Gregory v. Thorrez, 277 Mich. 197, 269 N.W. 142 (1936). See also Howard v. Kunto, 3 Wash.App. 293, 477 P.2d 210 (1970) for a good discussion of the meaning of privity and tacking.

18. 30 Ill.2d 258, 195 N.E.2d 619 (1964).

Statutes of limitation are of many kinds and obviously they will vary from state to state. They tend to fall into four categories: (1) the basic statute (typically fifteen to twenty years); (2) the short term statute (typically seven years); (3) the special purpose statutes designed to cure specific defects, such as stale mortgage claims, old restrictive covenants and conditions, etc.; and (4) the merchantability acts (typically forty years), passed to cure most defects of a certain age and to eliminate the disadvantages which have accumulated around the older, basic statutes. The latter two categories will be discussed in the following section which serves as a critique of modern methods of title assurance. We must clarify here, however, the distinctions between the first two categories.

The basic or twenty-year statute does not require the adverse claimant to pay taxes in order to perfect his title. In fact, the "true" owner could pay the tax bill throughout the period and still lose his title. Nor does this statute require the possessor to have color of title; he could be a naked trespasser with no more business on the land than a thief and still attain a valid title by adverse possession. It is true that the courts say he must have a *claim* of right, but this means no more than that he must indicate that he holds the land as against the whole world, including the "true" owner. Most adverse possessors can be said to claim a fee simple so this is the estate usually obtained, but the claim does mark the extent of the title and if it is only for a life estate or a lesser interest that is the property right secured.[19]

On the other hand, the short term statutes usually require a union of possession, tax payment, and color of title in order to be effective. If these three factors coincide it is easy to see why legislative policy calls for earlier relief for the claimant. The short or seven-year statutes are normally subject to the same disadvantages as the basic statutes (problems of proving adverse possession, effective only against present, possessory interests, disability provisions) so that while they bolster merchantability of title they do not assure it. There is usually no difficulty in determining who has paid the taxes, but color of title can be troublesome. Obviously, color does not mean the same thing as a good or valid title or there would be no need for the statute. Nor is it synonymous with claim of right, since the possessor who relies on this statute must have some basis for his actions. Color of title is that which has the appearance of title but is in fact none; normally, a writing is required and it should accurately describe the premises and purport to convey title. Frequently, color of title is sup-

19.   Ricard v. Williams, 7 Wheat. 59, 5 L.Ed. 398 (1822); Bond v. O'Gara, 177 Mass. 139, 58 N.E. 275 (1900).

plied by a court proceeding or an official conveyance, such as a tax deed or a master's deed, which appears valid on its face but is void or voidable because of defective procedure. Even a forged deed can constitute color of title so long as it is regular on its face and a b. f. p. has relied on its validity.[20] However, where a father purported to convey his children's interest as "father and natural guardian of . . . " color of title was lacking because it was apparent on the face of the deed that he had no power to make such a transfer without following the prescribed judicial procedure.[21]

Color of title is also important in the constructive adverse possession cases, where the deed describes a large area but the claimant in fact occupies only a small proportion of the whole. Normally, the adverse possessor can claim title only to the *pedis possessio*, the portion of the land actually occupied. But if he claims under color of title and the larger area is accurately described in the deed, he may assert ownership to the whole on the basis that he has constructively possessed the described land and that the deed has served as requisite notice to the world.[22]

It is not too difficult to establish the adverseness of a claim against strangers. The very fact that A occupies land owned by B, with no apparent reason for doing so, tends to show adverseness. The situation is more complex if A is a tenant of B, a purchaser under a contract of sale, or a cotenant of B. In the first two situations, the possession, initially at least, was based on consent and A must show a repudiation of that relationship and a "hoisting of his own flag" before the statute of limitations will begin to run. The third situation is covered succinctly in Simpson v. Manson.[23] "The rule is well settled that the mere possession by one tenant in common [or any other cotenant] who receives all the rents and profits and pays the taxes assessed against the property, no matter for how long a period, cannot be set up as a bar against the cotenants. In such case the possession of one tenant in common is in contemplation of law the possession of all the tenants in common. Such possession, however, may become adverse if the tenant in common by acts and conduct disseizes his cotenants by repudiating their title and claiming adversely to them. . . . Before the possession of one tenant in common can be adverse to the cotenant there must be a disseizin or ouster by some outward act of ownership of an unequivocal character, overt and notorious, and of such nature as to impart information and notice to the cotenant that an adverse possession and dis-

20. Bergesen v. Clauss, 15 Ill.2d 337, 155 N.E.2d 20 (1959).

21. Mercer v. Wayman, 9 Ill.2d 441, 137 N.E.2d 815 (1956). Comment, 1957 U.Ill.L.F. 120.

22. Note, 23 Harv.L.Rev. 56 (1909).

23. 345 Ill. 543, 551, 178 N.E. 250, 253 (1931). Cf. Nicholas v. Cousins, 1 Wash.App. 133, 459 P.2d 970 (1969).

seizin are intended to be asserted by the tenant in possession.
. . . Such notice need not, however, be formal in its nature
and if one tenant in common holds exclusive possession, claiming
the land to be his, and his conduct and possession are of such a
character as to give notice to his cotenant that his possession is
adverse, the statute of limitations will run."

SECTION 6. CRITIQUE OF MODERN METHODS OF TITLE ASSURANCE—SUGGESTIONS FOR CONVEYANCING REFORM [24]

"For whom does land law exist? For the land owner and
his neighbours, or for the conveyancer? Put in this way there
can surely be only one answer to the question. Yet to the land
owner, what is important is the substantive nature of his rights
and duties; of those rights, the right to convey is merely one,
and the technical method of exercising that right is to him of
secondary importance and a matter which hitherto he has been
content to leave in the hands of his technical advisers. If this be
the true perspective, the time has surely long since passed when
land law could be considered in the main as a secretion in the
interstices of conveyancing." [25]

Professor Hargreaves, who in all of his scholarly writings
has shown a rare instinct for the jugular, has asked the crucial
question. "For whom does land law exist?" The omission of
the word "land" leaves the query valid, but there is a peculiar
relevancy for the property lawyer in this simple cross-examina-
tion. Discussions at bar association meetings, abstracters' con-
ventions, title association gatherings, and some of the articles in
law reviews and such journals as *Title News*,[26] the official publication of the American Title Association, give the distinct impression that land law exists for the enrichment of the convey-

---

24. This section, with some changes,
first appeared as an article by the
author in 35 N.Y.U.L.Rev. 1291
(1960) under the title "Conveyancing Reform", as part of a symposium on the reform of real property
law.

25. The quote is from the late Professor Hargreaves' (University of

Birmingham) review of Potter, The
Principles of Land Law Under the
Land Registration Act (2d ed. 1948),
in 12 Modern L.Rev. 139, 143 (1949).

26. See, e. g., Audrain, Report of
Chairman of Judiciary Committee,
39 Title News 117, 119 (1960).

ancer and that the interest of the landowner is secondary. The relative merits of title examination by the lawyer, title insurance, and the Torrens system, as methods of title assurance for the landowner, are frequently lost to sight in the economic struggle for title business. Without preparing a brief for any "side," it seems clear that no useful social purpose is served by lawyers banding together for the sole purpose of preserving their historic monopoly in the face of encroaching title insurance, nor by insurance companies [27] competing in such a way that the landowner fails to receive the one thing he desires—a "good" title.

On the other side of the coin, any meaningful discussion of conveyancing reform must take into account the realities of modern methods of land transfer. It is useless to inveigh against the supposed "evils" inherent in title insurance if, in fact, the bulk of land transactions are to be handled by this device. It is equally futile to attack the admitted inefficiency of the laborious searching of the official records by a lonely, dust-covered attorney, wending his way back to a government patent, if this method is rapidly becoming passé.[28] What is wanted is a dispassionate analysis of our present methods of land transfer and a suggested program of reform, if one is called for,[29] that keeps in mind the key question posed by Professor Hargreaves.

A. CHANGING NATURE OF THE LAW OF LAND

It is trite to remark that Anglo-American property law is balanced precariously on its feudalistic base, but one must start from this obvious fact. While feudalism was never a system to those who lived through its dominant period in history, it now appears as a way of life, law, and government which was adequate for the needs of its day. Land was the central reality in the economy of feudalism and it is not surprising that a complex hierarchy of estates was spun from the concept of multiple inter-

---

27. This is not a blanket indictment of title insurance, but there is real danger in the way the industry is developing in some areas. The responsible title insurance companies are just as concerned as anyone else. See Tarpley, The Future of Title Insurance, 38 Title News 2, 4 (1959).

28. For the most recent attack of this type and a novel, if impractical, solution, see Comment, Enhancing the Marketability of Land: The Suit to Quiet Title, 68 Yale L.J. 1245 (1959).

29. It may be that conveyancing today represents the best of all possible worlds but many competent observers have felt otherwise. See, e. g., Payne, The Crisis in Conveyancing, 19 Mo.L.Rev. 214 (1954).

ests in a single *res*. Whether it was social security as exempli-
fied by dower and curtesy, borrowing as illustrated by the lowly
origin of the term of years, or national defense as reflected by the
knight's fee, land was made to serve the needs of a crude society.
Society lost some of its crudity, the needs changed, but the land
law retained much of its early form. As late as 1829, the English Real Property Commissioners still remarked that, "it [the
land law] appears to come almost as near to perfection as can be
expected in any human institutions." [30] Most of this human institution had been adopted by the colonies in North America but
not necessarily adapted to the nonfeudalistic society developing
in the wilderness.

This vast superstructure of property law was supported on
an antique conveyancing base that almost defies description. For
generations, livery of seisin, with its symbolic transfer of turf,
twig, or rock, had sufficed to make graphic that change of possession which was conceived to be the major ingredient in change
of ownership. Even the charter of feoffment was but a memorial
of the operative act and it took the Statute of Uses and the Statute of Frauds to make the conveyance a "paper" transaction.
The Statute of Enrollments could have given England a workable recording system but its clever evasion by secrecy minded
clients and lawyers, through the deed of lease and release, left
the conveyancing system in a chaotic state. The principal reliance came to be on the original title deeds which passed with the
land and were examined by each lawyer in turn.

By the end of the first World War, England was ready for
real property reform and this readiness became a movement
which culminated in the famous property legislation of 1925, designed to simplify the complicated structure. The substantive
changes wrought by the legislation are not within the scope of
this text but the avowed purpose behind it is central to our discussion. Professor Cheshire, then dean of the English property
bar, wrote:

"[I]t will be as well to state at the outset the main idea which
lay at the back of the legislation that resulted. *It was nothing
more than a desire to render the sale of land as rapid and simple
a matter as is the sale of goods or of shares.* . . .

"But the difference is inevitable, and the reason is that in
the great majority of cases the possessor of personal goods is
their absolute owner, and therefore able to pass a title which will
confer upon their deliveree an equally full and unencumbered
ownership. . . . But for a purchaser of land to be content
with the word of the vendor and with the appearance of owner-

30. First Report, p. 6.

ship which flows from his possession would be an act of sheer folly." [31]

The reform legislation was designed to usher in a system of title registration which would replace the cumbersome examination of title deeds with a modern, workable method of title assurance. (It should be noted that England does not have title insurance in the American sense. Individual defects may be insured against, e. g., a dormant restrictive covenant that *may* cause difficulty, but no blanket title policy is available.) Since 1925, in contrast to the atrophy of the Torrens system in the United States, title registration has had a remarkable success in England and elsewhere in the common-law world.

Meanwhile, the land law had taken a different direction in the United States. Although starting with a common heritage, which fortunately gave the various state laws a thread of consistency, the American bar never developed a reliance on title deeds, but instead turned at an early date to recording acts as a basis of title security. "The earliest mention of the record of a deed in the United States is found in the records of Plymouth Colony in 1627, where a contract of a bargain and sale of land is apparently required to be written into the book of the colony, not as a copy, but as an original, and signed therein by the parties." [32] Without attempting a history of the recording acts,[33] it is safe to conclude that they came to be the central core of the real estate transaction in America and the strengths and weaknesses of our title system are reflected in them. Whatever the faults of the recording acts, they represented a big improvement over the examination of title deeds and did form a public record on which a bona fide purchaser could, more or less safely, rely. They reversed the tyranny of "first in time, first in right" as a rule for determining priority and cut off the claims of those who slumbered on their rights and failed to record. They have worked well enough so that, more than three hundred years after the record of Plymouth Colony, they still play the dominant role in title assurance. Title insurance relies on the records just as much as the lone lawyer-examiner or the abstracter-lawyer team; only title registration has kicked over the traces and tried a different method. The big change in the United States has come about, not through any major reform in the laws of fifty separate jurisdictions, but through the growth of title insurance compa-

31. Cheshire, The Modern Law of Real Property 5–6 (8th ed. 1958).

32. 4 American Law of Property § 17.4 at 527 (Casner ed. 1952).

33. For good historical studies of the system, see Beale, The Origin of the System of Recording Deeds in America, 19 Green Bag 335 (1907), and Haskins, The Beginnings of the Recording System in Massachusetts, 21 B.U.L.Rev. 281 (1941).

nies [34] which add institutional security and an indemnity contract
to the opinion of an individual examiner.   Thus, it will be noted
that conveyancing has changed its character far less in the
United States than in England.   The crucial question remains:
Is there *need* for a radical change in this country?

What is important to the landowner is the substantive nature of his rights and duties, of which the right to convey is
merely one.   During the centuries the law of conveyancing has
been changed as just indicated, but a much greater evolution has
affected the substantive rights and duties of the man of property.

In Blackstone's day the law reflected society's emphasis on
the *rights* of the owner of land.   Blackstone's heavy emphasis on
rights was overdrawn even for his day and later writers have put
the matter in proper perspective.   "The right of property is an
exclusive right, but it has never been an absolute right.   In so
far as the right of property existed it was an exclusive right,
that is, it excluded others; but it was not a right without limitations or qualifications.   Notice the distinction between *exclusive*
and *absolute*." [35]   However, the fact remains that the earlier
common law was more concerned with the rights of the landowner than with his duties to his neighbors and to society.   If there
are two sides to private property, the individual side and the social side, it was the former which was dominant in the land law
of the nineteenth century and before.

The decades following World War I witnessed a major shift
in emphasis so that today it is clear that the duties of the landowner are of great importance.   Taxation has curtailed heavily
the ability of the individual to transmit his property to later
generations and makes restraints on alienation, the Rule Against
Perpetuities, and similar "anti-dead hand" doctrines seem old hat
as means of social control.   During life, the landowner is hedged
in by zoning, building restrictions, subdivision controls, etc., so
that Blackstone's "sole and despotic dominion" seems to belong
to another system of law entirely.   Today's lawyer cannot serve
his client simply by assuring him that his title is good; he must go
another mile and tell him how Blackacre fits into the land use
plan for his community.   "While it [property law] is the field
par excellence of certainty—for men and governments must arrange their affairs on the basis of expectations that will be honored—the law of property has proved over the centuries a marvel-

34. "There are approximately 160
     title insurance corporations issuing
     their own policies in the United
     States. The majority of these are
     'local' companies in the sense that
     they confine their insuring of titles
     to property within one state."

Grimes, The Lawyer, His Client and
Title Insurance, Student Law J., 4,
5 (1958).

35. 1 Ely, Property and Contract in
     Their Relations to the Distribution
     of Wealth 136 (1914).

ously flexible and supple instrument in accommodating new interests and wants."[36] If the previous statement is true (and it is) in the field of land use, is it any less true in conveyancing? Must the procedural aspects of land transfer lag behind the other areas of land law?

B. CHANGING NATURE OF LAND USE

Law seldom changes society; it only reflects and confirms changes that have already occurred. The shift from rights to duties as a focus of emphasis followed a major shift in land use from rural to urban. This shift, plus an exploding population which made land a scarce commodity in many areas, brought into play an old common law axiom, *sic utere tuo ut alienum non laedas,* and caused the ideas behind the court-developed law of nuisance to find new life in the legislature-centered law of zoning. These same changes in land use have great relevance for the law of conveyancing, even though that branch of the art has been slow to reflect them.

The principal change in land use of importance here is the relatively frequent ownership transfers which now occur for any given tract. We will take "textbook notice" [37] of the changing pattern of American life; not only is urbanization increasing apace but with it has come a high degree of personal mobility. When the family farm remained in a stable line for several generations (and even the city dweller often died in the house where he was born), title transfer by a search back to a government patent or some remote historical epoch was not unreasonable. Men made up their minds slowly and proceeded deliberately thereafter. It made sense to have a conveyancing system that operated at the same rate of speed. But today, when a big corporation moves a man from New York to California, he travels by jet and buys and sells land (or wants to) with split-second timing. Moreover, he doesn't deal in cash but in secured financing, and the lending institutions demand speed and accuracy before they make the kind of commitments required by present-day home buying. The simple truth is that land has become a commodity

---

36. Haar, Land-Use Planning at viii (1959).

37. This is the equivalent of judicial notice and saves the trouble of citing voluminous statistics to prove a self-evident fact.

that must move freely and easily in commerce. Does the law of conveyancing reflect this simple truth?

Of course, land cannot be equated with chattels, nor should it be. Land *is* unique, and its very immobility means that special laws are required for it and that its transfer will never be as simple as the purchase of a bag of apples at a supermarket. However, at this point we must remember that, in contemplation of law, property is composed of the legal relations among people in regard to a *res*, and not of the *res* itself. It would seem to follow that these legal relations can be so arranged by the law that even the most ponderous *res* may change ownership with relative ease. If this is what the changing nature of land use requires, then the law of conveyancing must provide it.

C. BASIC PRINCIPLES OF CONVEYANCING REFORM

Real property reform is no sport for the uninitiated. It is relatively easy to reform the law of land; it is difficult to be sure that the change represents progress. The law is so intricate and so entwined in ancient history that the cutting of an old root frequently has unforeseen results. Two illustrations will suffice.

The destructibility of contingent remainders was obviously a relic of a bygone age. When a testator left land to "*A* for life, remainder to those children of *A* who survive him," he clearly meant for *A* to have no more than a life estate. Yet if *A* was also the heir of the testator he could obtain the fee and destroy the contingent remainder in his children by a simple conveyance to *X* and return.[38] Even if the reversion passed to some person other than *A*, the two parties could combine to defeat the children's interest. The statutes which abolished the doctrine of destructibility [39] were hailed as a major step in real property reform, and so they were, as devices for giving greater effect to the testator's or grantor's intent. However, they had a side effect which was not a step forward in the law of conveyancing. The doctrine of destructibility allowed the elimination of contingent remainders in at least one situation and thus made land more freely alienable by putting in someone's hands the power to convey a fee simple. Since abolition of the doctrine, land is more likely to be tied up until the death of *A*, when his children's in-

---

38. For a relatively recent example, see Blocker v. Blocker, 103 Fla. 285, 137 So. 249 (1931).

39. For the present status of the doctrine, see 2 Powell, Real Property, § 314 (1950).

terests can finally vest. The ancient doctrine was not all bad; it defeated intent but it made land alienable at an earlier date.

Of course, defeating "legitimate" [40] interests in order to promote merchantability of titles seems unreasonable, but can't you have it both ways? Why not simply give the life tenant a power of sale, impress the proceeds with a trust, and let the parties have the same interests in the fund which they had in the land? This would protect the contingent remaindermen, carry out the intent of the testator (except that personalty rather than realty would pass to the children), and leave the land freely alienable. This is exactly what was done in the English property legislation of 1925, only on a much broader scale. The English abolished all legal estates in land except the fee simple absolute and the term of years, and, by creating a power of sale in the present owner of the freehold, made it possible for land to be more freely alienable while protecting the other diverse interests by giving them a share of the fund created by the sale. [41]

The Rule in Shelley's Case was even more barbarous than the doctrine of destructibility. [42] To hold that a grant to "*A* for life, remainder to his heirs" gave *A* a fee simple was absurd except as a lesson in feudal logic. But when the reformers abolished the rule and gave *A* a life estate, followed by contingent remainders in his heirs, they reduced alienability with the same stroke which resuscitated intent. The rule at least allowed *A* to convey a fee at once; its abolition tied up the land until his death.

These two illustrations are not intended to criticize the modernization of substantive rules of real property, but rather to develop the complex character of those rules and plead for care in the field of conveyancing reform. What are the basic principles which should be observed if we are to improve modern methods of land transfer?

First, the system must give adequate *security* for land titles. Unless the purchaser or mortgagee can be assured that his investment is sound, the particular method fails, whatever other virtues it may possess. Second, it must provide *speed* in the determination of title status so that the transaction can be closed with a minimum amount of cliff-hanging. Third, the method must be relatively *inexpensive* so that a disproportionate amount of the

---

40. A side issue: Are they legitimate?

41. For an excellent short account of the English law, see Hargreaves, Introduction to Land Law 128–37 (3d ed. 1952).

42. "That Rule is a relic, not of the horse and buggy days, but of the preceding stone cart and oxen days. . . . This Rule is only a trap and snare for the unwary, and should be repealed." Sybert v. Sybert, 125 Tex. 106, 110–11, 254 S.W.2d 999, 1001–02 (1953) (Griffin, J., concurring). The court nonetheless applied the rule! It has since been abolished in Texas.

purchaser's dollar is not channeled into title service. Our present conveyancing practice should be scrutinized in the light of these principles and all changes analyzed for contribution to security, speed, and lack of expense.

D. MODERN METHODS OF TITLE ASSURANCE— A CRITIQUE

There are essentially four modern methods of title assurance: personal covenants for title in a warranty deed, lawyer's title opinion based on the original records or an abstract therefrom, title registration (Torrens system), and title insurance. They are not mutually exclusive, since a warranty deed may be used in the latter three and a lawyer may, in effect, guarantee his own opinion, as in the so-called Florida plan.[43]

(1) Personal Covenants for Title

As a method of title assurance the warranty deed can never be more than an auxiliary weapon in the conveyancer's arsenal. It is speedily delivered; it can be drafted for a nominal fee; but it secures nothing other than the personal promise of the grantor and is no better than his solvency and availability at some future date when suit may be necessary. Apart from this weakness inherent in all the warranty deeds, the covenants used today are still needlessly technical and hedged about with ancient dogma as to whether they will run with the land, when the breach occurs, the amount of damages due in case of breach, etc. Modern statutory short-form warranty deeds, with their covenants incorporated by shorthand use of a mystical word or words,[44] are a vast improvement over their prolix ancestors, but no well-advised purchaser would rely on such a deed as his sole title security. A careful re-evaluation of covenants for title is overdue and legislation could improve their usefulness, but at best they are

43. See generally Carter, A New Role for Lawyers: The Florida Lawyers' Title Guaranty Fund, 45 A.B.A.J. 803 (1959).

44. See, e. g., Ill.Rev.Stat. ch. 30, § 8 (1973).

likely to remain a side show—the main attraction is in the big tent!

---

(2) LAWYER'S TITLE OPINION

Professor McDougal wrote, over thirty years ago: "To a foreign anthropologist land transfer in the United States would probably look, as one of my former students forcefully put it, much like an aboriginal, ritualistic clambake. Like most other objects of 'property,' land is transferred by symbols, pieces of paper; but, unlike many of the other symbols, these particular symbols do not pass freely from hand to hand—their circulation is accompanied by much dilatory, costly, and extra-necessitous behavior of wise men." [45] The lawyer's opinion of title lends itself to parody about as well as any phase of the practice of law. The long search back to a government patent or to some remote period, the "fly-specking tendencies" of the conveyancing bar, the repetition of this process each time the land is transferred, etc., can be ridiculed with ease. Fortunately, unlike covenants for title, the system of using lawyers' opinions for title assurance is not beset with inherent defects, and with proper improvements such opinions can continue to fulfill the needs of large areas of the country.

The title opinion, if carefully done and as bolstered by statutes of limitations which protect even the unwary, does give adequate security for land titles. True, the lawyer does not guarantee the title and since he is liable only for negligence the client *may* suffer loss. In the main, however, the "horrible awfuls" do not occur, and the client can sleep soundly in his bed without fearing the dower-claiming spouse of a former owner if a competent lawyer has passed on his title. There is, of course, a lack of uniformity in lawyers' opinions and the big institutional lenders which operate on a nation-wide scale do prefer the title insurance scheme.

The lawyer's opinion is relatively inexpensive and indeed in many smaller communities it is doubtful whether the fee is high enough to cover the attorney's efforts on any realistic basis. The biggest defect of this method may be its slowness. In an effort to gain maximum security for the title and to prevent the next

45. McDougal, Title Registration and Land Reform: A Reply, 8 U. Chi.L.Rev. 63, 65 (1940).

examiner from catching him in a technical error, the lawyer may spend an inordinate amount of time checking nonessentials. The long period of search currently required in most jurisdictions adds to this difficulty.

In brief, the lawyer's opinion, as presently being handled, leaves much to be desired, but it is susceptible to reform and should have a vigorous future in some areas of the country.

---

(3) TITLE REGISTRATION (TORRENS SYSTEM)

There is a strong temptation to overpraise the Torrens system. Theoretically, it is the best method of title assurance yet devised. In a law school property course, the student who brings a bright and inquiring mind, unhampered by the realities of the title world, to bear upon land transfer problems usually concludes that registration is the ideal system. It has been soundly praised by many impartial observers of the title parade. It has worked well in England and in the British Commonwealth countries and is considered to be the wave of the future in various parts of the world. It was the fair-haired child of property reformers in this country several decades ago when the legal literature rang with acclaim and denunciation.[46]

Even during the period when the greatest claims were being made for Torrens, some writers were already calling the system a failure.

"Explanations of this failure of registration to take hold are manifold. Much is to be attributed to inertia and ignorance, coupled with the fact that registration of land titles is entirely optional. Initial expense and time must have deterred some and insufficient assurance funds may have discouraged others. Title companies, which feel that they have only to lose by the adoption of the Torrens system, have done much to oppose stringent Tor-

---

46. The battle was joined when Professor Powell published a study critical of the Torrens system in New York. Powell, Registration of the Title to Land in the State of New York (1938). The champions of reform struck back in McDougal & Brabner-Smith, Land Title Transfer: A Regression, 48 Yale L.J. 1125 (1939), and in Fairchild & Springer, A Criticism of Professor Richard R. Powell's Book Entitled Registra-tion of Title to Land in the State of New York, 24 Cornell L.Q. 557 (1939). The running battle continued with Bordwell, The Resurrection of Registration of Title, 7 U. Chi.L.Rev. 470 (1940), versus McDougal, Title Registration and Land Reform: A Reply, 8 U.Chi.L.Rev. 63 (1940). The more serious troubles abroad seemed to quell the domestic struggle as the forties wore on.

rens legislation, and by their refusal to extend loans on registered titles have prevented the successful operation of the system." [47]

Torrens is not yet dead in the United States and it still provokes discussion in the law reviews.[48] But if burial is premature, rejoicing at a resurrection is equally out of place. The system exists to some extent in Colorado, Georgia, Hawaii, Illinois, Massachusetts, Minnesota, Nebraska, New York, North Carolina, Ohio, South Dakota, Tennessee, Utah, Virginia, and Washington.[49] In these jurisdictions three situations account for a substantial fraction of the registrations: first, it is a useful device for clearing a bad title; second, registration typically excludes adverse possession and is helpful where wild timber land and undeveloped mineral land might otherwise be lost by adverse possession; and third, registration of title in suburban developments has provided a relatively inexpensive evidence of title for purchasers.[50] Nowhere in the United States, however, has it become the dominant method of land transfer.

Professor Bade's succinct critique sums up the assets of Torrens. "Title registration is an obvious improvement over recorded titles. A registered title is a title that has been adjudicated in an officially directed and controlled proceeding in rem. The title is then kept clear by constant official supervision. There is no need thereafter to trace and examine the title from its origin. The present state of the title is normally represented on the face and obverse of an owner's certificate of title. When the title is transferred the former owner's certificate is cancelled and a new one is issued to the new owner. Subsisting encumbrances are carried forward to the new certificate. Those that have been eliminated by lapse of time, satisfaction, or other sufficient means, are not. Thus by examination of two sides of a certificate of title, in 99% of the cases, a competent lawyer should be able to examine a title in an hour or less. Furthermore, what appears on the certificate is not merely prima facie evidence of title, it is conclusive. If anyone is injured by errors of the Registrar of

47. Handler, Cases on Vendor and Purchaser 674 (1933).

48. See, e. g., Heinrich, The Case for Land Registration, 6 Mercer L.Rev. 320 (1955); Maher, Registered Lands Revisited, 8 W.Res.L.Rev. 162 (1957). The latter article concludes: "The registration of land in Ohio has largely been confined to the communities surrounding the larger cities, although a large minority of the counties have some registered titles. Whether additional land will be registered in the future is a matter of speculation, but it is not speculation that a practicing attorney must have a speaking acquaintance with the registered land statutes if he has much practice in real estate." Id. at 169.

49. 4 American Law of Property, § 17.39 (Casner ed. 1952). California repealed its title registration act in 1955. Cal.Gen.Laws Ann. Act 8589, § 1 (Deering Supp.1959).

50. Powell, Registration of the Title to Land in the State of New York (1938).

Titles, his recourse is not against the registered owner, but against a state administered assurance fund." [51]

One can agree wholeheartedly with the foregoing analysis and still conclude that Torrens has little or no future in the United States. If we were setting up a wholly new society in a virgin land we could forget the recording system and rely on registration. Its qualities are manifestly superior to the cumbersome system with which we are saddled. We *could* make the Torrens system work in the United States if we would pass legislation making registration compulsory for each parcel of land as soon as it is next transferred *inter vivos* to a new owner. This would have to be done in fifty states (if we wanted a nationally uniform system), over the combined opposition of most of the groups which make our present system operate, at a huge initial cost with state subsidy, and only after the personnel required for the new system had been adequately trained.[52] If we had no recording system and no title insurance, as in England, such a step would be required to keep pace with modern society. However, our title destiny lies in another direction, for it is impractical to expect a Torrens revolution short of an actual breakdown of the present machinery.

In brief, title registration provides maximum security, relative speed, and, after the initial charge, is not too expensive, but it remains too frail a reed to support modern conveyancing reform because other methods are so firmly embedded in our institutions of property.

---

(4) TITLE INSURANCE

"Title insurance is available in nearly all parts of the United States. The insurable title is steadily increasing in favor as the most acceptable title and the one affording maximum protection and security to the insured. Life insurance companies, which are large investors in real estate mortgages all over the country, prefer title insurance to other forms of title evidence. In New York City, Chicago, Cleveland, and Los Angeles, and their sub-

---

15. Bade, Cases on Real Property and Conveyancing 306 (1954).

52. This last point is of major importance. The Torrens system can-

not be efficiently operated with just anybody the political machine sees fit to appoint. Even England is proceeding slowly until personnel can be trained.

urban areas, title insurance predominates as a method of affording title protection.

"Title insurance is steadily growing in favor because it is a flexible form of title assurance, readily adaptable to the changing needs of lawyers and their clients in all types of transactions in real estate. It offers a degree of protection, security, and freedom from worry and expense no other kind of title evidence can match. More and more lawyers have come to recognize that title insurance complements and does not displace their services to their clients in real estate deals." [53] This quotation from Charles F. Grimes, formerly General Counsel and Secretary of the Chicago Title and Trust Company, one of the nation's leading title insurance companies, is an eloquent statement of the industry's claim to be the wave of the future.

Not all observers see title insurance through such rose-tinted glasses. Professor Bade would seem to damn it with faint praise. "Another device that is advocated by some as a remedy for the shortcomings of recorded title systems is 'Title Insurance.' In the first place the name of the thing is a misnomer. Titles are not insured. At most, named persons are insured against loss by reason of failure of title. But even in that aspect, it has its shortcomings. . . . It has been suggested that it insures only that the insurance company has made a careful examination of the title and has listed all serious defects in the exceptions from its coverage. . . . Generally, title insurance does not insure a marketable title. In addition to the limitations on coverage, they commonly require claim and suit to be brought under it within a short period of time. Insurance premiums are not low. The coverage is limited to those named or designated in the policy. Generally the policies are not assignable and do not pass with the land. New owners may have the policy endorsed in their favor, but must pay a further premium therefor. In contrast, title registration is permanent, and the benefit of it passes to each successive owner." [54]

It is possible to agree with Professor Bade's obvious preference for title registration, as a system, and still conclude that title insurance will be the dominant factor in the future of American conveyancing. The growth of title insurance has been phenomenal, particularly in the period since the end of World War II. "[T]itle insurance is now [1956] written by 147 companies, of which 77 have more than one outlet in their home state, 31 operate in more than one state, and 11 in 5 or more states. As an indication of the present size of the business, premiums on title insurance written in 1954 totalled about 100

---

53. Grimes, supra note 34, at 24.   54. Bade, supra note 51, at 306.

million dollars—representing at an average premium rate of
3½ dollars a thousand, 28½ billion dollars of title insurance
coverage. Although the extent of its use varies, being highest
on the Pacific Coast and least in New England, title insurance
has become the predominant method of title protection in many
metropolitan areas and has been written on some land in every
state." [55]

Although title insurance has been spreading rapidly, it is
still difficult to appraise its relative merits as a method of land
transfer. Exact information about its operation is difficult to
obtain, and most critiques have been prepared either by ardent
enthusiasts with a vested interest in its propagation or by strong
advocates of a rival system (lawyers' opinions or the Torrens
system). Moreover, the title companies themselves vary so
widely that generalizations are likely to be misleading. This
last point is particularly important. Some of the companies
are old, established corporations with highly professional staffs,
concerned with the efficient operation of modern conveyancing
and playing an important role in the development of the real
property law of their particular state or states. In many metropolitan areas, like Cook County in Illinois, title insurance has
the principal role in land transfer and few lawyers would wish
it otherwise. Such title insurance has met a need with the busi-
ness-like efficiency that the situation demanded. Unfortunately, not all title insurance is of this type.

The best impartial analysis of title insurance was made in
1957 by Professor Quintin Johnstone of Yale Law School. He
based his study on interviews and correspondence with leading
title insurers, lenders, and Torrens officials, plus data obtained
from state insurance commissions. His conclusions are significant. "There have been three major reasons for the growth
of title insurance in the United States: the life insurance companies' strong preference for it in their lending operations; the
efficiency with which title insurers having complete title plants
can search and examine titles, particularly in large cities; and
the aggressive promotion of title insurance by the insurers.
Because these factors are likely to continue, title insurance will
probably become even more successful in the future. The Torrens system offers no serious competition, and the lawyers have
shown surprisingly little opposition. Perhaps the lawyers will
resist title insurance more strenuously if it threatens to exclude

55. Johnstone, Title Insurance, 66
    Yale L.J. 492–93 (1957). Professor
    Johnstone points out that his
    premium and coverage figures are
    based on reported premiums in the
    1956 Directory of the American
    Title Association plus an estimate
    of unreported premiums and are
    rough approximations.

them from searches and examinations in small towns and rural areas. More state-wide and national companies may shift their emphasis from developing large networks of small volume agencies to heavy saturation of favorable areas, following the Pacific Coast and Illinois patterns. Finally, rigorous government regulation of the title insurance industry is unlikely, unless Public Law 15 [56] leads to more intensive regulation of all kinds of insurance or unless insolvency again threatens title insurers." [57]

Title insurance can give the necessary security (if the purchaser clearly understands the exclusions from coverage) and it operates with the requisite speed, but its Achilles' heel *may* be expense. Without making any present indictment, it is necessary to raise a warning flag. Both recording and registration operate as agencies of local government. This makes their cost to the purchaser of land low, and it does not seem unfair that the public should assume some of the cost of a system of land transfer. The lawyer's fee for examination of the records or of an abstract is based on a reasonable professional charge for service rendered and is kept within limits by the charges of his fellow practitioners. Thus far, title insurance has been forced to compete with at least one rival system, and in some areas two, so that charges have not been excessive. What will be the result if title insurance becomes a virtual monopoly? Land law exists for the benefit of the landowner and systems of conveyancing must serve him. Title insurance is a private business but it bases its services on public records and is affected with the public interest. If normal competition fails to keep the coverage adequate and the cost within bounds, it will be necessary for the state to regulate the industry like any other public utility. This could be the long range future of conveyancing in the United States—privately insured titles based on public records, with public control as to coverage and cost.

56. 59 Stat. 33 (1945), 15 U.S.C.A. §§ 1011–15 (declaring Congress in favor of continued state regulation of insurance).

57. Johnstone, supra note 55, at 518.

E. SUGGESTED REFORMS

In a recent critique of conveyancing in Virginia, Professor Spies of the University of Virginia Law School concluded that no radical changes were necessary. He suggested that a system of tract indexes be substituted for the cumbersome grantor-grantee indexes, that title standards be adopted as authoritative guides to lend uniformity to title opinions, and that a marketable title statute be passed in the state to give reasonable scope to title search. To implement these proposals, he recommended the appointment of a committee consisting of members of the bar and representatives of Virginia's four law schools.[58]

In contrast, an appraisal, nation-wide in scope, in the Yale Law Journal concludes: "In effect, this Comment has suggested that the objectives of the Torrens system be implemented within the framework of recordation." [59] This latter proposal envisages a series of periodic quiet title suits to cleanse the title chain of its accumulated debris. While this plan is far from revolutionary, it is more radical than the fence-patching suggestions of Professor Spies. The clarion call for sweeping reform has more impact on the printed page, but the laborious patchwork is, in this case at least, more likely to serve society's needs.

(1) GENERAL SUGGESTIONS

Four broad points need to be made before we move into the area of specifics. First, there is no real need for a completely uniform system of conveyancing on a national scale. Symmetry can be a false god. Land remains a creature of the local jurisdiction and some variation in conveyancing procedure is probably inevitable, even desirable, since it leads to experimentation which may then be helpful elsewhere. It is true that the national lending agencies exert a powerful force for uniform procedures and that the trend is in that direction, but this need not become the focal point for national legislation or even for uniform state laws. Obviously, this primacy of local law does not rule out the need for model acts which can serve as the basis for local reform.

58. Spies, A Critique of Conveyancing, 38 Va.L.Rev. 245, 262–63 (1952).

59. Comment, Enhancing the Marketability of Land: The Suit to Quiet Title, 68 Yale L.J. 1245, 1315 (1959).

Second, conveyancing reform is the responsibility of the state bar and each state should have active sections or committees working on the problems of the local jurisdiction, drafting legislation, preparing title standards, etc.

Third, some diversity in conveyancing method is desirable even in the same jurisdiction, i. e., there are situations where title insurance is called for, others where lawyers' opinions are preferable, and Torrens can always add a healthy leaven to the loaf. Moreover, so long as competitive methods are available the spectre of monopoly will be kept under control.

Fourth, since the recording system is the heart of modern conveyancing, the recording acts should be strengthened so that both lawyers' opinions and title insurance can flourish at maximum effectiveness. Certainly, the recording system should not be allowed to become so complex that all title business is forced into the hands of the insurance companies by default.

---

(2) SPECIFIC SUGGESTIONS

Once the decision is made to attack the problems of conveyancing by a revitalization of the recording system, two major works assume paramount importance—Professor Paul E. Basye's Clearing Land Titles, published in 1953, and Simes and Taylor's The Improvement of Conveyancing by Legislation, released in 1960. The latter book was prepared for the Section of Real Property, Probate and Trust Law of the American Bar Association and for the University of Michigan Law School.[60] One may safely predict that it will become the handbook for those states seriously interested in reform. It concludes that: "Title legislation, in order to accomplish its basic objectives and remain within the ambit of the existing recording system, should be in accord with one or more of the following propositions.

"(a) The records should include, as nearly as possible, all the facts required to determine the state of the title. . . .

"(b) So far as practicable, the record should be self-proving. . . .

"(c) The length of the record required for a marketable title should be shortened. . . .

"(d) Stale claims should be eliminated. . . .

"(e) Some future interests should be restricted in duration. . . .[61]"

60. Contributions to the research project were made by several title companies, the American Title Association, individuals, insurance companies, and foundations.

61. Simes & Taylor, The Improvement of Conveyancing by Legislation at xvii (1960).

All of these propositions are eminently sound and the model legislation which has been drafted to accomplish the basic objectives is worthy of careful study by state associations.

There are at least five varieties of reform by which our recording system may be restored to a reasonable degree of effectiveness. They are: (1) shortening the period of title search through merchantability of title acts or special statutes of limitation; (2) the elimination of purely technical objections by curative legislation; (3) making miscellaneous changes in the mechanical operation of the recording acts; (4) altering the substantive law of property so as to simplify title problems; and (5) the adoption by local bar groups of title standards or rules for the examination of abstracts. A brief look at each of these areas will point the way to a reasonable program of conveyancing reform.

(a) *Merchantability of Title Acts* [62]

The most hopeful device for bolstering the conveyancing system is a well drafted merchantability act which will restrict the period of search to a reasonable limit. A statute of limitations is an honored tool for giving stability in diverse areas of the law. Such statutes have for centuries—the first one goes back to 1275 in England—played a prominent role in real property law. As early as 1540, the modern method of measuring limitations was adopted and in 1623 the basic twenty-year period was established. Unfortunately, such statutes have never been of great help to the title examiner because they do not apply to claims of governmental units, contain exceptions for individuals under disability, do not run against future interests until such interests become possessory, and depend for their effectiveness on the proof of facts dehors the record, e. g., that the possession has been hostile, adverse, notorious, continuous, under claim of right, etc. What is needed is a statute which bars old claims solely because of the passage of time, unless there is a legitimate reason for keeping them alive. The various merchantability acts seek to fill this need.

When the recording acts were first passed, they had the effect of cutting off what would have been valid claims but for the

62. For a brief discussion of merchantability acts in the midwestern states, see Cribbet, A New Concept of Merchantability, 43 Ill.B.J. 778 (1955). See also Comment, Marketability Acts: A Step Forward for Title Examination Procedure in Illinois, 1957 U.Ill.L.F. 488. In Illinois, a state bar committee was appointed which led, in 1959, to the adoption of a forty-year merchantability act, Ill.Rev.Stat. ch. 83, §§ 12.1–4 (1961), discussed in Basye, Clearing Land Titles, § 173.

failure of the claimant to follow the dictates of the statute. That is still the effect of the acts and no one contends that this makes them unconstitutional or unfair. The great social value in an effective recording system outweighs the occasional loss to the individual who fails to record. The principal defect of the recording system lies in its failure to be self-cleansing; once a claim is of record, it tends to remain valid indefinitely. In the early years of the recording system this was no defect but now the system is becoming more cumbersome each decade. Fortunately, there is no reason for this defect to continue in its present form.

The simplest way to cleanse the records would be to provide a gross period beyond which no claim of ownership could be enforced against the present owner. This method has in fact been used for certain interests, such as equitable servitudes,[63] possibilities of reverter and powers of termination,[64] and for foreclosure of mortgages.[65] In sustaining the constitutionality of the Illinois act limiting the duration of a possibility of reverter or power of termination to fifty (now forty) years, the court stated: "It has been said that the Reverter Act was passed in recognition of the operation of possibilities of reverter as 'clogs on title, withdrawing property thus encumbered from the commercial mortgage market long after the individual, social or economic reason for their creation had ceased, and at a time when the heirs from whom a release could be obtained would be so numerous as to be virtually impossible to locate.' . . . The statute reflects the General Assembly's appraisal of the actual economic significance of these interests, weighed against the inconvenience and expense caused by their continued existence for unlimited periods of time without regard to altered circumstances. As a result of that appraisal, their potential duration has been limited to fifty years. . . . We are unable to say that that method offends the constitutional provisions relied upon."[66] This succinct statement of the public policy in favor of merchantability

63. For legislation restricting the effectiveness of covenants, conditions, and restrictions to thirty years, see Mass.Gen.Laws Ann. ch. 184, § 23; Minn.Stat.Ann. § 500.20(2); R.I.Gen. Laws Ann. § 34–4–21 (1956).

64. Ill.Rev.Stat. ch. 30, § 37e. The period was originally fifty years but was reduced to forty in 1959 to correspond with the forty-year period of the new merchantability act.

65. Ill.Rev.Stat. ch. 83, §§ 11b, 12 (1973), operates in twenty years from the due date where such date is determinable from the mortgage or in thirty years from the date of the instrument where the due date cannot be so ascertained.

66. Trustees of Schools of Tp. No. 1 v. Batdorf, 6 Ill.2d 486, 492, 130 N. E.2d 111, 114 (1955).

Note, however, that New York declared a similar statute unconstitutional on the grounds that it impaired the obligation of a contract and deprived an owner of his property without due process of law. Board of Education of Central Service District No. 1 v. Miles, 15 N.Y.2d 364, 259 N.Y.S.2d 129, 207 N.E.2d 181 (1965).

highlights the usefulness of the gross period of limitation in clearing titles.

It would be unfair, however, to bar *all* claims more than forty years old since substantial estates or interests of record, not yet matured, would thereby be extinguished. But is there any reason why the holder of these old interests should not be required to re-record the claim within a reasonable period or lose it? Must such old claims cloud the title forever? The merchantability acts are based on the simple premise that unless the stale claim is kept alive by a new recording within a gross period (with a saving clause for old claims in existence at the passage of the act), it ceases to be enforceable. No attempt will be made here to analyze the various statutes of this type since that has been done elsewhere,[67] but a few illustrations will show their usefulness. Typically, they apply against future interests and claimants under disability.

Assume a forty-year act of the Illinois type.[68]

O dies testate in 1928, leaving Blackacre to his son, S, for life, remainder to such children of S as should survive him. S is twenty-two at the time and unmarried. He promptly mortgages Blackacre, wastes his substance in riotous living, and allows the mortgage to be foreclosed the following year. The mortgagee is an individual rather than an institution and assumes that S was the fee simple owner. A buys at the foreclosure sale, taking a deed purporting to convey a fee. S leaves the state, marries and has one daughter, D. S dies in 1967 and in 1968 D returns to the old community to live. In the meantime, Blackacre has changed hands several times, usually by warranty deed, and each successive owner has been in possession of the tract. By 1970, V is the purported owner. In 1971, he contracts to sell Blackacre to P. Does V have a merchantable title?

In the absence of a Merchantability Act, no. P would search the title back to the 1928 will and find that S never had more than a life estate. The various statutes of limitation have not been running against D since she had a non-possessory future interest until S's death in 1967 (it is now 1973 for the purposes of this problem). Her contingent remainder did not vest until 1967 and she has a valid claim to the land. With a Merchanta-

67. See Simes & Taylor, supra note 25; Aigler, Clearance of Land Titles—A Statutory Step, 44 Mich. L.Rev. 45 (1945); Aigler, Constitutionality of Marketable Title Acts, 50 Mich.L.Rev. 185 (1951); Cribbet, supra note 62; Comment, supra note 59. For two recent cases of importance, see Tesdell v. Hanes, 248 Iowa 742, 82 N.W.2d 119 (1957), and Wichelman v. Messner, 250 Minn. 88, 83 N.W.2d 800 (1957).

68. See note 62 supra.

bility Act V would have merchantable title unless D, or someone in her behalf, had re-recorded notice of her claim within the 40 year period. V was justified in going back to the 1929 "root" deed from the mortgage foreclosure and has had a connected chain of title with no recorded defects for 40 years. All claims prior to that period are barred (even future interests) in the absence of their being brought back into the chain by re-recording.

This may seem unfair to D since she may not have known of the will or of the Act, but it is the price that must be paid for a shortened chain of title. Most claims that old will not be of great consequence in any case and should be barred in the interests of a better conveyancing system. Of course, if S had not mortgaged or sold the land, D's claim would not have been destroyed by the forty year period. The Act would not convert S's life estate into a fee regardless of how long he owned the estate. It is the rights of third parties who have relied on a forty year connected chain of title which are protected.

In a recent Iowa case, the court held a title to be merchantable despite an alleged break in the title chain due to a misdescription in a 1907 deed. Relying squarely on the Iowa act, the court stated: "Iowa was the first of several states to pass a statute which bars all claims to real property arising prior to a stated date without regard to the nature of any legal condition on the part of a possible claimant. . . . It will thus be observed there is a growing tendency to effectively bar potential claims arising out of irregularities in a chain of title to real property where no claim is filed based on said irregularity by the date stated in a particular statute." [69]

Merchantability acts are relatively new and there may be some "bugs" in them, but these can be ironed out by amendment and, as the bar becomes familiar with their operation, they should do a great deal to improve the efficiency of the recording system. Forty years is probably too long a period for most claims and the length of time should be reduced as soon as feasible. Actually, the twenty-year limitation of the old English act seems long enough, particularly since an active interest can always be protected by a vigilant claimant. Most old clouds on title are not, in fact, active and should be decently interred as soon as practicable. Some of the impetus for reform should now be directed toward the further shortening of the period of title search.

69. Tesdell v. Hanes, 248 Iowa 742, 747, 82 N.W.2d 119, 121–22 (1957). See also Chicago and Northwestern Railway Company v. City of Osage, 176 N.W.2d 788 (Iowa 1970).

(b) Curative Legislation

Nearly every title examination will disclose technical errors which tend to destroy merchantability but which could scarcely be the basis of a serious lawsuit. Examiners object to these defects largely out of fear that a successor examiner will mention the error and make the first lawyer appear careless. These defects constitute one of the principal areas of "fly-specking." [70] A typical example is the omission of a private seal on a deed or mortgage. Many states periodically pass curative or validating acts to heal these relatively minor abrasions, e. g., "All deeds or mortgages heretofore irregularly executed by the omission of a seal are validated and made effective as though such omitted seal had been affixed." [71]

The history, scope, and constitutionality of curative legislation has been thoroughly explored in the legal literature.[72] Any state which wishes to avail itself of this valuable tool for the improvement of conveyancing can find detailed precedents to follow. The principal difficulty here is keeping the legislation up to date and covering all of the necessary points. It is grubby business, not unlike the daily polishing of brass on a ship, and unless an alert merchantability committee keeps steadily on the job the technical defects will accumulate faster than they can be removed.

(c) Changes in Mechanical Operation of the Recording Acts

The recording acts originated in colonial times and were designed for a simpler society. While basically sound, they need to be examined in the light of today's needs. The major defect is faulty indexing. No record is worth much unless the examiner can find it quickly and accurately. There are two basic systems of indexing—the grantor-grantee and the tract. The present trend is to reduce the number of indexes and use only one gran-

---

70. Ward in his book, Illinois Law of Title Examination (2d ed. 1952), tells the story of the young examiner who objected because the President's wife had not joined in executing a patent from the government. Apocryphal but revealing!

71. Ill.Rev.Stat. ch. 30, § 34b (1973).

72. See, e. g., Basye, supra note 26, at §§ 201–364 (1953); Scurlock, Retroactive Legislation Affecting Interests in Land (1953); Day, Curative Acts and Limitations Acts Designed to Remedy Defects in Florida Land Titles (pts. 1–4), 8 U.Fla. L.Rev. 365 (1955), 9 id. at 145 (1956).

tor-grantee system, but many states have a separate index for each type of instrument (mortgagor-mortgagee, mechanic's lien, index to miscellaneous documents, etc.). For example, Idaho has twenty-four different indexes.[73] It is apparent that such a proliferation of indexes can lead only to delay and error. Moreover, since the grantor-grantee index is usually held to be the official system, the chain of title concept has developed and instruments of record that are outside the chain have been held to give no notice. The tract index is clearly superior and should be adopted whenever possible as the required, official system. This change plus a shorter period of search would go far toward restoring efficiency to the recording system.

Even when the indexing is adequate the acts may be defective in scope.[74] Since the acts reversed the common law scheme of priority, they are strictly construed and apply only to the instruments expressly described. This can mean that some legal documents which affect title to land do not have to be recorded and yet will be binding on a subsequent purchaser. Moreover, a title once obtained by adverse possession may survive to plague a subsequent purchaser even though the adverse possessor did not record any evidence of his claim and was not in possession at the time the alleged bona fide purchaser bought the land.[75] The problem of federal tax liens is notorious and leaves the unsuspecting purchaser at the mercy of secret claims, thus violating the whole basis of the recording system.

The solution to this part of the recording act problem is simple to state but difficult to achieve. *All* claims, interests, liens, etc., affecting real property should be placed on record or be forever lost. This should include government liens since the state, of all groups, should never be above the principle of the law. It should also include claims of adverse possession since the purported owner can at least place an affidavit on record giving notice of his claim. Many records affecting land, e. g., probated wills, state tax liens, judgments, etc., must be found at offices separate from that of the recorder of deeds. These should be held to an absolute minimum and, where they are causing difficulty in the particular jurisdiction, should be required to be filed, by transcript, in the recorder's office. The Torrens system requires nearly all such records to be filed with the registrar on the memorial of title or fail as notice; the recording acts should copy this page from their sister system.

73. Idaho Code Ann. § 31–2404 (1948).

74. Cf. 4 American Law of Property, § 17.8 (Casner ed. 1952).

75. See, e. g., Mugaas v. Smith, 33 Wash.2d 429, 206 P.2d 332 (1949).

(d) Changes in Substantive Law of Property

Some of the conveyancing difficulties have little to do with the recording system; they spring instead from archaic rules of property law that have not been revised to keep pace with changing times. High on the list are such marital interests as dower (or curtesy) and homestead. Designed as a kind of feudal social security, in the case of dower, and as a mid-nineteenth century statutory exemption for debtors, in the case of homestead, they have survived largely as clogs on title and as levers to pry better financial settlements out of straying spouses. Where the husband (or wife) fails to sign a conveyance, even inadvertently, or where the record fails to disclose the marital status of a grantor, the title may be clouded for years. Moreover, this can be a peculiarly difficult defect to correct in a fluid society when the parties move freely from state to state. If these marital interests still play a useful social role they should be retained and legislation designed to remove the cloud as soon as possible.[76] However, many jurisdictions [77] have concluded that these interests should join livery of seisin and socage tenure in limbo, thereby freeing land from one more tentacle of the past.

The whole panorama of future interests should be viewed with a modern eye since such estates are a prolific source of title difficulty. That problem is beyond the scope of this text. It should be noted, however, that statutes limiting the existence of possibilities of reverter and powers of termination to a gross period [78] have a direct effect both on the law of future interests and conveyancing.

The foregoing examples demonstrate the types of substantive property law problems that need study in any full-scale conveyancing reform. These problems vary from state to state and generalizations on a national basis can be misleading, but the bar of each state should make an inventory of its principal "traps for the unwary" and then modify them by appropriate legislation.

(e) Adoption of Title Standards

All of the preceding suggestions require legislative intervention; title standards, however, can be adopted by the cooperative effort of the bar itself. In 1942, the Section on Real Estate Law

------

76. For an example of how this can be done, see Ark.Stat.Ann. § 61–226 (1947).

77. Listed in 2 Powell, Real Property ¶217 (1950).

78. E. g., Ill.Rev.Stat. ch. 30, § 37e (1973).

of the Illinois State Bar Association adopted uniform rules for examination of abstracts. These rules do not purport to bind anyone but they serve as a guide for local bar associations and as a result have been influential with the title bar. The first rule sets the tenor: "An attorney making an examination of title should raise objections only to such matters as are substantial defects in the abstract of title, and should be prepared to show by legal authority that the matter complained of is of such character as would substantially affect the merchantability of the title and would interfere with the ability of the owner to readily dispose of the same." [79]

Many of the rules simply state the existing law, either statutory or decisional, and to that extent are useful only as a method of calling details to the attention of the title examiner. Others go beyond "the law" and set up matters of custom which help to eliminate trivial objections.

Paradoxically, the strength of title standards (improvement in conveyancing without the necessity of legislative action) is also their weakness. As a cooperative venture of the bar they are a long stride forward, but, because the standards lack the sanction of law, they tend to disintegrate in the face of stubborn opposition. The Nebraska legislature has adopted as law the entire set of standards previously passed by the state bar association,[80] and the Connecticut bar association has expressed hope that all states will give such standards the force of law.[81] Nonetheless, the future of title standards lies in their voluntary approach to abstract examination rather than in legislative coercion. Once frozen into code form they become inflexible and call for overly frequent revision. Michigan,[82] Iowa,[83] and Kansas[84] have comprehensive standards that should be studied by all bar groups embarking on this fruitful method of conveyancing reform.

79. Section on Real Estate Law, Ill. Bar Ass'n, Rules for Title Examinations, 31 Ill.B.J. 128 (1942). These rules have now been revised to reflect the new merchantability act in Illinois plus other recent legislative changes.

80. Neb.Rev.Stat. §§ 76–604 to 76–644 (1950).

81. Report of the Committee on Standards for Title Opinions, Proceedings of the ABA Section of Real Property, Probate and Trust Law 130, 132 (1939).

82. 35 Mich.S.B.J. 12–155 (1956).

83. Iowa Land Title Examination Standards (3d ed. 1955).

84. Committee on Title Examination, Kan.B.Ass'n Report, 27 J.B.A.Kan. 55 (1958).

F. THE LAWYERS' ROLE

Lawyers do not have the sole responsibility for the commercial transfer of real property. While the legal role is of great importance, many lay groups are involved in selling, financing, and title assuring. Since the economic stakes are unusually high, it is not surprising that conflicts have developed among the various interest groups serving the consuming public. All of the groups should remember that the goal is service to the public. This is particularly true of lawyers who are members of a learned profession and have been granted a kind of monopoly in the public interest. A desire to protect their own financial stake should not lead them into self-defeating attacks on real estate brokers, title insurance companies, and lending institutions, which may be able to provide adequate service at reasonable cost. Suits against real estate brokers and others for unauthorized practice of the law are probably doomed to failure in any case and only bring the bar into public disrepute.[85] It would seem the proper course for lawyers would be to concentrate on giving superior and more broadly based service and working out cooperative agreements with those other groups involved in commercial land transactions.[86]

85. See, for example, Chicago Bar Ass'n v. Quinlan and Tyson, Inc., 34 Ill.2d 116, 214 N.E.2d 771 (1966) and State ex rel. Indiana State Bar Ass'n v. Indiana Real Estate Ass'n, Inc., 244 Ind. 214, 191 N.E.2d 711 (1963), noting particularly Judge Arterburn's concurring opinion in the latter case. The two cited cases limited the drafting of deeds to lawyers but allowed real estate brokers to "fill in the blanks" in contracts of sale and related documents. After the Arizona Supreme Court held with the bar in a suit against lay groups, the public reversed the decision by a constitutional amendment (which passed about 4 to 1), allowing laymen to practice law in a limited way.

86. See Foreman, The Illinois Real Estate Broker—Lawyer Accord, 55 Ill.B.J. 284 (1966) and Proceedings, Section of Real Property, Probate and Trust Law, Part II, Real Property Law Division 187–193 (1964). The author of this text was chairman of the committee making the latter report.

Part Four

THE USE OF PROPERTY

According to the civil law,[1] property involves six rights: *jus possidende* or right of possessing; *jus prohibendi* or right of excluding others; *jus disponendi* or right of disposition; *jus utendi* or right of using; *jus fruendi* or right of enjoying the fruits and profits; and *jus abutendi* or right of destroying or injuring if one likes.[2] Accepting this listing as roughly correct for the common law, note how many of the rights relate to use of the *res* once it has been acquired. While we have touched on questions of use throughout this book (many use questions are settled by the estate which *X* owns), we now focus our attention on several specific problems in the use of property.

Here, again, personal property raises few difficulties. Most chattels are created to be consumed and once ownership is established the titleholder can do with them as he pleases. True, if he abuses his dog or whips his horse in public the Humane Society may call him to account, but there are few public policy issues

1. Pound, The Law of Property and Recent Juristic Thought, 25 A.B.A.J. 993, 996 (1939).

2. This last right is misleading, as see Ely, Property and Contract In Their Relation To The Distribution Of Wealth, Vol. 1, p. 135 (1914). "Furthermore, *property is exclusive in its nature and not absolute.* A phrase is found in Roman law which, as a definition of property, is misleading. The phrase is, "*Dominium est jus utendi et abutendi re.*" Some have said that it means that the right of property carries with it the right to use or to abuse a thing, and so it has been actually claimed that property is the right to use or misuse a thing, and that the right of property carries with it the right to make a bad use of things. But such an idea comes from bad translation. *Abutendi* means to use up or consume a thing, not to abuse it, and that has been conclusively shown by Knies in his discussion of the subject. While it means the right of using up or consuming, the Roman law never intended to give anyone the right of misusing a thing. This right might have existed in spite of the intent of the law, but it was contrary to the spirit of the law to give the right. It might have existed because it could not be prevented, but it was never sanctioned. Wagner also calls attention to the fact that, added to the phrase, '*Jus utendi et abutendi re*', is the generally ignored clause, '*quatenus juris ratio patitur*', 'in so far as the reason of law permits'. But Wagner claims that while *abutendi* may mean simply to consume, it does carry with it at least a suggestion or implication of misuse." This point has important implications for our philosophical approach to current environmental problems.

involved and the law seldom interferes. Occasionally, an owner
will sell or give his chattels to another and try to control their use
after they leave his possession but these are rare cases. Real
property, on the other hand, is not typically consumed by use and,
since the thin crust of soil on which all life depends is in limited
supply, there are many areas where public policy is involved in its
use. Frequently, owners transfer title to the land but seek to
maintain an interest in it or control its use long after it has left
their possession. We will discuss the legal principles involved
under three chapter headings: (1) rights in the land of another,
which obviously represent restrictions on use by the possessor-
owner, and include easements, profits, licenses, covenants, and
conditions; (2) natural rights, i. e., rights of use inherent in the
ownership of the land such as the right to prevent a nuisance,
the right to physical support of the soil, and water rights; and
(3) public regulation of land use, including planning, zoning, subdivision control, and environmental control.

Chapter 1

RIGHTS IN THE LAND OF ANOTHER

All of the so-called rights in the land of another are closely related and there is a strong temptation to discuss them in one homogeneous mass, sorting out detail as we move along. However, since they have distinct, although overlapping, legal functions it may be clearer to take them up separately with frequent cross references.

SECTION 1.   EASEMENTS AND PROFITS

An easement is a property right in a person or group of persons to use the land of another for a special purpose not inconsistent with the general property right in the owner of the land.[3] It is best illustrated by rights of way across another's land, public utility telephone lines and pipelines, and flooding privileges, but it can include a wide variety of novel and interesting rights.[4] A profit à prendre (to use the technically correct terminology) is an easement plus, i. e., it is the right to use another's land by removing a portion of the soil or its products. My favorite illustration is the right to go on the land of a seashore owner and collect seaweed for use as fertilizer on your own land. Much of the law of profits à prendre was developed in the old English seaweed cases but the right to remove gravel, minerals, and timber is more common today. There is no necessity for treating these two property interests separately since the same legal principles apply to both. In English law, there was a difference since easements could exist only as appurtenant to other land owned by the holder of the easement while profits could be owned separately from any

3. A more detailed and hence more accurate definition is found in Restatement, Property, § 450 (1944). "An easement is an interest in land in the possession of another which (a) entitles the owner of such interest to a limited use or enjoyment of the land in which the interest exists; (b) entitles him to protection as against third persons from interference in such use and enjoyment; (c) is not subject to the will of the possessor of the land; (d) is not a normal incident of the possession of any land possessed by the owner of the interest, and (e) is capable of creation by conveyance."

4. For a discussion of these novel easements see Drye v. Eagle Rock Ranch, Inc., 364 S.W.2d 196 (Tex. 1962).

other land, i. e., in gross. While some remnants of this meaningless distinction haunt us in this country it has little practical significance because easements too may now be in gross.[5]

Before proceeding to problems of creation, transfer, scope, and termination it may be useful to clarify a few terms. Easements may be classified in several ways: affirmative, allowing the holder to do acts on another's land, or negative, allowing the holder to prevent the owner from doing acts on his own land; appurtenant, benefiting other land owned by the holder, or in gross, not benefiting any other land owned by the holder; express, created by direct action of the parties, or implied, created by operation of law from the peculiar facts and circumstances involved; and several other categories, such as legal or equitable, of less importance. Easements are usually referred to in relation to dominant and servient tenements or tracts of land. The dominant tenement is the land benefited by the easement, the servient tenement is the land burdened by the easement. Thus, if *A* owns a tract north of *B* and has the right to cross *B's* land to reach a highway south of it, *A's* tract is the dominant tenement (benefited by the means of access) and *B's* tract is the servient tenement (burdened by having to allow *A* to cross his land). An easement is in gross when it burdens servient land but benefits no dominant land, e. g., telephone company wires.

A. CREATION

Easements can be created by express act of the parties, by implication, or by prescription.[6] At a very early date, even prior to the Statute of Uses when livery of seisin still ruled the roost for freehold estates, easements could be created by grant, an instrument under seal. Indeed, the old saw ran, those things which lie not in livery lie in grant. Today, "the formal requisites for the creation of an easement by conveyance inter vivos are (a) those required in a conveyance of an estate in land of like duration, and (b) subject to statutory modification, a written in-

---

5. Restatement, Property, § 450, special note (1944).

6. Perhaps custom should be added to this list, since the Supreme Court of Oregon, in an historic and fascinating decision, relied on custom to protect the "dry-sand" area of the Oregon beaches from private exploitation. State ex rel. Thornton v. Hay, 254 Or. 584, 462 P.2d 671 (1969). The court, in effect, found an easement in the public, based on immemorial usage or custom, dating back to the Indians. The facts were unique, however, and the case finds little support in American precedent.

strument under seal." [7]   Therefore, if *A* wishes to buy an easement across the land of *B*, he may enter into a transaction not unlike that involved in purchasing a fee and take conveyance by
means of a regular deed that describes the interest correctly.   The
parties must be careful to make their intent clear because there
can be ambiguity as to whether a fee simple title to a strip of land
or an easement only is being conveyed.   Thus, "a strip of land for
a right of way over and across Blackacre" may create a fee [8] or
virtually the same language may create an easement.[9]   The distinction becomes vital on abandonment of the way, as by a railroad, because if an easement only resulted the strip belongs to the
servient owner when the use ceases.   Failure to comply with formal requirements, such as a seal, may defeat the easement and
give the grantee a mere license which can be revoked by the grantor.[10]   However, if the grantee changes his position in reliance on
the grant, an easement still may result on the principle of estoppel.[11]

  In addition to a grant, easements may be created by express
reservation or exception.   For example, *A*, owning Blackacre in
fee simple, can convey to *B* but reserve or except an easement
across Blackacre for his own use so that he can reach retained
land from a highway.[12]   Technically, this would be a reservation
since a new interest in land is being created in the grantor (a man
cannot have an easement in his own land, so the interest came
into existence with the deed of the fee to *B*), but the old distinction between reservations and exceptions has little modern meaning.[13]   No attempt should be made to create an easement in a
third party, *C*, by this method since the necessary words of grant
would be missing and some courts would hold it ineffective.[14]

  Easements created by implication are of two basic types:
(1) easements implied from quasi-easements and (2) easements

---

7.   Note 5 supra, p. 467.

8.   Midland Valley Railroad Co. v.
     Arrow Industrial Manufacturing
     Co., 297 P.2d 410 (Okl.1956).

9.   Bernards v. Link, 199 Or. 579, 248
     P.2d 341 (1952).   See also Harvest
     Queen Mill and Elev. Co. v. Sand-
     ers, 189 Kan. 536, 370 P.2d 419
     (1962).

10.   Nelson v. American Tel. and Tel.
     Co., 270 Mass. 471, 170 N.E. 416
     (1930).

  Note, however, that the need for a
  seal has been abolished in most
  jurisdictions by statute.   Even
  where a seal is technically required

at law, equity may enforce a written grant which is unsealed, i. e., an
equitable easement results.   Baseball Publishing Co. v. Bruton, 302
Mass. 54, 18 N.E.2d 362, 119 A.L.R.
1518 (1938).

11.   Stoner v. Zucker, 148 Cal. 516, 83
     P. 808 (1906).

12.   Mitchell v. Castellaw, 151 Tex.
     56, 246 S.W.2d 163 (1952).

13.   See 3 Powell, Real Property 403
     (1952).

14.   See p. 165, supra ; Restatement,
     Property, § 472 (1944).

implied from necessity. It could be argued that no easement should ever be implied because this allows the creation of an interest in land without the writing demanded by the Statute of Frauds. However, the courts have consistently treated such easements as exceptions to the legislative ban and have rationalized the result by interpreting the description of the land conveyed to include the easement as an appurtenance.[15]

The easement implied from a quasi-easement arises when there is a severance of the unity of title where an obvious servitude has been imposed on one part of an estate. "The general rule may be expressed that where during the unity of title an apparent and obvious, permanent, continuous and actual servitude or use is imposed on one part of an estate in favor of another, *which at the time of severance of unity* is in use and is reasonably necessary for the fair enjoyment of the other, then upon a severance of such unity of ownership there arises by implication of law a grant of the right to continue such use even though such grant is not reserved or specified in the deed." [16] The implication is based on the probable intention of the parties in order to reach a fair and equitable result.

Thus, *A* owns Blackacre and has a house and farm dwellings on the north half, with a clearly defined road across the south half to a major highway. There is also a highway to the north so that *A* could have access by that route, but the highway itself is a poor one and the hilly, rocky soil makes such a way difficult. *A* cannot be said to have an easement across the south half of his own land, but he does have a quasi-easement and the north half is quasi-dominant land, the south half quasi-servient, i. e., the facts show an interest in the nature of an easement. If *B* buys the north half, he would undoubtedly expect to have the same access *A* had to the buildings. He *should* require *A* to make an express grant of such an easement across the retained half, but if the parties fail to do so a court will imply the easement by way of grant, unless the parties negative any intent to create such an interest. If *B* buys the south half of Blackacre rather than the north, the problem changes slightly. If any easement is implied, it must arise by way of reservation in *A*, since the quasi-servient land is being conveyed first. This would mean that *A* would be claiming an easement in derogation of his own grant and, if a warranty deed were used, would be creating an incumbrance against the terms of his deed. For this reason, most courts are more reluctant to imply an easement in favor of a grantor (by way of reservation) than in favor of a grantee (by way of grant) and will do so only if it is strictly

---

15. 3 Tiffany, Real Property 254 (3d ed. 1939).

16. Deisenroth v. Dodge, 7 Ill.2d 340, 346, 131 N.E.2d 17, 21 (1955).

necessary to the enjoyment of the land.[17] Some courts do not make this distinction and will imply an easement whenever it is reasonably required for the enjoyment of the land, regardless of whether it is a reservation or a grant.[18]

Easements may be implied by necessity, regardless of the prior use of the land, although such prior use may also be involved in the facts. In the previous hypothetical case, if no highway had existed to the north an easement would have been implied in favor of either party to prevent the creation of a land-locked tract. The right of way would have been *strictly* necessary for the enjoyment of the north half of Blackacre and would have been implied even if no roadway across the south half had existed at the time of severance. The key here is *strict* necessity although a practical, as distinguished from an absolute, necessity will suffice.[19] Easements implied from necessity are based upon the presumed intention of the parties and the implication will not be invoked unless both the dominant and servient tracts were once under a common ownership.[20] If, at one time, there had been unity of title, the way by necessity may lie dormant through many transfers of title and yet pass with each transfer as appurtenant to the dominant estate and be exercised at a much later date by the holder of the easement.[21] In spite of the emphasis on intent, it should be noted that public policy plays a large role and that full utilization of the land requires some sort of access to isolated tracts. Where this access can be furnished by a statute allowing eminent domain proceedings for land-locked owners, the judicial doctrine may be subject to change.[22]

If the easement was implied because of strict necessity, it will continue only so long as the necessity exists, whereas if it was implied from a quasi-easement it may continue indefinitely.[23] While most types of easements, including sewage disposal rights which can be very important,[24] may be created by implication, easements for light and air cannot arise in this country, either by implication or prescription. They can be created only by express agreement.[25] The doctrine of implied easements does have

17. Mitchell v. Castellaw, 151 Tex. 56, 246 S.W.2d 163 (1952).

18. Walker v. Witt, 4 Ill.2d 16, 122 N.E.2d 175 (1954).

19. Flood v. Earle, 145 Me. 24, 71 A.2d 55 (1950); 19 Ore.L.Rev. 362, 365 (1940).

20. Simonton, Ways By Necessity, 25 Col.L.Rev. 571, 575 (1925).

21. Finn v. Williams, 376 Ill. 95, 33 N.E.2d 226, 133 A.L.R. 1390 (1941).

22. Simonson v. McDonald, 131 Mont. 494, 311 P.2d 982 (1957).

23. Martinelli v. Luis, 213 Cal. 183, 1 P.2d 980 (1931).

24. Wiesal v. Smira, 49 R.I. 246, 142 A. 148, 58 A.L.R. 818 (1928).

25. Maioriello v. Arlotta, 364 Pa. 557, 73 A.2d 374 (1950). England has a doctrine of ancient lights which does allow such easements to be created by prescription. The Pennsylvania court did not rule out all possibility of an implied easement but they found no cases in which it had been allowed.

a pervasive quality, however, and even when public streets are vacated according to statutory authority an implied means of access may continue on a private basis for individuals fronting on the old street.[26]

Many easements are created by prescription or adverse user. If adverse possession for a statutory period can ripen into a fee simple title, it ought to follow that adverse use of a right of way, drain, support wall, etc., should create an easement. Interestingly enough, the statutes of limitation were usually drafted to apply only to possession, not to use, so that incorporeal rights were not necessarily created by long continued use of land for purposes in the nature of an easement. Fortunately, the courts have filled this legislative gap and the period of the basic statute has been adopted by analogy as a basis for presuming a grant of an easement.[27] Having seized the statute of limitation analogy, the courts have tended to adopt its refinements as well, so that tacking by successive adverse users is allowed, if privity is present between them, disabilities toll the running of the period, etc.

Prescription means literally, "before written", and the common-law theory was that since the use had continued for so long (at one stage the phrase immemorial usage was much in vogue) it must have been based on a lost grant. This made some sense in England, which had no recording system, but loses most of its appeal in this country where the writing should have been recorded, if it existed. Of course, it was only a fiction anyway and the cases are full of learned discussions as to the kind of presumption of lost grant raised by the passage of time.[28] This is of more than historical interest since it goes to the very principle on which prescription is based and has resulted in great confusion in the cases.

If a presumption of lost grant is the true basis, then acquiescence of the fee owner in the use is material since it strengthens the fiction that at some time such a right was granted to the user. A letter of protest, forbidding the use to continue, written while the easement was still inchoate, would thus seem to be fatal to a prescriptive right since it negatives acquiescence. In fact, many cases so hold, thereby drawing a sharp distinction between prescription and adverse possession.[29] However, if the true basis is the adverseness of the use, the protest would seem to strengthen the case for the claimant and would not prevent the acquisition of the easement. This latter view is more consistent with the theory

26. Highway Holding Co. v. Yara Engineering Corp., 22 N.J. 119, 123 A.2d 511 (1956). Comment, 55 Mich. L.Rev. 885 (1957).

27. Parker and Edgarton v. Foote, 19 Wend. (N.Y.) 309 (1838).

28. O'Banion v. Borba, 32 Cal.2d 145, 195 P.2d 10 (1948).

29. Dartnell v. Bidwell, 115 Me. 227, 98 A. 743, 5 A.L.R. 1320 (1916).

of the statutes of limitation, admittedly used by way of analogy, and would defeat claims based on permissiveness which should give rise, at best, to a mere license.[30] The cases continue to present this curious ambivalence and the lawyer relying on prescriptive rights would do well to analyze the decisions in his own jurisdiction before taking a firm stand on either side of the issue.

B. TRANSFER

At this point, distinctions between easements appurtenant and in gross and profits à prendre become relevant. The easement appurtenant is a parasite attached to its host land, the dominant estate, and it has no life separate from that estate. When the dominant estate is transferred the easement follows along with it, even if not mentioned in the deed either specifically or under the catch all, "and other appurtenances." [31] If the grantor of the dominant estate wishes to prevent the transfer of the appurtenant easement to his grantee, he can do so by a proper provision in the deed, but this has the effect of extinguishing the easement and relieving the servient land of its burden.[32] It will not normally change the easement into one in gross in the hands of the grantor.[33] Profits à prendre which are appurtenant to other land follow the same rules of transfer.

It is the right in gross which has caused the difficulty. The profit in gross was an inheritable and assignable interest even in the early days because, since it included the right to remove timber, soil, etc., from the land of another, it was in the nature of an estate in the land.[34] Easements in gross were treated, in England, as non-assignable and non-inheritable, dying with the individual holder. "In the United States there have been a few decisions and a considerable quantity of dicta to the same effect. In general, however, we have avoided the simple English rule, agreeing among ourselves that these easements in gross are some transferable and some not transferable, but disagreeing among ourselves

30. Lunt v. Kitchens, 123 Utah 488, 260 P.2d 535 (1953).

31. Stockdale v. Yerden, 220 Mich. 444, 190 N.W. 225 (1922).

32. Cadwalader v. Bailey, 17 R.I. 495, 23 A. 20, 14 L.R.A. 300 (1891).

33. "If the purpose of the provision is to change the easement appurtenant into an easement in gross, it will have this effect if, and only if, the manner or the terms of the creation of the easement permit such a change to be made." Restatement, Property, § 487, comment b (1944).

34. Post v. Pearsall, 22 Wend. (N.Y.) 422 (1839).

(quite violently at times) as to the criteria for separating the sheep from the goats." [35]

The English view has some merit. *A* grants a right of way across Blackacre to *B*, the owner of Whiteacre. Absent a contrary intent, this is a right attached to Whiteacre and its owner rather than to *B*, as an individual. Naturally, if Whiteacre is sold to *C* the easement trails along. However, if *A* grants *B* a right to cross Blackacre, unrelated to *B's* ownership of other land, this is a mere personal right and *B* should not be able to transfer it to others. Since certainty is one objective of property law, the simplest rule is to ban all transfers of easements in gross. However, certainty has a way of conflicting with social utility at times and the merit of the English rule becomes questionable if *B* is a railroad company, a public utility, etc., rather than a private person. Why shouldn't such vast commercial easements in gross be transferable like any other interest in land? American courts saw no reason to deny alienability generally and, while results have not always been consistent, they have made a case-by-case approach to the problem with satisfactory results. Most commercial easements in gross are readily assignable; non-commercial types may also be transferred if the grantor has evidenced the necessary intent, e. g., has used such words as "heirs and assigns." [36]

Once most easements in gross become transferable a new problem arises—surcharge of the servient tenement. All easements are a burden on the servient land and interfere with the full enjoyment of the fee. If transfer greatly increases this burden, it amounts to a surcharge and may be unfair to the owner of the land. There are no easy answers here and the courts must scrutinize the facts of each case. Frequently interests which are transferable will be held non-divisible, thus placing some limitation on free alienability. To prevent excessive use the transferees may be required to exercise the right "as one stock," i. e., use the easement as contemplated by the parties at the time of its creation.[37]

35. 3 Powell, Real Property 476– 477 (1952).

36. Miller v. Lutheran Conference and Camp Ass'n, 331 Pa. 241, 200 A. 646, 130 A.L.R. 1245 (1938).

37. Id.

C. SCOPE

Conflict between the holder of an easement and the owner of the servient land is built into this split of property rights. The easement may be indispensable to the owner of the dominant land and the pressure to increase the use may be irresistible as economic conditions change. The increase in benefit causes a corresponding increase in burden and a lawsuit develops. The best preventive medicine is a carefully drafted document which leaves little to judicial interpretation.

The essential problem in determining the scope of an express easement is the same as in most cases involving judicial interpretation of a deed, contract, etc.[38] The court looks at the four corners of the document and decides what the parties intended, frequently using the "rule of reason" as a basis of interpretation. This means that the court tries to place itself in the position of the parties when the document was drafted and give the words their reasonable meaning. "This rule of reason does not prevent the parties from making any contract regarding their respective rights which they may wish, regardless of the reasonableness of their wishes on the subject. The rule merely refuses to give unreasonable rights, or to impose unreasonable burdens, when the parties, either actually or by legal implication, have spoken generally." Thus, in Sakansky v. Wein,[39] where a right of way was given a definite location across servient land, the holder was entitled to insist on his rights, as clearly expressed, and did not have to accept a different route to reach his dominant estate. Even the servient owner's offer to leave eight feet of headroom for passage under a new building was not decisive without a showing that such amount of space was reasonable. Some of the cases may sound as if the holder of the easement is a "dog in the manger" insisting on excessive rights, but it must be remembered that an easement is an interest in land and its owner is entitled to full legal protection, no less than the fee simple owner.

38. In Herold v. Hughes, 141 W.Va. 182, 90 S.E.2d 451 (1955), an easement acquired by the State Road Commission for "public road purposes" was held to include the right to locate a gas transmission line beneath the road. The court said:

"We cannot assume that the grant was made and accepted for any limited purposes or methods of travel or transportation." A contrary conclusion was reached in Heyert v. Orange and Rockland Utilities, Inc., 17 N.Y.2d 352, 271 N.Y.S.2d 201, 218 N.E.2d 263 (1966). Cases involving similar problems are collected in Note, 58 A.L.R.2d 525 (1958).

39. 86 N.H. 337, 169 A. 1 (1933).

In most of the litigation involving scope, the court must try to balance the relative interests of the parties so that each can enjoy his property to the maximum extent. The servient owner can use his land for any purpose, so long as it does not unreasonably interfere with the easement. Some easements hinder the servient owner very little and, indeed, may benefit the land; others, such as railroads, will require exclusive possession of a part of the estate and leave little space for enjoyment by the fee owner.[40] The servient owner must allow the easement holder to come on the land and make necessary repairs, but the duty to repair rests on the holder.[41] If the alteration in the easement, such as lowering a pipeline where the terms did not state the depth at which it was to be buried, is made for the benefit of the servient owner then he must bear the expense.[42] Some flexibility in use is essential as times change and, subject always to interpretation of the grant, courts do allow altered and expanded activity, but the easement must benefit only the original dominant land and cannot be expanded to include other tracts purchased by the holder of the easement.[43]

It is even more difficult to determine the scope of a prescriptive easement since there is no document to interpret. Typically, the courts say that the nature of the use which established the easement sets its scope as well.[44] Thus, the hauling of timber for twenty years across the land of *A* will not necessarily allow access to the old timber tract if a circus is set up there. Again, a rule of reason must be applied and an easement acquired for horse drawn vehicles ought not to fail because automobiles have become the mode of transport.[45] It should be noted that an express easement may have its scope enlarged by adverse user for the prescriptive period.[46]

Surcharge of the servient land can be a material factor in determining scope, just as it is in deciding alienability. The fact situations can be complex but, in general, the division of the dominant tenement into smaller tracts allows each new owner to use

40. The grantor of the easement does retain the mineral rights, however, even though access may be hindered by the user. Magnolia Petroleum Co. v. Thompson, 106 F.2d 217 (8th Cir. 1939).

41. Guillet v. Livernois, 297 Mass. 337, 8 N.E.2d 921, 112 A.L.R. 1300 (1937).

42. Buckeye Pipeline Co. v. Keating, 229 F.2d 795 (7th Cir. 1956), certiorari denied 352 U.S. 830, 77 S.Ct. 44 (1956).

43. S. S. Kresge Co. v. Winkelman Realty Co., 260 Wis. 372, 50 N.W. 2d 920 (1952).

44. Bartholomew v. Staheli, 86 Cal. App.2d 844, 195 P.2d 824 (1948).

45. For a detailed discussion see 4 Tiffany, Real Property, § 1209 (3d ed. 1939).

46. Gehman v. Erdman, 105 Pa. 371 (1884).

the old easement since the possibility of subdivision should have been foreseen when the right was created.[47] However, this partition does not create additional ways across the servient land and if the burden is too great the court may decide that it goes beyond what the parties originally contemplated.[48]

D. TERMINATION

An easement may expire by its own terms. Like any other interest in land, it may be created for the life of the holder only or it may be designed for a particular purpose and end when the purpose is accomplished.[49] As previously noted, an easement implied from necessity will cease when the necessity ceases. Most easements, however, have a potentially unlimited duration and some specific action is required to terminate them. Mere non-use is not enough since property rights can lie fallow for years and then be reasserted.

The servient owner may strongly desire to be rid of the burden and he can purchase the easement from the holder and extinguish it by a conveyance. Sometimes, the cost is so high that the owner may simply purchase the dominant land and thus terminate the easement by unity of title. It is elementary that union of the dominant and servient estates in a single owner causes the easement to merge into the fee.[50] This is but another way of saying that a man cannot have an easement in his own land.[51]

Termination by estoppel, abandonment,[52] and prescription are all closely related. While non-use is not enough, if the servient owner thinks this means abandonment and makes substantial improvements on his estate, to the knowledge of the holder of the

47. Restatement, Property, § 488 (1944).

48. Wood v. Ashby, 122 Utah 588, 253 P.2d 351 (1952).

49. Griffin v. Dwyer, 181 Okl. 71, 72 P.2d 349 (1937).

50. Dimoff v. Laboroff, 296 Mich. 325, 296 N.W. 275 (1941).

51. Lake Bluff v. Dalitsch, 415 Ill. 476, 114 N.E.2d 654 (1953); Matteodo v. Ricci, 56 R.I. 208, 184 A. 573 (1936).

52. In Aggregate Supply Co. v. Sewell, 217 Ga. 407, 122 S.E.2d 580 (1961) the court held that a profit à prendre (in this case the right to remove sand and gravel from the land of another), being a corporeal interest, was not subject to termination by abandonment. This position conflicts with the Restatement of Property, § 450, Special Note, view that there are no significant distinctions in American law between easements and profits.

easement, the latter may be estopped to assert his rights in the future.[53] Abandonment is the most frequent method of termination of the three just mentioned, but it requires a proof of intent to release all rights and this can be a troublesome point.[54] Non-use is some evidence but overt physical acts by the holder, such as plowing the land formerly used to reach the easement or building a fence across the old way, are normally required. If non-use by the holder is coupled with an inconsistent use of the servient land for the statutory period by the servient owner, the easement will be extinguished by prescription.[55] Note that abandonment and estoppel do not require the passage of any particular period of time.

Destruction of the servient estate and failure to record an express easement may also lead to termination. The former type of extinguishment is most likely to arise in party wall situations or in easements of passage through a building subsequently destroyed by fire.[56] If a b. f. p. buys servient land subject to an unrecorded easement that is not apparent from physical evidence of its use the easement will be extinguished. However, since the recording system does not apply to easements created by prescription or implication and since there is no written instrument to record in either case, the purchaser, even without notice, will take subject to these interests.[57]

SECTION 2. LICENSES

The license is the least important of the rights in the land of another. A great deal has been written about this elusive interest but much of it turns out to be a lesson in semantics. Even that master of analysis, Professor Hohfeld, called it a "chameleon-hued term . . . a word of convenient and seductive obscurity."[58] It has been denied that it is an interest in land at

53. Trimble v. King, 131 Ky. 1, 114 S.W. 317 (1908).

54. Lindsey v. Clark, 193 Va. 522, 69 S.E.2d 342 (1952).

55. Glatts v. Henson, 31 Cal.2d 368, 188 P.2d 745 (1948).

56. Shirley v. Crabb, 138 Ind. 200, 73 N.E. 130 (1894) held that no easement attached to a new building erected on the old site, but Douglas v. Coonley, 156 N.Y. 521, 51 N.E. 283 (1898) seemed to indicate the easement would be suspended and would attach to a new building if and when one was constructed.

57. McKeon v. Brammer, 238 Iowa 1113, 29 N.W.2d 518, 174 A.L.R. 1229 (1947). See also p. 283 supra for a discussion of a similar point as to adverse possession.

58. Hohfeld, Faulty Analysis in Easement and License Cases, 27 Yale L.J. 66, 92 (1917).

all, e. g., it is not subject to the Statute of Frauds. Indeed, it has been stated that a licensee operating on the land of another is not entitled to legal protection from interference by third parties, but this seems incorrect on principle since even a naked trespasser receives some support against acts of a later trespasser.[59]

A license is a personal, revocable privilege to do an **act** or series of acts upon the land of another without possessing any estate or interest in that land. It is a defense against a suit in trespass by the owner of the land and, until revoked, it does smack of an interest in land since it carries the privilege of being on the premises. Termination at the will of the licensor is the key to the distinction between a license and an easement.[60] Failure to comply with the technical requisites for creating an easement may result in a license, despite the obvious intent of the parties, but this is only another way of saying that the easement is unenforceable.[61] Conversely, some cases hold that a license may become irrevocable because of acts done in reliance on its continuance, but this can only mean that an easement has been created by estoppel.[62]

A license can be created orally, in writing, or simply by default in trying to create a greater interest. It is subject to few, if any, conveyancing rules and questions of scope seldom arise since in the case of dispute the licensor can always terminate the "interest" entirely. Enough has been said to indicate the role of the license in the classification of property interests and to distinguish it from its more legally mature brothers.

SECTION 3.   COVENANTS AND CONDITIONS

Covenants and conditions have been discussed before in this book.[63] We approach them now from a new angle, but the earlier material should be reviewed to avoid confusion. Leases bristle with covenants and covenants for title are of the essence in a warranty deed, but our concern now is for the restrictive covenant in a deed which serves as a private control of the use of

59. See Note, 33 Yale L.J. 642 (1924).

60. Baseball Publishing Co. v. Bruton, 302 Mass. 54, 18 N.E.2d 362, 119 A.L.R. 1518 (1938).

61. Nelson v. American Tel. and Tel. Co., 270 Mass. 471, 170 N.E. 416 (1930).

62. Stoner v. Zucker, 148 Cal. 516, 83 P. 808 (1906).

63. See pp. 215, 268 supra.

land. *A* conveys tracts to *B*, *C*, and *D*, inserting covenants that the land shall be used solely for residential purposes. What legal problems arise from this attempt to control another's use of his own land? The condition is closely related but differs in the method of enforcement. *A* conveys to *B*, *C*, and *D*, inserting a condition so that the grantees receive only a defeasible fee, reserving a possibility of reverter, a power of termination, or an executory interest in a third person, depending on the form of language used. In event of breach, the estate of *B*, *C*, or *D* will be forfeited if a condition is used, whereas the covenant calls for damages, specific performance, or an injunction. Occasionally, the two are intermingled so that it is difficult to tell which device was intended.[64] The use of a condition is not normally desirable because of its drastic consequences for the grantee and because courts, abhorring forfeitures, may be astute to find no breach of the condition or that the breach has been waived. Most of the cases involve covenants and the bulk of our discussion will relate to them, with incidental references to conditions.

Note the affinity of covenants and easements. *A*, the covenantor, exacts a promise from *B*, the covenantee, not to build within twenty feet of the street. *A's* retained land is now the dominant tenement, *B's* land is the servient tenement; *A* has the benefit, *B* the burden. Typically, the covenant will bind both parties so that the burdens and benefits are mutual, but this does not change the analytical character of the interests. The covenant is like a negative easement because it gives *A* the right to prevent *B* from using his land in certain prescribed ways. Does *A* now have an interest in the land of *B*, appurtenant to his own land? For most purposes, he does have and the legal consequences are similar to those involved in easements and profits.

The law-equity split adds a dash of spice to this section. On breach, an action at law can be filed for money damages and the court will approach the problem as it would most contract matters, being much concerned as to whether the covenant will run with the land to bind successors in interest. Money damages will probably be inadequate and, in some cases, the covenant may be technically deficient at law, although adequate to touch the conscience of the chancellor, so that equity may take jurisdiction. That court will probably use the language of "equitable servitude" and point out that *B's* land is burdened by the servitude while *A's* is benefited by it. Chancery will be less concerned by the difficulty of binding successors in interest to an equitable servitude of which they had notice. This bifurcation will be discussed in more detail under "transfer" but you should remember

---

64. Scaling v. Sutton, 167 S.W.2d 275 (Tex.Civ.App.1942).

that, in a sense, covenants and equitable servitudes are but two sides of the same coin.

A. CREATION

In modern practice covenants have become detailed blueprints for the regulation of subdivision growth. Racial restrictions are no longer enforceable since Shelley v. Kraemer [65] and related cases, but any other restriction which is not illegal or offensive to public policy can be utilized. In view of their complex character, covenants should be carefully drafted and every possible ambiguity eliminated. [66] Clearly, they should be in writing and the covenants should be inserted into each deed delivered by the subdivider-grantor or they should be incorporated by reference to a recorded master list or to a recorded plat that indicates the restrictions. This latter method of creation is quite common and the title examiner must always look at any recorded plats to discover those covenants which may be binding on the purchaser.

The preceding paragraph represents the normal and ideal way to create covenants, but aberrational situations are bound to arise which may also result in binding covenants. The crux of the matter is the requirement of a writing. Since a covenant is an interest in land it falls under the Statute of Frauds and according to many cases is unenforceable unless in writing. [67] A few cases have taken a directly contrary position, holding that a covenant does not relate to an interest in land but merely to its use and hence oral covenants can be enforced. [68] Even if covenants do fall within the statute they may be enforced, in some instances, upon the grounds of estoppel or part performance. [69] The parol covenant issue is most likely to arise when a subdivider-grantor places written covenants in the first deeds out and promises orally to put similar covenants in the remaining deeds

---

65. 334 U.S. 1, 68 S.Ct. 836 (1948); Barrows v. Jackson, 346 U.S. 249, 73 S.Ct. 1031 (1953); Capitol Federal Savings and Loan Ass'n v. Smith, 136 Colo. 265, 316 P.2d 252 (1957).

66. See note 64, supra, for a case where detailed covenants were ambiguous on the key issue of covenant versus condition.

67. Sprague v. Kimball, 213 Mass. 380, 100 N.E. 622 (1913).

68. Thornton v. Schobe, 79 Colo. 25, 243 P. 617 (1925).

69. Williams Realty Co. v. Robey, 175 Md. 532, 2 A.2d 683 (1938). Note, 14 Ind.L.J. 372 (1939).

as they are delivered. If he fails to do so, his oral promise may not be binding because of the statute,[70] but since the first grantees ought to be able, on equitable principles, to enjoin a sale by the subdivider without the covenants, any subsequent purchaser with knowledge of the facts should also be bound by the covenant.[71]

The more intriguing question relates to implied covenants. In jurisdictions which follow the Statute of Frauds strictly, like Massachusetts,[72] the easy answer is to eliminate all such covenants. However, if easements can, under proper circumstances, be implied in spite of the statute why should we balk at covenants? The leading case on this point is Sanborn v. McLean.[73] *A*, a common grantor of *B* and *C*, conveyed lots in a subdivision and put covenants restricting the use to residential purposes in some of the deeds, including that to *B*, but not in others. *C*, a later purchaser had no covenant in his deed and proceeded to build a service station. *B* was able to enjoin the use by *C* on the theory that a covenant was implied in the latter's deed. Said the court: "If the owner of two or more lots, so situated as to bear the relation, sells one with restrictions of benefit to the land retained, the servitude becomes mutual, and, during the period of restraint, the owner of the lot or lots retained can do nothing forbidden to the owner of the lot sold. For want of a better descriptive term this is styled a reciprocal negative easement. It runs with the land sold by virtue of express fastening and abides with the land retained until loosened by expiration of its period of service or by events working its destruction. It is not personal to owners, but operative upon use of the land by any owner having actual or constructive notice thereof."

The court called this interest a "reciprocal negative easement," but this only gives further evidence of the semantic difficulties in this area because it is clearly an implied covenant. The case raises an additional problem since the covenant in *B's* deed would seem to be out of *C's* chain of title [74], but since a general building scheme or plan was apparent to *C* at the time he purchased he would have some difficulty in denying any knowledge of the restricted character of the subdivision. Indeed, this may well be the key to the whole case, i. e., the reluctance of the court to allow a subsequent purchaser to shut his eyes to the circumstances and cause loss to prior buyers by destroying a residential area. The reciprocal negative easement could be the peg on which to hang an equitable result. This belief is strengthened

70. Note 67, supra.

71. Johnson v. Mt. Baker Park Presbyterian Church, 113 Wash. 458, 194 P. 536 (1920).

72. Note 67, supra.

73. 233 Mich. 227, 206 N.W. 496, 60 A.L.R. 1212 (1925).

74. See p. 290, supra.

by a later Michigan case [75] which the dissenting judge thought was governed by the doctrine but which the majority distinguished, largely because there was no general plan of development.

The implication of covenants is a hazardous business which could work real hardship on subsequent purchasers unless carefully controlled. In view of the need for certainty in land titles and because every covenant is an incumbrance on the title, the doctrine should be restricted to situations where the original owner is still involved or where the notice to a subsequent purchaser is clear cut.

With very few exceptions, a covenant is viewed as appurtenant to land owned by the covenantee. It is made for the benefit of that land and should pass with the tract when it is transferred. It is difficult to visualize a covenant in gross which could be transferred apart from the land which it benefits. The closest we come to this concept is the Illinois case of Van Sant v. Rose [76], where a grantor conveyed all the land he owned to a grantee who covenanted to erect only single-family dwellings thereon. The grantor was allowed to enjoin the erection of an apartment house by a subsequent owner, even though he (the grantor) retained no land to be benefited. This comes close to being a covenant in gross, but the case has seldom been followed in other states and has been severely criticized, even in Illinois. [77] Moreover, the grantor in that case had not tried to transfer the benefit of the covenant to another party and presumably would have failed had he attempted to do so.

The moral of the preceding paragraph is that intent to benefit the land whose owner now seeks to enforce the covenant is a factor in the creation of an equitable servitude. If the covenantee retains no land to be benefited, most jurisdictions would deny that a servitude has been created since no one could enforce it. [78] Moreover, this makes good sense; there is no reason for fettering a grantee's land if no corresponding benefit is obtained for other land. To allow this type of restriction indiscriminately could play havoc with land use. Note, however, that this can be done by the employment of conditions since the grantor does not have to retain land in order to keep a possibility of reverter or a power of termination.

75. Buckley v. Mooney, 339 Mich. 398, 63 N.W.2d 655 (1954).

76. 260 Ill. 401, 103 N.E. 194 (1913).

77. Leesman, Covenants Running with the Land in Illinois, 14 Ill.L. Rev. 480, 486–500 (1920).

78. London County Council v. Allen, L.R. [1914] 3 K.B. 642, Ann.Cas. 1916C, 932. But see the discussion of Van Sant v. Rose where suit was allowed even though no land was retained by the covenantee.

Lack of intent to benefit can be a roadblock to the creation of servitudes in other ways. If the party suing has taken a conveyance *prior* to the time when covenants are inserted in deeds to subsequent grantees, it is sometimes difficult to find any intent by the grantor to benefit the earlier grantees. The converse of this is not true, since if a subsequent grantee sues it is clear that the covenants in the prior deeds were inserted for the benefit of the grantor's retained land, a portion of which the complainant now owns. Even in the former situation, the covenants will be effectively created if a general building scheme or plan is apparent from looking at the total area.[79] It is not always essential that the intent to benefit run solely to retained land since, in jurisdictions allowing third party beneficiary contracts, it is possible to create an equitable servitude in favor of a stranger to the conveyance, providing he owns land to be benefited and the intent to benefit him is clear.[80] This, of course, results in the creation of a covenant in favor of land not involved in the conveyance at all. Because of the importance of intent to benefit, good draftsmanship requires the spelling out of the intent in clear, succinct language rather than leaving it to judicial implication.

B. TRANSFER

The legal problem of transfer brings us face to face with an old friend (or enemy?)—the running of covenants with the land. The complexity of this problem can be appreciated only by reading Judge Clark's classic book on the subject.[81] Fortunately, the basic principles can be clarified without an exhaustive restatement of old controversies, many of which have lost modern significance. To begin with, a distinction must be drawn between the burden and the benefit. *A* conveys to *B*, who covenants to build only a single story, ranch type house on the tract. *A* covenants to put a similar restriction in the deed when he sells the retained land. *A* sells the retained tract to *C* and does, in fact, insert such a covenant. If *B* now tries to build an apartment building on his land and *C* sues him, we would be dealing with the running of a benefit to *C*. The burden has not moved and the

79. Snow v. Van Dam, 291 Mass. 477, 197 N.E. 224 (1935).

80. Vogeler v. Alwyn Improvement Corporation, 247 N.Y. 131, 159 N.E. 886 (1928).

81. Clark, Covenants and Interests Running With Land (2d ed. 1947).

sole issue is whether *C* can enforce the covenant even though the promise ran to *A* and not to *C*. If, however, *B* were to sell to *D*, who starts the prohibited construction, we would face the running of the burden as well, since *D* would be sued for violation of a covenant which he did not personally make, solely because he owns the burdened land. It is usually easy to determine whether we are dealing with the burden or the benefit (or both) and it is analytically important to do so because the courts have traditionally been freer in allowing the benefit to run than the burden.[82]

In addition to the burden-benefits distinction, the forum is important because, as mentioned earlier, equity is much freer in binding the parties to an equitable servitude than law is in allowing the covenant to run with the land. Equity's liberality may, in fact, make much of the legal dogma passé, but it cannot be wholly ignored. A final distinction is the age of the case. This is relevant in all phases of law, but it has added importance here because covenants used to be viewed mainly as incumbrances on the title and of little social utility, hence the courts were willing to throw up roadblocks against their runability. Today, they are a part of the pattern of land use and recognized as beneficial in the proper development of land. Not surprisingly, this attitude is reflected in the greater leniency of the courts.

In order for a covenant to run with the land at law five factors are involved: (1) the necessary formalities for creation of the covenant must be met; (2) the covenant must "touch and concern" the land; (3) the parties must intend that the covenant shall run with the land; (4) consideration must be given to whether the covenant is negative or affirmative; and (5) there must be privity, whatever that nebulous term means.

All of these factors are fairly clear except the last one. No covenant can run with the land if the promise itself is unenforceable between the original parties. The Statute of Frauds is the principal troublemaker (or troublesaver, depending on your point of view) here but lack of intent to benefit other land can also invalidate the covenant. "Touch and concern" is that same requirement so essential in leases [83], but it does not cause great difficulty here since most covenants as to the use of land clearly

---

82. "The theory upon which the benefit of promises respecting the use of land runs with land is not fundamentally different from that upon which the burden runs. That theory is that the successor to the land becomes identified for the purposes of the promise with his predecessor. But the running of the burden of a promise tends to reduce the alienability of the land with which it runs while the opposite is true with respect to the running of the benefit. Hence the rules respecting the running of benefits are less restrictive than those respecting the running of burdens." Restatement, Property, Introductory Note to Chapter 46 (1944).

83. See p. 192, supra.

"touch and concern" that land. The clearest indication of intent that the covenant shall run with the land is found where the parties spell it out in the body of the deed or other instrument, e. g., "these covenants shall run with the land" or "these covenants shall be construed as real covenants running with the land." Similarly, an express written statement that "these are personal covenants binding only on the original parties" is sufficient to prevent runnability. If the instrument is silent, the issue will be decided from the nature of the covenants and the probable intent of the parties. The mere expression of intent is not enough to cause the covenants to run if the other criteria are not met. Probably arising out of an age-old antipathy toward the enforcement of affirmative duties, the courts are friendlier to the running of negative than affirmative covenants. Since most land-use covenants are restrictive, and hence of the former type, this distinction does not become significant in the bulk of the cases.

This leaves privity as the principal hurdle on the law track. Privity is a requirement in two separate senses: (1) privity between the covenantor and his successor in interest and (2) privity between the covenantor and the covenantee. The first of these is the same requirement we are familiar with from landlord-tenant and covenants for title. The Restatement of Property provides: "The successors in title to land respecting the use of which the owner has made a promise are not bound as promisors upon the promise unless by their succession they hold (a) the estate or interest held by the promisor at the time the promise was made, or (b) an estate or interest corresponding in duration to the estate or interest held by the promisor at that time." [84] This requirement poses no difficulty if the fee simple title is transferred from the covenantor to the new grantee, but it forms another needless obstacle in cases where interests less than a fee are involved.

The real problem, however, is presented by privity in the second sense, i. e., between the covenantor and the covenantee. The cases and legal writers are far from agreed as to just what this means and it may be little more than a mystical way of saying that there must be a succession of interests in land between the promisor and the promisee, i. e., that binding promises running with the land cannot be effective where no interest in land passes between the parties. Thus, this requirement is satisfied any time an *inter vivos* conveyance is made of an estate in fee from one of the parties to the other, provided the promise is made at the time of the conveyance. A covenant made after a conveyance, though between the parties, lacks the requisite privity and the burden will not run.[85] The Restatement uses this language: "The suc-

84. Restatement, Property, § 535 (1944).

85. Wheeler v. Schad, 7 Nev. 204 (1871).

cessors in title to land respecting the use of which the owner has made a promise are not bound as promisors upon the promise unless (a) the transaction of which the promise is a part includes a transfer of an interest either in the land benefited by or the land burdened by the performance of the promise; or (b) the promise is made in the adjustment of the mutual relationships arising out of the existence of an easement held by one of the parties to the promise in the land of the other." [86]   Clause (a) is illustrated by the previous discussion, i. e., the covenant must be contemporaneous with the transfer.   Clause (b) is clarified by the Restatement's own example: "A conveys to B, the owner and possessor of Blackacre, an easement giving to B the privilege of taking mud deposits from a pond on Whiteacre, neighboring land owned by A, to be used as a fertilizer upon Blackacre.   Two months later A and B enter into a supplemental but independent contract whereby A agrees on behalf of himself, his successors and assigns, that he will draw the water out of the pond under certain stipulated conditions for the purpose of enabling B to secure the mud deposit." [87]

If the preceding discussion of privity seems a bit murky, I can only plead guilty to being a prisoner of an archaic doctrine and direct your attention to two modern cases which face the problem realistically—Neponsit Property Owners' Ass'n v. Emigrant Industrial Sav. Bank [88] and 165 Broadway Building, Inc. v. City Investing Co. [89]   In the former case Judge Lehman allowed suit by a property owners' association, organized for the purpose of enforcing the covenants, even though the promise called for the affirmative act of paying money for the upkeep of roads, parks, etc., in a subdivision.   All of the technical arguments against the running of the covenant were trotted in review, including the fact that the association owned no lands as such, and hence privity was lacking.   This masterful opinion breathed new life into covenants, concluding: "In substance if not in form the covenant is a restrictive covenant which touches and concerns the defendant's land, and in substance, if not in form, there is privity of estate between the plaintiff and the defendant."   The latter case gave Judge Clark [90] an opportunity to build on the Neponsit case and to launch another blow at the sagging doctrine of privity.   Said he: "That a requirement so anomalous should

86. Restatement, Property, § 534 (1944).

87. See Morse v. Aldrich, 36 Mass. 449 (1857).

88. 278 N.Y. 248, 15 N.E.2d 793, 118 A.L.R. 973 (1938). This has been a particularly influential case as see, e. g., Merrionette Manor Homes v. Heda, 11 Ill.App.2d 186, 136 N.E. 2d 556 (1956); Comment, 1956 U. Ill.L.F. 651.

89. 120 F.2d 813 (2d Cir. 1941).

90. This is the same Clark who had written the book cited in footnote 81, supra, while he was teaching at Yale Law School.

exist at all is therefore doubtful; the authorities tend to show that, if it is not to be rejected altogether, it is not applicable in any event to the running of the benefit of covenants, as here."

While the law courts were preoccupied with privity, equity had followed a different route. As early as 1848, in the famous case of Tulk v. Moxhay [91], the English Court of Chancery had decided to enforce a covenant against a subsequent purchaser with notice without worrying about privity. Said the Lord Chancellor: "It is said that, the covenant being one which does not run · with land, this Court cannot enforce it; but the question is, not whether the covenant runs with the land, but whether a party shall be permitted to use the land in a manner inconsistent with the contract entered into by his vendor, and with notice of which he purchased." Tulk v. Moxhay has been consistently followed in United States [92] and there is general agreement that privity of estate between the covenantor and the covenantee has no significance in equity. Even privity between the covenantor and his successors in interest has been ignored in some instances.[93] This does not mean that equity has no requirements for the running of covenants and, in fact, the formalities, the intent of the parties, "touch and concern", and the affirmative-negative distinction all have validity in chancery, although they will be determined with more flexibility than at law. Of course, it is always necessary to prove that the purchaser of the burdened land took with notice, actual or constructive, since this is the rationale of equitable servitudes as disclosed by Tulk v. Moxhay.

C. SCOPE

The sole problem as to the scope of restrictive covenants is the construction or interpretation of language. Easements may arise by implication or prescription and you will recall that these interests then raise exceedingly difficult questions of scope because there is no express language to construe. Covenants are infrequently implied and when they are, as in the doctrine of "reciprocal negative easements",[94] they must spring from express language in a prior deed which is then the subject of interpreta-

91. 2 Phillips 774 (1848).

92. Note 88, supra.

93. 5 Restatement, Property, § 539, Comment i (1944).

94. P. 350, supra.

tion.   Careful draftsmanship can eliminate most problems of scope, but there will always be situations in which the court must decide what the original parties had in mind.

As usual, the cases disclose certain principles which are ostensibly used to determine intent.   "However variously phrased, they are, in substance, that restrictions on the use of land are not favored by the law because they are an interference with an owner's free and full enjoyment of his property; that nothing will be deemed a violation of a restriction that is not in plain disregard of its express words; that there are no implied rights arising from a restriction which the courts will recognize [*quaere* "reciprocal negative easements"?]; that a restriction is not to be extended or enlarged by implication; that every restriction will be construed most strictly against the grantor and every doubt and ambiguity in its language resolved in favor of the owner." [95]

Within this general framework of principles, the cases fragment rather badly.   Since restrictions vary so widely in form the court has great discretion and, with the aid of counsel's ingenuity, can justify some odd interpretations.   For example, a restriction may be held to apply to the number and type of buildings which can be erected but not to the subsequent use of such buildings so that if built for a private dwelling they may end up being used for a convalescent or nursing home.[96]   As mentioned before in this book, the lawyer's role will depend largely on the stage at which he enters the case.   If he drafts the covenants, he must avoid all ambiguous language and spell out the restrictions so clearly that the chances of litigation are held to a minimum.[97]   However, if he is consulted by a client as to the meaning of an existing covenant, he must take the language as he finds it and puzzle out, through precedent and/or common sense, whether a ban on apartment houses includes boarding and lodging houses,[98] whether a prohibition on trade or business includes using a lot for parking space without charge but to serve a business on unrestricted land,[99] etc.   Since these restrictions affect the merchantability of title, the lawyer must always view them with a wary eye and, as title examiner, he must be sure to call them to the attention of the purchaser, and explain the interpretations in event of dispute.

95. Jones v. The Park Lane For Convalescents, Inc., 384 Pa. 268, 272, 120 A.2d 535, 537 (1956).

96. Id.

97. For suggestions as to drafting as well as a general discussion see McCarthy, Restrictive Covenants, 1955 U.Ill.L.F. 709.

98. David v. Bowan, 191 Ga. 467, 12 S.E.2d 873 (1941).

99. Bennett v. Consolidated Realty Company, 226 Ky. 747, 11 S.W.2d 910 (1928).

D. TERMINATION

However beneficial restrictive covenants may be to the developer and owner of land, they also constitute a burden on land and the question of their termination is frequently of prime importance. They are sometimes drafted so that they will expire by their own terms, i. e., made binding for twenty, thirty, or forty years only. This is a desirable practice because they tend to outlive their usefulness in about a generation and this builds in a device for the automatic clearing of the title with the passage of time. In the bulk of the cases this is not done, however, and the covenants therefore have a potentially infinite duration as an interest in land. Because of this fact, various statutes have been passed to eliminate stale restrictions after the passage of time. The legislation falls into four basic patterns: (1) the "substantial benefit" type, providing that if the restriction ceases to be of substantial benefit to the person for whom created, it is void; (2) the "fixed period of duration" type, terminating the restriction at the end of a gross period; (3) the "marketable title type," requiring a re-recording of the restrictions within a certain period in order for them to remain valid; and (4) the "inalienability type", prohibiting the transfer of the benefit.[1] Many states have no such legislation and the parties will have to rely on non-statutory methods of extinguishment, such as release, merger, waiver, abandonment, and change in neighborhood conditions.

The party who has the right to enforce a covenant may release that right just as any other interest in land may be surrendered to the fee owner. The difficulty, however, is that many people may be benefited by the covenant, as in the case of a subdivision, and the release must be given or acquiesced in by a large number of individuals. Since their own needs may be quite diverse, release may turn out to be a practical impossibility. Merger occurs when the title to property subject to the covenant is acquired by the owner of property for whose benefit the restriction was imposed. Resale of the previously burdened lots will not cause a resurrection of the covenant unless it is expressly created anew. A court of equity may refuse to enforce a covenant because of the acquiescence of the lot owners in such substantial violations as to amount to abandonment of the covenant or a waiver of the right to insist on compliance with its terms. Equity may also refuse to enforce the restriction because of such

1. Simes, Elimination of Stale Re-   A. Section on Real Property, Pro-
    strictions on the Use of Land, A.B.   bate and Trust Law (1954).

a change of conditions in the restricted area that it is impossible to secure, in any significant degree, the benefits sought to be realized by the covenant.[2]

This refusal by the chancellor to enforce the covenant is another example of equity's discretionary role and does not, in fact, terminate the covenant since it may still be possible to recover damages at law for the breach,[3] thus leaving the title in an unmerchantable state.   Moreover, if the covenant is construed as a condition, creating a possibility of reverter or a power of termination there is a serious question as to whether changed neighborhood conditions will affect the result.[4]   There is also a serious question as to whether the changes must occur *within* the restricted area or whether the general alteration in the community *outside* the area, but in close proximity to it, will suffice.[5]   Failure to require the changes to take place within the area can lead to destruction of the very plan for which the restrictions were created since once the buffer zone of border lots goes commercial, the pressures on the rest of the residential area become irresistible.

Covenants can be extinguished by condemnation of the burdened land, as where the city takes a tract in the heart of a residential area for municipal purposes.   Since the taking permits a use inconsistent with the continuance of the covenant, it is no longer effective as to the condemned land although the remaining land in the area may still be burdened.   The courts are split on the issue of compensation for thus depriving the neighboring landowners of the benefit of their covenants.[6]   Some courts indicate that the loss is *damnum absque injuria* because no property right in the strict sense, is involved; others are more pragmatic and see the requirement of compensation as an unnecessary burden on the sovereign right of eminent domain.   On principle however, compensation should be paid since a covenant is analytically like an easement which is clearly a property right.   Moreover, compensation is not limited to tangible property interests but includes the right of use and enjoyment.

2.   Cowling v. Colligan, 158 Tex. 458, 312 S.W.2d 943 (1958).   See also West Alameda Heights Homeowners Assoc. v. Board of Commissioners, 169 Colo. 491, 458 P.2d 253 (Colo.1969).

3.   St. Lo Construction Co. v. Koenigsberger, **174** F.2d 25 (D.C.Cir. 1949); Pound, The Progress of the Law, 1918–1919, 33 Harv.L.Rev. 813, 820 (1920).

4.   Goldstein, Rights of Entry and Possibilities of Reverter as Devices to Restrict the Use of Land, 54 Harv.L.Rev. 248 (1940).

Changed neighborhood conditions will not result in the termination of an easement.   Waldrop v. Town of Brevard, 233 N.C. 26, 62 S.E.2d 512 (1950).

5.   Downs v. Kroeger, 200 Cal. 743, 254 P. 1101 (1927).

6.   Wells v. City of Dunbar, 142 W. Va. 332, 95 S.E.2d 457; Comment, 1957 U.Ill.L.F. 133.

Although restrictive covenants can be extinguished by the power of the state, exercised through eminent domain, the police power, exercised through zoning regulations, does not ordinarily have this effect.[7]   The private covenants may be more restrictive than the zoning and if so, they continue to control. If the zoning is more restrictive it will control.   The development plan for the area, reflected in the zoning ordinances, may be used to show changing neighborhood conditions, however, and in that sense may lead to effective termination of the covenants.

As the discussion in this chapter indicates, society's attitude toward the restrictive covenant has changed considerably in the last few decades.   From being viewed essentially as a burden on the land, it has become an essential tool in private land use control.   The contemporary subdivision with its detailed set of covenants, to be enforced by a Property Owners' Association rather than by individual owners, has become a part of every community.   Indeed, the covenants look more and more like statutes, evidencing the fact that they represent a kind of private local government.[8]   Even the name, restrictive covenant, has frequently been replaced by the term, protective covenant, indicating the role they now seem to play.

Despite this generally favorable view of restrictive covenants today, they do impress a rigid control on the owner's use of Blackacre and hence he will frequently try to escape from their legal impact via some of the methods for termination just outlined.   One technique for obtaining greater flexibility should be resisted.   If the original grantor (usually a developer) reserves the power to dispense with restrictions, as he sees fit, by agreement with any individual grantee, he will negative the existence of a uniform development and, the restrictions will become mere personal covenants and will not run with the land.[9] This is true because no subsequent grantee would have any assurance, other than the personal integrity of the original grantor, that restrictions on any lot in the subdivision might not be annulled or altered at any time without his assent.   The grantor might achieve this result by using conditions which would leave him with a possibility of reverter or a power of termination, which he could enforce as he saw fit, but few grantees would accept this device since they lose all control over the subdivi-

---

7. See Berger, Conflicts Between Zoning Ordinances and Restrictive Covenants, 43 Neb.L.Rev. 103 (1964); Note, 24 Vand.L.Rev. 1031 (1971).

8. See Ellickson, Alternatives to Zoning: Covenants, Nuisance Rules,

and Fines as Land Use Controls, 40 U. of Chi.L.Rev. 681 (1973).

9. Suttle v. Bailey, 68 N.M. 283, 361 P.2d 325 (1961).

sion, having no right to enforce the condition themselves. The best solution would appear to be a set period during which the covenants would operate, followed by an option to continue them for another period, if a certain percentage of the owners wish to do so. If the land is unzoned at the time the covenants became effective, it might be desirable to provide that they cease to be binding once public land use controls are instituted or within a set period thereafter.[10]

10. See Smith v. Pindar Real Estate Co., 187 Ga. 229, 200 S.E. 131 (1938), where a statute provided that covenants restricting land should not run for more than 20 years in cities which have adopted zoning ordinances.

Chapter 2

NATURAL RIGHTS

————

A owns Blackacre in fee simple absolute, his title is merchantable, and no one else has the slightest claim against the land. Leaving aside the question of public controls like zoning and the residual power of eminent domain, is *A* free to do exactly as he pleases with Blackacre? If so, is *B*, owner of Whiteacre, an adjoining tract, equally free? Is *C* equally free, etc? To ask the question is to answer it. All freedom is relative and while *A* has the natural right to use Blackacre as he sees fit, for most purposes, that right is subject to *B's* rights and *C's* rights, etc.[1] This aspect of land use can be demonstrated by a discussion of nuisance, lateral and subjacent support, water rights, and air rights. The first two subjects will be treated briefly, the third and fourth will be given more extended coverage because of their great importance in contemporary society.

————

SECTION 1. NUISANCE

————

The law of nuisance is summed up in an old Latin maxim, *sic utere tuo ut alienum non laedas*—use your own property in such a manner as not to injure that of another. This states the principle but solves no problems. In fact, it assumes the very point in issue, if quoted as an explanation of why a given court has decided to enjoin specific acts as a nuisance. What use injures the property of another and at what point does that use become unreasonable? Each case tends to be unique and no hard and fast rule can be established to cover all situations. "A nuisance may be merely a right thing in the wrong place, like a pig in the parlor instead of the barnyard." [2]

1. "The social side [of property] limits the individual side, and as it is always present there is no such thing as absolute private property. An absolute right of property, as the great jurist, the late Professor von Ihering says, would result in the dissolution of society." Ely, Property and Contract in Their Relation to the Distribution of Wealth, Vol. 1, p. 137 (1914). Do you see why this statement is true?

2. Village of Euclid v. Ambler Realty Co., 272 U.S. 365, 388, 47 S.Ct. 114, 118, 71 L.Ed. 303, 311 (1926).

Most of the nuisance cases are decided in equity by a suit to enjoin, although money damages can be recovered at law in what would have been a common-law action of case. In the final analysis, most nuisance suits become a balancing of the equities, with the court trying to decide how much inconvenience and disturbance a land owner must endure as an incident of modern life. It is clear that the urban dweller cannot expect the peace and quiet of the countryside and if he prefers the advantages of community living he must experience some of the inconvenience. Smoke, odors, pollution, etc., which would be enjoined in an isolated hamlet will not move the conscience of the chancellor if they occur in the industrial area of Buffalo, New York.[3] It may be relevant too that the complaining party has "moved to the nuisance" rather than vice versa.[4]

Nuisances are classified as public, private, and mixed. The public nuisance affects an indefinite number of people, the public generally, and is normally abated by an officer, such as the state's attorney or attorney general, acting on behalf of the public. A private nuisance affects one or a small group of property owners in a manner different from its impact on the public generally and it is usually the subject of private litigation. Since the line of demarcation is hard to draw, many nuisances fall into the mixed category and may involve both public abatement and private suit for damages.[5] This classification makes more apparent the inherent weakness of the law of nuisance; it is really a kind of judicial zoning but carried out on a sporadic, hit-or-miss basis.[6] While the law of nuisance has had a distinguished past as a regulator of land use, in the days when life was less complex, it would appear to be of diminishing importance as legislative control by zoning takes over from the judiciary. It should be noted, however, that a land use allowed by zoning may still be a nuisance, if conducted in an improper fashion, and the old doctrines should not yet be consigned to the trash can.[7]

The increased emphasis on environmental problems has already caused a revitalized interest in the ancient law of nuisance and recent cases have demonstrated it can be an effective weapon for the environmentalist. Thus, in Boomer v. Atlantic Cement Company,[8] the New York Court of Appeals granted an

3. Bove v. Donner-Hanna Coke Corporation, 236 App.Div. 37, 258 N.Y. S. 229 (1932).

4. East St. Johns Shingle Co. v. Portland, 195 Or. 505, 246 P.2d 554 (1952).

5. Ozark Poultry Products, Inc. v. Garman, 251 Ark. 389, 472 S.W.2d 714 (1971).

6. Beuscher and Morrison, Judicial Zoning Through Recent Nuisance Cases, [1955] Wis.L.Rev. 440.

7 Comment, 54 Mich.L.Rev. 266 (1955); Comment, 34 Tex.L.Rev. 482 (1956).

8. 26 N.Y.2d 219, 309 N.Y.S.2d 312, 257 N.E.2d 870 (1970).

injunction against a cement company which was polluting the atmosphere but provided that it should be vacated upon payment by the defendant of such amounts of permanent damage to the respective plaintiffs as should be determined by the court. A dissenting judge would have issued an injunction, period, unless the defendant abated the nuisance within eighteen months. He viewed the majority decision as being a kind of private eminent domain and felt this "inverse condemnation" should not be invoked by a private person or corporation for private gain or advantage.[9]

SECTION 2.   LATERAL AND SUBJACENT SUPPORT

If private ownership means anything, surely *A* can dig holes on his own land (Blackacre) without consulting his neighbor prior to excavation. But *B*, owner of Whiteacre, may have a building close to the line and if it tumbles into *A's* excavation that is scarcely consistent with *B's* private rights, or is it? This is the stuff of the law of support. The owner of land has a right to the support of his soil in its natural state, both lateral, i. e., from adjoining land and subjacent, i. e., from the subsurface, so that the topsoil will not fall into a mine being operated by the owner of a mineral interest. The *extent* of this right to support is the heart of the matter.

Two closely related problems should be distinguished from the natural right to support. First, there is the question of negligence. If the excavator proceeds in a negligent fashion, so that adjoining property is damaged as the proximate result of poor engineering practice then the liability is clear.[10] This matter is controlled by the law of torts and the excavator is liable just as the owner of an automobile must respond in damages for negligent driving. The law of natural support deals with absolute liability, i. e., the situations in which one landowner has an absolute duty to support the land of another and is liable, with or without negligence, if harm results. Second, there is the matter of an easement of support. Thus, even though *A* has no natural duty to support *B's* land or only a limited duty, *B* can buy from *A*

---

9. See Juergensmeyer, Control of Air Pollution Through the Assertion of Private Rights, 1967 Duke L.J. 1126.

10. Of course, it is far from clear just what constitutes negligent withdrawal of support. See Restatement, Torts, § 819 (1939).

an easement of support which will require a certain standard of conduct. A party wall agreement is an example of this kind of easement. The natural right of support is not based on any such acquired easement, but is inherent in the ownership of the land. The converse of the above is also possible, i. e., the owner of the surface may sell his right of support to the subsurface owner so that the latter can mine at will with no concern for injury to the surface.[11]

The doctrine of lateral support, as applied in the majority of American jurisdictions, is limited to the right of a landowner to have his soil supported in its natural state by the land adjacent to it. Recovery will normally be granted only to the extent of injury to the land in its unimproved condition, i. e., without the weight of structures upon it.[12] This general principle seems to be based on the idea that to require the support of improved land would be an interference with the rights of the owner of unimproved land. Thus, if *A* built first, and *B* had an absolute duty to support both land and building, *B* might be limited in developing his own land. Therefore, he should be absolutely liable only for the land as it exists in a state of nature and the rest should be left to the law of negligence.[13]

This sounds simple enough but, as with most simple rules, the application muddies the water.[14] Suppose *B* withdraws support in a careful and workmanlike manner but the surface of *A's* land still subsides because it was resting on quicksand which flows into *B's* excavation. *B* is liable according to the law of sup-

11. See Pennsylvania Coal Company v. Mahon, 260 U.S. 393, 43 S.Ct. 158, 67 L.Ed. 326 (1922) for an example of this type of property interest and the effect of a Pennsylvania statute regulating mining on the private right.

12. Comment, The Doctrine of Lateral Support in Illinois, 1956 U.Ill. L.F. 646.

13. It is frequently said that the "right to lateral support is limited to land in its natural condition, and does not extend to filled ground." Jennemann v. Hertel, 264 S.W.2d 911 (Mo.App.1954). But in Bradley v. Valicenti, 185 Pa.Super. 403, 138 A.2d 238 (1958) the lapse of time (five years being deemed sufficient) was considered to convert filled land into "natural" land.

14. This is a somewhat subtle pun. If the only substance withdrawn is water, as opposed to soil, quicksand, etc., then the withdrawing party is not liable at all under the English Rule of absolute privilege in the use of ground water. Finley v. Teeter Stone, Inc., 251 Md. 428, 248 A.2d 106 (1968). The court also felt there would be no liability under the American Rule since the defendant in that case was conducting legitimate quarrying operations on his own land. See p. 373 infra. The court was not too happy with this result but believed any change was for the legislature, if public interest required it. Note the Restatement, Second, Torts § 818 (Tent.Draft No. 15, 1969) takes a position contrary to the Finley v. Teeter Stone, Inc. case. "One who is privileged to withdraw water, oil, minerals or other substances from under the land of another is not for that reason privileged to cause a subsistence of the other's land by such withdrawal."

port. Now suppose further that A has a building on his land but the surface would have dropped even without the weight of the building. Is B liable just for the damage to the land or must he also pay for injury to the building? Here the cases are in conflict and precedent can be marshalled, together with good reasons, for either view.[15] Some courts call this situation a qualification of the general rule and state: " . . . a landowner by building upon his land has not thereby lost his right to have his soil supported, and, when that right is invaded by his neighbor, and his land sinks, he is entitled to compensation for the direct results of such breach of duty, including any injury to buildings upon his land, when such injury is due to an interference with the lateral support of the soil, and cannot be ascribed to the weight and pressure of the buildings upon the land." [16] Of course, if the land would not have fallen but for the buildings there is no liability in the absence of negligence.

It is a tough question of fact as to whether the land would have fallen without the weight of the buildings and it is equally difficult to draw a fine line between absolute liability and negligence. While the analysis given in this section is theoretically accurate there is reason to doubt its practical effect. One writer has concluded: "As a practical matter, the cases seem to substantiate the proposition that the naked right of lateral support is of little legal significance. On the other hand, it appears that the excavator's primary concern has been and will continue to be the problem of avoiding negligence, a more fertile field of litigation. In any event, notice should be given of the nature and extent of the excavation and the probability of injury to the adjacent owner. The excavation and construction should then proceed in accordance with professionally accepted engineering standards. Where possible, it would seem advisable to conclude an agreement before hand with other interested parties as to the responsibility of each for any damages which might ensue." [17]

Most of the preceding discussion has dealt with lateral support but the same legal principles apply to subjacent support. There are, of course, different practical problems of proof and the latter cases arise only where there has been a severance of the subsurface interest so that two or more parties own estates on different physical planes. An intriguing question arises as to the statute of limitations in these cases. If A mines without proper supports, the surface, owned by B, will probably subside sometime, but it may remain unchanged for years. Does the statute begin to run when the subjacent support is withdrawn or

15. Prete v. Cray, 49 R.I. 209, 141 A. 609 (1928).

16. Id. at 213 and 612.

17. Note 12 supra at 650.

does it wait until collapse occurs? A minority of courts follow a theoretical approach and hold that the cause of action arises when the support is withdrawn since the wrong consists in failure to maintain the natural state.[18] Others take a more practical view and, in effect, make harm to the surface a part of the cause of action so that the statute runs from the date of subsidence.[19]

The common-law doctrine is sufficient to decide cases after the harm has been done, but it offers rather poor guidance to the property owner who is planning construction work requiring excavation on his own land. According to the leading case of Braun v. Hammack,[20] if a builder, seeing that a neighboring structure will topple into his excavation, goes on the adjacent land and shores it up he does so at his own expense, even though the excavator had no duty to support the adjoining land plus building. It was argued that the builder should recover in quasi-contract for the benefit conferred but, while the dissenting judge thought this was a good position, it did not sway the majority. This leaves the builder in a greater quandary than ever since he seems to be proceeding at his own peril at all stages. In an effort to alleviate some of the uncertainty, various ordinances and statutes have been passed. Some exonerate the excavator if he serves a statutory notice on his neighbor and is free from negligence; others add to his responsibility by making him strictly liable for structures as well as land; still others seek a middle ground by shifting the obligation between the parties depending on the depth of the excavation.[21] None of the legislative changes appear to be particularly satisfactory either to the engineers or the lawyers and a working agreement between the adjoining owners is probably the best solution.

18. Noonan v. Pardee, 200 Pa. 474, 50 A. 255 (1901).

19. Western Coal and Mining Co. v. Randolph, 191 Ark. 1115, 89 S.W.2d 741 (1936).

20. 206 Minn. 572, 289 N.W. 553 (1940).

21. See 5 Powell, Real Property, § 702 (1956).

For an interesting case involving a California land support statute see Holtz v. Superior Court of City and County of San Francisco, 3 Cal.3d 296, 90 Cal.Rptr. 345, 475 P.2d 441 (1970). The Supreme Court of California held the San Francisco Bay Area Rapid Transit District (Bart) strictly liable for damages to the plaintiffs' land and buildings injured in subway construction. (They were also liable for negligence if that could be proved). The court used "inverse condemnation" principles and socialized the loss as a cost to the public of building public improvements. See Van Alstyne, Inverse Condemnation: Unintended Physical Damage, 20 Hastings L.J. 431 (1969).

SECTION 3. WATER RIGHTS [22]

Water law at the present time is in a fluid state.[23] From coast to coast there is a deep concern about the future water supply of the United States. Of course the arid West has faced the greatest challenge and made the most complicated response but the humid East is also becoming restive in the face of frequent drouths, exploding population curves, and vastly increased use of water for industry and agriculture. Articles are appearing in newspapers, popular magazines, and the professional journals at a rapidly increasing rate. No attempt will be made to catalogue them here but a brief quote from an issue of *Harper's Magazine* typifies the tone of national urgency: "To most Americans today, pure palatable water in unlimited quantities is a kind of birthright, like citizenship, and not even the Supreme Court can ever take it away. No following generation of Americans is ever likely to share this luxurious attitude. We are rapidly running out of good water. More than a thousand cities and towns already have been forced to curtail their water service. Near Chicago, where artesian wells flowed under their own pressure a hundred years ago, new wells must go down 2,000 feet to reach the water table. Dallas is already pumping the salt-tainted Red River into its mains, and New York faces the likelihood that eventually it will have to purify the polluted Hudson to slake its growing thirst. In Mississippi, wells are now 400 feet deeper, on the average, than they were only ten years ago. Denver, eager for new industry, has been turning away manufacturers whose production processes involve a heavy use of water." [24]

Law has never pumped a single gallon of water but a rational system of legal rights is essential to proper allocation of the available supply. And as the demand comes closer to the supply the role of law becomes more and more apparent. The American people, with their great faith in law as a healer of the ills of the body politic, are bringing pressure for various changes in the existing structure. A permit system has been adopted in

---

22. This section is based on, and draws heavily from, a study prepared by the author of this text for the Illinois State Chamber of Commerce. See also Cribbet, Water as a Species of Private Property—The Illinois View, 47 Ill.B.J. 449 (1959).

23. This is a lousy pun and I would apologize except that it happens to be a true statement.

24. Robert and Leona Rienow, The Day the Taps Run Dry, Harper's Magazine 72 (October, 1958).

many Eastern states and is being considered in others.[25]   The
details of the various systems differ but the idea behind them is
similar and rather simple.   A permit must be obtained from a
state agency in order to take water for irrigation or such other
use as the statute specifies.   They give the state a check on water
use and thus provide a minimal form of control.   The interest
in permit systems reached a temporary peak with the approval,
in August 1958, of a Model Water Use Act [26] by the Commissioners on Uniform State Laws.   It is apparent that, with all of the
ferment in the area of water law, we should have a rather clear
picture of the present status of water rights in this country.

A.   CLASSIFICATIONS OF WATER LAW

In order to make the law manageable those who deal with it
professionally cut the "seamless web" at countless points and
put the pieces in separate compartments.   This may be necessary
but it has unfortunate results and frequently leads to inconsistent rules in closely related fields.   Water law has been plagued
by this problem.   Thus the scientist looks at water as a whole
and speaks of the hydrologic cycle—the endless process of evaporation, transpiration, condensation, precipitation, and flowage to
the sea.[27]   It would seem therefore that the law of water should
follow a single pattern but history has decreed otherwise.   In
fact, different rules have developed for the water in natural
watercourses (rivers, streams, and lakes), for diffused surface
water, and for groundwater (also called underground, subter-
ranean, and percolating water).   Our discussion will follow
these traditional categories, but first we must say a word about
the basic cleavage in American water law.

25. See, for example, Iowa Code
Ann. c. 455A;   Minn.Stat.Ann. §§
105.38–105.64;   Miss.Code Ann. §
51–3–1 et seq.;   Wis.Stat.Ann. 31.14.
seq.;   Wis.Stat.Ann. 31.14.

26. This Act was drafted by the Legislative Research Center, University
of Michigan School of Law.   See
44 A.B.A.J. 689 (1958).

27. Ecclesiastes 1:7 puts it this way:
"All the rivers run into the sea;
yet the sea is not full;   unto the
place from whence the rivers come,
thither they return again."

B. THE EAST-WEST DICHOTOMY

Oversimplification is rampant in water law and I am now about to add to that rampage. This is unfortunate, but an understanding of water law must spring from the background of the east-west division. The seventeen western states (Arizona, California, Colorado, Idaho, Kansas, Montana, Nebraska, Nevada, New Mexico, North Dakota, Oklahoma, Oregon, South Dakota, Texas, Utah, Washington, and Wyoming) represent the areas of relative scarcity and follow the doctrine of prior appropriation. The remaining states fall in the eastern group and represent the humid areas of relative plenty. They follow the common-law doctrine of riparian rights. Strictly speaking these two doctrines apply only to natural water courses but the philosophy also affects ground water and may even be reflected in diffused surface water. It must be stated that there is no uniformity within the basic groupings (even neighboring states may have pronounced differences) but there is a fundamental distinction between the East and the West.

C. RIPARIAN DOCTRINE

Although this is the recognized doctrine of the common law it was actually borrowed from the Roman law. In early common-law England there was little litigation over the use of water. "First come, first served" was the guiding principle and in those days it was an adequate rule. The Industrial Revolution altered the factual base of the law and inevitably changed the law itself. The United States was facing the same challenge to the then existing law and under the leadership of Justices Kent and Story, who were learned in the Code Napoleon (based on Roman law), this country developed the doctrine of riparian rights, adopting the word itself from the French. Story used the word riparian for the first time in Tyler v. Wilkinson [28] in 1827 and set out the rights of riparian proprietors, both individually and collectively. The doctrine was then adopted in England in the classic case of Embrey v. Owen [29] and, thus sanctified by Baron Parke, became the rule of the common law.

28. 4 Mason 397, Fed.Cas. No. 14,-   **29.** 6 Exch. 353 (1851).
312 (1827) ; 3 Kent Com. 439 (1828).

Briefly stated, a riparian proprietor is one who owns land bordering on a natural watercourse and hence has certain rights to use the water that flows therein. All other landowners are excluded from using the water except as they may contract with a riparian owner. Water does not belong to the public generally (except for certain rights in navigable streams and public waters) or to the state but constitutes a property interest to be adjusted among those who have access to the stream or lake from their own land. The doctrine embodies the principle that all riparian proprietors on a watercourse or lake have equal rights in respect to the use of the water, and that none can use to the extent of depriving others of an equal opportunity to use.[30] The application of this principle to concrete cases is not an easy task and the courts have differed widely in their efforts to solve the inevitable disputes. Some courts have followed the "natural flow or natural law theory"; others have adopted the "reasonable use theory." Frequently it is difficult to tell which view the court is following and the two theories tend to blend in many states.

D. PRIOR APPROPRIATION DOCTRINE [31]

While a form of prior appropriation was recognized in parts of the present southwestern United States during the period when they were under Spanish and Mexican rule, the modern doctrine originated after the California gold rush. The first man to stake out a good claim had a right against subsequent claimants and this right was extended to include the water supply needed to work the claim successfully. This idea was expanded until it applied to other water uses as well, including the vital matter of irrigation. "Basically, the resulting doctrine of prior appropriation provides a means by which an individual may acquire a right to divert a given quantity of water, at given times and from a given place, and—initially at least—for use at a given place (which of course need not be on riparian land) and for a given purpose. When there is insufficient water to meet the claims of all possessors of such appropriative rights, their positions

30. Restatement, Torts, Chapter 41 (1939). This chapter contains an excellent exposition of the basic principles of riparian rights. In particular, the Restatement develops (perhaps overly so) the distinction between the "natural flow" and "reasonable use" theories of the riparian doctrine.

31. See Hutchins, Selected Problems in the Law of Water Rights in the West, U.S.D.A.Misc.Pub. 418 (1942).

For a case explaining the doctrine of prior appropriation in Colorado see Coffin v. Left Hand Ditch Co., 6 Colo. 443 (1882).

depend on the dates when their respective rights were acquired. The system is based on the principle of 'first in time, first in right,' each appropriator being entitled to receive his full quantity of water before appropriators junior to him become entitled to any water at all. The value of an appropriative right then depends upon its place in the priority schedule.[32]

This western doctrine has been implemented by state administrative agencies with centralized control over the following areas: (1) adjudication of existing rights in cases of dispute; (2) procedures for acquiring new rights; and (3) methods for controlling the actual diversion of water in accordance with established rights. Of course, the details of administration vary from state to state but tend to follow the same general pattern.

The basic assumption of the prior appropriation doctrine is that the water resources of the state belong to the public generally rather than to the riparian owners, hence the administrative agency represents the people in establishing the right to use water and this right can be given to any individual or group quite apart from the ownership of adjacent lands. Once the right is given it becomes a vested property interest. It is readily apparent that any attempt to engraft the western doctrine on a well-established system of riparian rights will lead to constitutional as well as property law problems.[33]

E. THE COMMON LAW OF WATER RIGHTS

Water rights can be understood best by an analysis of the common-law doctrines. All statutory change (prior appropriation or otherwise) must start from this common-law base. Since the doctrine in the thirty-one eastern states tends to follow a similar pattern, the remainder of this section will focus primarily on the case law of one state (Illinois) in order to highlight the general principles at work in this field of property law.

Illinois is one of the eastern states for water law purposes and is firmly committed to a doctrine of riparian rights. As a

---

32. Marquis, Freeman and Heath, The Movement for New Water Rights Laws in the Tennessee Valley States, 23 Tenn.L.Rev. 797, 821 (1955).

33. For a discussion of this aspect of the problem in the western states that followed the California doctrine, see Hutchins, History of the Conflict between Riparian and Appropriative Rights in the Western States, Production Economics Research Branch, Agricultural Research Service, U.S.D.A. (1954).

matter of fact, the early cases squarely repudiate a prior appropriation doctrine and in the leading case of Evans v. Merriweather,[34] Justice Lockwood stated: "Mere priority of appropriation of running water, without such consent or grant, confers no exclusive right." There has been relatively little litigation in the East in the field of water consumption and use and many questions cannot be answered except by speculation or analogy. The bulk of the case law deals with water in natural watercourses but that area will be discussed last. We shall turn first to the law of ground water and diffused surface water.

---

(1) GROUND WATER [35]

The Illinois law of ground water rests on a single case decided in 1899. Edwards v. Haeger [36] is generally considered to place Illinois in the list of states following the English common-law rule laid down in Acton v. Blundell.[37] Under this English rule the landowner could do about as he pleased with the ground water under his land. He could pump out all he could reach and use it for any purpose on his own or any other land.[38] He could even waste the water if he chose and apparently the only limitation was that he must not maliciously injure his neighbor. This doctrine was based on the old Latin maxim, *cujus est solum, ejus est usque ad coelum et ad inferos* (to whomsoever the soil belongs, he owns also to the sky and to the depth), but ignored the scientific fact that percolating ground water moves as does surface water, although at a lesser rate. Moreover, each owner had similar rights and this doctrine could lead to a costly battle between deeper wells and larger pumps.

The conclusion that Illinois follows the English rule is based more on what the court said than on what they actually held.

34. 4 Ill. 492, 38 Am.Dec. 106 (1842). See also Bliss v. Kennedy, 43 Ill. 67 (1867).

35. For a detailed study of Illinois ground water see Control of Ground Water, Publication 88 of Illinois Legislative Council (May, 1948).

36. 180 Ill. 99, 54 N.E. 176 (1899).

37. 12 Mees. and W. 324, 152 Eng. Rep. 1223 (1843). That the writers have so interpreted Edwards v. Haeger, see note 34 supra at page 12; Liessmann, Miscellaneous Water Rights in Illinois, 9 Ill.L.Rev. 564 (1915); and 29 A.L.R.2d 1358.

The A.L.R. annotation contains an excellent discussion of the English rule and lists Illinois with the majority of states adopting such a rule. However, it calls the case *obiter*.

38. See Finley v. Teeter Stone, Inc., 251 Md. 428, 248 A.2d 106 (1968). The defendant had caused damage to the plaintiff's land (substantial subsidence) by pumping water from his own land to keep his quarry dry. This was a legitimate purpose and he was not maliciously injuring the plaintiff. Cf. the land support doctrines p. 365 supra.

Justice Boggs wrote: "Water which is the result of natural and ordinary percolation through the soil is part of the land itself and belongs absolutely to the owner of the land, and, in absence of any grant, he may intercept or impede such underground percolations, though the result be to interfere with the source of supply of springs or wells on adjoining premises. Upon this proposition there is, so far as we are advised, no dissension in the decisions of courts or in the writings of the authors of text books. Nor does appellee contend any different rule prevails, in the absence of a grant creating a right to percolating water in another than the owner of the soil." [39]

The case has been cited several times, but usually on other points and it has never been overruled, modified, or even explained by subsequent decisions. Nor have the appellate courts been called upon to decide on the use of percolating waters in later cases. Thus, the Illinois law in this area has a shaky foundation and no superstructure at all. One commentator [40] indicates that there would be no right to take ground water by force pumps, draining it from under a neighbor's land, and using it outside the owner's land. While this may be the law in some states, if they follow the reasonable use or correlative rights doctrines, there is no authority for even this limitation in Illinois.

It is clear that, in Illinois, an owner has no right to pollute ground water, even on his own land, in such a way that it causes harm to a neighbor's property interests.[41] Thus, in an appellate court case involving the pollution of wells with salt water from oil drilling operations, the court stated: "In this situation, the decisions are not uniform. Some states, such as Pennsylvania, hold that the salt water may be allowed to flow according to natural drainage, without resulting liability. Others (some by statute) hold that adjoining landowners and others downstream, have a right to water in its natural quality, both in their wells and in streams in which they have riparian rights. Illinois takes the latter view, as to pollution of waters in general. [Citing cases.] The Voss case specifically repudiates the Pennsylvania rule. For collected cases, see note 34 A.L.R. 266." [42]

These pollution cases are based on the law of nuisance which finds its origin in the Latin maxim, *sic utere tuo ut alienum non laedas.* Simply put, this boils down to reasonable use of the land, including the water supply. Note that this conflicts with the

39. Note 36 supra at p. 106.

40. Liessmann, Miscellaneous Water Rights in Illinois, 9 Ill.L.Rev. 564 (1915).

41. Wahle v. Reinbach, 76 Ill. 322 (1875) (pollution by privy); Belvi-dere Gaslight and Fuel Co. v. Jackson, 81 Ill.App. 424 (1898) (pollution by gas plant); Iliff v. School Directors, 45 Ill.App. 419 (1892) (pollution by privy).

42. Phoenix v. Graham, 349 Ill.App. 326, 332, 110 N.E.2d 669, 671 (1953).

English common-law rule of absolute ownership of percolating water.[43] That rule, which was supposedly adopted in Illinois in Edwards v. Haeger, would allow virtually any use, short of malice or intent to injure a neighbor. Of course, it is possible that the Illinois courts would follow one view with respect to pollution of ground water and another in regard to the use of such water. But it could be argued logically that the pollution cases modify the rigidity of the English common-law rule and that, given the proper set of facts, the Illinois courts would announce a doctrine of reasonable use in relation to the needs of adjoining owners. This is particularly so in view of the present state of scientific knowledge that demonstrates that ground water is not a static pool under a single owner's land but is in fact a slowly moving mass of water that affects an entire area. It seems, moreover, that the courts could adopt this view without overruling any previous cases and thus could state the reasonable use doctrine as the common law of Illinois. It is of further significance that England has itself changed the law of Acton v. Blundell by the passage of legislation in regard to ground water.[44]

In states following the reasonable use doctrine, malicious or wasteful use, even on the surface owner's land, would clearly be unreasonable as to neighboring owners. Although this result could be reached under the English rule as well, it is by no means clear that all courts would so conclude. Perhaps the major difference between the two rules arises out of use away from the surface owner's land. Under the English view of absolute ownership the water could be pumped and then sold or used for purposes away from the surface soil and a neighboring landowner could not successfully sue even if he suffered substantial damage.[45] By the reasonable use test, such activity would be privi-

43. Does it follow from the English rule on withdrawal of percolating water that a landowner would not be liable for polluting such water to the detriment of other landowners? See Gilmore v. Royal Salt Co., 84 Kan. 729, 115 P. 541 (1911); Nelson v. C. & C. Plywood Corp., 154 Mont. 414, 465 P.2d 314 (1970); Annotation, 38 A.L.R.2d 1265 (1954); Restatement, Second, Torts § 858B (Tent. Draft No. 17, 1917) (Note to Council concerning this section asserts that there is "no authority for the proposition stated in § 859 [1st Restatement] that 'unintentional' pollution of ground water is permissible if the polluter does not know he is causing harm.").

44. The basic rule of Acton v. Blundell remains the same, but legislation allows the Minister of Health to conserve water in the public interest. Waste or taking of water in excess of reasonable requirements may be prohibited. Water Act of 1945, 8 and 9 Geo. 6, c. 42; 26 Hals.Laws of England 786 (2d ed. 1951).

45. For an excellent case demonstrating the vigor of the English rule see Corpus Christi v. Pleasanton, 154 Tex. 289, 276 S.W.2d 798 (1955).

The Supreme Court of Texas followed the English Rule where water from artesian wells was being transported 118 miles with great loss by evaporation, seepage etc. enroute.

leged only if it caused no substantial damage to neighboring owners.[46] However, under the reasonable use test the landowner can apparently make any use of the water he desires on his own surface land (short of malice or waste), even to the point of exhausting the supply.

No clear-cut answer can be given as to the law of many American jurisdictions. Before 1922, at least twenty-eight states adopted by direct holding or by dicta the English rule of substantially unrestricted privilege. However, all but eight of these cases were decided prior to 1900, when the influence of the English common law was greater and when the present problems of water shortage did not exist.[47] It may not be a rash prediction to state that, as in the case of the riparian doctrine, the evolution is toward reasonable use. This trend could have a powerful influence on the various courts when they next face a specific problem.

What then is the common law as it affects ground water? No specific answer can be given. The law probably rests somewhere between the English common-law rule and the reasonable use doctrine. Perhaps it is a "brooding omnipresence in the sky," waiting to be pulled down and put to work when the proper cases arise. The simple truth is that until recently the East has had sufficient ground water for all use, reasonable or unreasonable, and without the problem of short supply and great demand the law has not had a chance to develop.

---

(2) DIFFUSED SURFACE WATER [48]

Diffused surface water requires only a brief general discussion to show its place in the scheme of water rights. Man's principal interest in surface water has been to "get rid of it." "Getting rid of it" has been no small undertaking and has given rise

There was a strong dissent but the majority felt any change in doctrine was for the legislature not the courts.

46. Bassett v. Salisburg Mfg. Co., 43 N.H. 249 (1862); Forbell v. City of New York, 184 N.Y. 522, 58 N.E. 644 (1900).

47. 5 Powell, Real Property 418 (1956).

48. For a clearly written statement on the Illinois law of drainage, see Hannah, Illinois Farm Drainage Law, Circular 751, University of Illinois, College of Agriculture (1956 Edition).

See generally, Maloney and Plager, Diffused Surface Water: Scourge or Bounty? 8 Nat.Res.J. 72 (1968).

to comprehensive drainage laws and codes. The drainage codes furnish a working example of statutory implementation of an inadequate common law and may supply some useful analogies for future legislation in the area of water use.

Illinois early adopted the law of natural drainage which derives from the old Roman code. The Supreme Court stated in Gormley v. Sanford: [49] "As water must flow, and some rule in regard to it must be established when land is held under the artificial titles created by human law, there can clearly be no other rule at once so equitable and so easy of application as that which enforces natural laws. There is no surprise or hardship in this, for each successive owner takes whatever advantages or inconvenience nature has stamped upon his land."

Not all states have followed the civil law principles and some use the so-called "common enemy" rule which gives a landowner an unrestricted right to deal with water coming on his land or the "reasonable use" rule which gives a landowner some right to restrict water coming on his land but limits that right to reasonable ditching, etc., in relation to his neighbor's land.[50] Obviously all of these views overlap at some points.

The Illinois principles of natural drainage are roughly as follows: (1) a lower landowner must receive surface water flowing naturally from higher ground; (2) a landowner may collect surface water, discharge it, and hasten its flow to lower ground, if good husbandry requires it; (3) a landowner may drain surface waters into watercourses; and (4) a lower landowner has no right to obstruct the flow of surface water by building an artificial structure that will interfere with the drainage of higher land. These principles are subject to interpretation by the courts and they are applied in a flexible fashion in order to do justice among the parties. Even so, the principles proved inadequate for some purposes and as early as 1885 the Agricultural Drainage

---

49. 52 Ill. 158, 162 (1869). Illinois still follows this view. See Mello v. Lepisto, 77 Ill.App.2d 399, 222 N.E.2d 543 (1966).

50. See Armstrong v. Francis Corporation, 20 N.J. 320, 120 A.2d 4 (1956) for a good discussion of all three rules.

The Supreme Court of New Jersey rejected both the civil law and common enemy rules and opted for a reasonable use test. Mr. Justice Brennan concluded:

"But while today's mass home building projects, of which the Francis development is typical, are assured-

ly in the social good, no reason suggests itself why, in justice, the economic costs incident to the expulsion of surface waters in the transformation of the rural or semi-rural areas of our State into urban or suburban communities should be borne in every case by adjoining landowners rather than by those who engage in such projects for profit. Social progress and the common well being are in actuality better served by a just and right balancing of the competing interests according to the general principles of fairness and common sense which attend the application of the rule of reason."

Act made certain changes which have carried over into the present Drainage Code. For example, the Code provides that an owner may extend his drains across the land of others when necessary to perfect his own drainage and provided he meets certain legal conditions. It also places a duty of repair on the builder of the drain, his heirs, and assigns, so that the drain will not injure the property through which it passes.

The law of natural drainage, even with the statutory changes just mentioned, was not adequate to meet the needs of all landowners in the state, particularly in river bottoms and flat prairie land. Here cooperative effort was necessary and in 1879 the legislature provided for drainage districts which would have the power to control drainage within their respective areas. This same legal device was retained in the new Drainage Code which became effective January 1, 1956.[51] The districts are established on a local basis to meet a local need and if an owner has adequate drainage under natural drainage principles and hence would not be benefited by a district he cannot be included against his wish.

In its treatment of diffused surface waters Illinois has retained its original common-law base, although codifying it, and has supplemented this base by cooperative action at the local level but within a legal framework established by the state. Moreover, it has followed the natural geographical facts in setting up the drainage districts, rather than attempting to force them into some pre-existing artificial unit. Thus, a drainage district cannot be organized to correspond with the boundaries of a township or other political unit unless such a unit constitutes a natural watershed and contains lands that can be efficiently connected by a continuous line of ditches or drains. Obviously this will seldom happen.

----

(3) WATER IN NATURAL WATERCOURSES

Rivers, streams, and lakes are the principal sources of water supply for most eastern residents. Ground water is of primary importance in many parts of the East but, taken as a whole, considerably more water from natural watercourses finds direct utilization for municipal, industrial, agricultural, and recreational purposes. Fortunately, the East is blessed by nature with abundant natural watercourses. As in the case of ground water, this bounty has led to a relatively meager set of laws and many questions cannot be answered with authority. The cases have tended to deal with matters of pollution and diversion rather than con-

51. Ill.Rev.Stat. ch. 42, Art. 1–12 (1973).

sumption but there are sufficient decisions to form at least a working base. For instance, it is quite clear that the East is committed to a system of riparian rights and apparently most courts have incorporated the theory of reasonable use as opposed to the natural flow theory.[52] In discussing this subject we will turn first to a leading case and then develop the refinements of doctrine which have followed through the years.

(a) Evans v. Merriweather [53]

In the law of any subject there are always a few key cases that influence the future growth of the law. Evans v. Merriweather is such a case in water law. Decided in 1842, it adopted the basic principles of the riparian doctrine and set forth a series of propositions that are being followed today. It is cited in many subsequent decisions on the subject and is frequently quoted by the judges. Therefore, it is important to have a clear understanding of the case itself.

The facts were simple. Two mills were located on a stream which in normal periods supplied sufficient water to run the machinery of both establishments. During a fall drouth, however, there was not enough water to run either mill all of the time. The defendant, who owned the upper mill on the stream, allowed his employees to build a dam across the watercourse and divert the water into his well for use in his mill. As a result the branch dried up below and the plaintiff was deprived of all water. He

---

52. The Restatement of Torts (4 Restatement, Torts, 341–350, 1939) makes a clear-cut distinction between the reasonable use and natural flow theories. It then lists a series of legal consequences which follow the adoption of a particular theory. One of the most important of these consequences is that under the natural flow theory any sensible or material change in the quantity or quality of the water may give rise to a cause of action for at least nominal damages whether the lower owner suffers actual damages or not. Thus, any use of water on non-riparian land which causes a sensible diminution of the stream would allow the lower owner to sue. On the other hand, under a reasonable use theory no right to sue would accrue unless actual damages can be shown and not even then if the use by the upper owner is reasonable under all of the facts and circumstances.

There is much reason to quarrel with these arbitrary distinctions, particularly since the courts mix up the results with little regard for nicely stated theories. It might be more accurate to say that the natural flow theory, if it ever existed in the pure state, has been refined to mean that the riparian owners are entitled to the natural flow of water subject to the reasonable use by each such owner. The discussion of the cases will attempt to clarify this point further. See also Mally v. Weidensteiner, 88 Wash. 398, 153 P. 342 (1915).

53. 4 Ill. 492, 38 Am.Dec. 106 (1842).

brought a suit at law for damages for obstructing and diverting a watercourse and obtained a judgment for $150 which was sustained on appeal.

The court, in reaching its decision, enunciated the following principles:

(1) "A watercourse begins *ex jure naturae,* and having taken a certain course naturally, cannot be diverted." This is the natural flow theory that all through whose land water naturally flows may enjoy the privilege of using it. This right to use depends on riparian ownership of land and is not a property right in the fluid itself but rather in the impetus of the water.

(2) Mere priority of appropriation of running water confers no exclusive right.

(3) Reasonable use determines the extent of the riparian owner's property right.[54] The court quotes with approval from Tyler v. Wilkinson.[55] "I do not mean to be understood as holding the doctrine that there can be no diminution whatever, and no obstruction or impediment whatever, by a riparian proprietor in the use of water as it flows; for that would be to deny any valuable use of it. There may be, and there must be, of that which is common to all, a reasonable use. The true test of the principle and extent of the use is, whether it is to the injury of the other proprietors or not. There may be diminution in quantity, or a retardation or acceleration of the natural current, indispensable for the general and valuable use of the water, perfectly consistent with the use of the common right. The diminution, retardation, or acceleration, not positively and sensibly injurious, by diminishing the value of the common right, is an implied element in the right of using the stream at all. The law here, as in many other cases, acts with a reasonable reference to public convenience and general good, and is not betrayed into a narrow strictness, subversive of common use, nor into an extravagant looseness, which would destroy private rights."

(4) Water uses are divided into natural and artificial uses. The former represents needs that must be supplied if man is to exist—drinking purposes, household wants, and water for his cattle or stock. To supply these wants the upper riparian owner may take all of the water he actually needs, even if it means that the lower owner is left without any supplies. In this instance, at least, the upper riparian owner does have a better right than a lower owner.

On the other hand, artificial uses are those which supply the comfort and increase the prosperity of the landowner—irrigat-

54. Note how in this leading case the court first states the traditional natural flow theory (point 1) and then modifies it by allowing the riparian owner a "reasonable use" of the water.

55. Note 28 supra.

ing lands or propelling machinery (i. e., agricultural and industrial uses). Water for artificial uses must be on a reasonable basis and one owner cannot deprive another of a proportionate use of the water for this purpose.

(5) Irrigation is not a natural use and stands on the same footing as industrial use. "In countries differently situated from ours, with a hot and arid climate, water doubtless is absolutely indispensable to the cultivation of the soil, and in them, water for irrigation would be a natural want. Here it might increase the products of the soil, but it is by no means essential, and cannot therefore be considered a natural want of man. So of manufactures, they promote the prosperity and comfort of mankind, but cannot be considered absolutely necessary to his existence; nor need the machinery which he employs be set in motion by steam."

(6) The issue of reasonable use by riparian owners is an issue of fact and must be decided by the jury. "Where all have a right to participate in a common benefit, and none can have an exclusive enjoyment, no rule, from the very nature of the case, can be laid down, as to how much each may use without infringing upon the rights of others. In such cases, the question must be left to the judgment of the jury, whether the party complained of has used, under all the circumstances, more than his just proportion."

The six principles just enumerated form the basic law of riparian rights. In succeeding sections we will trace their elaboration and application.

(b) When Does the Riparian Doctrine Apply?

The riparian doctrine comes into play only when a natural watercourse is involved, as opposed to diffused surface water or percolating ground water. In close cases there may be a question of fact as to whether a natural watercourse exists, but usually this will be quite obvious. A watercourse implies a stream having some ascertainable limits or boundaries within which the water habitually flows.[56] Thus, if the conformation of land is such that the surface water uniformly follows a definite course within reasonable limits as to width and is discharged upon servient land at a definite place, the line of flow is a watercourse.[57] Even where a slough or natural depression follows an irregular

56. Wills v. Babb, 123 Ill.App. 511 (1905), aff'd 222 Ill. 95, 78 N.E. 42 (1906).

57. Winhold v. Finch, 286 Ill. 614, 122 N.E. 53 (1919).

course from a pond to a creek, and there is considerable current in the slough bed in times of high water or freshets the course of the slough constitutes a natural watercourse.[58] What starts out as an artificial watercourse, constructed by the work of man, can ripen into a natural watercourse, subject to the usual riparian rules, if it is maintained for the necessary period of time (typically twenty years) and meets the test as to a prescriptive right.[59]

The doctrine of riparian rights applies to all flowing streams whether navigable or non-navigable. However, in the case of navigable streams, the right of the riparian owner is subject to a public easement to use the river for navigation purposes.[60]

The owner of land abutting on a river or stream is a riparian owner. Lessees and owners of rights of way or easements and grantees of riparian rights are also riparian owners, and, to the extent of their title, are endowed with all the accompanying rights.[61] Moreover, riparian rights may be acquired by prescription; that is, by use adverse to others for over twenty years.[62] A good statement of the general law appears in a recent issue of the *Iowa Law Review:* "The question sometimes arises, however, whether a riparian owner can purchase land contiguous to the riparian land, but apart from the stream, and claim riparian rights as to the newly acquired land which does not abut upon the stream. It is generally held that riparian rights do not accrue to subsequent additions to the original tract, but are limited to the smallest abutting tract held under one chain of title leading to the present owner. In any event, land which is outside the watershed of a stream is not considered riparian, nor is land riparian which is separated from the stream by a highway or railroad right of way." [63]

The rights of an owner of land abutting upon a lake or pond (except where the lake or pond is entirely enclosed by the owner's land) are similar to those of one who owns property next to a river or stream, except that they are technically called *littoral* rights rather than *riparian* rights. Littoral means belonging to

58. People ex rel. Road District No. 12 v. Cache River Drainage District, 251 Ill.App. 405 (1929).

59. Saelens v. Pollentier, 7 Ill.2d 556, 131 N.E.2d 479 (1956); Mauvaisterre District v. Wabash Ry. Co., 299 Ill. 299, 132 N.E. 559, 22 A.L.R. 944 (1921); Beidler v. Sanitary Dist. of Chicago, 211 Ill. 628, 71 N.E. 1118, 67 L.R.A. 820 (1904). See also Nixon v. Welch, 238 Iowa 34, 24 N.W.2d 476 (1946).

60. Leitch v. Sanitary District of Chicago, 369 Ill. 469, 17 N.E.2d 34

(1938); Braxon v. Bressler, 64 Ill. 488 (1872).

61. Indian Refining Co. v. Ambraw River Drainage Dist., 1 F.Supp. 937 (E.D.Ill.1932).

62. Ballard v. Struckman, 123 Ill. 636, 14 N.E. 682 (1888).

63. Davis, Water Rights in Iowa, 41 Iowa L.Rev. 216, 220 (1956); see also 5 S.C.L.Q. 178–81 (1952); 56 Am.Jur., Waters, §§ 277, 278, 280; Restatement Torts, §§ 843–44 (1939).

the shore, as of seas and great lakes. However, riparian is used coextensively with littoral and is so treated in this section. The point is well stated by the Iowa Supreme Court: " . . . [A] *riparian* owner is one whose land abuts upon a river. If his land abuts upon a lake, he is deemed to be a *littoral* owner. The distinction is wholly immaterial for the purpose of this case. The case law is the same whether the ownership be riparian or littoral, and such case law has been developed largely in riparian cases." [64]

(c) Riparian Rights Are Protected Property Rights

The extent of the riparian right, as measured by the reasonable use test, is at best vague and ill-defined, but whatever the extent, the right is carefully protected by law. For example, in the City of Kewanee v. Otley [65] the court stated: "The right to a stream of water is as sacred as a right to the soil over which it flows. It is a part of the freehold, of which the owner cannot be disseized except by due process of law, and the pollution of a stream constitutes the taking of property, which may not be done without compensation."

This statement is a shade too extreme. A stream of water is not a part of the freehold and that portion of the quotation was repudiated by a later decision.[66] In Illinois, cases involving a freehold could formerly be appealed directly from the trial court to the Supreme Court, by-passing the appellate tribunal. In Clark v. Lindsay Light Co.,[67] the Supreme Court transferred a stream pollution case to the appellate court because no freehold was involved. The riparian owner was said to have no property in the water of a natural stream, but to have a *usufruct* in the water while it passes. A *usufruct* was defined as "the right of enjoying a thing, the property of which is vested in another, and to draw from the same all the profit, utility and advantage which it may produce, provided it be without altering the substance of the thing." Similar rights are those to the light and air above the land. Concluded Justice Daily, "While we agree with appellants that the natural right to use the water of a stream is one

---

64. Peck v. Olsen Construction Co., 216 Iowa 519, 532–33, 245 N.W. 131, 137 (1931).

65. 204 Ill. 402, 417, 68 N.E. 388 (1903).

66. Clark v. Lindsay Light Co., 405 Ill. 139, 89 N.E.2d 900 (1950).

67. Id.

that cannot be taken without due process of law, we conclude that such right is but an incident of ownership, and not a portion of the land or freehold itself. We cannot say that the flowing waters of the stream in question were a part of appellants' freehold, any more than they were a part of the freehold of riparian owners above or below them."

Although the riparian right is usufructuary in character, it is none the less a property right and is therefore subject to the full protection of the law. It can be taken away from the owner only by due process of law, which means that adequate compensation must be paid and that only governmental units having the power of eminent domain would be able to take the right by condemnation proceedings.[68]

(d) *Reasonable Use As A Test Of Riparian Rights*

It is one thing to state glibly a rule of law; it is quite another to apply it to the concrete situations of life. What is the reasonable use of the water in a natural watercourse? This is the heart of the matter, but the question can never be answered except in relationship to a specific set of facts. General statements are useful as guiding principles, but they must not be taken as absolute rules of law. In this section we will try to define the problem by reference to several leading cases.

At the outset, it should be clear that Illinois, like most eastern states does not always restrict itself to the natural flow theory of riparian rights. There is language in some of the cases that might indicate that it does, but other decisions seem to apply a reasonable use test. The crucial issue is stated in Tetherington v. Donk Bros. Coal Co. [69]: "In a strict and highly technical sense any use of a stream of water may diminish the quantity or impair the quality in some infinitesimal degree, but it is not this sense in which the law assures the right of a riparian owner to the use of the stream. It would be of no avail to a landowner to give him such a right, for in turn the next lower riparian owner would have the same strict right to have the stream come to him in like condition, so that no one would have a right to do more than stand on the shore and see the stream flow by him. The right of each proprietor to use the stream is subject to a like reasonable right

---

68. Leitch v. Sanitary District of Chicago, 369 Ill. 469, 17 N.E.2d 34 (1938); The People v. Economy Power Co., 241 Ill. 290, 89 N.E. 760 (1909); Druley v. Adam, 102 Ill. 177 (1882); Eimers v. Cleveland, C. C. and St. L. Ry. Co., 158 Ill. App. 557 (1910).

69. 232 Ill. 522, 525, 83 N.E. 1048, 1049 (1908).

in other riparian owners, and each must submit to such *reasonable use* by his neighbor, so long as such use does not inflict substantial injury upon other owners who have a like right. When questions arise between riparian owners respecting the right of one to make a particular use of the water in which they have a common right, the right will generally depend on the *reasonableness of the use* and the extent of the detriment to the lower owner."

We will now discuss the reasonableness of use as it relates to diversion, pollution, and consumption.

---

1. Diversion

An owner of land has a right (i. e., it is reasonable) to change a water channel on his own land if he returns the water to the natural channel before it leaves his land, and if it causes no damage to the lower riparian owner.[70] However, any diversion that carries over into the lower land is likely to be treated as unreasonable. In Plumleigh v. Dawson,[71] three-fourths of the water in a stream was diverted to run a mill and was not returned to the natural channel before it left the diverter's land. The water was returned to the channel eventually, but at a point below the plaintiff's land. There was still enough water passing through the natural channel for agricultural and domestic uses and the plaintiff was unable to show any actual damage. The court stated the basic principles of riparian rights and then decided that no special damage need be shown in order to recover for a diversion. The defendant had no right to take three-fourths or any other specific proportion of the water as his share and divert it from the plaintiff's land. Said the court, "There are some few cases in which the doctrine seems to be sanctioned, that there must be proof of actual damage to entitle the plaintiff, in this and like cases, to a recovery. . . . But I think the doctrine well settled, that where a party is deprived of such a right, the law will imply some damage; for otherwise before the party might be able to prove actual damage, the wrong doer might acquire a right by prescription, or upon the presumption of a grant. Thus an injury is likely to ensue from such an invasion of his right, and which is sufficient damage to sustain this action for the recovery of nominal damages at least, and so establish his right."

70. Dettmer v. Illinois Terminal R.   **71.** 6 Ill. 544 (1844).
    Co., 287 Ill. 513, 123 N.E. 37 (1919).

Plumleigh v. Dawson was decided in 1844 but it has never been overruled and it has been cited with approval in numerous later cases. Of course, the diversion was of a major sort (three-fourths of the total supply) and even though the plaintiff was not presently damaged there was a clear invasion of his rights. However, the court did not restrict its doctrine to such large scale activities but said the defendant had no right to take "three-fourths *or any other specific proportion*" of the water. In view of the Dawson case it may be more accurate to say that here Illinois, at least, does follow the natural flow theory and that even slight diversions from the established channel are actionable. Apparently the statute of limitations starts to run as soon as the diversion occurs and the diverter would have a prescriptive right to maintain the new channel after a twenty-year period. It is important to note, however, that the plaintiff is entitled to only nominal damages to establish the existence of his right. Presumably he could not enjoin the diversion without showing actual damage. This may mean that he will win a hollow victory at best.

If a stream cannot be diverted without incurring liability to other riparian owners it follows that it cannot be obstructed by dams, bridges, etc., that cause a change in the flow of the water. There are a number of cases so holding.[72]

The case of Druley v. Adam [73] illustrates the strictness with which the courts treat the diversion problem. This was a suit involving the diversion of water in the Desplaines River. The defendant had an agreement allowing diversion for use in navigation on a canal. He had then added more water to the river by deepening the canal and was trying to remove some of the surplus water for use in ways other than navigation. The court interpreted the agreement strictly and refused to allow the diversion. Where a stream is natural, all waters which flow into it become a part of that stream, and subject to the same natural rights as the rest of the water. Even though the defendant put the additional water into the stream he could not later remove a like quantity on the theory that it was his. He might do so if the addition and diversion are both part of the same act, are done on his own land, and do not interfere with the amount and quality of water flowing to the lower owner's land. "This view is, however, manifestly inapplicable in an action at law, where the party adding the water, in a legal point of view, abandons it, so that the lower riparian proprietor has a legal right, technical though it may be, to have the added water flow down over his land as a part of the waters of the stream; for no common-law

72. Leitch v. Sanitary District of Chicago, 369 Ill. 469, 17 N.E.2d 34 (1938); Deterding v. Central Ill. Service Co., 313 Ill. 562, 145 N.E. 185 (1924).

73. 102 Ill. 177 (1882).

doctrine is settled more firmly by the concurrent judgments of common law courts, than that for every distinct invasion of a right, although the invasion itself may be productive of no actual injury, some damage is presumed."

2.　Pollution

Pollution of natural watercourses by municipal and industrial wastes is a major problem throughout the United States and is becoming increasingly serious.[74]　However, the legal principles involved are relatively simple.　The lower riparian owner is entitled to the flow of water with its quality undiminished. Obviously, this does not mean that no wastes can be dumped into natural watercourses, but it does mean that "reasonableness" is strictly applied and the upper riparian owner will be held to a high degree of care in treatment of sewage, industrial waste products, etc.　In Clark v. Lindsay Light and Chemical Co.,[75] the court refused an injunction against pollution because the damage was only nominal, but it indicated that if real damages were involved it would grant the relief even though it might cause disproportionate losses to the defendant in relation to the benefit conferred upon the plaintiff.

The principal difficulty in this area lies in the fact that the public interest in the control of the pollution of water cannot be adequately protected through the sporadic efforts of individual litigations.　For adequate protection, resort must be had to some sort of public administrative regulation.　In Illinois, for example, the Sanitary Water Board has the power to determine whether pollution exists in the waters of the state and then to act to correct the situation.[76]

3.　Consumption

Evans v. Merriweather established the classic test of natural versus artificial uses.　The former are always reasonable, or at least the upper riparian owner has the right to exhaust completely the available supplies in satisfying his own wants.　But how do you draw the line between artificial uses?

74.　A Report by the Presidential Advisory Committee on Water Resources Policy (December 22, 1955).

75.　341 Ill.App. 316, 93 N.E.2d 441 (1950).

76.　Ill.Rev.Stat. ch. 19, §§ 145.1– 145.18 (1973).

In Bliss v. Kennedy,[77] a case involving two factories on the same stream about one hundred yards apart, the court came as near to establishing a concrete test as can be found. Wrote Justice Breese: "A reasonable rule, and one which we desire to lay down, would seem to be this: That so far as the water is destroyed by being converted into steam, neither of these factories is entitled to its exclusive use; that it is to be divided between them as nearly as may be according to their respective requirements; that, if each factory requires the same quantity of water, it should be equally divided; but, while the water is incapable of being thus divided with mathematical exactness, if the jury should find that the upper factory has used more than its reasonable share, or has diverted the water after using it from its natural channel, or so corrupted it, as to deprive the lower proprietors of its use to such a degree as to cause a material injury to that factory, it would be ground for damages, and ultimately for an injunction." The most important thought here expressed is that ultimately the question of reasonableness must be decided by a jury.

To illustrate the vital role of the jury in the reasonable use test, reference must be made to W. H. Howell Co. v. Charles Pope Glucose Co. [78] Several factories were located on the Fox River and in the dry season of the year not enough water was available to furnish adequate supplies for all users. By custom the mills and factories shut down at night and on Sundays so that the water could accumulate for use at other times. The defendant disregarded this general agreement and operated his factory at all hours, thus exhausting the water and depriving the other owners of power. The plaintiffs sought an injunction but the court held that equity lacked jurisdiction until there had been a jury determination of the reasonableness of the use. Said the court: "Whatever may be the rule of law in other States, we think it is settled in this, that where there is a controversy between the owners of water power rights, growing out of what is claimed to be an unreasonable use of the power by one to the prejudice of others, equity will not extend its restraining arm until it has been determined by a court of law that the use complained of is unreasonable. The question of what is a reasonable or unreasonable use of water is one of fact to be determined by a jury from the evidence."

Sandusky Portland Cement Co. v. Dixon Pure Ice Co.[79] casts further light on the meaning of reasonable use. The plaintiff owned a large ice plant on the Rock River and cut the

77. 43 Ill. 67 (1867).

78. 61 Ill.App. 593 (1895), aff'd 171
      Ill. 350, 49 N.E. 497 (1898).

79. 221 F. 200 (7th Cir. 1915).

ice from the river opposite its plant during the winter. The defendant operated a cement factory upstream from the plaintiff. The cement factory used between 3,000,000 and 4,000,000 gallons of water a day for cooling purposes in connection with its condensing machinery. The water was returned to the stream, but heated to a temperature of from 50° to 60°. As a result the warm water moved downstream some 3,000 feet and kept the ice from freezing in front of the plaintiff's plant. The court stated the reasonable use test and pointed out that if the defendant's action was not unreasonable the plaintiff could not complain even though it had suffered some injury from the heated water. Apparently no jury was requested by either party and the trial judge decided the use was unreasonable and granted an injunction against the defendant's action. This holding was affirmed on appeal.

The Court of Appeals for the Seventh Circuit said: "But where, as in the present case, it is shown by the evidence that defendant's use of the river water, while essential for its own purposes, entirely destroys the right of complainant thereto, there can be no claim by defendant that its use thereof is reasonable. In other words, the emergency of defendant's needs is not the measure of its rights in the water."

A somewhat similar case in Iowa [80] is worth noting because it states principles which would undoubtedly apply elsewhere. The Iowa case involved the construction of a dam to create a pond from which to harvest ice in winter. The pond would take about two and one-half days to fill during which period a lower mill owner would be deprived of power. After that time the water would spill over the dam and turn the wheel as before. The court held that the building of the dam was not an unreasonable interference with the defendant's rights and stated several criteria for deciding such questions: "No statement can be made as to what is such reasonable use which will, without variation or qualification, apply to the facts of every case. But in determining whether a use is reasonable we must consider what the use is for; its extent, duration, necessity, and its application; the nature and size of the stream, and the several uses to which it is put; the extent of the injury to the one proprietor, and of the benefit to the other; and all other facts which may bear upon the reasonableness of the use."

80. Gehlen Brothers v. Knorr, 101 Iowa 700, 70 N.W. 757 (1897).

(e) The Key Factors in Determining Reasonable Use

The summation of the Iowa court demonstrates the genuine flexibility of the reasonable use doctrine. This very flexibility is a two-edged sword, however, for while it leaves the law relatively free to grow and respond to changing situations it furnishes a very poor basis for predictability. The lawyer has difficulty advising clients when the standards of conduct are so loosely phrased. In an attempt to give a greater degree of predictability the reasonable use test has been stated in terms of six critical factors: (1) the *purpose* of the questioned use; (2) the *destination* to which the water is taken for use; (3) the *extent* of the use; (4) the *pollution* of water by use; (5) use which involves an *alteration* in the manner of flow; and (6) *miscellaneous* types of conduct which may give rise to litigation.[81]

F. THE ROLE OF LEGISLATION

This Section on water rights has dealt primarily with the common law and the principal emphasis has been on the eastern portion of the United States. This approach does not indicate any lack of appreciation for the importance of the prior appropriation doctrines of the western states but there are enough differences between the various western jurisdictions so that a meaningful, general discussion is impossible in the space available in a short text. The prior appropriation doctrines are heavily statutory and administrative; the interested student will have to explore them on his own.[82]

The common-law doctrines have tended to treat water rights as a species of private property rather than as a natural resource belonging to society as a whole. Moreover, most of the cases have involved private litigation and the decisions, of necessity, reflect an ad hoc approach which can scarcely be said to reflect a rational policy for dealing with so important a national asset. This is true even in the growing area of weather modification where recent scientific advances open a whole new field of poten-

---

81. 5 Powell, Real Property 364–383 (1956).

82. For a major treatise see Clark, Waters and Water Rights (1967).

See also Trelease, Coordination of Riparian and Appropriative Rights to the Use of Water, 33 Tex.L.Rev. 24 (1954).

tial litigation.[83] This treatment of water rights as private property makes it imperative that the lawyer be aware of existing common-law doctrine as the legislative role moves to the center of the stage. For one thing, it raises constitutional issues of the taking of vested property interests when legislation changes the existing law. For example, in a case altering, by statute, the Texas law of drainage from the common-enemy rule to the civil-law rule, the Supreme Court of Texas said: "These rights of the owners of estates under the civil law are appurtenant to and a part of the land itself, and passed to them with the grants. The right of the owner of the upper estate to have the surface waters falling thereon to pass in their natural condition onto the lands of the lower estate is a servitude or natural right in the nature of an easement over the lower estate of his neighbor. It is a right of property, which inheres in the estate entitled to its benefit independent of any contractual or prescriptive right." [84] The court upheld the statute but it recognized the difficulties involved in altering established rules on which property owners may have relied. It would be economically impracticable to pay compensation for "taking" such water rights and yet it is clear that substantial changes must occur in traditional doctrine. Here, as in zoning, the police power will probably have to be used so that the changes can be viewed as regulation rather than taking.[85]

Fortunately, much of the statutory change moves in the same direction as the common law and is designed to make old doctrine more efficient and effective. For example, principles of nuisance, as well as of water rights, have long regarded pollution of water as non-privileged but the private remedies have been inadequate to preserve the quality of our rivers and lakes.

---

83. Southwest Weather Research, Inc. v. Rounsaville, 320 S.W.2d 211 (Tex.1958). In affirming this case, the Supreme Court of Texas said: "These causes involve complicated scientific problems, as well as the legal determination of the property rights of both the landowners on one hand and those engaged in a business enterprise on the other. Admittedly the case is not fully developed. It has not been tried upon the merits and the sole purpose of the temporary injunctions was to preserve the status quo until these complicated scientific problems and attendant legal questions can be fully considered and a final judgment rendered delineating and determining the rights of litigating parties." 327 S.W.2d 417 (1959). Noted, 73 Harv.L.Rev. 790 (1960). For background and discussion of the issues, see: Controlling the Weather (H. Taubenfeld ed. 1970); Ball, Shaping the Law of Weather Control, 58 Yale L.J. 213 (1949); Corbridge and Moses, Weather Modification: Law and Administration, 8 Nat.Res.J. 207 (1968); Davis, State Regulation of Weather Modification, 12 Ariz.L.Rev. 35 (1970); Oppenheimer, The Legal Aspects of Weather Modification, 1948 Ins.L.J. 314 (1958).

84. Miller v. Letzerich, 121 Tex. 248, 49 S.W.2d 404, 85 A.L.R. 451 (1932).

85. See pp. 399 to 401 infra.

State legislation, as previously discussed, has had some impact but the problem needed to be dealt with on a national basis. Riparian doctrines apply to navigable streams but they are subject to the overriding federal easement to protect the navigability of streams.[86] This federal power has provided the basis for a diverse set of regulations, designed to restore the quality of the nation's rivers and lakes.[87] It is too early to predict just how effective these federal and state acts will be but they represent a move in the right direction. Water law is too important to be left to the case by case approach of the common law.

Taken as a whole, the current legislation (state and federal) still does not disclose an adequate approach to the water problems of the nation. The various statutes furnish evidence of a legislative response to specific problems as the pressures have developed, but do not indicate a unified approach on a comprehensive basis to the monumental issues involved in twentieth century water use. Here is an ideal example of the need for inter-disciplinary action, based on cooperative research by lawyers and other specialist groups concerned with the quality of the nation's environment.

SECTION 4.   AIR RIGHTS

It is unorthodox to view air rights as one of the so-called natural rights since most of the problems deal with the invasions of air space by the airplane, particularly the modern jet plane. These invasions are normally thought of as torts, and covered in that course, or as administrative matters to be dealt with under the federal regulatory power. Nonetheless, an owner of Blackacre has a natural right to use the air space over his land just as he has a natural right to prevent a nuisance, to the support of his surface land, and to a usufruct in the water on his land. A discussion of basic principles would not provide the "big picture" of property law without a brief look at air rights. Moreover, air rights are of growing importance as they are severed from the surface rights and sold as separate interests in land. Many large buildings are built almost entirely on

86. United States v. Willow River Power Co., 324 U.S. 499, 65 S.Ct. 761, 89 L.Ed. 1101, 103 Ct.Cl. 797 (1945).

87. See, for example, the Water and Environmental Quality Improvement Act of 1970, Pub.L. 91–224, 91 St.Cong.2d Sess.

air rights with only minimal surface ownership to provide support for the structure. For example, the Prudential Building in Chicago is constructed over the Illinois Central Railroad right of way and the air rights were a valuable asset of the railroad. Incidentally, this type of construction can raise extremely interesting legal problems as to the nature of a railroad right of way. Is it owned in fee or is it only an easement across the land owned by another?[88] In Hickey v. Illinois Central Railroad Company,[89] the State of Illinois claimed it was the latter and hence the air rights belonged to the state, not the railroad. Without deciding that issue squarely, the Illinois Supreme Court held that while statutes of limitation do not normally apply against governmental units, the doctrine of laches may be used even against the state. Since for more than fifty years the state and the city of Chicago had disclaimed any interest in the air rights over the railroad and acted as if the lands were owned in fee by the railroad, they were estopped from asserting any claim to the air rights.

The legal problems of the Hickey case would not arise if the ownership of Blackacre was clearly in fee simple absolute. Then the owner could use the air space over his land in any reasonable way (including severing and selling it to others) so long as he did not violate zoning or other police power regulations.[90] The whole condominium concept is based on the subdivision of air rights with a vertical rather than a horizontal development of Blackacre.[91] Quite recently, Professor Costonis has suggested an imaginative plan for the preservation of historic buildings,[92] based on the transfer of air rights from one site to another, which illustrates that air rights will be of growing importance as American cities continue their explosive growth.

88. See p. 337 supra.

89. 35 Ill.2d 427, 220 N.E.2d 415 (1966).

90. Just how high can a landowner build a modern equivalent of the Tower of Babel? For an amusing possibility see Time Magazine: "In Chicago, testy old (87) Architect Frank Lloyd Wright casually disclosed his latest high-flown fantasy: A one-mile-high, 510 story office building for the Loop. Topped with a 330-ft. TV antenna, it would be four times taller than the Empire State Building. 'It's perfectly scientific, and perfectly feasible,' he said, brushing aside questions on how he would get 100,000 office workers in and out of the building on time, or what he would do about the planes that cross the area at considerably less than 5,600 ft. 'If you're going to have centralization,' Wright said, 'why not have it!' Told that Chicago's Mayor Richard J. Daley had been cautiously noncommittal about the proposition, Wright asked: 'Who's Daley? He couldn't be very bright if he's mayor of Chicago.'" Time Magazine, Sept. 10, 1956.

91. See pp. 239 to 262 supra.

92. Costonis, Space Adrift: Saving Urban Landmarks Through The Chicago Plan (Univ. of Ill. Press, 1974).

Law is a product of social problems; if there are few problems there is little law.   In Blackstone's day, a Latin maxim *cujus est solum, ejus est usque ad coelum et ad inferos*,[93] could sum up the legal principles of air rights.   There was little need to expand this simple doctrine until modern technology created the skyscraper and the airplane.[94]   Even then, the cases were few and far between until America moved from a rural to an urban society and air travel became a way of life for a fast moving population.   The inevitable conflicts thus arise in a virtually non-existent legal milieu.   The courts were forced to decide the cases by analogy to existing doctrines, such as nuisance and trespass, which frequently led to inconsistent results.   It was clear that the landowner had certain natural rights to the air space over Blackacre but the extent of those rights was far from clear.   He no longer owned from "heaven to hell" and the federal government soon made it clear that all navigable airspace was within the public domain, just as all navigable streams were subject to an overriding public easement.   In 1962, the Supreme Court of the United States [95] took specific notice of the Federal Aviation Act of 1958.[96]

"Following the decision in the Causby case, [United States v. Causby, 328 U.S. 256, 66 S.Ct. 1062, 90 L.Ed. 1206, 106 Ct.Cl. 854], Congress redefined 'navigable airspace' to mean 'airspace above the minimum altitudes of flight prescribed by regulations issued under this chapter, and shall include airspace needed to insure safety in take-off and land of aircraft.' . . . By the present regulations the 'minimum safe altitudes' within the meaning of the statute are defined, so far as relevant here, as heights of 500 or 1,000 feet, '[e]xcept where necessary for take-off or landing.'   But as we said in the Causby case, the use of land presupposes the use of some of the airspace above it."   Note particularly the final sentence of the quotation.   The owner of Blackacre has some air rights, even when his land lies near an airport, as it did in the *Griggs* case.   The tough question is how extensive are those rights and on what theory is he entitled to vindicate them?

Theories of nuisance and trespass are useful by analogy but they fall short of a clear chart to wisdom and can lead to odd results.   For example, in Batten v. United States [97] the majority

93. To whomsoever the soil belongs, he owns also to the sky and to the depths.

94. Note, Airspace: A New Dimension in Property Law, [1960] U. of I. Law Forum 303.

95. Griggs v. County of Allegheny, 369 U.S. 84, 82 S.Ct. 531, 7 L.Ed.2d 585 (1962).

96. 72 Stat. 737, 49 U.S.C.A. § 1301 (24) (Supp.1961).

97. 306 F.2d 580 (10th Cir. 1962).

of the court allowed recovery for direct overflights, on a trespass theory of invasion of the plaintiff's air rights but denied recovery for damages which were not caused by actual invasion of air space. Judge Murrah, in dissent, had difficulty with this narrow view of a landowner's rights. "It is my thesis that a constitutional taking does not necessarily depend on whether the Government physically invaded the property damaged."

While no legal theory can solve all of the problems, particularly the always troublesome factual issue of the amount of damages, the best approach was followed by the Supreme Court of Washington in Martin v. Port of Seattle.[98] In that case an inverse condemnation [99] action was brought by 196 property owners against the Port of Seattle, a municipal corporation, as owner of the Seattle-Tacoma International Airport. The owners sought damages for an alleged taking or damaging of their property for public use caused by nearby low altitude flights of jet aircraft landing and taking off from the airport. The court rejected the trespass theory: "We are unable to accept the premise that recovery for interference with the use of land should depend upon anything as irrelevant as whether the wing tip of the aircraft passes through some fraction of an inch of the airspace directly above the plaintiff's land. The plaintiffs are not seeking recovery for a technical trespass, but for a combination of circumstances engendered by the nearby flights which interfere with the use and enjoyment of their land."

Property was recognized as including the right to use, enjoy, and dispose of land. The Washington Constitution directed that just compensation be paid for the reduction in value of the land caused by the jet aircraft. This theory, inverse condemnation, avoided the inequities of the trespass theory and recognized the "propertyness" of air rights. A somewhat similar approach has been followed in *Griggs* [1] where the United States Supreme Court had required payment for an easement of air access to the airport, recognizing that the taxing agency must pay not only for the fee simple title to the land on which the airport was built but for the property interest represented by the easement of access. Mr. Justice Douglas noted: "Without the 'approach areas,' an airport is indeed not operable. Respondent

---

98. 64 Wash.2d 309, 391 P.2d 540 (1964).

99. Reference has been made several times to inverse condemnation. "Inverse condemnation is the popular description of an action brought against a governmental entity having the power of eminent domain to recover the value of property which has been appropriated in fact, but with no formal exercise of the power." Thornburg v. Port of Portland, 233 Or. 178, 376 P.2d 100 (1962).

1. Note 95, supra.

in designing it had to acquire some private property. Our conclusion is that by constitutional standards it did not acquire enough." However, the decision in *Martin* was broader than *Griggs,* since in the latter a direct overflight of the land would seem to be required. The point is that both cases treat air rights as a species of private property for which compensation must be paid under the appropriate circumstances.[2]

The legal protection of a landowner's air rights (really an incident of his natural rights in Blackacre) is important under our system of private property but it is a costly proposition for the state.[3] Other, and more promising, approaches to handling noise and other environmental impacts of airports include comprehensive planning of airport location and design, improvement of traffic control systems, coordination with other forms of transportation, construction of sound-resistant dwellings, and development of quieter aircraft engines.[4]

2. Stoebuck, Condemnation by Nuisance: The Airport Cases in Retrospect and Prospect, 71 Dick.L.Rev. 207 (1967); Spater, Noise and The Law, 63 Mich.L.Rev. 1373 (1965).

3. Note that similar protection has been denied when sought by landowners near major highways. See Northcutt v. State Road Dept., 209 So.2d 710 (Fla.App.1968).

4. See Airport and Airway Development Act of 1970, 49 U.S.C.A. § 1712 et seq.; Environmental Studies Board, National Academy of Sciences—National Academy of Engineering, Jamaica Bay and Kennedy Airport (1971).

Chapter 3

PUBLIC REGULATION OF LAND USE

The public interest has always played a role in the law of property, but until recent decades it has been exercised largely in a negative, hands-off fashion. It is a postulate of private property that the individual should have maximum freedom in the acquisition, transfer, and use of the material things of this earth. It was considered in the public interest to provide a stable framework for the settlement of disputes and a workable preventive law to keep those disputes at a minimum, e. g., the recording system was designed to provide notice; but only in the instances of intolerable conflict such as waste, nuisance, etc., did it appear necessary to tell the owner how he could use his property. The population explosion, our increasingly urban or suburban society, and the exhaustion of our natural resources have forced a more direct intervention by the state, representing the public interest, into the realm of private property.

The change which all of this has wrought in the law of property can be visualized best by a look at the diminishing fee simple. Today, the man who buys a tract in an urban area finds a smaller "bundle of sticks" than his counterpart of a century (or even a few decades) ago. Quite apart from private restrictive covenants and other controls previously discussed, he may find he can use his land for only one purpose, build only a certain type of structure, and occupy only a prescribed portion of the lot up to a designated height. The lawyer who examines the title and advises him in the purchase has done only half a job if he tells him the title is merchantable but neglects to point out problems of zoning, building ordinances, subdivision restrictions, etc.

It is the purpose of this chapter to point out those aspects of the public regulation of land use which are most important to a general knowledge of land law. This chapter includes sections on planning and zoning; control of subdivisions, streets, and parks; public development of land; and environmental controls.

SECTION 1.   PLANNING AND ZONING

Deep roots are among the glories of the law.   In an era of unprecedented scientific progress and continuous social, political, and economic ferment we are indeed fortunate that our legal system has so firm a base.   Except in periods of quiet reflection it is difficult to conceive of the distance we have travelled in a few decades.   Whole fields of law have been created—and then altered overnight; [1] other areas, formerly of importance, have faded to insignificance; and every phase of law has been vitally influenced by changing conditions.   Zoning furnishes a prime example of this last phenomenon.   As one authority puts it, "The years which have elapsed since . . . [1936] . . . have been eventful years for zoning in the courts.   These are the years in which zoning has really come into its own." [2]

Zoning is only one segment of the much broader area of community planning.   Indeed, one writer states, "Zoning is an implement of urban planning which seems old hat to a generation of professional city planners accustomed to talk in terms of slum clearance, low-cost housing, and such *ad hoc* programs as redevelopment authorities." [3]   However, it is an important tool in the hands of the community planners and a thorough knowledge of its capabilities is expected from the lawyer members of the planning team.

The roots of zoning go back to the Romans, who regulated the height of buildings, protected against street encroachments, and segregated some areas.   European cities were zoned to some extent before either England or United States adopted the practice.   In a sense, the ancient law of nuisance was a kind of zoning although admittedly of an unplanned sort and scarcely effective from a broad point of view.   Nevertheless, *sic utere tuo ut alienum non laedas* is still a forceful maxim in this area of the law.

"The late start of zoning in the United States has been attributed to many different causes, but the one most frequently mentioned, and perhaps most accurately, is the tendency of our courts down through the years to protect and preserve individual rights in property against the arbitrary control thereof by municipalities." [4]   Ironically enough, the American love of individ-

---

1. Witness the Internal Revenue Code of 1954 and subsequent changes, the rise of no-fault insurance, and the emerging environmental laws.

2. Yokley, Zoning Law and Practice 10 (2d ed. 1953).

3. Babcock, Classification and Segregation Among Zoning Districts, 1954 U.Ill.L.F. 186.

4. Note 2, supra, at 4.

ual freedom, and its protection by the courts, led, in the case of zoning, to ultimate loss to many individuals and to society as a whole.   Only as the courts realized that zoning, in the end, gave "the greatest amount of freedom and protection to the greatest number of people" did this implement of urban planning assume its present usefulness.[5]   A greater understanding of its potentialities is still called for; zoning has not yet outgrown its infantile repressions.   When one considers that the leading case in the field, Village of Euclid v. Ambler Realty Company,[6] was not decided until 1926, it is apparent that zoning's deep roots did not give rise to an early American harvest.

Clearly, planning is not the same as zoning, indeed you can have planning without zoning and zoning without planning, the latter usually resulting in a real hodgepodge, but they are closely related and go hand in hand.   The well-drafted enabling acts require the preparation of a master plan for the municipality before zoning ordinances can be effective.   At times, interim zoning ordinances must be passed to protect the municipality while the plan is being developed, but these interim ordinances may be void if the enabling act does not provide for this power.[7]   The planning may precede the actual zoning by months or years and, if it results in a land use map that shows the direction of urban growth and sketches in the zones which will ultimately be allowed, it may have considerable impact on the value of land in the community.   It may even raise troublesome questions as to merchantability of title where presently unzoned land lies in the path of a particular type of development.

A.   THE POWER TO ZONE

Zoning involves the regulation of the use and the density of occupation of real property.   It includes control of the activities permitted on the land, regulation of the size of buildings, and the location of structures in relation to side lines and street boundaries.   So extensive a regulation can be justified only un-

5. Not all commentators would agree that zoning is socially useful and serious doubts about its role are now being raised. See Siegan, Land Use Without Zoning (1972) for an attack on zoning principles as well as on the implementation of those principles.

6. 272 U.S. 365, 47 S.Ct. 114, 71 L. Ed. 303 (1926).

7. Kline v. City of Harrisburg, 362 Pa. 438, 68 A.2d 182 (1949); see also Miller v. Board of Public Works of City of Los Angeles, 195 Cal. 477, 234 P. 381, 38 A.L.R. 1479 (1925).

der the police power of the state. Therefore, the power to zone is vested in the legislature and can be exercised by it or by those municipal corporations (city, county, etc.) to which the power is delegated. This means that the state enabling act is the key to zoning authority and local ordinances which exceed its grant of power are void. In general, governmental restrictions on the use of private property can be imposed only if they are designed for the protection of the public health, safety, and welfare.

The basic power to zone was firmly established in Village of Euclid v. Ambler Realty Co., where the Supreme Court of the United States decided that a general attack on zoning ordinances as unconstitutional *per se* could not be sustained. The court gave this classic statement of the issue: "The question is the same under both Constitutions [United States and Ohio], namely . . . : Is the ordinance invalid, in that it violates the constitutional protection 'to the right of property in the appellee by attempted regulations under the guise of police power, which are unreasonable and confiscatory?' "[8] While the court gave a ringing "no" to this question, since the attack was on the power to zone as such, two years later in Nectow v. City of Cambridge [9] the same court made it clear that specific ordinances could be invalidated as applied to a complainant's land if the ordinance "has no foundation in reason and is a mere arbitrary or irrational exercise of power having no substantial relation to the public health, the public morals, the public safety or the public welfare in its proper sense."

Although this distinction seems to be a valid one, it is readily apparent that it opens the door to attacks on the constitutionality of any given ordinance as it applies to *X's* land. Since what is "arbitrary" and what constitutes "substantial relation to public health etc." is a matter on which reasonable men may differ, it is not surprising that the courts frequently upset the work of local legislative bodies and constitute themselves a kind of super zoning board of appeals. The United States Supreme Court has stayed out of the controversy since 1928, apparently feeling that the guidelines were well established, but the state supreme courts have been quite active. In some states judicial hostility has been sufficient to interfere with the functioning of the whole zoning process.[10]

A normally unarticulated premise of the power to zone is that Blackacre is being regulated under the police power, which

8. Note 6 supra at 386, 118, and 310.

9. 277 U.S. 183, 48 S.Ct. 447, 72 L.Ed. 842 (1928).

10. See Babcock, The Illinois Supreme Court and Zoning: A Study In Uncertainty, 15 U.Chi.L.Rev. 87 (1947).

requires no compensation,[11] rather than taken under the power of eminent domain, which requires the payment of fair market value for the property right transferred from private to public ownership. Since the principal value of land lies in its use, a certain amount of legal sophistry is involved in this distinction and the border line between the two governmental powers is a hazy gray area rather than a thin red line. Frequently, when a court invalidates a zoning ordinance as applied to X's land it seems to be saying that regulation has gone too far and become a taking, even though the exact rationale is couched in terms of unreasonableness or arbitrariness.[12] This is particularly true where the zoning, in effect, so restricts the landowner's use of Blackacre that the land loses its value.[13] It should help our thinking about zoning, and related police power controls, to realize that all regulation is, depending on the point from which you start, a kind of taking. Some is valid, some is not, but, unless the fee simple absolute is actually transferred from the landowner to the taking agency, the difference is likely to be one of degree rather than of kind.[14]

B. PRINCIPLES OF CLASSIFICATION [15]

The heart of the zoning ordinance is the decision by the local legislative body as to what uses will be permitted in the designated districts or zones. Stated another way, if the municipality must be divided according to classification, what are the proper determinates for the zones? It is fundamental that all property in like circumstances should be treated alike. The use restrictions should be general and uniform in a particular dis-

11. In zoning's infancy this premise was challenged and in Minnesota an attempt was made to compensate the landowner. See Burger v. City of St. Paul, 241 Minn. 285, 64 N.W.2d 73 (1954). This scheme was dropped both because of the cost factor and the difficulty of determining compensation.

12. See Indiana Toll Road Commission v. Jankovich, 244 Ind. 574, 193 N.E.2d 237 (1963), cert. denied 379 U.S. 487, 85 S.Ct. 493, 13 L.Ed.2d 439 (1965), holding invalid severe restrictions on the height of structures near airports (airport zoning).

13. Dooley v. Town Plan and Zoning Commission of Town of Fairfield, 151 Conn. 304, 197 A.2d 770 (1964), invalidating flood plain zoning as applied to X's land.

14. See Kusler, Open Space Zoning: Valid Regulation or Invalid Taking, 57 Minn.L.Rev. 1 (1972).

15. For a detailed statement see note 3, supra.

trict. Originally, zoning was viewed primarily as a device to keep residential areas free from commercial and industrial uses.[16] This was reflected in the practice of making all zones cumulative from residential "down" through industrial. Residences were generally permitted in commercial and industrial zones and most "higher" uses were permitted in the less limited areas. Thus the New Jersey court ordered a shopping center to be issued a permit in a light industrial zone although the local authorities had refused such permission.[17] There was a vigorous dissent by Mr. Justice Brennan, however, and there is growing evidence across the country that the old cumulative use districts are passé and that as zoning and planning techniques acquire maturity residential developments can be excluded from commercial and industrial districts.[18]

With the rise of non-cumulative zoning it became clear that specific land uses could be excluded from a wide range of zones to protect property values, increase the tax base of a community, and preserve land for industrial development. The courts continued to assert that land could not be zoned to protect established businesses from competition [19] but in many cases that was clearly an incidental effect of the classification. For example, in Forte v. Borough of Tenafly [20], the court said:

"The trial judge ruled, in effect, that since the avowed purpose of the ordinance was 'to protect the business district' it was invalid. We think that was too narrow a view. Zones are often created or uses therein curtailed in a manner which benefits other zones. The mere fact that this is one of the purposes of the ordinance does not make it invalid. An area desirable for industry may be zoned otherwise because industry would damage a nearby residential or business zone. Conversely, residential uses may be forbidden in or near industrial areas to encourage the full expansion of industrial plants therein without fear of complaint of nuisance. It is true that a municipality may not, by zoning or otherwise, exclude a particular use only because it will compete with an existing business or businesses (179 Duncan Ave. v. Jersey City, 122 N.J.L. 292, 5 A.2d 68

---

16. City of Aurora v. Burns, 319 Ill. 84, 149 N.E. 784 (1925).

17. Katobimar Realty Co. v. Webster, 20 N.J. 114, 118 A.2d 824 (1955).

18. Note 3 supra at 204–205.
See also Grubel v. MacLaughlin, 286 F.Supp. 24 (D.C. Virgin Islands, 1968) and Gruber v. Mayor and Township Committee of the Township of Raritan, 39 N.J. 1, 186 A.2d 489 (1962).

19. Pearce v. Village of Edina, 263 Minn. 553, 118 N.W.2d 659 (1962). See also Mandelker, Control of Competition as a Proper Purpose in Zoning, 14 Zoning Digest 33 (1962).

20. 106 N.J.Super. 346, 255 A.2d 804 (1969).

(1939)), but if the exclusion of competition happens to be an incident or effect of otherwise valid zoning, it does not invalidate it."

Of course, any specific exclusion from a given classification may be invalidated as unreasonable, arbitrary, or capricious and it is difficult to predict the outcome of any close case.[21] This is one reason for the large volume of litigation in the zoning field.

The two basic categories of classification are (1) types of land use and (2) intensity of land use. The traditional types include industrial, business and commercial, residential, agricultural, accessory uses and home occupations, and special uses. Each of these types can be further subdivided, e. g., light, medium, and heavy industrial or single family, multi-family, residential, etc. The courts have sustained all of these classifications and the only real difficulty is where the lines are to be drawn.

New concepts in classification are constantly being developed and the courts must scrutinize each one to see that it represents a reasonable exercise of the police power. For example, some ordinances attempt to exclude certain uses from a municipality. Favorite excludees are manufacturing uses, drive-in theatres, and trailer camps. Since these are not nuisances *per se,* serious questions arise as to the power to exclude. The ordinances have been sustained where the region as a whole can absorb the excluded use and leave the particular municipality residential in character,[22] but there are greater doubts if the exclusionary zoning is not based on regional planning and simply represents a desire to keep out an unwanted, but legitimate, use. Another new device for industrial areas is classification not in terms of products but by the degree of noise, dirt, smoke, and sewage pollution caused by the particular operation. This is called regulation by performance standards and the planners who advocate it would not restrict industry to a single, and often undesirable, land area, but would permit such use regardless of existing classifications if the use is not injurious to adjacent land or to the comprehensive plan of the city.[23] The courts have not

21. See Fogg v. City of South Miami, 183 So.2d 219 (Fla.App.1966), where the exclusion of a "drive-in operation" from a retail commercial district was held unreasonable. Cf. Vickers v. Township Committee of Gloucester Township, 37 N.J. 232, 181 A.2d 129 (1962), holding valid an ordinance excluding trailer camps from an entire municipality.

22. Duffcon Concrete Products, Inc. v. Borough of Cresskill, 1 N.J. 509, 64 A.2d 347 (1949).

23. See Horack and Nolan, Land Use Controls 81–84 (1955).

yet had much occasion to rule on this type of regulation but it is being used in several of the large metropolitan areas.[24]

Classification according to intensity of land use also has a well-developed judicial history with some newer concepts appearing in recent years. Of course, classification by intensity of use cuts across the type of land use and the two categories are not mutually exclusive. Thus, a residential zone will also have set-back lines and other restrictions in addition to the single-family, multi-family districting. The traditional regulations included set-back lines, side-yard lines, rear-yard lines, and height and area limitations. The bulk of these regulations apply only to residential land because it is usually conceded that, except for height restrictions, a maximum use of commercial and industrial property is permissible. The basic power to impose these restrictions was established in Gorieb v. Fox, where Mr. Justice Sutherland wrote that "front-yards afford room for lawns and trees, keeps the dwellings farther from the dust, noise, and fumes of the street, add to the attractiveness and comfort of a residential district, create a better home environment, and, by securing a greater distance between houses on opposite sides of the street, reduce the fire hazard; that the projection of a building beyond the front line of the adjacent dwellings cuts off light and air from them, and by interfering with the view of street corners, constitutes a danger in the operation of automobiles." [25]

The latest developments in zoning classification designed to regulate intensity of land use have to do with minimum lot size and minimum floor area. These requirements have common elements, although they are separate types of regulation. The minimum lot size is the older technique and originated as a reaction against the practice of real estate developers who squeezed as many lots as possible out of a given tract of land. From this genesis, however, the regulation has moved rather far afield and minimum lot sizes of one, two, three, and five acres have been sustained.[26] While such large tract zoning is not unreasonable *per se*, it may be unreasonable and hence void as applied to specific tracts in certain circumstances. This seems to be moving away from zoning solely to protect the public health, safety, and welfare and into the protection of the economic value of the land and close to regulation for aesthetic purposes. This does not necessarily mean that such controls are undesirable, but the change in purpose should be faced squarely by both the legisla-

24. See Haar, Land-Use Planning 210 (1971).

25. 274 U.S. 603, 609, 47 S.Ct. 675, 677, 71 L.Ed. 1228, 1231, 53 A.L.R. 1210 (1927).

26. Fischer v. Bedminster Tp., 11 N. J. 194, 93 A.2d 378 (1952).

tive and judicial branches of the government. It may be that land regulation of this type should be left to private restrictive covenants, put in by the subdivider or by agreements among adjoining owners, rather than enforced by the state's police power.

Minimum floor size carries this technique the next logical step by setting up detailed regulations as to the minimum size of dwellings. Lionshead Lake, Inc. v. Wayne Township [27] is the leading case sustaining this extension of the zoning power but a vigorous dissent felt such a provision "runs afoul of the fundamental principles of our form of government. It places an unnecessary and severe restriction upon the alienation of real estate. It is not necessary, it seems to me, in order to meet any possible threat to the general health and welfare of the community." [28] Some courts have refused to sustain minimum floor area requirements, but in Pennsylvania, after first invalidating such regulation, the court, four years later, sustained a similar ordinance and even gave its official nod to zoning for aesthetic purposes.[29] The traditional view, and still the stated position of most American courts, is that zoning for aesthetics is beyond the scope of the police power. This position is largely sabotaged, however, by the doctrine that if aesthetics is an incidental by-product rather than the main purpose there is no ground for objection.[30] More and more, the courts are recognizing that aesthetic standards are part and parcel of the planning and zoning objectives and clearly the individual municipalities are making beauty and symmetry a portion of their community goals.[31]

How far can classification based on aesthetics be extended? The outer limits seem to have been reached in Reid v. Architectural Board of Review of the City of Cleveland Heights.[32]   In

27. 10 N.J. 165, 89 A.2d 693 (1952).

28. Id. at 181 and 701. For some of the law review discussion see Haar, Zoning for Minimum Standards: the Wayne Township Case, 66 Harv. L.Rev. 1051 (1953); Nolan and Horack, How Small a House?—Zoning for Minimum Space Requirements, 67 Harv.L.Rev. 967 (1954); Haar, Wayne Township: Zoning for Whom?—In Brief Reply, 67 Harv. L.Rev. 986 (1954).

29. Medinger's Appeal, 377 Pa. 217, 104 A.2d 118 (1954); Bilbar Construction Co. v. Board of Adjustment, 393 Pa. 62, 141 A.2d 851 (1958).

30. In a case sustaining a billboard control law the court said: "Beauty may not be queen but she is not an outcast beyond the pale of protection or respect. She may at least shelter herself under the wing of safety, morality or decency." New York State Thruway Authority v. Ashley Motor Court, Inc., 10 N.Y.2d 151, 153, 176 N.E.2d 566, 569 (1961).

31. United Advertising Corp. v. Borough of Metuchen, 42 N.J. 1, 198 A.2d 447 (1964). See Dukeminier, Zoning for Aesthetic Objectives: A Reappraisal, 20 Law and Contemp. Prob. 218 (1955) and Note, Beyond the Eye of the Beholder: Aesthetics and Objectivity, 71 Mich.L.Rev. 1438 (1973).

32. 119 Ohio App. 67, 192 N.E.2d 74 (1963).

that case no residential structure could be built in a single-family residential district without prior approval of a board of architects, guided by loosely-stated design criteria. The purpose was obviously to maintain the architectural integrity of a conventional area filled with traditional, two to two-and-one-half story homes. The applicant wished to build a modern, single story home of unconventional design but was denied permission. The court sustained the denial of the application, stressing that such a dwelling might be an interesting home in a different environment but that its presence in this district would be a detriment to existing homeowners. A strong dissenting opinion argued that the permit was denied exclusively for aesthetic considerations, unrelated to requirements of public health, safety, or welfare and that this could not be done under Ohio law. However, similar ordinances have been upheld in Missouri [33] and Wisconsin [34]. On the other hand, Illinois invalidated an ordinance of this general type for failure to prescribe adequate standards.[35]

As in the case of minimum lot size and minimum floor area classifications, some critics believe this aesthetic control should not be exercised by government under the police power but should be left to private land use controls. Even if the device of restrictive covenants is used similar problems can arise. In Donoghue v. Prynnwood Corporation,[36] the court held that a covenant requiring a developer to approve plans should be construed as meaning that he must act reasonably and that he had unreasonably withheld approval of a modern flat roof design.[37] It should be noted that if the goal of the zoning ordinance is conformity not merely with existing structures, as in *Reid* and related cases, but also with local historic design, judicial reaction is likely to be even more favorable.[38]

Throughout legal history changes in the law can be seen to have had consequences not visualized by those who were responsible for the change. The Statute of Uses, you will recall, was a prime example. Designed as a simple revenue measure

33. State ex rel. Stoyanoff v. Berkeley, 458 S.W.2d 305 (Mo.1970).

34. State ex rel. Saveland Park Holding Corp. v. Wieland, 269 Wis. 262, 69 N.W.2d 217 (1955).

35. Pacesetter Homes v. Village of Olympia Fields, 104 Ill.App.2d 218, 244 N.E.2d 369 (1968).

36. 356 Mass. 703, 255 N.E.2d 326 (1970).

37. See Annotation, Validity and Construction of Restrictive Covenant Requiring Consent to Construction on Lot, 40 A.L.R.3d 864 (1971).

38. City of Santa Fe v. Gamble-Skogmo, Inc., 73 N.M. 410, 389 P.2d 13 (1964). See also Comment, Public Historic Preservation in Texas, 49 Tex.L.Rev. 267 (1971).

for a financially-strapped King Henry VIII, it altered the face of the law of land. Zoning has proved to be no exception to this historical principle. The zoning enthusiasts saw the police power as a reasonable way to regulate land use with a minimum of interference with the rights of private property. They knew that zoning would result in the reallocation of land values but this would occur in any case through the normal operation of the market and was simply one more factor to be considered in the development of urban areas. Zoning was designed to eliminate incompatible land uses and to allow planning and orderly growth to replace the chaotic patterns of the nineteenth century. To a considerable extent these goals were realized, but by the late 1960's the nation, at long last alert to the evils of racial discrimination and the problems of "the other America", discovered that zoning had a largely unforeseen side effect. It could be used to discriminate against those members of society who could not afford to live in areas classified for large lots and minimum floor areas. Of course, zoning was only one facet of discrimination in housing but it was based on the police power of the state and was therefore obnoxious to a legal system based on equality of opportunity.

Courts which had previously recognized the validity of large lot classifications, on community planning and aesthetic grounds, had second thoughts when the exclusionary character of such zoning was explicitly raised. One of the best examples is to be found in Pennsylvania, a state which in the 'fifties had embraced large lot classifications. In Appeal of Kit-Mar Builders, Inc.,[39] the court held an ordinance requiring one, two, and three acre lots unconstitutional. Said the court: "We decided in *National Land*[40] that a scheme of zoning that has an exclusionary purpose or result is not acceptable in Pennsylvania. We do not intend to say, of course, that minimum lot size requirements are inherently unreasonable. Planning considerations and other interests can justify reasonably varying minimum lot sizes in given areas of a community. 'At some point along the spectrum, however, the size of lots ceases to be a concern requiring public regulation and becomes simply a matter of private preference.' 419 Pa. at 524, 215 A.2d at 608. The two and three acre minimums imposed in this case are no more reasonable than the four acre requirements struck down in *National Land*. As we pointed out in *National Land*, there are obvious advantages to the residents of a community in having houses built on four- or three-acre lots. However, minimum lot

39. 439 Pa. 466, 268 A.2d 765 (1970).

40. National Land and Investment Co. v. Easttown Township Bd. of Adjustment, 419 Pa. 504, 215 A.2d 597 (1965).

sizes of the magnitude required by this ordinance are a great deal larger than what should be considered as a *necessary* size for the building of a house, and are therefore not the proper subjects of public regulation. As a matter of fact, a house can fit quite comfortably on a one acre lot without being the least bit cramped. Absent some extraordinary justification, a zoning ordinance with minimum lot sizes such as those in this case is completely unreasonable."

The Pennsylvania court did not rule out all large lot zoning but found it to be invalid under the circumstances and particularly so in the absence of regional planning since this might result in total exclusion of minority and lower income groups from a community. They refused to allow a township to use the police power to "keep out people, rather than make community improvements". The same court also held unconstitutional an ordinance which made no provision for apartments in the Philadelphia suburb of Nether Providence Township.[41]

The battle has now been joined nationwide and the full implications of exclusionary zoning must be faced.[42] This unforeseen (originally) and unwanted side effect of zoning does not argue against all zoning but it does go to the reasonableness of the classification and will require a re-thinking of much residential zoning.[43] It will probably give additional impetus to regional planning since the courts will wish to be assured that ample provision is being made for all groups in society.[44]

The problems of exclusionary zoning may be the tip of an iceberg, as zoning drifts further from its original anchor in nuisance theory and becomes, quite openly, a part of modern social planning. Recent cases in New Jersey, long a pacesetter in zoning law, have held that "the essence of zoning is to provide a balanced and well-ordered scheme of activity." [45]

If the goal of zoning is to provide a balanced community the door is open for controls undreamed of by the old zoning

41. Appeal of Girsh, 437 Pa. 237, 263 A.2d 395 (1970).

42. LaRussa, Exclusionary Zoning: An Overview, 47 Tulane L.Rev. 1056 (1973); Brigham and Bostwick, Exclusionary Zoning Practices: An Examination of the Current Controversy, 25 Vand.L.Rev. 1111 (1972).

43. See Allred v. City of Raleigh, 7 N.C.App. 602, 173 S.E.2d 533 (1970), reversed 277 N.C. 530, 178 S.E.2d

432 (1971); Aloi and Goldberg, Racial and Economic Exclusionary Zoning: The Beginning of the End? 1971 Urban Law Annual 9.

44. Note, Regional Planning—Zoning—Minimum Lot Size and the General Welfare, 58 Cornell L.Rev. 1035 (1973).

45. J. D. Construction Corp. v. Board of Adjustment of Freehold, 119 N. J.Super. 140, 147, 290 A.2d 452, 456 (1972).

pioneers. This was clearly illustrated in Golden v. Ramapo,[46] where the New York Court of Appeals upheld an ordinance even though the development of land could be prevented for a period of up to eighteen years. While the court conceded that land could not be *permanently* restricted without there being an unconstitutional taking, it characterized the ordinance as a *temporary* restriction and concluded the land could be put to a reasonable use within a reasonable time. By controlling development in this way the planners achieved a temporal balance that may well be wise but at a considerable cost to the landowner's traditional rights. It is unclear how many courts will go this far [47] but *Ramapo* indicates the new direction of planning for a balanced community. There is a strong temptation to explore this balanced community concept at some length but it lies beyond the purview of this basic text. The important point is that the power to zone is expanding and the next decade is likely to see major developments in this area, comparable to the previous decade's alterations in landlord-tenant law.[48] One commentator sketches the nature of this looming development as follows:

"Recent New Jersey judicial decisions have propounded the 'balanced community' as a standard of validity of zoning ordinances. The 'balanced community' standard is appealing to many planners in spite of the danger of ambiguity arising out of the diverse range of its meanings: (e. g., socio-economic balance, fiscal balance, ecological balance, regional balance, and temporal balance). Judicial acceptance of the 'balanced community' standard for zoning law validity would emphasize the need to evaluate the merits of competing land uses. It would enhance the importance of the planning process because the validity of zoning laws would depend on the *process* by which the merits of competing land uses are evaluated. Adoption of the 'community balance' standard would constitute judicial acceptance of planning principles of rational land-use allocation as criteria by which this evaluation is to be made." [49]

46. 30 N.Y.2d 359, 334 N.Y.S.2d 138, 285 N.E.2d 291 (1972). See Note, A Zoning Program For Phased Growth: Ramapo Township's Time Controls on Residential Development, 47 N.Y.U.L.Rev. 723 (1972).

47. Apparently New Jersey would not, as see Lomarch Corp. v. Mayor of Englewood, 51 N.J. 108, 237 A.2d 881 (1968), where the court held that an Official Map Act providing for a "freeze" on development of land for a *one-year* period would be an unconstitutional deprivation of property unless the owner was compensated for the "option" price of the "temporary taking".

48. See pp. 235 to 238 supra.

49. The interested student should read all of Rose, The Courts and the Balanced Community: Recent Trends in New Jersey Zoning Law, 39 J. of Am. Inst. of Planners, 265-276 (1973).

C. ALTERATIONS IN THE ZONING PLAN

If the basic planning is carefully done and if the zoning districts are established with wisdom and foresight, there will be relatively little need for alterations until major changes occur in community development. The first two "ifs" may not be satisfied and in recent years urban growth has been phenomenal. It follows that alterations are frequent and unless carefully controlled they can emasculate the original purpose of land use planning. These alterations are normally made by way of amendments, exceptions, and variances.

First, however, we should note that the zoning districts do not start life with one hundred per cent effectiveness. Only if the districts contain raw land can the use designation be fully enforced. Inevitably, a grocery store or a garage will be operating in a residential zone when the ordinance is adopted. To order its immediate elimination would raise questions of political expediency as well as constitutional power. The original assumption was that any attempt to remove nonconforming uses would be a deprivation of property without due process of law. Hence, they were allowed to remain islands of nonconformity in a sea of uniformity. Typically, they were hedged about with regulations which prohibited any extension of activity, any alteration other than towards conformity, any rebuilding if destroyed by fire, etc., and any renewal of the use if the premises were once abandoned.[50] The planners felt that this tight rein would soon cause the disappearance of the non-conforming use, but since they were left as monopolies in the areas they served there has been no rapid drying on the vine. This has led to the amortization of nonconforming uses (called time zoning) and many ordinances now require elimination of such uses within a specified period of time, depending on the nature of the use. Such legislation has been sustained as a reasonable exercise of the police power.[51]

In considering the validity, and indeed the advisability, of time zoning you must note that there are three very different types of nonconforming uses: (a) a nonconforming use in a con-

50. See Note, 102 U.Pa.L.Rev. 91 (1953).

51. City of Los Angeles v. Gage, 127 Cal.App.2d 538, 274 P.2d 34 (1954). This case involved elimination, in five years, of a nonconforming use (plumbing) but not of a nonconforming building.

For a contrary view, see Hoffman v. Kinealy, 389 S.W.2d 745 (Mo.1965), holding invalid an amortization ordinance requiring termination of use of a vacant lot for open storage of lumber within six years.

forming structure, (b) a nonconforming use in a nonconforming structure, and (c) a nonconforming use not involving a structure. It is easier to prohibit a specific use if the structure can still be utilized than it is to tell the owner that he must remove or alter his building within a set period of time. There is no quick solution to this problem and we shall have nonconforming uses with us for a long period, even if time zoning is on the statute books.

Since the zoning ordinance must be passed by the local legislative body, it follows that amendments may be made by the same group when required by changing conditions. It is not difficult to visualize the problems involved in the amending process. The original plan and the resulting ordinance and zoning map were supposedly based on a thorough study of the municipality's needs and represent a comprehensive scheme for land use. Amendments tend, however, to be the result of specific pressures brought by individual owners who feel the constricting force of the regulations. They are frequently passed without any real consideration of their effect on the comprehensive plan and thus cause a slow deterioration of the area.

In theory, an amendment is valid only if there was a significant error in the original plan or if the community has changed substantially since its adoption. If these conditions cannot be established, the amendment is unreasonable and a court should declare it void as "spot zoning", i. e., the conferring of a special benefit on a small tract without commensurate benefit to the community.[52] In fact, many amendments are void by judicial standards but if they are not challenged by the city or by affected owners they have the force of law. Moreover, even if challenged the amendments may have a presumption of validity which makes the court reluctant to interfere. What looks very much like "spot zoning", even to dissenting judges, is often sustained because "a court is without authority to substitute its own judgment for that vested by the statutes in a zoning authority." [53]

While amendments are made by the local legislative body (county or township board of commissioners, city council, etc.), its action is normally preceded by the recommendation of a professional planning official to the plan commission, an administrative agency established to develop a comprehensive plan for the community and to maintain its essential integrity when changes are sought. The plan commission (composed of lay citizens) holds public hearings, after proper notice, and sub-

---

52. See Horack and Nolan, Land Use Controls 53 (1955).

53. Bartram v. Zoning Commission of City of Bridgeport, 136 Conn. 89, 96, 68 A.2d 308, 312 (1949).

mits its findings to the legislative body for action. In the event of a court challenge, the ultimate result may depend on presumptions of validity and burden of proof. As indicated in the preceding paragraph, many courts do presume validity for the legislative act and thus sustain amendments against the judges' own better judgment. Other courts take a contrary view and put a heavier burden on the local legislature. In Roseta v. County of Washington,[54] the court found an amendment to be "spot zoning" and stated their view of the proper test. "In Smith v. County of Washington . . . we also laid down the principle that once the Board has established a zone and thereafter a change in character of the use is authorized, the usual presumption of legislative regularity is not recognized and in such a case the Board carries the burden of proving that there has been a change in the neighborhood in order to justify the rezoning of a small tract as an amendment in keeping with the comprehensive plan." This view may more readily allow the court to substitute its judgment for that of the local legislature but it has the merit of requiring the plan commission to build a strong case for amendments, justifying them in relation to the comprehensive plan, rather than yielding, willy nilly, to local pressure groups. Given the practical operation of most local legislatures in the zoning field, there seems little reason to accord zoning ordinances the normal presumption of legislative validity granted to acts of Congress and to statutes of state legislature. The courts should exercise restraint, lest they usurp the zoning function, but it seems fair for them to put the burden on the proponents for change in an existing plan.

Amendments involve a legislative change in the ordinance itself; variances and exceptions are "safety valves" built into the original ordinance to give flexibility to meet hardship cases. "An 'exception' in a zoning ordinance is one allowable when facts and conditions detailed in the ordinance, as those upon which an exception may be permitted, are found to exist. But zoning ordinances usually provide . . . for another kind of dispensation, also permitted by statute, by which a 'variance' from the terms of the ordinance may be authorized in cases where a literal enforcement of its provisions would result in unnecessary hardship."[55] The exceptions, then, are spelled out in the ordinance; churches, parks, schools, electric sub-stations, etc., are permitted in otherwise residential districts. There may even be specific exceptions for height and area requirements. Since they are specifically stated, the problem is mainly one of

54. 254 Or. 161, 458 P.2d 405 (1969).   55. Application of Devereux Foundation, Inc., 351 Pa. 478, 483, 41 A.2d 744, 746 (1945).

checking the proposed use against the ordinance to see if it fits the pattern.

Variances cause more difficulty than exceptions because they cannot be set forth in *haec verba* but must be left to the limited discretion of some administrative body. This body, variously called zoning board of appeals, board of adjustment, etc.,[56] acts on petition from the aggrieved property owner who alleges that he will suffer unnecessary hardship unless he is granted relief. The board has no power to amend the ordinance since that is a legislative function, but it may reach much the same result by granting a variance which will leave the form the same but change the substance of the zones. Variances are usually of two kinds: use variance and height, bulk, and area variance. The former is more destructive of the comprehensive plan since it may allow a grocery store in a residential area, a light industry in a commercial zone, etc., and in recent years many municipalities have refused to allow use variances by zoning boards of appeal and have narrowly restricted the scope of other variances as well.[57]

"In order to support a variance, it must be found that: (1) No diminution in value of surrounding properties would be suffered. (2) Granting the permit would be of benefit to the public interest. (3) Denial of the permit would result in unnecessary hardship to the owner seeking it. (4) By granting the permit substantial justice will be done. (5) The use must not be contrary to the spirit of the ordinance."[58] These are highsounding words and undoubtedly many zoning boards of appeal try to follow them, but the record also shows that such boards, like trial courts, are always at the point of incandescence and that theory bends in the search for the right solution.[59] Countless variations are made which result in "spot zoning" in fact, if not in theory, and the courts are helpless to police them all. Of course, the board's discretion cuts both ways and variances are frequently denied to the anguish of the petitioner. Courts hold that no person has a legal right to a variance and will not interfere to order relief for the petitioner unless the board's

56. These bodies should not be confused with the plan commission which is responsible for the comprehensive plan and for amendments to it.

57. Ziman v. Village of Glencoe, 132 Ill.App.2d 399, 270 N.E.2d 537 (1971).

58. Gelinas v. City of Portsmouth, 97 N.H. 248, 250, 85 A.2d 896, 898 (1952).

59. Anderson, The Board of Zoning Appeals—Villain or Victim? 13 Syracuse L.Rev. 353 (1962); Dukeminier and Stapleton, The Zoning Board of Adjustment: A Case Study in Misrule, 50 Ky.L.J. 273 (1952).

action appears to be unreasonable, whimsical, capricious, or arbitrary.[60]

D. FLEXIBLE ZONING

One permanent problem of zoning is its inflexibility. It tends to impress a straitjacket on the community that may interfere with the rational growth it hopes to promote. It can lead to overly segregated land uses and to residential areas that look like a collection of cheese boxes on a raft. Alterations in the plan can be made by amendments, exceptions, and variances but these are often cumbersome tools and the planners desire greater flexibility than they afford. This desire has led to such techniques as special uses, contract zoning, floating zones, and planned unit developments (PUD). Each of these techniques has run into difficulties with the courts, which frequently believe they allow too much administrative discretion and too little opportunity for judicial review to protect the rights of the individual property owner.

"The special use is a relatively new method of land use control. Zoning ordinances embodying this technique retain the usual residential, commercial, and industrial zones, specifying the uses permitted in each zone. For each zone, however, special uses are also established which are permitted within the zone only if approved by the zoning board or the governing legislative body." [61] The planners know they may someday wish to provide for the special use but they are not yet prepared to draw the actual lines and show where it will be. This technique gives notice to landowners that eventually a different use may be allowed in their zone [62] but doesn't spell out the details. When the blow falls, the landowner may well challenge the legality of the technique as well as the reasonableness of its employment in the specific case.[63] Illinois sustained the general legality

60. Pendergast v. Board of Appeals of Barnstable, 331 Mass. 555, 120 N.E.2d 916 (1954).

61. Kotrich v. County of DuPage, 19 Ill.2d 181, 166 N.E.2d 601 (1960).

62. Among the special uses may be colleges and universities, public outdoor recreational centers, rest homes, hospitals and sanitariums, planned developments of not less than 40 acres, and "public service uses" such as electric and telephone substations, filtration plants, and fire and police stations.

63. Assuming the validity of the special use device in principle, there remains the possibility that the

of special uses, even though the state enabling act did not specifically provide for them, but there was a vigorous dissent. The late Judge House wrote: "From the standpoint of zoning enthusiasts and administrators the special use device provides a flexible method disposing of troublesome 'unique' situations. On the other hand, its use in such cases as here (recreation center) is the further limiting of the rights of ownership of property under the guise of the much tortured and misused police power." Iowa, on the other hand, adopted the position of the Illinois dissent [64] and the special use remains a controversial device. On principle, the special use would appear to be a logical extension of the power to amend but it would seem desirable to include provision for it in the state enabling act, where proper standards and safeguards can be spelled out in some detail.

Contract zoning is even more controversial than the special use and for much the same reason. The planner needs it for flexibility; the landowner may see it as a further infringement on his rights, not specifically authorized by the enabling act. Anyone who has served on a plan commission knows the problem well.[65] A landowner wishes an amendment to the zoning ordinance so he can build a handsome shopping center. He produces scale models, detailed land use maps, etc. which show a center with all of the attractiveness of a college campus and far exceeding the minimum requirements of the ordinance. The amendment is approved and he builds a macadam jungle, barely meeting the guidelines of the zoning classification. Had he kept his promise he would have produced a community asset and the amendment would have been justified; he did not and "spot zoning" has destroyed the integrity of the comprehensive plan.

Contract zoning puts teeth into the amendment by requiring the developer to enter into restrictive covenants (with the benefit running to other land owned by the municipality) that provide for setback lines, landscaping, open space, etc. that exceed the requirements of the ordinance. It is a combination of zoning and private restrictive covenants that provides for "fine honing" not otherwise available to the planner. But is it legal? Can it be misused to force the developer into decisions he would not otherwise be required to make, a kind of duress? Does it

---

standards or their application may be invalid. See Pioneer Trust and Savings Bank v. County of McHenry, 41 Ill.2d 77, 241 N.E.2d 454 (1968), holding that lack of "public necessity" was not a sufficient basis for denial of a permit for a mobile home park and sales enterprise to an applicant who would suffer "substantial economic loss" from the denial.

64. Depue v. City of Clinton, 160 N. W.2d 860 (Iowa, 1968).

65. The author served for six years on the Champaign Plan Commission.

encourage "spot zoning" by allowing the local legislature to make amendments it would otherwise deny and which are contrary to the original plan for the area? Not surprisingly, the courts have given inconsistent answers to these questions when the frequently used device has been subjected to judicial challenge. In Sylvania Electric Products, Inc. v. City of Newton,[66] the Supreme Judicial Court of Massachusetts sustained the use of "contract zoning", in a case where it seemed justified on the facts, but it noted decisions to the contrary and there was a strong dissent. Other courts have sustained it by indulging in distinctions that seem to be unrealistic. For example, Wisconsin sustained restrictions when they were challenged by a subsequent owner of the burdened land, reasoning: "We hold that when a city itself makes an agreement with a landowner to rezone the contract is invalid; this is contract zoning. However, when the agreement is made by others than the city to conform the property in a way or manner which makes it acceptable for the requested rezoning and the city is not committed to rezone, it is not contract zoning in the true sense and does not vitiate the zoning if it is otherwise valid." [67] This sounds sensible but it may be relatively easy to get the developer to work out restrictions with private parties with the implicit knowledge that only when this is done will the amendment be granted. At the very least the courts should keep this technique under careful scrutiny.[68]

The so-called "floating zone" is a device not unlike the special use. In the latter a number of special uses are listed in the ordinance but their exact location is left open; in the former only one use may be involved but its location is left to "float" until such time as the planners feel it should be "anchored" in one of the existing zones. It has also been called "flexible selective zoning", perhaps a more descriptive term which discloses both its virtues and its vices. In Eves v. Zoning Board of Adjustment of Lower Gwynedd Township,[69] the Supreme Court of Pennsylvania held the device *ultra vires* the state enabling act, after 300 landowners in an "A" residential zone objected to anchoring a limited industrial district in their zone. Said the court: "The adoption of a procedure whereby it is decided which areas of land will eventually be zoned 'F–1' Limited Industrial Districts on a case by case basis patently admits that at the point of enactment of ordinance 28 there was no orderly plan of

66. 344 Mass. 428, 183 N.E.2d 118 (1962).

67. State ex rel. Zupancic v. Schimenz, 46 Wis.2d 22, 174 N.W.2d 533 (1970).

68. Comment, the Use and Abuse of Contract Zoning, 12 U.C.L.A.L.Rev. 897 (1965).

69. 401 Pa. 211, 164 A.2d 7 (1960).

particular land use for the community. Final determination under such a scheme would expressly await solicitation by individual landowners, thus making the planned land use of the community dependent upon its development. In other words, the development itself would become the plan, which is manifestly the antithesis of zoning 'in accordance with a comprehensive plan.'   .   .   .

"If the legislature contemplated such a novel scheme of zoning, withdrawing as it does a close standard of court review in the very delicate area of protecting property rights, and shifting as it does the focus from planned land use to individual solicitation, we are convinced it would have said so in more clear and exact terms than are found anywhere in the enabling legislation."

Other courts have reacted favorably to the "floating zone" technique [70] and it is difficult to see any essential difference between this device and the actual use of the amendment process in many states where changes are rather freely made in existing zones under the pressure of rapid community development. At least in the "floating zone" cases the landowners have notice that such a zone might come to rest in their area, whereas they are frequently lulled into a false sense of security by the more traditional use of the amendment process. Again, as in the case of the special use, it would be desirable to provide for the inclusion of this technique in the state enabling act. The real danger may be in the use of ad hoc methods dreamed up by the planners and employed without the authorization of the state legislature.

The planned unit development (PUD) is a less controversial tool than the three just discussed but it too is designed to give greater flexibility to the planners. It was clearly described by the Pennsylvania Supreme Court in Cheney v. Village of New Hope, Inc.[71] "Under traditional concepts of zoning the task of determining the type, density and placement of buildings which should exist within any given zoning district devolves upon the local legislative body. In order that this body might have to speak only infrequently on the issue of municipal planning and zoning, the local legislature usually enacts detailed requirements for the type, size and location of buildings within each given zoning district, and leaves the ministerial task of enforcing these regulations to an appointed zoning administrator, with

70. Huff v. Board of Zoning Appeals, 214 Md. 48, 133 A.2d 83 (1957); Rodgers v. Village of Tarrytown, 302 N.Y. 115, 96 N.E.2d 731 (1951); see Haar and Hering, The Lower Gwynedd Township Case: Too Flexible Zoning or an Inflexible Judiciary? 74 Harv.L.Rev. 1552 (1961).

71. 429 Pa. 626, 241 A.2d 81 (1968).

another administrative body, the zoning board of adjustment, passing on individual deviations from the strict district requirements, deviations known commonly as variances and special exceptions. At the same time, the overall rules governing the dimensions, placement, etc. of primarily public additions to ground, e. g., streets, sewers, playgrounds, are formulated by the local legislature through the passage of subdivision regulations. These regulations are enforced and applied to individual lots by an administrative body usually known as the planning commission.

"This general approach to zoning fares reasonably well so long as development takes place on a lot-by-lot basis, and so long as no one cares that the overall appearance of the municipality resembles the design achieved by using a cookie cutter on a sheet of dough. However, with the increasing popularity of large scale residential developments, particularly in suburban areas, it has become apparent to many local municipalities that land can be more efficiently used, and developments more aesthetically pleasing, if zoning regulations focus on density requirements rather than on specific rules for each individual lot. Under density zoning, the legislature determines what percentage of a particular district must be devoted to open space, for example, and what percentage used for dwelling units. The task of filling in the particular district with real houses and real open spaces then falls upon the planning commission usually working in conjunction with an individual large scale developer. See Chrinko v. South Brunswick Twp., Planning Bd., 77 N.J.Super. 594, 187 A.2d 221 (1963). The ultimate goal of this so-called density or cluster concept of zoning is achieved when an entire self-contained little community is permitted to be built within a zoning district, with the rules of density controlling not only the relation of private dwellings to open space, but also the relation of homes to commercial establishments such as theaters, hotels, restaurants, and quasi-commercial uses such as schools and churches. The present controversy before this Court involves a frontal attack upon one of these zoning districts, known in the trade as a Planned Unit Development (hereinafter PUD)."

The court sustained the use of PUD as a necessary weapon in the planning arsenal and some states have enacted statutes specifically authorizing planned unit development ordinances.[72] It has been viewed by many experts as one of the most useful recent developments in flexible zoning.[73] Other far reaching

---

72. See, e. g., N.J.Rev.Stat. § 40:55–54 (1967).

73. Krasnowiecki, Planned Unit Development: A Challenge to Estab-lished Theory and Practice of Land Use Control, 114 U.Pa.L.Rev. 47 (1965).

reforms are now under serious discussion in the planning field but they are beyond the scope of this basic text.[74]

E.   ENFORCEMENT AND REMEDIES

The legislative, administrative, and judicial procedures involved in zoning are of prime importance to the property lawyer. A large number of governmental units are involved in an understanding of this procedure: the state legislature must pass the enabling act; the city or county planning commission must develop the master plan and suggest ordinances and amendments to the local legislative body; that body must pass the ordinances; the zoning board of appeals must hear petitions for variances and special exceptions; the administrative official (typically the city engineer) charged with enforcement must issue building permits if the construction proposal complies with the ordinance; and the courts must occasionally be called upon to interpret the ordinance, to aid in enforcement, or to excuse the individual from compliance.

Usually the zoning regulations are enforced by proceeding directly against the owner or user of the land.[75] The enforcement may be by the governmental body charged with the duty of making the regulations or by private individuals who benefit from them.[76] The former will use (1) prosecution for violation, (2) direct police action, (3) denial of required permits, and (4)

74. See the three tentative drafts of the American Law Institute's Model Land Development Code: T.D. No. 1 (1968); T.D. No. 2 (1970); and T.D. No. 3 (1971).

75. Many writers believe that the primary liability should be on the builder or contractor. "Zoning laws are almost universally enforced against the wrong people and in the wrong way. . . . We should license building contractors. The terms of the license should include authority for its revocation in case of repeated violations and should require the posting of bonds for the faithful compliance with the zoning law. . . . With such provisions . . . the city would then have the authority to proceed against those persons who because of their training and business are the very ones which the public expects to know the law and comply with it. It would prevent the builder or contractor from proceeding without a permit because of his awareness of the city's reluctance to prosecute the land owner." Horack, 1954 Planning p. 146. American Society of Planning Officials.

76. For a detailed discussion of these matters see Graham, Legislative, Administrative and Judicial Procedure in Zoning, 1954 U.Ill.L.F. 242.

injunction. The latter may invoke (1) a complaint resulting in prosecution, (2) a complaint to an administrative officer or board, (3) mandamus directed to an administrative officer, and (4) injunction. This sounds like an impressive array of remedies but while they are used in extreme cases and particularly in the larger cities, they tend to be ignored to a large extent. The violator-owner is not considered a criminal and the cost of alteration often seems an excessive penalty. This causes public support for proper enforcement to lag and prosecution is thus politically inexpedient. Fortunately, most people comply with the ordinance and official action then becomes unnecessary.

The other side of the coin is represented by the owner who desires to use his land for a prohibited purpose but does not want to violate the ordinance. If he fails to obtain an amendment, variance, or special exception, he may attack the legality of the ordinance itself. Prior to the *Euclid* case the constitutionality of the entire ordinance was frequently challenged, either defensively as an answer to attempted enforcement or offensively by way of injunction against enforcement, declaratory judgment, mandamus against the proper official, etc., but this route offers little hope today. The individual's best chance is to contend that the ordinance is arbitrary or unreasonable as applied to his particular parcel. Even here, the chances are not very good since he must prove that the burden on his land is different or more intense than that imposed on other land similarly situated. Occasionally, however, the courts sustain such an attack in flagrant cases and this is sufficient to keep the spark of hope alive in all aggrieved property owners.[77]

SECTION 2. CONTROL OF SUBDIVISIONS, STREETS, AND PARKS

Some public regulation of land use is the only alternative to planless growth, inevitably resulting in urban chaos. Zoning will help solve many of the problems, but it is only one tool in the planner's kit. As we have seen, zoning is the segregation of the community into districts, classified by use types and by in-

---

77. This spark of hope frequently flares into extensive litigation. For a discussion of the problems see Krasnowiecki, Zoning Litigation and the New Pennsylvania Procedures, 120 U. of Pa.L.Rev. 1029 (1972).

tensity of land utilization. This does not control the size, construction, and use of streets, alleys, and walks, the platting of subdivisions, or the location of parks. Clearly, all of these items require careful planning and unless they are integrated into the zoning scheme the effectiveness of the whole process will be seriously impaired. Moreover, since much of a community's growth occurs on the periphery, outside the corporation limits, the subdivisions may set the standard of expansion without any public control at all. To meet this last problem, some states which do not allow a city to zone beyond its corporate limits will allow subdivision regulation of contiguous territory within a reasonable distance.[78]

Subdivision regulation and similar land use controls have received much the same treatment from the courts as that accorded to zoning. The enabling act is typically recognized as a valid exercise of the police power of the state and it is essential only that the legislature declare the governing principle and policy; the implementation may be left to the agency set up to administer the law.[79] However, the courts will scrutinize the application of the regulations in specific situations and may upset the ruling of the local administrative agency if it is based on a misapplication of law.[80] The bulk of the subdivision regulation relates to streets, alleys, sidewalks, gutters, curbs, etc., and the courts have allowed considerable leeway in these areas so that subdividers are frequently forced to dedicate portions of their land to public use in ways which approach the border line between the police power and the power of eminent domain.[81]

The zeal for subdivision regulation can go too far, however. When a village tried to require an owner to dedicate at least one-

78. See Ill.Rev.Stat., ch. 24, § 53-2 (1959) (one and one-half miles beyond the corporate limits). In 1961, the General Assembly granted the cities power to zone as well, in this one and one-half mile area, providing no county zoning was in effect.

79. Mansfield and Swett, Inc. v. Town of West Orange, 120 N.J.L. 145, 198 A. 225 (1938).

80. Id. at 159 and 233. In the Mansfield and Swett case a building permit was refused by the town because most of the landowners in the area objected to lower priced housing coming into a very exclusive subdivision. The court reversed, saying: "This evinces a palpable misconception of the law. The standard is not the advantage or detriment to particular neighboring landowners, but rather the effect upon the entire community as a social, economic and political unit." It would appear that such regulation should be taken care of by private covenants rather than by relying on public controls.

81. Ayres v. City Council of Los Angeles, 34 Cal.2d 31, 207 P.2d 1 (1949). The dissent in this case felt that the forced dedication of land to the city was based on a doctrine of "stateism" which he found abhorrent. To him, the case represented a taking rather than a regulating of property. The difficulty, of course, is that all regulation involves a taking of sorts since it cuts down on one basic attribute of property, i. e., use.

tenth of an acre for each acre of land in the subdivision for school purposes and without compensation, the court held the ordinance void and granted a writ of mandamus compelling the corporate authorities to issue the necessary permit without any dedication.[82] The court said: "The developer of a subdivision may be required to assume [only] those costs which are specifically and uniquely attributable to his activity and which would otherwise be cast upon the public." This test is easier to state than to apply, but it does furnish some guide as to how far such regulations can go. The court, in the same case, asked the key question: "Is it reasonable that a subdivider should be required under the guise of a police power regulation to dedicate a portion of his property to public use; or does this amount to a veiled exercise of the power of eminent domain and a confiscation of private property behind the defense of police regulations?"

In 1962, Illinois had invalidated a subdivision ordinance requiring dedication of land for park purposes, as discussed in the preceding paragraph. By 1971, the tide had turned and California was holding such ordinances valid.[83] Said the Supreme Court of California:

"Many of the issues raised by Associated have been discussed in the cases and law reviews.[84] The clear weight of authority upholds the constitutionality of statutes similar to section 11546. While Illinois has held an ordinance requiring a subdivider to dedicate land for park purposes to be unconstitutional (Pioneer Trust & Savings Bank v. Village of Mount Prospect, supra, 22 Ill.2d 375, 176 N.E.2d 799, 801–802 (1961)),[85]

---

82. Pioneer Trust and Savings Bank v. Village of Mount Prospect, 22 Ill.2d 375, 176 N.E.2d 799 (1961).

83. Associated Home Builders of the Greater East Bay, Inc. v. City of Walnut Creek, 4 Cal.3d 633, 94 Cal. Rptr. 630, 484 P.2d 606 (1971).

84. See, e. g., Zilavy, Comment, supra, 1961 Wis.L.Rev. 310; Cutler, Controlling Community Growth, 1961 Wis.L.Rev. 370, 387–391; Johnston, Subdivision Control Exactions, 52 Cornell L.Q. 871; Heyman and Gilhool, Increased Community Costs, 73 Yale L.J. 1121; Reps and Smith, Control of Urban Land Subdivision, supra, 14 Syracuse L.Rev. 405; Cunningham, Subdivision Control, 66 Mich.L.Rev. 1, 28; Taylor, Subdivision Control, 13 Hastings L.J. 344, 350. [Footnote by the Court.]

85. *Pioneer Trust* relied upon *Ayres*, interpreting it as holding that a developer may be compelled to provide the streets which are required by the activity within the subdivision but cannot be required to provide a major thoroughfare, the need for which stems from the total activity of the community. The court in *Pioneer Trust* goes on to state that in the light of this principle a dedication requirement may be upheld only if the burden cast upon the subdivider is specifically and uniquely attributable to his activity and that no such showing was made. The Ayres case cannot be interpreted in this manner. One commentator has written that *Pioneer Trust* completely misunderstood the holding of *Ayres*. (See Johnston, Subdivision Control Exactions, supra, 52 Cornell L.Q. 871, 907–908.) [Footnote by the Court.]

Montana has reached a contrary conclusion (Billings Properties, Inc. v. Yellowstone County, 144 Mont. 25, 394 P.2d 182 (1964)). New York and Wisconsin have affirmed the validity of statutes requiring either dedication or a fee in lieu thereof (Jenad, Inc. v. Village of Scarsdale, supra, 18 N.Y.2d 78, 271 N.Y.S.2d 955, 218 N.E.2d 673 (1966); Jordan v. Village of Menomonee Falls, supra, 28 Wis.2d 608, 137 N.W.2d 442 (1965)). In Connecticut the dedication requirement has been upheld but the requirement that a fee be paid in lieu of dedication was struck down on the ground that its use was not confined for the benefit of the subdivision but to the contrary the fees could be utilized to purchase park land for the residents of the entire town (Aunt Hack Ridge Estates, Inc. v. Planning Commission of Danbury, 27 Conn.Sup. 74, 230 A.2d 45, 47 (1967)).

"The rationale of the cases affirming constitutionality indicate the dedication statutes are valid under the state's police power. They reason that the subdivider realizes a profit from governmental approval of a subdivision since his land is rendered more valuable by the fact of subdivision, and in return for this benefit the city may require him to dedicate a portion of his land for park purposes whenever the influx of new residents will increase the need for park and recreational facilities. (Jordan v. Village of Menomonee Falls, supra, 28 Wis.2d 608, 137 N.W.2d 442, 448 (1965); Billings Properties, Inc. v. Yellowstone County, supra, 144 Mont. 25, 39 P.2d 182, 187 (1964).) Such exactions have been compared to admittedly valid zoning regulations such as minimum lot size and setback requirements. (Jenad, Inc. v. Village of Scarsdale, supra, 18 N.Y.2d 78, 271 N.Y.S.2d 955, 958, 218 N.E.2d 673 (1966).)"

Much earlier, Mr. Justice Holmes had sounded a warning in this area of the law when he wrote in Pennsylvania Coal Company v. Mahon: "The protection of private property in the Fifth Amendment presupposes that it is wanted for public use, but provides that it shall not be taken for such use without compensation. A similar assumption is made in the decisions upon the Fourteenth Amendment. . . . When this seemingly absolute protection is found to be qualified by the police power, the natural tendency of human nature is to extend the qualification more and more until at last private property disappears. But that cannot be accomplished in this way under the Constitution of the United States." [86] Despite the Holmes' warning, the trend is steadily in the direction of greater regulation under the police power, in pursuit of the concept of a balanced community.[87]

86. 260 U.S. 393, 415, 43 S.Ct. 158,   87. See p. 409 supra.
     160, 67 L.Ed. 322, 326 (1922).

The enabling acts are becoming broader [88] and the courts are sustaining them as a reasonable exercise of the police power.

The role of the official map or plan is particularly interesting. Two cases illustrate the problem. Following a legislative enabling act, the City of Rochester, New York, passed an ordinance which gave the city council power to establish an official map or plan showing streets, highways, and parks. Pursuant to the ordinance, the city adopted a plan and map which showed part of the plaintiff's land as being taken for a street widening program in the future. The plaintiff could thereafter build on or utilize that portion of the street bed only by securing a permit from the Zoning Commission. The purpose was to hold down the ultimate cost to the city, which did not have to pay anything until the land was actually taken. Without applying for a permit or showing any actual loss, the plaintiff attacked the constitutionality of the ordinance some ten years after it was passed. The court, stressing the public purpose of the enabling act and ordinance, the small portion of land actually involved for *street* purposes, and the lack of present injury to the plaintiff, dismissed the complaint.[89]

A similar ordinance was declared invalid in Pennsylvania when the map in question located a park area and provided that a private owner could not build there without the danger that if the park became an actuality he would fail to be compensated for his improvements.[90] The ordinance did provide that if the land were not taken for park purposes within three years the map would be null and void, but this gambit was not enough to save the plan. The court stated the issue succinctly: "It has long been well settled that the mere plotting of a *street* upon a city plan without anything more does not constitute a taking of land in a constitutional sense so as to give an abutting owner the right to have damages assessed. The doctrine is said to be founded upon equitable considerations and a wise public policy. . . . Shall this principle relating to streets, which are narrow, well defined and absolutely necessary, be extended to parks and play grounds which may be very large and very desirable but not necessary?"

The Pennsylvania court answered the question in the negative, but the hazy boundary between *taking* and *control* remains

88. For example, the Washington act provides that the planning agency shall consider all "relevant facts and determine whether the public interest will be served by the subdivision and dedication." Wash. Rev.Code Ann. 58.17.110. See Yearwood, Subdivision Law: Timing and Location Control, 44 J. Urban L. 585 (1967).

89. Headley v. City of Rochester, 272 N.Y. 197, 5 N.E.2d 198 (1936).

90. Miller v. City of Beaver Falls, 368 Pa. 189, 82 A.2d 34 (1951).

and the conflict between public and private interests will have to be worked out, after the method of the common law, on a case-by-case basis.[91] Zoning doctrine has long assumed that the structural use of land can be regulated, but that structures as such cannot be prohibited. It is becoming apparent, however, that in many instances the elimination of permanently affixed buildings is not only desirable but may be necessary. Flood-plain zoning to prevent the construction of buildings in the path of recurring rampages[92] and "green belts" around our major urban areas are but examples of a growing concern for better land utilization. The question is not whether these things need to be done, but how they are to be done within our concepts of property law. One solution is for the state, through some of its agencies, to buy the development rights of the owner so that property is not taken without compensation under the guise of regulation.[93]

SECTION 3. PUBLIC DEVELOPMENT OF LAND

By 1954, seventy per cent of the land area of the continental United States had passed into private ownership.[94] At one time the soil of the vast territories west of the Alleghenies was held in public ownership; it represented an asset more valuable and more extensive than that held by any European government. "It was characteristic of the spirit of America that it was never seriously considered to settle and cultivate these lands as publicly owned state farms, but that their orderly transfer into free private ownership and management was from the outset regarded as the very purpose of their temporary public owner-

91. Compare Lomarch Corp. v. Mayor and Common Council of City of Englewood, 51 N.J. 108, 237 A.2d 881 (1968), with Metro Realty v. County of El Dorado, 222 Cal.App. 2d 508, 35 Cal.Rptr. 480 (1963). Note that the mere existence of a plan showing projected public use of privately owned land is not a taking. State National Bank of Connecticut v. Planning and Zoning Commission of Town of Trumbull, 156 Conn. 99, 239 A.2d 528 (1968).

92. Vartelas v. Water Resources Commission, 146 Conn. 650, 153 A. 2d 882 (1959); Iowa Natural Resources Council v. Van Zee, 261 Iowa 1287, 158 N.W.2d 111 (1958). See Dunham, Flood Control Via the Police Power, 107 U.Pa.L.Rev. 1098 (1959).

93. See Kusler, Open Space Zoning: Valid Regulation or Invalid Taking, 57 Minn.L.Rev. 1 (1972).

94. 1956 Statistical Abstract of the United States 181.

ship".[95]   Actually, the most desirable lands were privately
owned by the end of the nineteenth century and government policy had begun to shift from disposition to conservation.   The
thirty per cent of the land still held by federal (21%), state,
and local governments can be developed more or less as those
governments see fit, i. e., it can be transferred gradually to private hands or managed for its value as timber, oil, water, grazing, and other natural resources of public importance.   While
the problems even in this area can be immense, they are not what
is meant by the public development of land as the term is used
in this section.   We are here concerned with the role of government in taking private land by eminent domain so that it can be
developed in the public interest.[96]

Let me state the question baldly: Can the state, under
proper circumstances, take land away from one private owner,
pay him just compensation for his loss, and turn it over to another private owner who will presumably develop the land more
in line with what is conceived to be the public interest?   The
answer is a qualified "yes", qualified that is by a legislative determination that the taking is for a public purpose and subject
to judicial review to curb excessive legislative zeal.[97]   This sweeping use of governmental power has evolved naturally from the
power to zone, to restrict nuisances, and to regulate subdivision
growth.   If the public interest, as expressed through the proper governmental agency, is best served by placing restrictions on
land use to prevent the worst aspects of urban chaos and by
planning to promote orderly growth in the future, it follows
that some attack will be required on the existing slums, obsolescent areas, and human wastelands which now haunt our major
cities.   Since any reasonable chance for success in urban renewal
requires the acquisition of large blocks of physical space which
must be cleared and redeveloped, it is not surprising that government has been called upon to do the job.   The wisdom of some of
the planning which has been going on as a part of our urban
redevelopment, renewal, and conservation programs may be
open to doubt,[98] but the legal power to proceed in this fashion
seems to be clear.

95. Rheinstein,   Inheritance   and
Property Rights, 93 Trusts and
Estates 223, 224 (1954).

96.   For an extended analysis of how
some European nations have dealt
with this problem see Cribbet, Some
Reflections On The Law of Land—
A View From Scandinavia, 62 N.W.
U.L.Rev. 277 (1967).

97.   For an interesting case in which
the local legislature went too far

and was accused of "palpable bad
faith" see Redevelopment Authority
of the City of Erie v. Owners Or
Parties In Interest, 1 Pa.Cmwlth.
378, 274 A.2d 244 (1971). There are
few such cases and normally the
taking is sustained.

98.   For a scathing attack which concludes that the trouble with city
planning is the planners, see Jacobs,
The Death and Life of Great American Cities (1961).

The key case in the public development of land is Berman v. Parker,[99] decided by the Supreme Court of the United States in 1954. Congress had passed the District of Columbia Redevelopment Act of 1945 which empowered a redevelopment land agency to acquire and assemble, by eminent domain and otherwise, real property for "the redevelopment of blighted territory in the District of Columbia and the prevention, reduction, or elimination of blighting factors or causes of blight." The plaintiff sought to enjoin the taking of his property as unconstitutional since it would deprive him of his land without due process of law. The plaintiff's property was in a "blighted area", but was not slum property as such since it was, in fact, a department store. Furthermore, he contended no public purpose was involved since the cleared land would be turned over to private owners to redevelop in line with a comprehensive land-use plan. The court held that this was a valid exercise of the governmental power and that the rights of the property owner were protected so long as he received that just compensation which the Fifth Amendment exacts as the price of taking. The legislature can plan on a broad as well as a piecemeal basis and it was reasonable to clear all of the land in a given area to carry out the public purpose.

The court stated that in these cases the legislature rather than the judiciary is the principal guardian of public needs and that the role of the judiciary in determining whether the power is being exercised for a public purpose is an extremely narrow one. Moreover, Mr. Justice Douglas struck a blow for aesthetic values as a basis for redevelopment when he wrote: "It is within the power of the legislature to determine that the community should be beautiful as well as healthy, spacious as well as clean, well-balanced as well as carefully patrolled. . . . If those who govern the District of Columbia decide that the Nation's Capital should be beautiful as well as sanitary, there is nothing in the Fifth Amendment that stands in the way." [1]

Berman v. Parker clarified the power to act under the Constitution of the United States but what about the state constitutions? The redevelopment laws of the several states, all depending on a heavy infusion of federal funds to make them more than pious expressions of intent, came under successive attacks. In some instances, the acts were struck down as authorizing a taking for a private purpose.[2] For example, in Edens v. City of Columbia [3] it was held that the law was valid to the extent

---

99. 348 U.S. 26, 75 S.Ct. 98, 99 L.Ed. 27 (1954).

1. Id. at 33, 102, and 38.

2. Adams v. Housing Authority of Daytona, 60 So.2d 663 (Fla.1952);

Housing Authority of Atlanta v. Johnson, 209 Ga. 560, 74 S.E.2d 891 (1953).

3. 228 S.C. 563, 91 S.E.2d 280 (1956).

that the condemned land would be used by the University of South Carolina, but invalid where it would be turned over to private developers to use for a light industrial area. The South Carolina Constitution allowed land to be taken for a public *use* only and the court felt that cases in states allowing a taking for a public *purpose* were not in point. Only an amendment of the constitution would allow this use of the power of eminent domain.

On the other hand, the majority of states followed the lead of the United States Supreme Court and sustained this extension of the power of eminent domain without much reference to the semantic distinction between public use and public purpose. They seemed to find sufficient justification for the power in the public interest served by the clearance of slum or blighted areas regardless of the ultimate use of the land, assuming, of course, that the use was in accordance with a valid comprehensive plan.[4] A series of Illinois cases handled this theme as well as any in the nation and concluded that even private industrial development is consistent with this use of governmental power.[5]

The use of the power of eminent domain to prevent slums as well as to eliminate them was upheld in Gutknecht v. Chicago.[6] Mr. Justice Schaefer went to the heart of the matter. "It is also contended that the 'line of demarcation between a public and private use in the employment of eminent domain to eliminate slum areas . . . must be the elimination rather than the prevention of slums.' But we are aware of no constitutional principle which paralyzes the power of government to deal with an evil until it has reached its maximum development. Nor is there force in the argument that if the use of eminent domain in the prevention of slums is permitted 'every piece of property within the city or State can be condemned to prevent it from becoming a slum.' Legitimate use of governmental power is not prohibited because of the possibility that the power may be abused."

The legal problems involved in urban renewal are immense and this brief discussion is designed solely to raise the curtain

---

4. See Mandelker, The Comprehensive Planning Requirement in Urban Renewal, 116 Pa.L.Rev. 25 (1967); Scheuer, Goldston and Sogg, Disposition of Urban Renewal Land—A Fundamental Problem in the Rebuilding of Our Cities, 62 Colum.L.Rev. 959 (1969).

5. Gutknecht v. City of Chicago, 414 Ill. 600, 111 N.E.2d 626 (1953);

Gutknecht v. City of Chicago, 3 Ill. 2d 539, 121 N.E.2d 791 (1954); People ex rel. Adamowski v. Chicago Land Clearance Commission, 14 Ill. 2d 74, 150 N.E.2d 792 (1958). Comment, 1958 U.Ill.L.F. 477. See also Cannata v. City of New York, 11 N.Y.2d 210, 227 N.Y.S.2d 903, 182 N.E.2d 395 (1962).

6. 3 Ill.2d 539, 121 N.E.2d 791 (1954).

and provide a glimpse of the drama which has been playing since the end of World War II.[7] For example, one of the most serious urban renewal problems is the relocation of residents of project areas in satisfactory housing. In Norwalk CORE v. Norwalk Redevelopment Agency [8], such residents were held to have standing to challenge an urban renewal plan as denying equal protection and failing to comply with statutory relocation requirements.[9] This important development should do much to enable the "poverty lawyer" to protect the rights of those who find themselves in the path of the bulldozer.

In all of the preceding cases, it is clear that the owner must receive adequate compensation before his property can be taken. In some public development it is not so clear that any property rights have been taken and the case turns, not on the exercise of the power, which is admitted, but on the compensation due. This problem is most acute in the building of super highways and expressways [10] and in the public regulation of navigable waterways. A discussion of these border line cases is impossible here, but the student should ponder well Mr. Justice Jackson's realistic appraisal of property rights in United States v. Willow River Power Co.[11] Said he: ". . . [N]ot all economic interests are 'property rights'; only those economic advantages are 'rights' which have the law back of them, and only when they are so recognized may courts compel others to forbear from interfering with them or to compensate for their invasion. . . . We cannot start the process of decision by calling such a claim as we have here a 'property right'; whether it is a property right is really the question to be answered. Such economic uses are rights only when they are legally protected interests."

7. For a general discussion of urban renewal and related programs, see National Institute for Education in Law and Poverty, Handbook on Housing Law, Ch. 3 (1970).

8. 395 F.2d 920 (2d Cir. 1968).

9. See McGee, Urban Renewal in the Crucible of Judicial Review, 56 Va. L.Rev. 826 (1970).

10. See, e. g., People v. Ricciardi, 23 Cal.2d 390, 144 P.2d 799 (1944) where an easement of view was held to be a valuable property right for which compensation was due when destroyed by a highway underpass. There was a strong dissent.

11. 324 U.S. 499, 65 S.Ct. 761, 764, 89 L.Ed. 1101, 1107, 103 Ct.Cl. 797, (1945).

SECTION 4.　ENVIRONMENTAL CONTROLS

Unfortunately, an extended discussion of law and the environment is impossible in a basic book on principles of the law of property. The subject is too extensive and the major developments too recent for meaningful treatment in a brief compass. These few paragraphs are included primarily to complete the "big picture" of a developing law of land. Concern about the environment is not new but awareness of the critical impact of man's abuse of nature's bounty is new. The realization of law's role in curbing the most egregious of those abuses is also relatively recent and therein lies the heart of the problem. As a society, we have waited until our rivers and lakes were polluted, our resources despoiled, and our scenic wonders mutilated before we decided to act. Thus our challenge is not only to protect against further depredations but to correct the errors of the past—a much more difficult task. Moreover, our present goal must be to deal with the very quality of life on this planet not just with the protection of open space and the preservation of material resources. It goes without saying that the quality of life involves issues far greater than the proper use of land, however important that may be.

In a general way, law has long been concerned with the environment. Principles of waste were developed to protect the remainderman or reversioner from the destruction of the freehold by the life tenant.[12] It could be argued that we are all life tenants, even when we own a fee simple absolute, and that the law should protect the land for the next generation of life tenants and so on ad infinitum.[13] In that sense, environmental controls are but the logical extension of a basic principle of property law to meet a newly recognized social need. Similarly, nuisance doctrines gave a limited protection to the environment, the common law of water curbed some pollution of the lakes and streams,[14] and police power regulations made life in the cities somewhat more tolerable.[15] But if the principles were there all along, their application to the concrete realities of an industrial society were woefully inadequate. The ad hoc measures of private litigation could not hope to stem, much less roll

12.　See p. 209 supra.

13.　This idea is embodied in the National Environmental Policy Act of 1969, 83 Stat. 852, 4 U.S.C.A. § 4321 et seq. (Supp.1970), which lists as its first goal "to the end that the nation may (1) fulfill the responsibilities of each generation as trustee of the environment for succeeding generations. . . ."

14.　See p. 368 supra.

15.　See p. 397 supra.

back, the inexorable tide.   The conservationists of an earlier era find their counterparts in the environmentalists of today.

By the late 1960's the quality of the environment had become a major issue in American society and the law of land had begun to develop a new set of remedies and a new vocabulary. The environmental impact statement took its place alongside the venerable nuisance doctrine as a weapon in the legal battle to protect the quality of American life.   The key charter in the zoning struggle had been the Standard State Zoning Enabling Act [16] and the Magna Charta of environment control, The National Environmental Policy Act of 1969 (NEPA),[17] may well play a somewhat similar role in the decades ahead.   The Act is too lengthy to reprint here, but a brief portion must be set out to establish the ambitious nature of the crusade on which the nation is now embarked.

"Purpose

"Sec. 2.   The purposes of this Act are: To declare a national policy which will encourage productive and enjoyable harmony between man and his environment; to promote efforts which will prevent or eliminate damage to the environment and biosphere and stimulate the health and welfare of man; to enrich the understanding of the ecological systems and natural resources important to the Nation; and to establish a Council on Environmental Quality.

"TITLE I

"DECLARATION OF NATIONAL ENVIRONMENTAL POLICY

"Sec. 101(a) The Congress, recognizing the profound impact of man's activity on the interrelations of all components of the natural growth, high-density urbanization, industrial expansion, resource exploitation, and new and expanding technological advances and recognizing further the critical importance of restoring and maintaining environmental quality to the overall welfare and development of man, declares that it is the continuing policy of the Federal Government, in cooperation with State and local governments, and other concerned public and private organizations, to use all practicable means and

16. It was drafted by an Advisory Committee on Building Codes and Zoning, appointed by the then Secretary of Commerce, Herbert Hoover.

17. Ftn. 13 supra.

measures, including financial and technical assistance, in a manner calculated to foster and promote the general welfare, to create and maintain conditions under which man and nature can exist in productive harmony, and fulfill the social, economic, and other requirements of present and future generations of Americans.

"(b) In order to carry out the policy set forth in this Act, it is the continuing responsibility of the Federal Government to use all practicable means, consistent with other essential considerations of national policy, to improve and coordinate Federal plans, functions, programs, and resources to the end that the Nation may—

(1) fulfill the responsibilities of each generation as trustee of the environment for succeeding generations;

(2) assure for all Americans safe, healthful, productive, and esthetically and culturally pleasing surroundings;

(3) attain the widest range of beneficial uses of the environment without degradation, risk to health or safety, or other undesirable and unintended consequences;

(4) preserve important historic, cultural, and natural aspects of our national heritage, and maintain, wherever possible, an environment which supports diversity and variety of individual choice;

(5) achieve a balance between population and resource use which will permit high standards of living and a wide sharing of life's amenities; and

(6) enhance the quality of renewable resources and approach the maximum attainable recycling of depletable resources.

(c) The Congress recognizes that each person should enjoy a healthful environment and that each person has a responsibility to contribute to the preservation and enhancement of the environment."

NEPA and its state progeny [18] plus a rash of related legislation [19] have made it abundantly clear that the legislative bodies, at least, are determined to meet the environmental problems head on. It is too soon to assess the effectiveness of this

18. See, for example, the Illinois Environmental Protection Act of 1970, Ill.Rev.Stat.1970, ch. 111½, § 1001 et seq., and the Michigan Environmental Protection Act of 1970, Public Act No. 127, Legislature of State of Michigan, Mich.Comp.Laws Ann. § 691.1201 et seq. (Current Material 1970). See also, Sax, Defending the Environment: A Strategy for Citizen Action (1971).

19. See Water and Environmental Quality Improvement Act of 1970, Pub.L. 91–224, 91 St.Cong., 2d Sess.

monumental legislative assault but it is already apparent that the courts will take their role seriously and attempt to put sharp teeth into the legislative mandate.   Thus, in Calvert Cliffs Coordinating Committee, Inc. v. Atomic Energy Commission [20], Judge Wright of the United States Court of Appeals for the District of Columbia wrote: "These cases are only the beginning of what promises to become a flood of new litigation—litigation seeking judicial assistance in protecting our national environment.   Several recently enacted statutes attest to the commitment of the Government to control, at long last, the destructive engine of material 'progress'.   But it remains to be seen whether the promise of this legislation will become a reality.   Therein lies the judicial role."   The court then proceeded to construe NEPA as a mandate to the old and new federal administrative agencies to carry out the broad purposes of the Act.   The Atomic Energy Commission's rules had not been rigorous enough in following the mandate and the case was remanded for further action by the Commission.   The exact details of the case are of less importance than the judicial attitude toward the importance of the new legislation.   The court had "read the election returns" and was responding, once again, to the prevailing mood of the people.

An important key to the success of NEPA is the environmental impact statement.   The Act does not require such a statement in every case in which a federal agency plans or finances a project.   Statements are required, however, if the proposed project is "major" and if it will have a "significant effect" upon the quality of the human environment.   The vital role of the statement is illustrated by Goose Hollow Foothills League v. Romney,[21] where a United States District Court in Oregon held up a $3,000,000 plus high-rise apartment building until a proper statement was filed.   The area presently had no high-rise buildings and, while the developers had presumably complied with zoning and subdivision controls, they had filed only a "negative statement", indicating that no environmental impact statement was necessary.   Since the Department of Housing and Urban Development (HUD) was loaning more than a million dollars for the project the development fell within the ambit of NEPA. The court did not decide that the structures could not be built but they did find that they would undoubtedly change the character of the neighborhood and hence that HUD must consider carefully the impact on the environment of housing a significant number of people (students in this case) in an area previously free from this kind of population concentration.   Where

20.   146 U.S.App.D.C. 33, 449 F.2d   **21.**   334 F.Supp. 877 (D.C.Or.1971).
1109 (1971).

projects fall under NEPA, or the related state legislation, this new environmental control assumes an importance equal to the other police power regulations.

NEPA applies to situations in which federal agencies must approve major projects which will have a significant effect on the environment. What is "major" and what is "significant"? These chameleon like terms will have to be defined by the normal judicial process and the courts will thus play a major role in the success or failure of the current generation of environmental controls. Moreover, the courts must decide on the adequacy of the administrative compliance with environmental legislation, while being careful not to usurp the administrative role by substituting judicial judgment for administrative discretion. This will be a complex process but the courts have dealt with this problem in other contexts and should prove adequate to the task.

NEPA and its state counterparts are important even if they are restricted to "public developments" but what about "private developments" that may have significant effect on the environment? In California a land developer began construction of a "mini-skyscraper" apartment building in an area of single-family cabins in the High Sierras. Led by Mrs. Andrea Mead Lawrence, a former Olympic skiing gold medalist, the residents of Mammoth Lakes sued to halt the project on the grounds that, even though it was a private development on private land, it harmed the surrounding environment. The Supreme Court of California held (6 to 1) that under the California Environmental Quality Act of 1970 the residents were entitled to relief.[22] State and local governmental agencies must complete environmental impact statements and make them public before they can approve private construction that may have a significant impact on the environment.

This was the first time that the idea of environmental impact statements had been directly applied to private developments and if this view prevails in California and other states (California has recently been a bellwether in the land use area) a vital weapon has been made available to the environmentalists. Again, it is too early to tell how far this changing pattern of land use controls will go although the *direction* of changes seems apparent. The California decision in *Friends of Mammoth* created a furor among builders, lenders, and unions [23] and led to immediate calls for changes in the legislation. The cities and

22. Friends of Mammoth v. Board of Supervisors of Mono County, 104 Cal.Rptr. 16, 500 P.2d 1360 (1972), modified on denial of rehearing 104 Cal.Rptr. 761, 502 P.2d 1049 (1972).

23. See, for example, an article in the Wall Street Journal, "California Court Ruling on Ecological Impact Throws Builders, Lenders and Unions for a Loss", page 26, October 9, 1972.

counties claimed that they didn't know how to make the necessary environmental impact studies, didn't have the necessary staff or funds, and didn't know how to define significant private construction. It does seem that additional clarity will have to be provided by the legislatures and that funding and qualified staff will have to be made available. Since such environmental controls are still in their infancy, legal statesmanship will be required to meet the demands of the new age. It should be a fertile field for the property lawyer, already steeped in the traditions of land-use planning. Some California lawyers for private developers are talking about abandoning any idea of seeking relief through injunctions or declaratory judgments and concentrating on the concept of inverse condemnation. They would not fight the regulations but would contend instead that property had been "taken" and seek damages for the loss in value. If this approach were to prevail in the courts, it could be the death knell of police power controls because of the fiscal problems involved. The answers to the long series of questions raised by the environmental controls and related land planning techniques will have to be provided in the years ahead.

SECTION 5.   CHANGING CONCEPTS IN THE LAW OF LAND USE

As this chapter on Public Regulation of Land Use has disclosed, the impact of governmental power on private rights in land has changed the very nature of the fee simple absolute. The modern principles of the law of property could no more be understood without a consideration of these changes than feudal principles could be grasped absent an understanding of tenure, the Statute of Uses, and the dichotomy between law and equity. Since the police power regulations are now the subject of considerable controversy, ranging from proposals to abolish zoning as a failure to suggestions that the police power be expanded to provide balanced communities, it seems desirable to trace the growth of the public regulation of land in a "free society" and provide a greater understanding of our present dilemma. At the risk of some repetition, this chapter concludes with an analysis of the changing concepts in the law of land use.[24]

24. This section is based on an article by the author in 50 Iowa L.Rev. 245 (1965).

Over three decades ago Professor Philbrick published his classic article, Changing Conceptions of Property in Law.[25]   Although his analysis preceded the explosive development of land-use planning and focused on property for power rather than on property for use,[26] it continues to be a foundation stone for any serious discussion of evolving property concepts.   Professor Philbrick wrote:

"Manifestly we need a modernized philosophy of property. No mere philosophy of words or aspirations, however.   In that respect the contrast between Mill and Comte—one looking to individualism to save society, the other to society to save the individual—is precisely the same as that which existed between Aristotle and Plato.   The first tenet of an adequate philosophy must be that property is the creature and dependent of law, including, of course, our constitutions —surely no radical doctrine!   On one hand, private property, though admitting that it can only exist by virtue of public protection, pleads payment of taxes as the whole price of that protection, and beyond that claims immunity from all social obligations.   On the other hand, the thought of the world for two generations has been tending toward collective Utopias.[27]"

In describing property as a creature of law, Professor Philbrick was being a good Benthamite.   "Property and law are born together, and die together.   Before laws were made there was no property; take away laws and property ceases." [28]   However, he recognized the vital truth that the law itself evolves only as it reflects the society it serves.   In his opening paragraph he noted: "The forces that change the law in other than trivial ways lie outside it.   It is to other things than law, therefore, that your attention must primarily be called." [29]   Thus, the pattern is complete: property is shaped and controlled by law but law is shaped and controlled by society.   Our search for changing concepts in the law of land use must involve an understanding of the changing nature of modern life, especially of those phases normally subsumed under the rubric "population explosion."

25.   86 U.Pa.L.Rev. 691 (1938).

26.   By property for use is meant property held for personal consumption; by property for power, property whose title is available for alienation—and which therefore involves potential control over the services of others whose necessities or desires impel them to an exchange of services for property. In particular, property for power involves control of the means of production.   Id. at 697.

27.   Id. at 728–29.

28.   Bentham, Theory of Legislation 113 (Dumont ed. Hildreth transl. 1864).

29.   Philbrick, Changing Conceptions of Property in Law, 86 U.Pa.L.Rev. at 691 (1938).

We *still* need a modernized philosophy of property. The concepts we have inherited, willy-nilly, from the past are inadequate for the vaguely glimpsed pressures of the future. Karl Marx revolted against the exaggerated individualism of absolutist concepts of private property and came up with communism as a cure for accumulated social maladjustments. This was a new, or at least a different, philosophy of property and economics, but we need not, "seeing the perversion of principles, follow the besetting fallacy of men and seek salvation from one evil in its opposite, as if the means of escaping death by fire were freezing to death." [30] We need a philosophy that recognizes both the *rights* and the *duties* of the individual landowner, a philosophy that can rationalize laws which will protect private ownership [31] without hamstringing the legitimate public interest. This is a big order and it is the purpose of this Section to explore only one facet of a modernized philosophy, i. e., the law relating to land use.[32] The discussion will revolve around three principal points: (1) past concepts—*laissez faire*; (2) concepts in transition—comprehensive zoning and its fellows; and (3) concepts for the future.

A.   PAST CONCEPTS—LAISSEZ FAIRE

Several generations of American lawyers were reared on Blackstone. As public leaders they translated his thought into social policy. His view of property was inaccurate even for his own day, but etched on the printed page it had the ring of

---

30. Lieber, On Civil Liberty and Government 19 (3d ed. 1911).

31. One German scholar states that ownership should be "merely the right, and the duty, to control and to use a thing in accordance with socially approved [*sittliche*] purposes." Schmidt, Der Principielle Unterscheid Zwischen dem Römischen und Germanischen Rechte 225 (1853).

32. The term "land use" is ambiguous. Within the last fifteen years American law schools have begun to offer courses and seminars variously entitled land-use controls, land-use planning, land utilization, or simply land use. The leading law school book in the field, Haar's Land-Use Planning, was published in 1959. Most of these courses include planning, zoning, subdivision controls, nuisance, urban renewal and redevelopment, private land-use controls, etc. It is in this specialized sense that the term "land use" is employed in this Section. Professor Philbrick had a broader vision of the term. "Question any man, and he will yield the opinion that the sole reason for owning property is to use or (which is enjoyment in another form) to sell it. He will agree that title is only a shell that covers and protects a kernel of enjoyments." Philbrick, supra note 29, at 701.

eternal truth: "There is nothing which so generally strikes the imagination, and engages the affections of mankind, as the right of property; or that sole and despotic dominion which one man claims and exercises over the external things of the world, in total exclusion of the right of any other individual in the universe." [33]   Amen!   This simplistic version of absolute private property had a great appeal to men struggling for rights against a powerful monarch.   The right of the poorest man in his cottage to be secure, castlelike, against the very King of England was a step forward in the age-old battle between crown and subject. Unfortunately, battle cries linger after the enemy is vanquished, and "sole and despotic dominion" means something quite different when arrayed against the public welfare operating under the police power.

Oddly enough, English land law did not originate with any such one-sided view of property.   Feudalism, which provided Anglo-American law with its concepts of estates, tenure, etc., was a curious blend of private land law with a system of government, but ownership of the fee was, from the beginning, a combination of rights and duties.   The knight had well-protected interests in his *feud,* but he owed clearly defined duties to his overlord.   Those duties became onerous, then unnecessary, and ultimately ridiculous so that the system itself dissolved, but the concept behind them was sound.   Ownership of land does involve participation in the affairs of society, and the use of land is of more than private concern.   "The disappearance of any long established social system must involve some losses.   And so, in the case of feudalism it is regrettable that there could not have been preserved the idea that all property was held subject to the performance of duties—not a few of them public." [34]   It may be that the wrong concepts of feudalism survived—that we threw out the baby and kept the bath.

------

(1) Theoretical Basis of Laissez Faire

It was not Blackstone, however, who provided the theoretical basis for *laissez faire* in the field of land use (and elsewhere). He may have been the preacher thundering from his pulpit, but sophisticated theologians were required to justify the thunder. John Locke with his view of property as a natural right, Adam Smith with his economics of individualism, and Jeremy Bentham

------

33. 2 Blackstone, Commentaries *1–2.   **34.** Philbrick, supra note 29, at 710.

with his rationalization of the social utility of private use, were the true fathers of *laissez faire.*[35]

John Locke (1632–1704) was not a lawyer, although his father was, but his social compact theory shows the influence of the common law. His two Treatises on Civil Government were directed against the divine right of kings and in support of the democratic and egalitarian principles of the Puritan revolution. His political theories provided the ideological justification for the English Revolution of 1688, the American Revolution of 1776, and to some extent for the French Revolution of 1789.[36] His comments on property were not a detached essay but part and parcel of his disquisition on civil government. He bolstered his attack on the tyranny of the House of Stuart by establishing the sanctity of private property with which the monarchs were interfering.

> "The great and chief end, therefore, of men's uniting into commonwealths, and putting themselves under government, is the preservation of property. . . . The supreme power cannot take from any man any part of his property without his own consent. For the preservation of property being the end of government, and that for which men enter into society, it necessarily supposes and requires that the people should have property, without which they must be supposed to lose that by entering into society, which was the end for which they entered into it, too gross an absurdity for any man to own. [37]"

Locke proceeded to justify property as ordained by God in such a way that men of substance and standing came to regard society as a kind of joint stock company established in the interest of property owners. Of course, not all men agreed, and Thomas Paine said, "The Creator of the earth did not 'open a land office from which the first title-deeds were issued.'" [38] In fact, Locke's full argument, and certainly the circumstances under which it was made, did not support the dominance of property over all other social interests. Indeed, at one point Locke contended: "As much as any one can make use of to any advantage of life before it spoils, so much he may by his labour

---

35. Of course, many other thinkers, including Hume, Kant, Spencer, et al., were involved, but the main pattern was set by the "influential three."

36. For a brief treatment of Locke's contributions see Patterson, Jurisprudence: Men and Ideas of the Law 358–62 (1953).

37. Locke, Of Civil Government, Second Treatise 102, 115 (Gateway ed. 1962).

38. Larkin, Property in the Eighteenth Century 129 (1930).

fix a property in; whatever is beyond this, is more than his share, and belongs to others. Nothing was made by God for men to spoil or destroy." [39] With the passage of time, however, men forgot what Locke meant, or even what he actually said, and made of his words a philosophic justification for the immunity of property from all but the most inoffensive regulation by the state. Locke exalted property to protect the liberties of a people against a king, but the emergence of parliamentary supremacy in England denied to property a place above the legislature. The same concept became enthroned in the constitutions (federal and state) of the New World, and a vastly expanded meaning of property, to include virtually all business enterprise, threatened to render powerless the government itself. This was an aspect of property for power which served as a battlefield in the 'thirties, and the role of the Lockian concept has been thoroughly explored by Professor Walton Hamilton and others.[40] This same concept had great staying power in the field of land use, and the fee simple owner felt free to use his own land virtually unimpeded even though it caused injury to his neighbor (short of common-law nuisance) and ran counter to the best interests of the community. Locke was right in stressing the importance of property, but his followers were wrong in assuming that property was an entity beyond the power of organized society. "Neither 'liberty' nor 'property' is antecedent to the state or beyond the domain of public control. Each is but a name for a cluster of prevailing usages,—certain to change and subject to amendment,—which binds the individual to the social order." [41]

Adam Smith (1723–1790) was a political economist and philosopher, but his classic work, Wealth of Nations, was regarded by him as, at least partially, a work on jurisprudence. He was too much of a realist to swallow whole the doctrine that property is natural and inviolable, but he certainly accepted the principle of *laissez faire* and helped create the classic economic theory of the nineteenth century which presupposed the existence of the *laissez faire* state. He believed in the inherently desirable economic equality of men and is forever associated with the economics of individualism. Professor Arnold Toynbee states: "Two conceptions are woven into every argument of the Wealth of Nations—the belief in the supreme value of individual liberty, and the conviction that man's self-love is God's providence, that the individual in pursuing his own interest is promoting the welfare of all." [42] These concepts meshed perfectly with Locke's

39. Locke, op. cit. supra note 37, at 25.

40. Hamilton, Property—According to Locke, 41 Yale L.J. 864 (1932).

41. Id. at 879.

42. Toynbee, Lectures on the Industrial Revolution 148 (1913).

ideas on property and further cemented the rights' side of ownership. Property was an individual right to be protected, not regulated, by the state. Duties there might be but they were minimal and could be handled by the *ad hoc* processes of the common law. Translated to the use of land, this meant the individual could develop it as he pleased and the public welfare would be served by the collective results of the individual's freedom of action.

Jeremy Bentham (1748–1832) was a student of Blackstone and he was not impressed. He was critical of the "frivolous" reasons that his teacher gave for the various rules of the common law, but they did serve to start him on a life-long search for better ones. He was influenced by both Locke and Smith but he did not fully accept the ideas of either. He recognized that there could be no absolute property rights. Such rights were at least subordinate to the needs of the state in maintaining security.[43] He viewed property as a creature of law, including legislation, rather than as an inalienable right stemming from God.[44] He accepted the economic concepts of the Wealth of Nations and with them the heavy emphasis on the individual rights of man. As the great utilitarian, Bentham believed in the "greatest happiness" principle and worked for legal reform which would produce the greatest happiness (absence from pain if not direct pleasure) for the individual. It was his theory that laws should be evaluated by estimating their social consequences to the interests of individuals. Like Adam Smith, he felt the social welfare was necessarily served when the individual prospered. "[H]e adopted *laissez faire* as the best means of securing the greatest total of community happiness; and he, also, assumed the concurrence of individual and social interests. They [Smith and Bentham] were therefore equally exalters of private initiative and—Bentham more directly—of private property." [45]

Since Bentham's ideas of property were more sophisticated than those of Locke, to say nothing of Blackstone, they have had even greater staying power. "Bentham conceived of property and contract as both founded on expectation: 'The idea of property consists in an established expectation; in the persuasion of being able to draw such or such an advantage from the thing possessed, according to the nature of the case.' This expectation can only be the work of the law, which gives it security." [46] This is sound doctrine, but whose expectations are we

43. Bentham, op. cit. supra note 28, at 124–26.

44. Id. at 112.

45. Philbrick, supra note 29, at 711–12.

46. Patterson, op. cit. supra note 36, at 454.

talking about—the individual's, society's, or both? To Bentham the answer was clear—the individual's. Society's expectations would follow in his train. The social utility of private use was *the* justification for private property, and anything more than minimal interference by the state was dangerous.

The stage was now set for the reception of these concepts of property and, hence, of land use into the New World. It has been frequently stated that the framers of the Constitution of the United States understood liberty as having to do primarily with property rights. It is perhaps of equal importance that the leaders of public thought in the new nation were heavily influenced by the property concepts of Blackstone, Locke, Smith, and Bentham. Stressing the views first of one, then another, sometimes of all four, property emerged as ordained of God, a natural, inalienable right, absolute, individualistic, and central to the *laissez faire* economy of the New Jerusalem. Property could be controlled by law, but legislative tampering must be viewed with suspicion since the individual's use of his own land was protected by the Constitution, the laws of God, and the writings of philosophers.

---

(2) Historic and Demographic Factors in the American Reception of Laissez Faire

Great ideas do shape the world,[47] but the world is frequently in such a shape that the ideas merely rationalize the inevitable. The land-use pattern in the New World would probably have been much the same without the concepts of Locke et al., but the explanations would have lacked elegance and style. Property rights, as both natural and individual, fitted America like a glove. Land was cheap, if not actually free, and the loose economic conditions gave maximum opportunity for the self-made man of property. There were no urban concentrations of any real significance (in 1790 the nation was without a city of 50,000), and the social problems of the failure in society could be solved by moving West. "Cheap land had as one of its consequences that of stimulating and universalizing acquisitive instincts and respect for property rights." [48]

The American view of property as an absolute right in the Blackstonian sense was strengthened by the colonial experience.

47. For a fascinating account of some of them see Downs, Molders of the Modern Mind (1961).

48. Philbrick, supra note 29, at 723.

England herself was emerging from the worst aspects of feudalism, and in 1660 the Statute of Tenures marked the end of the strictly feudal period of English land law.[49] The colonists had come to the New World for many reasons one of which was escape from a society they found oppressive. To set up a system of land holding filled with meaningless duties like those involved in military tenure would have been unthinkable. The idea of tenure, however, was deeply ingrained in English land law, and the original grants and charters provided that the estates be held of the crown in free and common socage. The Revolution severed even this weak tie and left the landowner free of any duties to an overlord. Mr. Justice Story described this absence of tenure as one of the significant forces in the life of the new nation:

> "In short, for most purposes, our lands may be deemed to be perfectly allodial, or held of no superior at all; though many of the distinctions of feudal law have necessarily insinuated themselves into the modes of acquiring, transferring, and transmitting real estates. One of the most remarkable circumstances in our colonial history is the almost total absence of leasehold estates. . . . The tenants and occupiers are almost universally the proprietors of the soil in fee simple. . . . The philosophical mind can scarcely fail to trace the intimate connexion, which naturally subsists between the general equality of the apportionment of property among the mass of a nation, and the popular form of its government." [50]

Some concepts of tenure did survive the Revolution, with the State taking the place of the King. As recently as 1934 a state court wrote: "Clearly the theory of law in the United States, then is that first and originally the state was the proprietor of all real property and last and ultimately will be its proprietor, and what is commonly termed ownership is in fact but tenancy, whose continuance is contingent upon legally recognized rights of tenure, transfer, and of succession in use and occupancy." [51] However, this case dealt only with a question of escheat, and there is little evidence that tenure, if it exists at all, has had any impact on land use. It seems safe to conclude, with Chancellor Kent, that in the United States "every

---

49. For an excellent, brief account of English feudalism and its effect see Hargreaves, Introduction to the Principles of Land Law (4th ed. 1963).

50. 1 Story, Commentaries on the Constitution of the United States 159–60, 166 (1833).

51. In re Estate of O'Connor, 126 Neb. 182, 252 N.W. 826 (1934).

real vestige of tenure is annihilated." [52]   In general, the annihilation was both useful and desirable; the law can accomplish everything from an allodial base which it can from a tenurial one.   Once again, however, it had a curious side effect. Freed from duties to a superior lord (king, noble, *or* society), the owner not only felt but believed that the land was his to do with as he saw fit.   Intrusions by the government were not only unwelcome but unconstitutional.

If the newly formed United States had been restricted to the Atlantic seaboard, these property concepts would have been put to an early test, but "manifest destiny" decreed otherwise. As the course of empire rolled westward, new land seemed always available on the frontier.   At one time the soil of the vast territories west of the Alleghenies was held in public ownership; it represented an asset more valuable and more extensive than that held by any European government.   This natural resource could have formed a basis of public policy which would have altered radically the inherited concepts of private property. Public policy was clearly present, as the statutes from the period 1785–1934 reveal.[53]   Public education and private transportation were promoted, but principally the policy was to get public lands into private hands, free of the control of government.   Professor Rheinstein puts it succinctly: "It was characteristic of the spirit of America that it was never seriously considered to settle and cultivate these lands as publicly owned state farms, but that their orderly transfer into free private ownership and management was from the outset regarded as the very purpose of their temporary public ownership." [54]   By 1954, seventy per cent of the land area of the continental United States had passed into private ownership.[55]   The lands remaining in public control can, of course, be managed and developed as the governments (federal, state, and local) see fit.   Since some of this land is valuable for timber, oil, water, grazing, and other natural resources, basic land-use issues are involved, but this discussion is concerned solely with property in private ownership.   The significant fact is that *laissez faire* had controlled from start to finish—from colonial days to the disposition of land on the frontier.   Now the frontier was no more;

---

52.   4 Kent, Commentaries *24. For a short discussion of tenure in the United States, with references to the leading articles and books, see 1 American Law of Property 57–60 (Casner ed. 1952).

53.   For a good selection of these statutes see Haar, Land-Use Planning 25–41 (2d ed. 1971).

54.   Rheinstein,   Inheritance   and Property Rights, 93 Trusts & Estates 223, 224 (1954).

55.   U.S. Bureau of the Census, Dep't of Commerce, Statistical Abstract of the United States 181 (77th ed. 1956).

the forces that would ultimately lead to megalopolis were at work in society. Would these "forces outside the law" change the concept of property and of land use? But first, what were the consequences of *laissez faire*?

---

(3) The Consequences of Laissez Faire

The principal consequence of *laissez faire* was to continue the tradition that had characterized Anglo-American law for a long time—the tradition of entrusting the protection of vital social interests to private contract or to essentially private litigation.[56] Minerals could be exploited, forests could be destroyed, streams could be polluted, water could be wasted, air could be contaminated, and buildings could be constructed in growing cities without regard to elementary principles of health (to say nothing of aesthetics), all in the sacred name of private property.[57] If the prevailing concept of property could have been viewed as a bundle of sticks representing rights (the favorite visual aid of property professors), most of them would have been labelled "private" although an occasional fragile straw would have borne the sign "public—to be activated by private initiative." These straws, representing the doctrine of nuisance, were real tokens in the wind. They demonstrated that even at their most extreme development property rights could not be absolute. Professor Cohen phrased it well:

> "To permit anyone to do absolutely what he likes with his property in creating noise, smells, or danger of fire, would be to make property in general valueless. To be really effective, therefore, the right of property must be supported by restrictions or positive duties on the part of the owners, enforced by the state as much as the right to exclude others which is the essence of property." [58]

To phrase it differently, a second consequence of *laissez faire* was to demonstrate that property rights could not be absolute. They had to be relative to the rights of others. "There is no absolute property, i. e., property that is freed from taking into consideration the interest of the community, and history has taken care to inculcate this truth into all peoples." [59] The

---

56. See Pound, The Spirit of the Common Law 13–15 (1921).

57. This is not the place to explore these consequences in depth. It has, of course, been done in magnificent detail elsewhere. For a highly readable account see Udall, The Quiet Crisis (1963).

58. Cohen, Property and Sovereignty, 13 Cornell L.Q. 8, 21 (1927).

59. Jhering, Der Geist des Römischen Rechts auf den Verschiedenen Stufen Seiner Entwicklung 7 (4th ed. 1878).

seeds of a new concept were contained in the fruits of the old. The community interest under *laissez faire* was protected on an *ad hoc* basis by the law of nuisance, public and private.[60] However adequate this may have been in the nineteenth century, it was soon to prove woefully inadequate for the problems of the twentieth. The breach had been made, however, and society had a legitimate interest, under the proper circumstances, in the property of the individual.[61] It now remained for "forces outside the law" to affect the concept itself. The period of transition was about to begin, and comprehensive zoning was to be its handmaiden.

B. CONCEPTS IN TRANSITION—COMPREHENSIVE ZONING AND ITS FELLOWS

Legal concepts do not change overnight. Nor do they evolve in isolation from the general intellectual climate of society. New ideas of land use were part and parcel of new ideas about property and its role in the community. In Germany, Rudolf von Jhering, starting from a base of Roman law, rejected the idea that the owner has unlimited power over his own property. "The principle of the inviolability of property means the delivery of society into the hands of ignorance, obstinacy and spite." [62] In France, Leon Duguit launched an attack upon the individualistic conception of private property found in the Code Napoléon. "Property is no longer the subjective right of the proprietor, but the social function of the holder of wealth." [63] In the United States, economists like Richard T. Ely, Simon Patten, and John R. Commons questioned the doctrine of *laissez faire* as sufficient for the new age. The American Economic

60. For a good collection of cases, articles, and other materials on nuisance see Haar, op. cit. supra note 53, at 133–155 (2d ed. 1971).

61. For a spirited contemporary justification of nineteenth-century, *laissez faire* property see Dietze, In Defense of Property (1963). This is a curious book which starts off as a defense of private, individualistic property (apparently the author feels even the doctrines of nuisance were an unwarranted interference with individual rights) and ends up as an attack on much of modern life. He feels the country began to slide downhill with Wilson's New Freedom and is now on a precipitous slope. One can agree with some of what he says without understanding how a return to Blackstone's view of property would save us!

62. Jhering, Law as a Means to an End 389 (Husick transl. 1913).

63. Duguit, Transformations du Droit Privié 158 (1912).

Association was established in 1885, and it favored the adjustment of property rights to the new social conditions. The state was viewed not as an enemy to be feared but as an agency whose positive assistance would be required to achieve human progress.

The bench, too, was looking at the constitution, law, and society with new eyes. Mr. Justice Holmes, in dissent, in Lochner v. New York stated it best:

> "This case is decided upon an economic theory [*laissez faire*] which a large part of the country does not entertain. . . . The liberty of the citizen to do as he likes so long as he does not interfere with the liberty of others to do the same, which has been a shibboleth for some well-known writers, is interfered with by school laws, by the Post Office, by every state or municipal institution which takes his money for purposes thought desirable, whether he likes it or not. The Fourteenth Amendment does not enact Mr. Herbert Spencer's Social Statics. . . . [A] constitution is not intended to embody a particular economic theory, whether of paternalism and the organic relation of the citizen to the State or of *laissez faire*." [64]

The Supreme Court declared a New York statute restricting the working hours for bakers unconstitutional and upheld the traditional view of freedom of contract (the freedom of acquiring property?), but the very concept the majority supported was slipping away. If Holmes was right and the state had a legitimate concern in the sacrosanct freedom of contract, did it not follow that the state also had a stake in how the land within its jurisdiction was used?

------

(1) Early Zoning Concepts

As suggested earlier,[65] Blackstone's reference to property rights as "sole and despotic dominion" to the exclusion of others never was accurate. It only seemed so because the text writers in property concentrated on the creation of estates and interests in land, the rights of the owners thereof, and the laws relating to their transfer, both inter vivos and at death. The slowly developing law of land use was handled by torts writers almost as a species of personal injury.[66] In fact, an Act for Re-

------

64. 198 U.S. 45, 75 (1905).

65. See text accompanying notes 33–34 supra.

66. Only in the last twenty years have property writers seriously included materials on land-use control. For the best example of the

building the City of London [67] was passed in 1679; an Act for Prevention of Common Nuisances Arising by Slaughterhouses, etc. was enacted by the Province of Massachusetts Bay in 1692; [68] and Pennsylvania sustained an act to bar wooden buildings from populous parts of Philadelphia in 1799.[69] Apart from this type of land-use legislation, there was the doctrine of public and private nuisance, which did something to curb the worst abuses and established the key principle that a man could not do *exactly* as he pleased with his own. Still, the prevailing concept was *laissez faire*, and even the early zoning was not viewed as any major interference with the essentially individual rights in property.

By the turn of the century, the American myth of the superabundance of natural resources had acquired a hollow ring and the forces of conservation had begun to fight back with the idea that government controls were needed to prevent people from exploiting mother earth fully as much as constitutional safeguards were required to prevent government from exploiting people.[70] At the same time, the urban thinkers were beginning to discover that *laissez faire* might not be the best way to build beautiful, healthful, spacious cities. The first City Planning Conference was held in 1909, and, although zoning received scant attention [71] at this session, the stage was set for the rapid growth of land-use regulation. By 1916, New York City had enacted the first comprehensive zoning ordinance and other municipalities were quick to follow suit. In 1922, one writer reported that zoning had taken the country by storm with twenty enabling acts, fifty ordinances, and nearly one hundred zoning plans in progress.[72] A major influence in this amazing popularity was the Standard State Zoning Enabling Act which was adopted, in whole or in part, by nineteen states in 1925. It had been drafted by an Advisory Committee on Building Codes and Zoning appointed by Secretary of Commerce Herbert Hoover, and it remains the model for much state enabling legislation.

new trend see 6 Powell, Real Property (1958). The same attitude has been present in curriculum planning in the law schools. Even now, many basic real property courses fail to grapple with land-use problems, thus giving the student a feeling that property is all history and individual rights.

67. 1679, 19 Car. 2, c. 3.

68. Province of Mass. Bay Acts & Resolves 1692, ch. 23.

69. Respublica v. Duquet, 2 Yeates 493 (Pa.1799).

70. See Udall, The Quiet Crisis passim (1963).

71. Ford, The Scope of City Planning in the United States, S.Doc.No. 422, 61st Cong., 2d Sess. 70 (1910).

72. Review of Planning in the United States, 1920–1921, 11 Nat'l Munic. Rev. 27, 32 (1922).

Prior to 1926, the struggle for legal recognition of zoning regulations was being fought in the state courts, and it was "a near thing." The judiciary was reluctant to sanction this invasion of traditional property rights, and some states felt required to pass constitutional amendments to remove any doubts about the validity of zoning.[73] There was always the lurking suspicion that the whole scheme was unconstitutional under the Fourteenth Amendment to the United States Constitution and that some day the Supreme Court would invalidate all of the acts, ordinances, and plans.

The big showdown came in 1926 in the now historic case of Village of Euclid v. Ambler Realty Co.[74] Mr. Justice Sutherland[75] deserted his fellow conservatives (Van Devanter, McReynolds, and Butler) to write the majority opinion sustaining the Euclid, Ohio, ordinance. The Court found the justification in the police power of the state, asserted for the public welfare. However, it was clear that the analogy to nuisance law carried the day.

> "In solving doubts, the maxim *sic utere tuo ut alienum non laedas,* which lies at the foundation of so much of the common law of nuisances, ordinarily will furnish a fairly helpful clew. And the law of nuisances, likewise, may be consulted, not for the purpose of controlling, but for the helpful aid of its analogies in the process of ascertaining the scope of, the power. . . . Under these circumstances, apartment houses, which in a different environment would be not only entirely unobjectionable but highly desirable, come very near to being nuisances." [76]

The courts in the absence of legislation could act to prevent nuisances; the legislature could itself declare an area to be a public nuisance and act to abate it; [77] and now the state could pass an

---

73. Ga.Const. art. III, § 7, par. 23; La.Stat.Ann.—Const. art. 14, § 29; Mass.Const. Amend. art. 60; N.J. Const. art. 4, § 6, par. 2.

74. 272 U.S. 365 (1926). For a somewhat flamboyant account of that controversy by one of the participating lawyers, see 1 Metzenbaum, Law of Zoning 54–61 (2d ed. 1955).

75. There is subtle irony in Mr. Justice Sutherland's role, since in 1923 he had written the opinion invalidating a minimum wage law for women. See Adkins v. Children's Hosp., 261 U.S. 525 (1923). He then wrote: "To sustain the individual freedom of action contemplated by the Constitution, is not to strike down the common good but to exalt it; for surely the good of society as a whole cannot be better served than by the preservation against arbitrary restraint of the liberties of its constituent members." Id. at 561.

76. Village of Euclid v. Ambler Realty Co., 272 U.S. 365, 387–88, 394–95 (1926).

77. This had been done in Dingley v. City of Boston, 100 Mass. 544 (1868), more than fifty years before.

enabling act, activated by local ordinances, to prevent a nuisance from arising in the first place. Justice Sutherland must have felt certain that the Court's view was consistent with his concepts of the private use of property, and his concepts were *laissez faire* and individualistic in the nineteenth-century sense.[78] These new zoning laws were justified on the basis of self-protection; they rearranged the rules for the protection of private property, but they did not materially alter the concept. The public interest, the planning function, the social welfare might all be involved, but the principal value to be conserved was the economic worth of the individual tract of land.

Two years later, in 1928, the Supreme Court took another case, Nectow v. City of Cambridge,[79] for the apparent purpose of clarifying its position in *Euclid*. The earlier decision meant that comprehensive zoning was not unconstitutional per se, but it was still possible for a given regulation to be unconstitutional as applied to a specific piece of land. "The governmental power to interfere by zoning regulations with the general rights of the land owner by restricting the character of his use, is not unlimited, and other questions aside, such restriction cannot be imposed if it does not bear a substantial relation to the public health, safety, morals, or general welfare." [80] The Court did not follow this warning with continued supervision of the zoning power [81] but left the constitutional scrutiny to the state courts, which, in general, accepted the "passed buck" with alacrity.[82] Today, attacks on the validity of an entire ordinance have all but ceased, whereas the struggles against specific applications as arbitrary and unreasonable seem to have increased in intensity.

---

(2) Changing Zoning Concepts

Prior to *Euclid*, urban land use was determined by economic forces and individual preferences. After *Euclid*, the forces and

78. See note 75 supra.

79. 277 U.S. 183 (1928).

80. Id. at 188.

81. See Johnson, Constitutional Law and Community Planning, 20 Law & Contemp.Prob. 199, 208 (1955).

82. In some states the highest court seemed to view its function as a kind of state-wide board of appeals and treated as constitutional issues which, at best, were close questions of fact. See Babcock, The Illinois Supreme Court and Zoning: A Study in Uncertainty, 15 U.Chi.L. Rev. 87 (1947). With the adoption of a new judicial amendment in Illinois the supreme court has served notice that it will no longer hear the mine run of cases but will leave them to the intermediate appellate courts. See First Nat'l Bank & Trust Co. v. City of Evanston, 30 Ill.2d 479, 197 N.E.2d 705 (1964).

preferences remained dominant, but the owner had to consider the land-use pattern established by the community for his own (and its) benefit.   Euclidean zoning was based on several assumptions about desirable land use, demands of the market, and economic and social changes.

> "It saw the ideal city as a great pattern of contrasting districts, rigidly separating incompatible types of land uses. It assumed that similar uses naturally tend to congregate in homogenous areas, that development takes place lot-by-lot on small parcels, that shifts of social groups and land values come about slowly, and that where and when and how development takes place can be predicted and regulated in advance.   It did not reckon with the swift advances in technology, transportation, and communication, and the dynamic growth of American cities, which have wrought changes in every old neighborhood and rung in new kinds of suburban development." [83]

In short, Euclidean zoning bears an interesting resemblance to feudalism.   On receiving his feud the ancient knight took the land subject to duties to his overlord.   He might not like them, but at least they were clear and certain.   The modern purchaser of a fee simple takes his plot subject to restrictions on its use, but he knows what they are when he buys.   In a sense, all zoning is retroactive because someone owns the land when the controls are imposed, but only if the loss is too great or the unfairness too apparent does the law protect the owner, as in the case of a nonconforming use.   Even then, the pressure is great for conformity, and the use may be terminated if properly amortized.[84]   Subject to this caveat on retroactivity, zoning creates a mold for the future and helps guide the growth of the area.   The word "mold" is used advisedly because the virtue of Euclidean zoning is also its vice.   It tends to be certain, but it tends also to be inflexible and needs a mechanism to allow for growth and change.

From the beginning the flexibility was provided by three methods—amendment, special exceptions, and variances.   All of them are necessary, but they are also subject to abuse, and many of the criticisms of zoning are directed at its administration

---

83.   Dukeminier & Stapleton, The Zoning Board of Adjustment: A Case Study in Misrule, 50 Ky.L.J. 273, 339–40 (1962).

84.   City of Los Angeles v. Gage, 127 Cal.App.2d 442, 274 P.2d 34 (2d Dist. 1954); Harbison v. City of Buffalo, 4 N.Y.2d 553, 152 N.E.2d 42, 176 N.Y.S.2d 598 (1958).   For comment on the latter case see Anderson, Amortization of Nonconforming Uses—A Preliminary Appraisal of Harbison v. City of Buffalo, 10 Syracuse L.Rev. 44 (1958).

rather than at its basic concept.[85]   Some of the critics, however, see the defect as more fundamental and doubt if tinkering alone is enough.   "Some of these remedies [for reforming the zoning board of adjustment] have merit.   But none of them goes to the basic problem: a Euclidean zoning system which, at the age of fifty, is showing signs of old age.   We are not sure that hardening of the arteries can be cured by small, or even massive, doses of Geritol." [86]

The heart of the matter is that the zoning concept itself has changed since *Euclid*.   Justice Sutherland justified zoning on the nuisance principle for the self-protection of the landowner, but now land-use controls are frequently justified by the benefits which inure to the whole community.   The fee simple is diminishing [87] in the hands of the individual, and the "withdrawn sticks" are showing up in the public pile.   The lawyer tends to see zoning as a restriction on the private property of his client, conflicting frequently with the views of property he learned in law school;   the planner tends to see zoning as one weapon in the battle for a better society and the private landowner as a cantankerous individual who is always objecting about his rights and cares little for his duties.[88]   It is the planners, not the lawyers, who have the most influence on the shape of zoning regulations since they are the key advisers to the planning commissions and the experts who are best trained in the fine art of city planning.   They see zoning in the light of the master plan for the community, and, while nuisances must be prevented, the principal aim is to achieve community goals.[89]   The original concept of zoning was preventive; the new concept is creative. The tough question is whether this view of property as a social asset is consistent with the concept of property as an individual right.

A detailed discussion of zoning is beyond the scope of this Section.[90]   However, four brief examples should suffice to illustrate the change in Euclidean concepts—zoning for minimum

85.   Babcock, The Unhappy State of Zoning Administration in Illinois, 26 U.Chi.L.Rev. 509 (1959).

86.   Dukeminier & Stapleton, supra note 83, at 350.

87.   See Cross, The Diminishing Fee, 20 Law & Contemp.Prob. 517 (1955).

88.   For an excellent illustration of the respective viewpoints see Haar, op. cit. supra note 53, at 745–58 (2d ed. 1971).

89.   "For, whatever the form of structure of government, one of its purposes—given the philosophy of society that I have set forth—must be the achievement of a better society." Howard, The Planner in a Democratic Society—A Credo, 21 J. of the American Institute of Planners 62 (1955).

90.   See Cunningham, Land-Use Control—The State and Local Programs, 50 Iowa L.Rev. 367, 368–414 (1965).

lot and house size, aesthetic zoning, noncumulative zoning, and "flexible" zoning. In Lionshead Lake, Inc. v. Township of Wayne,[91] the New Jersey court upheld a zoning ordinance which fixed the minimum size for dwellings in an entire township. Other cases have sustained minimum lot sizes as large as five acres in a semirural residence district.[92] Undoubtedly, this protects existing land values for those who prefer large lots and substantial houses, but it goes far beyond the original zoning concept of sorting out noncompatible uses.[93] Justice Jacobs in his concurring opinion placed heavy reliance on the relationship of adequate living space to mental and emotional health and cited the testimony of a professor of public health from Yale University. The king could not enter an Englishman's humble cottage against the owner's will, but an American township can keep the cottage from being built.

The prevailing American view is still against aesthetic zoning, but this ban is more apparent than real. No state court of last resort has upheld a zoning ordinance directed *solely* at aesthetic ends, but a number of decisions contain dicta supporting such ordinances and several lower court opinions have taken this position.[94] It is becoming quite clear that beauty is not beyond the pale of protection by the police power, and for our present purposes this represents another facet of a changing concept.[95]

Cumulative zoning was a necessary corollary of the nuisance concept. If residences had their own districts from which industry was excluded, that was sufficient to protect the landowner. Those individuals who chose (or were forced by economic circumstances) to live in an industrial zone were certainly free

91. 10 N.J. 165, 89 A.2d 693 (1952), appeal dismissed, 344 U.S. 919 (1953).

92. Fisher v. Township of Bedminster, 11 N.J. 194, 93 A.2d 378 (1952).

93. For a detailed analysis of the case see a series of law review articles: Haar, Zoning for Minimum Standards: The Wayne Township Case, 66 Harv.L.Rev. 1051 (1953); Nolan & Horack, How Small a House?—Zoning for Minimum Space Requirements, 67 Harv.L.Rev. 967 (1954); Haar, Wayne Township: Zoning for Whom?—In Brief Reply, 67 Harv.L.Rev. 986 (1954).

94. For a good collection of cases and a recent analysis see Comment,

Zoning, Aesthetics, and the First Amendment, 64 Colum.L.Rev. 81 (1964). See also Agnor, Beauty Begins a Comeback: Aesthetic Considerations in Zoning, 11 J.Pub.L. 260 (1962); Dukeminier, Zoning for Aesthetic Objectives: A Reappraisal, 20 Law & Contemp.Prob. 218 (1955).

95. The "historic district" cases are good examples of rigid controls established primarily for aesthetic reasons. See Opinion of the Justices to the Senate, 333 Mass. 773, 128 N.E.2d 557 (1955). See also Reid v. Architectural Bd. of Review, 119 Ohio App. 67, 192 N.E.2d 74 (1963), where the court sustained a refusal by the zoning board to allow a unique one-story home in a two-story area.

to do so. Thus, all "higher" uses were permitted in "lower" use districts, and the scheme became hallowed by custom. If, however, the master plan called for restricted industrial areas, not to protect homeowners alone but to preserve needed space for new companies, then the cumulative principle would defeat zoning's own ends. In a New Jersey case, Katobimar Realty Co. v. Webster,[96] the court clung to old standards and allowed a shopping center in an industrial zone after it had been excluded by a new type ordinance, but Justice Brennan, in dissent, saw the issue clearly and urged judicial approval of the zoning plan. A Connecticut court saw the issue in still a different light, as the following exchange discloses:

> "The Court: Well the witness, I have inferred, takes the position that good zoning requires that this particular property holder in the suppositious case I have made should be protected against himself.

> "The Witness: That is exactly it—protected against himself.

> "The Court: Whether that is valid is the point we have to decide in this case." [97]

Both New Jersey and Connecticut seemed hostile to noncumulative zoning because of the facts of the particular cases, but other courts have been more receptive and the principle seems well on its way to judicial acceptance.[98] This type of zoning may protect land values, but it is scarcely based on nuisance doctrines except in the sense of "father knows best." Basically, it protects the community at large by preserving land areas for industrial expansion and, hence, for civic growth.

The greatest change in concept shows up in so-called "flexible" zoning. Euclidean zoning requires the local authorities to be far-seeing prophets and establish a zoning plan for land as yet undeveloped. It would be much simpler to freeze all land in its present use and then decide each application for a changed use on its merits as the occasion arises. In Rockhill v. Township of Chesterfield [99] the township passed an ordinance authorizing agricultural uses and then allowed a permitted series

96. 20 N.J. 114, 118 A.2d 824 (1955).

97. Record on Appeal, Corthouts v. Town of Newington, 140 Conn. 284, 99 A.2d 112 (1953) (quoted in Haar, Land-Use Planning 219 (2d ed. 1971)).

98. Roney v. Board of Supervisors, 138 Cal.App.2d 740, 292 P.2d 529 (1st Dist. 1956); People ex rel. Skokie Town House Builders, Inc. v. Village of Morton Grove, 16 Ill. 2d 183, 157 N.E.2d 33 (1959); Note, Industrial Zoning to Exclude Higher Uses, 32 N.Y.U.L.Rev. 1261 (1957).

99. 23 N.J. 117, 128 A.2d 473 (1957).

of special uses *if* the planning board decided they were desirable and in the best interests of the township. Boundary lines were not drawn and zones were not established. In holding the ordinance void under the enabling act, the court said: "The scheme of the ordinance is the negation of zoning. It overrides the basic concept of use zoning by districts, that is to say, territorial division according to the character of the lands and structures and their peculiar use suitability and a comprehensive regulatory plan to advance the general good within the prescribed range of the police power." [1] Actually, a variation of this practice has been common for a long time by the simple expedient of drawing the zones to fit existing land use and then allowing easy amendment or variance as the need arises. The New Jersey ordinance was more blatant about it and gave the authorities open discretion without any apparent guidelines. In other states, the special-use technique has been allowed even without specific authorization in the enabling act. Thus, a series of Illinois cases has refused to outlaw the practice despite vigorous opposition by judges who recognize that this is a considerable departure from Euclidean concepts.[2] These judges doubt the constitutionality of the practice even if authorized by the enabling act. "Zoning, as the name itself imports, is regulation by districts and not by individual pieces of property. . . . Even if there were a statute purporting to authorize ordinances such as the one in this case its constitutionality would be open to serious question." [3]

The special-use device is not unlike the so-called floating-zone technique which appears as the second stage of a two-step process. First, the entire community is zoned in the traditional manner, but certain uses are allowed to "float" and only come to rest when the planning authority grants a special permit as the need arises. Note that this differs from "special exceptions" which are spelled out in the ordinance itself. In a leading Pennsylvania case [4] this technique too was disapproved, largely because it did not satisfy the statutory requirement that zoning be in accordance with a comprehensive plan.[5] There does ap-

---

1. Id. at 127, 128 A.2d at 478.

2. Ward v. Village of Skokie, 26 Ill. 2d 415, 186 N.E.2d 529 (1962). See particularly the specially concurring opinion by Justice Klingbiel, which discusses prior cases in Illinois and elsewhere. See also Huff v. Board of Zoning Appeals, 214 Md. 48, 133 A.2d 83 (1957).

3. Ward v. Village of Skokie, supra note 2, at 421, 422, 186 N.E.2d at 531, 532.

4. Eves v. Zoning Bd. of Adjustment, 401 Pa. 211, 164 A.2d 7 (1960).

5. For a detailed discussion of the problem see Haar & Hering, The Lower Gwynedd Township Case: Too Flexible Zoning or an Inflexible Judiciary?, 74 Harv.L.Rev. 1552 (1961).

pear to be a difference between the floating-zone ordinance of the *Gwynedd Township* case and the more sweeping delegation of discretion involved in the *Chesterfield Township* case. In the former, the ordinance establishes basically compatible uses and then allows modifications (not unlike amendments or variances) as conditions change. In the latter, there is little advance determination, and permission is granted or withheld in terms of the individual uses and the circumstances at the time the development is sought. This approach

> "does not so much modify the zoning concepts long prevailing in this country as move away from them toward an adaptation of the English approach embodied in the Town and Country Planning Act, 1947, under which each change of use must be preceded by permission. Although advance determinations are made and embodied in the development plan for the area, they are not binding on the administrator, and each application is considered on its own merits. Such a technique is a far cry indeed from the floating-zone variant of Euclidean zoning." [6]

The floating-zone variant itself is considerably removed from the nuisance theory of zoning and demonstrates the increased emphasis on flexibility at the expense of certainty. Surely this is a changing concept in the law of land use.

----

(3) Changing Concepts Aside From Zoning

Zoning has been discussed in some detail because it is the principal land-use regulator at the command of the planning groups. It is also the control device with which most people are familiar and which has the greatest impact on the day-to-day use of land. No less dramatic, however, have been the shifting concepts in other, closely related, areas. Four such areas require brief exploration before turning to concepts for the future: (1) building and housing codes; (2) subdivision regulations; (3) official maps and open-space controls; and (4) urban renewal legislation.

----

6. Id. at 1572. The ordinances involved in the Illinois cases are of the *Gwynedd Township* type rather than the *Chesterfield Township* variety. It is not clear what the Supreme Court of Illinois would do with the latter type. Certainly the dissenting justices, at least, would be even more disturbed.

(a) Building and Housing Codes

Although terminology in this area can be confusing, building and housing codes are of two basic types. A building code establishes standards for new construction and includes detailed structural requirements. A housing code sets minimum standards for occupancy of all buildings, including those already in existence. Codes of both types operate under the police power and constitute direct restraints on the owner's freedom to use his land as he sees fit. These codes are vital to a program of effective urban rehabilitation. "Without question, the failure to enact, improve, soundly administer, and effectively enforce adequate local codes, more than any other single cause, accounts for the huge tasks of the present urban renewal effort." [7]

The codes are not a new idea; their genesis may be found in seventeenth-century England.[8] As a serious attempt to control urban environment, however, the real story begins in the twentieth century. That story has been carefully told elsewhere,[9] and our concern here is solely with the concept.

> "Various means, increasingly sophisticated, have been employed by governments in an attempt to control the maturation, aging, death and resurrection of our city neighborhoods. From simple fire and health regulations, government activity has extended to zoning, comprehensive building and housing codes, electrical and plumbing codes, to public housing, slum clearance and finally to programs designed to encourage the conservation and rehabilitation of existing buildings." [10]

As the regulations have moved from the simple to the complex, there have been constitutional challenges hurled against this invasion of "sole and despotic dominion." [11] With few exceptions, the police power has been broad enough to withstand the challenge, and the housing inspector has the right to enter, which was to the king denied.[12] "A man's house may be his castle,

---

7. Osgood & Zwerner, Rehabilitation and Conservation, 25 Law & Contemp.Prob. 705, 719 (1960).

8. See 1679, 19 Car. 2, c. 3.

9. See, e. g., Abbott, The Tenements of Chicago, 1908–1935 (1936); Jacobs, The Death and Life of Great American Cities (1961); Riis, A Ten Years' War (1900); Sert, Can Our Cities Survive? (1944).

10. Comment, Building Codes, Housing Codes and the Conservation of Chicago's Housing Supply, 31 U. Chi.L.Rev. 180 (1963).

11. See Miner, Some Constitutional Aspects of Housing Legislation, 39 Ill.L.Rev. 305 (1945); Note, 7 Geo. Wash.L.Rev. 520 (1939).

12. Note, Housing and Health Inspection: A Survey and Suggestions in Light of Recent Case Law, 28 Geo.Wash.L.Rev. 421 (1960).

but that castle no longer sits on a hill surrounded by a moat. The modern 'castle' is connected to a central water system, a garbage collection system, and frequently to houses on either side." [13] The role of the sanitary inspector has been commented on in England too, where it has been noted that few public officials are invested with such power to search and inspect. In principle, says one writer, the power of entry is a direct negation of the rights of private individuals as established in the common law.[14]

Due to the difficulty of enforcement, some ordinances, such as the New York Multiple Dwelling Law, put the burden directly on the owner, and if he refuses to make the alterations the city can make them for him, the cost becoming a lien upon the property. This assumption of decision making for the owner has been sustained except where the lien was given priority over existing mortgages and the mortgagees were not required to be notified before the improvements were made.[15] This technique not only recognizes the duty of the landowner to meet minimal social standards but, in effect, provides for specific performance of that duty. It seems clear that prior mortgagees (and other lien holders) could be subjected to the same social responsibility if the law were drafted to give them notice and an opportunity to make the alterations or see that the owner makes them. Even without this notice the legislation would probably be sustained if the buildings were in a dangerous rather than merely a substandard condition.[16]

The codes, like zoning, have been plagued by their rigid character. They apply to an entire city, and frequently it is impossible to enforce them vigorously in some areas because the standards set are unrealistically high. Yet, these standards may be necessary in another section of the city in order to carry out urban renewal policies. The result has been unequal enforcement of the codes, and some urban renewal experts have even recommended this as a matter of policy.[17] The logical next step is to propose a zoned housing code which would achieve different standards in different areas by means of legislation rather than by discretionary enforcement. Such a proposal was

13. Brief for the Member Municipalities of the National Institute of Municipal Law Offices as Amici Curiae, p. 6, Frank v. Maryland, 359 U.S. 360 (1959).

14. Clay, The Sanitary Inspector's Handbook 26 (5th ed. 1942).

15. Central Sav. Bank v. City of New York, 279 N.Y. 266, 18 N.E.2d 151 (1938).

16. In the Matter of City of New York (Jefferson Houses), 208 Misc. 757, 143 N.Y.S.2d 346 (Sup.Ct.1955).

17. See, e. g., Nash, Residential Rehabilitation: Private Profits and Public Purposes 107 (1959).

in fact made in 1947 by the Health Commissioner of Milwaukee, Wisconsin, but the bill was not presented to the legislature because the corporation counsel advised that it would be unconstitutional. At the present time it seems to be generally agreed that a zoned code would be invalid because it would be a denial of equal protection of the laws.[18] However, proposals of this type, no less than the floating zones discussed in the previous section, show which way the winds of doctrine are blowing.

(b) Subdivision Regulations

Ownership rights certainly include the power of alienation. Indeed, this power to transfer to another is so thoroughly stressed in common-law countries that land law and conveyancing have tended to become synonymous. As late as 1949, Professor Hargreaves felt compelled to state: "[T]he time has surely long since passed when land law could be considered in the main as a secretion in the interstices of conveyancing." [19] It follows that a man can split up his acres as he will and sell the parcels to whom he will. More accurately, it followed in the nineteenth century that this was so. The encouragement of land subdivision was the natural policy during the period of westward expansion. The land was there to be developed (exploited?), and it mattered not whether it was timber to be removed, stone to be quarried, or urban land to be subdivided and sold. The congressional legislation disposing of the federal lands imposed few restrictions, and the landowner was left with a free hand.

It was not until the second decade of the twentieth century that the disastrous consequences of this *laissez faire* policy became apparent.[20] Since 1928, when the United States Department of Commerce published a model law for subdivision control, there has been a heavy increase in state enabling acts and local ordinances. Whereas the model zoning act served to create uniformity in the state legislation, the subdivision controls have tended to follow diverse paths, ranging from little more than pious exhortations to detailed commands with heavy sanctions.

18. Note, Municipal Housing Codes, 69 Harv.L.Rev. 1115 (1956).

19. Book Review, 12 Modern L.Rev. 139, 143 (1949).

20. The depression of the 1930's set forth in bold relief some of the consequences of careless subdivision planning. The resulting tax sales, unmarketable titles caused by premature platting, etc., continue to plague American cities. Some of the urban renewal legislation now on the books was required to clear up these old mistakes. See People ex rel. Gutknecht v. City of Chicago, 414 Ill. 600, 111 N.E.2d 626 (1953).

In general, these regulations have been sustained by the courts, frequently in language that recognizes that they were long overdue.

> "We are surrounded with the problems of planless growth. The baneful consequences of haphazard development are everywhere apparent. There are evils affecting the health, safety and prosperity of our citizens that are well-nigh insurmountable because of the prohibitive corrective cost. To challenge the power to give proper direction to community growth and development . . . is to deny the vitality of a principle that has brought men together in organized society for their mutual advantage." [21]

The enabling acts typically allow the municipalities to require that the subdivision be adequately drained, that the streets be of sufficient width and suitable grade, that curbs, sidewalks, gutters, street lights, etc. be satisfactory, and that the street design conform to that shown in the master plan.[22] In order to make the controls effective, the municipality can frequently impose its authority several miles beyond the corporate limits,[23] a power that has been traditionally denied to zoning authorities.[24] The net result of the subdivision regulations is the inclusion of community planning as one of the factors to be considered by the real estate developer. No longer can he establish a subdivision with his eye solely on the economic return; he must consider the public interest as well as his own. Usually these tend to coincide and the landowner has no quarrel with the basic requirements, but sometimes he is forced to dedicate portions of his land to public use in a way which comes close to, or crosses, the hazy line between the police power and eminent domain.[25]

The tendency is for the controls to move further and further into the area of private volition so that the community not only regulates the way in which the land is to be subdivided but whether it is to be subdivided at all. Thus, the Washington act provides:

> "The city, town, or county authority shall inquire into the public use and interest proposed to be served by the es-

21. Mansfield & Swett, Inc. v. Town of West Orange, 120 N.J.L. 145, 150–51, 198 Atl. 225, 229 (Sup.Ct. 1938).

22. E. g., N.J.Stat.Ann. § 40:55–1.20 (Supp.1963).

23. The model act set the limit at five miles. U. S. Dep't of Commerce, Standard City Planning Enabling Act § 12 (1928).

24. In 1963, Illinois, for the first time, allowed cities to zone 1½ miles beyond the corporate limits if there were no county zoning. Ill. Ann.Stat. ch. 24, § 11–13–1 (Smith-Hurd). This is still relatively rare.

25. See the discussion at p. 421 supra.

tablishment of the plat, subdivision, or dedication. It shall see that appropriate provision is made in the plat or subdivision for streets and other public ways, parks, playgrounds, sites for schools and school grounds, and *shall consider all other facts deemed by it relevant and designed to indicate whether or not the public interest will be served by the platting, subdividing, or dedication.*" [26]

In a Connecticut case, the planning commission was held not to have the power (under the enabling act) to deny a subdivision because it would cause "an unbearable financial burden" to the town in providing schools, roads, and police and fire protection.[27] In a recent Michigan case,[28] a city zoning ordinance (as opposed to a subdivision regulation) required a minimum lot size for the purpose of limiting future density of population in proportion to sewage capacity. The ordinance was declared arbitrary, unreasonable, unrelated to the present needs of the community, and, therefore, invalid. However, three judges dissented in the Michigan case, and the Connecticut decision was based on lack of power in the enabling act, not on the unconstitutionality of an act like that in Washington. Quite apart from the desirability or even the necessity of controlling the tempo and sequence of city growth through subdivision regulation,[29] it is apparent that this is a far cry from the *laissez faire* concept of land use.

(c) Official Maps and Open-Space Controls

As our land-use concepts move from *laissez faire* through nuisance prevention to the regulation of land as a social asset, the public planning side of property looms larger and larger. At the heart of planning lies a flexible blueprint for community development. If this blueprint is made concrete in the form of an official map, private land may be regulated in a way which comes close to a taking without compensation.[30] So long as the map plots the course of community growth but does not deny the rights of the private developer no legal problem arises, but

26. Wash.Rev.Code Ann. § 58.16.060 (1961). (Emphasis added.)

27. Beach v. Planning & Zoning Comm'n, 141 Conn. 79, 103 A.2d 814 (1954).

28. Christine Bldg. Co. v. City of Troy, 367 Mich. 508, 116 N.W.2d 816 (1962), 62 Mich.L.Rev. 131 (1963).

29. See Fagin, Regulating the Timing of Urban Development, 20 Law & Contemp.Prob. 298 (1955).

30. For a detailed analysis of a specific map act see Waite, The Official Map and the Constitution in Maine, 15 Me.L.Rev. 3 (1963).

if the owner cannot build in designated areas without a permit, except at the risk of no compensation for improvements when the land is later taken for a street or park, it is a different story. Despite the constitutional challenges, the official-map technique has widespread judicial approval, and apparently no enabling act has been declared unconstitutional in the past fifty years.[31] Only occasionally has a local ordinance gone so far as to be declared invalid.[32] This may seem like a relatively mild interference with private property concepts, but to the extent that the official map freezes land development and deprives an owner of profits he could realize by making further developments, a portion of the community's costs for highways, parks, etc. is being paid by the private landowner.

As urban sprawl eats further into the countryside, the need for open space in and near megalopolis becomes more apparent. Some of the demand can be satisfied by outright purchases or gifts of park lands, forest preserves, etc., but, due to the capital outlay required, it seems doubtful that this method will ever be adequate. The natural tendency is to turn to techniques which have been successful elsewhere and think in terms of official maps designating areas for future acquisition or area-wide zoning which will freeze land use to agricultural pursuits. This might accomplish the purpose, but it would be a greater inroad on private rights than our property concepts have so far allowed. The English experience furnishes a valuable guide in open-space regulation, and a book by Professor Mandelker explores the "greenbelt" problem in depth.[33] He concludes:

> "American planning is currently much attracted to the greenbelt concept. As in England, however, the motivations for the programs are not entirely clear, and the idea has not been precisely defined. . . . [I]n the United States the dominant trend is to seek the purchase of open space either through the acquisition of the freehold or through the purchase of an easement in the development rights, a scheme that is reminiscent of the 1947 English experiment. Unless the American programs are well financed, however, English experience under the 1938 Green Belt Act suggests that public purchase is not adequate to the task. At the same time, the use of planning powers

31. Headley v. City of Rochester, 272 N.Y. 197, 5 N.E.2d 198 (1936); Waite, supra note 30, at 6 n. 14.

32. Miller v. Beaver Falls, 368 Pa. 189, 82 A.2d 34 (1951). See p. 420 supra.

33. Mandelker, Green Belts and Urban Growth (1962).

to impose restrictive controls on new developments in substantial green-belt areas presents complicating questions of constitutionality and of administration, especially since the drawing of the green-belt boundary has such substantial effects on land values." [34]

The federal government has now entered the arena, and Title VII of the Federal Housing Act of 1961 provides for limited federal aid to state and local programs for the preservation of open space.[35] It is still too early to tell what effect green-belt thinking will have on private property concepts, but it is safe to predict that it will start no stampede back to *laissez faire*.

(d) Urban Renewal Legislation

Nowhere are changing concepts better illustrated than in slum clearance and urban renewal. Zoning, subdivision regulations, official maps, and green belts are all designed to prevent the worst mistakes of the past from recurring. Essentially preventive in character, they cannot remedy the errors of yesterday, but the philosophy behind them calls for affirmative action by the community to improve the living conditions of its citizens. The major surgery required in modern megalopolis necessitates the acquisition of land (at least temporarily) in order to clear the slums and blighted areas so that the natural resource can be returned to productive social use. Again, the feudal analogy is not inapt. If the possessor of the *feud* failed to meet the prevailing standards, the land could be forfeited to the king or lord and regranted to another who would conform. The rules were different but the principle was similar. Clearly, this result cannot be accomplished in the United States under the police power alone. The land has to be condemned and taken for a valid public use or purpose. The power of eminent domain is an attribute of sovereignty. It is an inherent power of the state, not derived from, but limited by, the fundamental principles of the constitution. Traditionally, the power was involved in the acquisition of roads, parks, sites for public buildings, etc. —land which was to be retained by the taking agency and used by the public. Today, however, the land is cleared of slums or

---

34. Id. at 153, 154.

35. For an analysis of American open-space problems see Krasnowiecki & Paul, The Preservation of Open Space in Metropolitan Areas,

110 U.Pa.L.Rev. 179 (1961); Comment, Control of Urban Sprawl or Securing Open Space: Regulation by Condemnation or by Ordinance?, 50 Calif.L.Rev. 483 (1962).

blight and then sold for private development. Is this a constitutional use of the power of eminent domain?

It was long assumed that one thing which the state could
not do was take one individual's property and give it to another,
with or without compensation.[36] Like many other assumptions
about property, this was only partially true. Many legal rules
have the effect of curtailing one man's activity for the benefit
of his fellows, and in this sense take from one to give to another.
Perhaps the best example is found in the equitable doctrine of
"balancing conveniences." If a landowner commits acts which
are clearly a nuisance but equity refuses to enjoin them in order
to protect the dominant business interest in the state (mining
in Pennsylvania, lumbering in California, copper smelting in
Tennessee and Georgia), this may virtually destroy a neighbor's
land and leave him only unsatisfactory money damages or the
opportunity to sell, against his wishes, to the wrongdoer.[37]
While the result may be socially desirable, it is a kind of private
eminent domain which violates the absolutist view of private
property. The courts seldom refer to this aspect of the problem, and little hue and cry has been raised against invasion of
individual rights of ownership. Of course, the aggressor (taker) in these cases is a private landowner, usually a corporation,
and the state's role, through the courts, is seen as a mediator,
not as an active participant in the process. As in the nuisance-
zoning analogy, government in urban renewal moves to a more
dominant position.

In the period since World War II, the old assumption has
been revised, and it now seems clear that carefully drafted legislation utilizing the power of eminent domain as an instrument
for forced land transfer from one private owner to another will
be sustained. Berman v. Parker [38] cleared the way under the
federal constitution with its classic statement: "The rights of
these property owners are satisfied when they receive that just
compensation which the Fifth Amendment exacts as the price
of the taking." [39] Occasionally by constitutional amendment
but usually by judicial interpretation, the public use or purpose
was found to exist in the taking itself, i. e., the clearing of the
slum or blighted area for a more productive social use. The

36. For a good development of this
point see Philbrick, Changing Conceptions of Property in Law, 86 U.
Pa.L.Rev. 691, 724–25 (1938).

37. These cases are legion and good
collections can be found in any of
the standard equity casebooks. See,
e. g., Cribbet, Cases on Judicial

Remedies 379 (1954). For a particularly frank statement of "economic
balancing" see Rose v. Socony-
Vacuum Corp., 54 R.I. 411, 173 A.
627 (1934).

38. 348 U.S. 26 (1954).

39. Id. at 36. See p. 425 supra.

struggle over the changing concept goes on, but now it appears mainly in dissent, as in a recent Washington case. In that case the dissent voiced its disapproval of an urban renewal act, saying in part:

> "The constitution of the state is a document designed to protect minorities against the appetites and power of majorities. Without the constitution, the safeguarding of the lives, liberties, and properties of minorities would be lost. Unless the people are willing to change the constitution so as to permit it, one man's property should not be taken by the government and turned over to another to aid in the fulfillment of a utopian ideal of the state.
>
> The urban renewal act as it is now written authorizes the appropriation of private property for private use, and as such runs afoul of amendment 9, Art. 1, § 16, of the Washington constitution." [40]

A majority of the Washington court sustained the legislation.

Thus, the state, under proper circumstances, can take land from one private owner, pay him just compensation for his loss, and turn the land over to another private owner who presumably will develop it more in line with what is conceived to be the public interest. As the use of this power continues to expand under the pressures of an exploding population, the role of "just compensation" assumes a new importance.[41] Land is only one species of property, and society, acting through the legislature, is deciding that its owner can be forced to trade it for another species—money. Under earlier concepts this could be done infrequently; today, as the public sticks in the bundle grow in number, it can be done quite frequently. The courts must make every effort to see that the owner receives fair market value for his land. To give him more will be a breach of faith with the tax-paying public; to give him less will make even further changes in our concepts of private property and lead to partial expropriation in violation of the federal and state constitutions.

40. Miller v. City of Tacoma, 61 Wash.2d 374, 402–03, 378 P.2d 464, 481 (1963), 62 Mich.L.Rev. 1065 (1964). This case contains a detailed discussion of the whole problem, including a table of cases from the various states.

41. For a good collection of materials on this point see Haar, Land-Use Planning 478–560 (2d ed. 1971). Professor Haar wisely calls this section of his book "The Riddle of Just Compensation."

C. CONCEPTS FOR THE FUTURE

Our legal concepts of land use have moved from *laissez faire* to *savoir faire*.   Once society agrees on goals the law is a ready tool to be used in achieving them.   The police power regulations are under serious attack for defects in their administration,[42] but few responsible voices are being raised for a return to the nineteenth century.   Forces outside the law have changed our view of property and law has adjusted to the change.   "The influence of the metropolis upon the concepts, rules and institutions relating to property is not unique.   It follows the historical pattern of evolutionary adaptation of the law to the interests of the group to which it is applicable." [43]   Nothing can be more certain than that the evolutionary adaptation will continue and that our concepts for the future will build on, but be different from, our concepts of the past.[44]

A glimpse into the future was furnished by Planning 1963, a collection of selected papers from the national conference of the American Society of Planning Officials held in Seattle in May, 1963.   A leading speaker came directly to the point: "What I am suggesting to you is that large-scale social developments in our culture in the last generation have made many of our institutions of land use control obsolete." [45]   He grants that, in light of the purposes it was designed to serve, zoning has proved to be a remarkably successful instrument, especially in the stabilization of property values, and he admits that all of the police power devices will continue to be useful in the future.   However, he believes they are inadequate for the magnitude of the task and calls for a new set of Federalist Papers, a dialogue by politically sophisticated men who will explore the subtle kinds of intergovernmental relationships into which our urban problems are pushing us.   He suggests abandonment of the struggle

42. "The question must be asked seriously whether zoning, as it is currently being practiced, is endangering our democratic institutions. A second question stemming from the first is: 'Is zoning increasingly becoming the rule of man rather than the rule of law?' I would be inclined to answer both questions affirmatively." Blucher, Is Zoning Wagging the Dog?, in 1955 Planning 96; Babcock, The Unhappy State of Zoning Administration in Illinois, 26 U.Chi.L.Rev. 509 (1959).

43. Reeve, The Influence of the Metropolis on the Concepts, Rules, and Institutions Relating to Property 204 (1954).

44. For an example of how this evolutionary adaption is progressing see The American Law Institute's Model Land Development Code, Tentative Draft No. 2 (1970).

45. Doebele, Key Issues in Land Use Controls, in 1963 Planning 8.

for metropolitan government of the Miami and Toronto type, except in special situations, but he would "move toward a Common Market in the allocation of metropolitan land, that is, a situation in which any industry, any shopping center, and, most important of all, any family of whatever size or income, can locate freely within the metropolis without concern for municipal boundaries that have become technologically meaningless." [46]

A study of the Planning 1963 papers and of the voluminous literature on land-use planning published since then makes the following questions pertinent, albeit a few of them rhetorical. Will there be a growing need for large-scale planning in an increasingly urbanized society? Will there be a similar need for proper conservation and utilization of agricultural, timber, mineral, and recreational land? Will there be a need for increasing public acquisition of land? Will there be a need for regional as well as local planning? Assuming the answer to the previous questions is yes, what is likely to be the form of controls employed to make such large-scale planning effective? Will it be possible to continue to encourage socially desirable land use or will it become necessary to coerce the individual to use his land for the benefit of society? What effect will such controls have on concepts of individual rights in property? Is such comprehensive planning of land use consistent with American political and social institutions?

Is land use planning a local matter or should the federal government play a larger role in the proper utilization of a scarce resource? If a larger federal role is necessary and desirable what should that role be? Similar questions were asked in England following the passage of the Town and Country Planning Act of 1947 with its far-reaching impact on English land law. Mr. R. E. Megarry,[47] a respected English barrister and writer, responded: "The right to use property in a particular way is not in itself property. The fee simple in land remains the same fee simple as before. 'All that has happened is that the fruits of ownership have become less sweet; but that is nothing new in land law.'" [48] The last sentence, at least, is amply supported by English history going back to copyhold tenure "in the merrie years of Henry VIII and Elizabeth I." [49]

46. Id. at 11.

47. Now Sir Robert Megarry, a High Court Justice in the Royal Courts of Justice of England. Incidentally, these questions are still being asked in England and the answers given by the Conservatives and Labor were issues in the 1974 general election where Labor called for further "nationalization" of land, albeit without spelling out exactly what the party had in mind.

48. Megarry, A Manual of the Law of Real Property 616 (3d ed. 1962).

49. Tefft, Book Review, 31 U.Chi.L. Rev. 204, 207 (1963).

However, the first sentence challenges even present-day concepts of property in this country, to say nothing of traditional views. The right to use can be reasonably regulated, but at some point regulation becomes taking and constitutional guarantees come into play. Locating the point is no mean accomplishment, but Chief Judge Murrah of the Court of Appeals for the Tenth Circuit suggests a test:

> "As I reason, the constitutional test in each case is first, whether the asserted interest is one which the law will protect; if so, whether the interference is sufficiently direct, sufficiently peculiar, and of sufficient magnitude to cause us to conclude that fairness and justice, as between the State and the citizen, requires the burden imposed to be borne by the public and not by the individual alone.[50]"

A test like this will have to be kept in mind and flesh added to its spirit by concrete cases or our concept of property will evolve into something entirely different.

Professor Dunham has approached the problem in a way somewhat similar to the Megarry view:

> "In constructing a theory about the relation of property law to planning, we are not interested in the formal shape of property law—in such matters as estates, future interests, and formalities of transfer. Bentham tells us that property is nothing more than the expectation of deriving a certain advantage from a thing which the law allows us. . . . If property is the established expectations which the law gives an owner, then as long as the owner is not commanded to use his property in a particular way and is secured some freedom of choice as to its use, it cannot be said that government restriction on land use has in it any denial of private property.[51]

As Professor Dunham recognizes, this is the curtain-raiser to the deeper question: "What expectations should the law allow a private citizen?"

This brings us to the crux of our changing concepts of land use. We are not abandoning our historical emphasis on individual rights in property, but we are expanding our emphasis on public rights to such an extent that we do, indeed, have a diminishing fee simple absolute. The law of property, like the law generally, can be divided into substantive and adjective sides. On the substantive side, property consists of a bundle of rights and duties that could be described with some degree of accuracy

50.   Batten v. United States, 306 F.2d 580, 587 (10th Cir. 1962).

51.   Dunham, Property, City Planning, and Liberty, in Law and Land 28, 30 (Haar ed. 1964).

at any given moment in time and space.[52] Viewed from this side the "propertyness" of Blackacre in Blackstone's England and Traynor's California presents some stunning contrasts. However, as this Section has attempted to demonstrate, the content of the bundle has always been subject to fluctuation. "[W]hile 'property rights' under American law enjoy a reputation for permanence, they are in fact more highly relative and more sensitive to changing economic factors and social opinion than most other legal concepts."[53] Of course, the quantum of private rights could be so reduced that the owner would be left with the hollow shell of title and the privilege of paying taxes. Presumably, before this point is reached the courts will apply Judge Murrah's test and require the state to take, not regulate.[54] It is obviously impossible to freeze the contents of the bundle at any given period of time, and it is exceedingly difficult to describe the *ideal* contents even at the present time. One may wish for the ample expectations of the country squire but be faced by the spectre of a Harlem slum. If those population experts who visualize a day in the future when each man on earth will have but a square foot of soil are correct, then the contents of the bundle will be slim indeed. In that situation, forces outside the law, perhaps resulting in compulsory birth control, would have more to do with our concepts of land use than all the writings of jurists and philosophers.

It is the adjective side of property that presents the greatest challenge to the property statesman of our day. Granting that changes in substance are inevitable, if not desirable, it is *how* they are made which will have the greatest impact on our political and social institutions. Sometimes it will be necessary for land to be used in one certain way for the benefit of society. In those cases the land should be taken under an expanding concept of public purpose and the owner should receive just compensation for his loss. The owner should not be coerced, under the guise of regulation, into using his land in one particular way which may be socially desirable but personally nonproductive.[55]

52. Note in this connection that property does not have the same meaning at any one time in different places. Different rules apply in neighboring states, and even within a state local variations can be sizable. Thus, in Texas, Houston has no zoning at all, while all of the other major cities in the state have highly developed police power regulations.

53. Netherton, Control of Highway Access 80 (1963). For a review of this excellent book see 4 Natural Resources J. 205 (1964).

54. This is exactly what does happen in the zoning cases when the planners become too zealous. For a classic case see Arverne Bay Constr. Co. v. Thatcher, 278 N.Y. 222, 15 N.E.2d 587 (1938).

55. The courts have usually been alert to this problem, see Robertson v. City of Salem, 191 F.Supp. 604 (D.Or.1960); Vernon Park Realty,

Moreover, as public purpose encompasses fields far beyond the traditional view of public use it would seem wise to expand our concepts of just compensation and include incidental losses in arriving at a final award.[56]   In the great bulk of the situations the owner will be left with a reasonable freedom of choice as to land use (or else he will not care, as is true when he buys industrially zoned land for an industrial use), and the basic issue becomes how the police power regulations are passed, modified, and made effective.   Property is the established expectations which the law gives an owner; those expectations cannot be static, but neither can they be subject to the whim and caprice of the community.   The community must act under established rules so that property is subject to the rule of law, not of men.[57] This concept must not change!

It is precisely at this juncture that the police power regulations are already subject to justifiable attack.   Sound in concept, they have often been weak in administration.   "Whether through ignorance of the law, political influence, the belief that mistakes in legislation can be cured through administrative relief, or magnification of power for purposes of prestige, the board of appeals in many cities has become a device of danger rather than safety." [58]   The public has legitimate rights in private property, but those rights must be exercised with extreme caution.   Government, of all groups, must never be above the law it administers.

We have much to learn from the English experience since 1947, and fortunately the triumphs and defeats of planning in that tight little island are well documented.[59]   The English started with extreme flexibility, centralized control over local action, "undivinable" administrative review, and almost no judicial review (none on the merits of a specific proposal).   At about the same time, the American pattern was certainty (called rigidity by some), local autonomy, and judicial review of local action.[60] Today "it is clear that the English approach and the American

Inc. v. City of Mount Vernon, 307 N.Y. 493, 121 N.E.2d 517 (1954), but not always. See McCarthy v. City of Manhattan Beach, 41 Cal.2d 879, 264 P.2d 932 (1953).

56. See Comment, Eminent Domain Valuations in an Age of Redevelopment: Incidental Losses, 67 Yale L. J. 61 (1957).

57. Of course, all laws are made and administered by men but they must not be allowed to act in an arbitrary or capricious fashion.

58. Reps, Discretionary Powers of the Board of Zoning Appeals, 20 Law & Contemp.Prob. 280, 282 (1955). See also note 42 supra.

59. See Haar, Law and Land (Anglo-American Planning Practice) (Haar ed. 1964); Mandelker, Notes From the English: Compensation in Town and Country Planning, 49 Calif.L. Rev. 699 (1961).

60. This analysis is from Babcock, Key Issues in Land Use Controls, in 1963 Planning 15–16.

approach are going to meet each other half way and, as in so many things, the true . . .   position will probably be found precisely midway between the extremes of rigidity on the one hand and complete fluidity on the other." [61]

Undoubtedly, we must have regional land-use planning in this country because the little fiefdoms of municipal power are stifling the very logic of public rights in private land.[62]   However, we should keep all possible decisions at the local level and utilize the metropolitan area or region only when absolutely necessary. We should avoid the English concept of centralized control because it does not fit our society or our needs. As we modify the rigid line-drawing of Euclidean zoning, we must develop new techniques which will enable the owner to ascertain with some certainty what the permissible land uses will be. The private owner, no less than the public, needs to plan for the future. Finally, we must develop an administrative expertise which will give property owners some of the same confidence in planning commissions and boards of adjustment that they now feel in the courts. Until that can be done we should continue a high degree of judicial surveillance over all of the tools of land-use control.

D. CONCLUSION

Although this Section has been devoted to the changing concepts in the law of land use from the days of John Locke to the days of Lewis Mumford, it is arguable that our *underlying* concepts have altered very little. The linguistic philosophers at Oxford [63] have thought it intellectually profitable to spend their productive lives clarifying the meaning of such broad generalizations as justice, truth, beauty. They reason that if the words themselves can be made precise cutting instruments, much of the ancient controversy will disappear and intelligent men will find new areas of agreement. It would be intriguing to have such an analysis of the emotion-laden words "private proper-

---

61. Id. at 20.

62. The courts recognize this even when local legislatures do not. See Borough of Cresskill v. Borough of Dumont, 15 N.J. 238, 104 A.2d 441 (1954).

63. For a critical account of linguistic philosophy see Gellner, Words and Things (1959). For an illustration of this approach in the law see Hart, The Concept of Law (1961).

ty."   If one could arrive at the essence of this concept he might find that while conditions have changed greatly in the world since Blackstone wrote of "sole and despotic dominion," the concept of private property is still remarkably intact.   There may be universal principles in the law and perhaps they alter not; it may be our way of looking at them from a particular platform in time and space that changes.   If this be so, perhaps we still conceive of "absolute" dominion over the Blackacres of this planet but recognize that the term "absolute" too is relative and must be redefined to include the public interest in order to make the individual's interest meaningful.

Part Five

CONCLUSION

The law of property is one of the most fundamental areas of jurisprudence to be found in any society. Property, as an institution, is a principal foundation of any stable civilization. Nowhere does the lawyer render greater service to society than in providing the professional skill necessary to the smooth functioning of our property system. Land reform has long been a first step in any revolution and widespread discontent with an existing property structure is a prime cause of social turmoil.

We, in the United States, are the inheritors of the most sophisticated, yet practical, system of property law developed in the world thus far. But nothing in life is static and Anglo-American law needs constant scrutiny lest its arteries harden and senility creep in. Balanced precariously on a feudal base, our land law, particularly, must slough off its archaic rules after they have served their purpose and we, as lawyers, must be alert to new social needs and aspirations. Change for the sake of change can produce chaos, but reasoned improvement of the law is more than a casual luxury, it is a prime necessity. In this sense, reform, far from being ivory tower, is of the essence of practicality.

Just as we must understand law before we can practice it successfully, so must we understand our property system before we try to reform it. Most legal principles are founded on reason, but it may be the reason of history, not the logic of the present. In property law, these reasons tend to run more deeply into the past than elsewhere and we must be careful not to disrupt a viable institution when we sever a particularly noxious root. Research and planning should precede reform so that all change is responsible change, paying respect to our great traditions of the past as we move into the future.

Property clearly has two sides—an individual side and a social side. The two are so intertwined that it is never possible to deal with one without affecting the other. Property rights, like all rights, are relative and just as the common law of nuisance once limited the fee simple owner of Blackacre in the activities on his own land, so today the law of zoning and its brothers limits the absoluteness of the fee. But this law that restricts also expands, and the right to run a filling station in a residential area, lost by *A*, is restored to him in the right to live in a quiet suburb free from *B's* service station. Who, today, would want to live in New York, Chicago, or Los Angeles, subject only to the property law of Coke's time?

If we are Benthamites and agree that property is a creature of law,[1] then we are members of a profession which bears a heavy responsibility in maintaining the correct balance between the rights of the individual and the power of the state. What that correct balance may be will differ as our own consciences, beliefs, and motivations differ, but we must search for a consensus within the Western tradition of freedom and justice. This will require statesmen in the field of property and you must prepare to be one of them.

1. See p. 4 supra.

TABLE OF CASES

References are to Pages

INDEX

END OF VOLUME